Traversing the Ethical Minefield

ASPEN PUBLISHERS

Traversing the Ethical Minefield

Problems, Law, and Professional Responsibility

Second Edition

Susan R. Martyn

Stoepler Professor of Law and Values
University of Toledo College of Law

Lawrence J. Fox

Partner, Drinker Biddle & Reath
I. Grant Irey Adjunct Professor
University of Pennsylvania Law School

Wolters Kluwer
Law & Business

AUSTIN   BOSTON   CHICAGO   NEW YORK   THE NETHERLANDS

Aspen Publishers
Attn: Permissions Department
76 Ninth Avenue, 7th Floor
New York, NY   10011-5201

To contact Customer Care, e-mail customer.care@aspenpublishers.com, call 1-800-234-
1660, fax 1-800-901-9075, or mail correspondence to:

Aspen Publishers
Attn: Order Department
PO Box 990
Frederick, MD 21705

Printed in the United States of America.

1 2 3 4 5 6 7 8 9 0

ISBN 978-0-7355-6962-1

Library of Congress Cataloging-in-Publication Data

Martyn, Susan R., 1947-
    Traversing the ethical minefield : problems, law, and professional responsibility / Susan
R. Martyn, Lawrence J. Fox.—2nd ed.
        p. cm.
    Includes index.
    ISBN 978-0-7355-6962-1 (hardcover : alk. paper) 1. Legal ethics—United States. 2.
Attorney and client—United States. I. Fox, Lawrence J., 1943- II. Title.

KF306.M37 2008
174'.30973—dc22

2007049847

About Wolters Kluwer Law & Business

Wolters Kluwer Law & Business is a leading provider of research information and workflow solutions in key specialty areas. The strengths of the individual brands of Aspen Publishers, CCH, Kluwer Law International and Loislaw are aligned within Wolters Kluwer Law & Business to provide comprehensive, in-depth solutions and expert-authored content for the legal, professional and education markets.

CCH was founded in 1913 and has served more than four generations of business professionals and their clients. The CCH products in the Wolters Kluwer Law & Business group are highly regarded electronic and print resources for legal, securities, antitrust and trade regulation, government contracting, banking, pension, payroll, employment and labor, and healthcare reimbursement and compliance professionals.

Aspen Publishers is a leading information provider for attorneys, business professionals and law students. Written by preeminent authorities, Aspen products offer analytical and practical information in a range of specialty practice areas from securities law and intellectual property to mergers and acquisitions and pension/benefits. Aspen's trusted legal education resources provide professors and students with high-quality, up-to-date and effective resources for successful instruction and study in all areas of the law.

Kluwer Law International supplies the global business community with comprehensive English-language international legal information. Legal practitioners, corporate counsel and business executives around the world rely on the Kluwer Law International journals, loose-leafs, books and electronic products for authoritative information in many areas of international legal practice.

Loislaw is a premier provider of digitized legal content to small law firm practitioners of various specializations. Loislaw provides attorneys with the ability to quickly and efficiently find the necessary legal information they need, when and where they need it, by facilitating access to primary law as well as state-specific law, records, forms and treatises.

Wolters Kluwer Law & Business, a unit of Wolters Kluwer, is headquartered in New York and Riverwoods, Illinois. Wolters Kluwer is a leading multinational publisher and information services company.

For Angela & Joshua, and Sarah & Aaron
For Carrie & Tony, and Emily & Peter

Summary of Contents

Contents

PART II: LAWYERS AND CLIENTS: FIDUCIARY DUTY

PART III: LAWYERS AND JUSTICE: THE LIMITS OF ADVOCACY

PART IV: LAWYERS AND SOCIETY: THE PROFESSION

Chapter 13: Self-Regulation   509

Chapter 14: Being a Lawyer   547

Preface

This book represents a unique collaboration between a law professor with extensive academic experience (Susan Martyn) and a long-time practitioner who has dealt with most of the issues in this book (Larry Fox). We suspect that our casebook is unlike many you have encountered so far in law school, and therefore we begin your study by introducing you to our pedagogical goals as well as several distinctive features of the book you are about to use.

In this second edition we again hope to accomplish four goals. First, we have updated the problems, cases, and materials to engage you in a fascinating and dynamic subject. Second, we have added two chapters (Control and Communication and Judicial Ethics) to teach you more about the rapidly expanding law governing lawyers. Third, we have included a series of notes to focus on practice context. Here we examine the ethical challenges unique to specialized areas of practice, including criminal and insurance defense, as well as representing organizations, governments and pro bono clients. Fourth, throughout these materials, we continue to invite you to recognize good lawyering, or the need to develop practical ethical judgment, a task that requires more than just compliance with the law. Overall, we hope that our combination of problems, cases, short stories, and continuing notes will engage and assist you in your study of the law governing lawyers.

The Problems

The short problems that introduce each section of the book ask you to evaluate the actions of a hypothetical law firm, Martyn & Fox. Each set of problems is followed by citations to the relevant professional code provisions and sections of the Restatement of the Law Governing Lawyers found in your rules supplement. You should prepare for each class by formulating answers to the problems after considering these provisions along with the relevant cases and other materials in the book.

As you address the dilemmas faced by Martyn & Fox, you will discover that the firm is capable of great inconsistency. At times, the lawyers at Martyn & Fox may seem wise and capable. On other occasions, you will wonder at their fallibility. In many situations, you may identify with their confusion and angst. Most often, the firm can be rescued from disaster by sage advice.

We intend these problems to promote all of our pedagogical goals, so you should expect to approach them on several levels. First, we hope they will engage you in interesting issues faced by modern lawyers. Second, we want them to motivate you to study the relevant provisions in various lawyer codes, the

Restatement of the Law Governing Lawyers, and the cases and other materials that explain and construe them. Third, we anticipate that the relative brevity of each problem will lead you to conclude that the answer "depends on" additional facts that might change the advice you offer Martyn & Fox. Indeed, issues of professional responsibility often require careful attention to facts as well as law. We invite you to articulate your assumptions and to anticipate how additional facts might change your answer. For example, does it matter whether Martyn & Fox is a two- or two-hundred-person law firm? Whether it focuses primarily on litigation or transactional work? Whether its practice is located in a rural area or a major city? Whether the lawyer is a partner or an associate? Whether Martyn & Fox's client is an individual or an entity? How much Martyn & Fox's client can pay?

Finally, once you get into the law that governs the situation described in a problem, you will discover occasions when Martyn & Fox has a range of options. In these instances, you should identify the discretion ceded to the lawyer's individual moral conscience and articulate how you believe that discretion should be exercised. Here, we hope to assist you in developing practical ethical judgment as well as learning the law.

The Cases

Most people new to this subject are surprised at the vast array of cases that explain and expand on the professional code provisions and other remedies that make up the law governing lawyers. We offer you a rich assortment of these cases, emphasizing those decided in the past decade. Each of the 55 cases in this book has been edited for clarity. We use ellipses or brackets to indicate omissions from the court's opinion, but omitted citations and footnotes are not identified.

The Short Stories

The short stories in this book offer you the opportunity to engage in a difficult issue of legal ethics from the viewpoint of the lawyers confronting the situation. Larry wrote these stories to offer you an alternative way to learn some substantive law. Primarily, however, we intend these excerpts to show you the human face of some of the legal issues raised in the story. The extended detail of the story will enable you to understand more fully the context in which the lawyer must make a practical ethical judgment.

The Continuing Notes

Unlike the note material in most casebooks, the notes in this book are short essays organized around six general themes. These notes provide transitions between various topics in the materials, further explanation of a case or series of cases, and an opportunity to explore a topic at an accessible but more advanced level. They also serve as occasions to connect and integrate the basic ideas and themes that the courts have woven throughout the law governing lawyers.

In the first set of continuing notes, entitled **Lawyers' Roles**, five notes make explicit the often-unnoticed roles lawyers assume when they represent clients, with particular emphasis on the legal risks created by each of these roles. We hope these notes prod you to think about why some of the lawyers who became the subject of cases in this book got into trouble, as well as encourage you to consider the kind of lawyer you want to be.

The second series of continuing notes, entitled **The Law Governing Lawyers**, encompasses seven notes where we explore the fiduciary obligations lawyers assume when they say "yes," or agree to represent clients, and the remedies provided by the cases and materials when these obligations are ignored.

In the third group of notes, entitled **The Bounds of the Law**, six notes explain when lawyers may or must say "no" to clients, because of some external legal control that imposes a limit on the lawyer's advocacy.

In these notes, we explore the vast law of fraud, the ever-expanding criminal law, procedural sanctions, and the impact of the Constitution on the regulation of lawyer conduct. Each of these bodies of general law has been read into the professional codes to create an explicit boundary beyond which lawyers tread only at great risk both to themselves and to their clients.

The fourth series of continuing notes, entitled **Practice Pointers**, offers you practical advice about how to avoid or mitigate the legal consequences raised in the problems, cases, and other materials. Here we showcase six topics:

The fifth set of notes, entitled **Lawyers and Other Professionals**, examines whether the courts treat lawyers and other professionals consistently. Here we examine five issues that confront a variety of professionals:

The final set of notes, entitled **Lawyers and Clients**, focuses on legal representation in five common practice settings. Here, we examine specialized legal regulation of the client's rights and responsibilities, which in turn shapes a lawyer's advocacy on behalf of the client.

The Combination

Overall, we intend the problems, rules, cases, stories, and continuing notes in this book to serve as a guide to identifying, understanding, and avoiding the minefields and mistakes that the lawyers in these materials have confronted. We also hope you enjoy this study as much as we have enjoyed preparing it.

Susan Martyn and Larry Fox
February 2008

Acknowledgments

We could not have completed this casebook without the accumulated wisdom of hundreds of lawyers who have taught and refined our understanding of these issues. In particular, we thank our colleagues who served as reporters and advisors to the American Law Institute's Restatement (Third) of The Law Governing Lawyers and those who served with us on the ABA Ethics 2000 Commission. We also are indebted to many at the ABA Center for Professional Responsibility, who provided us with research data and information about recent developments exactly when we needed it.

The two of us first met in 1987 in a windowless conference room at the American Law Institute during a meeting of the advisors to the Restatement of the Law Governing Lawyers. These meetings clearly are an acquired taste. The Reporters to Restatement projects circulate a draft weeks before each meeting, then sit on a raised dais facing a semicircle of 25 or 30 judges, professors, and lawyers to defend each section, comment, and example line by line, usually for several days at a time. Only the good will and good humor of the participants can make such a process bearable, and we soon found that we were providing large doses of both for each other. From our 13-year sojourn with the ALI, a broad friendship developed that also took us into new adventures, including CLE programs and the ABA's Ethics 2000 project in which we both served as Commissioners to undertake a stem-to-stern review of the ABA Model Rules of Professional Conduct.

For us, nothing has been quite like our work on this volume. After Larry returned from a stay in Ithaca, Susan learned of the problems he had developed for his Professional Responsibility course at Cornell Law School and decided they could form the backbone of a casebook. Susan selected and edited the cases, organized the materials, and wrote the continuing notes in the book while teaching the materials to students at Toledo, Marquette, and George Washington Law Schools. Larry contributed to the second edition while teaching at the University of Pennsylvania and Harvard Law Schools, providing several chapters of short stories from his previously published works. In short, we could not have completed this book without each other, and we both feel free to blame the other for the flaws that remain.

The faculties and students at six law schools—Cornell, George Washington, Harvard, Marquette, the University of Pennsylvania, and the University of Toledo—contributed to these materials by consulting, arguing, and correcting many of our mistakes. Others across the country also commented on and helped us formulate our ideas. Special thanks to Harry Bryants, James Caruso,

Kathleen Clark, Roger Cramton, Leslie Griffin, Mark Harrison, Geoffrey Hazard, Barbara and Charles Hicks, Andrew Kaufman, Margaret Love, Nancy Moore, Tom Morgan, Mitt Regan, Becky Stretch, Robert Tuttle, Brad Wendel, and Leah Wortham. We also received able research assistance from Erika Ban, Ryan Bricker, Amy Granger, Cara Hanson, Juan Peña, Jeanne Whalen, and Robert White. Our ideas never would have taken shape without the capable, cheerful, and knowledgeable assistance of Bea Cucinotta.

Susan would not have had the time to devote to this project without the assistance of the Eugene N. Balk Fund, which provided the funds to carry out most of the research in the continuing notes. Larry never would have been able to develop the problems if it were not for the invitation from Charles Wolfram to escape practice and teach at the Cornell Law School.

Finally, our thanks to the following for permission to reproduce all or portions of their work:

American Bar Association, Formal Opinions 93-379, 94-389, 04-433. © 1993, 1994, 2004 by the American Bar Association. All rights reserved. Reprinted by permission of the American Bar Association. Copies of ABA Ethics Opinions are available from Service Center, American Bar Association, 321 N. Clark Street, Chicago, IL 60610, 1-800-285-2221.

American Bar Association, *Legal Tender: A Lawyer's Guide to Handling Professional Dilemmas* by Lawrence J. Fox (1995) pp. 85-96, 122-125, 157-166. Reprinted by permission.

American Bar Association, *Raise the Bar: Real World Solutions for a Troubled Profession*, Lawrence J. Fox, ed. (2007) pp. 15-29. Reprinted by permission.

American Bar Association, *I Did Not Sleep With That Vice-President* by Lawrence J. Fox, 15 No. 2 The Professional Lawyer 1 (2004). Reprinted by permission.

Cardozo Law Review, *Why Lawyers Are Unhappy* by Martin E.P. Seligman, Paul R. Verkuil & Terry H. Kang, 23 Cardozo L. Rev. 33-53 (2001).

The Cartoon Bank, for permission to use the New Yorker Cartoons in Chapters 6, 8, 10, and 12 of this volume.

District of Columbia Bar Association Opinion 329 (2005).

Matthew Bender & Co., a member of the LexisNexis Group, *Understanding Lawyers' Ethics* by Monroe H. Freedman & Abbe Smith, pp. 7-8, 45, 46-47, 53-54, 62, 63, 71, 72 (3d ed. 2004). Reprinted with permission, © 2004, Matthew Bender & Co., a member of the LexisNexis Group. All rights reserved.

Nebraska Law Review, *In Defense of Client-Lawyer Confidentiality . . . And Its Exceptions . . .* by Susan R. Martyn, 81 Neb. L. Rev. 1320-1350 (2003).

Oxford University Press and Deborah L. Rhode, *In the Interests of Justice: Reforming the Legal Profession* © by Deborah L. Rhode, pp. 49-50, 53-58, 64-67, 77, and 79 (2001). Used by permission of Oxford University Press, Inc.

The University of Chicago Press and James Boyd White, *The Edge of Meaning*, © by The University of Chicago, pp. 223-226, 250-251 (2001).

Utah State Bar Association, Utah Ethics Advisory Opinion 99-04, by the Utah State Bar Association Ethics Advisory Opinion Committee (1999).

Traversing the Ethical Minefield

Part I

Introduction

Chapter 1

Lawyers, Role, and Law

A. Lawyers and Role

Problems

1-1. Should Martyn & Fox file a claim on behalf of a client after the statute of limitations has expired? What if we are fairly sure the opposing party will not be represented?

1-2. During negotiations, a lawyer on the other side agrees on behalf of his client to pay an extra $50,000 because the land is zoned for ten lots. Martyn & Fox knows that the lawyer is mistaken. Should Martyn & Fox close the deal without correcting the mistake?

1-3. Should Martyn & Fox advise its client to sign an agreement in a divorce case that settles property division and child support where the opposing lawyer mistakenly believes that alimony can later be negotiated, but we know that the law will bar such a later claim? What if the opposing lawyer is a best friend and has not handled many divorces?

1-4. Should Martyn & Fox tell a client the chances of her getting caught doing something illegal, e.g., deducting the cost of a child's wedding as a business expense? How about failing to produce a document in response to a legitimate request for production of documents?

Consider: Model Rules Preamble and Scope
Restatement of the Law Governing Lawyers §1

Monroe H. Freedman & Abbe Smith
Understanding Lawyers' Ethics
pp. 7-8, 45, 46-47, 53-54, 62-63, 71, 72 (3d ed., Lexis-Nexis 2004)

. . . In expressing the distinctive feature of ethics in the legal profession, we would identify the client not as "this other person, over whom I have power," but as "this other person whom I have the power to help." In this view, the central concern of lawyers' ethics is not (as Schaffer says, quoting Plato) how my client "can be made as good as possible."* Rather, it is how far we can ethically go—or how far we should be required to go—to achieve for our clients full and equal rights under law.

Put otherwise, Shaffer thinks of lawyers' ethics as being rooted in moral philosophy, while we think of lawyers' ethics as being rooted in the moral values that are expressed in the Bill of Rights. . . .

Can you be a good lawyer and a good person at the same time? The question implies that serving your clients competently and zealously will require you to violate your personal morality in at least some instances.

At the heart of that issue is whether it is the lawyer or the client who should make the moral decisions that come up in the course of the representation. As it is frequently put: Is the lawyer just a "hired gun," or must the lawyer "obey his own conscience, not that of his client?" . . .

In an article that has been widely cited with approval,[6] Wasserstrom recalls John Dean's list of those involved in the Watergate coverup. Dean placed an asterisk next to the names of each of the lawyers on the list, because he had been struck by the fact that so many of those implicated in wrongdoing were lawyers. Wasserstrom concludes that the involvement of lawyers in Watergate was "natural, if not unavoidable," the "likely if not inevitable consequence of their legal acculturation." Indeed, on the basis of Wasserstrom's analysis the only matter of wonder is why so many of those on John Dean's list were *not* lawyers. What could possibly have corrupted the non-lawyers to such a degree as to have led them into what Wasserstrom sees as the uniquely amoral and immoral world of the lawyers? "For at best," Wasserstrom asserts, "the lawyer's world is a simplified moral world; often it is an amoral one; and more than occasionally perhaps, an overtly immoral one."

Wasserstrom considers "role-differentiated behavior" to be the root of the problem. As he says, the "nature of role-differentiated behavior . . . often makes it both appropriate and desirable for the person in a particular role to put to one side considerations of various sorts—and especially various moral considerations—that would otherwise be relevant if not decisive."

Illustrative of how Wasserstrom thinks lawyers should make moral considerations relevant is his suggestion that a lawyer should refuse to advise a wealthy client of a tax loophole provided by the legislature for only a few wealthy taxpayers. If that case were to be generalized, it would mean that the legal profession can properly regard itself as an oligarchy, whose duty is to nullify decisions made by the people's duly elected representatives. . . .

Nevertheless, Wasserstrom suggests that lawyers should "see themselves less as subject to role-differentiated behavior and more as subject to the demands of *the* moral point of view." Is it really that simple? Is there a single point of view that can be identified as "the" moral one? . . .

In day-to-day practice, the most common instances of amoral or immoral conduct by lawyers are those occasions in which lawyers preempt their clients'

---

* *See* Thomas Shaffer, *Legal Ethics and the Good Client*, 36 Cath. U. L. Rev. 319, 320 (1987).
6. Richard Wasserstrom, *Lawyers as Professionals: Some Moral Issues*, 5 ABA Human Rights 1 (1975).

moral judgments. That occurs in two ways. Most often lawyers assume that the client wants her to maximize his material or tactical position in every way that is legally permissible, regardless of non-legal considerations. That is, lawyers tend to assume the worst regarding the client's desires, and act accordingly. Much less frequently, we believe, a lawyer will decide that a particular course of conduct is morally preferable, even though not required legally, and will follow that course on the client's behalf without consultation. In either event, the lawyer fails in her responsibility to maximize the client's autonomy by providing the client with the fullest advice and counsel, legal and moral, so that the client can make the most informed choice possible. . . .

One of the essential values of a just society is respect for the dignity of each member of that society. Essential to each individual's dignity is the free exercise of his autonomy. Toward that end, each person is entitled to know his rights with respect to society and other individuals, and to decide whether to seek fulfillment of those rights through the due processes of law.

The lawyer, by virtue of her training and skills, has a legal and practical monopoly over access to the legal system and knowledge about the law. The lawyer's advice and assistance are often indispensable, therefore, to the effective exercise of individual autonomy.

Accordingly, the attorney acts both professionally and morally in assisting clients to maximize their autonomy, that is, by counseling clients candidly and fully regarding the clients' legal rights and moral responsibilities as the lawyer perceives them, and by assisting clients to carry out their lawful decisions. Further, the attorney acts unprofessionally and immorally by depriving clients of their autonomy, that is, by denying them information regarding their legal rights, by otherwise preempting their moral decisions, or by depriving them of the ability to carry out their lawful decisions.

Until the lawyer-client relationship is contracted, however—until, that is, the lawyer chooses to induce another to rely upon her professional knowledge and skills—the lawyer ordinarily acts entirely within the scope of her own autonomy. Barring extraordinary circumstances, therefore, the attorney is free to exercise her personal judgment as to whether to represent a particular client. Since a moral choice is implicated in such a decision, however, others are entitled to judge and to criticize, on moral grounds, a lawyer's decision to represent a particular client or cause. . . .

Closely related to the concept of client autonomy is the lawyer's obligation to give "entire devotion to the interest of the client, warm zeal in the maintenance and defense of his rights and the exertion of [the lawyer's] utmost learning and ability."[1] This ethic of zeal is a "traditional aspiration" that was already established in Abraham Lincoln's day, and zealousness continues today to be "*the* fundamental principle of the law of lawyering," and "the dominant standard of lawyerly excellence."

Client autonomy refers to the client's right to decide what her own interests are. Zeal refers to the dedication with which the lawyer furthers the client's interests. The ethic of zeal is, therefore, pervasive in lawyers' professional

---

1. ABA Canons of Prof. Ethics 15 (1908).

responsibilities, because it infuses all of the lawyer's other ethical obligations with "entire devotion to the interest of the client." . . .

The obligation of "entire devotion to the interest of the client [and] warm zeal in the maintenance and defense of his rights" is not limited to the role of the lawyer as advocate in the courtroom. . . . It is important to remember, however, that any lawyer who counsels a client, negotiates on a client's behalf, or drafts a legal document for a client must do so with an actual or potential adversary in mind. When a contract is negotiated, there is a party on the other side. A contract, a will, or a form submitted to a government agency may well be read at some later date with an adversary's eye, and could become the subject of litigation. The advice given to a client and acted upon today may strengthen or weaken the client's position in contentious negotiations or in litigation next year. In short, it is not just the advocate in the courtroom who functions in an adversary system, and it is not just the client currently in litigation who may both require and be entitled to "warm zeal in the maintenance and defense of his rights."

Deborah L. Rhode
In the Interests of Justice: Reforming the Legal Profession
pp. 49-79 (Oxford University Press 2000)*

The Advocate's Role in the Adversary System

My first legal case was almost my last. It brought home Dostoevski's definition of an advocate as "a conscience for hire." And it made me wonder about putting mine on the market.

The insight came when I was interning at the Washington, D.C., public defender's office after my first year in law school. Two of the office's juvenile clients had stomped an elderly "wino" to death, just for the fun of it. They confessed to my supervising attorney and to the arresting officer; indeed, they appeared somewhat proud of their accomplishment. However, the police committed a number of constitutional and procedural violations in obtaining the confession and other inculpating evidence. My supervisor was able to get the case dismissed on what the public would consider a "technicality." He also was proud of his accomplishment. The clients were jubilant and unrepentant. I had no doubt that the office would see them again. Nor did I doubt that I was utterly unsuited to be a criminal defense lawyer. I wasn't sure I was ready to be a lawyer at all.

Now, with the benefit of a quarter century's hindsight, I think both my supervisor and I were right. He was providing an essential and ethically defensible safeguard for constitutional values. And I was right to feel morally troubled by the consequences. I had assisted a process that sent the wrong messages to guilty clients: some lives are cheap; a gifted lawyer can get you off.

This is one of the "hard cases" in legal ethics. Its moral tensions arise from deeply rooted conflicts in America's commitments to both individual rights and social responsibilities. This conflict plays out in many law-related contexts, and legal ethics is no exception. When lawyers straddle these cultural contradictions, the public both demands and condemns their divided loyalties.

---

* By permission of Oxford University Press, Inc.

Defense of disempowered clients and unpopular causes earns lawyers their greatest respect but also their sharpest criticism. The clash between lawyers' responsibilities as officers of the court and advocates of client interests creates the most fundamental dilemmas of legal ethics. All too often, the bar has resolved this conflict by permitting overrepresentation of those who can afford it and underrepresentation of everyone else. The result is to privilege the profession's interests at the expense of the public's. . . .

The Premises of Partisanship

The standard ethical justifications for the advocate's role rest on two major premises. The first assumption, drawing on utilitarian reasoning, is that an adversarial clash between opposing advocates is the best way of discovering truth. The second assumption, based on individual rights, is that morally neutral partisanship is the most effective means of protecting human freedom and dignity. Both claims unravel at several key points.

The truth-based rationale for the advocate's role assumes that the "right" result is most likely to occur through competitive presentations of relevant law and facts. As a report by the Joint Conference of the American Bar Association and the Association of American Law Schools emphasized, only when a decision-maker "has had the benefit of intelligent and vigorous advocacy on both sides" can society have confidence in the decision. This faith in partisan process is part of a broader worldview that underpins America's basic social and economic institutions. Robert Kutak, chair of the ABA commission that drafted the Model Rules of Professional Conduct, observed that our commitment to the advocate's role in an adversarial framework reflects "the same deep-seated values we place on competition" in other contexts.

A second defense of neutral partisanship involves the protection of rights and the relationships necessary to safeguard those rights. Here again, the priority we give to personal liberties is rooted in more general cultural commitments. In a highly legalistic society, preservation of personal dignity and autonomy requires preservation of access to law. According to bar leaders, individual freedom would be severely compromised if the profession began screening cases on the basis of their moral merit. The result would be an "oligarchy of lawyers," in which "saints [would] have a monopoly on lawsuits," and lawyers would have a monopoly on determining who qualified for sainthood. The legal profession has no special claim to righteousness and no public accountability for their view of justice. By what right should they "play God" by foreclosing legal assistance or imposing "their own views about the path of virtue upon their clients"?

If advocates assumed such authority, bar leaders further claim that ethical professionals would refuse to assist those clients most in need of ethical counseling. And if advocates were held morally accountable for their clients' conduct, less legal representation would be available for those most vulnerable to popular prejudice and governmental repression. Our history provides ample illustrations of the social and economic penalties directed at attorneys with unpopular clients. It was difficult enough to find lawyers for accused communists in the McCarthy era and for political activists in the early southern civil rights campaign. Those difficulties would have been far greater without the principle that legal representation is not an endorsement of client conduct.

These rights-based justifications of neutral partisanship assume special force in criminal cases. Individuals whose lives, liberty, and reputation are at risk deserve an advocate without competing loyalties to the state. Ensuring effective representation serves not only to avoid unjust outcomes but also to affirm community values and to express our respect for individual rights. Guilt or innocence should be determined in open court with due process of law, not in the privacy of an attorney's office. The consequences of an alternative model are readily apparent in many totalitarian countries. Where defense lawyers' role is to "serve justice," rather than their clients, what passes for "justice" does not commend itself for export. Often the roles of counsel for the defendant and the state are functionally identical and the price is paid in innocent lives. A case in point involves China's celebrated prosecution of the Gang of Four following the Cultural Revolution of the 1960s. The attorney appointed to defend Mao Tse Tung's widow chose not to honor his client's request to assert her innocence or to conduct any investigations, present any witnesses, or challenge the government's case. According to the lawyer, such advocacy was unnecessary because "the police and the prosecutors worked on the case a very long time and the evidence they found which wasn't true they threw away."

This country has had similar experiences when the crime has been especially heinous or the accused has been a member of a particularly unpopular group. To take only the most obvious example, for most of this nation's history, southern blacks accused of an offense against a white victim stood little chance of anything approximating zealous advocacy or a fair trial. Despite substantial progress, racial and ethnic bias in legal proceedings remains common, as most Americans and virtually every bar task force agree. The risk of abuse is significant in other contexts as well. Perjury, fabrication of evidence, and suppression of exculpatory material by law enforcement officials remain pervasive problems. Such abuses were present in some two-thirds of the sixty-odd cases involving defendants facing the death penalty who recently have been exonerated by DNA evidence. . . .

Although these rationales for zealous advocacy have considerable force, they fall short of justifying current partisanship principles. A threshold weakness is the bar's overreliance on criminal defense as an all-purpose paradigm for the lawyer's role. Only a small amount of legal work involves either criminal proceedings or civil matters that raise similar concerns of individual freedom and governmental power. An advocacy role designed to ensure the presumption of innocence and deter prosecutorial abuse is not necessarily transferable to other legal landscapes. Bar rhetoric that casts the lawyer as a "champion against a hostile world" seems out of touch with most daily practice. The vast majority of legal work assists corporate and wealthy individual clients in a system that is scarcely hostile to their interests. When a Wall Street firm representing a Fortune 500 corporation squares off against understaffed regulators or a victim of unsafe practices, the balance of power is not what bar metaphors imply.

A similar problem arises with traditional truth-based justifications for neutral partisanship. Their underlying premise, that accurate results will emerge from competitive partisan presentations before disinterested tribunals, depends on factual assumptions that seldom hold in daily practice. Most legal representation never receives oversight from an impartial decision maker. Many disputes never reach the point of formal legal complaint, and of those that do, over 90 percent settle before trial. Moreover, even cases that end up in court seldom resemble the bar's idealized model of adversarial processes. That model presupposes adversaries with roughly equal incentives, resources, capabilities, and access to relevant information. But those conditions are more the exception than the rule in a society that tolerates vast disparities in wealth, high litigation costs, and grossly inadequate access to legal assistance. As a majority of surveyed judges agreed, a mismatch in attorneys' skills can distort outcomes; a mismatch in client resources compounds the problem. In law, as in life, the haves generally come out ahead. . . .

For similar reasons, the bar's traditional rights-based justifications offer inadequate support for prevailing adversarial practices. Such justifications implicitly assume that clients are entitled to assistance in whatever the law permits. This assumption confuses legal and moral rights. Some conduct that is socially indefensible may remain lawful because adequate prohibitions appear unenforceable or because decision-making bodies are too uninformed or compromised by special interests to impose effective regulation. An ethic of undivided client loyalty in these contexts has encouraged lawyers' assistance in some of the most socially costly enterprises in recent memory, the distribution of asbestos and Dalkon Shields, the suppression of health information about cigarettes, and the financially irresponsible ventures of savings and loan associations.

Defenders of neutral partisanship typically respond that protection of client rights is ethically justifiable despite such consequences because individual liberty and autonomy are of paramount value in a free society. Moral philosophers generally make no such mistake. As David Luban notes, this standard justification for zealous advocacy blurs an important distinction between the "desirability of people acting autonomously and the desirability of their autonomous acts." It is, for example, morally desirable for clients to make their own decisions about whether to attempt to defeat a needy opponent's valid claim through a legal technicality; it is not morally desirable for them actually to do so. Autonomy does not have intrinsic value; its importance derives from the values it fosters, such as individual initiative and responsibility. If a particular client objective does little to promote those values, or does so only at much greater cost to third parties, then the ethical justification for zealous advocacy is less convincing. . . .

Professional Interests and Partisan Practices

Whatever their inadequacies in serving the public interest, prevailing adversarial practices have been reasonably effective in serving professional interests. They permit all the justice that money can buy or a client who can afford it, and they impose few responsibilities on those who cannot. . . .

The Price of Partisanship

Yet these financial and psychological comforts come at a price. The avoidance of ethical responsibility is ultimately corrosive for lawyers, clients, and the legal framework on which they depend. For many practitioners, the neutral partisan role undermines the very commitments that led them to become lawyers. . . . The submersion of self into a role too often leaves the advocate alienated from his own moral convictions. When professional action becomes detached from ordinary moral experience, the lawyer's ethical sensitivity erodes. The agnosticism that neutral partisanship encourages can readily spill over into other areas of life and undercut a lawyer's sense of moral identity. . . .

Neither lawyers' nor clients' long-term interests are served by eroding the institutional frameworks on which an effective rule of law depends. Taken to its logical extreme, a professional role that gives primary allegiance to client concerns can undermine the legal order. Yale law professor Robert Gordon gives an example: "[T]ake any simple case of compliance counseling; suppose the legal rule is clear, yet the chance of detecting violations low, the penalties small in relation to the gains from non compliance, or the terrorizing of regulators into settlement by a deluge of paper predictably easy. The mass of lawyers who advise and then assist with noncompliance in such a situation could, in the vigorous pursuit of their clients' interests, effectively nullify the laws." . . .

The bar has similar responsibilities concerning core cultural values. Norms like good faith, honesty, and fair dealing are essential for efficient markets and effective regulatory systems. These values depend on some shared restraint in the pursuit of short-term client interests. Legal processes present frequent opportunities for obstruction, obfuscation, and overreaching. An advocacy role that imposes few practical constraints on such behavior erodes expectations of trust and cooperation. These expectations are common goods on which clients as a group ultimately depend. In the short term, free riders can profit by violating norms that others respect. But these values cannot survive if deviance becomes a routine and acceptable part of the advocate's repertoire. Over the long run, a single-minded pursuit of clients' individual self-interests is likely to prove self-defeating for clients as a group. . . .

An Alternative Framework

An alternative framework for the advocate's role needs to be ethically justifiable in principle and consistently reinforced in practice. At its most basic level, such a framework would require lawyers to accept personal responsibility for the moral consequences of their professional actions. Attorneys should make decisions as advocates in the same way that morally reflective individuals make any ethical decision. Lawyers' conduct should be justifiable under consistent, disinterested, and generalizable principles. These moral principles can, of course, recognize the distinctive needs of lawyers' occupational role. . . .

However, unlike the bar's prevailing approach, this alternative framework would require lawyers to assess their obligations in light of all the societal interests at issue in particular practice contexts. . . . Respect for law is a fundamental value, particularly among those sworn to uphold it. Adherence to generally accepted rules also serves as a check against the decision maker's own bias or self-interest. But attorneys may confront cases in which the applicable rules are so indeterminate or inadequate that reference to broader moral principles is necessary.

Most ethical dilemmas arise in areas where the governing standards already leave significant room for discretion. Individual attorneys can decide whether to accept or withdraw from representation and whether to pursue certain tactics. In resolving such questions, lawyers need to consider the social context of their choices. They cannot simply rely on some idealized model of adversarial and legislative processes. Rather, lawyers must assess their action against a realistic backdrop, in which wealth, power, and information are unequally distributed, not all interests are adequately represented, and most matters will never reach a neutral tribunal. The less confidence that attorneys have in the justice system's capacity to deliver justice in a particular case, the greater their own responsibility to attempt some corrective.

. . . At one end of the spectrum are those who believe that lawyers have responsibilities to pursue substantive justice and that such responsibilities may sometimes authorize noncompliance with formal legal requirements. In defending this position, William Simon analogizes to the decisions of judges or juries when they nullify a law. Our system accepts their refusal to enforce an outmoded statute or to convict a guilty defendant when necessary to avoid serious injustice. In Simon's view, we should grant lawyers similar discretion to disregard legal rules that appear plainly wrong and that compromise fundamental values. Under his analysis, rules that irrationally withhold minimal welfare support might justify such noncompliance. At the other end of the spectrum are ethics experts who deny that the equities for clients should define the responsibilities for attorneys. According to Harvard law professor Andrew Kaufman, "Being on the wrong side of the entitlement line does not seem to me to give the welfare mother any moral claim to the lawyer's assistance." Geoffrey Hazard similarly argues that the appropriateness of lawyers' strategies in divorce cases should not "turn on the underlying merits." From these commentators' perspective, respect for formal rules is essential for effective legal processes. If these rules result in substantial injustice, a lawyer should work publicly for their reform, not subvert them privately for particular clients.

An intermediate position, and the one most compatible with the contextual ethical framework proposed here, seeks ways of advancing justice without violating formal prohibitions. Lawyers taking this position may pursue a result that is morally but not substantively justified as long as they refrain from illegal conduct such as knowing presentation of perjury or preparation of fraudulent documents. . . .

. . . [T]he aim of this alternative framework is for lawyers to make the merits matter and to assess them from a moral as well as a legal vantage. Not all poor clients would be entitled to unqualified advocacy. But neither would factors like poverty be irrelevant if they affect the justice of a particular claim. Of course, in a profession as large and diverse as the American bar, different lawyers will make different judgments about what is in fact just. Although such judgments should be defensible under accepted ethical principles, their application will necessarily reflect individuals' own experiences and commitments. . . . But the framework proposed here does not demand that lawyers reach the same results in hard cases. It demands rather that lawyers recognize that such cases *are* hard and that they call for contextual moral judgments. . . .

▨ Lawyers' Roles:
The Client-Lawyer Relationship

Close your eyes and try to imagine yourself as the lawyer for a potential client. You meet this prospective client for the first time. First, do you envision an individual or an organizational client? Second, how do you decide whether to undertake this representation? Is your primary concern whether and how much the client can pay? Are you at all concerned about the effect of this legal representation upon society as a whole? Third, assuming you decide to handle the matter, think of what you will do for the client. Do you see yourself as a legal technician who will execute the client's instructions? Or are you more comfortable imagining yourself as a guardian of the rule of law whose job it is to explain the legal realities of the situation to the client? Will you talk to the client about the moral as well as the legal implications of the client's chosen course of action? Finally, imagine the place where this meeting occurs and what it conveys about the answers to these questions.

In this series of notes entitled "Lawyers' Roles," we will examine these questions, focusing on the way lawyers articulate their own sense of role in relation both to clients and the legal system. Professors Freedman, Smith, and Rhode all understand lawyers' ethics as a function of the social role a lawyer assumes in representing a client. They believe that the lawyer professional codes should foster a distinct model of the client-lawyer relationship.

Professors Freedman and Smith endorse what has been labeled the "dominant" or the adversary ethic. This view emphasizes that lawyers have fiduciary duties to represent clients zealously, motivated by and focused on the client's values and goals. Legal rights exist to protect human autonomy, which is essential to human dignity. Lawyers do the right thing by serving what is essentially human in others. Justice is defined in terms of the legal rights granted to citizens. The legal system should protect and reinforce the individual decisions that people are best able to make for themselves, rather than any competing version of social welfare or outcome.

To a philosopher, this view is "relentlessly deontological," that is, focused on the duties of lawyers in relation to clients, rather than on any particular outcome those relationships create.[1] The lawyer's morality depends primarily on her role as an advocate, which in turn requires two primary virtues. The lawyer must be simultaneously neutral (because her client's interests should prevail), and partisan (to promote those interests). Amoral advocacy becomes the guiding norm of the adversary ethic.[2]

Commentators have characterized this view in a number of colorful ways.[3] A lawyer who adopts some form of the dominant or adversarial ethic has been labeled "client-centered," as well as called an "amoral instrument," "hired gun," "plumber," "puppet," or "prostitute." This lawyer can overidentify with clients and can lack the independent judgment necessary to provide proper legal advice.

---

1. Timothy P. Terrell, *Turmoil at the Normative Core of Lawyering: Uncomfortable Lessons from the "Metaethics" of Legal Ethics*, 49 Emory L.J. 87 (2000); Stephen L. Pepper, *The Lawyer's Amoral Ethical Role: A Defense, a Problem, and Some Possibilities*, 1986 Am. Bar Found. Research J. 613.
2. *See* David Luban, *Lawyers and Justice: An Ethical Study* at xx (Princeton U. Press 1988).
3. *See* James E. Moliterno, *Ethics of the Lawyer's Work* 129-130 (2d ed., West 2003); Symposium, *Client Counseling and Moral Responsibility*, 30 Pepp. L. Rev. 591 (2003).

Professor Rhode criticizes the neutral partisanship this role seems to require. She argues instead for a public interest ethic that would require lawyers to be subject to personal moral responsibility for the results of their actions. Although she agrees with Professors Freedman and Smith that deontological or rights-based justifications have special force in criminal cases where individuals can be overwhelmed by governmental power, she questions why lawyers should apply the same ethic to powerful interests like wealthy individuals and large corporations. She also defines justice in terms of distributive fairness rather than individual rights, meaning that lawyers should consider the social harm they help clients foist on unrepresented persons or interests.

A philosopher might label Professor Rhode's view teleological or utilitarian, that is, focused on the ultimate goal or consequences of individual client-lawyer relationships. According to this view, lawyers should assess the consequences of each legal representation, envisioning their social role as connected to some larger conception of the public interest. This lawyer ultimately will need to accept personal moral responsibility for distributive fairness, or "justice in the long run."[4]

Commentators note that this view can represent another extreme, and have labeled it in equally colorful ways as "directive," "traditional," "authoritarian," or "parentalist."[5] Expert lawyers, familiar with the legal system, may presume they know what is best and act as authorities in all aspects of the relationship. These lawyers can underidentify with clients and can assume a judgelike perspective, ignoring fiduciary duties that demand advice, obedience to client instructions, and zealous advocacy.

Lawyers as Instruments

Instrumental lawyers tend to focus on providing individual client representation and adversarial advocacy. Some pride themselves in representing almost any client who seeks their assistance, on the theory that every point of view deserves legal representation. Others, like Professors Freedman and Smith, prefer to exercise moral judgment about which clients to represent, because they are not willing to devote their legal skills to advocate every point of view.

Once they agree to take on a representation, instrumental lawyers rightly recognize fiduciary duties of control over the goals of the representation, communication, competence, confidentiality, and conflict of interest resolution to clients.[6] But their preference for client autonomy may tempt them to suppress their own moral judgment and cede all authority to the client in the process. Single-minded loyalty to a client then becomes transformed into a narrow-minded, unquestioning devotion to that client's will. The client's value system

---

4. *See* William H. Simon, *The Practice of Justice: A Theory of Lawyers' Ethics* 53-76 (Harvard U. Press 1998).
5. Professors Shaffer and Cochran divide this category into two parts. They call the first the lawyer as "Godfather," where the lawyer controls the representation and seeks client victory, and the second the lawyer as "guru" where the lawyer controls the representation and seeks client goodness. Thomas L. Shaffer & Robert F. Cochran, Jr., *Lawyers, Clients, and Moral Responsibility* 7-9, 32-39 (West 1994).
6. David A. Binder, Paul B. Bergman, Susan C. Price & Paul R. Trembly, *Lawyers as Counselors: A Client-Centered Approach* 9-11 (2d ed. West 2004).

controls the representation, and the lawyer escapes any moral accountability for either the outcome or the means employed.

Lawyers who prefer an instrumental view of their role see only one limit to client advocacy: the bounds of the law and the legal system itself. Yet these legal bounds may be unclear to an instrumental lawyer, because law itself may be viewed as a malleable means to pursue the client's desires.[7] If the legal system exists to promote individual welfare, then law can be envisioned primarily as a process that provides clients with a means to challenge or take advantage of the existing order.[8] It follows that, if the client has an arguable legal right, the lawyer should or must pursue it.

Instrumental lawyers tend to view the social fabric as relatively strong, capable of withstanding most challenges to the existing limits of the law or other majoritarian interests. At the same time, however, focusing primarily or exclusively on client interests may cause them to lose opportunities to explain a legal or moral boundary to clients or even to discover a client's true intention. Worse, these lawyers can become blind to a clear legal limit that may subject the client and the lawyer to severe sanctions. The result may be serious harm to others as well as to the client and the lawyer.

Professor Wasserstrom warns, for example, that assuming such role-differentiated behavior also may transform a lawyer's entire personality. Lawyers who see their role in instrumental terms may be unrelenting and unwilling to compromise, even when the client seeks settlement. Lawyers who live an amoral professional life may be tempted to assume an amoral personal existence as well. Such lawyers also may incorporate those qualities deemed essential to accomplishing their task, such as competitive, aggressive, ruthless, and pragmatic behavior rather than cooperative, accommodating, compassionate, and principled action.[9]

Lawyers as Directors

Directive lawyers tend to focus on their roles as officers of the legal system and members of a profession. Some pride themselves in taking on any client, because they care little or not at all about the client's goals or viewpoint. Others, accustomed to relying on their own judgment, tend to lean on their own personal values in deciding which clients to represent. This may mean, for example, that the client's willingness to pursue a particular legal goal, or the client's ability to pay, become dominant factors in determining whether to take on a matter.

Once they agree to take on a representation, directive lawyers nod to basic fiduciary duties, but are apt to regard themselves as legal experts capable of determining how to handle the matter with little client consultation. Their

---

7. Of course, this statement vastly oversimplifies the complexity of various philosophies of law, which may shape any lawyer's practice. *See* Gerald B. Wetlaufer, *Systems of Belief in Modern American Law: A View from Century's End*, 49 Am. U. L. Rev. 1 (1999).
8. Professor Wetlaufer includes some legal realists and the proponents of contemporary critical theory in this category and describes these lawyers as generally skeptical about the fairness and legitimacy of the existing order, the possibility of the rule of law, the use of reason, and the use of language to convey stable and determinate meaning. *Id.* at 61-62.
9. Richard Wasserstrom, *Lawyers as Professionals: Some Moral Issues*, 5 Human Rights 1 (1975).

preference for legal solutions may tempt them to underidentify with clients, whom they see as lacking the lawyer's experience and judgment or as too emotionally close to the matter to consider the short- and long-term consequences of their decisions. The lawyer's legal expertise then can generalize and transform into a moral judgment about the proper outcome for a client. Here, the lawyer cedes little authority to the client and the lawyer's values control the representation.

Lawyers who believe they know more than their clients also may find it relatively easy to impose limits on client advocacy. The lawyer's own view of the law and its limits can be seen as an objective datum not subject to argument or modification. Directive lawyers may envision the legal system as a means to promote social order and stability, and the law as the categorization of principles, rules, and procedures that shape client expectations.[10] They may see law as necessary to preserve a relatively thin social fabric that easily could unravel without constant tending by lawyers.

At the same time, focusing on legal outcomes means that the directive lawyer can lose an opportunity to challenge a legal rule or apply it in a different context. More extreme is the tendency to limit client advocacy by imposing the lawyer's own social agenda on the client's matter. Even worse, knowing what is best may be confused with preferring a lawyer's own personal agenda (often a monetary goal) over the client's interests. The client then becomes an object to be used to pursue the lawyer's goals, rather than a subject who deserves individual respect. If this occurs, lawyers who believe they know best can become blind to basic fiduciary duty, which requires them to consult and obey client instructions.

Like the instrumental lawyer, the directive lawyer may assume personality characteristics that permeate the lawyer's life. Directive lawyers who define their role as conciliatory, for example, may pressure a client to settle or compromise when the client wishes to vindicate an important right. Such lawyers also can be judgmental, controlling, even patronizing and overbearing in their professional and personal life. They also may be impatient and have trouble listening to others. Directive lawyers may share the pragmatism of instrumental lawyers, but they often will prefer tangible legal standards to less clearly articulated individual facts or emotional feelings.

Lawyers as Collaborators

The risks that accompany both ends of this spectrum of behavior point to a golden mean that most lawyers adopt most of the time. The lawyer who heeds both fiduciary duty and the limits of the law but steers clear of the instrumental and directive extremes can be characterized as a "collaborator,"[11] "translator,"[12]

---

10. Professor Wetlaufer attributes this view to those he calls "Team Faithful" because of their faith in the fairness and legitimacy of the existing social order. He includes legal formalists, natural law proponents, positivists, as well as the legal process and law and economics schools of thought in this group. Wetlaufer, *supra* note 7, at 61-63, 72.
11. Robert F. Cochran, Jr., John M. A. DiPippa & Martha M. Peteres, *The Counselor-at-Law: A Collaborative Approach to Client Interviewing and Counseling* (2d ed., Lexis-Nexis 2006).
12. Clark D. Cunningham, *The Lawyer as Translator, Representation as Text: Towards an Ethnography of Legal Discourse*, 77 Cornell L. Rev. 1298 (1992).

"wise counselor,"[13] teacher,"[14] "statesman,"[15] or "friend."[16] Collaborative law-yers create enough professional distance to offer objective advice, but foster a relationship that enables the client to articulate the ends and means of the representation. Clients are seen as best able to make decisions for themselves, but need the expertise and perspective of lawyers to consider fully both their own interests as well as the effect of their decisions on others.

Philosophically, this model of the client-lawyer relationship acknowledges both a deontological and a utilitarian view, but also can rely on practical wisdom and a relational ethic of care.[17] Collaborative lawyers adopt a deontological viewpoint because they respect and see it as their duty to promote the individual autonomy of each client. Collaborative lawyers also care about the utilitarian legal and nonlegal consequences of a client representation, both for the client and those that the client might affect. Beyond professional duties and client rights, many collaborative lawyers also exhibit character traits such as empathy and compassion in order to discern the client's full scope of interests. In de-ciding how to proceed, this means that the lawyer weighs heavily the significant obligation to favor the client's interests as articulated by the client.

To enable clients to articulate their interests, collaborative lawyers believe that they should join with clients in the representation, but neither dominate nor be dominated by a client's values. The relationship itself is participatory,[18] deliberative, or collaborative. At the same time, collaborative lawyers care about integrating personal and professional morality, which may lead them to ques-tion, or even challenge, the goals of the representation as well as the client's values. Lawyer and client might even be characterized as friends, who "wrestle with and resolve the moral issues" in the representation.[19] Individual clients should be respected as subjects, not treated as objects, though entity clients may be more objectified.

Lawyers as collaborators recognize the law itself as more than formless process, but less than categorical command. They understand that many legal norms are definitive and may dictate some of the representation. At the same time, they appreciate the fact that applicable legal norms may conflict and that law must be applied to individual circumstances. Overall, they view law as deeply embedded with moral norms that address some of the most significant issues in human existence. They understand and value the contribution of these

---

13. Lon L. Fuller & John D. Randall, *Professional Responsibility: Report of the Joint Conference of the American Bar Association and the Association of American Law School*, 44 ABA J. 1159, 1161 (1958).
14. William F. May, *Beleaguered Rulers: The Public Obligation of the Professional* (Westminster John Knox Press 2001).
15. Anthony T. Kronman, *The Lost Lawyer: Failing Ideals of the Legal Profession* (Harvard 1993).
16. Shaffer & Cochran, *supra* note 5, at 44-54; Stephen R. Morris, *The Lawyer as Friend: An Aristotelian Inquiry*, 26 J. Legal Prof. 55 (2002). Some commentators have used this appellation to describe the instrumental lawyer. *See, e.g.,* Charles H. Fried, *The Lawyer as Friend*, 85 Yale L.J. 1060 (1976), which has been criticized by a number of commentators. *See, e.g.,* Charles J. Ogletree, Jr., *Beyond Justifications: Seeking Motivations to Sustain Public Defenders*, 106 Harv. L. Rev. 1239 (1993); Edward A. Dauer & Arthur A. Leff, *Correspondence, The Lawyer as Friend*, 86 Yale L.J. 573 (1977).
17. *See* Kronman, *supra* note 15, at 40-46; Stephen Ellmann, *The Ethic of Care as an Ethic for Lawyers*, 81 Geo. L.J. 2665 (1993).
18. Douglas E. Rosenthal, *Lawyer and Client: Who's in Charge?* (Russell Sage Found. 1974).
19. Shaffer & Cochran, *supra* note 5, at 42-54.

norms to the social welfare, but remain willing to challenge existing majoritarian interests when those interests do not respect the individual rights of a client. In short, collaborative lawyers seek to act as translators of the moral norms of the law to their clients as well as translators of their client's moral interests back to the legal system.[20]

Collaborative lawyers believe that they assume joint moral accountability with their clients for the representation. They feel free to express their own moral and legal judgment, but remain subject to the client's final determination of which interests to pursue, within the limits or bounds of the law. They attempt to steer clear of directive behavior by focusing on fiduciary duties to their clients, and they try to avoid instrumental tendencies by being aware of the bounds of the law. They listen to clients but also refuse to exclude their own personal values from a client's representation.

In practice, individual lawyers may fall anywhere on a spectrum between instrumental and directive behavior. In fact, conscientious lawyers may find themselves falling at different places on the spectrum not only as to different representations, but during the same representation. Many lawyers borrow from all three models, just as many morally reflective persons rely on a combination of deontological, utilitarian, virtue, and relational moral theories to assess right and wrong. As you study the materials in this book, consider how the lawyers involved characterized their roles. If a lawyer ended up in trouble, think about whether that lawyer's view of his role contributed to the problem. Consider also whether one point of view may be more helpful in some representations, such as litigation or transactional practice, or with some clients, such as individuals or entities. As you assess what the lawyers in these cases and materials did well or poorly, you may be able to begin to formulate your own concept of the kind of relationships you want to establish with your clients.

B. Lawyers and Law

Every other course you take in law school is designed to improve your ability to assist your clients in achieving their goals, by articulating their interests, asserting their rights, and defending their positions. Only in this course are you provided with the tools to recognize your own obligations and professional responsibilities, the limitations on your own conduct, as well as your rights as a lawyer, an officer of the legal system, and a citizen.

Our experience indicates that many legally educated professionals (practicing lawyers and academics) are less than fully aware of some of the most crucial concepts covered in this course. Our purpose is to ensure that this will not be the case for you. As we examine the law governing lawyers, we will encounter two very interesting dimensions. First, the "legal" in legal ethics means that this is a typical law school class, which examines lawyer codes, as well as the application of general law (constitutional, criminal, and civil) to lawyer conduct. Second, the "ethics" in legal ethics indicates that both this

---

20. Cunningham, *supra* note 12.

course and the law governing lawyers addresses moral questions, questions of what is right and wrong.

■ The Law Governing Lawyers: *Sources of Law*

In this series of notes entitled "The Law Governing Lawyers," we consider the substantive standards, remedies, and sanctions embedded in the various strands of law that, taken as a whole, constitute the law governing lawyers. Professional responsibility or legal ethics is the study of what is required for a lawyer to provide a professional service to another. The client simultaneously empowers the lawyer to act and becomes subject to the lawyer's power, which is a function of the lawyer's specialized knowledge and ability to access the legal system. The law governing lawyers regulates this relationship and also creates obligations to the legal system that act as limits on a lawyer's conduct on behalf of a client. The law governing lawyers also provides for a variety of remedies when lawyers violate professional norms.

Sources of Law

The law governing lawyers includes two vast bodies of law, the lawyer codes and general law applied to lawyers. The Restatement (Third) of the Law Governing Lawyers brings together these two bodies of law. Although each body of law imposes its own legal consequences, the lawyer codes and general law applied to lawyers have developed in parallel paths and cross-fertilized each other over the past century. For example, courts often rely on professional code provisions that embody general legal obligations of lawyers (such as fiduciary duty) to create standards of conduct outside of professional discipline (such as malpractice). Similarly, the drafting of lawyer codes has been heavily influenced by a lawyer's common law responsibilities (such as confidentiality and loyalty).

Lawyer Codes Lawyers are the only professional group licensed and controlled by the judicial rather than the legislative branch of government. Lawyer codes are promulgated by the highest state court in each jurisdiction to control lawyer conduct after state licensure. Courts have exercised the power to license and regulate lawyers for several centuries, which includes the prerogative to admit and discipline lawyers, to establish official lawyer codes, to define the practice of law, to require continuing legal education, and to levy monetary assessments to fund bar admission and discipline.[1]

Once a lawyer is admitted to practice, the lawyer code of that jurisdiction applies to that lawyer's conduct.[2] In the past century, the American Bar Association has promulgated various model professional codes and recommended them to the highest courts in each jurisdiction.[3] Each state and federal court in

---

1. Charles W. Wolfram, *Modern Legal Ethics* 22-25 (West 1986).
2. Bar admission authorities appointed by the highest state courts also refer to the lawyer codes in considering the fitness of an applicant to practice law.
3. The American Bar Association is a private organization of lawyers. At any given time, one-third to more than one-half of licensed U.S. lawyers are members.

turn enacted its own version of an official lawyer code, usually in the form of court rules. Violation of a lawyer code provision subjects a lawyer to professional discipline, with sanctions ranging from private or public reprimand, to fines, suspensions, or even permanent disbarment from legal practice.[4] Disciplinary proceedings are usually administrative in nature, require a high burden of proof (clear and convincing evidence), and allow for an appeal to the highest state court.[5]

The idea of a lawyer code began as an annual series of lectures on legal ethics by retired Judge George Sharswood, at the University of Pennsylvania Law School in the mid-nineteenth century.[6] Later publication of his essays influenced the development of the first model professional code, adopted by the ABA in 1908, called the Canons of Professional Ethics ("Canons"). The Canons consisted of largely aspirational standards, and soon was officially adopted by nearly every jurisdiction in this country. The ABA Model Code of Professional Responsibility ("Model Code," or "CPR") superseded the Canons in 1969. Nearly every jurisdiction soon followed the ABA's recommendation, replacing the Canons with the Model Code. The Model Code retained the aspirational language of the Canons in statements called Ethical Considerations, and added black letter mandatory standards, called Disciplinary Rules.

In 1983, the ABA recommended that the Model Rules of Professional Conduct ("Model Rules") replace its Model Code. The Model Rules significantly expanded the provisions of the Model Code and changed its structure to mirror other uniform codes: black letter rules followed by comments. To date, all but a few jurisdictions have adopted some version of the Model Rules, often adding their own amendments. In 1997, the ABA established the Ethics 2000 Commission to update and recommend changes to the Model Rules. The ABA adopted these revisions in 2002; this adoption has prodded the vast majority of jurisdictions to study and update their own professional codes.

The substantive provisions of these various lawyer codes evolved in a slow hundred-year process by applying general legal and moral concepts found in other bodies of law to lawyer behavior. For example, First Amendment principles shaped the law of lawyer advertising and solicitation, the law of agency delineated a lawyer's obligations to avoid conflicts of interest, the evidentiary attorney-client privilege informed duties of confidentiality, contract law dictated some of the law on lawyer fees, and competence duties were borrowed from tort law.

Generally Applicable Law   As courts were adopting and revising lawyer codes, they also were applying general legal concepts and rules to lawyer conduct in an evolving common law process. In civil cases, the common law has been called on to address issues such as fiduciary duties, the formation of a client-lawyer relationship, fee arrangements, malpractice liability for professional errors, and

---

4. *See, e.g., ABA Standards for Imposing Lawyer Sanctions* (1986).
5. *See, e.g., ABA Model Rules for Lawyer Disciplinary Enforcement* (1996).
6. George Sharswood, *An Essay on Professional Ethics* (5th ed., T & J. W. Johnson & Co. 1884). Sharswood's essays were influenced by David Hoffman's "Resolutions in Regard to Professional Deportment" in *A Course of Legal Study Addressed to Students and the Profession Generally* 752-775 (2d ed., J. Neal 1836).

the attorney-client privilege. In criminal cases, the constitutional rights of defendants have shaped prosecutorial obligations of fairness, as well as the standards of competence for defense counsel. Most of these cases sought civil and criminal remedies apart from, and in addition to, professional discipline, such as civil liability, reversal of a criminal conviction, disqualification, and fee forfeiture. In cases that seek these judicial remedies, courts often rely on lawyer codes to assist them in articulating common law principles, and the appropriate standard of behavior in a civil or criminal case. This explains the general rule that violation of a lawyer code provision may be "evidence of breach of the applicable standard of conduct" in a civil suit or other judicial remedy.[7]

Legal Remedies and Sanctions

Professional Discipline   Professional discipline can be imposed for violation of a lawyer code and is probably the most serious consequence a lawyer may suffer, because it involves both the potential loss of a license to practice as well as a loss of professional reputation.[8] Professional disciplinary systems are becoming increasingly well funded and staffed, which increases the number of lawyers disciplined each year.

When lawyers are unsure about the meaning or application of a lawyer code provision, they can ask a local, state, or national bar association for an ethics opinion.[9] Opinions are written by volunteer members of an ethics committee, who issue both informal opinions addressed to a discrete circumstance or lawyer, and formal opinions addressed more broadly to many similarly situated lawyers. Unless written by an official disciplinary agency, ethics opinions are advisory, that is, not binding on courts. However, courts that subsequently disagree with an ethics opinion rarely discipline a lawyer for following the committee's advice.[10]

Judicial Remedies   Beyond discipline, lawyers increasingly worry about other consequences that follow from the breach of obligations to clients, third parties, and tribunals, such as the threat of a malpractice suit, nonclient reliance on an opinion letter, or discovery abuse. Courts recognize a wide array of additional judicial remedies that create new pitfalls for lawyers. For example, lawyers can be held liable in tort to clients for malpractice or breach of fiduciary duty. They are accountable to nonclients for misrepresentation, and can be subject to monetary sanctions for violating procedural rules (such as Federal Rule of Civil Procedure 11 or 26). Moreover, judges now exercise their power to "fire" lawyers representing clients by disqualifying them if the lawyer's conduct threatens to taint a trial process, or enjoining them from continuing representation outside of court. Courts also dismiss claims and defenses, grant new trials, deny the admission of evidence, exercise their contempt power, sanction and fine lawyers, and order fee forfeiture.[11]

---

7. Model Rules, Preamble and Scope ¶20; RLGL §52(2).
8. RLGL §5.
9. *See* Peter A. Joy, *Making Ethics Opinions Meaningful: Towards More Effective Regulation of Lawyer's Conduct*, 15 Geo. J. Leg. Ethics 313 (2002).
10. *See, e.g.,* Morrell v. St., 575 P.2d 1200 (Alaska 1978).
11. RLGL §6.

Multiple Consequences The parallel development and influence of the lawyer codes and general civil and criminal law applied to lawyers can result in multiple legal consequences for the same conduct. For example, because the lawyer codes incorporate some general legal obligations (such as competence or confidentiality) as well as some general legal prohibitions (against fraud or frivolous lawsuits), lawyers who are professionally disciplined also may suffer criminal or civil accountability for the same conduct.[12]

Your Study of the Law Governing Lawyers

Understanding the sources of the law governing lawyers will help you analyze the rest of the problems in this book. In preparing your answers to these problems, notice whether a question asks you about professional discipline or other remedies. If it asks only about professional discipline, then the answer should be found in a lawyer code. The fact that most jurisdictions have enacted some form of the ABA Model Rules of Professional Conduct makes the most recent version of the Model Rules the focus of our study in this course.

Most of the problems in this book will ask more generally whether a lawyer "may" or "should" take a specific action. In that case, you should refer both to the relevant lawyer code sections and to the general law applied to lawyers, including the cases and other materials that follow each set of problems as well as the applicable sections of the Restatement of the Law Governing Lawyers ("RLGL").[13] When you move beyond the lawyer codes, remember that you are examining other legal remedies that might exist, or other consequences that may befall an errant lawyer or law firm, such as civil or criminal liability, litigation sanctions, fee forfeiture, or judicial disqualification.

In seeking legal answers to the problems confronting Martyn & Fox, you will discover that the law governing lawyers, like all law, often embodies moral judgments. You should therefore feel free to question the moral choices that Martyn & Fox lawyers contemplate, as well as the rules that govern their conduct. As the problems in this chapter demonstrate, you also will realize that the

---

12. *E.g.*, In re Halverson, 998 P.2d 833 (Wash. 2000) (lawyer who had sexual relationship with client suspended from practice for six months, five years after he settled a civil suit by the client for a "substantial sum"); People v. Sichta, 948 P.2d 1018 (Colo. 1998) (lawyer convicted of security and wire fraud disbarred); Dodrill v. Exec. Dir., Comm. on Prof. Conduct, 824 S.W.2d 383 (Ark. 1992) (lawyer who filed repeated frivolous complaints and motions in bankruptcy court violated FRCP 11, held in criminal contempt and suspended for one year); In re Perl, 407 N.W.2d 678 (Minn. 1987); Gilchrist v. Perl, 387 N.W.2d 412 (Minn. 1986) (lawyer who employed opposing party's adjuster on other matters suspended from practice for one year and forfeited some or all of $705,000 fee to 128 plaintiffs in *Dalcon Shield* litigation); In re Conway, 301 N.W.2d 253 (Wis. 1981); and Ennis v. Ennis, 276 N.W.2d 341 (Wis. App. 1979) (lawyer who represented wife in divorce against former client/husband disqualified from further representation of wife, denied fee award, and publicly reprimanded).

13. This usage parallels the use of the term "may" in the Multistate Professional Responsibility Examination, where "may" "asks whether the conduct referred to or described in the question is professionally appropriate in that it:"

    a. would not subject the lawyer . . . to discipline; and

    b. is not inconsistent with the Preamble, Comments or text of the ABA Model Rules of Professional Conduct . . . ; and

    c. is not inconsistent with generally accepted principles of the law of lawyering."

law in this course, unlike much of the law you study in law school, directly addresses your own personal concept of what it means to be a lawyer in modern society. In traversing the law governing lawyers and the choices of the lawyers involved in these materials, try to identify the moral discretion inherent both in the rules and in the answers you articulate.

Ultimately, the stories of lawyers that run throughout this book should help you consider whether you wish to follow their examples. We see the law governing lawyers as a map that will help you understand your professional responsibilities and avoid the ethical minefields that await you in law practice. At the same time, we see the "ethics" in legal ethics as an integral part of the lawyer's practical moral wisdom that is essential to make modern law practice meaningful. We hope that as you study the law governing lawyers your explorations also will help you map out the kind of lawyer you want to be.

Chapter 2

Judicial and Professional Regulation of Lawyers

This chapter focuses on two aspects of the inherent power of the judicial branch of government to regulate the practice of law: admission to practice and professional discipline. The last note in Chapter 1 indicated that lawyers are subject to licensure and control by the judicial rather than the legislative branch of government. In some states, constitutions explicitly grant the judicial branch this power to regulate lawyers. In most jurisdictions, courts claim an inherent power to license and regulate lawyers implied from the constitutional recognition of the separation of powers because lawyers are necessary to ensure the proper administration of justice.

Few give a second thought to the special power that a law license provides. Yet, only lawyers can file complaints on behalf of clients, an awesome power that triggers, with no more than the act of the lawyer, the machinery of the system of justice. This includes the start of time limits that require the response of others and ultimately adjudication of the claim, whether for damages, an injunction, incarceration, or even execution of a defendant. Similarly, only lawyers can serve discovery requests requiring others to gather thousands or even millions of documents, answer intrusive interrogatories, or respond to requests for admissions. Equally significant is the power of lawyers to force both parties and party representatives, simply by filing a notice of deposition, to sit for hours or days of testimony under oath in a lawyer's office and to force these witnesses to bring documents with them.

Beyond litigation, only lawyers can provide the legal opinions that a corporation is duly formed, that stock is properly issued and non-assessable, that corporate action is duly authorized, that security interests have been perfected, and the multiple other legal opinions that must be issued every day to permit transactions to be consummated and the wheels of commerce to turn smoothly.

The fact that lawyers exercise all these powers—and others—regularly should not lessen our appreciation of the fact that a law license grants them exclusively to members of our profession.

A. Bar Admission

Problem

2-1. Martyn & Fox represent Mary Moore, who is about to graduate from law school.

(**a**) Should Moore be denied admission to the bar because she included as text, and without attribution, seven direct quotations, three from cases and four from law review articles in a seminar paper in law school?

(**b**) What if Moore pled guilty to drunk driving five years ago and again last year?

(**c**) What if Moore believes in White supremacy and has announced plans to become General Counsel to the KKK Council?

Consider: Model Rules 8.1, 8.4
　　　　　　　Model Code DR 1-101, 1-102

In re Application of Converse
602 N.W.2d 500 (Neb. 1999)

PER CURIAM.

Paul Raymond Converse appeals a decision of the Nebraska State Bar Commission (Commission) denying his request to take the July 1998 Nebraska bar examination. For the reasons that follow, we affirm the decision of the Commission. . . .

[As part of the application process, Converse's law school dean certified that he had completed law school and checked "yes" when asked whether the BAR Examiners should inquire further regarding his moral character, which triggered a Commission hearing revealing the following facts.] After he received a grade he believed to be unjustified by his performance in the appellate advocacy course, Converse wrote letters to May and to the USD law school dean, Barry Vickrey, requesting assistance with an appeal of that grade. In addition to writing letters to Vickrey and May, Converse also sent a letter to the South Dakota

Supreme Court regarding the appellate advocacy course professor's characterization of his arguments, with indications that carbon copies of the letter were sent to two well-known federal court of appeals judges. . . . Despite all such correspondence, Converse testified at the hearing that no formal appeal of the grievance was ever filed. Converse's grade was never adjusted.

The evidence showed that following the grade "appeal," Converse prepared a memorandum and submitted it to his classmates, urging them to recall an "incident" in which yet another professor lashed out at him in class, and to be cognizant of the image that incident casts "on [that professor's] core professionalism" prior to completing class evaluations. Converse also wrote a letter to a newspaper in South Dakota, the Sioux Falls Argus Leader, regarding a proposed fee increase at the USD law school. Converse immediately began investigating the salaries of USD law professors and posted a list of selected professors' salaries on the student bulletin board, as well as writing a letter that accused Vickrey of trying to pull a "fast one."

Converse's next altercation at the USD law school involved a photograph of a nude female's backside that he displayed in his study carrel in the USD law library. The picture was removed by a law librarian. In response to the removal of this photograph, Converse contacted the American Civil Liberties Union (ACLU) and received a letter indicating that his photograph might be a protected expression under the First Amendment. Once again, Converse went to the student newspaper to alert the student body of the actions of the law school authorities, accusing them of unconstitutional censorship.

Converse redisplayed the photograph once it was returned by the law librarians. Vickrey received several complaints about the photograph from other students, classifying Converse's behavior as "unprofessional and inappropriate." Upon Converse's redisplay of the photograph, Vickrey sent him a memorandum explaining that the picture would not be removed only because Vickrey did not want to involve the school in controversy during final examinations. Converse testified that he redisplayed the photograph in order to force the alleged constitutional issue. . . .

The Commission also heard testimony regarding Converse's attempt to obtain an internship with the U.S. Attorney's office in South Dakota. Converse arranged for the internship on his own, only to have his request subsequently rejected by the law

[handwritten note: Focus on problems / Research Guide / Bloomberg]

his denial, ... ent to all of ... members. ...verse's in... ecause he ... law school's procedures regarding internships. Converse then contacted the chairperson of the law school committee of the South Dakota State Bar Association with his complaint, expressly referring to Vickrey as being "arrogant." There is no indication of a response from the chairperson in the record.

The issue next considered by the Commission was that of various litigation threatened by Converse. Converse indicated that he would "likely" be filing a lawsuit against Vickrey for violations of his First Amendment rights. Converse was also involved in a dispute with other law students, in which he threatened to file a lawsuit and warned the students that all lawsuits in which they were involved would need to be reported to proper authorities when they applied to take a bar examination. Further, Converse posted signs on the bulletin board at the law school denouncing a professor, in response to the way in which Converse's parking appeal was handled, and then went to the student newspaper to criticize the process and those involved in that appeal.

One of the final issues addressed by the Commission in its hearing was that of a T-shirt Converse produced and marketed on which a nude caricature of Vickrey is shown sitting astride what appears to be a large hot dog. The cartoon on the shirt also contains the phrase "Astride the Peter Principle," which Converse claims connotes the principle that Vickrey had been promoted past his level of competence; however, Converse admits that the T-shirt could be construed to have certain sexual overtones. Converse admitted that the creation of this T-shirt would not be acceptable behavior for a lawyer.

In response to not being allowed to post signs and fliers at the law school, Converse sent a memo to all law students in which he noted to his fellow students that his "Deanie on a Weenie" T-shirts were in stock. In that same memo, Converse included a note to his schoolmates:

> So far 4 causes of action have arisen, courtesy Tricky Vickrey. [He then listed what he believed the causes of action to be.] When you pass the SD Bar, if you want to earn some atty [sic] fees, get hold of me and we can go for one of these. I've kept evidence, of course.

Vickrey asked Converse not to wear his T-shirt to his graduation ceremony, and Converse decided that "it would be a better choice in [his] life not to go to that commencement." Converse acknowledges that Vickrey's request was made in a civil manner.

The evidence also revealed that prior to law school, Converse, in his capacity as a landlord, sued a tenant for nonpayment of rent and referred to the tenant as a "fucking welfare bitch." At the hearing, in response to questioning from the Commission, Converse testified at great length as to how he tends to personally attack individuals when he finds himself embroiled in a controversy.

After the Commission notified Converse on December 18, 1998, that he would not be allowed to sit for the Nebraska bar examination, Converse appealed the adverse determination to this court. . . .

Converse first assigns as error that the Commission's determination should not stand because it is based in large part upon speech that is protected by the First Amendment. In Konigsberg v. State Bar, 366 U.S. 36 (1961), the bar applicant argued that when the California bar commission forced him to either answer questions about his affiliation with the Communist Party or to face the repercussions of not being certified as possessing the required moral character to sit for the bar, the commission violated his First Amendment rights. The Supreme Court disagreed, [and] . . . balanced the effect of allowing such questions against the need for the state to do a complete inquiry into the character of an applicant and concluded that questions about membership would not chill association to the extent of harm caused by striking down the screening process. The Court held that requiring the applicant to answer the questions was not an infringement of the applicant's First Amendments rights. . . .

Converse conceded at oral argument that the Commission's decision cannot be based solely on an applicant's exercise of First Amendment freedoms but that it is proper for the Commission to go behind the exercise of those freedoms and consider an applicant's moral character. That is exactly what was done by the Commission in the instant case. An investigation of Converse's moral character is not a proceeding in which the applicant is being prosecuted for conduct arguably protected by the First Amendment, but, rather, "an investigation of the conduct of [an applicant] for the purpose of determining whether he shall be [admitted]." . . .

Were we to adopt the position asserted by Converse in this case, the Commission would be limited to conducting only cursory investigations of an applicant's moral character and past conduct. [I]n Law Students Research Council v. Wadmond, 401 U.S. 154 (1971), [the majority], noted that the implications of such an attack on a bar screening process are that no screening process would be constitutionally permissible beyond academic examination and an extremely minimal check for serious, concrete character deficiencies. "The principal means of policing the Bar would then be the deterrent and punitive effects of such post-admission sanctions as contempt, disbarment, malpractice suits, and criminal prosecutions." . . .

We conclude that the Commission properly considered Converse's conduct as it reflects upon his moral character, even if such conduct might have been protected by the First Amendment. . . .

Converse next contends that the Commission violated his due process rights by not making him aware of all of the "charges" against him in these proceedings. . . .

There is no question that "[a] state can require high standards of qualification, such as good moral character or proficiency in its law, before it admits an applicant to the bar. . . ." Schware v. Bd. of Bar Examiners, 353 U.S. 232, 239 (1957). The Court has also stated that it must be "kept clearly in mind . . . that an applicant for admission to the bar bears the burden of proof of 'good moral character' a requirement whose validity is not, nor could well be, drawn in question here." Konigsberg v. St. Bar, 366 U.S. 36, 40-41 (1961). "If at the conclusion of the proceedings the

evidence of good character and that of bad character are found in even balance, the State may refuse admission. . . ."

With that in mind, we commence our analysis with the standards for moral character required for admission to the Nebraska bar as set out in our rules governing the admission of attorneys. Neb. Ct. R. for Adm. of Attys. 3 (rev. 1998) governs this situation, which provides in pertinent part:

An attorney should be one whose record of conduct justifies the trust of clients, adversaries, courts, and others with respect to the professional duties owed to them. A record manifesting a significant deficiency by an applicant in one or more of the following essential eligibility requirements for the practice of law may constitute a basis for denial of admission. In addition to the admission requirements otherwise established by these Rules, the essential eligibility requirements for admission to the practice of law in Nebraska are:

(a) The ability to conduct oneself with a high degree of honesty, integrity, and trustworthiness in all professional relationships and with respect to all legal obligations; . . .

(c) The ability to conduct oneself with respect for and in accordance with the law and the Code of Professional Responsibility; . . .

(j) The ability to conduct oneself professionally and in a manner that engenders respect for the law and the profession.

Under rule 3, Converse must prove that his past conduct is in conformity with the standards set forth by this court, and the record in this case compels the conclusion that he has failed to do so.

We considered an appeal of a similarly situated bar applicant in In re Appeal of Lane, 544 N.W.2d 367 (Neb. 1996). *Lane* involved an individual seeking readmission to the Nebraska bar whose past included confrontations with law school faculty, the use of strong and profane language with fellow students at his bar review course, the use of intimidating and rude conduct directed at a security guard at the place where he was taking his bar review course, and some controversial interactions with females. We held that, taken together, "these incidents show that Lane is prone to turbulence, intemperance, and irresponsibility, characteristics which are not acceptable in one who would be a counselor and advocate in the legal system," and we upheld the denial of his application.

We explained in . . . *Lane* that the "requisite restraint in dealing with others is obligatory conduct for attorneys because 'the efficient and orderly administration of justice cannot be successfully carried on if we allow attorneys to engage in unwarranted attacks on the court [or] opposing counsel. . . . Furthermore, " 'an attorney who exhibits [a] lack of civility, good manners and common courtesy . . . tarnishes   the . . . image of . . . the   bar. . . .' " . . . We   held in . . . *Lane* that "abusive, disruptive, hostile, intemperate, intimidating, irresponsible, threatening, or turbulent behavior is a proper basis for the denial of admission to the bar." . . .

The evidence in this case shows that Converse's numerous disputes and personal attacks indicate a "pattern and a way of life which appear to be [Converse's] normal reaction to opposition and disappointment." *See Lane*. The totality of the evidence clearly establishes that Converse possesses an inclination to personally attack those with whom he has disputes.

Such inclinations "are not acceptable in one who would be a counselor and advocate in the legal system."

In addition to Converse's tendency to personally attack those individuals with whom he has disputes, his pattern of behavior indicates an additional tendency to do so in arenas other than those specifically established within the legal system. This tendency is best exemplified by observing Converse's conduct in situations where there were avenues through which Converse could have and should have handled his disputes, but instead chose to mount personal attacks on those with whom he had disputes through letters and barrages in the media. . . .

Converse is 48 years old, and his actions cannot be excused as isolated instances of youthful indiscretions.

Taken together with the other incidents previously discussed, the evidence clearly shows that Converse is prone to turbulence, intemperance, and irresponsibility; characteristics which are not acceptable in one seeking admission to the Nebraska bar. . . . In light of Converse's admission that such conduct would be inappropriate were he already an attorney, we reiterate that we will not tolerate conduct by those applying for admission to the bar that would not be tolerated were that person already an attorney. Furthermore, Converse has consistently exhibited a tendency to cause disruption and then go to some arena outside the field of law to settle the dispute, often to an arena not specifically designed for dispute resolution. . . .

The record before us reflects that the Commission conducted such an inquiry and, at the conclusion thereof, correctly determined that Converse possessed a moral character inconsistent with one "dedicated to the peaceful and reasoned settlement of disputes," see 401 U.S. at 166, but, rather, more consistent with someone who wishes to go outside the field of law and settle disputes by mounting personal attacks and portraying himself as the victim and his opponent as the aggressor. Such disruptive, hostile, intemperate, threatening, and turbulent conduct certainly reflects negatively upon those character traits the applicant must prove prior to being admitted to the Nebraska bar, such as honesty, integrity, reliability, and trustworthiness.

The result might have been different if Converse had exhibited only a "single incident of rudeness or lack of professional courtesy," see In re Snyder, 472 U.S. 634, 647 (1985), but such is simply not the case. The record clearly establishes that he seeks to resolve disputes not in a peaceful manner, but by personally attacking those who oppose him in any way and then resorting to arenas outside the field of law to publicly humiliate and intimidate those opponents. Such a pattern of behavior is incompatible with what we have required to be obligatory conduct for attorneys, as well as for applicants to the bar.

Converse has exhibited a clear lack of self-restraint and lack of judgment, and our de novo review of the record leads us to independently conclude that Converse has exhibited such a pattern of acting in a hostile and disruptive manner as to render him unfit for the practice of law in Nebraska. We conclude that the Commission's determination to deny Converse's application was correct. . . .

▨ Lawyers and Other Professionals: *Professional Licensure*

In this series of notes entitled "Lawyers and Other Professionals," we will examine the legal restraints on various groups of professionals, comparing the law governing lawyers with similar bodies of law that regulate other professionals, such as health care providers, accountants, design professionals, and mental health practitioners (psychiatrists, psychologists, and counselors).

Professionals control and influence nearly every aspect of modern life. Most commentators agree that three features identify a professional. Professionals (a) "profess" a body of knowledge, (b) provide a valuable social service to someone else, and (c) are subject to the standards of that professional group of colleagues.[1] Professionals are distinguished from technicians by their level of knowledge and required study and their internal professional standards designed to serve the public.[2]

---

1. William M. Sullivan et al., *Educating Lawyers: Preparation for the Practice of Law* 21 (John Wiley & Sons 2007); William F. May, *Beleaguered Rulers: The Public Obligation of the Professional* 7 (Westminster John Knox Press 2001).
2. This may explain why courts addressing the issue of whether a defendant is a professional now generally agree that nurses qualify, but are less sure about social workers, teachers, and funeral directors. *See* Frank J. Cavico and Nancy M. Cavico, *The Nursing Profession in the 1990's: Negligence and Malpractice Liability*, 43 Clev. St. L. Rev. 557 (1995); Michael J. Polelle, *Who's On First, and What's a Professional?* 33 U.S.F. L. Rev. 205 (1999). *See also* Steven Mark Levy, *Liability of the Art Expert for Professional Malpractice*, 1991 Wis. L. Rev. 595.

Most professionals are licensed by state legislation, which often creates an administrative agency to manage professional licensure according to statutory criteria. Lawyers, however, are the only professionally licensed group regulated by the judicial branch of government. The highest state court in each jurisdiction sets licensing criteria through court rules and administers bar admission through designated administrative agencies or bar associations.

Becoming a Licensed Professional

In the past century, professionals have become licensed by state laws designed to admit those qualified to practice and to exclude all others. State statutes define the scope of practice for most professionals, and typically make unlicensed practice a crime.[3] All professional groups have used professional licensing as a means to limit competition.[4] For lawyers, unauthorized practice committees established by state courts have official power to bring legal actions for injunctive relief against laypersons engaged in unlicensed practice. State administrative agencies charged with licensing other professional groups have similar authority to bring administrative actions against those who practice without licensure.[5]

Most state licensure provisions require that a person who seeks a professional license satisfy at least three criteria: age, education, and/or experience, and examination.[6] In addition, some professions in some jurisdictions add a fourth requirement discussed in *Converse* that applies to all lawyers: good moral character.[7] Further, unlike other professionals, lawyers also are required to take an oath.

For lawyers, *Converse* illustrates that bar applicants bear the burden of proving the requisite character and fitness. Most courts apply criteria like those relied on in *Converse,* including honesty, respect for law, and the ability to act professionally. To facilitate consideration of character, applicants are required to complete a lengthy questionnaire that canvasses relevant topics related to these criteria. For example, concerns about an ability to act honestly may be evidenced by a criminal record, academic misconduct, or neglect of professional

---

3. Because lawyers are licensed by the judicial branch, definitions of the practice of law typically are found in court opinions. *See, e.g.,* Birbrower, Montalbano, Condon & Frank P.C. v. Superior Court, *infra* p. 535.

4. *See, e.g.,* In re Guess, 393 S.E.2d 833 (N.C. 1990) (physician who practiced homeopathic medicine disciplined for engaging in unprofessional conduct). *But see* N.C. Gen. Stat. §90-14(6) (2007) ("The Board shall not revoke the license of or deny a license to a person solely because of that person's practice of a therapy that is experimental, nontraditional, or that departs from acceptable and prevailing medical practices unless, by competent evidence, the Board can establish that the treatment has a safety risk greater than the prevailing treatment or that the treatment is generally not effective.").

5. *E.g.,* St. Bd. of Nursing v. Ruebke, 913 P.2d 142 (Kan. 1996) (lay midwife not engaged in unauthorized practice of nursing or medicine); Hunter v. St., 676 A.2d 968 (Md. 1996) (lay midwife engaged in unauthorized practice of nursing).

6. For descriptions of Federal and State professional licensing requirements, *see* David P. Bianco, ed., *Professional and Occupational Licensing Directory* (2d ed., Gale Research Inc. 1996).

7. *E.g.,* Ga. Code §43-3-6 (2007) (CPAs); 225 Ill. C. S. §25/11 (2007) (Dentists); 32 Me. R. S. §13732 (2007) (Pharmacists); N.J. Stat. §45:11-26 (2007) (Nurses); 59 Okla. Stat. §46.24 (2007) (Architects); 26 Vt. Stat. §1391 (2007) (Physicians).

or financial obligations.[8] Bar examiners treat any lack of candor in the bar admission application itself as equally serious.[9] The ability to act professionally in a manner that engenders respect for law and the profession may be evidenced by letters of reference, reports of law school administrators, or by the absence of a history of drug or alcohol dependence or mental illness, or successful treatment for these conditions.[10]

In deciding whether an applicant has met the necessary criteria, most courts look at how these factors predict future ability to practice. They also consider whether past conduct would have violated a professional code requirement if the candidate had been licensed at the time. If so, the applicant usually will not succeed in showing the requisite character and fitness to practice law.[11] Most obvious are prior criminal convictions, where applicants must show rehabilitation to be admitted.[12] Less obvious are troubling patterns of behavior, like those in *Converse*, which indicate disruptive characteristics that probably will cause future trouble with clients, opponents, and tribunals.[13]

Converse also illustrates how courts respond when confronted with First Amendment challenges. The court relied on a series of cases that held that bar admissions officials may ask about membership in specific associations, as long as it is relevant to fitness to practice. For example, Communist Party membership may indicate a shared belief specifically contrary to a lawyer's ability to represent

---

8. *E.g.,* In re Application of Chapman, 630 N.E.2d 322 (Ohio 1994) (consent decree in civil action by State Attorney General against bar applicant alleging deceptive and unconscionable sales practices in connection with a business demonstrated recent pattern of highly questionable and outright illegal behavior that justified rejection of bar applicant; renewed application that would demonstrate substantial change in applicant's conduct may allow for admission at a later date).
9. *E.g.,* Radtke v. Bd. of Bar Examrs., 601 N.W.2d 642 (Wis. 1999) (lawyer who misstated material fact on his bar application about his earlier plagiarism did not satisfy character and fitness requirement).
10. *E.g.,* In re Ralls, 849 N.E.2d 36 (Ohio 2006) (two DUI convictions during law school combined with failure to accept responsibility for alcohol abuse precluded applicant from admission until he demonstrated sustained period of compliance with alcohol treatment programs); In re Covington, 50 P.3d 233 (Or. 2002) (three years of sobriety not enough time to establish that applicant's past abuse of drugs and alcohol would not recur).
11. *E.g.,* In re Mustafa, 631 A.2d 45 (D.C. App. 1993) (because applicant's conduct by a lawyer would have resulted in disbarment for at least five years, applicant should wait for a similar period of time from proven misconduct before good moral character can be established).
12. Courts look to the timing, number, and nature of the convictions as well as the applicant's recognition of the wrongfulness of the conduct and change in behavior over a period of time since the criminal activity. In re R.M.W., 428 F. Supp. 2d 389 (D. Md. 2006) (adopting uniform procedure and criteria for applicants with prior criminal convictions); In re Hamm, 123 P.3d 652 (Ariz. 2005) (no person ever convicted of first degree murder has been able to make the extraordinary showing of good moral character for bar admission); In re Prager, 661 N.E.2d 84 (Mass. 1996) (sixteen years of marijuana use, international smuggling, and living as a fugitive not outweighed by seven years of a credible work history, successful completion of probation and law school, but applicant could reapply in five years).
13. For a case where a lawyer was disbarred for conduct strikingly similar to Converse's, *see* Off. of Disc. Counsel v. Baumgartner, 796 N.E.2d 495 (Ohio 2003) (lawyer who "repeatedly harmed her client's interests, manipulated the legal system, and publicly accused dozens of people of criminal wrongdoing" and whose "actions were done as a means to retaliate against anyone who defied her" disbarred). *See also* Grievance Adminstr. v. Fieger, 719 N.W.2d 123 (Mich. 2006), *cert. denied*, 127 S. Ct. 1257 (2007) (lawyer who castigated appellate judges in radio broadcasts, calling them Nazis and "three jackass Court of Judges," and announcing that they deserved anal violation publicly reprimanded).

clients in this country's legal and political institutions.[14] On the other hand, a question that asks candidates to list memberships in all organizations during law school is overbroad and not rationally related to the ability to practice law.[15]

These Supreme Court decisions also shaped the analysis of the Illinois Bar's Committee on Character and Fitness in the case of bar applicant Matthew Hale. Hale readily admitted that he headed an organization called the World Church of the Creator, which did not sanction violence, but called for white racial supremacy and the use of political power to provide for the deportation of all other races, including Jews, blacks, and other "mud races" so that the United States could then become a "white race" only country. He claimed he would follow the law until he could change it by peaceable means. A hearing panel correctly focused on Hale's conduct, rather than his beliefs, denying him admission because he had admitted he would follow the Rules of Professional Conduct "only when he felt like it." They held that he was "absolutely entitled to his beliefs, but at the same time the public and the bar are entitled to be treated fairly and decently by attorneys."[16]

The Supreme Court has invalidated two licensure requirements states used to impose, citizenship and residency, on constitutional grounds. It first barred citizenship requirements for lawyers on Equal Protection grounds. The state could not prove a compelling interest that would overcome the strict scrutiny required by the Fourteenth Amendment to protect resident aliens.[17] The Court explained that lawyers, while "officers of the court," are not state officers in any political sense, simply "by virtue of being lawyers."[18] The Court subsequently relied on this precedent to overturn citizenship requirements for notaries public,[19] engineers,[20] and real estate brokers.[21] At the same time, citizenship requirements for probation officers,[22] state police,[23] and public

---

14. Law Students Civ. Rights Research Council, Inc. v. Wadmond, 401 U.S. 154 (1971) (upholding an inquiry into whether the applicant specifically intended to further an organization's advocacy of violent overthrow of the government while a member of the organization.); Schware v. Bd. of Bar Examrs. of N.M., 353 U.S. 232, 246-247 (1957) (Communist Party membership prior to WWII could not be used as the basis to infer moral unfitness to practice law because such past membership had no rational connection to evil purposes or illegal conduct); Konigsberg v. St. Bar of Cal., 366 U.S. 36, 52 (1961) (state can inquire about current Communist Party membership and can deny bar admission to an applicant who refused to answer, because of the state's interest "in having lawyers who are devoted to the law in its broadest sense, including . . . its procedures for orderly change").
15. Baird v. St. Bar of Ariz., 401 U.S. 1 (1971) (overturning a general inquiry not connected to knowing membership); In re Stolar, 401 U.S. 23 (1971).
16. W. Bradley Wendel, *Free Speech for Lawyers*, 28 Hastings Const. L.Q. 305 (2001). The Illinois Supreme Court refused to hear the case on appeal, but one justice dissented, characterizing Hale's conduct as "open advocacy of racially obnoxious belief." In re Hale, 723 N.E.2d 206 (Ill. 1999), *cert. denied sub nom.* Hale v. Comm. on Character and Fitness of the Ill. Bar, 530 U.S. 1261 (2000). Since being denied bar admission, Hale has been convicted of soliciting the murder of a federal judge. Natasha Korecki & Frank Main, *Supremacist Gets 40 Yrs.; Hale Given Maximum for Trying to Have Judge Murdered*, Chicago Sun-Times (Apr. 7, 2005).
17. In re Griffiths, 413 U.S. 717 (1973).
18. *Id.* at 729.
19. Bernal v. Fainter, 467 U.S. 216 (1984).
20. Examining Bd. of Engrs., Architects & Surveyors v. Flores de Otero, 426 U.S. 572 (1976).
21. Ind. Real Est. Commn. v. Satoskar, 417 U.S. 938 (1974).
22. Cabell v. Chavez-Salido, 454 U.S. 432 (1982).
23. Foley v. Connelie, 435 U.S. 291 (1978).

school teachers,[24] designed to serve political rather than economic functions, have been upheld.

The Supreme Court also has overturned residency requirements, under the privileges and immunities clause in Art. IV, §2 of the Constitution, concluding that the state could require lawyers to be familiar with local law, obey the jurisdiction's professional codes, participate in pro bono work, or be available to appear in court, but could not use residency as a surrogate for such restrictions.[25] The same principles were applied to federal court residency requirements in *Frazier v. Heebe*, where the Court exercised its inherent power to invalidate a local district court residency requirement.[26] Similar residency requirements have been overturned in cases involving engineers,[27] pharmacists,[28] real estate brokers,[29] and construction workers.[30]

The net result of these decisions is that states remain free to impose admission requirements on residents and non-residents alike, as long as the prerequisites do not favor resident lawyers. So, for example, the Third Circuit has upheld New Jersey's requirement that both resident and non-resident lawyers maintain a local bona fide office and attend continuing legal education courses.[31] Several courts also have upheld similar prerequisites to *pro hac vice* admissions (a tribunal's permission to represent a client in one particular matter).[32]

Maintaining a Professional License

Once qualified for a professional license, professionals become subject to additional state licensure provisions and are subject to professional discipline for violating relevant statutory or administrative standards. For lawyers regulated by the judicial branch of government, these standards are embodied in official court rules adopted by the highest state court.

Common grounds for professional discipline in other professions generally parallel those found in lawyer codes: incompetence, conviction of a crime, or other "unprofessional conduct."[33] Some states add specific offenses relevant to a particular practice, such as unlawful sale of drugs, impairment due to substance

---

24. Quintero de Quintero v. Aponte-Roque, 974 F.2d 226 (1st Cir. 1992).
25. Piper v. S. Ct. of N.H., 470 U.S. 274 (1985). *See also* Barnard v. Thorstenn, 489 U.S. 546 (1989) (invalidating similar residency requirements in the Virgin Islands); S. Ct. of Va. v. Friedman, 487 U.S. 59 (1988) (invalidating residency requirements as a condition of admission on motion).
26. 482 U.S. 641 (1987).
27. Tetra Techs. Inc. v. Harter, 823 F. Supp. 1116 (S.D.N.Y. 1993).
28. Natl. Pharms. Inc. v. De Melecio, 51 F. Supp. 2d 45 (D.P.R. 1999).
29. Baker v. MacLay Props. Co., 648 So. 2d 888 (La. 1995).
30. A.L. Blades & Sons v. Yerusalim, 121 F.3d 865 (3d Cir. 1997).
31. Tolchin v. S. Ct. of N.J., 111 F.3d 1099 (3d Cir. 1997), *cert. denied*, 522 U.S. 977 (1997).
32. *See, e.g.,* Paciulan v. George, 229 F.3d 1226 (9th Cir. 2000) (residents not admitted to the bar not allowed to appear *pro hac vice*); Mowrer v. Warner-Lambert Co., 1998 U.S. Dist. LEXIS 12746 (E.D. Pa. 1998) (local counsel of record required for *pro hac vice* admission); Parnell v. S. Ct. of App., 926 F. Supp. 570 (N.D. W. Va. 1996) (lawyer admitted in the state must maintain office in the state to qualify as "responsible local attorney" to support another lawyer's *pro hac vice* admission).
33. Barry R. Furrow et al., *Health Law* 82 (2d ed., West 2000).

abuse, commission of child abuse or neglect, or failure to report an adverse malpractice judgment or settlement to the licensing agency.[34]

Occasionally, lawyers and other professionals have challenged broad disciplinary rules as being void for vagueness. Courts have generally upheld these provisions, including competency standards,[35] prohibitions against sexual abuse,[36] "habitual intemperance,"[37] as well as statutory definitions of practice such as "nurse midwifery."[38] Lawyers have been equally unsuccessful in challenging for vagueness lawyer code provisions such as Model Rule 8.4(d) (conduct prejudicial to the administration of justice).[39]

Both medicine and law have developed national practitioner databases to assure that any change in licensure in one jurisdiction will be reported to another. For physicians and dentists, Congress established the National Practitioner Data Bank, which has provided this information to hospitals and state licensing boards since 1990.[40] For lawyers, the American Bar Association has created a similar National Discipline Data Bank, which provides reciprocal discipline information to disciplinary and bar admission officials. Like the physician data bank, the lawyer data base is available only to officials charged with bar admissions and discipline and may not be used by others.[41]

Finally, like lawyers, other professionals have relied on the Americans with Disabilities Act to force accommodations in both admission and discipline, such as those discussed in *Busch* in the next section of this chapter. Consistent with

---

34. *Id.* at 82-83.
35. *E.g.*, Braun v. Bd. of Dental Examrs., 702 A.2d 124 (Vt. 1997) (statute that prohibits delegating "diagnosis, treatment planning and prescription" to persons other than licensed dentists not void for vagueness); Rathle v. Grote, 584 F. Supp. 1128 (M.D. Ala. 1984) (statute that prohibited "practicing medicine . . . in such a manner as to endanger the health of the patients of the practitioner" not void for vagueness).
36. *E.g.*, Haley v. Med. Disc. Bd., 818 P.2d 1062 (Wash. 1991) (statute that prohibits "the commission of an act of moral turpitude, dishonesty or corruption relating to the practice of person's profession, whether the act constitutes a crime or not. . . ." not void for vagueness as applied to physician who had a sexual relationship with a former patient who was a minor); Adams v. Tex. St. Bd. of Chiropractic Examrs., 744 S.W.2d 648 (Tex. App. 1988) (statute that prohibits "grossly unprofessional conduct or dishonorable conduct likely to deceive or defraud the public" not void for vagueness as applied to chiropractor who engaged in sexual misconduct with patients).
37. Colo. St. Bd. of Med. Examrs. v. Hoffner, 832 P.2d 1062 (Colo. 1992).
38. St. v. Kimpel, 665 So. 2d 990 (Ala. Crim. App. 1995); People v. Rosburg, 805 P.2d 432 (Colo. 1991) ("midwife" not unconstitutionally vague).
39. Fla. Bar v. Zamft, 814 So. 2d 385 (Fla. 2002) (ex parte communication with a judge by a lawyer who did not represent either party in the matter); In re Stanbury, 561 N.W.2d 507 (Minn. 1997) (refusing to pay a law-related judgment and make payment on a court filing fee); In re Stuhff, 837 P.2d 853 (Nev. 1992) (intentionally interfering with sentencing of a criminal defendant by filing a disciplinary complaint against a judge just before the sentencing hearing); In re Haws, 801 P.2d 818 (Or. 1990) (failure to respond to bankruptcy trustee's inquiry and disciplinary complaint); St. of Neb. ex rel. Neb. Bar Assn. v. Kirshen, 441 N.W.2d 161 (Neb. 1989) (failing to respond to bar complaint and properly supervise office staff); In re Jones, 534 A.2d 336 (D.C. App. 1987) (failure to respond to inquiries of bar counsel).
40. 42 U.S.C. §§11101-11152 (2000); 45 C.F.R. §§60.1-60.14 (2003). Hospitals are required to report adverse actions regarding institutional privileges, licensure agencies are required to report most disciplinary outcomes, and insurers must report adverse settlements or judgments over $10,000. 42 U.S.C. at §11131.
41. ABA Recommendations for the Evaluation of Disc. Enforcement, Recommendation 20 (1992).

Busch, courts have found a judicial nominating commission[42] as well as state licensing boards subject to Title II of the ADA.[43] Health care professionals also have raised ADA claims (though often deemed to be without merit) against public professional schools,[44] residency programs,[45] and public hospitals in disputes over staff privileges.[46]

The Future

Lawyers have led the way in successfully challenging both citizenship and residency licensure requirements. Two trends in other professions, especially medicine, may have some future influence on lawyers as well. As specialization has grown, physicians have moved to national specialty exams, though licensing has remained a state prerogative. Some predict similar trends toward national specialization for lawyers.[47] At the same time, related health care professionals, such as nurse practitioners, osteopaths, and chiropractors, have sought related and separate licensing to distinguish and legitimate their own practice.[48] Lawyers are working out similar boundary issues with accountants and real estate brokers.[49] Some foresee similar turf battles for lawyers, including professional licensure for lay legal practitioners, such as paralegals or court clerks.[50]

B. Professional Discipline

Problems

2-2. Fox meets his close friend and law school roommate, Prosecutor, for dinner. Prosecutor tells Fox that he's just learned he has only months to live before he dies of colon cancer. After several drinks, he also confides that two years ago he suppressed exculpatory blood evidence in order to obtain a murder conviction. What should Fox do?

2-3. Martyn & Fox are successor counsel for Client, and discover that Client's former lawyer stole client's money from his trust account. What should Martyn & Fox recommend?

2-4. Martyn discovers that an associate in the firm has been charging clients for phantom travel expenses, thereby generating money that he has used to fund a gambling addiction. Martyn tells Fox she has investigated, the associate has repaid the money, and the associate has joined Gamblers Anonymous. Should Fox accept that solution?

---

42. Doe v. Jud. Nominating Commn., 906 F. Supp. 1534 (S.D. Fla. 1995).
43. *E.g.,* Hason v. Med. Bd., 279 F.3d 1167 (9th Cir. 2002) (denial of license to practice medicine); Firman v. Dept. of St., 697 A.2d 291 (Pa. Commonwealth 1997) (revocation of nursing and midwifery licenses).
44. *E.g.,* Darian v. U. of Mass., 980 F. Supp. 77 (D. Mass. 1997) (nursing student); Wong v. Regents of the Univ. of Cal., 192 F.3d 807 (9th Cir. 1999) (medical student).
45. Swanson v. Univ. of Cin., 268 F.3d 307 (6th Cir. 2001).
46. Menkowitz v. Pottstown Meml. Med. Ctr., 154 F.3d 113 (3d Cir. 1998).
47. *See, e.g.,* Fred C. Zacharias, *Reform or Professional Responsibility as Usual: Whither the Institutions of Regulation and Discipline?* 2003 Ill. L. Rev. 1505, 1519-1521.
48. *E.g.,* Sermchief v. Gonzales, 660 S.W.2d 683 (Mo. 1983) (legislative revision of nursing practice act immunizes nurse practitioners from charges of unauthorized practice of medicine).
49. Katherine D. Black & Stephen T. Black, *A National Tax Bar: An End to the Attorney-Accountant Tax Turf War,* 36 St. Mary's L.J. 1 (2004).
50. *Id.;* Deborah L. Rhode, *Access to Justice* 189-191 (Oxford U. Press 2004).

Consider: Model Rules 1.6, 3.8, 5.1, 8.3, 8.4
Model Code DR 1-102, 1-103, 4-101, 7-103
RLGL §5

ABA *Formal Opinion 04-433*
American Bar Association Standing Committee on Ethics and Professional Responsibility

OBLIGATION OF A LAWYER TO REPORT PROFESSIONAL MISCONDUCT BY A LAWYER NOT ENGAGED IN THE PRACTICE OF LAW

A lawyer having knowledge of the professional misconduct of another licensed lawyer, including a non-practicing lawyer, is obligated under Model Rule 8.3 to report such misconduct if it raises a substantial question as to that lawyer's honesty, trustworthiness, or fitness as a lawyer. The professional misconduct must be reported even if it involves activity completely removed from the practice of law. If the report would require revealing the confidential information of a client, the lawyer must obtain the client's informed consent before making the report.

This opinion explores a lawyer's duty under the Model Rules of Professional Conduct to report the misconduct of a licensed but non-practicing lawyer. This situation can arise in a variety of contexts. For example, a lawyer practicing in a corporation may learn of misconduct by a fellow employee who is a licensed lawyer but employed by the corporation in a nonlegal capacity. A lawyer in private practice may discover misconduct by an employee of her firm (such as the firm's in-house accountant) who the lawyer knows is admitted to law practice. In addition, there are circumstances in which the lawyer observing the misconduct may herself not be engaged in active law practice, as in the situation in which she serves on the faculty of a law school and learns of misconduct by another law professor who is a licensed lawyer exclusively engaged in teaching.

Conduct Encompassed by Model Rule 8.4 Most, but by no means all, ethical duties under the Model Rules spring from a lawyer's representation of clients. A lawyer also may violate the Model Rules when he or she engages in misconduct unrelated to the practice of law. Model Rule 8.4(a) provides that it is professional misconduct for a lawyer "to violate or attempt to violate the Rules of Professional Conduct, knowingly assist or induce another to do so, or do so through the acts of another." Model Rule 8.4(c) provides that it is professional misconduct for a lawyer "to engage in conduct involving dishonesty, fraud, deceit or misrepresentation."

The most obvious, and perhaps the most serious type of misconduct in which a non-practicing lawyer might engage, is criminal activity. Criminal conduct by a lawyer is addressed in Rule 8.4(b), which indicates that lawyers are subject to professional discipline for criminal conduct if the conduct "reflects adversely on the lawyer's honesty, trustworthiness or fitness as a lawyer in other respects." Lawyers committing the crimes of stalking,[4] harassing,[5] and willfully failing to file a tax form[6] have been found to have violated Rule 8.4(b). Similarly, crimes involving the use of alcohol or drugs, sex-related crimes, and crimes of violence, including domestic violence, can result in a violation of the Model Rules whether or not the lawyer is convicted or even charged with a crime.[7] Even criminal conduct that is arguably minor or personal may be found to fall within the Rule if a court finds that such conduct tends to exhibit a disregard of legal obligations.[8] Whether the conduct exhibits such a disregard will depend upon the nature of the act and the circumstances of its commission.[9]

Isolated minor infractions do not necessarily trigger disciplinary action. On the other hand, the repetition of even minor violations "can indicate indifference to legal obligation."[10]

Rule 8.4(c) addresses conduct that may or may not be criminal in nature, and prohibits a very broad range of dishonest, fraudulent,[11] or deceitful conduct, or misrepresentation. This expansive provision reaches any activity or aspect of the lawyer's personal or professional life. For example, willful and material misrepresentations on the lawyer's personal applications for employment, credit, or insurance would violate Rule 8.4(c),[12] as would personal insurance claims fraudulently submitted by the lawyer.[13]

A Lawyer's Duty to Report Misconduct of Licensed but Non-practicing Lawyers

We now examine the duty of a lawyer to report to the appropriate disciplinary authorities the misconduct of licensed but non-practicing lawyers.[14]

---

4. *See* Attorney Grievance Comm'n of Maryland v. Thompson, 786 A.2d 763, 768-69 (Md. 2001) (conviction for stalking thirteen-year-old boy reflects adversely on trustworthiness and fitness as lawyer notwithstanding lawyer's arguments that his practice was limited to areas not involving minors and that stalking was not in course of representing clients).

5. *See* In re Muller, 659 N.Y.S.2d 255, 255-56 (App. Div. 1997) (lawyer made harassing phone calls to former girlfriend and posed as clerk to federal court judge to harass her at law school and gain information about her).

6. *See* Arizona State Bar Op. 87-26 (Dec. 30, 1987), available at *http:// www.myazbar.org/Ethics/ pdf/87-26.pdf.*

7. *See Annotated Model Rules Of Professional Conduct*, 605-07 (5th ed. 2002).

8. *See id.* at 605 ("Offenses Covered").

9. Restatement (Third) of The Law Governing Lawyers §5 cmt. g (2000) (hereinafter "Restatement").

10. *Annotated Model Rules of Professional Conduct* at 604 (citing Rule 8.4 cmt. 2).

11. The Model Rules define "fraud" and "fraudulent" expansively. Rule 1.0(d) indicates that either term "denotes conduct that is fraudulent under the substantive or procedural law of the applicable jurisdiction and has a purpose to deceive." Comment [5] to Rule 1.0 elaborates that fraud "does not include merely negligent misrepresentation or negligent failure to apprise another of relevant information. For purposes of these Rules, it is not necessary that anyone has suffered damages or relied on the misrepresentation or failure to inform."

12. *See, e.g.,* In re Courtney, 538 S.E.2d 652, 653 (S.C. 2000) (lawyer, inter alia, filed false credit application and prepared false title opinion letter in order to obtain real estate mortgage loan); In re Capone, 689 A.2d 128, 129 (N.J. 1997) (lawyer knowingly made false statement on loan application).

13. *See, e.g.,* In re Bennett, 975 P.2d 262, 263 (Kan. 1999) (lawyer submitted itemized claim to his homeowner's insurance company for purportedly burglarized items still in his possession).

14. There are few reported decisions where a lawyer has been disciplined solely for failing to report the misconduct of another lawyer. These decisions are not particularly instructive in the

Because the legal profession enjoys the privilege of regulating itself, it is critically important that its members fulfill their responsibility to stand guard over the profession's integrity and high standards. Rule 8.3(a) implements this responsibility. It states: "[a] lawyer who knows that another lawyer has committed a violation of the Rules of Professional Conduct that raises a substantial question as to that lawyer's honesty, trustworthiness or fitness as a lawyer in other respects, shall inform the appropriate professional authority."

The Committee is mindful of the awkwardness and potential discomfort of reporting the misconduct of a colleague. The difficulty confronting the lawyer in that situation may be even more acute if the lawyer to be reported is a superior of the lawyer making the report. Whether employed in a law firm, a corporate law department, on a law school faculty, or elsewhere, the lawyer may be facing the same dilemma: jeopardize her career by making the report, or jeopardize it by remaining silent in violation of the rules of ethics.[15] In this regard, however, the Committee notes the instruction of the Preamble to the Model Rules, Comment [12]: "Every lawyer is responsible for observance of the Model Rules of Professional Conduct. A lawyer should also aid in securing their observance by other lawyers. Neglect of these responsibilities compromises the independence of the profession and the public interest which it serves."

Thresholds for Reporting

When Rule 8.3 is read in conjunction with Rule 8.4, then it is apparent that lawyers must report a wide variety of misconduct. Two thresholds must be reached, however, before the lawyer's obligation arises: the lawyer must "know" of the violation; and the misconduct must raise a "substantial question" as to the lawyer's honesty, trustworthiness or fitness as a lawyer. Therefore, we now turn to a discussion of those two requirements.

Rule 1.0(f) in the Terminology section of the Model Rules states that the term "knows" denotes "actual knowledge of the fact in question. A person's knowledge may be inferred from circumstances."

Most cases and ethics opinions conclude that "knowledge" is determined by an objective standard. The following analysis by the Mississippi Supreme Court typifies this approach: "The standard must be an objective one . . . not tied to the subjective beliefs of the lawyer in question. The supporting evidence must be such that a reasonable lawyer under the circumstances would

---

context of this opinion. The most widely known decision is In re Himmel, 533 N.E.2d 790 (Ill. 1988). *Himmel*, however, was not decided under the Model Rules, but rather under the Illinois version of the Model Code of Professional Responsibility. The Illinois Supreme Court limited the confidentiality afforded by the Illinois Code to information protected by the attorney-client privilege. This is much narrower than the scope of protection afforded to confidential information by the Model Rules. . . .
15. *See* Lindsay M. Oldham & Christine M. Whitledge, *Current Developments 2001-2002: The Catch-22 of Model Rule 8.3*, 15 Geo. J. Legal Ethics 881 (2002) (discussing ethics rule requiring lawyers to report other lawyers' unethical conduct and how violations of that rule are prosecuted, as well as associate's causes of action for termination after reporting co-worker's unethical behavior); Douglas R. Richmond, *Associates as Snitches and Rats*, 43 Wayne L. Rev 1819, 1838-47 (1997) (discussing problems facing law firm associates who learn of professional misconduct by other lawyers in their firms).

have formed a firm opinion that the conduct in question had more likely than not occurred."[16]

If a lawyer "knows" that another licensed lawyer violated the Rules, she must report such misconduct only if the violation raises a "substantial[17] question" as to the lawyer's honesty, trustworthiness or fitness as a lawyer in other respects. As Comment [3] to Rule 8.3 points out, "[t]he term 'substantial' refers to the seriousness of the possible offense and not the quantum of evidence of which the lawyer is aware."

Criminal conduct that violates Rule 8.4(b) often will raise a "substantial question" as to the lawyer's fitness. Whether particular non-criminal conduct raises such a question, however, will almost invariably require "a measure of judgment."[18]

If the lawyer, after assessing all of the circumstances,[19] remains uncertain whether she has a duty to report, she nevertheless may opt to do so. Voluntary reporting made in good faith always is permissible, subject to the guidance of Rule 8.3(c) regarding information protected by Rule 1.6 or gained by a lawyer or judge while participating in an approved lawyers assistance program.[20]

Rule 1.6 and the Duty of Confidentiality

Rule 1.6(a) provides in relevant part that "[a] lawyer shall not reveal information relating to the representation of a client unless the client gives informed consent. . . ." Read together with Rule 8.3, this means that, if a report of misconduct would reveal information relating to the representation of a client, a lawyer must obtain the client's informed consent before making such a report. . . . Stated more bluntly, Rule 1.6 trumps Rule 8.3.

Although paragraph (b) of Rule 1.6 sets forth a number of exceptions to the prohibition contained in paragraph (a), those exceptions seldom will come into play in the context of reporting the misconduct of another lawyer. For example, Rule 1.6(b)(1) allows a lawyer to reveal information relating to the representation of a client, but only "to prevent reasonably certain death or substantial bodily

---

16. Attorney U. v. Mississippi Bar, 678 So.2d 963, 972 (Miss. 1996). The Restatement also supports an objective standard: "[K]nowledge is to be assessed on an objective standard. . . . Knowledge exists in an instance in which a reasonable lawyer in the circumstances would have a firm opinion that the conduct in question more likely than not occurred." Restatement §5 cmt. i. *But see* Rhode Island Eth. Adv. Panel Op. 95-41 (Sept. 14, 1995) ("[T]he determination as to whether another attorney has violated an ethical rule . . . is one which involves [a] credibility determination that is largely subjective and is therefore one to be made by the attorney witnessing such conduct. . . .").
17. "'Substantial' when used in reference to degree or extent denotes a material matter of clear and weighty importance." Rule 1.0(l).
18. *See* Rule 8.3 cmt. 3.
19. *See* District of Columbia Bar Op. 246 (adopted Apr. 19, 1994; revised Oct. 18, 1994) ("In the end, however, it is for the inquiring lawyer to determine, in light of all the facts of the situation as she knows them, whether in her judgment a particular disciplinary violation raises a 'substantial question' about another lawyer's fitness, so as to trigger her own ethical obligation to report it. It is and should be a solemn and unenviable task.").
20. *See* New York State Bar Ass'n Committee on Prof. Eth. Op. 635 (Sept. 23, 1992) ("As a general proposition, a lawyer is always free to report evidence of what may constitute improper conduct by another attorney, subject to the obligations to preserve client confidences and secrets. The lawyer need not have actual proof of misconduct; a good faith belief or suspicion that misconduct has been committed is a sufficient basis for making a report.").

harm," a circumstance that will most likely be rare. The exception in paragraph (b)(4), which permits revelations "to comply with other law or court order," also is of limited application in the present context. "Other law" refers to law extraneous to the Model Rules, such as the substantive or procedural law of the jurisdiction.

We also note that Rule 1.6 is not limited to communications protected by the attorney-client privilege or work-product doctrine. Rather, it applies to all information, whatever its source, relating to the representation. Indeed, the protection afforded by Rule 1.6 is not forfeited even when the information is available from other sources or publicly filed, such as in a malpractice action against the offending lawyer.[21]

Within a corporate environment, the reach of Rule 1.6 is particularly wide. Its protection includes any information relating to the representation of any client or any communication with the organization's lawyer by a constituent of the organization in the constituent's organizational capacity.[22]

As a practical matter, clients have the ultimate authority when it comes to protecting confidential information. Hence, however salutary and indeed important the reporting of misconduct of lawyers may be, under the Model Rules the hands of lawyers are often effectively tied in these situations by the wishes or even whims of their clients.[23]

Seeking Informed Consent to Disclose the Confidences of Clients

If the lawyer determines that the information necessary to report the misconduct is protected by Rule 1.6, what should the lawyer do? Comment [2] to Rule 8.3 entreats a lawyer to "encourage a client to consent[24] to disclosure where prosecution would not substantially prejudice the client's interests." Any discussion of consent to disclosure, therefore, must include the potential adverse impact that disclosure may have on the client, including the effect on the client's ultimate recovery in a malpractice action, for example.

Clients may have a variety of reasons for not wanting to consent to disclosure of information. For example, they may be embarrassed by the matter, hesitant to become entangled in the controversy, or simply want the matter to come to an end. As a practical matter, there may be little benefit for the client in consenting to report the misconduct to the disciplinary authorities.

Nevertheless, we believe it would be contrary to the spirit of the Model Rules for the lawyer not to discuss with the client the lawyer's ethical obligation

---

21. See District of Columbia Bar Op. 246 ("Thus, even if the client has authorized the lawyer to file a lawsuit charging another lawyer with malpractice, this does not mean that the client cannot expect the lawyer to keep the matter confidential for other purposes.").

22. See Rule 1.13 cmt. 2 ("When one of the constituents of an organizational client communicates with the organization's lawyer in that person's organizational capacity, the communication is protected by Rule 1.6.").

23. See In re Ethics Advisory Panel Op. 92-1, 627 A.2d 317, 321 (R.I. 1993) ("Rhode Island's version of Rule 1.6 does not authorize an attorney to second guess a client's decision to refuse disclosure of otherwise confidential information.").

24. See Annotated Model Rules Of Professional Conduct at 93 ("Informed Consent to Disclosure") ("Informed consent means that a client's decision to disclose information is based upon an understanding of the risks and benefits that may result from the disclosure and nondisclosure. In the context of Rule 1.6, relevant issues include whether disclosure could result in the attorney-client privilege being waived, or the information being disclosed to others or used to the client's disadvantage.").

to report violations of the Rules. In essence, this would allow the lawyer to circumvent them.[25]

Conclusion

We interpret Rule 8.3 as requiring a lawyer to report professional misconduct committed at any time by a licensed but non-practicing lawyer. Even misconduct arising from purely personal activity must be reported if it reflects adversely on the lawyer's fitness to practice law. A lawyer violates the Model Rules and is subject to professional discipline when she fails to report such professional misconduct, in circumstances in which Rule 8.3 requires such reports.

State ex rel. Oklahoma Bar Association v. Busch
919 P.2d 1114 (Okla. 1996)

SUMMERS, J.:

The Oklahoma Bar Association filed a six-count formal complaint against Respondent Michael Busch alleging neglect of client matters, failure to adequately keep the client informed, failure to appeal twice, and intentional misrepresentation as to the status of a case, both to the court and the client. After a hearing the Professional Responsibility Tribunal recommended discipline in the form of an eighteen month suspension, and that after the period of suspension Respondent be subject to monitoring for his mental condition, Attention Deficit Disorder. Both

parties have filed briefs, the Bar seeking a two year suspension, and the Respondent urging he be allowed to continue his practice subject to medication and supervision.

All incidents giving rise to this complaint involved Respondent's handling of Connie Bateman's medical malpractice claim.[1] Respondent filed on behalf of Bateman and her daughter a lawsuit against the doctor who delivered Bateman's daughter. The daughter, now an adult, suffers permanent physical and mental handicaps, allegedly caused by the doctor's negligence. On November 9, 1989, Bateman's motion for default judgment was granted, giving her a

---

25. *See* Geoffrey C. Hazard & William Hodes, *The Law of Lawyering* §64.8 at 64-18 (3rd ed. 2002 and Supp. 2003) ("Good faith decisions by a client to withhold information from the disciplinary process must be respected, but it should be regarded as a violation of Rule 8.3 for a lawyer to manipulate a client into making that choice. If the violation that should be reported is serious enough, the lawyer has at least a moral duty—even putting aside the ethical duty—to urge the client to come forward (or to permit the lawyer to come forward) in the public interest.").

1. Count I of the complaint alleges violation of Rule 1.1 and 1.3 by signing a letter agreeing not to pursue the personal assets of the doctor. Count II alleges that he failed to appeal the district court's ruling. Count III alleges violations of Rules 1.4(a) and (b) in failing to inform Bateman of his decision not to appeal. Count IV alleges violations of Rule 1.1 and 1.3 in failing to timely appeal from the ruling in favor of the hospital. Count V alleges that he failed to inform his client that the appeal had been dismissed. Count VI alleged intentional misrepresentation to a court regarding the status of the case.

judgment against the doctor for ten million dollars. The doctor made no attempt to set aside the judgment.

A few months later Respondent sent the doctor a letter, stating that Respondent would not execute on any personal assets, but would instead collect from any insurance proceeds available. Respondent testified that a brief investigation led him to believe that the doctor had insurance and did not have substantial personal assets. Bateman testified that she did not agree to having such a letter sent. In response to this letter the doctor wrote to his insurance carrier, admitting negligence and making demand that it pay the policy limits. The carrier refused to pay. After further contact the insurer stated that no coverage was in effect at the time of the incident.

When it was later discovered by Respondent that the doctor had substantial amounts of money in several different bank accounts, as well as a ranch which was not his homestead and a collection of valuable antique cars, Respondent attempted to execute against his personal assets. But the letter from Respondent was upheld in a state court as being a valid covenant not to execute.

Bateman was thus barred from executing against the personal assets of the doctor and has, to this date, received nothing on her ten million dollar judgment. Bateman told Respondent to appeal the state court ruling and he agreed. He filed a Notice of Intent to Appeal. However, he failed to file a Petition in Error. He did not notify Bateman of this, and later testified that he decided not to file the appeal because he felt the chances of winning were slim.

In 1990 Respondent filed a second lawsuit for Bateman against Drum-right Memorial Hospital, alleging negligence on the part of the hospital for permitting the doctor to have hospital privileges. The hospital filed a motion for summary judgment, which was sustained. Bateman asked Respondent to appeal. He agreed and filed a Petition in Error. However, due to his preoccupation with another case he filed the Petition in Error a day late. In 1991 this Court dismissed the appeal as being out of time. He did not notify Bateman of these events.

In February, 1993, Respondent appeared in front of District Judge Woodson, in a hearing to determine the enforceability of the covenant not to execute. Judge Woodson specifically questioned Respondent as to the status of the lawsuit against the hospital, and Respondent stated that the appeal was pending and he "expected a decision shortly."

During this ongoing attorney-client relationship with Bateman, she testified that he repeatedly refused to return her calls as to the status of her case. Respondent's secretary confirmed this, and stated that she repeatedly urged Respondent to tell Bateman of its status. Bateman was in the courtroom when he told Judge Woodson that the appeal was pending. She did not know it had been dismissed until she inquired with the Supreme Court Clerk's office.

Respondent testified that in June and July 1993 he was diagnosed as having Attention Deficit Disorder. Since that time he has been on medication, and the problem has, for the most part, resolved itself. He continues to seek counseling for other problems in his personal life which have resulted from his disorder. He believes that his handling of the Bateman case was a direct result of Attention Deficit Disorder.

His psychiatrist testified on his behalf, stating that Respondent has done well since the implementation of a regime of medication. He stated that the general symptom of ADD is impulsive and inattentive behavior. When asked specific questions by the trial panel, he testified that ADD does not create an inability to tell the truth. However, ADD does cause impulsive and stupid behavior without thought to the consequences. He specifically stated that "Lying is not a symptom of ADD."

At the request of the trial panel the psychiatrist also submitted, in written form, a proposed program to help attorneys in Respondent's situation. The first step, and most critical, is to maintain a steady course of medication. The second step includes surveillance and monitoring of the professional practice of Respondent. The doctor suggests that someone who does not have ADD must oversee his workload. The third step includes monitoring for periods of "flooding."[2] During these periods, Respondent would need another attorney to take over his case load. This last step requires that Respondent continue his involvement with Lawyers Helping Lawyers. The doctor did not believe it necessary to inform Respondent's clients of his problem.

As for Respondent's prior history of discipline, he received a private reprimand in 1990 for his failure to respond to a grievance, a public censure in 1992 for his neglect of a client matter, and a 90 day suspension in 1993 with one years probation for neglect of a client matter. State ex rel. Oklahoma Bar Assn. v. Busch, 853 P.2d 194 (Okla. 1993).

The trial panel determined that Respondent's conduct violated the Rules of Professional Conduct. Specifically, the panel found: As to Counts I, II and IV Respondent violated Rules 1.1 and 1.3 with regard to his actions (sending the letter agreeing not to execute on personal assets from the judgment in the first case, and failing to appeal the district court's rulings as to both cases) which bar Bateman from executing on the doctor's personal assets. As to Count III Respondent violated Rule 1.4(a) and (b) by failing to keep Bateman informed about her case and in failing to explain the legalities. As to Count V Respondent violated Rule 1.4 and 8.4(c) by failing to inform Bateman that the appeal against the hospital had been dismissed and misleading her to believe it was still pending. As to Count VI, Respondent violated Rules 3.3(a)(1) and 8.4(c) by making a false statement to Judge Woodson. The trial panel continued by finding that Respondent's conduct in Counts I, III, V and VI were not a result of his disorder, and "do not relate to his diagnosis [of attention deficit disorder]." It found, however, that Counts II and IV do relate to the symptoms of his disorder. The trial panel concluded that Respondent should be disciplined for his conduct in Counts I, III, V, and VI, and that after his period of suspension, Respondent should be subject to the guidelines set forth by his doctor.

This Court's review of a disciplinary proceeding is de novo. As the licensing court exercising exclusive

---

2. Flooding is described as a neurologic phenomenon in which a person with ADD cannot focus, despite medication and extra effort.

jurisdiction, it is the duty of this Court to review the evidence presented, along with the trial panel report, to determine whether the allegations have been proven by clear and convincing evidence. "The nondelegable, constitutional responsibility to regulate both the practice and the ethics, licensure, and discipline of the practitioners of the law is solely vested in this Court." State ex rel. Okla. Bar Assn. v. Downing, 804 P.2d 1120, 1122-3 (Okla. 1990).

Respondent asserts that the trial panel erred in its imposition of discipline by failing to follow the mandates of the American with Disabilities Act (ADA). See 42 U.S.C. 12101 et seq. He asserts that as an individual with a disability recognized under the ADA,[3] he is entitled to a "reasonable accommodation" for his disability, and that the trial panel's imposition of punishment is not a "reasonable accommodation." ...

Prior to the enactment of the Americans with Disabilities Act, courts traditionally held that mental illness did not prevent attorney discipline. Because of the importance of maintaining the integrity of the bar, courts held that discipline was necessary regardless of the reason for unfitness. However, mental infirmity might be a basis for mitigation. See Matter of Hoover, 745 P.2d 939 (Ariz. 1987) (manic depression was not a complete bar to discipline but was a factor to consider when decid-

ing the punishment); Carter v. Gonnella, 526 A.2d 1279 (R.I. 1987) (bipolar disorder did not prevent bar discipline); Matter of Hein, 516 A.2d 1105 (N.J. 1986) (alcoholism was not a defense to bar discipline). To hold otherwise would erode the public's confidence in the bar. The sympathy felt for those with mental illnesses does not extend "to the point of lowering the barriers to the protection we have attempted to give to that portion of the public who are clients, especially clients who entrust their money to lawyers."

The Americans with Disabilities Act, enacted 1990, states as its goal "equality of opportunity, full participation, independent living and economic self-sufficiency" for disabled individuals. 42 U.S.C. §12101(8). It has been described as a "nationwide mandate to provide reasonable accommodations for disabled persons." Petition of Rubenstein, 637 A.2d 1131, 1136 (Del. 1994) quoting Morrissey, The Americans With Disabilities Act: The Disabling of the Bar Examination Process, The Bar Examiner, May 1993.

Relevant to this case is Subchapter II of the ADA which deals with "public entities." 42 U.S.C. 12131 et seq. "Public entity" is defined to include "any State or local government" and "any department, agency, special purpose district or other instrumentality of a State or States or local government." Id. This definition has

3. We note that the Bar Association does not dispute that Respondent's disorder is recognized under the ADA. After conducting our independent research, the ADA defines "disability" as "a physical or metal impairment that substantially limits one or more of the major life activities of such individual. ... " 28 C.F.R. §35.104 interprets this definition to include "any mental or psychological disorder such as mental retardation, organic brain syndrome, emotional or mental illness, and specific learning disabilities." Respondent's psychiatrist testified that ADD is a neurological disorder, and is recognized in the Diagnostic and Statistical Manual. He also stated that it does fall within the Americans with Disabilities Act and is mentioned in the Individuals with Disabilities Education Act of 1979.

been interpreted to include many instrumentalities of the courts, such as Boards of Bar Examiners, judicial nominating commissions, and disciplinary committees. In Section 12132, public entities are prohibited from discrimination on the basis of a disability.

The Bar Association urges that the ADA is inapplicable to the association in general and more specifically, the Professional Responsibility Tribunal. The basis for this argument is that the Bar Association is not an "employer" of attorneys. However, the ADA has three subchapters. The first deals with employers, the second with public entities and the third with public accommodation. It is the second subchapter—public entities—which is involved here. . . . Clearly, the ADA applies to the Oklahoma Bar Association, an arm of this Court.

Because the parties do not dispute that the Respondent's disability falls within the purview of the ADA, and because the Oklahoma Bar Association is subject to the ADA, we next must decide what impact this Act has on Respondent's disciplinary proceeding. . . .

Two states have been called upon to reconcile the duty of the bar association in monitoring and disciplining its members with the mandate of the ADA. The Florida Supreme Court, in Florida Bar v. Clement, 662 So. 2d 690 (Fla. 1995), addressed the issue when an attorney who was suffering from bipolar disorder (manic depression) was accused of ethical violations. The disciplinary referee recommended disbarment, but the attorney disputed the recommendation, urging that it violated the ADA. The Florida Supreme Court disbarred the attorney

although his sickness was one recognized by the ADA.

The Court held that "the ADA does not prevent this Court from sanctioning [an attorney]." This holding was based on two grounds. First, the conduct complained of (misuse and misappropriation of client funds) was not causally connected to his mental illness. Second, even if the conduct has been causally related:

> [T]he ADA would not necessarily bar this Court from imposing sanctions. . . . Clement is not "qualified" to be a member of the Bar because he committed serious misconduct, and no "reasonable modifications" are possible. . . .
>
> Thus, while the ADA applies to the Bar, it does not prevent this Court from taking disciplinary action against Clement. . . .

A slightly different result has occurred when the issue is bar admission rather than attorney discipline. These attacks have focused on either the questions asked on the bar application or on the examination process itself. In Petition of Rubenstein, 637 A.2d 1131 (Del. 1994), the Court held that once a disability is established which meets the criteria of the ADA, the public entity must make reasonable accommodations to facilitate the disabled person. As an instrumentality of the court, the Board of Bar Examiners was subject to the "reasonable accommodation" standard of the ADA. Extra time for the taking of the examination was considered a reasonable accommodation.

In McCready v. Illinois Board of Admissions to the Bar, 1995 WL 29609 (N.D. Ill. 1995), an applicant alleged violations of the ADA when he was denied admission to the bar after passing the examination. The denial was based on his mental health history which included prolonged problems with drug addiction and other mental disorders. The court held that the denial of admission was proper and did not violate the ADA.

Under Title II, the protected class is limited to "qualified individuals with a disability." By protecting "qualified individuals with a disability" (and not all individuals with disabilities), the ADA expressly recognizes that, in some cases, an individual may be unqualified by reason of the disability.... It is not enough to be qualified "but for" a disability; "the right inquiry is whether the person can satisfy the program's requirements despite his handicap."...

The ADA clearly applies to the Oklahoma Bar Association, as an arm of this Court. However, unlike *Rubenstein*, we see no "reasonable accommodation" which can be made with regard to Respondent's neglect of client matters and deceit in court which would accomplish the purpose of maintaining the integrity of the Bar and promoting the public's confidence in the state's many attorneys. This Court has a constitutional duty in overseeing the Bar to insure that its members are fit to practice.

Our case is closer to *Clement*. As the Florida Supreme Court stated, the ADA does not prevent the discipline of attorneys with disabilities.... It is undisputed that Respondent failed to pursue an appeal in the first case and failed to timely file the petition in error in the second. We find the evidence to be clear and convincing that Respondent agreed—without his client's knowledge or permission—to pursue the ten million dollar judgment only against the doctor's insur-

ance rather than against the doctor's personal assets. We similarly find that he told Judge Woodson that an opinion in the appeal was expected soon, when, in fact, Respondent knew that the appeal had been dismissed as untimely.

As mitigation we find that Respondent was suffering from Attention Deficit Disorder, that he is now being treated for this illness, and take that into account in the imposition of our discipline. We also note that Respondent has worked with Lawyers Helping Lawyers because of his illness.

We would be shirking our duty as the guardians of the state's bar were we to permit Respondent to avoid discipline. Such would surely erode public confidence in the bar. Respondent's client testified that due to Respondent's gratuitous letter she has received no compensation for her daughter's injuries in spite of the fact that she obtained a ten million dollar judgment. We find no excuse for Respondent's deceitful behavior in a court of this state. While his neglectful behavior may have been influenced by his ADD, his physician testified that lying is not a direct result of the illness. Because we find that the Bar Association has proven by clear and convincing evidence all counts as alleged in the complaint, we agree that discipline is necessary.

Taking his neurological deficit, now under control, into account as mitigation, Respondent is hereby suspended from the practice of law for two years and one day. After completion of the suspension, if Respondent resumes his practice, he shall be subject to the guidelines set forth by Dr. Dodson in his letter of August 1, 1995. This plan shall include Respondent's involvement with Lawyers Helping Lawyers. If disagreement as to the plan arises, Lawyers Helping Lawyers shall immediately contact the office of the General Counsel for the Oklahoma Bar Association. We also find that Respondent should be, and is hereby, assessed costs in this matter totalling $2,272.54 to be paid within thirty days of the date this opinion becomes final. . . .

OPALA, J., with whom SIMMS and WATT, JJ., join, concurring in part and dissenting in part.

I concur in the court's view that respondent breached professional discipline and that the A.D.A. does not pose a legal impediment to imposition of sanctions; I dissent from today's suspension. I would order respondent's disbarment.

◼ The Law Governing Lawyers: *Professional Discipline*

ABA Formal Opinion 04-433 and *Busch* illustrate aspects of the system of professional discipline that forms the backbone of the professional regulation of lawyers. We will see additional examples of lawyer discipline for violations of applicable lawyer code provisions throughout these materials.

Over the past 40 years, state and federal courts have extensively reformed the substance of lawyer codes, updated the procedures for disciplinary enforcement, and implemented guidelines to standardize disciplinary sanctions. The result has been more extensive discipline for a wider variety of professional misconduct. At the same time, because professional discipline continues to reach only a small fraction of client and third-party complaints, other remedies, such as malpractice, fee forfeiture, disqualification, and procedural sanctions also have expanded to fill the regulatory void.

The Emergence of Modern Disciplinary Systems

Courts have inherent power to regulate the practice of law. They do so by establishing substantive lawyer codes and procedures for professional discipline, which are *sui generis*, neither civil nor criminal in nature.[1] The potential for loss of professional license is less serious than loss of liberty, but a more severe penalty than civil damages. These realities explain why the Supreme Court has required procedural due process guarantees such as notice of the charge,[2] and the right to invoke a Fifth Amendment privilege against self-incrimination in disciplinary proceedings.[3] At the same time, the Fifth Amendment protection

---

1. ABA Model R. for Law. Disc. Enforcement, R. 18(A) (1999). *See also* Fred C. Zacharias, *The Purposes of Lawyer Discipline*, 45 Wm. & Mary L. Rev. 675 (2003).
2. In re Ruffalo, 390 U.S. 544 (1968) (lawyer entitled to notice of charge in disbarment proceeding). The adequacy of due process in a state disciplinary proceeding also determines whether a federal court can impose reciprocal discipline for the same conduct without plenary review. *See* Selling v. Radford, 243 U.S. 46 (1917); In re Ruffalo, 390 U.S. at 550; In re Edelstein, 214 F.3d 127 (2d Cir. 2000).
3. Spevack v. Klein, 385 U.S. 511 (1967) (lawyer may not be disbarred for properly invoking the Fifth Amendment privilege against self-incrimination in disciplinary proceeding). A federal court

against double jeopardy does not apply, because the purpose of a disciplinary proceeding is not to punish the lawyer but to protect the public.[4] The unique nature of the process further justifies the use of a jurisdiction's rules of civil procedure and evidence, a requirement of clear and convincing evidence, adjudication by judges or other lawyers rather than a jury, and a right to appeal a hearing committee decision.[5] The Supreme Court also has applied the *Younger* abstention doctrine to state disciplinary proceedings, requiring federal courts to refrain from considering constitutional challenges to pending state proceedings that afford the lawyer an opportunity to present the constitutional issues.[6]

In 1970 and 1992, two ABA commissions evaluated the efficacy and efficiency of disciplinary enforcement nationwide.[7] Both reported inadequately funded and understaffed disciplinary systems, decentralized organization, and delay that required the "immediate attention of the profession."[8] Lawyers disciplined in one jurisdiction could be admitted elsewhere, and those convicted of serious crimes sometimes continued to practice for years before any disciplinary action occurred.[9] Although some agencies handled serious matters well, many state courts continued to delegate control over lawyer discipline to bar associations, a practice that created real and apparent conflicts of interest and impropriety.[10] Secret disciplinary procedures and lack of immunity for complainants shielded too many errant lawyers in most jurisdictions. Equally important, an outsized number of disciplinary complaints filed by clients that alleged neglect, incompetence, or failure to communicate were being dismissed by disciplinary authorities as minor infractions. This meant nothing was done to correct the lawyer's behavior or compensate the client.[11]

Most of these problems have been addressed by continual improvements in state and federal disciplinary proceedings. Professional staff, largely in statewide offices, now administers lawyer discipline. Many states now conduct public

---

has added the constitutional right to clear and convincing evidence, In re Medrano, 956 F.2d 101 (5th Cir. 1992).

4. *See, e.g.,* In re Cardwell, 50 P.3d 897 (Colo. 2002); In re Caranchini, 160 F.3d 420 (8th Cir. 1998); In re Brown, 906 P.2d 1184 (Cal. 1995); Disc. Counsel v. Campbell, 345 A.2d 616 (Pa. 1975).

5. ABA Model R. for Lawyer Disc. Enforcement, *supra* note 1, R. 11 and R. 18.

6. Middlesex County Ethics Comm. v. Garden St. Bar Assn., 457 U.S. 423 (1982). *See also* Allstate Ins. Co. v. W. Va. St. Bar, 233 F.3d 813 (4th Cir. 2000) (*Rooker-Feldman* doctrine prevents federal court review of state bar committee's ruling regarding unauthorized practice of law).

7. ABA, Special Comm. on Evaluation of Disc. Enforcement, *Problems and Recommendations in Disciplinary Enforcement* (Final Draft, 1970) (The Clark Commission); ABA, *Lawyer Regulation for a New Century: Report on the Commission on Evaluation of Disciplinary Enforcement* xiv (1992) (The McKay Commission).

8. The Clark Commission at 2; McKay Commission at xvi-xx. *See also* In re Atty. Disc. Sys., 967 P.2d 49 (Cal. 1998) (state supreme court has inherent authority to assess a fee from each licensed lawyer to fund disciplinary functions).

9. The Clark Commission at 116-135.

10. In the first seven decades of the 20th century, bar disciplinary proceedings were used inappropriately against several groups of lawyers, including immigrants, plaintiff's lawyers, antiwar activists, civil rights lawyers, and legal aid lawyers. *See* James E. Moliterno, *Politically Motivated Bar Discipline*, 83 Wash. U. L.Q. 725 (2005).

11. The McKay Commission at xvii.

disciplinary hearings[12] and most grant immunity to complainants.[13] The ABA's Center for Professional Responsibility administers a National Lawyer Regulatory Data Bank, which has enabled jurisdictions to share information about public lawyer regulatory sanctions and thus enhance reciprocal discipline (sanctions based on prior discipline in another jurisdiction).[14] The acceptance of the ABA Model Rules for Lawyer Disciplinary Enforcement and Standards for Imposing Lawyer Sanctions also has encouraged uniform procedures and expanded the range of sanctions.[15] One example is interim suspension, which now routinely occurs for conviction of a serious crime or where serious harm to the public is threatened, such as by a lawyer who abandons a law practice.[16] A few jurisdictions have expanded the scope of professional regulation even further by making law firms as well as individual lawyers subject to disciplinary sanctions.[17]

The scope of public protection has been further expanded by the judicial branch's addition of complementary agencies, such as client protection funds, fee arbitration, mediation of malpractice complaints, law practice assistance, and substance abuse counseling.[18] These additional agencies address issues that may be dismissed as less serious than those that warrant formal discipline; by doing so, they respond to a greater number of legitimate client complaints that cannot otherwise be addressed by the disciplinary system.

Today, more states could benefit the public by mandating additional client protections, such as financial record keeping, trust account maintenance and overdraft notification, random audits of trust accounts, the maintenance of malpractice insurance, and a program of recertification.[19]

---

12. Landmark Commun. Inc. v. Va., 435 U.S. 829 (1978) (state law that made it a crime to disclose information about grievance proceedings violates First Amendment); R.M. v. N.J. Supr. Ct., 883 A.2d 369 (2004) (rule that required confidentiality in grievance records unconstitutional prior restraint on free speech).

13. St. v. Rutherford, 863 So. 2d 445 (Fla. 4th Dist. App. 2004) (absolute civil immunity for complainants did not bar criminal perjury charges).

14. *E.g.,* Gadda v. Ashcroft, 377 F.3d 934 (2004), *cert. denied,* 543 U.S. 876 (federal law does not preempt state regulation of lawyers and allows for disbarment by the state of California, and reciprocal disbarment by federal board of immigration appeals, as well as Ninth Circuit); Atty. Grievance Commn. v. McCoy, 798 A.2d 1132 (Md. 2002) (lawyer disbarred in Delaware disbarred in Maryland for the same conduct); In re Monaghan, 743 N.Y.S.2d 519 (App. Div. 2002) (state court imposed reciprocal discipline following federal court's earlier determination that lawyer committed misconduct).

15. McKay Commission at xix, 93, 108.

16. ABA Model R. for Law. Disc. Enforcement, *supra* note 1, R. 19 and 20; Ex parte Case, 925 So. 2d 956 (Ala. 2005) (lawyer entitled to procedural due process guarantees before interim suspension except when convicted of a serious crime or genuine emergency exists).

17. *See, e.g.,* N.Y. Code of Prof. Resp. DR 1-102(a) (2003). *See also* Ted Schneyer, *Professional Discipline for Law Firms?* 77 Cornell L. Rev. 1 (1991). *Cf.,* Julie Rose O'Sullivan, *Professional Discipline for Law Firms? A Response to Professor Schneyer's Proposal,* 16 Geo. J. Leg. Ethics 1 (2002).

18. ABA, *A National Action Plan on Lawyer Conduct and Professionalism* 80 (1999). ABA Model R. for Law. Disc. Enforcement, *supra* note 1 at R. 1(A). For a discussion of the impact of practice assistance programs as an alternative to discipline, *see* Diane M. Ellis, *A Decade of Diversion: Empirical Evidence that Alternative Discipline Is Working for Arizona Lawyers,* 52 Emory L.J. 1221 (2003).

19. *National Action Plan, supra* note 18, at 37 (1999).

Which Lawyers Are Disciplined?

Complaints to disciplinary authorities can come from clients, judges, other lawyers, or third parties. In 2005 (when the total lawyer population was 1,323,723), state disciplinary agencies received 128,294 complaints, investigated 82,316 of them, and imposed public and private sanctions against 5,673 lawyers.[20]

Long-standing commentary and empirical evidence indicates that solo practitioners and small firm lawyers are subject to discipline much more often than their large firm or inside counsel counterparts.[21] A California State Bar study found that solo practitioners and small firm lawyers accounted for 95 percent of the investigations opened, and nearly 98 percent of the completed disciplinary cases, but only 56 percent of the lawyer population.[22] Two-thirds of client's complaints were made against solo practitioners, resulting in 68 percent of investigations opened and 78 percent of completed disciplinary prosecutions.[23]

The report identified several "factors unique to the practice environment" that explain this result. First, lawyers in large firms tend to represent clients with more money and power—very often, large institutions. If these clients become dissatisfied, they have the ability to change lawyers, negotiate reduced fees, or litigate. On the other hand, clients of small firm lawyers tend to be individuals who often lack the money or power to leverage such alternatives. They therefore are more likely to seek the assistance of bar authorities when something goes wrong.

Beyond clients, lawyers in large firms also have a great deal more peer assistance available to them. Colleagues can cover for lawyers who become ill or overwhelmed. Larger firms are more likely to institutionalize procedures and policies that can prevent many violations, such as those dealing with client trust funds and conflicts of interest. Small firm lawyers may lack such support systems or office procedures. Financial pressures may induce some small firm or solo practitioners to "borrow" from client trust accounts. Time pressures may cause missed deadlines, failure to communicate with clients, or lack of documentation that could assist in defending against unfounded allegations.

The California study candidly admits that budget difficulties characteristic of most disciplinary systems have forced administrators to set priorities among complaints. The first step ferrets out "non-serious, minor, and technical allegations," which would likely not result in discipline. These include many fee disputes and failures to communicate. Once an investigation is undertaken in a more serious matter, "the main determinants of the outcome of the investigation are whether there is harm to a client or the public, whether the burden of proof can be sustained, and the appropriate level of disposition in accordance with case law and [other] standards."[24]

---

20. West Virginia did not provide data for the report. ABA, Standing Comm. on Lawyer Disc., *Survey on Lawyer Discipline Systems 2005*. Available at *www.abanet.org/cpr/discipline/sold/home. html*. Last visited July 9, 2007.
21. E.g., Sharon Tisher, Lynn Bernabei and Mark Green, *Bringing the Bar to Justice: A Comparative Study of Six Bar Associations* 102-106 (Pub. Citizen 1977).
22. St. Bar of Cal., *Investigation and Prosecution of Disciplinary Complaints Against Attorneys in Solo Practice, Small Size Law Firms and Large Size Law Firm* (June 2001). Available at *http:// calbar.ca.gov/calbar/pdfs/reports/2001_SB143-Report.pdf*. Last visited, July 7, 2007.
23. *Id.* at 14.
24. *Id.* at 13.

Of course, sustaining the burden of proof can be a function of the scope and power of the defense mounted against an allegation. Here the report notes that lawyers in large firms cooperate with the disciplinary authorities, and usually hire counsel to assist them. This means both that large firm lawyers probably will not be the subject of disciplinary complaints unless the evidence appears strong, and when it is, that counsel will advise them to make personal or professional changes to prevent further malfeasance. It may also be the case that some practices of some large firms, like billing fraud, have not yet come to the attention of disciplinary authorities.[25] On the other hand, the report finds that the "vast majority of non-cooperating and defaulting attorneys in the discipline system are solo practitioners,"[26] who may lack retained counsel and therefore not be able to present a substantial defense or benefit from advice that could salvage an otherwise threatened career.

What Behavior Triggers Discipline?

ABA Opinion 04-433 makes clear that lawyers are not required by Model Rule 8.3 to report every violation of the Rules of Professional Conduct.[27] First, a lawyer must "know" that another lawyer has committed a violation of the professional rules. Second, the violation should raise a "substantial question as to that lawyer's honesty, trustworthiness or fitness as a lawyer in other respects," that is, the misconduct should be significant. Both cases and bar regulations offer some guidance to lawyers faced with determining the magnitude of a violation. For example, Florida provides five categories of serious conduct that are likely to result in a serious sanction and presumably raise a substantial question regarding a lawyer's fitness to practice law.[28] These include misappropriation of a client's funds or property, misconduct that resulted in actual loss of money or legal right to a client or third person, prior discipline, misconduct that includes dishonesty and, last, the commission of a felony.[29] Cases and ethics opinions in other jurisdictions generally follow these definitions.[30] Less serious matters, such as a single act of incompetence or conflicts of interest that do not cause harm, have been found not to trigger the reporting requirement.[31]

---

25. *See, e.g.,* Lisa G. Lerman, *Blue-Chip Bilking: Regulation of Billing and Expense Fraud by Lawyers,* 12 Geo. J. Leg. Ethics 204 (1999); Lisa G. Lerman, *Lying to Clients,* 138 U. Penn. L. Rev. 659 (1990), discussed in Practice Pointers: Fee Agreements, *infra* p. 446.
26. Cal. Bar Report, *supra* note 22 at 18.
27. Judges have identical obligations to report misconduct by lawyers and judges. ABA Model Code of Judicial Conduct Rule 2.15.
28. Fla. Bar. Reg. Rule 3-5.1 (2007).
29. *Id.*
30. *See, e.g.,* Prue v. Statewide Grievance Commn., 690 A.2d 898 (Conn. 1995) (failure to safeguard client's funds); Iowa Supr. Ct. Bd. Prof. Eth. & Conduct v. Miller, 568 N.W.2d 665 (Iowa 1997) (former lawyer's demand to repurchase her shares of stock bordered on extortion); St. Bar of Ariz. Op. 94-09 (1994) (excessive fee charged by another lawyer); Assn. of the Bar of the City of N.Y. Formal Op. 1995-5 (pattern of neglect of matters); Atty. Grievance Commn. of Md. v. Brennan, 714 A.2d 157 (Md. 1998) (suspended lawyer misrepresented his status to clients); St. Bar of Wis. Op. E-85-11 (1985) (billing client for fictitious expenses); In re Dowd, 559 N.Y.S.2d 365 (App. Div. 1990) (kickbacks to city officials); Conn. Bar Assn. Informal Op. 94-11 (1994) (cocaine use, spousal abuse); Pa. Bar Assn. Op. 92-8 (1992) (threats of physical violence).
31. *E.g.,* Conn. Bar Assn. Informal Op. 97-8 (1997) (probable malpractice); Pa. Bar. Assn. Informal Op. 97-40 (1997) (dual representation that does not adversely affect a lawyer's relationship with either client).

Third, in those cases where a lawyer knows of a violation that does raise a substantial question, Model Rule 8.3(c) further conditions disclosures on the requirements of client confidentiality in Model Rule 1.6. The ABA opinion summarizes the approach of nearly all jurisdictions on this point: Where a lawyer gains information about another lawyer's misconduct while representing a client, the duty of confidentiality trumps the duty of disclosure.[32] However, if an exception to confidentiality (such as client consent) allows the disclosure, Model Rule 8.3 then requires it.[33]

The ABA Opinion also states that Model Rule 8.4(a) makes every lawyer code rule violation, as well as every attempted rule violation, grounds for professional discipline.[34] Lawyers may not be required to report every violation, but clients and judges can, and do. Most jurisdictions also authorize disciplinary authorities to investigate matters without a request for investigation. The remaining chapters in this book will provide a number of examples of lawyers who violated a myriad of these professional code provisions.

Model Rule 8.4(a) also prohibits inducing others to violate the rules of professional conduct. For example, lawyers who use an agent to solicit cases or to make contact with a represented person have been disciplined under this provision,[35] as have those who direct others, such as legal assistants or secretaries, to do acts that violate the professional rules.[36]

In notes to come, we will examine the provisions of Model Rule 8.4(b), which prohibits lawyers from committing criminal acts that reflect adversely on their ability to practice law,[37] and Model Rule 8.4(c), which prohibits dishonesty, fraud, deceit, and misrepresentation.[38] Note that these provisions apply to lawyer conduct whether inside or outside of law practice.[39]

Model Rule 8.4(d), which prohibits conduct prejudicial to the administration of justice, also has been applied in a wide variety of contexts,[40] for example, to

---

32. The one exception appears to be Illinois. Ill. R. Prof. Conduct 8.3(c) (2007); Ill. St. Bar Assn. Advisory Op. 96-09 (1997); In re Himmel, 533 N.E.2d 790 (Ill. 1988).

33. Conn. Bar Assn. Informal Op. 95-17 (1995) (Conn. exception to Rule 1.6 that permits disclosure to rectify the consequences of a client's criminal or fraudulent act requires disclosure under Rule 8.3).

34. *E.g.,* Columbus Bar Assn. v. Ashton, 840 N.E.2d 618 (Ohio 2006) (lawyer who failed to advise clients of lack of professional liability insurance).

35. *E.g.,* In re Brass, 696 So. 2d 967 (La. 1997) (lawyer who paid investigator to refer personal injury and criminal cases suspended for two and one-half years); Emil v. Miss. Bar, 690 So. 2d 301 (Miss. 1997) (lawyer who asked highway patrol officer to refer automobile injury cases in exchange for 15 percent of eventual settlements indefinitely suspended).

36. *E.g.,* In re Ositis, 40 P.3d 500 (Or. 2002) (lawyer who directed a private investigator to pose as a journalist to interview a potential opposing party to a legal dispute suspended for 30 days); In re Morris, 953 P.2d 387 (Or. 1998) (lawyer who directed legal assistant to alter and file final account in a probate matter after it had been signed and notarized suspended for 120 days); Disc. Counsel v. Bandy, 690 N.E.2d 1280 (Ohio 1998) (lawyer who tried to validate a will naming himself as beneficiary six years after its execution by requesting that his former secretary, who was not present when the will was signed, nevertheless, sign it as an additional witness suspended for two years).

37. The Bounds of the Law: Criminal Conduct, *infra* p. 254.

38. The Bounds of the Law: Lawyer Dishonesty, Fraud, Deceit and Misrepresentation, *infra* p. 139.

39. *E.g.,* St. ex rel. Okla. Bar Assn. v. Pacenza, 136 P.3d 616 (Okla. 2006) (lawyer's deceit in sale of a home suspended for two years and one day); In re Barrett, 852 N.E.2d 660 (Mass. 2006) (lawyer served as corporate executive and took company funds suspended for two years).

40. Former President Bill Clinton was suspended from law practice in Arkansas for violating this rule. Jones v. Clinton, 36 F. Supp. 2d 1118 (E.D. Ark. 1999). After he was found in contempt of court by the trial judge, Clinton admitted "he knowingly gave evasive and misleading answers," but

lawyers who abandon law practice without notifying clients,[41] and prosecutors who seriously misuse their discretion.[42] The Rule has provided the basis for discipline for misconduct during litigation, such as shoving another lawyer in the courtroom,[43] making court appearances while intoxicated,[44] or making insulting remarks during a deposition[45] or in a trial brief.[46] Lawyers have been uniformly unsuccessful in challenging Model Rule 8.4(d) as void for vagueness.[47]

Model Rules 8.4(e) and (f) further prohibit specific kinds of conduct that are prejudicial to the administration of justice. Model Rule 8.4(e) proscribes conduct that suggests a lawyer can obtain results by improperly influencing a governmental agency or official.[48] The rule also has been applied to judges who misuse their positions.[49] Model Rule 8.4(f) further prohibits lawyers from assisting judges in violating the rules of judicial conduct, for example, by making loans to judges before whom they appear.[50]

Some jurisdictions have added additional grounds for discipline to Model Rule 8.4. For example, Massachusetts and New York prohibit lawyers from engaging in "any other conduct that adversely reflects on the lawyer's fitness to practice law."[51] Colorado, California, and Florida provisions make nonpayment of child support obligations grounds for license suspension.[52]

---

would not admit to lying. He did, however, agree to a five-year suspension from practice for violating Rule 8.4(d), rather than the more specific dishonesty standard in Rule 8.4(c). Tom Brune, *No Clinton Indictment; President Makes a Deal*, Newsday A 05 (Jan. 20, 2001).

41. *E.g.,* In re Kendrick, 710 So. 2d 236 (La. 1998) (lawyer who moved without notifying bankruptcy client, resulting in repossession of client's vehicles, suspended from practice for one year and a day and ordered to pay restitution); People v. Crist, 948 P.2d 1020 (Colo. 1997) (lawyer who left state, abandoning law practice of 60 pending cases, disbarred).

42. In re Christoff, 690 N.E.2d 1135 (Ind. 1997) (prosecutor and chief deputy prosecutor who renewed a long dormant criminal investigation against another lawyer who sought the prosecutor's job suspended for 30 days and publicly admonished).

43. In re Jaques, 972 F. Supp. 1070 (E.D. Tex. 1997) (lawyer who, inter alia, assaulted a person and verbally abused another lawyer during a deposition suspended).

44. In re Wyllie, 952 P.2d 550 (Or. 1998).

45. In re Golden, 496 S.E.2d 619 (S.C. 1998) (lawyer who made threatening and degrading comments during two depositions publicly reprimanded).

46. In re Abbott, 925 A. 2d 482 (Del. 2007) (lawyer who made unfounded accusations in trial court brief that trial court might rule other than on the merits publicly reprimanded).

47. *See, e.g.,* Fla. Bar v. Zamft, 814 So. 2d 385 (Fla. 2002) (ex parte communication with a judge by a lawyer who did not represent either party in the matter); In re Stanbury, 561 N.W.2d 507 (Minn. 1997) (refusing to pay a law-related judgment and make payment on a court filing fee); In re Stuhff, 837 P.2d 853 (Nev. 1992) (intentionally interfering with sentencing of a criminal defendant by filing a disciplinary complaint against a judge just before the sentencing hearing); In re Haws, 801 P.2d 818 (Or. 1990) (failure to respond to bankruptcy trustee's inquiry and disciplinary complaint); St. of Neb. ex rel Neb. Bar Assn. v. Kirshen, 441 N.W.2d 161 (Neb. 1989) (failing to respond to bar complaint and properly supervise office staff).

48. Disc. Counsel v. Cicero, 678 N.E.2d 517 (Ohio 1997) (lawyer who led prosecutor and client-defendant to believe he was having a sexual relationship with a judge after she recused herself from the case suspended from practice for one year); Disc. Proceedings Against Bennett, 376 N.W.2d 861 (Wis. 1985) (lawyer who, inter alia, told his client a bankruptcy matter could be handled in some "extra-legal" way suspended for six months).

49. *E.g.,* In re Yaccarino, 564 A.2d 1184 (N.J. 1989) (judge who contacted police and prosecutor about the arrest of his daughter and who conspired to obtain property that was the subject of a lawsuit over which he presided properly removed from office and subject to disbarment).

50. Lisi v. Several Attys., 596 A.2d 313 (R.I. 1991) (lawyers who made loans to judges before whom they appeared subject to suspension and reprimand).

51. Mass. R. Prof. Conduct 8.4(h) (2007); N.Y. Code of Prof. Resp. DR 1-102(a)(7) (2007).

52. Cal. Bus. & Prof. Code §490.5 (2007); Colo. R. C. P. §251.8.5(b) (2007); Fla. R. Prof. Conduct 4-8.4(h) (2007).

   Several jurisdictions also have enacted express prohibitions against discrimination. California prohibits "Discriminatory Conduct in a Law Practice";[53] the District of Columbia prohibits discrimination in employment;[54] Illinois, New York, and Ohio forbid unlawful discrimination;[55] Michigan requires lawyers to treat persons involved in the legal process "with courtesy and respect";[56] Minnesota prohibits harassment "on the basis of sex, race, age, creed, religion, color, national origin, disability, sexual preference or marital status;"[57] and Texas prohibits lawyers from manifesting "by words or conduct bias based on race, color, national origin, religion, disability, age, sex, or sexual orientation."[58] Courts have not had trouble disciplining lawyers for similar, truly outrageous conduct under the more general language of Model Rule 8.4(d), conduct prejudicial to the administration of justice.[59]

Defenses and Sanctions

The best defense to a disciplinary complaint is to demonstrate that disciplinary counsel failed meet the burden of proof.[60] Once that burden has been met, however, disciplinary sanctions differ from jurisdiction to jurisdiction. An increased range of sanctions and sanction uniformity have been encouraged by the ABA Standards for Imposing Lawyer Sanctions, relied on by several courts whose cases are found in these materials.[61] These Standards recognize a wide spectrum of sanctions, including disbarment, suspension, reprimand, admonition, probation, restitution, assessment of costs, limitation upon practice, appointment of a receiver, requiring that a lawyer take continuing legal education or retake all or part of a bar examination, and any other requirement deemed "consistent with the purposes of lawyer sanctions."[62] In determining the appropriate sanction, the Standards list four factors to be considered by a court:

---

53. Cal. R. Prof. Conduct 2-400 (2007).
54. D.C. R. Prof. Conduct 9.1 (2003).
55. Ill. R. Prof. Conduct 8.4(a)(9)(A) (2003) (discrimination in violation of federal, state, or local law); N.Y. Code of Prof. Resp. DR 1-102(a)(6) (2007); Ohio R. Prof. Conduct 8.4(g) (2007).
56. Mich. R. Prof. Conduct 6.5 (2003).
57. Minn. R. of Prof. Conduct 8.4(g) (2007). Rule 8.4(h) also forbids discriminatory acts prohibited by federal, state, or local law.
58. Tex. Disc. R. Prof. Conduct 5.08 (2007). The ABA opted to address these issues in Comment [3] to Rule 8.4 rather than in black letter.
59. *E.g.,* In re Monaghan, *supra* note 14 (race-based abuse of opposing counsel at a deposition was conduct prejudicial to the administration of justice and unlawful discrimination); Fla. Bar v. Martocci, 791 So. 2d 1074 (Fla. 2001) (sexist, racial, and ethnic insults constituted conduct prejudicial to the administration of justice); In re Charges of Unprofessional Conduct, 597 N.W.2d 563 (Minn. 1999) (prosecutor who sought to disqualify defense counsel solely on the basis of race engaged in conduct prejudicial to the administration of justice).
60. *See, e.g.,* In re Karr, 722 A.2d 16 (D.C. 1998) (state bar counsel did not prove by clear and convincing evidence that lawyer was guilty of neglect rather than acting in consideration of an ethical dilemma caused by his client's perjury). Of course, constitutional challenges also have met with some success. *See* The Bounds of the Law: The Constitution, *infra* p. 523. Laches and entrapment also have been raised on rare occasions in disciplinary proceedings. *See, e.g.,* In re Carson, 845 P.2d 47 (Kan. 1993) (ten-year delay in disciplinary proceedings not available as a defense where no prejudice to lawyer occurred); In re Porcelli, 397 N.E.2d 830 (Ill. 1979) (entrapment not available as a defense to a lawyer who paid a police officer to alter a client's blood alcohol report).
61. In re Halverson, *infra* p. 305; In re Sather, *infra* p. 425.
62. ABA, *Standards for Imposing Lawyer Sanctions,* Standards 2.1-2.8 (1991).

the duty violated, the lawyer's mental state, the actual or potential injury caused by the misconduct, and the existence of aggravating and mitigating factors.[63]

Aggravating factors include past discipline, dishonest or selfish motive, a pattern of misconduct or multiple offenses, obstruction of a disciplinary proceeding, refusal to acknowledge responsibility, a vulnerable victim, substantial experience in law practice, and illegal conduct.[64] Mitigating factors encompass personal and emotional problems, physical or mental disability, the absence of prior disciplinary violations or selfish motive, timely efforts to rectify harm, a cooperative attitude toward the disciplinary board, delay in the disciplinary proceedings, inexperience in law practice, good character and reputation, other penalties or sanctions imposed for the same conduct, remorse, and remoteness of prior offenses.[65] Advice of counsel is not a defense, but may be evidence of mitigation if the lawyer disclosed all relevant facts and followed the advice.[66]

One disability that plagues lawyers—substance abuse—has been the cause of a large number of disciplinary complaints. Here, most courts regard successful treatment for substance abuse as a mitigating factor, and failure to seek treatment as an aggravating circumstance.[67]

Busch also illustrates how a disability may mitigate a disciplinary sanction, but only if the disability caused the problem and can be accommodated to prevent it in the future. Recall that the court distinguished Busch's dishonesty, which was not caused by his disability, from his incompetence and failure to communicate, which arguably was. Unfortunately, three years later the same court faced similar misconduct by the same lawyer. This time, Busch was disbarred.[68]

---

63. *Id.* at Standard 3.0.
64. *Id.* at Standard 9.2.
65. *Id.* at Standard 9.32.
66. Disc. Counsel v. Levine, 2006 Haw. LEXIS 118 (reliance on advice may be a mitigating factor, but is not a defense to practicing law while suspended from practice); Atty. Grievance Commn. of Md. v. Johnson, 876 A.2d 642 (Md. 2005) (lawyer cannot rely on advice of counsel defense or use it as mitigation when she failed to show she disclosed all facts to her lawyer).
67. *Standards for Imposing Lawyer Sanctions* at Standard 9.32 (mental disability or chemical dependency are mitigating factors only when they caused the misconduct, have been confirmed by medical evidence, and recovery is demonstrated by a meaningful and sustained period of successful rehabilitation, which arrested the misconduct and makes recurrence unlikely).
68. St. ex rel. Okla. Bar Assn. v. Busch, 976 P.2d 38 (Okla. 1998).

Part II

Lawyers and Clients: Fiduciary Duty

A lawyer who agrees to represent a client also agrees to be bound by five basic fiduciary duties: client control concerning the goals of the representation, communication, competence, confidentiality, and conflict of interest resolution (the 5 Cs). This part of the book explores these obligations and the various remedies available to clients if these duties are breached. Since none of these obligations exists until a client-lawyer relationship has been created, the chapters in Part II also address the basic question of what factors determine when lawyers have created client-lawyer relationships and their concomitant fiduciary duties. In this chapter, we explore court appointments and lawyer choice as two ways that lawyers assume professional duties to clients, including service *pro bono publico,* for the public good.

Chapter 3

Beginning the Client-Lawyer Relationship

Problems

3-1. Should Martyn & Fox represent Credit Suisse in a case brought by descendants of Holocaust victims who deposited money in the bank before the war? Would you be willing to have us limit our representation to a statute of limitations motion?

3-2. Should Martyn & Fox represent an anti-gay and lesbian group that pickets the funerals of deceased soldiers from the Iraq War as a way of protesting the armed forces' willingness to recruit gays and lesbians under the "don't ask, don't tell" policy?

3-3. Should Martyn & Fox represent a client who wants to disinherit an adult child because he married a person of a different race and religion? Would it make a difference if the prospective client is near death and Martyn & Fox is the only available law firm?

3-4. Should Martyn & Fox represent a defendant on death row who brutally abused and then stabbed two young girls? How should we respond if a court appoints us to represent the defendant?

3-5. Should Martyn & Fox represent an indigent tenant who says she is being evicted because she tried to force her landlord to repair the building she lives in? What if she has no money to pay a lawyer? What if the housing court appoints us to represent her pro bono?

3-6. Should Martyn & Fox ghostwrite a brief for a pro se litigant?

Consider: Model Rules 6.1, 6.2

A. Court Appointments

Bothwell v. Republic Tobacco Co.
912 F. Supp. 1221 (D. Neb. 1995)

PIESTER, Magistrate Judge.

Before me for consideration is a motion, submitted by plaintiff's appointed counsel, Paula Metcalf, seeking reconsideration and vacation of my order appointing her to represent plaintiff in this case. . . .

BACKGROUND

In March 1994 plaintiff Earl Bothwell, who at the time was incarcerated at the Hastings Correctional Center, submitted to this court a request to proceed in forma pauperis, a civil complaint, and a motion for appointment of counsel. . . .

In his complaint plaintiff alleged that he "immediately ceased" purchasing and smoking factory-manu- factured cigarettes after Congress enacted the Federal Cigarette Label- ing and Advertisement Act of 1969 ("FCLAA"), 15 U.S.C. §1333 et seq, which mandated that a warning label be conspicuously placed on packages of such cigarettes. Plaintiff alleged that he thereafter switched to "roll your own" cigarettes, which were not covered by the FCLAA. . . . Plaintiff alleged that he switched to the defendants' products on the belief that, because the government had not mandated warning labels on loose tobacco and because the defendants had not voluntarily issued such warnings, those products were not harmful or hazardous. Plaintiff al- leged that in 1986 he became aware that he suffered from emphysema, asthma, heart disease, and "bronchial and other respiratory diseases." He later learned that the loose tobacco products he had been using "were stronger that [sic] [factory-produced] cigarettes and were twice as harmful and deadly." . . .

DISCUSSION

In her brief in support of her mo- tion to reconsider and vacate, Met- calf contends that my order appointing her as counsel is "contrary to law and clearly erroneous" because "a federal court has no statutory or inherent authority to force an attor- ney to take an ordinary civil case for no compensation."

Statutory Authority

Insofar as concerns statutory au- thority, Metcalf is correct. Plaintiff in this case is proceeding in forma pau- peris pursuant to 28 U.S.C. §1915(d). In Mallard v. U.S. Dist. Ct., 490 U.S. 296 (1989), the United States Su- preme Court held, in a 5-4 decision, that section 1915(d) does not autho- rize a federal court to require an un- willing attorney to represent an indigent litigant in a civil case. In so holding, the Court focused on the language of section 1915(d), which provides that a court may "request" an attorney to accept a court appoint- ment. . . . However, the Court in *Mal- lard* left open the question of whether federal courts possess the inherent power to require an unwilling attorney to accept an appointment. . . .

Inherent Authority . . .

Since its inception the federal ju- diciary has maintained that federal courts possess inherent powers which are not derived from statutes or rules. These inherent powers vest in the courts upon their creation. . . .

. . . [T]he power to conscript law- yers to represent the indigent . . . exists for two primary purposes: (1) to ensure a "fair and just" adjudicative process in individual cases; and (2) to maintain the integrity and viability of the judiciary and of the entire civil justice system. These two purposes mirror the dual functions that law- yers serve in the civil justice system.

First, they act as advocates in individual cases working to peacefully resolve civil disputes between citizens. Second, by their ready availability to act in that capacity, they preserve the credibility of the courts as a legitimate arm of the civil justice system. . . .

(1) "Fair and Just" Process in Individual Cases . . .

While it is established that a plaintiff has no constitutional right to counsel in a civil case, counsel nevertheless may be necessary in a particular civil proceeding to ensure fairness and justice in the proceeding and to bring about a fair and just outcome.

The American legal system is adversarial in nature. Gideon v. Wainwright, 372 U.S. 335, 344 (1963). The adversarial system has been embraced because it is believed that truth is best divined in the crucible of cross examination and adversarial argument. Attorneys, because they are trained in the advocacy skills of cross-examination and argument, are a necessary component in a properly functioning adversarial system. Thus, the notion that the adversarial system is an effective method for ferreting out the truth presumes that both sides have relatively equal access to adequate legal assistance from those trained in the art of advocacy. . . .

If the lack of legal representation is the free choice of the unrepresented party or if it results from factors unrelated to the indigency of the plaintiff, our system is not offended. Where, however, one party is unable to obtain legal representation because of indigency, the resulting disparity of advocacy skills clearly offends the principle of "equality before the law" underlying our system. Further, a substantial disparity in access to legal representation caused by the indigency of one of the parties threatens the adversarial system's ability to produce a just and fair result.

Access to legal representation in this country is gained primarily through the private market. For the most part, the market is an effective mechanism for providing legal services to those who need them. However, the market sometimes fails to provide counsel regardless of the merits of the claims at issue. Where the person whose claims have been rejected by the private market is indigent, he or she may seek representation through a legal aid organization. However, the ability of such organizations to meet the needs of the indigent has taken a serious hit over the past fifteen years in the form of reduced funding to the Legal Services Corporation ("LSC"), the federal entity responsible for funding state and local legal aid offices. . . . Compounding the problem of legal access for the poor is the growing apathy of the private bar to the plight of many indigent litigants. The inevitable net result of these factors is that the poor, indeed most of the so-called "middle class," have less realistic access to advocacy services from lawyers. . . .

. . . I conclude that, when indigency is the principal reason for disparate access to the civil justice system in an individual case, a federal court does possess the inherent authority to bring about a fair and just adjudicative process by conscripting an unwilling lawyer to represent the indigent party. . . .

(2) *Preserving the Integrity of the Civil Justice System*

The very purposes for the establishment of the judicial branch of government included the peaceful resolution of private disputes between citizens and the protection of the minority from loss of their rights to the majority, either at the ballot box or through force.

In order to be viable in delivering on these goals, a justice system must be both trustworthy and trusted. The judicial branch of our government was created powerless to enforce its own decisions; it relies on the respect of litigants for adherence to the law it declares, or, if necessary, actions of the executive branch. It is, to be sure, a living example of "the consent of the governed." To be accorded respect among the people it serves, it must be perceived as fair. If it is not trusted, it will not be seen as a legitimate means to serve its purposes of peacefully resolving disputes and protecting minority rights. . . .

Lawyers as Officers of the Court . . .
. . . Because the ready availability of lawyers is necessary to ensuring the perception, and indeed the reality, of fairness, their accessibility as officers of the court is necessary not only to the preservation of the justice system itself but to the ordered liberty of our society. . . .

Monopoly of Lawyers
A further justification which has been advanced for the view that attorneys are obligated to comply with court-ordered appointments is the monopoly theory. Under that theory, attorneys must provide legal services to indigents without compensation by virtue of the exclusive privilege they have been granted to practice law. . . .

[C]ritics claim that other groups enjoying monopolies as a result of state licensing, such as doctors, nurses, teachers, insurance agents, brokers, and pharmacists, do not bear an obligation to provide free services to the poor. While that is true, it misses the point. The practice of law—that is, the representation of others before the civil courts —is not simply a private enterprise. It is, in addition, a contribution to society's ability to manage its domestic affairs, a necessary condition of any civilized culture. Attorneys have a unique relationship to government not shared by other licensed groups. This relationship, which has been described as "symbiotic," places attorneys in "an intermediary position between the court and the public" where they are "inextricably linked to the public sector despite [their] dual position as a private businessperson."

By virtue of this special relationship between the bench and the bar, courts are dependent upon attorneys to aid in carrying out the administration of justice. While other professions also contribute to private gain and to the betterment of society's standards of living, no other group holds the exclusive key to meaningful participation in a branch of government and the protection of rights. This monumental difference between attorneys and other licensed groups justifies imposition of different conditions on the practice of the profession.

Ethical Obligation of Lawyers

An additional justification for the court's exercise of inherent power to compel representation is the ethical obligation of attorneys to provide representation to indigent litigants.... [The court cites Model Rule 6.1.]

While these obligations are not expressed in mandatory terms, they clearly indicate that service to the indigent is an essential characteristic of any ethical attorney. Two aspects deserve further attention.

First, these moral and ethical obligations to provide legal services to the poor do not exist merely to prompt the practicing lawyer to be a "good" person, respected in the profession. Rather, they are a recognition of the critical role of the lawyer in ensuring the fair and just adjudication of disputes, and the need for such advocacy in ensuring the existence of the system.

Second, these obligations are not self-executing.... It makes little sense to give only lip service to these ideals while the legitimacy of the court system is being challenged by other means of resolving private disputes. If our society is to have a legitimate civil justice system, the courts must be empowered to take necessary measures to create and maintain it. In a more genteel and public-spirited time, the mere suggestion by a court that a private attorney should provide free representation might be met with acceptance of the duty as a necessary means to ensure fairness and the justice system itself; perhaps that history contributes to the lack of mandatory requirements today....

Necessity of Exercising Authority

In deciding whether to exercise the authority to compel representation I first note that a court must exercise its inherent powers "with restraint and discretion." The common thread running through inherent powers jurisprudence is the concept of necessity. Thus, while this court possesses the inherent power to compel representation of an indigent plaintiff, the power should be exercised only where reasonably necessary for the administration of justice. In other words, the appointment of counsel must be necessary to bring about a fair and just adjudicative process.

... [W]hen determining whether counsel should be appointed for an indigent plaintiff, the court should consider such factors as (1) the factual complexity of the case, (2) the ability of the plaintiff to investigate the facts, (3) the existence of conflicting testimony, (4) the plaintiff's ability to present his claims and (5) the complexity of the legal issues. In re Lane, 801 F.2d 1040, 1043-44 (8th Cir. 1986). An additional factor ... is the plaintiff's ability to obtain counsel on his own....

... I conclude that the plaintiff's failure to obtain private counsel was not the result of his indigency but rather a result of the "marketability," or lack thereof, of his claims. This "marketability" analysis, which I believe to be a proper additional consideration in determining whether to appoint counsel, involves ... several steps.

The first step in the "marketability" analysis is to ask whether, realistically, there is a "market" of lawyers who practice in the legal area of the plaintiff's claims. Many indigent litigants, particularly prisoners, raise civil rights claims pursuant to 42 U.S.C. §1983. There are relatively few private attorneys who practice in the area of civil rights. Also, there are few, if any, lawyers willing to assume cases on a contingent-fee basis where the indigent plaintiff primarily seeks forms of relief other than monetary damages, such as injunctive or declaratory relief. As a result, in many cases, there simply is no true "market" to look to when determining whether an indigent plaintiff should be appointed counsel. In such cases, there should be no further inquiry into the "marketability" of a plaintiff's claims. Rather, the appointment of counsel should rest on those other factors commonly used in determining whether to appoint counsel. *See* In re Lane, *supra*.

In cases where such a "market" of lawyers is found to exist, a second question must be addressed: Does the plaintiff have adequate access to that market? This inquiry is necessary for two major reasons. First, many indigent litigants are physically unable to access private counsel regardless of the merits of their claims. This is especially true where the litigant is incarcerated. . . . Second, there may be communication barriers of language or language skills; barriers of physical, emotional, or mental disabilities; or educational or cultural barriers that block understanding between attorney and client. . . . Where a "market" of attorneys exists but a party does not have adequate, realistic access to it, no further "marketability" inquiry is necessary because such inquiry could not yield a reliable conclusion regarding the involvement of indigence as a factor in the litigant's failure to obtain counsel. In such situations,

the appointment of counsel should be analyzed using factors from In re Lane, *supra*.

If there is a market and the litigant had realistic access to it, the third step in the "marketability" analysis must be performed. That step requires an examination of the typical fee arrangements used in the particular area of the law implicated by the indigent plaintiff's complaint. Specifically, if contingent-fee or other low-cost financing arrangements are generally available in the area of law and would be feasible for the plaintiff, further examination is proper. . . .

Once it is determined that an accessible market exists, that the plaintiff has the ability to access that market, and that feasible fee arrangements are available, the final and most important step in the analysis must be performed. The court must determine whether the market's rejection of the party's claims was the result of indigency, for, as noted above, indigency is the touchstone which authorizes the court to exercise the inherent power to correct unequal access to advocacy services. There are many factors to consider when a lawyer is approached about taking a person's claims into litigation. These factors might include, but would not be limited to, the merits of the claims; the existence of precedent to support the claims; the costs of investigating the claims, handling the discovery needed to prepare the case for trial, and trying the case; the relationship of those costs to the amount of a likely recovery, discounted by the probability of recovery; the lawyer's time available to pursue the claims and the impact upon his/her other practice obligations, as well as upon those of partners or associates; the likeability of the litigant;[18] the popularity of the claims; and the potential settlement value of the claims. So long as the market's rejection of the claims was based on the interplay of these and other such factors, and not on the indigency of the plaintiff, the notions of equal justice discussed above are not offended and compelling an attorney to represent that plaintiff is not necessary to the achievement of a fair and just adjudicative process.

Applying the foregoing "marketability" analysis to this case, I first conclude that there was an adequate "market" of lawyers practicing in the general area of plaintiff's claims. Plaintiff raises product liability claims, as opposed to civil rights claims under 42 U.S.C. §1983. As such, a greater number of private attorneys were available to represent him than would be for a typical indigent litigant. The potential for joining a class action lawsuit against the tobacco companies further enhanced the "market" that was available to plaintiff. In sum, there was a realistic "market" of lawyers who could litigate the claims raised by plaintiff.

I further conclude that plaintiff had ready access to that "market" of lawyers. Plaintiff is not incarcerated nor has he alleged any other substantial barriers[20] which might have prevented him from communicating with private attorneys. He thus had the unfettered ability to communicate with private attorneys in his im-

mediate locale and elsewhere. Additionally, many of the attorneys who work in products liability and personal injury claims do so on a contingent fee basis. . . . Under a contingent fee arrangement, there typically is no requirement that the plaintiff advance costs, although the plaintiff would remain liable for them ultimately. Thus, despite plaintiff's indigency, there were feasible fee arrangements available to plaintiff.

The foregoing factors indicate that, unlike most cases initiated by indigent litigants, there was a "market" of private attorneys for plaintiff's claims and that, unlike most indigent litigants, plaintiff had open access to that market and has, in fact, accessed that market, albeit unsuccessfully. It thus is proper to determine whether that market's rejection of plaintiff's claims was the result of his indigency.

I conclude that it was not. The mere existence of indigency as a condition of the plaintiff did not prevent him from suggesting to lawyers that they consider his claims. Rather, he has had the same opportunity as middle- or upper-class plaintiffs to subject his claims to the scrutiny of tort attorneys. That this "market" of attorneys has thus far rejected his claims is the result of factors unrelated to his indigency. Primary among these factors is undoubtedly the enormous cost of litigating claims against tobacco companies. . . .

Plaintiff asserts that most of the attorneys he contacted requested payment of a retainer which he was unable to afford. However, due to the

---

18. While even the most despicable character is, by rights, entitled to the same access to the courts to voice his grievances as is the most attractive, wealthy, and urbane individual, the private market may exclude the former from access because of this intangible factor. It is not inappropriate for a court to consider this factor in determining whether the plaintiff's personal characteristics might have been a force behind the market's rejection of his claims.

20. While plaintiff has alleged health problems, he presents no evidence indicating that these problems would inhibit him from seeking out counsel either in person or via telephone or mail.

enormous costs involved in this type of litigation and the unlikelihood of settlement, the amount of money required for an adequate retainer would likely be so great that even a middle-class or upper-middle-class citizen would be unable to afford it. As such, the rejection of plaintiff's claims was not based on his indigency, but rather on marketability factors such as the expenses involved and the unlikelihood of settlement.

Because it is the lack of marketability of his claims, as opposed to his indigency, which has prevented plaintiff from obtaining counsel, the notions of equal justice discussed above have not been offended. As such, it is not reasonably necessary to the administration of justice for this court to compel Metcalf to represent plaintiff. Accordingly, I shall not exercise this court's inherent authority to do so.[22]

B. *Pro Bono* Service

■ Lawyers and Clients: *Service* Pro Bono Publico

This series of notes, entitled "Lawyers and Clients," focuses on five groups of clients served by substantial numbers of lawyers. In each situation, we will examine the same three topics: who are the clients?; the "5 C" fiduciary duties lawyers owe these clients; and the bounds of the law, including specialized legal regulation of the client's rights and responsibilities, which may shape and limit a lawyer's advocacy on behalf of the client. We begin by turning our attention to that large segment of the public served by a far too small group of lawyers: those without access to lawyers due to their modest means.

Access to justice in America remains elusive for most of the poor and much of the middle class. This concern is not new. In 1919, Reginald Heber Smith wrote that without equal access to the law, "[t]he system not only robs the poor of their only protection, but it places in the hands of their oppressors the most powerful and ruthless weapon ever invented."[1]

There are three different approaches that can be employed to address these needs. The first accepts public responsibility for access to justice, a goal that can be accomplished by creating legal rights to representation, publicly funding legal services programs, and simplifying legal procedures. The second approach focuses on a duty of individual lawyers to serve as court-appointed counsel or

---

22. Because I decline to exercise the court's inherent authority, I need not address Metcalf's contention that the exercise of that authority in this case would contravene the Fifth and Thirteenth Amendments of the Constitution. However, the majority of courts which have addressed those issues have found no constitutional violations. *See* Williamson v. Vardeman, 674 F.2d 1211 (8th Cir. 1982) (collecting federal and state cases); In re Amendment to R. Reg. the Fla. Bar, 573 So. 2d 800, 805 & n.11 (citing federal appellate cases); Bradshaw v. U.S. Dist. Court, 742 F.2d 515, 517 n.2 (9th Cir. 1984); Family Div. Trial Lawyers v. Moultrie, 725 F.2d 695, 712 (D.C. Cir. 1984); United States v. Dillon, 346 F.2d 633 (9th Cir. 1964), *cert. denied*, 382 U.S. 978 (1965); . . . To the extent these constitutional claims attack the very existence of the inherent power itself, I also reject them.
1. Reginald Heber Smith, *Justice and the Poor, A Study of the Present Denial of Justice to the Poor and of the Agencies Making More Equal Their Position Before the Law with Particular Reference to Legal Aid Work in the United States* 9 (Carnegie Found. 1919).

provide free or reduced rate services *pro bono publico,* for the common good. *Bothwell* illustrates both of these approaches by accepting public judicial responsibility for counsel to preserve the credibility of the courts as a legitimate civil justice system and by appointing counsel to serve without pay, both to achieve justice in a particular case. The third approach stresses deregulation, which would permit unlicensed persons or institutions to provide some kinds of legal assistance. To date, none of these strategies has gone far enough in its implementation to alleviate the lack of access to justice in civil cases.

The Clients

The disparity between lawyers available to paying clients and those available to serve the poor explains why, for at least the past century, judges have exercised their inherent power to offset this imbalance, first in criminal and then occasionally in civil cases.[2] In civil cases, *Bothwell* represents the modern trend, which recognizes inherent judicial power to appoint lawyers in individual cases when necessary to ensure the principle of equality before the law.[3] Model Rule 6.2 reflects these developments by requiring lawyers to accept such appointments unless the lawyers can present very weighty reasons to decline.

Although America has no overall shortage of lawyers, the access gap between rich and poor continues to expand simply because access to lawyers is determined largely by market forces.[4] Currently, only one legal service lawyer is available to serve 6,861 eligible persons. This compares unfavorably with one lawyer for every 525 persons who are able to pay.[5] In the past decade, private funding from foundations, charitable gifts, and state Interest on Lawyer Trust Accounts (IOLTA) programs have made up for some of the loss of federal money

---

2. Other countries have recognized a right to counsel in some civil cases. *See, e.g.,* New Brunswick (Minister of Health and Community Servs.) v. G.(J.), [1999] 177 D.L.R. (4th) 124 (indigent parents have constitutional right to state-funded counsel when government seeks a judicial order suspending parental custody); Airey v. Ir., 32 Eur. Ct. Hum. Rights (series B) 305 (1979) (government-appointed counsel required for indigent woman who sought judicial separation from her husband by European Convention on Human Rights guarantee of access to the courts). In this country, such a right has been found only by state courts pursuant to state constitutional guarantees. *See, e.g.,* Lassiter v. Dept. of Soc. Serv., 452 U.S. 18 (1981) (no due process right to appointed counsel in termination of parental rights proceedings); In re K.L.J., 813 P.2d 276 (Alaska 1991) (state due process clause required appointment of counsel to indigent biological father in waiver of consent to adoption cases); Salas v. Cortez, 593 P.2d 226 (Cal. 1979), *cert. denied,* 444 U.S. 900 (1979) (state due process clause required provision of counsel to indigent defendants in paternity proceedings brought by the state).
3. *See also* Burke v. Lewis, 122 P.3d 533 (Utah 2005) (absent physician defendant in medical malpractice case entitled to court-appointed counsel in order to preserve rights against malpractice insurer); Zimmerman v. Hanks, 766 N.E.2d 752 (Ind. App. 2002) (prison inmate had statutory right to appointed counsel in civil case).
4. In 1960 (when voluntary legal aid projects served less than 1 percent of those in need), the ratio of lawyers available to poor clients (those at or below the poverty level) was 1:120,000. By 1980, when legal services funding reached its height, the ratio had improved to 1:5,000. Today, substantial cutbacks in federal funding have been only partially offset by private grants. National Legal Aid & Defender Association, History of Civil Legal Aid. Available at *http://www.nlada.org/ About/About_HistoryCivil.* Last visited July 23, 2007.
5. Legal Services Corporation, *Documenting the Justice Gap in America* 15 (2005). Available at *http://www.lsc.gov/press/documents/LSCJusticeGap_FINAL_1001.pdf* at 16. Last visited July 23, 2007.

originally pledged to fund the Legal Services Corporation.[6] But in spite of these innovative alternative funding approaches, dozens of well-executed empirical studies conducted over the past two decades document that the existing legal services network simply does not meet the need for civil legal services for low- and moderate-income persons.[7]

The most extensive analysis, published by the American Bar Association in 1994, found that 71 percent of those in low income households and 61 percent of those in moderate-income households with serious legal claims never brought them to the civil justice system.[8] These neglected legal matters most frequently involved personal finances and consumer issues, housing and real property matters, domestic, and employment related problems.[9] This lack of legal counsel is rendered more tragic when one is reminded of what every law student and lawyer knows: those able to obtain a lawyer get significantly better results.[10]

Similar studies in nearly every state document that, even with the best voluntary pro bono programs and creatively financed legal services offices, lawyers typically address only 15 to 20 percent of the legal needs of the poor.[11]

The 5 Cs: Fiduciary Duties

Both lawyer codes and common law impose five fiduciary duties on lawyers who agree to represent clients, regardless of their ability to pay. Lawyers owe clients affirmative duties of control over the objectives of the representation, commu-

---

6. IOLTA funds, discussed in more detail in Chapter 10, also help fund criminal defense representation by public defender offices in many jurisdictions. In Brown v. Legal Found. of Wash., 538 U.S. 216 (2003), the Supreme Court held that state use of IOLTA funds to pay for legal services for those in need qualified as a taking for a "public use" justifying the state's authority to confiscate private property under the Just Compensation Clause of the Fifth Amendment. The Court nevertheless upheld the continuing viability of state IOLTA requirements by finding that no Fifth Amendment violation occurred because the value of the client's "just compensation" was zero in a properly administered fund.

7. Public funding for legal services exists in some form in most western democratic countries. Geoffrey C. Hazard & Angelo Dondi, *Legal Ethics: A Comparative Study* 248 (Stanford 2004).

8. ABA Consortium on Legal Services and the Public, *Legal Needs and Civil Justice: A Survey of Americans* 23 (1994). Low Income Households were defined as those at 125 percent of the official U.S. poverty line or less, Moderate Income Households as those just above this mark but earning less than $60,000 per year in 1992. *Id.* at 1. Also available at *http://www.abanet.org/legalservices/ downloads/sclaid/legalneedstudy.pdf.* Last visited July 23, 2007.

9. Over half of those persons, especially those who tried to handle the matter themselves or did nothing, were dissatisfied with the result. On the other hand, those few who did take a serious legal matter to the civil justice system reported the highest satisfaction with the result, 48 percent for low-income individuals and 64 percent for those of moderate means. *Id.* at 17-18.

10. *E.g.,* Carroll Seron, Gregg Van Ryzin & Martin Frankel, *The Impact of Legal Counsel on Outcomes for Poor Tenants in New York City's Housing Court: Results of a Randomized Experiment,* 35 Law & Socy. Rev. 419 (2001) (legal counsel provided to poor tenants produced large differences in outcome independent of the merits of the case).

11. Consumer, housing, public services, medical, and family problems are the most frequently mentioned needs. Reports issued by various states are available at *http://www.nlada.org/Civil/ Civil_SPAN/SPAN_Library/document_list?topics=000055&list_title=State+Legal+Needs+Studies% 3A+Reports.* Last visited July 23, 2007. For other state reports, *see, e.g., The Path to Equal Justice: A Five-Year Status Report on Access to Justice in California* (Cal. Commn. on Access to Just. 2001). Available at *http://www.calbar.ca.gov/calbar/pdfs/accessjustice/2002-Access-Justice-Report.pdf.* Last visited July 23, 2007. Massachusetts Legal Need Survey, *Findings from a Survey of Legal Needs of Low Income Households in Massachusetts* (2003). Available at *http://www.masslegalservices.org/ docs/Data_report_final.pdf.* Last visited July 23, 2007.

nication, competence, confidentiality, and conflict of interest resolution. Several of these fiduciary obligations take on special significance in providing legal services to persons of limited means.

Control, Communication, and Competence

To provide more clients with legal services, some lawyers are experimenting with unbundling legal services, delivering legal services à la carte rather than assuming full-service representations.[12] They might, for example, help a pro se litigant with a discrete task, such as preparation of pleadings or a trial court brief, or assist a person in drafting a letter or document. Lawyers who offer unbundled services often refer to themselves as "client coaches" who perform some, but not all, aspects of a legal representation. Some lawyers provide such services free of charge as part of a nonprofit or court-annexed limited legal services program or hotline.[13]

Unbundling proponents encourage lawyers to break down current legal services into discrete tasks, such as advice, legal research, fact gathering, negotiation, document drafting, or court representation. Proponents also seek to break up legal representation by issues, such as custody, visitation, property valuation (real, personal, business, investments, pensions, etc.), and insurance benefits.[14] Clients then are offered a menu of these separate tasks and issues, and are given the opportunity to select those that fit the client's budget, or reject those the client most thinks he or she can handle alone.

Unbundling implicates three core fiduciary duties: control, communication, and competence. First, unbundling assumes that clients will assume control over more aspects of a matter. Second, it requires special communication obligations of lawyers so that clients can take charge. Third, because unbundling means less than a full representation, the lawyer's duty of competence must be fulfilled in a unique manner. Model Rule 1.2(c) recognizes the ability of client and lawyer to agree to these limited scope representations, but only if the limitation is reasonable and the client gives informed consent.[15]

Indeed, the success of unbundling depends on a competent lawyer who is able to identify all aspects of the matter, clarify that handling less than all aspects is reasonable, and communicate "adequate information" about the risks and alternatives to unbundled service to obtain the client's "informed consent."[16] In short, lawyers must provide competent representation with respect to

---

12. *See* Forrest S. Mosten, *Unbundling Legal Services: A Guide to Delivering Legal Services a la Carte* (ABA Law Prac. Mgt. 2000).
13. *See, e.g.,* N.C. Formal Op. 10 (2005) (Virtual Law Practice and Unbundled Legal Services). Hotlines offer effective service when callers understand what they are told to do and follow the advice given. Follow-ups with written instructions also improve client success. But certain kinds of cases, such as dealing with government agencies and those involving family law matters, often require more extensive assistance. Special protocols are necessary for non-English speaking callers, those with very low education levels, and those who report no income. Center for Policy Research, Final Report—The Hotline Outcomes Assessment Study (2002). Available at *http://www.nlada.org/DMS/Documents/1037903536.22/finalhlreport.pdf.* Last visited July 23, 2007.
14. Mosten, *supra* note 12 at 50, 51.
15. MR 1.2(c); RLGL §19.
16. MR 1.0(e).

those items the client cedes to the lawyer and adequate advice to the client about how to accomplish the rest.[17]

Some lawyers asked to provide certain pro bono services express concerns about their competence because they fear a lack of ability to handle a pro bono client legal matter outside of their regular practice parameters. Although such fears are much less often expressed with respect to new matters required by paying clients, in some cases those concerns are real. As a result, lawyers and judges have created a number of innovative voluntary pro bono programs, all of which provide education and support for lawyers seeking to provide competent pro bono services.[18] Similar programs encourage or require pro bono participation in law school.[19]

These voluntary pro bono projects have helped many, but they have never been enough. This is why another alternative, mandatory pro bono service, has been proposed.[20] Vehement opposition by lawyers has followed each proposal, which has led to current Model Rule 6.1's admonition that lawyers "should," but are not required to, render such service. This basic duty remains aspirational, but the text has been changed to quantify the recommended service at 50 hours per year,[21] and in 2002, the rule was amended to add language that tiptoes close to a mandate: "Every lawyer has the professional responsibility to provide legal services to those unable to pay."

Although mandatory pro bono service has not been officially adopted by any jurisdiction,[22] proponents agree with *Bothwell* that one basis for such a duty is the monopoly on the provision of legal services (including access to justice) that

---

17. Mosten, *supra* note 12, at 29, 92-97; D.C. Op. 330 (2005) (duties that generally attach to lawyer-client relationships also apply to lawyer who provides unbundled services, including duties of competent service, diligence, loyalty, communication, confidentiality, and avoidance of conflicts of interest).

18. *See, e.g., The Support Center for Child Advocates, http://www.advokid.org/*, last visited July 23, 2007, an innovative Philadelphia-based program that provides lawyers for children who find themselves parties to family court proceedings and whose interests otherwise might go unrepresented; *American Bar Association Death Penalty Representation Project, http://www. abanet.org/deathpenalty/*, last visited July 23, 2007, which has provided lawyers to hundreds of prisoners on death row who have no counsel to represent them in habeas corpus proceedings; *The ABA Litigation Assistance Partnership Project, http://www.abanet.org/litigation/committees/ probono/lapp.html*, last visited July 23, 2007, which matches public interest law firms and legal services offices with private firms so that the latter can help the former handle litigation, particularly complex cases that strain the resources of the public service community; *Community Economic Development Law Program, http://www.clccrul.org/projects/community_economic_ development_law_project.html*, last visited July 23, 2007, a Chicago project which offers a full scope of transactional representation and strategic legal advice to community organizations to build affordable housing, to set up job-training programs, and to work with individuals starting their own small businesses; *Corporate Pro Bono*, a program that works with in-house counsel to encourage their participation in community pro bono efforts, *http://www.corporateprobono.org/*, last visited July 23, 2007.

19. One empirical study indicates that lawyers accustomed to pro bono service in law school offer much more pro bono service as lawyers than do students who attended law schools where pro bono was ignored or encouraged, rather than required. Deborah L. Rhode, *Pro Bono in Principle and in Practice: Public Service and the Professions* 154-165 (Stanford U. Press 2005).

20. The first mandatory pro bono proposal was made in 1980 when the ABA's Kutak Commission circulated a discussion draft of Rule 6.1 that proposed a mandatory pro bono service requirement.

21. For a chart that details each state pro bono rule, *see* Judith L. Maute, *Pro Bono Publico in Oklahoma: Time for a Change*, 53 Okla. L. Rev. 527, 597-609 (2000).

22. Some local bar groups have adopted mandatory pro bono requirements. *See, e.g.,* Dauphin County, PA, available at *http://www.dcba-pa.org/pages/probono.html*, last visited August 30, 2007.

lawyers enjoy.[23] Most state proposals also seek to avoid begrudgingly provided forced service by including a buyout provision, which would enable an individual lawyer to make a payment to a legal services agency in lieu of personally providing legal services.

An intermediate option, mandatory reporting of pro bono activity, has been adopted in several states.[24] These reporting requirements do not require any pro bono representation, but have, in fact, increased voluntary pro bono service.[25]

Confidentiality and Conflict of Interest Resolution

Private lawyers who offer pro bono services face the prospect that information from or service to a pro bono client, just like the representation of a paying client, could mean professional responsibility implications for their representation of private clients, because pro bono clients are entitled to the same measure of confidentiality[26] and loyalty[27] due all other clients.[28] Three Model Rules address specific conflicts of interest that have arisen in pro bono service. Model Rule 6.3 allows lawyers who serve on legal services organizations' boards or projects to disregard any general adverse interests of their paying clients, but prohibits them from participating in specific decisions incompatible with their obligations to either private or legal services organization clients. Model Rule 6.4 creates similar provisions for lawyers who serve on the boards of law reform organizations. Model Rule 6.5 facilitates limited-term legal services programs, such as hotlines or help desks. It encourages private lawyers to provide pro bono service to clients in these programs by temporarily suspending some conflict of interest requirements. Lawyers who recognize a conflict with a private client cannot offer advice, but otherwise, lawyers are not required to do a conflicts check of a law firm database before rendering this assistance.

The Bounds of the Law

A number of solutions to remedy the problem of access to justice go beyond public payment and lawyer pro bono service. Many argue that legal procedures and rules that govern recurring situations should be simplified. Proposals include increased use of court personnel to assist pro se litigants, more small claims courts, more accessible ADR procedures such as mediation, or plain English regulations that simplify current complex legal provisions or remedies.[29]

---

23. Rhode, *Pro Bono in Principle and Practice, supra* note 19 at 26.
24. *See, e.g.,* Ill. S. Ct. R. 756(f) (2007); Schwarz v. Kogan, 132 F.3d 1387 (11th Cir. 1998) (upholding the constitutionality of Florida's rule that requires a report of compliance on each annual bar dues statement with its aspirational goal of 20 hours or a contribution of $350 to a legal aid organization).
25. Rhode, *Pro Bono in Principle and in Practice, supra* note 19 at 45.
26. MR 1.6, 1.8(b); RLGL §§59, 60, 68, 87; Dept. of Children & Family Servs. v. Shadonna, 58 Cal. Rptr. 3d 173 (Cal. App. 2007) (former client of publicly funded nonprofit law office can seek disqualification if she shows a reasonable possibility that material confidential information relating to the former representation has been obtained).
27. MR 1.7-1.10, 1.18; RLGL §§121-135.
28. *See, e.g.,* Tenn. Formal Op. 2005-F-151 (ethical responsibilities of legal services organization lawyers in pilot program to provide limited legal services to otherwise pro se litigants in domestic relations matters).
29. Deborah L. Rhode, *Access to Justice* 189-191 (Oxford U. Press 2004).

Some courts have recognized that court rules create obstacles to unbundled pro se representation.[30] Typical provisions require the lawyer who offers any assistance to a litigant to enter an appearance on behalf of a client, thereby creating a full-scale representation. FRCP 11 and state equivalents require lawyers who prepare pleadings to sign them. But a pro se litigant or a lawyer may wish to prepare a pleading that the litigant herself signs,[31] or a lawyer may wish to ghostwrite a trial court brief for a client. Some jurisdictions require lawyers to notify the court about their assistance, because failure to do so is characterized as a fraudulent practice.[32] Others recognize a limited appearance, either by only requiring disclosure of the limited assistance,[33] or by exempting lawyers who perform specific tasks from any disclosure obligation.[34]

Other proposals recommend changes to current unauthorized practice rules that prevent nonlawyers from providing legal services.[35] One way to do this is to recognize the ability of nonprofits to hire lawyers to pursue their mission through direct client service.[36] Although the ABA has recommended that jurisdictional practice limitations be eased on lawyers during major disasters,[37] deregulation that would allow nonlawyers to compete with lawyers will undoubtedly continue to prove unacceptable to the practicing bar.[38] Complete deregulation might mean that nonlawyers could offer all kinds of legal assistance outside of court proceedings, such as drafting wills and tax forms, handling corporate and real estate transactions, collecting debts, and providing divorce or adoption services. Most of these measures would require reversal of current unauthorized practice restrictions, discussed in Chapter 13. On the other hand,

---

30. ABA Standing Committee on the Delivery of Legal Services, *An Analysis of Rules that Enable Lawyers to Serve Pro Se Litigants* 4 (2005). Available at *www.abalegalservices.org/delivery*. Last visited July 23, 2007. Pro se representation is especially common in high volume state courts, such as traffic, housing, and small claims, but increasing in other civil matters as well. *Id. See also* Winkelman v. Parma City Sch. Dist., 127 S. Ct. 1994 (2007) (parents of disabled children may pursue lawsuit and appeal on behalf of child pro se).
31. In some jurisdictions, signing a pleading indicates entering an appearance in the matter, a result neither lawyer nor client desire. Signing a pleading also triggers affirmations about fact and law checking that the client, but not the lawyer, has undertaken. *See* ABA Standing Committee on the Delivery of Legal Services, *An Analysis of the Rules that Enable Lawyers to Serve Pro Se Litigants* (2005).
32. *E.g.,* Colo. C.R.C.P. 11(b) (2007); Wash. C.R. 11(b) (2007).
33. *E.g.,* Nev. R. Prac. 5.28(a) (2006) (limitations on scope of the representation must be disclosed in the first paragraph of the first paper or pleading filed); Fla. R. Prof. Conduct 4-1.2 comment (2006) (lawyer who assists a pro se litigant not required to sign document, but is required to state "prepared with the assistance of counsel"); Me. R. Prof. Conduct 3.4(i) (2007) (lawyer may file a limited appearance on behalf of a client); N.M. R. Prof. Conduct 16-303(e) (2007) (limited appearance must be disclosed to court).
34. *E.g.,* Tenn. Formal Op. 2007-F-153 (lawyers who help pro se litigants draft pleadings are not required to disclose their involvement to opponent or court so long as there is no continuing aid that will mislead others); Cal. R. Ct. 5.70(a) (2007) (lawyer who drafts documents in family law case not required to disclose involvement).
35. *See, e.g.,* Deborah L. Rhode, *Access to Justice, supra* note 29.
36. *E.g.,* Mo. Formal Op. 121 (2006) (nonprofit battered woman's shelter may employ lawyers to provide legal services to its clients as long as no fee is charged and the nonprofit does not interfere with client-lawyer relationship).
37. *See Model Court Rule Relaxing Licensing Requirements During Major Disasters.* Available at: *http://www.abanet.org/cpr/clientpro/Recom_Report_Katrina.pdf.* Last visited July 23, 2007.
38. *See, e.g.,* ABA, *Nonlawyer Activity in Law-Related Situations: A Report with Recommendations* (1995).

the grudging acceptance by the legal profession of accountants and realtors who have established unique but overlapping turf with lawyers might mean that other allied professionals could one day become separately licensed or certified with distinct roles in the legal system.

The Future

As long as the "practice of law" is limited to licensed lawyers and government funds are inadequate to pay for civil legal services, lawyers will be left to shoulder the responsibility for the public's access to justice. Current voluntary pro bono efforts, while innovative, still fall far short of meeting the need for legal services. Most commentators see a continuing need for a network of alternatives.[39] Nearly all proposals see lawyer and law student pro bono work as an indispensable element of an overall plan,[40] and many argue that mandatory pro bono would not only provide more legal services to those unable to pay, but also would provide lawyers with a sense of personal and professional fulfillment that many are not able to achieve in practice.[41] Most proposals also focus on increased public funding, through federal and state grants, IOLTA, filing fee surcharges or service taxes on for-profit legal services, allocating punitive damage or unpaid class actions funds to a civil justice fund, and improved fee awards for successful poor claimants who establish entitlement to public benefits.[42] Many experts also envision simplified legal processes, alternative dispute resolution procedures, and the certifying of paraprofessionals.[43]

To date, the simple truth is that we lack the political will to provide equal access to justice, just as we lack the political will to provide equal access to housing, health care, child care, and education. Yet the lack of access to justice differs from the lack of access to these other essential services because providing legal services nearly always depends on advocating a particular point of view that will affect at least one other person's interest. This means that lack of legal representation not only deprives the poor and middle class of access to redress for a legal wrong, but also creates the opportunity for dishonest or exploitive conduct by those in a position to capitalize on this disparity. This is why some argue that lawyers who assist paying clients in a system fraught with misdistribution of legal services have a moral obligation to either provide legal services to those who lack access or to consider the impact of their work on those without representation.[44]

Ultimately, *Bothwell* reminds us that the fairness of the legal representation provided by a largely market driven system will be affected by the economic

---

39. Roger C. Cramton, *Delivery of Legal Services to Ordinary Americans*, 44 Case W. Res. L. Rev. 531 (1994).
40. *Id.*; Deborah L. Rhode, *Access to Justice, supra* note 29; *Recommendations of the Conference on the Delivery of Legal Services to Low-Income Persons*, 67 Fordham L. Rev. 1751 (1999). On law students, *see http://www.equaljusticeworks.org/*. Last visited June 26, 2007.
41. *See, e.g.,* Lawrence J. Fox, *Should We Mandate Doing Well By Doing Good?* 33 Fordham Urb. L.J. 249 (2005); Rhode, *Pro Bono in Principle and in Practice, supra* note 19, at 29-31.
42. Talbot D'Alemberte, *Tributaries of Justice: The Search for Full Access*, 25 Fla. St. U. L. Rev. 631 (1998).
43. *E.g.,* Deborah L. Rhode, *Access to Justice, supra* note 29.
44. Kathleen Clark, *Legal Ethics: The Lawful and the Just: Moral Implications of Unequal Access to Legal Services*, 2 J. Inst. Stud. Leg. Eth. 289 (1999).

differences among those it serves. Because lawyers benefit substantially from this system, we cannot avoid the reality of this unequal access. As you work through the materials that follow, consider how a lawyer's role depends on a reasonably just legal system, and how lack of access to that system undermines confidence in the justice the legal system produces.

Chapter 4

Control and Communication

This chapter explores two of the most basic fiduciary duties that lawyers owe clients: control and communication. Four themes run throughout this chapter. First, clients repose trust in lawyers, which gives lawyers power and makes them fiduciaries. Second, the authority vested in a lawyer to represent a client always remains subject to the client's control over the goals of the representation. Third, lawyers assume a fiduciary duty of communication to assure that the client's interests are properly identified and well served. Fourth, the law governing lawyers provides for multiple remedies when professional duties of control or communication are breached. Multiple remedies reinforce the reality that standards of conduct for lawyer-fiduciaries are kept at a higher level, which forces lawyers to focus on the best interests of each client-principal.

The client-lawyer relationship is one of the oldest examples of an agency relationship. An agent (the lawyer) agrees to act on behalf of a principal (the client). The agreement between principal and agent confers power and imposes the "5 C" fiduciary duties (client control, communication, competence, confidentiality, and conflict of interest resolution) on the agent, all designed to assure that the agent acts on the principal's behalf.[1] Lawyer-agents owe client-principals the 5 Cs to ensure that the client's moral values control the agency relationship, to make certain that lawyers avoid benefiting someone other than the client, and to protect clients from lawyers who might take advantage of the trust and power reposed in them.

The key to understanding these foundational fiduciary duties is to remember that the lawyer must initiate all conversations. Failure to do so leaves a lawyer vulnerable to multiple remedies available to clients for breaching some or all of the 5 Cs. In this chapter, we explore two of these remedies: professional discipline and civil liability. Recall that *Busch* in Chapter 2 involved the remedy of professional discipline for one major instance of a failure to communicate with a

---

1. *Restatement (Third) of Agency* §1.01 (Tentative Draft No. 2, 2001).

client as well as lawyer incompetence. Civil actions for both legal malpractice and breach of fiduciary duty also provide redress when breaches of the duty to communicate cause harm.

A. Control

Like other agents, lawyers have a duty to act on the client's behalf, subject to the client's right to control the objectives of the representation.[2] At the same time, most clients defer to and rely on their lawyers' expertise regarding the means to accomplish client goals. Lawyer codes and the law of agency recognize three spheres of authority between client and lawyer. In the first two, clients and lawyers each retain sole authority to make certain decisions that cannot be overridden by the other. In the third, client and lawyer decision-making authority overlap.

In the first sphere, clients retain sole authority to make decisions concerning the outcome of the representation, including whether and when to settle or appeal a matter, and in criminal cases, how to plead, whether to waive a jury trial, and whether to testify.[3] Clients may authorize their lawyers to make a particular decision within this sphere, but the ultimate authority of clients to decide may not be completely ceded to their lawyers.[4]

In the second sphere, lawyers retain sole authority to make some decisions during their representation of clients. A lawyer must refuse to perform, counsel, or assist an unlawful act of a client,[5] a topic we develop in greater detail in these materials in notes entitled "The Bounds of the Law." Second, in spite of client preferences to the contrary, a lawyer may take actions in tribunals he or she reasonably believes to be required by law or court order.[6]

These spheres of authority reserved exclusively to clients or lawyers place equally clear affirmative duties of communication on lawyers during a representation. Whenever a client decision arises, the lawyer must promptly inform and consult with the client about the decision.[7] Whenever a client insists on

---

2. *Restatement (Third) Agency* §1.01 (Tentative Draft No. 2, 2001).

3. MR 1.2(a); RLGL §22(1).

4. Mattioni, Mattioni & Mattioni, Ltd. v. Ecological Ship. Corp., 530 F. Supp. 910 (E.D. Pa. 1981) (provision in contingent fee contract that required lawyer's consent before settling case invalid and voided entire fee contract; lawyer reduced to quantum meruit recovery for fee); Abbott v. Kidder Peabody & Co., Inc., 42 F. Supp. 2d 1046 (D. Colo. 1999) (lawyers representing 200 individual plaintiffs disqualified because of contract that gave settlement authority to a select group of plaintiffs; each individual client's approval is essential); In re Lansky, 678 N.E.2d 1114 (Ind. 1997) (lawyer who included provision in retainer agreement that authorized lawyer "to settle this matter for any amount he determines is reasonable without further oral or written authorization" violated MR 1.2(a) and was suspended 30 days); In re Lewis, 463 S.E.2d 862 (Ga. 1995) (lawyer whose client signed a retainer agreement giving lawyer full authority to take all actions on client's behalf in a personal injury case and then settled her case without her express authority suspended for 18 months).

5. MR 1.2(d); RLGL §23(1).

6. MR 3.3; RLGL §23(2).

7. MR 1.2(a), 1.4(a)(1); RLGL §20(3).

illegal conduct, the lawyer must promptly inform the client that the conduct is not permitted, and must explain why.[8]

The third sphere of authority includes all other decisions not reserved solely to clients or lawyers. Here, the lawyer must reasonably consult with the client about the means to be used to achieve the client's goals, keep the client reasonably informed about the status of the matter, promptly respond to client requests for information, and provide enough information to enable the client to make informed decisions regarding the representation.[9] In other words, within this sphere of shared authority, lawyers and clients may bargain for broad delegation of authority to a lawyer, close continuing consultation with a client, or some measure of each.[10]

The outcome of this agreement creates the express terms of the engagement or actual authority, which obligates lawyers to obey the client's lawful instructions and empowers lawyers to act on behalf of the client.[11] Actual authority includes implied authority, which encompasses the authority to act in a manner that will further the client's objectives, as long as the lawyer reasonably believes the client desires such action.[12] Once reasonable consultation has occurred, lawyers are impliedly authorized to take lawful measures to advance the client's objectives.[13]

The scope of a client's control and the lawyer's authority also impacts the client's relationship with third parties. A lawyer-agent who acts within this scope legally binds the client-principal.[14] A client also can be bound by a lawyer's apparent authority, that is, authority "traceable to the principal's manifestations" that causes another to reasonably believe the lawyer-agent had the requisite authority to act on behalf of the client.[15]

Problems

4-1. Plaintiff retained Fox in a personal injury case. A few weeks later, Fox proudly informed Plaintiff that he had settled the case for a tidy sum. Plaintiff replied that she would never settle for that amount and refused to sign a release. What should Fox do? Does it matter if Fox agreed to the settlement during a mandatory court-annexed mediation?

4-2. Martyn represented Defendant, who was charged with first degree sexual assault. During the trial, Defendant and Martyn discussed the pros and cons of whether to ask the court for a lesser-included jury instruction for assault, and Martyn decided against such a request. After the jury convicted Defendant, Martyn believes she made a mistake and recalls that Defendant wanted her to ask for the lesser-

---

8. MR 1.4(a)(5); RLGL §20(1).
9. MR 1.4; RLGL §20.
10. *Id. See also* MR 1.2(a), 1.4.
11. *Restatement (Third) Agency* at §8.09 (Tentative Draft No. 2, 2001); RLGL §21 Comment d.
12. *Id.* at Comment b; *Restatement (Third) Agency* §2.01 (Tentative Draft No. 2, 2001).
13. MR 1.2(a); RLGL §21(3).
14. RLGL §26.
15. *Restatement (Third) Agency* §2.03 (Tentative Draft No. 2, 2001); RLGL §27.

included instruction. If these facts can be established on appeal, should Defendant prevail?

Consider: Model Rules 1.2, 1.4
          Model Code DR 7-101
          RLGL §§20-23, 25-27

Machado v. Statewide Grievance Committee

890 A.2d 622 (Conn. App. 2006)

GRUENDEL, J.

The plaintiff, Arthur D. Machado, an attorney, appeals from the judgment of the trial court dismissing his appeal from the reprimand issued to him by the defendant, the statewide grievance committee. . . .

. . . The plaintiff is an attorney licensed by the state of Connecticut and was retained by the complainant, Scott V. Adams, to represent him in a bankruptcy proceeding. The plaintiff initially met with Adams in January, 2000, while Adams was in prison. At the meeting, Adams instructed the plaintiff to communicate with Kendra Cihocki because, as a prisoner, Adams had limited means of communication. Subsequent to the meeting, Cihocki delivered an $850 check to the defendant as a retainer for Adams' bankruptcy filing.

Thereafter, Cihocki instructed the plaintiff to obtain the release of a sales tax lien that had been placed on a business owned by Adams and Cihocki. The plaintiff provided legal services in connection with the removal of the sales tax lien and, in so doing, depleted the retainer. Shortly thereafter, Cihocki picked up the file from the plaintiff's office and

retained new counsel. No funds were left to pursue Adams' bankruptcy, and the plaintiff took no further action on the bankruptcy. Furthermore, the plaintiff did not inform Adams that he no longer was pursuing the bankruptcy proceeding on his behalf.

In August, 2000, the plaintiff decided to close his office, and he released his last staff member the following month. By March, 2001, the lease on the plaintiff's office expired. During that time, Adams attempted to contact the plaintiff by telephone and mail regarding the status of his bankruptcy.[4] Adams never received a response to his telephone messages or letters.

On March 19, 2002, Adams filed a complaint with the defendant, alleging, among other things, that the plaintiff had failed to respond to letters and telephone calls made by Adams in 2000 and 2001. Adams also claimed that the plaintiff owed him [$850] because the plaintiff did not perform work on the bankruptcy as initially agreed by both parties. . . .

The plaintiff first . . . argues that Cihocki was Adams' agent and, therefore, the plaintiff was obliged to follow her orders in assisting with

---

4. Adams claimed that he spoke with the plaintiff's secretary, left messages and wrote a letter to the plaintiff outlining how he wanted to proceed with the bankruptcy. The plaintiff contended that he never received any telephone calls or correspondence from Adams during that time.

releasing a sales tax lien. We are not persuaded. . . .

First, in its February 14, 2003 decision, the reviewing committee found by clear and convincing evidence that "[Adams] retained the [plaintiff] to represent him in his bankruptcy." The reviewing committee further determined that Cihocki was indeed Adams' agent for the bankruptcy filing, but ceased being Adams' agent when she directed the plaintiff to release a sales tax lien on property owned by her and Adams. "The [plaintiff's] failure to abide by [Adams'] decision to file for bankruptcy and failure to consult with [Adams] regarding the change in the scope of representation from bankruptcy to release of a sales tax lien constituted a violation of rule 1.2 (a) of the Rules of Professional Conduct."

Second, the reviewing committee determined that the plaintiff did not keep Adams reasonably informed about the status of the bankruptcy. "By not informing [Adams] that his agent had instructed the [plaintiff] to change the scope of representation from bankruptcy to release of the sales tax lien, the [plaintiff] violated rule 1.4 (a) of the Rules of Professional Conduct."

In his brief, the plaintiff claims that Cihocki had both actual and apparent authority[8] to redirect his actions to release the sales tax lien. The plaintiff argues that Cihocki had actual authority because Adams gave her a power of attorney and told the plaintiff to follow her instructions. The plaintiff also contends that Cihocki had apparent authority because it was reasonable for him to assume that Cihocki's authority extended to the redirection of his work to encompass the sales tax lien. In support of his contention, the plaintiff lists a number of facts, including that he "spoke to Ms. Cihocki on an almost daily basis" and "spoke with Adams at his initial meeting and at least once by telephone regarding the tax liens. . . ." He also claims that "the tax liens were among the debts to be discharged in the bankruptcy. . . ." We are not persuaded by those arguments. . . .

In the present case, . . . the reviewing committee determined that the plaintiff failed to abide by Adams' decision to file for bankruptcy and failed to inform Adams regarding the change in the scope of representation from bankruptcy to release of a sales tax lien. Indeed, the plaintiff admitted that he was mistaken in not having a new fee agreement document prepared when Cihocki asked him to do work on the tax issue.[9] . . .

The plaintiff further argues that . . . he was discharged by Adams

---

8. "Actual authority may be express or implied. . . . Implied authority is actual authority circumstantially proved. It is the authority which the principal intended his agent to possess. . . . Implied authority is a fact to be proven by deductions or inferences from the manifestations of consent of the principal . . . and [the] agent." "Apparent authority is that semblance of authority which a principal, through his own acts or inadvertences, causes or allows third persons to believe his agent possesses. . . . Consequently, apparent authority is to be determined, not by the agent's own acts, but by the acts of the agent's principal. . . . The issue of apparent authority is one of fact to be determined based on two criteria. . . . First, it must appear from the principal's conduct that the principal held the agent out as possessing sufficient authority to embrace the act in question, or knowingly permitted [the agent] to act as having such authority. . . . Second, the party dealing with the agent must have, acting in good faith, reasonably believed, under all the circumstances, that the agent had the necessary authority to bind the principal to the agent's action."
9. According to the plaintiff, Adams had signed a flat fee retainer agreement in connection with a chapter 7 bankruptcy petition.

and therefore could not have violated rules 1.2 (a) and 1.4 (a). Specifically, the plaintiff claims he was discharged when Cihocki picked up Adams' file from the plaintiff's office and retained new counsel. The plaintiff's argument is without merit.

. . . [T]he reviewing committee found by clear and convincing evidence that Cihocki no longer was Adams' agent when she directed the plaintiff to work on the release of a sales tax lien. In addition, the court noted that the plaintiff's failures to abide by Adams' decision to file for bankruptcy and to consult with Adams regarding the change in the scope of representation occurred prior to the removal of the file from the plaintiff's office. Even if the plaintiff was discharged when the file was picked up, the plaintiff already had violated rules 1.2 (a) and 1.4 (a). . . .

III

The plaintiff's third claim is that the court improperly determined that scienter was not necessary to constitute a violation of rules 1.2 (a) and 1.4 (a) of the Rules of Professional Conduct. In Statewide Grievance Committee v. Presnick, 559 A.2d 220 (Conn. App. 1989), this court observed that a finding of bad faith or corrupt motive is not necessary to constitute a professional misconduct violation. . . .

The fact that the plaintiff may not have acted in bad faith plays no part in determining whether he violated rules 1.2 (a) and 1.4 (a) of the Rules of Professional Conduct. Therefore, regardless of the plaintiff's scienter at the time that he worked on Adams' bankruptcy, substantial evidence exists in the record that the plaintiff violated the two rules.

The judgment is affirmed.

▨ Lawyers and Other Professionals: *Informed Consent*

Machado makes clear that the lawyer's failure to consult with his client throughout the representation caused Machado to mistake the nature and scope of the representation (bankruptcy or tax lien). The same lack of communication caused Machado to misunderstand the scope of his client's agent authority in directing the goals of the representation.

The law governing lawyers relies heavily on the notion of informed consent as a means to enable clients to maintain control and to prevent lawyers from breaching fiduciary duties. The Model Rules of Professional Conduct also define the requirement and impose the obligation on lawyers as a precondition to receiving instructions from a client,[16] to limiting the scope of a representation,[17] to disclosing or using confidential information,[18] and to resolving conflicts of interest.[19] Although the idea of informed consent can be linked to centuries-old concepts of fiduciary obligation, it is better known in recent legal literature as a doctrine that governs the conduct of physicians and other health care providers.

---

16. MR 1.2(a), 1.4.
17. MR 1.2(c).
18. MR 1.6(a), 1.9(a), 1.18(d).
19. MR 1.7(b)(4), 1.8-1.12, 2.3(b).

In this note, we trace the similarities as well as the distinctive features of the law of informed consent in both professions.

Autonomous Authorization

The recognition of a professional's legal obligation to disclose information to clients or patients emphasizes the importance of autonomy, or self-governance. The law of informed consent reflects the belief that persons make a real choice only if they have (1) understood information, (2) appreciated the consequences of a choice, and (3) used reason to evaluate this information. The law of informed consent imposes dual duties on professionals as a means of promoting the autonomous choices of those they serve: an obligation to provide information and deference to client choice.

Morally, respect for autonomy has deontological roots. Autonomy is essential to both religious and philosophical notions of respect for the dignity of the human person.[20] For example, Kant envisioned persons as inherently valuable because we are self-legislating agents capable of shaping our own destinies.[21] Making decisions requires an application of personal values to determine a future course, which in turn depends upon a view of humans as being free and rational. We respect a human person by relying on that person's own self-determined choices. To withhold or skew relevant information, even for a person's own good, is to treat him or her as an object to be manipulated.[22]

Autonomy also has been promoted on utilitarian grounds, because it promotes rational decision making. For example, John Stuart Mill argued that individuality was an element of well-being and that we further have affirmative obligations to actively strengthen autonomous expression by arguing with those who have mistaken views.[23] Lawyers and physicians often are unable to know what values their clients and patients place on alternative courses of action. The subjectivity of weighing possible consequences and the reality that the client must live with the eventual result of the decision lead many to argue that informed consent maximizes the benefit of decision making to clients, professionals, and the institutions they work in.

There is also considerable empirical evidence for this conclusion. In law, a study of New York City personal injury plaintiffs concluded that clients who actively participated in the conduct of their claim got significantly better results than those who passively delegated decision-making responsibility.[24] Similar studies in medicine validate the efficacy of informed consent in clinical decision making.[25]

---

20. *See* Marcy Strauss, *Toward a Revised Model of Attorney-Client Relationship: The Argument for Autonomy,* 65 N.C. L. Rev. 315, 336 (1987).
21. *See* Jessica W. Berg et al., *Informed Consent: Legal Theory and Clinical Practice* 22, 31 (2d ed., Oxford 2001).
22. *See* Isaiah Berlin, *Four Essays on Liberty* 137 (Oxford 1969).
23. Tom L. Beauchamp & James F. Childress, *Principles of Biomedical Ethics* 64 (5th ed., Oxford 2001).
24. Douglas E. Rosenthal, *Lawyer and Client: Who's In Charge?* 61 (Russell Sage Found. 1974).
25. Berg et al., *supra* note 21 at 26-30; Susan R. Martyn, *Informed Consent in the Practice of Law,* 48 Geo. Wash. L. Rev. 307, 340-343 (1980).

Lawyers

For lawyers, agency law imposes the obligation of informed consent. The requirement that a lawyer has an affirmative duty to advise a client "promptly whenever he has any information to give which it is important the client should receive"[26] originated in nineteenth-century agency cases where lawyers breached client confidentiality, failed to disclose a conflicting personal interest, or neglected to notify their clients about material facts in a transaction. These courts characterized the breach as a constructive fraud, because the client acted without sufficient information.[27] Many of these early cases focused on when such disclosure must be made, creating the foundation for our current understanding that disclosure is required to avoid breaching fiduciary duties of obedience, confidentiality, and loyalty. None of these cases required any expert testimony to establish the breach of fiduciary duty. It was enough if the lawyer failed to disclose sufficient information to allow the client to make an autonomous choice.

In this chapter, we encounter lawyers who did not clarify their clients' instructions or did not obey them, and in chapters to come we will also encounter lawyers who disclosed confidential information that harmed their clients,[28] and lawyers who used confidential information from their clients for the benefit of others.[29] We will also see situations where the lawyer's disclosures to clients have been insufficient to overcome a presumption of undue influence,[30] to justify a sexual relationship with a client,[31] to legitimate a joint representation,[32] or to collect a contingent fee.[33] In all of these cases, the special knowledge and skill of the lawyers gave them the power inadvertently or intentionally to abuse the trust of their clients. The courts' recognition of a fiduciary duty of disclosure and obedience protected these clients' right to individualized representation of their best interests. At the same time, proper consent of the clients could have prevented some of these breaches.

The Model Rules require that lawyers initiate the information and consent process on six different occasions.

- When decisions require client consent about the objectives of the representation, such as the decision to settle or appeal a matter.[34]
- When seeking any waiver of a client fiduciary obligation, especially confidentiality and conflicts of interest.[35]
- When decisions require client consent about the means to be used to accomplish client objectives. This could include, for example, whether to

---

26. Baker v. Humphrey, 101 U.S. 494, 500 (1879).
27. Martyn, *supra* note 25 at 323.
28. Perez v. Kirk & Carrigan, *infra* Chapter 6; In re Pressly, *infra* p. 189.
29. Matter of Anonymous, *infra* Chapter 6; Maritrans GP Inc. v. Pepper, Hamilton & Scheetz, *infra* p. 285.
30. Monco v. Janus, *infra* p. 294.
31. In re Halverson, *infra* p. 305.
32. Anderson v. O'Brien, *infra* p. 350.
33. Burrow v. Arce, *infra* p. 333.
34. *See* MR 1.2(a); RLGL §22.
35. *See* MR 1.4(a)(1), 1.6-1.12; RLGL §§20, 60-62, 121-135.

litigate, arbitrate, or mediate a matter; whether to stipulate to a set of facts; or whether to consult with another lawyer.[36]

- When necessary to periodically update clients on the status of a matter, including information about important developments in the representation itself, as well as changes in the lawyer's practice, such as a serious illness of the lawyer or a merger with another law firm.[37]
- When the client requests information.[38]
- When the client expects assistance but the lawyer cannot give it due to legal limitations on the lawyer's conduct, such as the obligation not to counsel or assist client crimes or frauds.[39]

The most difficult part of understanding the duty of informed consent for lawyers and other professionals involves knowing how much and what kind of information to disclose. Most cases require complete disclosure of all information that may be relevant to the lawyer's representation.[40] The disclosure must include both material facts as well as an explanation of their legal significance. Lawyer codes gradually have come to reflect a similar obligation to disclose and explain all material relevant information.[41]

The current Model Rules recognize the importance of both disclosure and explanation of relevant information by creating a uniform "informed consent" standard.[42] A client's agreement constitutes informed consent if the lawyer has communicated "adequate information and explanation" about two matters: "the material risks of and reasonably available alternatives to the proposed course of conduct."[43] Disclosure requirements for specific conflicts also have been clarified.[44] Labeling this obligation "informed consent" restates the lawyer's fiduciary obligation recognized in several centuries of cases.[45] Defining the content

---

36. *See* MR 1.2(a), 1.4(a)(2), 2.1; RLGL §21. In some matters, such as trials, lawyers have inherent authority to act for clients when the legal system demands an immediate decision without time for consultation. RLGL §23, Comment d. This exception roughly correlates to the emergency exception to physician informed consent. *See* note 71 *infra.*
37. RLGL §20, Comment c; MR 1.4(a)(3).
38. RLGL §20, Comment d; MR 1.4(a)(4).
39. RLGL §22, Comment c; MR 1.4(a)(5).
40. Ronald E. Mallen & Jeffrey M. Smith, *Legal Malpractice* §14.19, 616 (5th ed., West 2000).
41. *See, e.g.,* ABA Canons of Prof. Ethics, Canon 6 (1908) (With respect to conflicting interests, lawyer had a duty to disclose "all of the circumstances of his relations to the parties, and any interest in or connection with the controversy, which might influence the client . . ." and to acquire "express consent of all concerned given after a full disclosure of the facts."); ABA Model Code of Professional Responsibility (1983) ("full disclosure" required to reveal or use confidential information, DR 4-101(C)(1), and to obtain adequate consent to conflicts of interest, DR 5-101(A); DR 5-104(a); DR 5-107(A)). The original Model Rules replaced this full disclosure mandate with a "consent following consultation" standard, with consultation meaning "communication of information reasonably sufficient to permit the client to appreciate the significance of the matter in question." Model Rules, Terminology ¶2 (1983).
42. MR 1.0(e) (informed consent).
43. *Id.*
44. *Id.,* MR 1.5(e) (fee division with another lawyer), 1.8(i) (business transactions with clients), 1.8(g) (aggregate settlements), 2.4(b) (third-party neutral). The RLGL generally follows the same approach. In many places the Restatement adopted a "consent following consultation" standard borrowed from the original Model Rules. But it developed an informed consent standard for client waivers of conflicts of interest. *See, e.g.,* RLGL §§16, 20, 62, 122(1).
45. *See, e.g., Metrick v. Chatz,* 639 N.E.2d 198, 201 (Ill. App. 1994) (allegations that lawyers failed to disclose available options for alternative legal solutions, as well as to explain the

of required disclosure to include material risks and reasonably available alternatives parallels the same standard that has emerged in the last quarter century
in medicine.[46]

Health Care Providers

A patient's consent to a health care provider authorizes what would otherwise be
considered a harmful physical invasion of that person's body. While any action
or words can convey this authorization, the person's consent is not informed
unless he or she first understands the nature and purpose of the invasion and its
probable results. Courts have recognized this right in civil actions that allege
battery, lack of informed consent, and violation of constitutional liberty rights.[47]

Speaking many years ago in a battery case, Judge Cardozo said: "Every
human being of adult years and sound mind has a right to determine what shall
be done with his own body."[48] The idea that a legally valid consent can only
occur following the provision of information about foreseeable complications or
risks of a medical procedure came later.[49] In the landmark case of *Canterbury v.
Spence*, the D.C. Circuit Court of Appeals first articulated a negligence theory
for an informed consent cause of action.[50] The court held that the "fiducial
quality" of the doctor-patient relationship gave rise to a duty to disclose that
depended on patient need rather than medical custom. This duty required
disclosure of material risks and side effects as well as alternatives to the proposed treatment. Risks are material "when a reasonable person, in what the
physician knows or should know to be the patient's position, would be likely to
attach significance to the risk. . . ."[51] Failure to disclose a material risk constitutes breach of the duty to secure informed consent. To prove causation in
informed consent cases, the plaintiff must show that a reasonably prudent
person in the plaintiff's position would have decided otherwise if they had been
informed. Damages are established by showing that the undisclosed risk materialized.[52]

In the past quarter century, this standard of informed consent based on
patient need has been adopted in about half of American jurisdictions.[53] The

---

foreseeable risks and benefits of each, amount to "nothing more than an application of the long-
standing rule pertinent to a cause of action for medical negligence premised upon a lack of
informed consent").

46. Martyn, *supra* note 25.

47. *See, e.g.,* Wash. v. Glucksberg, 521 U.S. 702, 724-727 (1997); Cruzan v. Director, 497 U.S.
261, 279 (1990); *id.* at 287 (O'Connor, J., concurring); Ruth R. Faden & Tom L. Beauchamp, *A
History and Theory of Informed Consent* 114-150 (Oxford 1986). Recognition of a constitutional
right opens the door to a civil rights action against state or federal actors. *See, e.g.,* In re
Cincinnati Radiation Litig., 874 F. Supp. 796 (S.D. Ohio 1995).

48. Schloendorff v. Socy. of N.Y. Hosp., 105 N.E. 92, 93 (1914).

49. Shortly after the mid-twentieth century, courts begin to hold that physicians who failed to
disclose potential complications of treatment to patients committed a "technical battery," because
the consent given did not contemplate the risk that materialized. *See, e.g.,* Gray v. Grunnagle, 223
A.2d 663 (Pa. 1966); Scott v. Wilson, 396 S.W.2d 532 (Tex. Civ. App. 1965), *aff'd,* Wilson v.
Scott, 412 S.W.2d 299 (Tex. 1967); Bang v. Charles T. Miller Hosp., 88 N.W.2d 186 (Minn.
1958).

50. 464 F.2d 772 (D.C. Cir. 1972). *See also* Cobbs v. Grant, 502 P.2d 1 (Cal. 1972).

51. *Canterbury,* 464 F.2d at 787.

52. *Id.* at 790-791.

53. Dan B. Dobbs, *The Law of Torts* 655 (West 2000).

other half recognizes custom-based informed consent; that is, the plaintiff must introduce expert testimony that establishes the appropriate standard of care regarding disclosure by similarly situated physicians.[54] Topics of disclosure include information about the nature of the procedure, the material risks and side effects of the proposed intervention, and alternatives to the proposed treatment, including the alternative of no medical intervention.[55] The duty applies not only to situations involving physician-proposed treatment, but also when withholding consent to a diagnostic test or intervention creates a material risk.[56] Recent decisions address whether physicians also have a duty to disclose physician-specific information, such as the extent of their experience with a given procedure, and the alternatives of other more skilled practitioners.[57]

One group of informed consent cases against physicians parallels those based on breach of fiduciary duty against lawyers. In cases of "economic informed consent," plaintiffs allege that personal and economic interests of the physician conflict with therapeutic motivations. Where this conflict arises in the context of a physician who conducts research on a patient, both federal regulations and common law impose a full disclosure standard.[58] More generally, courts impose a duty on physicians to disclose "personal interests unrelated to the patient's health, whether research or economic, that may affect the physician's professional judgment."[59] Failure to provide this information constitutes both a lack of informed consent and a breach of fiduciary duty.

This theory has been relied on to create duties to disclose economic incentives in managed care plans. The recent trend has been for courts to deny

---

54. *E.g.,* Tashman v. Gibbs, 556 S.E.2d 772 (Va. 2002).
55. Berg et al., *supra* note 21 at 53-61. *E.g.,* Matthies v. Mastromonaco, 733 A.2d 456 (N.J. 1999) (risk of femur displacement and never walking again from bed rest following hip fracture compared to risk of surgical intervention to pin hip).
56. *E.g.,* Truman v. Thomas, 611 P.2d 902 (Cal. 1980) (risk of death from not consenting to a pap smear).
57. *E.g.,* Johnson v. Kokemoor, 545 N.W.2d 495 (Wis. 1995) (duty to disclose that physician had never done the procedure before and the availability of other, more skilled nearby practitioners); Hidding v. Williams, 578 So. 2d 1192 (La. App. 1991) (duty to disclose personal chronic alcohol abuse). *But see* Duttry v. Patterson, 771 A.2d 1255 (Pa. 2001) (no duty to disclose physician-specific information, even when patient asks for it). *See also* Aaron D. Twerski & Neil B. Cohen, *The Second Revolution in Informed Consent: Comparing Physicians to Each Other,* 94 Nw. U. L. Rev. 1 (1999).
58. *See, e.g.,* Blaz v. Michael Reese Hosp. Found., 191 F.R.D. 570 (N.D. Ill. 1999) (duty to warn of results of research discovered at a later time); Kus v. Sherman Hosp., 644 N.E.2d 1214 (Ill. App. 1995) (cause of action for battery and lack of informed consent stated for physician and hospital's failures to monitor informed consent to research); In re Cincinnati Radiation Litig., *supra* note 46 (plaintiffs denied procedural and substantive due process by professionals who did not inform them they were the subjects of radiation experiments); Mink v. U. of Chic., 460 F. Supp. 713 (N.D. Ill. 1978) (plaintiffs state cause of action for battery and lack of informed consent against physicians who failed to inform them they were part of a double-blind experiment with DES). Federal regulations require that the patient be told that he or she is a subject of a research protocol, given a description of the research project, its risks, benefits, and alternatives to the research, and that participation is voluntary and may be ended at any time. 45 C.F.R. §46.116 (2005).
59. Moore v. Regents of the U. of Cal., 793 P.2d 479 (Cal. 1990). This translated into a duty to inform the patient that the physician had used tissue from the patient's surgically removed spleen to develop a patented cell line, worth millions of dollars. The court left the issue of damages open, but specifically held that the patient had no right to claim all the profits based on a cause of action for conversion.

such a separate cause of action, finding it more appropriate to focus on whether any medical malpractice occurred in the treatment.[60] Some suggest that the insurer rather than the physician should have such a duty.[61]

The Limits of Informed Consent

Both professions' doctrines of informed consent also agree that consent validates most, but not all, proposed conduct by professionals. First, in some circumstances the potential for undue influence makes voluntary consent nearly impossible. Some conflicts of interest, like sexual relationships between professionals and their clients or patients, cannot be legitimated by client consent.[62] Lawyers prohibit many other conflicts as well.[63] Similarly, federal regulations governing medical research also classify some interventions as too risky to be the subject of any informed consent.[64] Other clearly established professional duties also are not negotiable because their absence typically would cause great harm to clients or patients. For lawyers, this includes the requirement that client property be held in trust,[65] obligations to courts[66] and third parties,[67] and obligations to supervise staff.[68] For physicians, it includes proper sterilization techniques, instrument and sponge counts in surgery, and prescribing the correct medications.[69]

Finally, both professions recognize limited circumstances when clients or patients lack the capacity to give an authentic informed consent, but probably will benefit from an intervention. In medicine, this occurs most often in emergencies when action must be taken to prevent harm before consent can be obtained.[70] Here, the law of consent presumes that most patients would consent if able, and allows an implied consent rationale based on the physician's view of the best interests of the patient, as long as that person has not indicated otherwise.[71] In law, this same notion of best interests in the face of incapacity also justifies action on behalf of clients with diminished capacity who face imminent harm,[72] and organization clients whose managers fail to refrain from unlawful activity, threatening substantial harm to the organization.[73]

---

60. *See, e.g.,* Pegram v. Herdrich, 530 U.S. 211 (2000) (no cause of action for breach of fiduciary duty under ERISA); Neade v. Portes, 739 N.E.2d 496 (Ill. 2000) (breach of fiduciary duty claim duplicates medical malpractice claim).
61. *Id.* at 504, citing an American Medical Association opinion that requires disclosure of "any financial inducements that may tend to limit the diagnostic and therapeutic alternatives that are offered to patients or that may tend to limit patients' overall access to care," but allows physicians to satisfy this duty "by assuring that a managed care plan makes adequate disclosure to those enrolled in the plan."
62. *See Lawyers and Other Professionals: Sexual Relationships with Clients, infra* p. 311.
63. *See, e.g.,* MR 1.7(b)(2)-(3), 1.8(c)-(f).
64. *See* Basic HHS Policy for Protection of Human Research Subjects, 45 C.F.R. pt 46 (2005).
65. *E.g.,* MR 1.15.
66. MR 3.1-3.9.
67. MR 4.1-4.4.
68. MR 5.1-5.3.
69. Berg et al., *supra* note 21 at 133.
70. *Restatement (Second) of Torts* §892(D). Some cases articulate another exception that has rarely been applied, the so-called therapeutic exception, where disclosure would menace the patient's health. *See also* Dobbs, *supra* note 53, 656-657.
71. *Id.*
72. MR 1.14(b).
73. MR 1.13(c).

Informed Consent in the Practice of Law and Medicine

Both law and medicine envision informed consent as validating what would otherwise constitute a potentially harmful professional action. This explains why each profession's articulation of informed consent has influenced the other. The notion of informed consent as a means to avoid breaches of fiduciary duty by lawyers has influenced and may continue to inform similar duties for health care professionals. At the same time, the doctrine of informed consent in medicine continues to enlighten duties of disclosure for lawyers.

For lawyers, fiduciary duty means that disclosure must occur whenever the client has a right to decide; specifically, reasonable disclosure of material risks and alternatives must occur to enable the clients to determine the goals of the representation (as did not occur in either *Machado,* or in *dePape* below), and to legitimate any potential breach of confidentiality or loyalty. Many of these loyalty cases involve personal financial interests of the lawyer that conflict with those of the client. Physicians have not yet seen full implementation of such an economic theory of informed consent. They can benefit from understanding the admonition of lawyer conflict of interest cases that prohibit the lawyer from putting her own welfare above that of the client. When health care providers acquire a particular financial interest that conflicts with the health of a patient, they should be required to disclose that interest.[74]

At the same time, lawyers have learned and benefited from the articulation of the informed consent doctrine in medicine. Although fiduciary notions make clear when a lawyer must disclose, they have not always clearly articulated what must be said. Analogizing to health care cases has assisted such an analysis. It is not yet clear the extent to which lawyer-specific information, such as lack of experience with similar cases, must be disclosed. Cases that allege a parallel duty of lawyers may rely on cases against physicians that alleged similar failures to disclose.

B. Communication

The duty to communicate with clients is essential to every aspect of every fiduciary duty lawyers owe clients. Clients cannot control the goals of the representation without information about feasible options. Lawyers cannot act competently unless they initiate communication with clients to understand the initial scope of the relationship and what the clients wish to accomplish. Lawyers must communicate with clients about confidentiality so that clients can decide when to disclose information. They must search for and discuss with clients potential as well as actual conflicts of interest in order to proceed with a representation.

---

74. *See* Grant H. Morris, *Dissing Disclosure: Just What the Doctor Ordered,* 44 Ariz. L. Rev. 313 (2002); Nancy J. Moore, *What Doctors Can Learn from Lawyers About Conflicts of Interest,* 81 B.U. L. Rev. 445 (2001).

Problems

4-3. In representing Employer, Martyn & Fox forgot to insert a non-compete clause into an employment agreement for a new key employee, even though Employer had specifically requested that protection. Any problem? What if Martyn & Fox forgot to advise Employer that a covenant not to compete could be included?

4-4. Client retains Martyn to handle a contract dispute with an important customer of Client. Martyn files suit, warns Client of the risks of going to trial, is unable to settle the case, and the case ends in an adverse jury verdict. Disgruntled Client called Martyn several weeks later. "I've been talking to one of my lawyer friends. He couldn't understand why we didn't mediate this dispute. We could've gotten a great settlement and I wouldn't have lost a customer." Should Martyn have offered Client the option of mediation or arbitration?

> Consider: Model Rules 1.2, 1.4, 2.1
> Model Code EC 7-8
> RLGL §§16, 20-23, 49

dePape v. Trinity Health Systems, Inc.

242 F. Supp. 2d 585 (N.D. Iowa 2003)

BENNETT, Chief Judge . . .

The plaintiff in this breach-of-contract and legal malpractice case, Dr. Gregory dePape, is a Canadian citizen who completed his medical studies and training in Canada. Thousands of miles away in the small city of Fort Dodge, Iowa, Trimark Physicians Group, Ltd. ("Trimark") [a wholly owned subsidiary of Trinity Health Systems, Inc.] sought a family physician to fill a vacancy and to meet the burgeoning needs of the Fort Dodge medical community. Through a consulting firm, Trimark successfully recruited Dr. dePape to fill this vacancy, and in March of 1999, Trimark and Dr. dePape, while still living and working in Canada, entered into a five-year employment contract.

As part of the contract negotiations process, the parties discussed immigration matters and the fact that

Dr. dePape needed to obtain a visa for lawful entry and permission to work in the United States prior to beginning employment. In order to obtain such permission, Trimark engaged the services of a St. Louis, Missouri law firm, Blumenfeld, Kaplan & Sandweiss, P.C. . . .

On April 23, 1999, one month after Trimark and Dr. dePape entered into their employment contract, Blumenfeld held an initial conference regarding its representation of Trimark and Dr. dePape. Partners A and B of the Blumenfeld firm, [and representatives of Trimark] participated in this initial conference. Notably, Blumenfeld did not advise Dr. dePape to participate, nor did it even inform him of the conference. At this conference, Blumenfeld outlined Dr. dePape's immigration options. At the time of this conference, Blumenfeld learned (1) that Dr. dePape had a five-year employment contract with Trimark; (2) that both Dr. dePape and Trimark expected an employment relationship that would endure longer than five years and, ideally, the entirety of Dr. dePape's medical career; and (3) that Dr. dePape had not taken a three-stage set of examinations, known as the USMLE's, [United States Medical Licensing Examination] which precluded him from receiving one of the two visas available to foreign physicians—namely, the H-1B visa. . . .

After holding the initial conference, Partner A sent [Trimark] an engagement letter on April 26, 1999, confirming the parties' agreement and Blumenfeld's commitment to represent Trimark *and* Dr. dePape throughout the immigration process. . . . The engagement letter specifically states that both Trimark and Dr. dePape are Blumenfeld's clients, but Partner A sent a copy of the letter only to Trimark. . . . The engagement letter outlines Dr. dePape's immigration options; yet Blumenfeld did not send a copy to him, nor did Blumenfeld advise Trimark to forward the engagement letter to Dr. dePape, who . . . did not see the letter until preparing for this trial. . . .

It is undisputed that an H-1B visa is the preferred method of bringing a foreign physician into the United States. . . .

In order to perform direct patient care on an H-1B visa, the foreign physician must have successfully completed the USMLE's.

. . . Blumenfeld never attempted to ascertain whether Dr. dePape would complete the USMLE's, nor did it advise Dr. dePape that completion of the USMLE's was a necessary prerequisite to obtaining an H-1B visa and would be in his best interest. . . . Dr. dePape declined that

option because he held misconceptions about the length of time that it took to complete the exams. Dr. dePape believed that the USMLE's could not be completed in fewer than two years, while Partner A and Partner B testified that the process could be completed in six to eight months, [which Dr. dePape could have completed while waiting for his Iowa medical license]. . . .

[Eight months later when] Blumenfeld belatedly ascertained that Dr. dePape could not enter the country on an H-1B visa, it switched gears and began working on a TN visa. . . .

When Blumenfeld began work on a TN visa for Dr. dePape, it knew that the position described in his Employment Agreement would not pass muster as an acceptable TN classification job description. . . . Because Dr. dePape had a contract that outlasted the duration of the TN visa and was for a job that was not permitted by the visa, Blumenfeld, without consulting its clients, concocted a fictitious job title and description. Blumenfeld labeled this position "Physician Consultant" and described the duties of this position as a "community health care needs assessment." Blumenfeld did not discuss with Dr. dePape or Trimark the newly created position or the fact that Dr. dePape could not enter the United States and practice family medicine on the TN visa. . . .

. . . [W]hile Blumenfeld was billing for an H1B visa for which Dr. dePape was not qualified and preparing its sham TN application, Dr. dePape . . . worked in Canada doing locum tenens, which is temporary substitution work for vacationing physicians.

When Dr. dePape learned that he would be granted his Iowa medical license, he and Trimark ... then worked with Blumenfeld to arrange a June 8, 2000 entry at the Peace Bridge in Buffalo, New York, which Blumenfeld chose because of its arrangement with a particular INS officer. Dr. dePape ended his lease, shipped all of his belongings and his vehicle to Fort Dodge, and terminated his locum tenens. He and his fiancée ... flew from Vancouver to Toronto, and then rented a car to drive to Buffalo, New York. They planned to drive across the border, drop the car off at the rental station in Buffalo, and then fly to Fort Dodge, Iowa, where Dr. dePape intended to begin his new life. ...

Because the costs of accompanying Dr. dePape to his INS interview at the Peace Bridge were prohibitively high, Blumenfeld, consistent with its usual practice, retained its local immigration lawyer, Mr. Eiss, to assist Dr. dePape. Mr. Eiss met Dr. dePape at a coffee shop near the INS office in Fort Erie, Canada on the morning of June 8, 2000. There, for the first time, Dr. dePape was shown the letter describing his position as a Physician Consultant and told that he could not work in the United States as a family physician. ...

... During this short meeting, Mr. Eiss played the role of an immigration officer and asked Dr. dePape what he was planning on doing in the United States. Dr. dePape responded that he was going to be a family physician. Mr. Eiss shook his head and handed Dr. dePape the TN application letter. Dr. dePape was shocked, surprised, and outraged by the letter's description of his position and its temporary nature because, as far as he knew, he was permanently moving to Fort Dodge to be a doctor, not a temporary Physician Consultant doing a community health care

needs assessment—something he had never heard about or even knew what it was. Dr. dePape was skeptical and concerned about the lawfulness of representing to INS that he intended to perform a community health care needs assessment and then return to Canada. However, Mr. Eiss convinced Dr. dePape that the community health care needs assessment was legal and only a mere technicality that would not impede him from practicing medicine. Hesitant but confident in the legal advice of his attorney, Dr. dePape proceeded with Mr. Eiss to the INS office to attempt Dr. dePape's entry under TN status.

There, the INS official interviewing Dr. dePape did not believe that Dr. dePape sought entry to perform a community health care needs assessment. When the INS official asked Dr. dePape directly why he was going to the United States, Dr. dePape truthfully answered that he intended to practice family medicine. Because the TN visa does not permit this, the INS official turned Dr. dePape away and sent him back to Canada. Mr. Eiss did not return with Dr. dePape to counsel him further.

Devastated and shocked by his failed entry and with no direction from Mr. Eiss or the Blumenfeld firm, Dr. dePape found a pay phone and called [a Trimark representative, who] advised him to wait thirty minutes and to try to enter the United States as a visitor. If he accomplished that, she instructed him to drop the rental car off at the Buffalo airport and to fly to Fort Dodge in order to work out a "plan B." Dr. dePape and his fiancée followed [this] advice, but the INS officials immediately recognized Dr. dePape. The officials not only interrogated him and accused him of being a liar, they searched his car and belongings and

Dr. dePape and his fiancée felt as if they were being treated like criminals. INS again denied Dr. dePape entry to the United States, told him not to come back, and escorted him back to Canada. Dr. dePape felt helpless, humiliated, and angry.

When that entry attempt failed, Dr. dePape was literally stranded. He had no job, no home, and no possessions—not even his medical bag. Fortunately, he had a credit card with him and, at his own expense, he and his fiancée drove back to Toronto, where they paid over two thousand U.S. dollars for last-minute plane tickets back to Vancouver. Throughout this entire ordeal, there was no backup contingency plan and no advice from Blumenfeld.

Ultimately, Dr. dePape returned to British Columbia and, in his words, "re-started his life." He made several attempts to contact Trimark, [whose representative eventually] implored Dr. dePape to attempt another entry in Buffalo, New York, but he refused. She then asked if he was willing to take the USMLE's, but because he labored under the impression that the exams would have taken years to complete, he refused that option as well. Instead, Dr. dePape explored his employment options in Canada and ultimately began his own private practice in October of 2001.

Shockingly, no one at Blumenfeld ever attempted to contact Dr. dePape after his failed entry attempt on June 8, 2000. . . . [The court dismissed all of Dr. dePape's claims against Trinity and Trimark.]

D. COUNT IV: LEGAL MALPRACTICE . . .

It is well established that an attorney-client relationship may give rise to a duty, the breach of which may be legal malpractice. In a legal malpractice case, the plaintiff must demonstrate:

(1) the existence of an attorney client relationship giving rise to a duty, (2) the attorney, either by an act or failure to act, violated or breached that duty, (3) the attorney's breach of duty proximately caused injury to the client, and (4) the client sustained actual injury, loss, or damage.

In this case, there is no dispute that an attorney-client relationship (the first element) existed between Dr. dePape and Blumenfeld. . . .

1. Failure to pursue H-1B visa . . .

There is no question that Dr. dePape was not eligible for an H-1B visa because he had not taken the requisite examinations—the USMLE's. There is also no question that Blumenfeld was negligent when it failed to advise Dr. dePape of the consequences of not taking the USMLE's and failed to correct his misconception about the length of time the exams took to complete.

However, the record is devoid of any evidence establishing that Dr. dePape would have taken the USMLE's and become eligible for an H-1B visa if Blumenfeld had advised him to do so. Thus, this claim fails for lack of causation. . . .

2. Failure to communicate and advise

a. Breach of duty . . .

"An attorney breaches the duty of care owed to the client when the attorney fails to use 'such skill, prudence and diligence as lawyers of ordinary skill and capacity commonly possess and exercise in the performance of the task which [is undertaken].'" Expert testimony is generally required to establish that an attorney's conduct is negligent, but, when the negligence is so obvious that a layperson can recognize or infer it, such testimony is unnecessary.

In this case, the plaintiff offered the deposition testimony of Bart Chavez to establish Blumenfeld's negligence. The court has reviewed Mr. Chavez's deposition, and his testimony strongly supports a finding of negligence in this case. Moreover, the court finds that Blumenfeld's breach is of the ilk that does not necessitate expert testimony because it is so obvious and outrageous that a lay person could easily recognize it without the assistance of an expert. Even in the absence of Mr. Chavez's expert testimony, which clearly identifies and articulates a standard of care that Blumenfeld failed to meet, the court is not without guidance in assessing the level of care Blumenfeld is charged with maintaining. Although violations of [the Rules of Professional Conduct] do not create a private cause of action for a client, the rules provide guidance in determining the fiduciary duty owed to a client by an attorney. . . .

Accordingly, the minimum communication Blumenfeld should have maintained with Dr. dePape is: [The court cites Model Rule 1.4 and Comment 5.]

In fact, Blumenfeld itself understands the importance of communication with its clients, and it prides itself on maintaining regular client contact. Indeed, the "letterhead" on each link of Blumenfeld's webpage advertises that Blumenfeld "recognize[s] the importance of personal contact with clients as an integral

part of being a responsive firm." www.bks-law.com. . . .

That Blumenfeld breached its duty of communicating with and advising Dr. dePape does not present the court with a close call. Because Dr. dePape had no information, he indisputably lacked sufficient information upon which to make an informed decision about his immigration. A 20 minute meeting with Mr. Eiss at the border on the morning of Dr. dePape's entry attempt, which was preceded by months of silence, did not cure Blumenfeld's failure to communicate with Dr. dePape because, by that time, it was too late for Dr. dePape to make an informed decision regarding his immigration to the United States. Moreover, the only decision Dr. dePape was ever allowed to make was the one he was faced with at the border—lie and proceed with the immigration charade or tell the truth and be rejected. . . .

While there are a myriad of ways Blumenfeld could have fulfilled its obligation to Dr. dePape, there is no question that Blumenfeld's failure to communicate at all with Dr. dePape is inadequate to meet its obligation under any conceivable option. For example, Blumenfeld could have (1) sent a copy of the retention letter to Dr. dePape, (2) written Dr. dePape a follow-up letter to the initial conference explaining the requirements of the TN and the H-1B visas, (3) followed-up the written explanation with a telephone call to ensure that Dr. dePape understood the visa requirements and to answer any questions that Dr. dePape may have had, and (4) if it was not intended to be a sham, explained the community health care needs assessment to the hospital to determine if they needed or wanted it and to Dr. dePape to determine if he was ready, willing, and able to perform it. Because Blumenfeld failed to do anything to explain Dr. dePape's immigration options and their requirements and, in addition, sprung the community health care needs assessment on Dr. dePape at the border, the court finds that Blumenfeld breached its duty to communicate with and advise Dr. dePape. . . .

b. Causation

. . . "The burden of proving proximate cause in a legal malpractice action is the same as any other negligence action. To recover, the injured must show that, but for the attorney's negligence, the loss would not have occurred." As applied to this situation, the plaintiff must demonstrate that, but for Blumenfeld's failure to communicate with and advise Dr. dePape, Dr. dePape would have (1) gained entry to the United States or (2) would have chosen to pursue other employment options in Canada instead of attempting to immigrate to the United States. . . .

. . . [B]ecause of Blumenfeld's implausible interpretation of "temporary entry" and because of its exceedingly broad interpretation of the level of patient care permissible under the TN classification, the court finds that Blumenfeld attempted to perpetrate a fraud on the INS by representing that Dr. dePape sought entry to the United States as a Physician Consultant. . . .

However, this conclusion does not relieve Blumenfeld of liability because the court also finds that, had Dr. dePape been informed of his immigration options at the outset, he would have pursued other employment in Canada. Therefore, he would

have been able to start his own practice or to begin work in an established practice as soon as he was licensed in Canada.

c. Damages . . .

i. Lost income. . . . The court previously found that, had Blumenfeld explained the implications of this to him, Dr. dePape would have chosen to remain in Canada and would have started his practice as soon as possible. . . .

The difference between the net income Dr. dePape could have earned during the damages period and what he actually earned is . . . $203,736.20 United States dollars in lost income.

ii. Emotional distress. . . . "Under the tort theory of negligence, there is no general duty of care to avoid causing emotional harm to another. However, where the parties assume a relationship that is contractual in nature and deals with services or acts that involve deep emotional responses in the event of a breach, [Iowa courts] recognize a duty of care to protect against emotional distress."

In this case, Dr. dePape shares a special relationship with Blumenfeld that gives rise to a duty to avoid causing Dr. dePape emotional harm. This is not the sort of legal malpractice case in which mental distress damages are not recoverable. In Lawrence v. Grinde, 534 N.W.2d 414, 422 (Iowa 1995), the Iowa Supreme Court held that a legal malpractice plaintiff could not recover mental distress damages in his legal malpractice action because his distress was too remote to be reasonably foreseeable. There, the plaintiff's attorney failed to disclose a recent settlement on a bankruptcy petition, and the United States government subsequently indicted the plaintiff for bankruptcy fraud. The plaintiff was acquitted, but his indictment and trial gave rise to considerable media coverage.

In that case, the mental distress damages sought were indistinguishable from the damages sought for the plaintiff's alleged damages to his reputation. But because the damage to the plaintiff's reputation as a result of the indictment was one-step removed from the defendant's negligent act in preparing the bankruptcy petition, the Iowa court held that the plaintiff's claim for mental distress damages failed on causation.

Here, Blumenfeld was retained to assist Dr. dePape with his immigration, but instead of assisting Dr. dePape, Blumenfeld's negligence placed Dr. dePape directly in harm's way. It should be noted that Blumenfeld would not be liable for the mental distress that might have accompanied a failed legitimate entry attempt because it would be unfair under those circumstances to hold a lawyer responsible for the independent decision of an independent governmental entity. But in this case, Blumenfeld not only failed to provide Dr. dePape with sufficient information for him to make an informed decision about his immigration, moments before the entry attempt, Blumenfeld (through Mr. Eiss) counseled Dr. dePape to lie to INS officials in order to gain entry to the United States under false pretenses.

Aside from being unethical, this conduct directly led to the INS official's decision to deny Dr. dePape's visa request and formed the basis of the INS official's accusation that Dr. dePape was a liar. . . . Thus, the emotional distress damages resulting from Blumenfeld's negligence in this case are not one-step removed, and Dr. dePape may recover for them.

The court finds that, while short-lived, Dr. dePape suffered severe and intense emotional distress. He was ambushed at the United States border, asked to perpetrate a fraud on the United States government in order to gain entry, and then sent on his way without even the courtesy of a phone call from his lawyers. At the border, INS officials degraded Dr. dePape, and he felt extraordinarily humiliated. Moreover, he had spent the past fifteen months planning to begin his professional career with Trimark and had made the arrangements to do so. . . .

Fortunately, Dr. dePape is a person of strong character and incredible integrity. While he was setback by the emotional turmoil surrounding the ambush at the border, he was able to move on and begin anew. Accordingly, the court finds that Dr. dePape is entitled to $75,000 USD for emotional distress to compensate him for the severe level of mental anguish directly caused by Blumenfeld's negligence. . . .

THEREFORE, upon consideration of the evidence and the parties' arguments, the court finds (1) that there is no basis in fact or in law to hold Trinity or Trimark liable for Dr. dePape's damages; and (2) that Blumenfeld was extraordinarily negligent in failing to inform and communicate with Dr. dePape concerning his immigration and in counseling him to perpetrate a fraud on the INS in order to gain entry to the United

States; and (3) that, as a result of the damages caused by this negligence, Dr. dePape is entitled to recover from defendant Blumenfeld a total of $278,736.20 USD for his lost income and emotional distress. . . . [13]

■ The Law Governing Lawyers: *Actual and Accidental Clients*

In Chapter 1, Professor Wasserstrom pointed out that lawyers engage in role-differentiated behavior, that is, lawyers rightly favor the interests of clients over the interests of others. Choosing to take on a client means taking on fiduciary obligations to stay focused on the client's best interests as those interests are refined in discussions between client and lawyer and then determined by the client.

Actual Clients

In most situations, like *dePape*, lawyers know who their clients are because they have expressly agreed to represent them. No payment is necessary to establish a client-lawyer relationship as long as both lawyer and client agree that the lawyer should provide legal services to that client.[1] The law firm in *dePape* clearly agreed to take on two actual clients: the potential employer/clinic, Trimark, and the potential employee, Dr. dePape. The case illustrates how fiduciary duties automatically attach to each client-lawyer relationship once a lawyer agrees to represent a client.

Increasingly, however, the law governing lawyers also has recognized what lawyers may think of as "accidental" clients, those a lawyer did not expect, but those recognized by law as being owed the same fiduciary duties lawyers owe clients they intend to represent. *dePape* illustrates one situation where accidental clients may lurk: joint representation. When lawyers agree to represent more than one client in the same matter, they have to guard against assuming or favoring one client's interest over another.

It is possible that the law firm in *dePape* may have erred because it viewed and treated one of its two clients as "accidental" or "incidental" to its services. The law firm may have ignored its physician client because it viewed him as a

---

13. The evidence in this case strongly supports an award of punitive damages against Blumenfeld. Dr. dePape was bushwhacked at the border by Blumenfeld's egregious breach of duty and its willful and wanton disregard for Dr. dePape's rights. The plaintiff did not request punitive damages in his prayer for relief, and the court recognizes its authority to award them when supported by the evidence, even in the absence of a specific prayer for punitive damages. *See* Boeckmann v. Joseph, 889 F.2d 1094 (9th Cir. 1989) (table op.) (affirming district court's award of punitive damages in absence of request because plaintiff plead fraud and, therefore, the defendant was on notice because a finding of fraud supports an award of punitive damages).

In Iowa, the standard for punitive damages is "Whether, by a preponderance of clear, convincing, and satisfactory evidence, the conduct of the defendant from which the claim arose constituted willful and wanton disregard for the rights or safety of another." Iowa Code §668A.1 (1)(a). The court has carefully reviewed the plaintiff's initial and amended complaints but finds that Dr. dePape did not plead sufficient facts to put Blumenfeld on notice that punitive damages were at issue. Therefore, despite the overwhelming evidence to support an award of punitive damages in this case, the court will not impose them.
1. RLGL §14(1).

kind of "secondary" client, or a client it represented as an "accommodation" to its other "primary" client, Trimark, which was paying the bill and had all of the contact with the lawyers. If so, the case illustrates that a lawyer can never rely on one client to fully express the interests of another, or create levels of duty to clients based on the degree to which they pay or communicate directly to the lawyer. Here, the law governing lawyers is clear: Once a legally recognized client-lawyer relationship begins, full fiduciary duties attach.[2] *dePape* also teaches that lawyers who ignore the presence of any legally recognized clients set themselves up for trouble, including multiple and overlapping remedies such as professional discipline, malpractice, breach of fiduciary duty, and disqualification.

Accidental Clients

Joint representation is just one of at least ten situations where lawyers may take on incidental, accidental, or even unintended representations that bind them legally.

1. Court Appointments   In the last chapter, *Bothwell* instructs that client-lawyer relationships can be created involuntarily by court appointment. As an officer of the courts, lawyers have a duty to accept court appointments unless that lawyer can convince the judge that it would violate some other provision in the lawyer code, such as competence, confidentiality, or loyalty.[3]

2. Implied Client-Lawyer Relationships   Courts also find implied client-lawyer relationships when nonlawyers reasonably rely on legal advice or assistance.[4] For example, lawyers could find that they have accidentally taken on a client when they offer informal consults or give advice during public speeches or at social gatherings.[5] Lawyers also may find that advertising and websites can create accidental client-lawyer relationships if unknown persons reasonably rely on the information therein provided.[6] This law imposes a pre-contractual duty of

---

2. RLGL §16.
3. MR 6.2; RLGL §14(2).
4. *See, e.g.*, Togstad v. Vesely, Otto, Miller & Keefe, *infra* p. 102; The Law Governing Lawyers: Tort Liability to Clients, *infra* p. 109.
5. *See* Utah St. Bar Ethics Advisory Opinion 99-04, *infra* p. 517 (discussing the ethical implications of lawyers who conduct legal seminars, provide legal information to groups, conduct open houses, set up trade booths, or participate in bar-sponsored question and answer sessions).
6. *E.g.*, D.C. Op. 316 (2002) (lawyers may participate in chat rooms, but should avoid giving specific legal advice). *See also* Cal. St. Bar Op. 2005-168 (lawyer utilizing website for client contact and acquisition may disclaim duty of confidentiality to potential clients only if disclaimer is sufficiently plain to defeat potential client's reasonable belief in confidentiality); Assn. of the Bar of the City of New York Comm. on Prof. and Judicial Ethics Op. 2001-1 (when website does not disclose that information transmitted by potential clients is not considered by firm to be confidential, firm must treat information as confidential and cannot disclose or use to benefit another adverse client); N.C. Formal Op. 3 (2000) (a lawyer may respond to inquiries sent through Internet, but must disclose the extent of the lawyer-client relationship and specifically limit the extent if they wish to ensure that a lawyer-client relationship is not created); Barton v. U.S. Dist. Ct., 410 F.3d 1104 (2005) (holding that responding to a law firm's Internet questionnaire can create a lawyer-client relationship if the respondent reasonably believed that in filling out the form he/she was entering into a lawyer-client relationship).

good faith on lawyers by looking back on the matter from a reasonable nonlawyer perspective. As a result, a lawyer's memory of what was said or promised may not be the version that ultimately prevails.

3. Prospective Clients   When prospective clients discuss the possibility of obtaining legal services with lawyers, implied client-lawyer relationships can develop. Though prospective clients may not always become full-fledged clients, they become clients to the extent that they reasonably rely on a lawyer's legal advice. Even when lawyers make it clear that they will not take on a representation, if a lawyer offers legal advice and gains information from such a person, two duties, however limited, attach to such an encounter: competence in any advice offered and confidentiality that cloaks anything the lawyer learns. [7]

In addition to the formal prospective client-lawyer meeting, prospective clients lurk in many other circumstances as well, including:

- Beauty Contests, where prospective clients essentially audition lawyers by interviewing several before deciding whom to hire.[8]
- Public Speeches, where lawyers offer general legal information, but often are asked specific questions about specific facts. Especially dangerous is a response that begins with "There is no case/redress/cause of action in that circumstance," because a listener who takes no further action in reliance on such an option may fail to seek other legal help before a statute of limitations expires.
- Advertising, when lawyers offer advice about specific facts. Stating that no person should rely on this ad for advice (because every case differs, or the law provides for certain defenses, etc.) invites further inquiries, and also explains why reliance on the ad alone is not reasonable.
- E-lawyering, where lawyers offer advice or invite specific nonlawyer inquiries on websites. Lawyers who want to offer persons legal advice online should know who they are giving it to and do a conflicts check before offering the advice.[9]
- Consulting with other lawyers, where a lawyer seeks advice for a client, or advice for the lawyer in dealing with the client. In the right circumstances, either the lawyer or the lawyer's client can become clients of the consulting lawyer.[10]
- Splitting fees with other lawyers, where eligibility for payment depends on assuming "joint responsibility" for the representation.[11]
- Dealing with unrepresented persons where they seek advice or services from another person's lawyer.[12]
- Family members or social friends, where they seek and reasonably rely on legal advice.

---

7. MR 1.18; RLGL §15.
8. *Id.*
9. We discuss conflicts checking in Practice Pointers: Implementing a Conflicts Control System, *infra* p. 382.
10. ABA Formal Op. 97-406.
11. MR 1.5, Comment [7].
12. MR 4.3.

■ Limited-Term Pro Bono Service, where nonlawyers seek legal information from volunteer lawyers.[13]

4. Joint Clients   Clients often cluster in groups, and lawyers may be consulted and paid by one client for the representation of two or more. The communication duty breached in *dePape* represents one pitfall of incorrectly identifying and inadequately responding to each and every one of such clients. An even more common problem is loyalty, or resolving conflicts of interest that nearly always occur in joint representations. A lawyer must identify the conflict and obtain each client's informed consent to continue with the joint representation.[14] Some joint client conflicts are not consentable, which means that the lawyer must tell the parties that he or she cannot represent all of them. We examine these issues in more detail in Chapters 6 and 8.[15]

5. Third-Person Direction   Third-person nonclients who pay for or attempt to direct the representation of a client also can tempt a lawyer to treat these third parties as if they control the representation. But in law practice, he who pays the piper does not always call the tune. For example, the parent who hires and pays a lawyer to represent her child in a juvenile court is not a client. Neither is the son who hires and pays a lawyer to write Dad's will. In some situations, it may not be clear whether a lawyer has agreed to take on two clients (as in *dePape*), or has agreed to represent only one, with the other paying the bill. *Machado* illustrates another variation on this theme: A client designates an agent to communicate with the client's lawyer. Once again, the law governing lawyers imposes the burden of clarification on the lawyer, who must initiate communication to clarify the identity of the client(s), and remain loyal to the actual client, not the person paying or speaking with the lawyer.[16]

6. Insurance Defense   Lawyers who are hired by insurers to represent insureds confront a situation often fraught with similar ambiguity. Typical liability policies promise to "defend" covered persons when they are sued for a covered event. The policy obligates an insurer to hire a lawyer to provide this defense. Less clear is whether a joint representation also has been created. As we shall see in Chapter 8, jurisdictions are split over whether the lawyer represents one client, the insured, or two clients, the insured and the insurer, in such a circumstance.[17] Everyone agrees that lawyers owe fiduciary duties to their client-insureds. And even less clear than client identity is the extent to which lawyers may take direction from the insurer, whether client or not.

---

13. *See* Lawyers and Clients: Service *Pro Bono Publico, supra* p. 66.
14. MR 1.7; RLGL §130.
15. *See, e.g.*, Perez v. Kirk & Carrigan, *infra* p. 165 (employee-client had valid claim for breach of confidentiality against lawyers who represented employee and employer following employee's truck driving accident); Anderson v. O'Brien, *infra* p. 350 (lawyer who represented multiple parties in real estate transactions liable for reckless breach of fiduciary duty).
16. MR 1.8(f); RLGL §134.
17. MR 1.7, Comment [13], 1.8, Comments [11] & [12]; RLGL §134, Comment f; Paradigm Ins. Co. v. The Langerman Law Offices, P.A., *infra* p. 319; Lawyers and Clients: Insurance Defense Representation, *infra* p. 324.

7. Organizations   Lawyers who represent organizations can face dozens of accidental clients. In representing a publicly held corporation, family business, or governmental unit, a lawyer must deal with individual agents who manage and direct the organization, but the lawyer does not represent any of these individuals. In some circumstances (such as those of *dePape*) the lawyer can represent both an employer and employee, but again, the lawyer shoulders the burden of adequate communication, protection of confidential information, and appropriate conflicts waivers. Consistent with the law governing other accidental client-lawyer relationships, the lawyer must clarify any doubtful situations, especially those where an individual might reasonably believe the lawyer represents his or her interests as well as those of the organization.[18]

8. Clients Who Morph   The practice of law is dynamic, and accidental clients can occur when clients change. Individual clients marry, divorce, and die.[19] If lawyers do not notice, they may communicate with the wrong person or bring a lawsuit in the wrong name. Some clients have fluctuating capacities, which requires their lawyers to evaluate capacity before critical decisions can be made.[20] Organizational clients change their personnel, governance structure, or their status, for example, by merging or filing for bankruptcy, at which point a new decision maker may reverse a prior decision.[21] The class in class actions may be represented by named plaintiffs, but class identification and lawyer loyalty may change as the matter progresses and class(es) are certified by courts.[22] Finally, when lawyers complete a representation, each client morphs from a current client to a former client, a characterization that changes but does not extinguish a lawyer's fiduciary duties.[23]

9. Quasi-Clients   If lawyers owe fiduciary duties to clients, it seems axiomatic that they owe no such duties to nonclients. Yet some nonclients can be characterized as quasi-clients because of their relationship to clients. For example, intended third-party beneficiaries of client representations are owed some of the same duties of competence owed clients.[24] Similarly, lawyers who represent client-fiduciaries such as trustees, guardians, corporate directors, or partners also need to be mindful of the fiduciary obligations their clients owe others.[25] Representing such a client-fiduciary requires advice about the broad scope of duty owed by the fiduciary to third parties, duties that lawyers are obliged to assist their client-fiduciaries in fulfilling.[26]

---

18. MR 1.13; RLGL §§96, 97; Lawyers and Clients: Representing Organizations, *infra* p. 181.
19. *E.g.*, In re Forrest, *infra* p. 259.
20. MR 1.14; RLGL §24.
21. *E.g.*, In re ACC/Lincoln Savings & Loan Securities Litigation, *infra* p. 220.
22. RLGL §14, Comment f.
23. *E.g.*, Maritrans v. Pepper, Hamilton & Scheetz, *infra* p. 285.
24. *E.g.*, Greycas v. Proud, *infra* p. 134.
25. RLGL §14, Comment f, §51, Comment h.
26. *E.g.*, Fickett v. Superior Court, 558 P.2d 988 (Ariz. App. 1976) (lawyer for guardian owed duty of care to ward to prevent misappropriation of guardianship assets); Chem-Age Industries, Inc. v. Glover, *infra* p. 145; Lawyers and Other Professionals: Duties to Nonclients, *infra* p. 152.

10. Imputed Clients   Although some lawyers practice solo, most practice in association with others. The law governing lawyers imputes the obligations of one lawyer in a law firm to all other lawyers in that firm as well.[27] It also extends these law firm obligations to law firm employees, including temporary lawyers and student law clerks.[28]

Lawyers who do not share an employment relationship may nevertheless look or act like they have done so. For example, lawyers from different firms who intend to split a legal fee usually are required to assume joint responsibility for the representation, whether or not they work on the matter.[29] This creates a client-lawyer relationship with each lawyer. Similarly, lawyers who share office space may not share fees, but may act as a firm, by consulting on cases, using the same letterhead, or sharing file access. If so, they may be held to constitute a "firm" with imputed client-lawyer relationships.[30] Likewise, lawyers from different firms who participate in joint defense agreements may share enough confidential information that their conflicts will be imputed to each other.[31]

Conclusion

Lawyers cannot recognize or solve any legal ethics issue until they first learn to identify their clients, including those they may consider to be "accidental" clients. Accidental clients can appear when lawyers least expect them and can impose some or all of the same fiduciary duties on lawyers that intended clients can. Lawyers who understand that their fiduciary duty extends to identifying clients will be in a position to avoid client-lawyer relationships they do not wish to create, and to recognize the moment when fiduciary duties attach to client-lawyer relationships they intend to undertake. In other words, the first step to addressing any legal ethics issue is to know your clients, so that you will be able to observe the 5 Cs for all legally recognized clients and avoid interference by those who are not.

---

27. MR 1.10; RLGL §123.
28. MR 5.1, 5.3; RLGL §11.
29. MR 1.5(e); RLGL §47.
30. MR 1.0(c) and Comments [2]-[4]; RLGL §123, Comment e.
31. *E.g.*, Wilson P. Abraham Constr. Corp. v. Armco Steel Corp., 559 F.2d 250 (5th Cir. 1977) (lawyer who represented codefendant in prior criminal investigation disqualified to protect nonclient's shared confidences in joint defense arrangement); Analytica, Inc. v. NPD Research, Inc., 708 F.2d 1263 (7th Cir. 1983) (law firm disqualified where co-counsel relationship gave it access to potentially relevant confidential data).

Chapter 5

Competence

This chapter explores another basic fiduciary duty that lawyers owe their clients: competence. We emphasize here two common themes. First, the various yet related definitions of the competence requirement included in several distinct bodies of law, and second, the multiple remedies provided by the law governing lawyers when professional duties of competence are breached.

The problems in the first three sections of this chapter explore three of the possible multiple remedies that may be available to clients to redress incompetence: professional discipline, civil liability, and, in criminal cases, reversal of a conviction or sentence for ineffective assistance of counsel. We have already encountered the remedy of professional discipline in *Busch* in Chapter 2 for one major instance of incompetence and failure to communicate with a client. In Chapter 4, *dePape* further introduced us to civil actions, such as legal malpractice and breach of fiduciary duty. The last section of this chapter addresses various tort duties to nonclients.

A. Introduction

Problem

5-1. Martyn & Fox is asked whether the firm can file a patent application for a new gene therapy on behalf of the inventor. No one at Martyn & Fox took biology in college or ever filed a patent application. At a partners' new business meeting, Fox declares, "Let's take it, it can't be that hard; thousands are filed each year. We'll let the inventor teach us the science." How should Martyn respond?

Consider: Model Rule 1.1
         Model Code DR 6-101
         RLGL §16

B. Malpractice and Breach of Fiduciary Duty

Problems

5-2. Martyn interviewed a prospective client about a potential personal injury case and told him that it wasn't the kind of matter Martyn & Fox handled. Two months later the same person called, leaving a message that he wanted to check on the "status of his case." Before returning the call, Martyn noted that the applicable statute of limitations on the claim had run three weeks earlier. Martyn thinks she warned the prospective client about the statute when they met. What should Martyn do?

5-3. What if Martyn agreed to take the case when she first met with the prospective client?
(a) Must she tell the client that the statute has run?
(b) Can Martyn be disciplined?
(c) Can Martyn & Fox be disciplined?
(d) Will Martyn & Fox be liable for malpractice?

5-4. Martyn & Fox provided Client with tax advice regarding a settlement of $1 million to Client in a Ford Explorer rollover case. Later, Client learned about a similar case that ended in a jury verdict of $3 million. Can Client recover the difference from Martyn & Fox? What if Martyn & Fox had been retained to advise regarding the advisability of the settlement?

Consider: Model Rules 1.1-1.4, 1.18, 5.1
Model Code DR 6-101
N.Y. DR 1-102(a)
RLGL §§11, 14, 15, 19, 20, 52, 53

Togstad v. Vesely, Otto, Miller & Keefe
291 N.W.2d 686 (Minn. 1980)

PER CURIAM.

This is an appeal by the defendants from a judgment of the Hennepin County District Court involving an action for legal malpractice. The jury found that the defendant attorney Jerre Miller was negligent and that, as a direct result of such negligence, plaintiff John Togstad sustained damages in the amount of $610,500 and his wife, plaintiff Joan Togstad, in the amount of $39,000. . . .

In August, 1971, John Togstad began to experience severe headaches and on August 16, 1971, was admitted to Methodist Hospital where tests disclosed that the headaches were caused by a large aneurism of the left internal carotid artery. The attending physician, Dr. Paul Blake, a neurological surgeon, treated the problem by applying a Selverstone clamp to the left common carotid artery. The clamp was surgically implanted on August 27, 1971, in Togstad's neck to allow the gradual closure of the artery over a period of days. . . .

In the early morning hours of August 29, 1971, a nurse observed that Togstad was unable to speak or move. . . . Togstad is now severely paralyzed in his right arm and leg, and is unable to speak.

Plaintiff's expert, Dr. Ward Woods, testified that Togstad's paralysis and loss of speech was due to a lack of blood supply to his brain . . . [which] resulted from the clamp being 50% closed and that the negligence of Dr. Blake and the hospital precluded the clamp's being opened in time to avoid permanent brain damage. . . .

Dr. Blake and defendants' expert witness . . . both alleged that the blood clots were not a result of the Selverstone clamp procedure. . . .

About 14 months after her husband's hospitalization began, plaintiff Joan Togstad met with attorney Jerre Miller regarding her husband's condition. Neither she nor her husband was personally acquainted with Miller or his law firm prior to that time. John Togstad's former work supervisor, Ted Bucholz, made the appointment and accompanied Mrs. Togstad to Miller's office. Bucholz was present when Mrs. Togstad and Miller discussed the case.

Mrs. Togstad had become suspicious of the circumstances surrounding her husband's tragic condition due to the conduct and statements of the hospital nurses shortly after the paralysis occurred. One nurse told Mrs. Togstad that she had checked Mr. Togstad at 2 a.m. and he was fine; that when she returned at 3 a.m., by mistake, to give him someone else's medication, he was unable to move or speak; and that if she hadn't accidentally entered the room no one would have discovered his condition until morning. Mrs. Togstad also noticed that the other nurses were upset and crying, and that Mr. Togstad's condition was a topic of conversation.

Mrs. Togstad testified that she told Miller "everything that happened at the hospital," including the nurses' statements and conduct which had raised a question in her mind. She stated that she "believed" she had told Miller "about the procedure and what was undertaken, what was done, and what happened." She brought no records with her. Miller took notes and asked questions during the meeting, which lasted 45 minutes to an hour. At its conclusion, according to Mrs. Togstad, Miller said that "he did not think we had a legal case, however, he was going to discuss this with his partner." She understood that if Miller changed his mind after talking to his partner, he would call her. Mrs. Togstad "gave it" a few days and, since she did not hear from Miller, decided "that they had come to the conclusion that there wasn't a case." No fee arrangements were discussed, no medical authorizations were requested, nor was Mrs. Togstad billed for the interview.

Mrs. Togstad denied that Miller had told her his firm did not have expertise in the medical malpractice field, urged her to see another attorney, or related to her that the statute of limitations for medical malpractice actions was two years. She did not consult another attorney until one year after she talked to Miller. Mrs. Togstad indicated that she did not confer with another attorney earlier because of her reliance on Miller's "legal advice" that they "did not have a case."

On cross-examination, Mrs. Togstad was asked whether she went to Miller's office "to see if he would take the case of [her] husband. . . ." She replied, "Well, I guess it was to go for legal advice, what to do, where shall we go from here? That is what we went for." Again in response to defense counsel's questions, Mrs. Togstad testified as follows:

Q And it was clear to you, was it not, that what was taking place was a preliminary discussion between a prospective client and lawyer as to whether or not they wanted to enter into an attorney-client relationship?

A I am not sure how to answer that. It was for legal advice as to what to do.

Q And Mr. Miller was discussing with you your problem and indicating whether he, as a lawyer, wished to take the case, isn't that true?

A Yes.

On re-direct examination, Mrs. Togstad acknowledged that when she left Miller's office she understood that she had been given a "qualified, quality legal opinion that [she and her husband] did not have a malpractice case."

Miller's testimony was different in some respects from that of Mrs. Togstad. Like Mrs. Togstad, Miller testified that Mr. Bucholz arranged and was present at the meeting, which lasted about 45 minutes. According to Miller, Mrs. Togstad described the hospital incident, including the conduct of the nurses. He asked her questions, to which she responded. Miller testified that "the only thing I told her [Mrs. Togstad] after we had pretty much finished the conversation was that there was nothing related in her factual circumstances that told me that she had a case that our firm would be interested in undertaking."

Miller also claimed he related to Mrs. Togstad "that because of the grievous nature of the injuries sustained by her husband, that this was only my opinion and she was encouraged to ask another attorney if she wished for another opinion" and "she ought to do so promptly." He testified that he informed Mrs. Togstad that his firm "was not engaged as experts" in the area of medical malpractice, and that they associated with the Charles Hvass firm in cases of that nature. Miller stated that at the end of the conference he told Mrs. Togstad that he would consult with Charles Hvass and if Hvass's opinion differed from his, Miller would so inform her. Miller recollected that he called Hvass a "couple days" later and discussed the case with him. It was Miller's impression that Hvass thought there was no liability for malpractice in the case. Consequently, Miller did not communicate with Mrs. Togstad further.

On cross-examination, Miller testified as follows:

Q Now, so there is no misunderstanding, and I am reading from your deposition, you understood that she was consulting with you as a lawyer, isn't that correct?

A That's correct.

Q That she was seeking legal advice from a professional attorney licensed to practice in this state and in this community?

A I think you and I did have another interpretation or use of the term "Advice." She was there to see whether or not she had a case and whether the firm would accept it.

Q We have two aspects; number one, your legal opinion concerning liability of a case for malpractice; number two, whether there was or wasn't liability, whether you would accept it, your firm, two separate elements, right?

A I would say so. . . .

Kenneth Green, a Minneapolis attorney, was called as an expert by plaintiffs. He stated that in rendering legal advice regarding a claim of medical malpractice, the "minimum" an attorney should do would be to request medical authorizations from the client, review the hospital records, and consult with an expert in the field. John McNulty, a Minneapolis attorney, and Charles Hvass testified as experts on behalf of the defendants. McNulty stated that when an attorney is consulted as to whether he will take a case, the lawyer's only responsibility in refusing it is to so inform the party. He testified, however, that when a lawyer is asked his legal opinion on the merits of a medical malpractice claim, community standards require that the attorney check hospital records and consult with an expert before rendering his opinion.

Hvass stated that he had no recollection of Miller's calling him in October 1972 relative to the Togstad matter. He testified that:

A . . . [W]hen a person comes in to me about a medical malpractice action, based upon what the individual has told me, I have to make a decision as to whether or not there probably is or probably is not, based upon that information, medical malpractice. And if, in my judgment, based upon what the client has told me, there is not medical malpractice, I will so inform the client.

Hvass stated, however, that he would never render a "categorical" opinion. In addition, Hvass acknowledged that if he were consulted for a "legal opinion" regarding medical malpractice and 14 months had expired since the incident in question, "ordinary care and diligence" would require him to inform the party of the two-year statute of limitations applicable to that type of action.

This case was submitted to the jury by way of a special verdict form. The jury found that Dr. Blake and the hospital were negligent and that Dr. Blake's negligence (but not the hospital's) was a direct cause of the injuries sustained by John Togstad; that there was an attorney-client contractual relationship between Mrs. Togstad and Miller; that Miller was negligent in rendering advice regarding the possible claims of Mr. and Mrs. Togstad; that, but for Miller's negligence, plaintiffs would have been successful in the prosecution of a legal action against Dr. Blake; and that neither Mr. nor Mrs. Togstad was negligent in pursuing their claims against Dr. Blake. The jury awarded damages to Mr. Togstad of $610,500 and to Mrs. Togstad of $39,000. . . .

1. In a legal malpractice action of the type involved here, four elements must be shown: (1) that an attorney-client relationship existed; (2) that defendant acted negligently or in

breach of contract; (3) that such acts were the proximate cause of the plaintiffs' damages; (4) that but for defendant's conduct the plaintiffs would have been successful in the prosecution of their medical malpractice claim. . . .

We believe it is unnecessary to decide whether a tort or contract theory is preferable for resolving the attorney-client relationship question raised by this appeal. The tort and contract analyses are very similar in a case such as the instant one,[4] and we conclude that under either theory the evidence shows that a lawyer-client relationship is present here. The thrust of Mrs. Togstad's testimony is that she went to Miller for legal advice, was told there wasn't a case, and relied upon this advice in failing to pursue the claim for medical malpractice. In addition, according to Mrs. Togstad, Miller did not qualify his legal opinion by urging her to seek advice from another attorney, nor did Miller inform her that he lacked expertise in the medical malpractice area. . . . [W]e believe a jury could properly find that Mrs. Togstad sought and received legal advice from Miller under circumstances which made it reasonably foreseeable to Miller that Mrs. Togstad would be injured if the advice were negligently given. Thus, under either a tort or contract analysis, there is sufficient evidence in the record to support the existence of an attorney-client relationship.

Defendants argue that even if an attorney-client relationship was established the evidence fails to show that Miller acted negligently in assessing the merits of the Togstads' case. They appear to contend that, at most, Miller was guilty of an error in judgment which does not give rise to legal malpractice. . . . However, this case does not involve a mere error of judgment. The gist of plaintiffs' claim is that Miller failed to perform the minimal research that an ordinarily prudent attorney would do before rendering legal advice in a case of this nature. The record, through the testimony of Kenneth Green and John McNulty, contains sufficient evidence to support plaintiffs' position. . . .

There is also sufficient evidence in the record establishing that, but for Miller's negligence, plaintiffs would have been successful in prosecuting their medical malpractice claim. Dr. Woods, in no uncertain terms, concluded that Mr. Togstad's injuries were caused by the medical malpractice of Dr. Blake. Defendants' expert testimony to the contrary was obviously not believed by the jury. Thus, the jury reasonably found that had plaintiff's medical malpractice action been properly brought, plaintiffs would have recovered. . . .

---

4. Under a negligence approach it must essentially be shown that defendant rendered legal advice (not necessarily at someone's request) under circumstances which made it reasonably foreseeable to the attorney that if such advice was rendered negligently, the individual receiving the advice might be injured thereby. *See, e.g.,* Palsgraf v. Long Island R.R. Co., 162 N.E. 99 (N.Y. 1928). . . . A contract analysis requires the rendering of legal advice pursuant to another's request and the reliance factor, in this case, where the advice was not paid for, need be shown in the form of promissory estoppel. *See* . . . Restatement (Second) of Contracts, §90.

▓ Practice Pointers:
Engagement, Nonengagement, and Disengagement Letters

Togstad illustrates that misunderstandings between lawyers and clients can create real problems for both. Commentators recommend various types of engagement letters to remedy these potential differences. In their treatise entitled Legal Malpractice, Ronald Mallen and Jeffrey Smith identify four basic situations in which such a misunderstanding can occur. We have already run across the first two in these materials, and we will encounter the last two later in this chapter.[1]

- The lawyer wants to decline a specific request for representation (*Togstad*);
- The lawyer wants to specify which parties to a transaction the lawyer agrees to represent (*dePape*);
- The lawyer wants to prevent a claim for negligent misrepresentation (*Greycas*, p. 134); and
- The lawyer wants to prevent reliance by unrepresented third parties who are beneficiaries of the lawyer's service to another client (*Glover* p. 145).

Nonengagement Letters

The first situation involves facts like those in *Togstad*: the lawyer thinks he has declined representation, but the prospective client believes she has received legal advice. In that circumstance, a simple nonengagement letter such as the one below, recommended by Professors Munneke and Davis, can clarify any misunderstandings.[2] Consider how you would modify this form to address the facts in *Togstad*.

> [Letterhead]
> [Date]
> [Prospective Client]   Certified Mail No.
>   Return Receipt Requested
> Re: Potential Engagement Regarding [Matter]
> Dear [Name]
>
> Thank you for your visit today. As we discussed, although I have not investigated the merits of your matter, I do not feel it would be appropriate for [me/Law Firm Name] to represent you in your possible [matter]. In declining to undertake this matter, [I am/law firm is] not expressing an opinion on [the likely outcome of the matter].
>
> Please be aware that whatever claim, if any, that you have may be barred by the passage of time. Because deadlines may be critical to your case, I recommend that you immediately contact another lawyer/law firm for assistance regarding your matter. [*Optional:* For your information, the telephone number of the legal referral service of the (State) Bar Association is:_____.]

---

1. Ronald E. Mallen & Jeffrey M. Smith, *Legal Malpractice* §2.12 (2007 ed., West).
2. Gary A. Munneke & Anthony E. Davis, *The Essential Formbook: Comprehensive Management Tools for Lawyers* 280 (ABA, L. Prac. Mgt. Sect. 2004).

Thank you again for your interest in [me/Law Firm Name]. *Optional:* We appreciate your having approached us regarding your matter. If you ever have need of legal assistance in the field of (practice concentration), we hope that you will think of us again in that context. (We enclose a copy of our brochure describing our practice in that area.)

Sincerely,

[Your Name/Firm Name]

Engagement Letters

Just as nonengagement letters can help clarify the absence of a duty to a prospective client, engagement letters are intended to prevent misunderstandings by clarifying the scope and basis for undertaking a client representation. But an engagement letter also can be used to address other issues that might arise during the course of the representation. A complete list is probably impossible to compile, but commentators offer the following topics as candidates for inclusion in an engagement letter:[3]

- Identification of the client, adverse parties, and related parties;
- Definition of the scope of the engagement;
- Description of the respective responsibilities of the client and the lawyer;
- Identification and consents to conflicts of interest;
- Resolution of confidentiality issues, especially in multiple representations;
- Identification of goals of the representation;
- Proposed staffing, including agents of the client and lawyer;
- Methods of communication;
- Identification of third-party neutrals, such a judges, arbitrators, or mediators;
- Fee agreement and billing schedule;
- Grounds for withdrawal or termination;
- Policy on file retention; and
- Methods of dispute resolution between client and lawyer.

New York's professional code requires engagement letters in all cases except those for which the lawyer charges a fee of less than $3,000 or the "attorney's services are of the same general kind as previously rendered to and paid for by the client."[4] The letter must address the following matters: (1) explanation of the scope of the legal services to be provided; (2) explanation of attorney's fees to be charged, expenses, and billing practices; and (3) information about the client's right to arbitrate fee disputes.[5]

---

3. Mallen & Smith, *supra* note 1, §2.10; Munneke & Davis, *supra* note 2, 141-144.
4. N.Y. Ct. Rules §§1215.1, 1215.2 (2007). In domestic relations matters, New York requires lawyers to provide clients with both a Statement of Client's Rights and Responsibilities and a written retainer agreement, regardless of the fee charged. *Id.* at §§1400.2, 1400.3.
5. *Id.* at §1215.1(b).

Disengagement Letters

To prevent misunderstandings at the close of a matter, commentators also recommend a disengagement letter. Disengagement letters can be helpful when a lawyer completes a matter, decides to withdraw, is fired by the client, or when lawyers leave law firms and do not intend to continue work on a matter. The letter should make clear the reason the relationship has ended, and include appropriate warnings about unfinished work and time deadlines.[6] The letter also can address whether the client wishes the lawyer to communicate with successor counsel, and can provide for the orderly transmission of client files and documents.[7]

Disengagement letters essentially transform a current client into a former client and thereby limit (but, as we will see in succeeding chapters, do not extinguish) the duties the lawyer continues to owe that person or entity. Although the use of a disengagement letter can clarify the lawyer's lack of continuing obligation to the client, it is not an unmixed blessing. The lawyer also may hope that the client will call on the lawyer or the law firm for other services in the future. For this reason, the termination letter should be clear, but also can convey a willingness to serve in additional matters.

▧ The Law Governing Lawyers:
Tort Liability to Clients

dePape and *Togstad* make clear that lawyers agree by express or implied contract to assume fiduciary duties in representing clients. Agents who breach contracts or fiduciary duties may be liable in both contract and tort. The contract remedy usually is reserved for cases where a lawyer disobeys a clear and legal instruction of the client or acts contrary to the client's clear interests.[1] Tort remedies include intentional torts, such as fraud[2] and battery.[3] But because intentional torts are not covered by malpractice insurance, clients typically seek recovery against lawyers on a breach of fiduciary duty or malpractice theory.

Breach of Fiduciary Duty and Malpractice

In some cases, such as *dePape,* courts identify a breach of fiduciary duty remedy to redress a lawyer's failure to observe a basic fiduciary duty, such as a failure to

---

6. *See, e.g.,* Gilles v. Wiley, Malehorn & Sirota, *infra* p. 454 (client stated cause of action against former lawyers who withdrew at the last minute without adequately warning her that the statute of limitations was about to run on her medical malpractice case).

7. Mallen & Smith, *supra* note 1, §2.13.

1. *E.g.,* Interclaim Holdings, Ltd. v. Ness, Motley, Loadholt, Richardson & Poole, 298 F. Supp. 2d 746 (N.D. Ill. 2004) (upholding compensatory damages of $8.3 million and punitive damages of $27.7 million upheld on breach of contract theory against law firm that settled claims and released frozen assets without client's consent).

2. *See* The Bounds of the Law: Lawyer Fraud, *infra* p. 139.

3. *See, e.g,* Barbara A. v. John G., 193 Cal. Rptr. 422 (Cal. App. 1983) (lawyer who told client he "couldn't possibly get anyone pregnant" liable for battery and fraud after client suffered a tubal pregnancy, which resulted in permanent sterility).

obey,[4] inform (*dePape*), keep confidences,[5] or respond to and remedy conflicts of interest.[6] In these situations, the client has been deprived of a basic fiduciary obligation designed to protect the client's interests,[7] and the lawyer has acted "outside the scope of authority granted by the client."[8] Some courts describe this cause of action as constructive fraud, because the failure to communicate information the principal is entitled to know in a fiduciary relationship constitutes fraud.[9] Other courts, like *dePape*, seem to assume that breach of fiduciary duty is a species of malpractice that does not require expert testimony to show duty and breach.[10]

Most of the situations where clients seek a tort remedy do not involve such clear breaches of fiduciary duty. Instead, the client alleges a breach of the duties of care or competence—that the lawyer should have known more, should have had more experience, or should have exercised better judgment in accomplishing the client's goals. These situations, such as *Togstad*, commonly allege legal malpractice and usually require expert testimony.

Since World War II, both the number and complexity of malpractice cases against all professionals has grown.[11] The exact numbers are difficult to determine, because insurers report claims, and many lawyers do not carry malpractice insurance.[12] In Oregon, the only state that mandates malpractice insurance for lawyers, statistics for the past 20 years indicate that each year 8.7 to 13.2

---

4. *See, e.g.*, Olfe v. Gordon, 286 N.W.2d 573 (Wis. 1980) (no expert testimony required to show that lawyer breached fiduciary duty to client by failing to draft a first mortgage client specifically requested).
5. *E.g.*, Perez v. Kirk and Carrigan, *infra* p. 165.
6. *E.g.*, Wolpaw v. Gen. Accident Ins. Co., *infra* p. 348; Lawyers and Other Professionals: Sexual Relationships with Clients, *infra* p. 311.
7. RLGL §49; Roy Ryden Anderson & Walter W. Steele, Jr., *Fiduciary Duty, Tort and Contract: A Primer on the Legal Malpractice Puzzle*, 47 S.M.U. L. Rev. 235 (1994).
8. Kilpatrick v. Wiley, Rein & Fielding, 909 P.2d 1283, 1290 (Utah 1996).
9. RLGL §40, Comment a; *Restatement (Second) Torts* §551(2)(a).
10. *E.g.*, Est. of Fleming v. Nicholson, 724 A.2d 1026 (Vt. 1998) (no expert testimony necessary to establish negligence as a matter of law against lawyer who failed to inform client about a permit violation discovered during a title search on land the client wished to purchase, despite lawyer's claim that state had a nonenforcement policy concerning that type of violation). *See also* Charles W. Wolfram, *A Cautionary Tale: Fiduciary Breach as Legal Malpractice*, 34 Hofstra L. Rev. 689 (2006).
11. The vast array of treatises concerning other professionals also attests to this growth. *See, e.g.*, Dan L. Goldwasser & Thomas Arnold, *Accountants' Liability* (Practicing L. Inst. 2003); James Acret, *Architects and Engineers* (3d ed., Shepard's McGraw-Hill 1993); Norman L. Schafler, *Dental Malpractice: Legal and Medical Handbook* (3d ed., John Wiley & Sons, Inc. 1996); Ronald E. Mallen & Jeffrey M. Smith, *Legal Malpractice* (2007 ed., West); Warren Freedman, *Malpractice Liability in the Helping and Healing Professions* (Quorum Books 1995); David W. Louisell & Harold Williams, *Medical Malpractice* (Lexis-Nexis 2001); Lawrence E. Lifson & Robert I. Simon, eds., *The Mental Health Practitioner and the Law: A Comprehensive Handbook* (Harv. U. Press 1998); Nancy J. Brent, *Nurses and the Law: A Guide to Principles and Applications* (2d ed., W. B. Saunders Co. 2001); David B. Brushwood, *Pharmacy Malpractice: Law and Regulations* (2d ed., Aspen L. & Bus. 1998).
12. For example, one commentator estimates that 11-50 percent of lawyers do not carry malpractice insurance. Manuel R. Ramos, *Legal Malpractice: The Profession's Dirty Little Secret*, 47 Vand. L. Rev. 1657, 1672 (1994). *See also* Ronald E. Mallen & Robert J. Romero, eds., *Legal Malpractice: The Law Office Guide to Purchasing Legal Malpractice Insurance* (West 1999). A growing number of jurisdictions require lawyers to inform clients if they lack insurance. *E.g.*, N.H. R. of Prof. Conduct 1.17 (2006); Ohio R. of Prof. Conduct 1.4(c) (2007); R. of the S. Ct. of Va., Part 6, §IV, ¶18 (2007). Several jurisdictions also require malpractice insurance for lawyers who form professional corporations. RLGL §58, Comment c.

percent of Oregon lawyers have claims filed against them. Nationally, between 1979 and 1986, the number of legal malpractice cases doubled and the average settlement rose from $3,000 to $45,000.[13] Some think that the annual claims rate for lawyers is "probably closer to 20% or more."[14]

In formulating both breach of fiduciary duty and legal malpractice standards, courts rely on an extensive body of precedent.[15] To establish legal malpractice, for example, *dePape* and *Togstad* illustrate that a plaintiff must prove four elements: the existence of a client-lawyer relationship, breach of a professional duty of care, causation (actual and proximate), and damages. The requirement that a plaintiff establish a relationship with the professional is an application of the *Palsgraf* rule, that the plaintiff must be foreseeable, or in other words, the one to whom a duty is owed.[16] Expert testimony is not only admissible but is nearly always required to establish breach of the standard of care. Causation rules may be modified due to the special expertise of professionals or the kind of harm professionals can cause. Finally, proof of damages often requires more precision than that demanded by ordinary negligence cases.

Professional-Client Relationship

A breach of fiduciary duty or malpractice suit requires a showing of a professional relationship that creates a professional duty.[17] In *dePape*, there was no dispute that an express client-lawyer relationship existed, because the law firm deliberately agreed to represent Dr. dePape, and therefore owed him a duty of care as well as a fiduciary duty to communicate. *Togstad* illustrates how courts find that implied client-lawyer relationships create duties to prospective clients[18] when such parties reasonably rely on a lawyer's advice.[19] Most courts

---

13. Ramos, *supra* note 12, at 1678.
14. Ramos, *supra* note 12, at 1664. This estimate explains Ramos' conclusion that legal malpractice may be a "tip of the iceberg" problem, while medical malpractice more likely involves "a few bad apples." *See also* Manuel E. Ramos, *Legal Malpractice: No Lawyer or Client Is Safe*, 47 Fla. L. Rev. 1, 17 (1995).
15. Cases against lawyers can be traced to 1767. John W. Wade, *The Attorney's Liability for Negligence*, 12 Vand. L. Rev. 755 (1959). Those against physicians can be traced to 1374. *See* Allan H. McCoid, *The Care Required of Medical Practitioners*, 12 Vand. L. Rev. 549, 550 (1959).
16. *See* Palsgraf v. Long Is. R.R. Co., 162 N.E. 99 (N.Y. 1928).
17. In fact, most courts hold that a legal malpractice cause of action is not assignable to a third person. *See, e.g.,* Michael Greene, P.A. v. Leasing Assocs., Inc., 935 So. 2d 21 (Fla. App. 2006) (agreement to pursue malpractice claim in name only with promise to pay proceeds to a third party violates public policy against assignment of legal malpractice claims because it injures sanctity of client-lawyer relationship and treats malpractice actions as commodities to be exploited); Gurski v. Rosenblum & Filan, LLC, 885 A.2d 163 (Conn. 2005) (legal malpractice claims cannot be assigned to adversary in litigation); Rosby Corp. v. Townsend, Yosha, Cline & Prince, 800 N.E.2d 661 (Ind. App. 2003) (client's assignment of a legal malpractice claim barred regardless of whether assigned to an adversary). *Cf.,* Parrett v. Natl. Century Fin. Enters., Inc., 2006 U.S. Dist. LEXIS 16982 (S.D. Ohio) (general rule against assignment of legal malpractice claims does not apply to bankruptcy, where debtor's representative can pursue suit for benefit of creditors).
18. These implied relationships are one example of accidental clients, discussed in The Law Governing Lawyers, Accidental Clients, *supra* p. 96.
19. *See, e.g.,* DeVaux v. Am. Home Assurance Co., 444 N.E.2d 355 (Mass. 1983) (secretary who spoke to prospective client and told her to write a letter asking for representation and have a physician document injuries had actual or apparent authority to create client-lawyer relationship).

agree that prospective clients are limited-term clients to whom the duties of confidentiality and competence are due.[20] A limited-term implied client-lawyer relationship also has been found to exist in situations where a lawyer for one party to a transaction voluntarily provides services to other parties who reasonably rely on the lawyer's assistance.[21]

Duty

Plaintiffs must prove not only that a client-lawyer relationship existed, but also that it existed with respect to the acts or omissions that form the basis of a malpractice suit.[22] This rule recognizes that client and lawyer can agree to limit the scope of representation to certain specific matters.[23] Once both the client-professional relationship and the scope of representation are established, courts require lawyers to "exercise the competence and diligence normally exercised by lawyers in similar circumstances."[24] The general malpractice standard grants lawyers professional discretion, but only within the range of choices made by reasonably competent practitioners under similar circumstances.[25] Because jurors usually lack familiarity with what a particular professional should do, the duty requirement in professional malpractice cases nearly always requires expert testimony to establish the professional standard of care.[26]

The reality of state licensure of lawyers translates in malpractice suits into the admissibility of expert testimony of any lawyer licensed to practice in that state.[27] As lawyers specialize, the recognition of specialty areas also has become a component of the standard of care.[28] So, for example, lawyers as well as physicians have been held responsible for failing to understand the intricacies of a specialized task, or for failing to refer to a specialist who can competently provide the service.[29] Specialty designations can be established by state

20. See RLGL §§14, 15, 51(1).
21. Persons claiming such an implied client-lawyer relationship must reasonably believe that the lawyer represented their interests. E.g., Kremser v. Quarles & Brady, L.L.P., 36 P.3d 761 (Ariz. App. 2001) (corporation's lawyers undertook responsibility to perfect nonclient creditor's security interest); Nelson v. Nationwide Mortgage Corp., 659 F. Supp. 611 (D.D.C. 1987) (lawyer volunteered to answer questions and explain document).
22. See, e.g., Kates v. Robinson, 786 So. 2d 61 (Fla. App. 2001) (lawyer hired only to execute a judgment not responsible for recognizing other potential defendants). Cf., Nichols v. Keller, 19 Cal. Rptr. 2d 601 (Cal. App. 1993) (initial lawyer consulted by injured worker had duty to advise about availability of third-party action as well as worker's compensation claim, but second lawyer who undertook only workers' compensation case had no duty to advise).
23. See MR 1.2(c); RLGL §19.
24. Id.
25. Id., at Comment b; Equitania Ins. Co. v. Slone & Garrett P.S.C., 191 S.W.3d 552 (Ky. 2006) (lawyer can be liable for error in judgment that deviates from the standard of care); Jerry's Enters., Inc. v. Larkin, Hoffman, Daly & Lindgren, Ltd., 711 N.W.2d 811 (Minn. 2006) (lawyer must act with some level of reasonable care to be protected by honest error in judgment rule).
26. RLGL §52.
27. See, e.g., Russo v. Griffin, 510 A.2d 436 (Vt. 1986).
28. Ronald E. Mallen & Jeffrey M. Smith, Legal Malpractice, §19.4 (2007 ed., West).
29. Horne v. Peckham, 158 Cal. Rptr. 714 (Cal. App. 1979) (lawyer who acknowledged the need for expertise in tax had duty to refer client to an expert practitioner or to comply with the specialty standard of care).

regulations, by expert testimony, or by a lawyer who claims to practice in a specialized area.[30]

The power of professional custom also plays a role in mitigating the doctrine of negligence per se in malpractice cases. In ordinary negligence cases, courts treat relevant safety statutes as conclusive proof of the standard of care.[31] *dePape* illustrates the view of the majority of courts, which hold that such a violation is relevant and admissible to prove breach of the professional standard of care, but does not constitute negligence per se.[32] Courts often allow or require expert testimony to explain the Model Rule standard and its application.[33]

Breach

Once qualified as an appropriate expert, an expert witness's testimony must clearly articulate the standard of care or customary practice of the profession.[34] The jury then determines whether the defendant breached this standard of practice. *dePape* illustrates another aspect of legal malpractice cases: the common knowledge exception to the requirement of expert testimony.[35] This exception was created to address situations where expert opinion was not necessary to help the jury understand the alleged duty and breach, because the professional's error was not related to advanced skill, knowledge, or judgment.[36]

In legal malpractice actions, courts recognize three common knowledge exceptions for which juries do not need an expert to assess whether the lawyer failed to perform a basic duty owed to the client. The first involves breaches of fiduciary duty such as in *dePape*, and *Perez* in the next chapter. The second group of cases involves lawyers who miss obvious statutory time deadlines, such as statutes of limitations.[37] Finally, some courts have concluded that plaintiffs

---

30. *See, e.g.,* Battle v. Thornton, 646 A.2d 315 (D.C. 1994) (absent proof that the defendants held themselves out as specialists in Medicaid fraud defense, or that jurisdiction or profession recognizes such a specialty, lawyer is required to exercise skill and care of lawyers acting under similar circumstances).
31. *See, e.g.,* Martin v. Herzog, 126 N.E. 814 (N.Y. 1920). *Restatement (Second) of Torts* §286.
32. Model Rules, Scope ¶20; RLGL §52(2).
33. *See, e.g.,* Smith v. Haynsworth, Marion, McKay & Geurard, 472 S.E.2d 612 (S.C. 1996) (bar rules intended to protect a person in the client's position or addressing the particular harm are admissible to assess the legal duty of a lawyer).
34. *See, e.g.,* Clark v. D.C., 708 A.2d 632 (D.C. 1997) (expert witness's personal opinion not sufficient to establish the standard of care for medical malpractice); Childers v. Spindor, 754 P.2d 599 (Or. App. 1988) (expert witness's general discussion of deposition practice not sufficient to establish standard of care for legal malpractice).
35. In medical malpractice cases, the common knowledge exception applies where physicians operate on or injure a remote body part or leave surgical implements inside a patient's body. *See, e.g.,* Toy v. Mackintosh, 110 N.E. 1034 (Mass. 1916) (dentist allowed unconscious plaintiff to inhale an extracted tooth); Jefferson v. United States, 77 F. Supp. 706 (D. Md. 1948) (surgeon left towel in patient's abdominal cavity following gallbladder surgery).
36. *E.g.,* Valentine v. Watters, 896 So. 2d 385 (Ala. 2004) (trier of fact did not need expert to determine whether lawyer breached duty by misrepresenting his qualifications and missing a time deadline).
37. *See, e.g.,* Barnes v. Turner, 606 S.E.2d 849 (Ga. 2004) (lawyer who failed to safeguard client's security interest in the sale of a business, by renewing the security interest as required by statute five years after the sale); George v. Caton, 600 P.2d 822 (N.M. App. 1979) (statute of limitations).

do not need expert testimony to prove that lawyers should perform two basic functions: research applicable law[38] and investigate relevant facts.[39]

Causation

Once breach of a duty is established, courts require plaintiffs who allege legal malpractice to prove both actual and proximate causation. The "but-for" standard of actual causation and the foreseeable risk rule in proximate causation can present formidable obstacles.[40] Dr. dePape, for example, was unable to prove malpractice based on a duty of the law firm to pursue an H-1B visa, because he did not establish that he would have taken the medical exams that were required to qualify for it. He was, however, able to establish that he would have started his medical practice in Canada 15 months sooner had the law firm properly informed him of his legal options.

When a claim is based on the expiration of a time period such as a statute of limitations, plaintiffs who allege legal malpractice are required to prove a "case within a case," as was done in *Togstad*.[41] Some commentators, analogizing to medical malpractice, argue that some sort of increased risk doctrine should be applied in such situations.[42] A few courts have begun to recognize an alternative option: using expert testimony to prove what might have happened at trial.[43] This would mean that plaintiffs could recover if a negligent lawyer caused them to lose a chance of recovery, with the value of the loss measured by the settlement value of the underlying matter as established by expert testimony.[44]

---

38. *See, e.g.,* Smith v. Lewis, 530 P.2d 589 (Cal. App. 1973) (lawyer who failed to research law, which would have indicated a potential, though unclear, client claim in a divorce).
39. *See, e.g.,* Schmitz v. Crotty, 528 N.W.2d 112 (Iowa 1995) (lawyer who failed to investigate property descriptions in valuing estate taxes after he was put on notice they were inaccurate).
40. *E.g.,* Ambase Corp. v. Davis Polk & Wardwell, 866 N.E.2d 1033 (N.Y. 2007) (record provides no support for plaintiff's assertion that "but for" law firm's failure to advise it properly, a large loss reserve would have been removed earlier and client would not have suffered loss of business opportunities).
41. *E.g.,* Viner v. Sweet, 70 P.3d 1046 (Cal. 2003) (case within a case proof required for errors in transactional work as well as litigation); Bevin v. Fix, 42 P.3d 1013 (Wyo. 2002) (summary judgment granted against client who proved that former lawyer breached fiduciary duty but did not allege facts indicating that the underlying divorce action would have been more favorable to him); Winskunas v. Birnbaum, 23 F.3d 1264 (7th Cir. 1994) (former client must prove that lawyer who failed to file appeal of state court action would have gotten his loss reversed on appeal). The rule also burdens persons convicted of crimes, who must have their convictions reversed or prove their innocence to establish causation. *Cf.,* Whitley v. Chamouris, 574 S.E.2d 251 (Va. 2003) (jury question whether client proved merits of underlying case, no expert testimony required). See Lawyers and Clients: Criminal Defense, *infra* p. 124.
42. John Leubsdorf, *Legal Malpractice and Professional Responsibility,* 48 Rutgers L. Rev. 101, 149-150 (1995).
43. Garcia v. Kozlov, Seaton, Romanini & Brooks, P.C., 845 A.2d 602 (N.J. 2004) (expert testimony sufficient to establish actual cause against lawyer who negligently failed to investigate accident claim and join one of responsible drivers); Wolpaw v. Gen. Accident Ins. Co., *infra* p. 348.
44. *Cf.,* Jones Motor Co. Inc. v. Holtkamp, Liese, Beckemeier & Childress, P.C., 197 F.3d 1190 (7th Cir. 1999) (malpractice plaintiff who alleged former lawyer's failure to make a timely jury trial request failed to prove causation using a lawyer-expert witness whose opinion of probable jury verdicts was unsubstantiated by actual verdicts in comparable cases).

Damages

Since malpractice is a species of negligence, damages must be shown. For example, even if the jury determines that the plaintiff would have prevailed in a previous case, a defendant who can show that any judgment won would have been uncollectible will be relieved from being accountable for that portion of the verdict.[45] Traditionally, proving damages meant proving monetary or physical injury. Increasingly, clients and patients who allege foreseeable emotional harm also may be able to recover from the professional who caused it.[46] For example, the court in *dePape* recognized the availability of damages for emotional harm against some lawyers, at least where their breach of fiduciary duty is egregious and directly causes severe emotional distress.[47] *dePape* also illustrates the willingness of modern cases to extend punitive damages to professionals where their conduct is grossly negligent or outrageous in character.[48] Query whether Dr. dePape's malpractice lawyers themselves committed malpractice by failing to plead punitive damages.[49]

Defenses

Professionals often allege several defenses to malpractice suits. Increasingly, they seek to implead or be granted contribution from other professionals who provided services to the client.[50] Statutes of limitations may differ for breach of contract, fiduciary duty, and malpractice, and are also commonly alleged as defenses.[51] Most courts agree that because clients depend on professionals, the statute is tolled during the time the professional-client relationship continues.[52] Most courts also apply the "discovery rule" to lawyers; the statutory time period

---

45. *See, e.g.,* RLGL §53, Comment b. *Cf.,* Garretson v. Miller, 121 Cal. Rptr. 2d 317 (Cal. App. 3d Dist. 2002) (plaintiff must prove that judgment would be collectible).
46. *See, e.g.,* RLGL §53, Comment g. For a similar result in medical practice, *see, e.g.,* Oswald v. LeGrand, 453 N.W.2d 634 (Iowa 1990).
47. *See, e.g.,* Perez v. Kirk & Carrigan, p. 165 *infra,* which upheld emotional distress damages against lawyers whose breach of confidentiality caused a multiple-count criminal indictment against their client. *See also* Lawyers and Clients: Criminal Defense, *infra* p. 124. *Cf.,* Long-Russell v. Hampe, 39 P.3d 1015 (Wyo. 2002) (damages for emotional distress not recoverable in malpractice case alleging negligent legal advice about child custody). *See also* Lawrence v. Grinde, 534 N.W.2d 414 (Iowa 1995), cited in *dePape.*
48. RLGL §53, Comment h.
49. Courts differ on whether clients can recover punitive damages that a lawyer negligently failed to pursue. *E.g.,* Tri-G Inc. v. Burke, Bosselman & Weaver, 856 N.E.2d 389 (Ill. 2006) (clients cannot recover punitive damages lawyer might have recovered if case not dismissed due to lawyer's negligence); Jacobsen v. Oliver, 201 F. Supp. 2d 93 (D.D.C. 2002) (terrorism victim in legal malpractice case could recover punitive damages if his lawyer negligently failed to raise the issue in the underlying action).
50. *E.g.,* Sheetz, Inc. v. Bowles Rice McDavid Graff & Love, PLLC, 547 S.E.2d 256 (W. Va. 2001) (predecessor and successor law firms may be joint tortfeasors); Parler & Wobber v. Miles & Stockbridge, P.C., 756 A.2d 526 (Md. 2000) (lawyer being sued by former client may implead or obtain contribution or indemnification from successor lawyer).
51. A few states also have statutes of repose for malpractice suits, which start to run on the date of the act or omission. *See, e.g.,* Sorenson v. L. Off. of Theodore Poehlmann, 764 N.E.2d 1227 (Ill. App. 2001) (six-year statute of repose time stricture applies even where underlying acts only produce injury after that period of time).
52. *See, e.g.,* Shumsky v. Eisenstein, 750 N.E.2d 67 (N.Y. 2001) (analogizing to the continuous treatment rule in medical malpractice cases); Lima v. Schmidt, 595 So. 2d 624 (La. 1992).

does not begin until the plaintiff reasonably should have discovered the elements of the cause of action.[53]

Courts follow similar reasoning when deciding whether comparative negligence should apply. A lawyer cannot claim comparative fault as a defense in a case such as *dePape* where the client's failure to understand has been caused by the lawyer's negligent explanation or the client's reasonable reliance.[54]

Overall, courts apply fairly consistent rules to govern tort suits against lawyers. The development of this law has made malpractice suits a primary means of addressing professional incompetence. Understanding the remedy can help you avoid liability in practice.

C. Ineffective Assistance of Counsel

Problems

5-5. Is Fox in trouble because he failed to inform a criminal defendant client about a plea bargain offered by the prosecutor? What if Fox considered the offer "ridiculous"? What if Client told Fox, "I'll never cop a plea"? What if the defendant was eventually convicted and sentenced to five years and the plea bargain would have resulted in a two-year sentence?

5-6. Is Fox in trouble for letting his criminal defendant client take the stand to tell his side of the story, when by all accounts the testimony was a disaster? How about Fox's failure to cross-examine the 80-year-old victim, who, though slightly senile, left the jury in tears on direct?

Consider: Model Rules 1.1-1.4
            Model Code DR 6-101, 7-101
            RLGL §§21-23, 53 comment d

Roe v. Flores-Ortega
528 U.S. 470 (2000)

Justice O'CONNOR delivered the opinion of the Court.

In this case we must decide the proper framework for evaluating an ineffective assistance of counsel claim, based on counsel's failure to file a notice of appeal without respondent's consent.

---

53. *E.g.*, Feddersen v. Garvey, 427 F.3d 108 (1st Cir. 2005) (discovery rule applies but did not toll the statute of limitations where client could have reasonably discerned that he suffered some harm caused by the lawyer at an earlier point in time); Neel v. Magana, Olney, Levy, Cathcart & Gelfand, 6 Cal. 3d 176 (1971) (a cause of action for legal malpractice does not accrue until plaintiff knew, or should have known, all material facts essential to show the elements of the claim).

54. *See, e.g.*, RLGL §54, Comment d. On the other hand, a client who defrauded a third party was not entitled to indemnification from his lawyers, because "fraudfeasors" cannot hold others liable for harm caused by their own fraudulent conduct. Trustees of the AFTRA Health Fund v. Biondi, 303 F.3d 765 (7th Cir. 2002); Clark v. Rowe, 701 N.E.2d 624 (Mass. 1988) (upholding jury verdict that client was 70 percent negligent in refinancing a loan).

I

The State of California charged respondent, Lucio Flores-Ortega, with one count of murder, two counts of assault, and a personal use of a deadly weapon enhancement allegation. In October 1993, respondent appeared in Superior Court with his court-appointed public defender, Nancy Kops, and a Spanish language interpreter, and pleaded guilty to second-degree murder. The plea was entered pursuant to a California rule permitting a defendant both to deny committing a crime and to admit that there is sufficient evidence to convict him. . . . In exchange for the guilty plea, the state prosecutor moved to strike the allegation of personal use of a deadly weapon and to dismiss both assault charges. On November 10, 1993, respondent was sentenced to 15 years to life in state prison. After pronouncing sentence, the trial judge informed respondent, "You may file an appeal within 60 days from today's date with this Court. If you do not have money for Counsel, Counsel will be appointed for you to represent you on your appeal."

Although Ms. Kops wrote "bring appeal papers" in her file, no notice of appeal was filed within the 60 days allowed by state law. (A notice of appeal is generally a one-sentence document stating that the defendant wishes to appeal from the judgment.) Filing such a notice is a purely ministerial task that imposes no great burden on counsel. During the first 90 days after sentencing, respondent was apparently in lockup, undergoing evaluation, and unable to communicate with counsel. About four months after sentencing, on March 24, 1994, respondent tried to file a notice of appeal, which the Superior Court Clerk rejected as untimely. Respondent sought habeas relief from California's appellate courts, challenging the validity of both his plea and conviction, and (before the California Supreme Court) alleging that Ms. Kops had not filed a notice of appeal as she had promised. These efforts were uniformly unsuccessful.

Respondent then filed a federal habeas petition pursuant to 28 U.S.C. §2254, alleging constitutionally ineffective assistance of counsel based on Ms. Kops' failure to file a notice of appeal on his behalf after promising to do so. The United States District Court for the Eastern District of California referred the matter to a Magistrate Judge, who in turn ordered an evidentiary hearing on the limited issue of whether Ms. Kops promised to file a notice of appeal on respondent's behalf. At the conclusion of the hearing, the Magistrate Judge found:

"The evidence in this case is, I think, quite clear that there was no consent to a failure to file [a notice of appeal]. . . .

"It's clear to me that Mr. Ortega had little or no understanding of what the process was, what the appeal process was, or what appeal meant at that stage of the game.

"I think there was a conversation [between Ortega and Kops] in the jail. Mr. Ortega testified, and I'm sure he's testifying as to the best of his belief, that there was a conversation after the pronouncement of judgment at the sentencing hearing where it's his understanding that Ms. Kops was going to file a notice of appeal.

"She has no specific recollection of that. However, she is obviously an extremely experienced defense counsel. She's obviously a very meticulous person. And I think had Mr. Ortega requested that she file a notice of appeal, she would have done so.

"But, I cannot find that he has carried his burden of showing by a preponderance of the evidence that she made that promise." . . .

The Court of Appeals for the Ninth Circuit reversed. . . . We granted certiorari . . . to resolve a conflict in the lower courts regarding counsel's obligations to file a notice of appeal. . . .

II

In Strickland v. Washington, 466 U.S. 668 (1984), we held that criminal defendants have a Sixth Amendment right to "reasonably effective" legal assistance, and announced a now-familiar test: A defendant claiming ineffective assistance of counsel must show (1) that counsel's representation "fell below an objective standard of reasonableness," and (2) that counsel's deficient performance prejudiced the defendant. Today we hold that this test applies to claims, like respondent's, that counsel was constitutionally ineffective for failing to file a notice of appeal.

A

As we have previously noted, "no particular set of detailed rules for counsel's conduct can satisfactorily take account of the variety of circumstances faced by defense counsel." Rather, courts must "judge the reasonableness of counsel's conduct on the facts of the particular case, viewed as of the time of counsel's conduct," and "judicial scrutiny of counsel's performance must be highly deferential." We have long held that a lawyer who disregards specific instructions from the defendant to

file a notice of appeal acts in a manner that is professionally unreasonable. This is so because a defendant who instructs counsel to initiate an appeal reasonably relies upon counsel to file the necessary notice. Counsel's failure to do so cannot be considered a strategic decision; filing a notice of appeal is a purely ministerial task, and the failure to file reflects inattention to the defendant's wishes. At the other end of the spectrum, a defendant who explicitly tells his attorney not to file an appeal plainly cannot later complain that, by following his instructions, his counsel performed deficiently. *See* Jones v. Barnes, 463 U.S. 745, 751 (1983) (accused has ultimate authority to make fundamental decision whether to take an appeal). The question presented in this case lies between those poles: Is counsel deficient for not filing a notice of appeal when the defendant has not clearly conveyed his wishes one way or the other? . . .

In those cases where the defendant neither instructs counsel to file an appeal nor asks that an appeal not be taken, we believe the question whether counsel has performed deficiently by not filing a notice of appeal is best answered by first asking a separate, but antecedent, question: whether counsel in fact consulted with the defendant about an appeal. We employ the term "consult" to convey a specific meaning—advising the defendant about the advantages and disadvantages of taking an appeal, and making a reasonable effort to discover the defendant's wishes. If counsel has consulted with the defendant, the question of deficient performance is easily answered: Counsel performs in a professionally unreasonable manner only by failing to follow the defendant's express instructions with respect to an appeal. . . . If counsel has not consulted with the defendant, the court must in turn ask a second, and subsidiary, question: whether counsel's failure to consult with the defendant itself constitutes deficient performance. That question lies at the heart of this case: Under what circumstances does counsel have an obligation to consult with the defendant about an appeal?

Because the decision to appeal rests with the defendant, we agree with Justice Souter that the better practice is for counsel routinely to consult with the defendant regarding the possibility of an appeal. *See* ABA Standards for Criminal Justice, Defense Function §4-8.2(a) (3d ed. 1993). In fact, California imposes on trial counsel a per se duty to consult with defendants about the possibility of an appeal. *See* Cal. Penal Code Ann. §1240.1(a) (West Supp. 2000). Nonetheless, "prevailing norms of practice as reflected in American Bar Association standards and the like . . . are only guides," and imposing "specific guidelines" on counsel is "not appropriate." And, while States are free to impose whatever specific rules they see fit to ensure that criminal defendants are well represented, we have held that the Federal Constitution imposes one general requirement: that counsel make objectively reasonable choices. . . . We cannot say, as a constitutional matter, that in every case counsel's failure to consult with the defendant about an appeal is necessarily unreasonable, and therefore deficient. . . . We therefore reject a bright-line rule that counsel must always consult with the defendant regarding an appeal.

We instead hold that counsel has a constitutionally-imposed duty to consult with the defendant about an appeal when there is reason to think either (1) that a rational defendant would want to appeal (for example, because there are nonfrivolous grounds for appeal), or (2) that this particular defendant reasonably demonstrated to counsel that he was interested in appealing. In making this determination, courts must take into account all the information counsel knew or should have known. . . . Although not determinative, a highly relevant factor in this inquiry will be whether the conviction follows a trial or a guilty plea, both because a guilty plea reduces the scope of potentially appealable issues and because such a plea may indicate that the defendant seeks an end to judicial proceedings. Even in cases when the defendant pleads guilty, the court must consider such factors as whether the defendant received the sentence bargained for as part of the plea and whether the plea expressly reserved or waived some or all appeal rights. Only by considering all relevant factors in a given case can a court properly determine whether a rational defendant would have desired an appeal or that the particular defendant sufficiently demonstrated to counsel an interest in an appeal. Rather than the standard we announce today, Justice Souter would have us impose an "almost" bright-line rule and hold that counsel "almost always" has a duty to consult with a defendant about an appeal. . . . The relevant question is not whether counsel's choices were strategic, but whether they were reasonable. We expect that courts evaluating the reasonableness of counsel's performance using the inquiry we have described will find, in the vast majority of cases, that counsel had a duty to consult with the defendant about an appeal. We differ from

Justice Souter only in that we refuse to make this determination as a per se (or "almost" per se) matter.

B

The second part of the *Strickland* test requires the defendant to show prejudice from counsel's deficient performance.

1

In most cases, a defendant's claim of ineffective assistance of counsel involves counsel's performance during the course of a legal proceeding, either at trial or on appeal. *See, e.g.*, 466 U.S. at 699 (claim that counsel made poor strategic choices regarding what to argue at a sentencing hearing); United States v. Cronic, 466 U.S. 648, 649-650 (1984) (claim that young lawyer was incompetent to defend complex criminal case); Penson v. Ohio, 488 U.S. 75, 88-89 (1988) (claim that counsel in effect did not represent defendant on appeal); Smith v. Robbins, 528 U.S. 259 (2000) (claim that counsel neglected to file a merits brief on appeal); Smith v. Murray, 477 U.S. 527, 535-536 (1986) (claim that counsel failed to make a particular argument on appeal). In such circumstances, whether we require the defendant to show actual prejudice— "a reasonable probability that, but for counsel's unprofessional errors, the result of the proceeding would have been different," —or whether we instead presume prejudice turns on the magnitude of the deprivation of the right to effective assistance of counsel. That is because "the right to the effective assistance of counsel is recognized not for its own sake, but because of the effect it has on the ability of the accused to receive a fair trial, or a fair appeal." . . .

2

In some cases, however, the defendant alleges not that counsel made specific errors in the course of representation, but rather that during the judicial proceeding he was—either actually or constructively—denied the assistance of counsel altogether. "The presumption that counsel's assistance is essential requires us to conclude that a trial is unfair if the accused is denied counsel at a critical stage." The same is true on appeal. Under such circumstances, "no specific showing of prejudice [is] required," because "the adversary process itself [is] presumptively unreliable."

Today's case is unusual in that counsel's alleged deficient performance arguably led not to a judicial proceeding of disputed reliability, but rather to the forfeiture of a proceeding itself. According to respondent, counsel's deficient performance deprived him of a notice of appeal and, hence, an appeal altogether. Assuming those allegations are true, counsel's deficient performance has deprived respondent of more than a fair judicial proceeding; that deficiency deprived respondent of the appellate proceeding altogether. In *Cronic, Penson*, and *Robbins*, we held that the complete denial of counsel during a critical stage of a judicial proceeding mandates a presumption of prejudice because "the adversary process itself" has been rendered "presumptively unreliable." . . . The even more serious denial of the entire judicial proceeding itself, which a defendant wanted at the time and to which he had a right, similarly demands a presumption of prejudice. Put simply, we cannot accord any "'presumption of reliability,'" to judicial proceedings that never took place.

3

The Court of Appeals below applied a per se prejudice rule, and granted habeas relief based solely upon a showing that counsel had performed deficiently under its standard. Unfortunately, this per se prejudice rule ignores the critical requirement that counsel's deficient performance must actually cause the forfeiture of the defendant's appeal. If the defendant cannot demonstrate that, but for counsel's deficient performance, he would have appealed, counsel's deficient performance has not deprived him of anything, and he is not entitled to relief. *Cf.* Peguero v. United States, 526 U.S. 23, (1999) (defendant not prejudiced by court's failure to advise him of his appeal rights, where he had full knowledge of his right to appeal and chose not to do so). Accordingly, we hold that, to show prejudice in these circumstances, a defendant must demonstrate that there is a reasonable probability that, but for counsel's deficient failure to consult with him about an appeal, he would have timely appealed.

In adopting this standard, we follow the pattern established in *Strickland* and *Cronic*, and reaffirmed in *Robbins*, requiring a showing of actual prejudice (i.e., that, but for counsel's errors, the defendant might have prevailed) when the proceeding in question was presumptively reliable, but presuming prejudice with no further showing from the defendant of the merits of his underlying claims when the violation of the right to counsel rendered the proceeding presumptively unreliable or entirely nonexistent. . . . [W]e hold that when counsel's constitutionally deficient performance deprives a defendant of an appeal that he otherwise would have taken, the defendant has made

out a successful ineffective assistance of counsel claim entitling him to an appeal. We believe this prejudice standard breaks no new ground, for it mirrors the prejudice inquiry applied in Hill v. Lockhart, 474 U.S. 52 (1985), and Rodriquez v. United States, 395 U.S. 327 (1969). In *Hill*, we considered an ineffective assistance of counsel claim based on counsel's allegedly deficient advice regarding the consequences of entering a guilty plea. Like the decision whether to appeal, the decision whether to plead guilty (i.e., waive trial) rested with the defendant and, like this case, counsel's advice in *Hill* might have caused the defendant to forfeit a judicial proceeding to which he was otherwise entitled. We held that "to satisfy the 'prejudice' requirement [of *Strickland*], the defendant must show that there is a reasonable probability that, but for counsel's errors, he would not have pleaded guilty and would have insisted on going to trial." Similarly, in *Rodriquez*, counsel failed to file a notice of appeal, despite being instructed by the defendant to do so. We held that the defendant, by instructing counsel to perfect an appeal, objectively indicated his intent to appeal and was entitled to a new appeal without any further showing. . . .

As with all applications of the *Strickland* test, the question whether a given defendant has made the requisite showing will turn on the facts of a particular case. Nonetheless, evidence that there were nonfrivolous grounds for appeal or that the defendant in question promptly expressed a desire to appeal will often be highly relevant in making this determination. We recognize that the prejudice inquiry we have described is not wholly dissimilar from the inquiry used to determine whether counsel performed deficiently in the first place; specifically, both may be satisfied if the defendant shows nonfrivolous grounds for appeal. . . . But, while the performance and prejudice prongs may overlap, they are not in all cases coextensive. To prove deficient performance, a defendant can rely on evidence that he sufficiently demonstrated to counsel his interest in an appeal. But such evidence alone is insufficient to establish that, had the defendant received reasonable advice from counsel about the appeal, he would have instructed his counsel to file an appeal.

By the same token, although showing nonfrivolous grounds for appeal may give weight to the contention that the defendant would have appealed, a defendant's inability to "specify the points he would raise were his right to appeal reinstated," will not foreclose the possibility that he can satisfy the prejudice requirement where there are other substantial reasons to believe that he would have appealed. . . . We similarly conclude here that it is unfair to require an indigent, perhaps pro se, defendant to demonstrate that his hypothetical appeal might have had merit before any advocate has ever reviewed the record in his case in search of potentially meritorious grounds for appeal. Rather, we require the defendant to demonstrate that, but for counsel's deficient conduct, he would have appealed.

III

The court below undertook neither part of the *Strickland* inquiry we have described, but instead presumed both that Ms. Kops was deficient for failing to file a notice of appeal without respondent's consent and that her deficient performance prejudiced respondent. Justice Souter finds Ms. Kops' performance in this case to

have been "derelict," presumably because he believes that she did not consult with respondent about an appeal. But the Magistrate Judge's findings do not provide us with sufficient information to determine whether Ms. Kops rendered constitutionally inadequate assistance. Specifically, the findings below suggest that there may have been some conversation between Ms. Kops and respondent about an appeal (Ms. Kops wrote "'bring appeal papers'" in her file), but do not indicate what was actually said. Assuming, arguendo, that there was a duty to consult in this case, it is impossible to determine whether that duty was satisfied without knowing whether Ms. Kops advised respondent about the advantages and disadvantages of taking an appeal and made a reasonable effort to discover his wishes. Based on the record before us, we are unable to determine whether Ms. Kops had a duty to consult with respondent (either because there were potential grounds for appeal or because respondent expressed interest in appealing), whether she satisfied her obligations, and, if she did not, whether respondent was prejudiced thereby. Accordingly, the judgment of the Court of Appeals is vacated, and the case is remanded for further proceedings consistent with this opinion. . . .

Justice SOUTER, with whom Justice STEVENS and Justice GINSBURG join, concurring in part and dissenting in part.

I join Part II-B of the Court's opinion, but I respectfully dissent from Part II-A. As the opinion says, the crucial question in this case is whether, after a criminal conviction, a lawyer has a duty to consult with her client about the choice to appeal. The majority's conclusion is sometimes; mine is, almost always in those cases in which a plea of guilty has not obviously waived any claims of error.[1] It is unreasonable for a lawyer with a client like respondent Flores-Ortega to walk away from her representation after trial or after sentencing without at the very least acting affirmatively to ensure that the client understands the right to appeal. . . .

While *Strickland*'s disclaimer that no particular set of rules should be treated as dispositive respects the need to defer to reasonable "strategic choices" by lawyers, no such strategic concerns arise in this case. Strategic choices are made about the extent of investigation, the risks of a defense requiring defendant's testimony and exposure to crossexamination, the possibility that placing personal background information before a jury will backfire, and so on. It is not, however, an issue of "strategy" to decide whether or not to give a defendant any advice before he loses the chance to appeal a conviction or sentence. The concern about too much judicial second-guessing after the fact is simply not raised by a claim that a lawyer should have counseled her client to make an intelligent decision to invoke or forgo the right of appeal or the opportunity to seek an appeal.

The Court's position is even less explicable when one considers the condition of the particular defendant claiming *Strickland* relief here. Flores-Ortega spoke no English and had no sophistication in the ways of the legal system. The Magistrate Judge found that "it's clear . . . that Mr. Ortega had little or no understanding of what the process was, what the appeal process was, or what appeal meant." To condition the duty of a lawyer to such a client on whether, inter alia, "a rational defendant would want to appeal (for example, because there are nonfrivolous grounds for appeal)," is not only to substitute a harmless-error rule for a showing of reasonable professional conduct, but to employ a rule that simply ignores the reality that the constitutional norm must address.[2] Most criminal defendants, and certainly this one, will be utterly incapable of making rational judgments about appeal without guidance. They cannot possibly know what a rational decisionmaker must know unless they are given the benefit of a professional assessment of chances of success and risks of trying. And they will often (indeed, usually) be just as bad off if they seek relief on habeas after failing to take a direct appeal, having no right to counsel in state postconviction proceedings.

---

1. I say "almost" always, recognizing that there can be cases beyond the margin: if a legally trained defendant were convicted in an error-free trial of an open-and-shut case, his counsel presumably would not be deficient in failing to explain the options. This is not what we have here. Nor is this a case in which the judge during the plea colloquy so fully explains appeal rights and possible issues as to obviate counsel's need to do the same; such a possibility is never very likely and exists only at the furthest reach of theory, given a defendant's right to adversarial representation. . . . Finally, of course, there is no claim here that Flores-Ortega waived his right to appeal as part of his plea agreement; although he pleaded guilty, the record shows that he and the State argued before the trial court for different sentences, and he had little understanding of the legal system. The fact of the plea is thus irrelevant to the disposition of the case.

2. The Court holds that a duty to consult will also be present if "this particular defendant reasonably demonstrated to counsel that he was interested in appealing." Because for most defendants, and certainly for unsophisticated ones like Flores-Ortega who are unaware even of what an appeal means, such a demonstration will be a practical impossibility, I view the Court as virtually requiring the defendant to show the existence of some nonfrivolous appellate issue.

▨ Lawyers and Clients:
Criminal Defense

Roe offers us a portal through which to glimpse the reality of criminal defense representation in America. In most criminal cases today, defendants have a constitutional right to counsel, but the dream that every person charged with a serious crime "will be capably defended . . . sure of the support needed to make an adequate defense"[1] remains illusory.[2] This is especially true for death penalty cases, where the cost of error is high to the accused and the government.[3]

The recognition of constitutional rights to defense counsel created the need for large numbers of lawyers qualified to handle criminal trials.[4] That need has accelerated over the past few decades, as the number of those charged and convicted of crimes has increased dramatically.[5] Initially, courts relied on appointed counsel. The need for specialized expertise hastened the development of public defender offices. In the late 1960s, the American Bar Association adopted basic standards for providing defense counsel, and for the administration of criminal justice intended to assist lawyers in criminal practice.[6] Today, about two-thirds of those accused of a felony are poor enough to qualify for appointed counsel.[7] As a result, lawyers in public defender offices often shoulder huge caseloads.[8] At the same time, private appointed counsel, because

---

1. Anthony Lewis, *Gideon's Trumpet* 205 (Random House 1964).
2. Mary Sue Backus & Paul Marcus, *The Right to Counsel in Criminal Cases, A National Crisis*, 57 Hastings L.J. 1031 (2006); ABA Standing Committee on Legal Aid and Indigent Defendants, *Gideon's Broken Promise: America's Continuing Quest for Equal Justice* (2004). Available at *http:// www.abanet.org/legalservices/sclaid/defender/brokenpromise/*. Last visited June 7, 2007.
3. James S. Liebman, *The Overproduction of Death*, 100 Colum. L. Rev. 2030, 2102-2110 (2000) (state and federal courts reversed 68 percent of the capital judgments they fully reviewed over the past 25 years); Stephen B. Bright, *Counsel for the Poor: The Death Sentence Not for the Worst Crime but for the Worst Lawyer*, 103 Yale L.J. 1835 (1994). In capital cases, ineffective defense lawyers are part of, but not the entire problem. *See* Edward Connors, Thomas Lundregan, Neal Miller & Tom McEwen, *Convicted by Juries, Exonerated by Science: Case Studies in the Use of DNA Evidence After Trial* (U.S. Dept. of Just. 1996).
4. For a history of the American tradition of an independent criminal defense bar, *see* Susan P. Koniak, *The Law Between the Bar and the State*, 70 N.C. L. Rev. 1389, 1448-1460 (1992).
5. Arrest rates (per 100,000 inhabitants) have increased from 897 in 1971 to 954 in 1998, but were over 1,100 from 1987 to 1995. Ann L. Pastore & Kathleen Maguire, eds., *Sourcebook of Criminal Justice Statistics* 339 (U.S. Dept. of Just. 1999); incarceration rates (the number of prison and jail inmates per 100,000 U.S. residents) have more than doubled, from 313 in 1985 to 682 in 1999. *Id.* at 497.
6. ABA, *Standards for Criminal Justice, Providing Defense Services* (3d ed. 1993); ABA, *Standards for Criminal Justice, The Defense Function* (3d ed. 1993).
7. Deborah H. Rhode, *In the Interest of Justice: Reforming the Legal Profession* 61 (Oxford 2000).
8. Although most courts find that the Sixth Amendment does not provide the basis for overturning convictions on the basis of completely inadequate institutional funding or assignment systems, *see* United States v. Cronic, 466 U.S. 648 (1984), a few have done so, *e.g.,* State v. Peart, 621 So. 2d 780 (La. 1993) (although entire defender system was not constitutionally inadequate, lawyer who represented 70 active felony cases and had represented 418 defendants in the past seven months, entering 130 guilty pleas at arraignment rebuttably presumed not able to provide effective assistance). The courts' continuation of this rebuttable presumption until caseloads were reduced "prompted the Louisiana legislature to increase indigent funding by $5 million over the next two years." Note, 113 Harv. L. Rev. 2062, 2074 (2000). *See also* Miranda v. Clark County, Nev., 319 F.3d 465 (9th Cir. 2002) (en banc) (upholding civil rights action under §1983 for deliberate indifference to Sixth Amendment rights of defendants against county's public defender system, which assigned recently graduated lawyers to death penalty cases).

of inadequate fee schedules, often face an "inherent conflict between remaining financially solvent and the defendant's need for vigorous advocacy."[9] These workload and financial pressures present a huge impediment to the provision of effective legal assistance.[10]

The Clients

Judicial recognition of a constitutional right to counsel was recognized first in some,[11] and then in all felony cases, on the ground that defense lawyers "are necessities, not luxuries," both to protect against the risk of wrongful conviction and to provide due process of law.[12] Rights to counsel in juvenile and certain misdemeanor cases followed.[13] Today, a person accused of a crime has a right to retained or appointed counsel at all "critical stages"[14] of both criminal felony prosecutions and misdemeanor cases in which the defendant could be sentenced to a term of imprisonment.[15] In addition, a person convicted of a crime has a Fourteenth Amendment right to counsel for capital sentencing hearings and for the first appeal of right.[16] The right to counsel includes a right to counsel of choice, but only to defendants who can afford to hire or otherwise find a lawyer willing to represent the defendant without charge.[17] Indigent defendants have a right to counsel, but no right to counsel of choice.[18]

The 5 Cs

Although the Supreme Court has always recognized that the Sixth Amendment requirement of counsel presupposed *effective* assistance of counsel, it did not

---

9. *Report of the Committee to Review the Criminal Justice Act,* reprinted at 52 Crim. L. Rptr. 2265, 2284-2285 (1993); David Cole, *No Equal Justice* 81-89 (The New Press 1999). *See also* Olive v. Maas, 811 So. 2d 644 (Fla. 2002) (lawyers in capital cases may petition the court for additional compensation beyond mandatory fee cap to preserve right to counsel).
10. *See* Cole, *supra* note 9.
11. Powell v. Ala., 287 U.S. 45, 60 (1932) (Sixth Amendment requires counsel if fundamental unfairness would result). *See also* Johnson v. Zerbst, 304 U.S. 458 (1938) (Sixth Amendment requires counsel in all federal criminal proceedings).
12. Gideon v. Wainwright, 372 U.S. 335, 344 (1963) (Sixth Amendment requires right to counsel in all felony cases).
13. In re Gault, 387 U.S. 1 (1966) (Sixth Amendment requires counsel for juvenile proceedings that may lead to commitment in state institutions); Argersinger v. Hamlin, 407 U.S. 25 (1972) (Sixth Amendment requires counsel in misdemeanor cases where defendant is imprisoned); Ala. v. Shelton, 535 U.S. 654 (2002) (Sixth Amendment requires counsel in misdemeanor cases where defendant receives a suspended sentence).
14. Critical stages include preliminary hearings, some pretrial identification proceedings and questioning by prosecutor or police designed to elicit inculpatory statements. Wayne R. LaFave, Jerold H. Israel & Nancy J. King, *Criminal Procedure* 569 (3d ed., West 2000).
15. Scott v. Ill., 440 U.S. 367 (1979) (counsel not required in misdemeanor cases where defendant fined but not imprisoned); Nichols v. United States, 511 U.S. 738 (1994) (defendant can receive enhanced term of incarceration under federal sentencing guidelines even if prior misdemeanor conviction resulted in a fine where no counsel was provided).
16. Douglas v. Cal., 372 U.S. 353 (1963); Ross v. Moffit, 417 U.S. 600 (1974) (no right to counsel for discretionary state appeals); Pa. v. Finley, 481 U.S. 551 (1987) (no right to counsel in state habeas corpus proceedings).
17. United States v. Gonzalez-Lopez, 126 S. Ct. 2557 (2006). An absolute right to counsel of choice is subject to several limitations: Counsel must be a member of the bar in good standing, and not subject to a conflict of interest. Wheat v. United States, 486 U.S. 153, 159 (1988).
18. *Id.*

provide a framework to evaluate the adequacy of counsel until 1984 in Strickland v. Washington[19] and United States v. Cronic.[20] In these opinions, the Court found that the Sixth Amendment right to effective assistance of counsel included the right to a lawyer who would play "a role that is critical to the ability of the adversarial system to produce just results."[21] As *Roe* indicates, it then established a two-prong test to assess whether a defendant had been deprived of the effective assistance of counsel. The first prong, "that counsel's representation fell below an objective standard of reasonableness" parallels the duty-breach analysis in legal malpractice suits. The second, "that counsel's deficient performance prejudiced the defendant" parallels the "but-for" actual causation requirement and functions like a harmless error analysis in criminal appeals. In subsequent case law, the Supreme Court has interpreted both prongs to create very difficult proof burdens for defendants.

Control and Communication The alleged failure of Roe's lawyer to allow him to control the decision to appeal by failing to communicate appeal options or implementing his decision illustrates a decades-long debate about the scope and value of per se categories of reversible error in criminal cases. Those who favor the per se approach argue that a per se rule creates clear standards that protect indigent defendants from incompetence. Per se rules also prevent the time and cost of further fact-finding and act to counterbalance institutional incentives that foster incompetence, such as huge caseloads, poor funding, and lack of time. The absence of such a categorical approach gives defense counsel little incentive to honor basic fiduciary duties such as consultation and investigation, and allows such errors by counsel to be labeled "strategic choices," which current jurisprudence prevents the courts from second-guessing.

    Roe is typical of a wide variety of cases that have rejected per se rules because of a preference to uphold convictions unless the conduct falls so far below the standard of care that no possible reason can justify it. As *Roe* points out, case-by-case determinations are preferred to prevent distractions from the central focus of advocacy, which should be dictated by the particular facts and circumstances of the case. As a result, unless the accused can show total deprivation of counsel at a critical stage of the proceeding, the Sixth Amendment requires no such per se rule.[22]

Competence Criminal defense lawyers who face huge caseloads have affirmative obligations to refuse new appointments or seek leave to withdraw from existing cases in order to provide competent representation.[23] Whenever clients

---

19. 466 U.S. 668 (1984).
20. United States v. Cronic, *supra* note 8.
21. Strickland v. Washington, *supra* note 19, at 685. The defendant also has the alternative of representing herself, if she knowingly and intelligently waives her Sixth Amendment right. *See* Faretta v. Cal., 422 U.S. 806 (1975). Standby counsel can be appointed to assist the defendant. *Id.*; McKaskle v. Wiggins, 465 U.S. 168 (1984).
22. Of course, a state can impose per se rules as a matter of state constitutional or statutory law, as California had done in *Roe*. But such a breach will be irrelevant in a federal habeas corpus proceeding that alleges violation of the United States Constitution. *See, e.g.,* Bell v. Cone, 535 U.S. 685 (2002).
23. ABA Formal Op. 06-441 (Ethical Obligations of Lawyers Who Represent Indigent Criminal Defendants When Excessive Caseloads Interfere with Competent and Diligent Representation).

initially raise the issue of competence of counsel on appeal of their convictions or in a habeas corpus petition, they run into the *Strickland* two-prong standard.[24] The first competence prong of the *Strickland* test, that counsel's performance fell below an objective standard, requires defendants first to identify the precise error or errors of defense counsel and then to present some kind of expert testimony that those errors should not have occurred.[25] To meet this requirement, a defendant may offer testimony from an expert criminal defense practitioner or rely on what the Supreme Court in *Roe* referred to as evidence of "prevailing norms of practice as reflected in American Bar Association standards and the like." *Roe* typifies cases that find such standards (including the Model Rules) relevant, and on occasion very persuasive, but not determinative of the appropriate standard of care.

This prong of the *Strickland* test has proved difficult to meet, however, because *Strickland* further instructed courts to "indulge in a strong presumption that counsel's conduct falls within the wide range of reasonable professional assistance." This essentially invites courts to evaluate whether any established error was due to a strategic decision or came about because of an inexcusable lack of attentiveness.[26] If counsel errs following a reasonably complete investigation of the law and facts, deference usually wins the day. For example, a number of cases have alleged ineffective assistance because counsel failed to perform a more complete investigation prior to a capital punishment sentencing hearing. In most of these cases, despite finding that counsel failed to perform a more complete investigation into mitigating evidence, the courts have found that these less than thorough efforts constituted a reasonable strategic decision.[27] A few more recent cases indicate that the Court may be willing to take a more careful look when the death penalty is at stake, defense counsel has departed from clear standards of care, and reversal of a sentence rather than a conviction is sought.[28]

---

24. Most states limit direct appeals to issues raised on the face of the trial record. Because lawyer omissions often require additional investigation, and because trial counsel often handles the appeal, most ineffective assistance of counsel claims are not raised or identified until collateral habeas corpus proceedings. Massaro v. United States, 538 U.S. 500, 504-505 (2003).

25. A claim of ineffective assistance often requires an evidentiary postconviction hearing to develop more fully what happened and why. *See, e.g.,* Rompilla v. Beard, 545 U.S. 374, 385 note 3 (2005).

26. Joshua Dressler, *Understanding Criminal Procedure* 621-622 (3d ed., Lexis-Nexis 2002).

27. *E.g.,* Schriro v. Landrigan, 127 S. Ct. 1933 (2007); Burger v. Kemp, 483 U.S. 776 (1987). Some cases reasoned that only the complete failure to discover or offer any mitigation evidence was unreasonable, presumably because it indicated no attempt at developing a strategy. *See, e.g.,* Williams v. Taylor, 529 U.S. 362 (2000); Silva v. Woodford, 279 F.3d 825 (9th Cir. 2002); St. v. Koedatich, 548 A.2d 939 (N.J. 1988) (conviction reversed where defense counsel presented no mitigating evidence during penalty phase of death penalty case even though defendant instructed counsel to present no evidence and defendant signed a statement waiving his rights to present mitigating evidence).

28. *See, e.g.,* Rompilla v. Beard, *supra* note 25 (failure of defense counsel to review prosecutor's planned use of prior conviction record constituted unreasonable behavior under all the circumstances); Wiggins v. Smith, 539 U.S. 510 (2003) (counsel's failure to compile a social history of the defendant and expand investigation beyond pre-sentence report and social service records fell short of ABA Standards and constituted ineffective assistance). *But see* Schriro v. Landrigan, *supra* note 27 (district courts not required to grant evidentiary hearings to make out colorable ineffective assistance of counsel claim about inadequate mitigating evidence at capital sentencing).

When defendants have met the first prong of *Strickland*, they then face equal difficulty establishing the second prong, prejudice. This prong approximates the but-for causation test, by requiring the defendant to show that the professional mistake of counsel actually caused a "fundamentally unfair" conviction, sentence, or failure to appeal.[29] Typically, courts find that counsel's errors are harmless and refuse to grant relief under this prong.[30] However, in rare cases courts find the standard met, for example, where it was determined that if an adequate investigation into mitigating evidence had been completed, it would have caused defense counsel to introduce the evidence in the penalty phase of a capital trial, and "had the jury been confronted with this considerable mitigating evidence, there is a reasonable probability that it would have returned with a different sentence."[31]

Like *Roe*, most cases refuse to presume prejudice, because per se rules require that the circumstances must be "so likely to prejudice the accused that the cost of litigating their effect in a particular case is unjustified."[32] The "sleeping lawyer" cases illustrate the significant proof required to reach this threshold. When defense lawyers nap during a trial, courts have held that one episode of inattention or sleep does not alone rise to the level of a breakdown in the adversary process necessary to presume prejudice.[33] However, repeated periods of unconsciousness may become the equivalent of no counsel at all so that prejudice can be presumed.[34] The Supreme Court also has presumed prejudice where counsel has been actually or constructively denied during a critical stage of the proceeding, or counsel's error led to forfeiture of an appeal, as in *Roe*.

This law informed the result in *Roe* on remand. Initially, the district court found that the public defender did not consult with Mr. Flores-Ortega, but if she had done so, she would have advised against filing an appeal because there were no nonfrivolous grounds to support it. The Ninth Circuit reversed, finding that it was unlikely the public defender would have written "bring appeal papers" unless her client had expressed an interest in filing an appeal. Once this was established, the court presumed prejudice as a matter of law because it led to forfeiture of the proceeding. In other words, the defendant had shown that counsel failed to consult with him about an appeal, and that if consulted, he would have chosen to appeal.[35]

---

29. Lockhart v. Fretwell, 506 U.S. 364, 372 (1993). *See, e.g.,* Glover v. United States, 531 U.S. 198 (2001) (defense counsel's failure to group charges under Federal Sentencing Guidelines, which increased defendant's sentence by 6-21 months, constituted prejudice).

30. *E.g.,* Lockhart v. Fretwell, *supra* note 29 (counsel's incompetence, failing to raise an objection to inadmissible evidence in a sentencing hearing, did not prejudice the defendant because the claim was based on precedent that was subsequently overruled); St. v. Hongo, 706 So. 2d 419 (La. 1998) (failure to object to an erroneous jury instruction constituted harmless error); Melancon v. St., 66 S.W.3d 375 (Tex. App. 2001) (failure to subpoena alibi witness not prejudicial because witness's testimony not presented to prove it would have helped).

31. Wiggins v. Smith, *supra* note 28, at 536.

32. United States v. Cronic, *supra* note 8, at 658.

33. *E.g.,* Fellman v. Poole, 1994 U.S. App. Lexis 22667.

34. *See, e.g.,* Burdine v. Johnson, 231 F.3d 950 (5th Cir. 2000), *rev'd en banc*, 262 F.3d 336 (5th Cir. 2001); *cert. denied sub. nom.* Cockrell v. Burdine, 535 U.S. 1120 (2002).

35. Flores-Ortega v. Roe, 39 Fed. Appx. 604 (9th Cir. 2002). The court ordered the district court to "issue a conditional writ of habeas corpus releasing Flores from state custody, unless the state

Confidentiality Criminal defense lawyers have special confidentiality obligations. In the area of candor to the tribunal, Model Rule 3.3 requires all lawyers to take reasonable remedial measures, including disclosure, to correct false evidence. Lawyers are not allowed to knowingly offer false evidence, and may refuse to offer evidence they reasonably believe to be false.[36] The one exception is criminal defense. A lawyer who reasonable believes, but does not know, that his or her client/defendant will testify falsely must bow to the client's choice.[37] And, even when she knows, she may be required to permit the client to testify in an alternative narrative format.[38]

Conflict of Interest Resolution *Roe* illustrates that trial lawyers often file a notice of appeal for convicted defendants. Trial counsel may be disqualified from handling the appeal, however, because of an obvious personal conflict of interest that prevents him or her from identifying his or her own ineffective assistance of counsel as a basis for reversing the client's conviction.[39]

In cases where a lawyer's conflict of interest becomes the basis for asserting ineffective assistance, the courts again draw fine distinctions between presumed and actual prejudice. Courts have faced a number of recurring situations where conflicts have been alleged, including the joint representation of co-defendants, previous representation of the victim or other significant prosecution witness, fee arrangements including payment by one co-defendant for others or potential royalties to counsel that may accrue after the trial, investigation or possible prosecution of counsel for the same crime, or counsel who might be called as a prosecution witness. In Holloway v. Arkansas,[40] the Supreme Court held that the failure of a judge to inquire into a multiple concurrent representation conflict was enough to presume prejudice.[41] However, when previous representation of the victim was not raised on the record, prejudice was not presumed even when the defendant was unaware of the conflict, and it was known by the prosecutor, defense lawyer, and the trial judge.[42]

If prejudice is not presumed, defendants must show "actual" conflicts of interest that compelled defense counsel to compromise his or her duty of loyalty.[43] Courts have restricted this actual conflict category to a small list of flagrant conflicts such as a lawyer who was implicated in the defendants' crime,[44]

---

permits Flores to initiate and prosecute a direct appeal from his conviction within a reasonable period of time as determined by the district court." *Id.* at 606. The dissent questioned whether a defendant "still suffered prejudice if he or she has no non-frivolous issue to raise on appeal." *Id.* at 608.

36. MR 3.3 (a)(3); RLGL §120.

37. *Id.* We deal with this issue in more detail in Chapter 7. *See* The Bounds of the Law: Client Fraud, *supra* p. 237.

38. *See, e.g.,* Wisconsin v. McDowell, *infra* p. 271.

39. *See, e.g.,* St. v. Veale, 919 A.2d 794 (N.H. 2007) (reviewing per se, actual conflict and hybrid approaches to disqualification of appellate counsel).

40. 435 U.S. 475 (1978).

41. The trial judge can grant a motion to disqualify defense counsel if necessary to guarantee a fair trial. *See, e.g.,* United States v. Edwards, 39 F. Supp. 2d 716 (M.D. La. 1999).

42. Mickens v. Taylor, 535 U.S. 162 (2002).

43. Cuyler v. Sullivan, 446 U.S. 335 (1980).

44. United State v. Fulton, 5 F.3d 605 (2d Cir. 1993).

representation of co-defendants,[45] and a trial judge's direction to counsel to pull his punches if he wished his fee approved and to receive subsequent appointments from the court.[46] For the defendant who can demonstrate that an actual conflict existed, he or she need prove only that it "adversely affected" the lawyer's performance at trial instead of the usual but-for prejudice requirement.[47] In all other situations, however, the defendant must return to the traditional *Strickland* two-prong standard, establishing both the nature of the conflict and prejudice.[48]

The Bounds of the Law

Reversing Convictions This brief review of the law of ineffective assistance of counsel leads to the observation that despite frequent allegations of ineffective assistance of counsel in criminal appeals, very few defendants succeed in overturning convictions. Part of this is because over 90 percent of criminal convictions result from a guilty plea,[49] a situation where far less scrutiny of counsel's performance is usually possible, and where, even when it is, courts have been especially reluctant to reverse convictions.[50] Of course, the difficulty of satisfying both prongs of the *Strickland* test means that very few convictions are reversed for trial error as well.[51]

Yet despite these hurdles, state and federal cases do indicate several categories of failings by defense counsel that constitute constitutional error in some cases. Most obvious is a lawyer who failed to inform his client that he no longer represented the client in an appeal, essentially depriving the accused of any lawyer at all.[52] Similarly, when counsel is present, but fails to test the prosecution's case, for example, by conceding the defendant's guilt to the jury when the defendant consistently maintained his innocence,[53] or by a total lack of effort and explanation,[54] courts have no trouble finding a violation. Following a

---

45. *E.g.,* Moss v. United States, 323 F.3d 445 (6th Cir. 2003); Duvall v. St., 923 A. 2d 81 (Md. 2007) (conflict of interest found where same public defender's office represented both defendant, and, in an unrelated case, the man the defendant claimed was the crime's true perpetrator).

46. Walberg v. Isreal, 766 F.2d 1071 (7th Cir. 1985).

47. *See, e.g.,* Perillo v. Johnson, 205 F.3d 775 (5th Cir. 2000).

48. *See, e.g.,* Beets v. Collins, 65 F.3d 1258 (5th Cir. 1995).

49. *See* Ann L. Pastore & Kathleen Maguire, *supra* note 5, at 429, 460 (guilty or *nolo contendere* pleas occurred in 95 percent of federal criminal convictions and in 94 percent of state court convictions in 75 largest counties).

50. Bruce A. Green, *Judicial Rationalization for Rationing Justice: How Sixth Amendment Doctrine Undermines Reform,* 70 Fordham L. Rev. 1729 (2002).

51. Several Supreme Court justices have pointed out the "impotence" of the *Strickland* standard. In a dissent to a denial of certiorari, Justice Blackman chronicled the denial of ineffective assistance claims in death penalty cases where the clients were executed. The lawyers in these cases were addicted to drugs and incarcerated on federal drug charges a few weeks following the client's trial, suspended from practice on unrelated grounds, and unaware of a recent Supreme Court decision that would have reduced a client's death sentence. They committed errors such as failing to present any evidence at the penalty phase of the case and failing to appear for oral argument. One lawyer, asked to name a criminal case, could cite only "Miranda and Dred Scott," yet survived two challenges in state court. McFarland v. Scott, 512 U.S. 1256 (1994) (Blackmun, J., dissenting to the denial of *certiorari*). *See also* Mitchell v. Kemp, 483 U.S. 1026 (1987) (Marshall, J., dissenting to the denial of *certiorari*).

52. Fields v. Bagley, 275 F.3d 478 (6th Cir. 2001).

53. *E.g.,* Florida v. Nixon, 543 U.S. 175 (2004); St. v. Carter, 14 P.3d 1138 (Kan. 2000).

54. *E.g.,* People v. Bass, 636 N.W.2d 781 (Mich. App. 2001) (defense counsel had no memory of trial, lost most of the file, and offered no reason for failing to call witnesses); People v. Spann, 765

fact-specific inquiry, courts also have found counsel ineffective for failing to adequately investigate facts,[55] failing to find or understand relevant law,[56] giving defective advice about whether to testify or accept a plea bargain,[57] and failing to object to improper evidence or procedures.[58]

Malpractice   Convicted defendants also can bring a legal malpractice action against their former lawyers.[59] Theoretically, such a case should not differ much from ordinary malpractice litigation. Yet courts have created some special doctrines that make malpractice recovery against criminal defense lawyers very difficult to secure. Consider, for example, whether the facts in *Roe* would justify a successful malpractice claim.

In such a suit, Mr. Flores-Ortega would first be confronted with the defense of governmental immunity. Although the courts agree that publicly employed lawyers such as prosecutors should be protected from suit by governmental immunity,[60] they generally do not grant such immunity to appointed counsel[61] and are split about whether public defenders share similar immunity.[62] Thus, depending on the jurisdiction, his suit may be completely barred.[63]

N.E.2d 1114 (Ill. App. 2002) (defense counsel failed to challenge defective indictment, move to quash arrest or suppress evidence, give opening statement, or cross-examine the only witness against the defendant); Wenzy v. St., 855 S.W.2d 47 (Tex. App. 1993) (when not allowed to withdraw, counsel refused to take an active role in defense).

55. *E.g.,* Rompilla v. Beard, *supra* note 25; Wesley v. St., 753 N.E.2d 686 (Ind. App. 2002) (failure to get psychiatric record of victim who had a history of false accusations); In re K.J.O., 27 S.W.3d 340 (Tex. App. 2000) (failure to conduct investigation into juvenile's defense); People v. Truly, 595 N.E.2d 1230 (Ill. App. 1992) (failure to investigate and present alibi).

56. *E.g.,* Kimmelman v. Morrison, 477 U.S. 365 (1986) (mistake as to defense counsel's obligation to request discovery); Dando v. Yukins, 461 F.3d 791 (6th Cir. 2006) (trial counsel's failure to consult an expert and otherwise investigate the validity of a duress defense based on Battered Woman's Syndrome); Stanford v. Stewart, 554 S.E.2d 480 (Ga. 2001) (appellate counsel failed to recognize the significance of an error in jury instructions); Pena-Mota v. St., 986 S.W.2d 341 (Tex. App. 1999) (failure to object to jury instruction resulted in a double jeopardy violation).

57. *E.g.,* Ross v. Kemp, 393 S.E.2d 244 (Ga. 1990) ("fractured" defense by two lawyers who failed effectively to help defendant decide whether to testify); St. v. Donald, 10 P.3d 1193 (Ariz. App. 2000) (receipt of a fair trial did not cure rejection of favorable plea bargain due to counsel's ineffective assistance); Crabbe v. St., 546 S.E.2d 65 (Ga. App. 2001) (defense counsel did not advise defendant that guilty pleas would remove the possibility of parole).

58. Kimmelman v. Morrison, *supra* note 56 (failure to move to suppress due to a total failure to conduct pre-trial discovery); Dawkins v. St., 551 S.E.2d 260 (S.C. 2001) (failure to object to hearsay statements of victim); St. v. Crislip, 785 P.2d 262 (N.M. App. 1989) (failure to protect defendant against unsworn, out-of-court accusation by co-defendant); St. v. Scott, 602 N.W.2d 296 (Wis. App. 1999) (failure to object to prosecutor's breach of plea bargain); Alaniz v. St., 937 S.W.2d 593 (Tex. App. 1996) (failure to object to seating of a juror excused for cause); Evans v. St., 28 P.3d 498 (Nev. 2001) (failure to challenge prosecutor's remarks during penalty phase of trial); Ross v. St., 726 So. 2d 317 (Fla. App. 1999) (failure to object to improper remarks of prosecutor made during closing argument).

59. *See* Gregory G. Sarno, *Legal Malpractice in Defense of Criminal Prosecution,* 4 A.L.R.5th 273 (1992).

60. *See, e.g.,* Durham v. McElynn, 772 A.2d 68 (Pa. 2001).

61. *See, e.g.,* Ferri v. Ackerman, 444 U.S. 193 (1979) (federal law does not immunize appointed defense lawyers); Mossow v. United States, 987 F.2d 1365 (8th Cir. 1993) (federal law does not bar malpractice suit against military lawyer).

62. *See, e.g.,* Barner v. Leeds, 13 P.3d 704 (Cal. 2000) (public defenders not protected by statutory immunity for discretionary acts); Johnson v. Halloran, 742 N.E.2d 741 (Ill. 2000) (public defenders not protected by sovereign immunity). *But see* Public and Appellate Defender Immunity Act, 745 ILCS 19/1 (2000); Wooton v. Vogele, 769 N.E.2d 889 (Ohio App. 2001) (Ohio

Even if not barred by immunity, the statute of limitations also must be confronted. Most courts hold that the statute begins to run at the time of the reversal of the conviction.[64] Others prefer to reason that the cause of action accrues at the time of the conviction, or when the client reasonably should know of the wrongful conduct, which may require that the defendant bring the civil suit while his appeal is still pending to prevent the statute of limitations from running.[65]

If Mr. Flores-Ortega could surmount these defenses, proof of breach of the professional duty of care would not be as problematic. He most likely would be able to present expert testimony regarding the duty to consult, and he also could rely on the ABA Criminal Defense Standards as well as Model Rules 1.2(a) and 1.4 to establish such a duty.[66] In fact, his case arguably fits within the common knowledge exception explained in *dePape*, because his lawyer apparently breached a basic fiduciary duty of consultation, obedience, or both.

On the other hand, proving causation in Mr. Flores-Ortega's case would be impossible in most jurisdictions. The majority of courts require proof of actual causation by a showing that, but for the error of counsel, the defendant would not have been convicted. These courts further require that the defendant's conviction must be reversed in order to show that his lawyer's error actually caused him harm.[67] This means that defendants like Flores-Ortega who do not seek to reverse convictions will not succeed.[68] And some jurisdictions require even more: an affirmative proof of innocence.[69] A few jurisdictions do allow alternative proof, especially on facts like *Roe*, where the lawyer's error leads to a longer sentence or lost appeal. Consistent with *Roe*, they hold that defendant need only show that he would have accepted the plea (or appeal) if it had been presented to him.[70]

Tort Immunity Statute protects public defenders from suit); Dziubak v. Mott, 503 N.W.2d 771 (Minn. 1993) (public defenders protected from suit by judicial immunity).

63. Public defenders have been held not to act under color of state law under 42 U.S.C. §1983 because they act contrary to the government's interests. Polk County v. Dodson, 454 U.S. 312 (1981); Miranda v. Clark County, Nev., *supra* note 8 (assistant public defender who represented defendant in a traditional role, was not a state actor, but administrative head of public defender office, who determined how resources were spent was amenable to suit under §1983). *See also* Catherine R. Lazuran, *Court-Appointed Attorney as Subject to Liability Under 42 U.S.C. §1983*, 36 A.L.R. Fed. 594 (1978).

64. *E.g.*, Schreiber v. Rowe, 814 So. 2d 396 (Fla. 2002).

65. *E.g.*, Burnett v. South, 2007 Tenn. App. LEXIS 277; Gebhardt v. O'Rourke, 510 N.W.2d 900 (Mich. 1994).

66. ABA Standards for Criminal Justice, *Defense Function* §§4-5.2, 4-8.2 (3d ed. 1993); RLGL §22(1).

67. RLGL §53, Comment d. In guilty plea cases, the issue of claim preclusion—whether the defendant's admission of guilt precludes a subsequent malpractice suit—raises a similar issue. *See, e.g.*, Mrozek v. Inta Fin. Corp., 699 N.W.2d 54 (Wis. 2005).

68. *E.g.*, Canaan v. Bartee, 72 P.3d 911 (Kan. 2003); Gibson v. Trant, 58 S.W.3d 103 (Tenn. 2001); *cf.*, Falkner v. Foshaug, 29 P.3d 771 (Wash. App. 2001) (*Alford* plea, which allowed client to plead guilty without admitting guilt, did not preclude later proof of client's innocence in malpractice action against defense counsel).

69. *E.g.*, Bloomer v. Gibson, 912 A.2d 424 (Vt. 2006); Schreiber v. Rowe, *supra* note 64; Rodriguez v. Nielsen, 650 N.W.2d 237 (Neb. 2002) (allegation that defendant acted in self-defense does not establish actual innocence); Wiley v. County of San Diego, 966 P.2d 983 (Cal. 1998); Glenn v. Aiken, 569 N.E.2d 783 (Mass. 1991); Carmel v. Lunney, 511 N.E.2d 1126 (N.Y. 1987).

70. *See, e.g.*, Krahn v. Kinney, 538 N.E.2d 1058 (Ohio 1989); Levine v. Kling, 123 F.3d 580 (7th Cir. 1997) (innocence need not be shown where defendant alleges error such as failure to press double jeopardy defense).

In the few cases where causation can be shown, courts do not hesitate to approve recovery for emotional distress due to incarceration caused by the lawyer's negligence.[71]

Professional Discipline Of course, a defendant who complains about incompetent defense counsel also may file a disciplinary complaint against his former lawyer. In most of the cases where discipline has occurred, the lawyer exhibited a pattern or practice of incompetence. For example, lawyers have been disciplined for abandoning criminal clients,[72] failing to appear after being retained to do so,[73] and repeated incompetence in handling criminal matters.[74] Very few cases address the issue of whether incompetence in one criminal matter also can constitute a violation of the Model Rules. In one case involving an experienced defense lawyer whose client's felony conviction was reversed for ineffective assistance of counsel, the Arizona Supreme Court suspended the lawyer for violating Model Rules 1.1, 1.3, and 1.4.[75] The court held that the prior finding of ineffective assistance did not necessarily indicate that the lawyer should be subject to discipline, but at the same time, it recommended that when such a determination has been made "trial judges and appellate courts look to the circumstances and determine whether there is arguably some infraction that should be called to the attention of the appropriate bar authorities."[76]

Conclusion

Most criminal defense lawyers function in a system that is underfunded and overworked. They often labor under difficult conditions where the stakes are exceedingly high. *Roe* illustrates that the law of ineffective assistance of counsel produces few counterincentives to these difficult circumstances. State courts have created similar and often more extensive barriers to recovery in legal malpractice cases. Professional discipline, while possible, also rarely occurs. At the same time, the number of cases where allegations of ineffective assistance of counsel is alleged suggests continuing problems of quality in criminal defense representation. Further, the number of cases (such as *Roe* on remand) that have granted relief despite these considerable proof burdens suggests a continuing wide range of deficient conduct that raises serious questions about whether our constitutional guarantee of right to counsel is a truly meaningful one.

---

71. *E.g.,* Holiday v. Jones, 264 Cal. Rptr. 448 (Cal. App. 1989); Gautam v. De Luca, 521 A.2d 1343 (N.J. Super. 1987); Bowman v. Doherty, 686 P.2d 112 (Kan. 1984). In capital cases where the death sentence is reversed and the defendant's sentence is reduced to life imprisonment, no harm caused by the lawyer can be demonstrated.
72. *E.g.,* In re Mohling, 2001 Ariz. LEXIS 84.
73. In re Lewis, 689 A.2d 561 (D.C. App. 1997).
74. In re Fox, 522 N.E.2d 1229 (Ill. 1988); Atty. Grievance Commn. v. Middleton, 756 A.2d 565 (Md. 2000); Law. Disc. Bd. v. Turgeon, 557 S.E.2d 235 (W. Va. 2000).
75. In re Wolfram, 847 P.2d 94 (Ariz. 1993).
76. *Id.* at n.5. The State Bar of Arizona later clarified that when criminal defense lawyers execute an affidavit acknowledging their own ineffective assistance to assist in a defendant's appeal, Model Rule 8.3 requires any other lawyer who is aware of such an affidavit to report the conduct to the disciplinary authorities if the content of the affidavit raised a "substantial" question regarding the averring lawyer's "honesty, trustworthiness, or fitness as a lawyer in other respects." St. Bar of Ariz. Formal Op. 98-02.

D. Duties to Nonclients

1. Misrepresentation

Problem

5-7. In giving an opinion to Cheltenham Township on the issuance of bonds to finance a shopping center, Martyn & Fox inserted the usual boilerplate: "This issuance complies with all applicable law." Martyn & Fox forgot that there were new IRS regulations governing the tax-exempt status of such special purpose bonds. Any problems?

> Consider: Model Rules 1.1, 2.3, 4.1, 8.4(c)
> Model Code DR 1-102(A)(4), 6-101, 7-102(A)(5)
> RLGL §51

Greycas, Inc. v. Proud
826 F.2d 1560 (7th Cir. 1987), cert. denied, 484 U.S. 1043 (1988)

POSNER, Circuit Judge.

Theodore S. Proud, Jr., a member of the Illinois bar who practices law in a suburb of Chicago, appeals from a judgment against him for $833,760, entered after a bench trial. The tale of malpractice and misrepresentation that led to the judgment begins with Proud's brother-in-law, Wayne Crawford, like Proud a lawyer but one who devoted most of his attention to a large farm that he owned in downstate Illinois. The farm fell on hard times and by 1981 Crawford was in dire financial straits. He had pledged most of his farm machinery to lenders, yet now desperately needed more money. He approached Greycas, Inc., the plaintiff in this case, a large financial company headquartered in Arizona, seeking a large loan that he offered to secure with the farm machinery. He did not tell Greycas about his financial difficulties or that he had pledged the machinery to other lenders, but he did make clear that he needed the loan in a hurry. Greycas obtained

several appraisals of Crawford's farm machinery but did not investigate Crawford's financial position or discover that he had pledged the collateral to other lenders, who had perfected their liens in the collateral. Greycas agreed to lend Crawford $1,367,966.50, which was less than the appraised value of the machinery.

The loan was subject, however, to an important condition, which is at the heart of this case: Crawford was required to submit a letter to Greycas, from counsel whom he would retain, assuring Greycas that there were no prior liens on the machinery that was to secure the loan. Crawford asked Proud to prepare the letter, and he did so, and mailed it to Greycas, and within 20 days of the first contact between Crawford and Greycas the loan closed and the money was disbursed. A year later Crawford defaulted on the loan; shortly afterward he committed suicide. Greycas then learned that most of the farm machinery that Crawford had pledged to it had previously been pledged to other lenders.

The machinery was sold at auction. The Illinois state court that determined the creditors' priorities in the proceeds of the sale held that Greycas did not have a first priority on most of the machinery that secured its loan; as a result Greycas has been able to recover only a small part of the loan. The judgment it obtained in the present suit is the district judge's estimate of the value that it would have realized on its collateral had there been no prior liens, as Proud represented in his letter.

That letter is the centerpiece of the litigation. Typed on the stationery of Proud's firm and addressed to Greycas, it identifies Proud as Crawford's lawyer and states that, "in such capacity, I have been asked to render my opinion in connection with" the proposed loan to Crawford. It also states that "this opinion is being delivered in accordance with the requirements of the Loan Agreement" and that

> I have conducted a U.C.C., tax, and judgment search with respect to the Company [i.e., Crawford's farm] as of March 19, 1981, and except as hereinafter noted all units listed on the attached Exhibit A ("Equipment") are free and clear of all liens or encumbrances other than Lender's perfected security interest therein which was recorded March 19, 1981 at the Office of the Recorder of Deeds of Fayette County, Illinois.

The reference to the lender's security interest is to Greycas's interest; Crawford, pursuant to the loan agreement, had filed a notice of that interest with the recorder. The excepted units to which the letter refers are four vehicles. Exhibit A is a long list of farm machinery—the collateral that Greycas thought it was getting to secure the loan, free of any other liens. . . .

Proud never conducted a search for prior liens on the machinery listed in Exhibit A. His brother-in-law gave him the list and told him there were no liens other than the one that Crawford had just filed for Greycas. Proud made no effort to verify Crawford's statement. The theory of the complaint is that Proud was negligent in representing that there were no prior liens, merely on his brother-in-law's say-so. No doubt Proud was negligent in failing to conduct a search, but we are not clear why the misrepresentation is alleged to be negligent rather than deliberate and hence fraudulent, in which event Greycas's alleged contributory negligence would not be an issue (as it is, we shall see), since there is no defense of contributory or comparative negligence to a deliberate tort, such as fraud. . . . Proud did not merely say, "There are no liens"; he said, "I have conducted a U.C.C., tax, and judgment search"; and not only is this statement, too, a false one, but its falsehood cannot have been inadvertent, for Proud knew he had not conducted such a search. The concealment of his relationship with Crawford might also support a charge of fraud. But Greycas decided, for whatever reason, to argue negligent misrepresentation rather than fraud. It may have feared that Proud's insurance policy for professional malpractice excluded deliberate wrongdoing from its coverage, or may not have wanted to bear the higher burden of proving fraud, or may have feared that an accusation of fraud would make it harder to settle the case. . . . In any event, Proud does not argue that either he is liable for fraud or he is liable for nothing.

He also does not, and could not, deny or justify the misrepresentation; but he argues that it is not actionable under the tort law of Illinois, because he had no duty of care to Greycas. . . . He argues that Greycas had an adversarial relationship with Proud's client, Crawford, and that a lawyer has no duty of straight dealing to an adversary, at least none enforceable by a tort suit. In so arguing, Proud is characterizing Greycas's suit as one for professional malpractice rather than negligent misrepresentation, yet elsewhere in his briefs he insists that the suit was solely for negligent misrepresentation—while Greycas insists that its suit charges both torts. . . . So we shall discuss both.

Proud is undoubtedly correct in arguing that a lawyer has no general duty of care toward his adversary's client; it would be a considerable and, as it seems to us, an undesirable novelty to hold that every bit of sharp dealing by a lawyer gives rise to prima facie tort liability to the opposing party in the lawsuit or negotiation. The tort of malpractice normally refers to a lawyer's careless or otherwise wrongful conduct toward his own client. Proud argues that Crawford rather than Greycas was his client and . . . we shall assume for purposes of discussion that Greycas was not Proud's client.

Therefore if malpractice just meant carelessness or other misconduct toward one's own client, Proud would not be liable for malpractice to Greycas. But in Pelham v. Griesheimer, 440 N.E.2d 96 (1982), the Supreme Court of Illinois discarded the old common law requirement of privity of contract for professional malpractice; so now it is possible for someone who is not the lawyer's (or other professional's) client to sue him for malpractice. The court in Pelham was worried, though, about the possibility of a lawyer's being held liable "to an unlimited and unknown number of potential plaintiffs," so it added that "for a nonclient to succeed in a negligence action against an attorney, he must prove that the primary purpose and intent of the attorney-client relationship itself was to benefit or influence the third party." That, however, describes this case exactly. Crawford hired Proud not only for the primary purpose, but for the sole purpose, of influencing Greycas to make Crawford a loan. The case is much like Brumley v. Touche, Ross & Co., 487 N.E.2d 641, 644-45 (Ill. App. 1985), where a complaint that an accounting firm had negligently prepared an audit report that the firm knew would be shown to an investor in the audited corporation and relied on by that investor was held to state a claim for professional malpractice. In Conroy v. Andeck Resources '81 Year-End Ltd., 484 N.E.2d 525, 536-37 (1985), in contrast, a law firm that represented an offeror of securities was held not to have any duty of care to investors. The representation was not intended for the benefit of investors. Their reliance on the law firm's using due care in the services it provided in connection with the offer was not invited.

All this assumes that Pelham governs this case, but arguably it does not, for Greycas, as we noted, may have decided to bring this as a suit for negligent misrepresentation rather than professional malpractice. We know of no obstacle to such an election; nothing is more common in American jurisprudence than overlapping torts.

The claim of negligent misrepresentation might seem utterly straightforward. It might seem that by addressing a letter to Greycas intended (as Proud's counsel admitted at argument) to induce reliance on the statements in it, Proud made himself prima facie liable for any material misrepresentations, careless or deliberate, in the letter, whether or not Proud was Crawford's lawyer or for that matter anyone's lawyer. Knowing that Greycas was relying on him to determine whether the collateral for the loan was encumbered and to advise Greycas of the results of his determination, Proud negligently misrepresented the situation, to Greycas's detriment. But merely labeling a suit as one for negligent misrepresentation rather than professional malpractice will not make the problem of indefinite and perhaps excessive liability, which induced the court in *Pelham* to place limitations on the duty of care, go away. So one is not surprised to find that courts have placed similar limitations on suits for negligent misrepresentation —so similar that we are led to question whether, . . . these really are different torts, at least when both grow out of negligent misrepresentations by lawyers. For example, the *Brumley* case, which we cited earlier, is a professional-malpractice case, yet it has essentially the same facts as Ultramares Corp. v. Touche, Niven & Co., 174 N.E. 441 (N.Y. 1931), where the New York Court of Appeals, in a famous opinion by Judge Cardozo, held that an accountant's negligent misrepresentation was not actionable at the suit of a lender who had relied on the accountant's certified audit of the borrower.

The absence of a contract between the lender and the accountant defeated the suit in *Ultramares*—yet why should privity of contract have been required for liability just because the negligence lay in disseminating information rather than in designing or manufacturing a product? The privity limitation in products cases had been rejected, in another famous Cardozo opinion, years earlier. *See* MacPherson v. Buick Motor Co., 111 N.E. 1050 (N.Y. 1916). . . . So when in Rozny v. Marnul, 250 N.E. 2d 656 (Ill. 1969), the Supreme Court of Illinois, joining the march away from *Ultramares*, . . . was careful to emphasize facts in the particular case before it that limited the scope of its holding—facts such as that the defendant, a surveyor, had placed his "absolute guarantee for accuracy" on the plat and that only a few persons would receive and rely on it, thus limiting the potential scope of liability.

Later Illinois cases, however, influenced by section 552 of the Second Restatement of Torts (1977), . . . hold that "one who in the course of his business or profession supplies information for the guidance of others in their business transactions" is liable for negligent misrepresentations that induce detrimental reliance. Whether there is a practical as distinct from a merely semantic difference between this formulation of the duty limitation and that of *Pelham* may be doubted but cannot change the outcome of this case. Proud, in the practice of his profession, supplied information (or rather misinformation) to Greycas that was intended to guide Greycas in commercial dealings with Crawford. Proud therefore had a duty to use due care to see that the information was correct. He used no care. . . .

There is no serious doubt about the existence of a causal relationship between the misrepresentation and the loan. Greycas would not have made the loan without Proud's letter. Nor would it have made the loan had Proud advised it that the collateral was so heavily encumbered that the loan was as if unsecured, for then Greycas would have known that the probability of repayment was slight. . . .

Proud argues, however, that his damages should be reduced in recognition of Greycas's own contributory negligence, which, though no longer a complete defense in Illinois, is a partial defense, renamed "comparative negligence." It is as much a defense to negligent misrepresentation as to any other tort of negligence. . . .

But we think it too clear to require a remand for further proceedings that Proud failed to prove a want of due care by Greycas. Due care is the care that is optimal given that the other party is exercising due care. It is not the higher level of care that would be optimal if potential tort victims were required to assume that the rest of the world was negligent. A pedestrian is not required to exercise a level of care (e.g., wearing a helmet or a shin guard) that would be optimal if there were no sanctions against reckless driving. Otherwise drivers would be encouraged to drive recklessly, and knowing this pedestrians would be encouraged to wear helmets and shin guards. The result would be a shift from a superior method of accident avoidance (not driving recklessly) to an inferior one (pedestrian armor).

So we must ask whether Greycas would have been careless not to conduct its own UCC search had Proud done what he had said he did —conduct his own UCC search. The answer is no. The law normally does not require duplicative precautions unless one is likely to fail or the consequences of failure (slight though the likelihood may be) would be catastrophic. One UCC search is enough to disclose prior liens, and Greycas acted reasonably in relying on Proud to conduct it. Although Greycas had much warning that Crawford was in financial trouble . . . , that was a reason for charging a hefty interest rate and insisting that the loan be secured; it was not a reason for duplicating Proud's work. It is not hard to conduct a UCC lien search; it just requires checking the records in the recorder's office for the county where the debtor lives. *See* Ill. Rev. Stat. ch. 26, para. 9-401. So the only reason to backstop Proud was if Greycas should have assumed he was careless or dishonest; and we have just said that the duty of care does not require such an assumption. Had Proud disclosed that he was Crawford's brother-in-law this might have been a warning signal that Greycas could ignore only at its peril. To go forward in the face of a known danger is to assume the risk. But Proud did not disclose his relationship to Crawford. . . .

A final point. The record of this case reveals serious misconduct by an Illinois attorney. We are therefore sending a copy of this opinion to the Attorney Registration and Disciplinary Commission of the Supreme Court of Illinois for such disciplinary action as may be deemed appropriate in the circumstances. AFFIRMED.

▨ The Bounds of the Law:
Lawyer Dishonesty, Fraud, Deceit, and Misrepresentation

Lawyers are trained to give legal advice, that is, to inform clients just how close to the limits of the law their proposed conduct will take them. Yet, some lawyers, like those in *dePape* and *Greycas,* seem unaware that generally applicable law also applies to their own personal conduct. This series of notes, entitled "The Bounds of the Law," borrows its title from a century-old ethical canon repeated in today's Model Rules: The lawyer has an "obligation zealously to protect and pursue a client's legitimate interests, within the bounds of the law."[1] In these notes we will examine several bodies of generally applicable law that limit a lawyer's representation of a client. We focus here on when a lawyer must say "no" to a client to avoid violating a legal limitation on the lawyer's own conduct. Lawyers who exceed these bounds of the law face at least three consequences: criminal accountability, civil liability, and professional discipline.

In this note, we pause to consider the legal limits on a lawyer's behavior created by various bodies of law concerning deceitful conduct. In *Greycas,* Judge Posner made clear that the law of fraud limits the legally acceptable conduct of lawyers, just as it constrains the behavior of any other citizen. He further indicated that facts that support relief in tort also reveal "serious misconduct by an Illinois attorney," and referred the matter to the appropriate state disciplinary commission. In *dePape,* the court characterized the lawyer's "implausible interpretation" of the law as an attempt to perpetrate a fraud on the INS. Both cases illustrate how crucial it is for lawyers to understand the law of fraud.

The Model Rules

The Model Rules of Professional Conduct include four provisions, Model Rules 1.2(d), 3.3, 4.1(a), and 8.4(c), that incorporate nearly all of the general civil and criminal law of fraud and misrepresentation into professional obligations. Model Rule 1.2(d) requires that lawyers assess their clients' conduct as well as their own, by prohibiting lawyers from counseling or assisting a client in conduct the lawyer knows to be criminal or fraudulent.[2] Model Rules 3.3 and 4.1(a) provide that lawyers can be disciplined for knowingly making false statements of "material fact or law" to a tribunal, or to a third person when representing clients. Model Rule 8.4(c) broadens these prohibitions, by forbidding lawyers from engaging in any "conduct involving dishonesty, fraud, deceit or misrepresentation," both in representing clients and in private life.

---

1. Model Rules, Preamble ¶[9]. This language first appeared in Canon 15 of the 1908 Canons of Ethics, titled "How Far a Lawyer May Go in Supporting a Client's Cause" ("The lawyer owes entire devotion to the interest of the client, warm zeal in the maintenance and defense of his rights . . . [b]ut it is steadfastly to be borne in mind that the great trust of the lawyer is to be performed within and not without the bounds of the law.") and was the title of Canon 7 in the 1969 ABA Model Code of Professional Responsibility ("A Lawyer Should Represent a Client Zealously, Within the Bounds of the Law").
2. *See* The Bounds of the Law: Client Fraud, *infra* p. 237.

With respect to lawyer frauds on tribunals,[3] Model Rule 3.3 prohibits lawyers from making false statements in court,[4] in depositions,[5] as well as in written submissions,[6] and applies whether the lawyer acts as a party or a representative of a party.[7] Lawyers have been disciplined under this rule for a wide variety of false statements, including the location of a client,[8] reasons the lawyer was unprepared,[9] and false offers of proof.[10]

Model Rule 4.1 applies to all statements lawyers make to third parties in the course of representing clients. It prohibits intentional misstatements made by lawyers in documents, as in *Greycas*,[11] as well as oral statements made in the course of negotiating or closing a transaction or settlement.[12] Lawyers have been found to violate this rule by lying in the course of debt collection efforts, and while acting as escrow agents.[13] Courts also have relied on Model Rule 4.1(a) to grant other relief, such as tort or contract damages.[14] Model Rule 8.4(c) both overlaps with and expands upon the scope of Model Rules 3.3 and 4.1. It prohibits all fraud, deceit, dishonesty, and misrepresentation, whether before a tribunal or in other contexts. For example, it applies to dishonesty with clients, such as billing or expense fraud,[15] and lies about the status of a case.[16] It also

---

3. The term "tribunal" has been applied to adjudicative or trial-type proceedings, including courts, as well as arbitration and mediation proceedings. Disc. Action Against Zotaley, 546 N.W.2d 16 (Minn. 1996). *But see* MR 1.0(m), which excludes mediation from the definition of tribunals. Model Rule 3.9 extends the antifraud provision of Model Rule 3.3 to nonadjudicative proceedings such as legislative or administrative hearings.

4. In re Neitlich, 597 N.E.2d 425 (Mass. 1992).

5. In re Porter, 449 N.W.2d 713 (Minn. 1990) (false deposition testimony by a lawyer).

6. In re Lowell, 784 N.Y.S.2d 69 (App. Div. 2004); In re Lowell, 835 A.2d 679 (N.J. 2003) (six fraudulent promissory notes signed by client attached to application for pendent lite relief); In re Celsor, 499 S.E.2d 809 (S.C. 1998) (false notarization of client's signature).

7. People v. Kolbjornsen, 917 P.2d 277 (Colo. 1996) (lawyer testified falsely); In re Barratt, 663 N.E.2d 536 (Ind. 1996) (lawyer who was party to civil action testified falsely).

8. In re Fletcher, 694 N.E.2d 1143 (Ind. 1998).

9. In re Chovanec, 640 N.E.2d 1052 (Ind. 1994) (lawyer who was not prepared falsely told court he was too sick to proceed); Disc. Proceedings Against Urban, 574 N.W.2d 651 (Wis. 1998) (lawyer who failed to prepare documents falsely told several probate judges that he was waiting for resolution of tax disputes).

10. *E.g.*, Disc. Proceedings of Phelps, 637 F.2d 171 (10th Cir. 1981); Edward L. Raymond, Jr., *Attorney's Misrepresentation to Court of His State of Health or Other Personal Matter in Seeking Trial Delay as Ground for Disciplinary Action*, 61 A.L.R.4th 1216 (1988).

11. *E.g.*, In re Apt, 946 P.2d 1002 (Kan. 1997) (real estate deed); In re Holland, 713 A.2d 227 (R.I. 1998) (foreclosure deed).

12. *E.g.*, Ky. Bar Assn. v. Geisler, 938 S.W.2d 578 (Ky. 1997) (lawyer settled personal injury case without disclosing client's death); In re Bennett, 501 S.E.2d 217 (Ga. 1998) (lawyer lied about representing a client in order to receive insurance settlement); Slotkin v. Citizens Casualty Co. of New York, 614 F.2d 301 (2d Cir. 1979) (defense lawyer who lied about excess insurance coverage liable for fraud); Disc. of Granham, 395 N.W.2d 80 (Minn. 1986) (lawyer in a real estate transaction lied to parties about sending their deed to the county recorder's office).

13. *E.g.*, In re Eliasen, 913 P.2d 1163 (Idaho 1996) (debt collection lawyer lied to debtor about consequences of debt); Disc. Action Against Pyles, 421 N.W.2d 321 (Minn. 1988) (lawyer serving as escrow agent promised to pay money when account had been closed).

14. *E.g.*, Copp v. Breskin, 782 P.2d 1104 (Wash. App. 1989) (law firm that assured expert witness he would be paid could not later claim it was client's responsibility); Malewich v. Zacharias, 482 A.2d 951 (N.J. App. 1984) (lawyer who promised but did not inform opposing counsel if case was not adjourned violated Model Rule 4.1, subjecting lawyer to damages).

15. Lisa G. Lerman, *Blue-Chip Bilking: Regulation of Billing and Expense Fraud by Lawyers*, 12 Geo. J. Leg. Ethics 205 (1999).

16. Atty. Grievance Commn. v. Lane, 790 A.2d 621 (Md. 2002); Welts' Case, 620 A.2d 1017 (1993).

applies to lying to other lawyers, including bar officials,[17] as well as all other private dishonest behavior of lawyers. Examples of violations include a lawyer who represented that he was a notary public when he knew he was not,[18] a lawyer who knowingly provided a false answer on a handgun permit application,[19] and another who postdated and then stopped payment on a check to a travel agent.[20] Lawyers also have been disciplined under this provision for deceit committed as a trustee[21] and as a corporate board member.[22] Because of its breadth, courts often cite Model Rule 8.4(c) in combination with other rules in discipline cases.[23] In addition to expanding the scope of the disciplinary rules to all lawyer fraudulent conduct, the broad language of Model Rule 8.4(c) also "can be envisioned as designed to catch violations of *civil* law norms."[24] Together, these include all intentional, reckless, and negligent misrepresentations.[25] Judge Posner no doubt had this provision in mind when he referred Proud to the Illinois Disciplinary Commission.

The Law of Fraud

This brief review indicates that the lawyer codes provisions incorporate the external law of fraud, which is vast, both in its depth and in its breadth.[26]

17. Conduct of Wyllie, 957 P.2d 1222 (Or. 1998) (imposing two-year suspension for submitting fraudulent MCLE forms and failing to cooperate with investigation); In re Porter, 890 P.2d 1377 (Or. 1995) (imposing 63-day suspension for misrepresenting intentions to opposing counsel); In re Siegel, 627 A.2d 156 (N.J. 1993) (lawyer who defrauded his own law firm disbarred).
18. Conduct of Kluge, 27 P.3d 102 (Or. 2001).
19. In re Kotok, 528 A.2d 1307 (N.J. 1987).
20. Fla. Bar v. Schultz, 712 So. 2d 386 (Fla. 1998).
21. Disc. Counsel v. Kurtz, 693 N.E.2d 1080 (Ohio 1998).
22. Disc. Action Against Shinnick, 552 N.W.2d 212 (Minn. 1996).
23. E.g., In re Mozingo, 497 S.E.2d 729 (S.C. 1998); In re Hyde, 950 P.2d 806 (N.M. 1997). The disbarment of F. Lee Bailey provides an example. Bailey's client entrusted millions of dollars of stock to him, which the client intended to forfeit to the United States. Bailey claimed most of the money as his fee, spent the money in defiance of several court orders, and then falsely denied that he was aware of the orders. When the client fired him, Bailey wrote *ex parte* letters to the judge disparaging the client in an effort to protect his interest in the money. The Florida Supreme Court disciplined him for violating Rule 8.3(c) and several other rules, finding that he "committed multiple counts of egregious misconduct, including offering false testimony, engaging in *ex parte* communications, violating a client's confidences, violating two federal court orders, and violating trust account regulations by commingling and misappropriation." Fla. Bar v. Bailey, 803 So. 2d 683 (Fla. 2001).
24. Geoffrey C. Hazard, Jr. & W. William Hodes, The Law of Lawyering §65.5 (3d ed., Aspen Publishers, Inc. 2002).
25. Some courts view "dishonesty" as connoting a lack of trustworthiness and integrity and therefore view it as being broader than "fraud" and "deceit." E.g., In re Leonard, 784 P.2d 95, 100 (Or. 1989); In re Servance, 508 A.2d 178 (N.J. 1986) (lawyer represented investments were sound although "he knew little or nothing about them"). Other courts require that reckless or knowing misrepresentations be established to violate Model Rule 8.4(c). E.g., Disc. Counsel v. Anonymous Atty. A, 714 A.2d 402 (Pa. 1998); Disc. Matter Involving West, 805 P.2d 351 (Alaska 1991).
26. Stuart P. Green, Lying, Cheating, and Stealing: A Moral Theory of White Collar Crime 148-160 (Oxford 2006). Historically, the law of fraud can be traced to biblical times. The tort of misrepresentation developed in the thirteenth century with the writ of deceit, which was used to provide relief from deceptive practices before courts. The writ was extended to include out-of-court transactions and gradually developed into a civil remedy for fraudulent acts that caused actual harm. The criminal law responded to frauds in court by prohibiting perjury, and responded to frauds on the public outside of court by creating the offense of common law cheat, committed by using a false weight or measure.

Morally, the law of fraud reflects the fact that those who lie to gain a benefit should be responsible for harm caused when a victim trusts the honesty of the statement and reasonably relies on the speaker's misrepresentations.[27] Sissela Bok calls liars "free riders": persons who hope to gain from everyone else's honesty while unjustly benefiting from their own deviation from social norms.[28] The law reflects this common sense morality and addresses deceit in a wide variety of contexts, including criminal and tort accountability.[29] In the past century, frauds on courts, on the government, and between private parties all have become the subject of state and federal criminal law.[30] Many of these statutes also recognize civil actions by private parties.[31] State law, such as the Uniform Commercial Code, incorporates the common law of fraud in a number of provisions.[32] The common law has expanded to provide tort damages for misrepresentations that cause harm, regardless of whether they were committed intentionally, recklessly, or negligently.[33] Dishonest conduct also creates defenses to claims based upon contract and arising from other transactions. Fraud invalidates an otherwise lawful consent in tort, property, and contract law. As one early treatise writer put it: "Fraud vitiates everything, even judgments and orders of the Court."[34]

Criminal Fraud

The modern law of criminal fraud includes both general and specific statutes.[35] The general provisions prohibit conduct such as "conspiracy to defraud,"[36] mail fraud,[37] and wire fraud.[38] The mail and wire fraud statutes prohibit "schemes to defraud" committed by using the mail or wires, including radio and television. They have been used to address a wide variety of frauds, including insurance, securities, franchise, and even divorce mill fraud.[39] Specific fraud statutes have grown in the past century to address dishonest conduct that occurs in a specific context. Examples include access device fraud,[40] bankruptcy fraud,[41] bank fraud,[42]

27. *Id.* at 39, 149; Tamar Frankel, *Trust and Honesty: America's Business Culture at a Crossroad* 1-24 (Oxford 2006).
28. Sissela Bok, *Lying: Moral Choice in Public and Private Life* 23 (2d ed., Vintage Books 1999).
29. *E.g.,* Anthony Arlidge, Jacques Parry & Ian Gatt, *Arlidge and Parry on Fraud* (2d ed. Sweet & Maxwell 1996); Melville M. Bigelow, *The Law of Fraud* (Little Brown 1877).
30. Ellen S. Podgor, *Criminal Fraud*, 48 Am. U. L. Rev. 729, 736 (1999).
31. Dan B. Dobbs, *The Law of Torts* 1343 (West 2000).
32. Peter A. Alces, *The Law of Fraudulent Transactions* 1-7 (Warren Gorham & Lamont 1989).
33. *Restatement (Second) of Torts* §§525-552 (1977).
34. Sydney Edward Williams, *Kerr on Fraud and Mistake* 4 (Sweet & Maxwell Ltd. 1928). For an example of fraud vitiating a court judgment, *see* Spaulding v. Zimmerman, *infra* p. 204.
35. For a compilation of some of the major federal antifraud provisions, *see* Milton Eisenberg, ed., *Lawyers' Desk Book on White-Collar Crime* 325-494 (Nat'l. Leg. Ctr. for Pub. Interest 1991).
36. 18 U.S.C. §371 (2006) ("Conspiracy to Commit Offense or to Defraud United States").
37. 18 U.S.C. §1341 (2006) ("Frauds and Swindles").
38. 18 U.S.C. §1341 (2006) ("Frauds and Swindles").
39. Podgor, *supra* note 30, at 753-754, citing United States v. Edwards, 458 F.2d 875, 879 (5th Cir. 1972) (promise to mail valid divorce papers for a fee as part of a scheme to defraud).
40. 18 U.S.C. §1029 (2006). Access devices include credit cards and personal identification numbers used to access accounts in order to obtain money or services. 18 U.S.C. §1029(1). *See generally* Jerry Iannacci & Ron Morris, *Access Device Fraud and Related Financial Crimes* (CRC Press 2000).
41. 18 U.S.C. §157 (2006).
42. 18 U.S.C. §1344 (2006).

computer fraud,[43] food stamp fraud,[44] health care fraud,[45] marriage fraud,[46] securities fraud,[47] and tax fraud.[48] Most states also prohibit a wide variety of specific frauds, including insurance[49] and consumer fraud.[50]

Tort Liability: Misrepresentation

Greycas makes clear that the tort of misrepresentation includes intentional, reckless, negligent (and occasionally innocent) misstatements of material fact that cause harm to certain foreseeable third parties who reasonably rely on the false statements.[51] In tort, "fraud" includes both intentional and reckless misrepresentation. To be liable for fraud, a defendant such as Proud need not intend harm to the plaintiff. It is enough if he knows he is lying, the misrepresentation concerns a material fact, and reasonable reliance causes harm. This explains why Proud's knowing lie (that he had conducted a UCC search) combined with reasonable reliance, was enough to subject him to liability. When a misrepresentation is fraudulent, the lawyer's liability extends beyond a client to all foreseeable third persons who reasonably relied on the false information.[52]

Lawyers are also vulnerable to tort damages for negligent misrepresentation. Proud also could have been held liable for negligent (but not intentional) misrepresentation if he completed the search, but negligently examined the wrong files or database. In that case, he would not have lied about a material fact, but his legal opinion (that no liens existed on the property) would have been based on a failure to exercise reasonable care in obtaining the information.[53] In most jurisdictions, his liability would extend only to those in a limited class of persons "for whose benefit and guidance he intends to supply the information or knows the recipient intends to supply it,"[54] not to any person who reasonably relied on the information.

---

43. 18 U.S.C. §1030 (2006).
44. 7 U.S.C. §2015(b) (2006).
45. 18 U.S.C. §1347 (2006). *See generally* Carrie Valiant & David E. Matyas, *Legal Issues in Healthcare Fraud and Abuse: Navigating the Uncertainties* (2d ed., American Health Lawyers Association 1997).
46. 8 U.S.C. §1325(c) (2006). This statute prohibits "sham marriages" intended to evade immigration laws.
47. 15 U.S.C. §§78j(b), 78ff(a) (2006); 17 C.F.R. §240.10b-5. *See generally* Alan R. Bromberg & Lewis D. Lowenfels, *Bromberg & Lowenfels on Securities Fraud and Commodities Fraud* (2d ed., West 2001).
48. 26 U.S.C. §7206 (2006). *See generally* Ian M. Comisky, Lawrence S. Feld & Steven M. Harris, *Tax Fraud and Evasion* (6th ed., Warren, Gorham & Lamont 1995).
49. H. Brent Brennenstuhl, *Negligent Misrepresentation as "Accident" or "Occurrence" Warranting Insurance Coverage*, 58 A.L.R.5th 483 (1998).
50. Debra T. Landis, *What Constitutes "Fraudulent" or "Unconscionable" Agreement or Conduct Within Meaning of State Consumer Credit Protection Act*, 42 A.L.R.4th 293 (1985).
51. *Restatement (Second) of Torts* §§525-552C.
52. *Restatement (Second) of Torts* §531; Ultramares Corp. v. Touche, Niven & Co., 174 N.E. 441 (N.Y. 1931).
53. *Restatement (Second) of Torts* §552. Most courts refuse to extend the concept of innocent misrepresentation to lawyers who are sued by nonclients, because the misrepresentations have not been made in a transaction between the parties as required by *Restatement (Second) of Torts* §552C. *E.g.*, Garcia v. Rodey, Dickason, Sloan, Akin & Robb, 750 P.2d 118 (1988); Pasternak v. Sagittarius Recording Co., 617 F. Supp. 1514 (E.D. Mich. 1985), *aff'd*, 816 F.2d 681 (6th Cir. 1987).
54. *Restatement (Second) of Torts* §552(2).

Although the law of misrepresentation usually requires an affirmative mis-representation, there are a few occasions when failure to speak can create lia-bility as well. Fiduciary duties create obligations to disclose, which means that lawyers, who owe fiduciary duties to clients, have affirmative duties to disclose material information to clients.[55] A duty to disclose also arises when previously true statements become untrue, misleading, or material.[56] For example, a lawyer would have a duty to disclose tax liens to a prospective purchaser at a foreclosure sale if the buyer was induced to bid by the lawyer's prior incomplete repre-sentations in that regard.[57]

Misrepresentation and Client Advocacy

Like everyone else, lawyers are subject to the law of fraud and misrepresenta-tion. Lawyers who misrepresent a material fact can be held criminally or civilly accountable, or lose a benefit they lied to obtain. Beyond these consequences, lawyers, unlike others, can be professionally disciplined for acts of misrepre-sentation or dishonesty, whether they involve client representation or conduct of the lawyer apart from law practice. Understanding the law of fraud in any of its many permutations can help you avoid suffering any or all of these adverse consequences.

2. Aiding and Abetting

Problem

5-8. Client and Partner co-own a parcel of land. Martyn & Fox repre-sented Client in a settlement between them. Partner transferred her share in the parcel to Client who sold it. But instead of giving Partner her share as provided in the agreement, Client, on Martyn & Fox's advice, refused on the ground that Partner still owes Client $200,000 on an earlier deal. Partner sues Client and Martyn & Fox. Is Martyn & Fox in trouble?

---

55. *E.g.*, Baker v. Dorfman, 239 F.3d 415 (2d Cir. 2000) (lawyer who lied in his resume about the extent of his legal experience to a client liable for fraud, including compensatory, emotional distress, and punitive damages). Clients have multiple remedies in such a case, including a suit for fraud, malpractice, and breach of fiduciary duty, as occurred in *dePape*.
56. *Restatement (Second) of Torts* §551. *E.g.*, In re Alcorn, 41 P.3d 600 (Ariz. 2002) (trial lawyers who made a secret agreement with opposing counsel to dismiss action against their client fined and disciplined for failing to disclose agreement to trial judge who indicated he did not want any sweetheart deals or anything "crafted" that "would be misleading" to him); People v. Rolfe, 962 P.2d 981 (Colo. 1998) (lawyer who stated that a social worker had "begun" her investigation of the matter, but failed to inform the court about the existence of social worker's letter that concluded no abuse could be substantiated, censured for violating MR 3.3 (a)(1)).
57. Gerdin v. Princeton St. Bank, 371 N.W.2d 5 (Minn. App. 1985).

Consider: **Model Rules 1.1, 1.2(d), 4.1, 8.4(c)**
    Model Code DR 1-102(A)(4), 6-101, 7-102(A)(5)
    RLGL §51

Chem-Age Industries, Inc. v. Glover
652 N.W.2d 756 (S.D. 2002)

KONENKAMP, Justice

We are confronted with the question whether a lawyer who incorporates a business on behalf of an individual client owes any duty of care to the corporation thus created and to its director-investors who have no contractual relationship with the lawyer. While obtaining substantial funds and credit from two investors, the client had his attorney incorporate a business, naming the two investors as incorporators and directors. Then the client misappropriated the investors' funds and gave some money and property to the lawyer. The investors and the corporation sued the lawyer, his client, and others to recover all the funds and property, alleging fraud, conversion, malpractice, and breach of fiduciary duty. . . .

A. BACKGROUND

In the past twenty years, attorney Alan F. Glover of Brookings, South Dakota, has represented Byron Dahl, a Watertown entrepreneur, in various transactions and lawsuits around the country. In March 1997, Dahl interested two Watertown businesspersons, Roger O. Pederson and Garry Shepard, in investing in a start-up firm, under the name Chem-Age Industries. Dahl would contribute equipment and expertise; Pederson, and, to a lesser extent, Shepard, would contribute capital. . . .

Sometime during their business engagement (the exact timing is disputed), Pederson obtained a report from a private investigator warning him that Dahl was a "crook." According to Pederson, the report indicated that Dahl "had done this all over the country. He had done it on the east coast, he done it in Las Vegas. Guy lost his home in Las Vegas. The guy out east lost 300,000."

Pederson executed two "Stock Agreements" and a "Subscription Agreement and Letter of Investment," and despite this report continued to invest thousands of dollars in Dahl's enterprise. According to the terms of the stock agreements as prepared by Dahl, Pederson was to receive 48 shares of common stock in exchange for his investments. Pederson had originally given Dahl $25,000, but both Pederson and Shepard wanted the business to be incorporated before they invested more money. They pressed Dahl to get an attorney involved to set up the corporation. At some point between March and October 1997, Pederson, Shepard, and Dahl decided that Chem-Age Industries would be incorporated under the name "Chem-Age Industries, Inc." Pederson and Shepard agreed to serve as incorporators and directors of the corporation; Dahl agreed to serve as chief executive officer. With this understanding, Dahl engaged Glover to draw up articles of incorporation.

Glover prepared the articles and faxed them, either to Dahl alone or to both Pederson and Shepard: the parties disagree on this point. In either case, Dahl secured the signatures of Pederson and Shepard. The articles were dated October 30, 1997. When Dahl delivered the signed articles to him, Glover notarized Pederson's and Shepard's signatures, despite the fact that they had not signed the document in his presence.[1] On the same day, Glover signed a Consent of Registered Agent, agreeing to act as registered agent for "Chem-Age Industries, Inc." Soon thereafter, at Dahl's request, Glover filed the articles with the South Dakota Secretary of State. On November 6, 1997, the Secretary of State issued a Certificate of Incorporation. Glover then sent a letter to the company, attaching an application to obtain a federal tax identification number for the corporation.

On November 7, 1997, the day after Chem-Age Industries, Inc., was issued its Certificate of Incorporation, Sam's Club approved a "Business Membership-Credit Application" for "Chem-Age Industries" as a corporation. Pederson, in his capacity as President of Chem-Age, had completed and signed the document on the previous day, listing Dahl as "Billing Representative." By that date, Chem-Age had obtained a "Resale-Tax ID number." Soon thereafter, Pederson had acquired for the company a Bank One credit card, an American Express Optima card, and a charge account at Office Max. Pederson also obtained loans from Nor-

west Bank to provide operating capital for Chem-Age Industries, Inc. These amounted to some $140,000. It was the understanding of the Bank's representatives that the money was to be used by the corporation. With the number of judgments and liens against Dahl, the bankers would not have loaned him the money.

In March 1998, Glover received a desk as a "gift" from Dahl. It was charged on the Chem-Age corporate credit card for $1,113. In August 1998, Sioux Valley Cooperative commenced a lawsuit against Chem-Age, Inc.; Glover was engaged as the attorney for the defendant in that case, serving and filing an answer and counterclaim on behalf of Chem-Age, Inc.

By early fall of 1998, Pederson and Shepard became suspicious that they were being swindled: Dahl had accumulated large balances on the company's credit cards for what appeared to be personal items.[2] They engaged attorney John L. Foley of Watertown for legal advice. According to Foley's affidavit, a meeting was held in his office in October 1998. Present were plaintiffs Pederson and Shepard as well as defendants Glover and Dahl. At that meeting, Glover stated that he was representing "the corporation, Chem-Age Industries, Inc.," and that Dahl owned that entity. Foley also reported that Glover and Dahl were negotiating the sale of "the business" to New Age Chemical, Inc., a Wisconsin corporation. In Glover's presence, Dahl told Pederson and Shepard that "they would be paid

---

1. "It is a Class 2 misdemeanor for any notary public to affix his official signature to documents when the parties have not appeared before him." SDCL 18-1-11.
2. Items charged included "Hamburger Helper"; "Bailey's 750 ml"; and "Food & Beverage" at the "Princess Tower Hotel, Freeport, Bahamas."

out of the sale of the business." Pederson and Shepard claim that Glover led them to believe that he would be representing Chem-Age in this sale. Nonetheless, in a document entitled "License Agreement," dated November 11, 1998, the Chem-Age assets were sold to the Wisconsin business, under the name "Byron Dahl d/b/a BMD Associates, a South Dakota sole proprietorship." Glover represented Dahl in that transaction. When later questioned, Glover was not sure of the relationship between Chem-Age Industries, Inc., and BMD Associates. . . .

B. FRAUD . . .

Glover's past experience with Dahl in representing him in disputes with investors is not enough to create a question of material fact on whether Glover acted directly to defraud plaintiffs or on whether he knew or should have known that the incorporation documents he prepared would be used as a vehicle to bilk the investors. Without proof of a lawyer's complicity, a client's wrongful behavior, however egregious, may not be imputed to the lawyer. We conclude that the record is insufficient to show that Glover defrauded plaintiffs either alone or in concert with Dahl.[5] . . .

C. CONVERSION

Conversion is the unauthorized exercise of control or dominion over personal property in a way that repudiates an owner's right in the property or in a manner inconsistent with such right. . . .

Plaintiffs allege that Glover converted their corporate property, specifically, $1,800 in attorney's fees and $1,113 in office furniture. The attorney's fees apparently were paid either out of the loan money that Pederson secured for Chem-Age from the bank or from a cash advance on the American Express Optima credit card issued to Chem-Age Industries. Dahl obtained the furniture from Interstate Office Products in March 1998 by using the corporate Optima card, but the resulting debt was not paid by Dahl either personally or through Chem-Age. It seemingly remains a debt of the corporation, but Roger Pederson is also personally liable for it. Copies of cashed corporate checks attest to Glover's having received payment for attorney's fees. The record also shows that Glover remains in possession of the furniture because he contends that it was a gift from Dahl. . . .

Material questions of fact exist on whether Glover converted property belonging to the corporation. Thus, summary judgment for Glover on this issue is reversed, and the matter is remanded for trial.

D. LEGAL MALPRACTICE . . .

1. Corporation as Client

Dahl hired Glover to organize the business as a corporation. By his own admission, Glover's involvement with Dahl was directly related to that incorporation, notwithstanding Dahl's earlier engagement of Glover on

---

5. Because we hold that plaintiffs have not established a cause of action for fraud, it does not mean that plaintiffs cannot proceed on their claim for punitive damages. Conversion and breach of fiduciary duty may give rise to punitive damages, and plaintiffs may proceed to seek such damages if they succeed in either of those claims.

personal matters before and independent of the events at issue here.
As we concluded above, the business
was incorporated. Glover contends
nonetheless that he did not represent
the corporation. This is clearly a
question of material fact. In the absence of some indication otherwise,
Glover can be deemed the attorney
for the corporation, even if he was
also representing Dahl personally. An
attorney may represent both a corporation and individuals in the corporation. Plaintiffs offered evidence,
albeit disputed, that Glover not only
set up the corporation as a legal entity, but also held himself out as the
company's attorney, both in personal
conversations with outside parties
and in a formal appearance in another court action.

If it is shown that he represented
the corporation, then it follows that
Glover had a duty to the client corporation. Plaintiffs contend that
Glover, along with Dahl, improperly
arranged for the sale of corporate
assets and that those assets were
converted to personal use by Dahl.
Consequently, plaintiffs assert that
the company suffered losses....
Here, plaintiffs have alleged sufficient facts to take this case beyond
the reach of summary judgment....

2. Individual Constituents as Clients...

Here, the individual plaintiffs
sought no advice from Glover. Corre-
spondingly, Glover never agreed to
advise or assist them.... Beyond a
brief introduction to Pederson and
Shepard, Glover's only communication was with his long-time client,
Dahl. Glover had no personal consultation with Pederson and Shepard in
creating the corporation. All their

dealings were with Dahl. True, Glover
notarized Pederson's and Shepard's
signatures, without having them before him. However unlawful that was,
it did not create an attorney-client relationship. Furthermore, nothing in
the record suggests that the purpose of
Glover's arrangement with Dahl was
to confer the benefit of legal advice for
plaintiffs. We conclude that the record
is insufficient to show a contractual
arrangement wherein Glover agreed to
represent anyone other than Dahl and
the corporation....

Certainly there may be unique
circumstances, outside the ordinary
corporate arrangement, where shareholders with equal interest in a close
corporation who have ongoing contact with corporate counsel may reasonably believe that counsel is
representing each of them. But in the
absence of any professional contact
between Glover and the individual
plaintiffs, those singular circumstances do not exist here....

3. Nonclient Third Party Beneficiaries...

There are several reasons courts
are reluctant to relax the rule of
privity in attorney malpractice cases.
First, the rule preserves an attorney's
duty of loyalty to and effective advocacy for the client. Second, adding
responsibilities to nonclients creates
the danger of conflicting duties.
Third, once the privity rule is relaxed,
the number of persons a lawyer might
be accountable to could be limitless.
Fourth, a relaxation of the strict
privity rule would imperil attorney-
client confidentiality....

Perhaps cognizant that legal malpractice is one of the last citadels of
the privity doctrine, the Restatement
(Third) of the Law Governing Law-

yers [§51] sanctions limited instances where a lawyer owes a duty of care to nonclients. . . .

As to Subsection (2), unquestionably Glover's client, Dahl, did invite Pederson and Shepard to rely on Glover's services to effect incorporation, and their reliance was, at least arguably, reasonable. However, the routine act of incorporating a business is a function distinct and separate from advising and warning individual constituents of all the consequences and dangers inherent in investing in a corporation. Pederson and Shepard never asked for any advice and never met with Glover regarding the process of incorporation. There is no evidence that Glover acquiesced in any invitation Dahl may have made to these investors to rely on Glover's opinion or to provide some additional legal service other than incorporating the business.

As to Subsection (3), we find no evidence in the record to establish that the primary purpose for Dahl's contacting an attorney to incorporate the business was to benefit plaintiffs. . . . Thus, an incidental benefit to a nonclient is not sufficient.

E. BREACH OF FIDUCIARY DUTY

1. Direct Breach of Fiduciary Duty to Nonclients . . .

Plaintiffs Pederson and Shepard have submitted no evidence to show how they were in a confidential relationship with Glover, where they depended on him specifically to protect their investment interests, and where Glover exercised dominance and influence over their business affairs. On the contrary, they never consulted with Glover during the time he is alleged to have breached a fiduciary duty to them. Aside from simple avowals that they believed Glover was watching out for their interests, their claim that Glover was entrusted with explicit responsibility for their investments is "factually unsupported." Likewise for the corporation: outside the existence of an attorney-client relationship, we detect no facts justifying a fiduciary duty owed to the company. We conclude that there was no direct fiduciary relationship between Glover and plaintiffs.

2. Aiding and Abetting Breach of Fiduciary Duty

Although he may not have directly breached a fiduciary duty, if Glover assisted Dahl in a breach of Dahl's fiduciary duty, Glover may still be subject to liability. Plaintiffs' complaint alleges that both Dahl and Glover breached their fiduciary duties. [The court cites Restatement (Second) of Torts §876 (Persons Acting in Concert) and Comment [11] to MR 1.2.] Legal authorities . . . are unanimous in expressing the proposition that one who knowingly aids another in the breach of a fiduciary duty is liable to the one harmed thereby. That principle readily extends to lawyers. . . . In Granewich v. Harding, 985 P.2d 788, 793-94 (Or 1999), the defendant attorneys provided substantial assistance to the controlling shareholders to squeeze out the minority shareholder in breach of the fiduciary duties the majority shareholders owed to the minority shareholder. Unlike the fraud allegations against Glover, which require proof of misrepresentations, liability for aiding and abetting breach of a fiduciary duty requires only the giving of substantial assistance and encouragement.

Dahl, as the operating officer of the corporation, owed a fiduciary duty to the company and to its investors. Like controlling shareholders, officers and directors possessing discretion in the management of a company have a fiduciary duty "to use their ability to control the corporation in a fair, just, and equitable manner." For summary judgment purposes, the evidence that Dahl breached his fiduciary duties to the corporation and the investor-directors remains wholly uncontradicted. He used corporate funds for personal expenditures; he failed to deliver promised stock issues; he sold corporate assets and kept the proceeds. . . .

Holding attorneys liable for aiding and abetting the breach of a fiduciary duty in rendering professional services poses both a hazard and a quandary for the legal profession. On the one hand, overbroad liability might diminish the quality of legal services, since it would impose "self protective reservations" in the attorney-client relationship. Attorneys acting in a professional capacity should be free to render advice without fear of personal liability to third persons if the advice later goes awry. On the other hand, the privilege of rendering professional services not being absolute, lawyers should not be free to substantially assist their clients in committing tortious acts. To protect lawyers from meritless claims, many courts strictly interpret the common

law elements of aiding and abetting the breach of a fiduciary duty.

The substantial assistance requirement carries with it a condition that the lawyer must actively participate in the breach of a fiduciary duty. *See* Spinner v. Nutt, 631 N.E.2d 542, 556 (Mass 1994) (allegation that trustees acted under legal advice of defendants, without more, is insufficient to give rise to claim that attorney is responsible to third persons for fraudulent acts of clients). Merely acting as a scrivener for a client is insufficient. A plaintiff must show that the attorney defendant rendered "substantial assistance" to the breach of duty, not merely to the person committing the breach.[13] In *Granewich*, the lawyers facilitated the squeeze-out, not just by providing legal advice and drafting documents, but by sending letters containing misrepresentations and helping to amend by-laws eliminating voting requirements that protected the minority shareholder's interest.

Another condition to finding liability for assisting in the breach of a fiduciary duty is the requirement that the assistance be "knowing." Restatement (Second) of Torts §874 cmt c (1979). Knowing participation in a fiduciary's breach of duty requires both knowledge of the fiduciary's status as a fiduciary and knowledge that the fiduciary's conduct contravenes a fiduciary duty.

---

13. It has been suggested that an element of wrongful intent should be included as part of the "substantial assistance" requirement. One example of wrongful intent would be when a lawyer aids and abets the breach of a fiduciary duty in furtherance of the lawyer's own self-interest. The receipt of legal fees may be a basis for concluding that an attorney "participated" in the client's breach of fiduciary duty for the attorney's own financial gain. *See* Weingarten v. Warren, 753 F. Supp. 491, 496 (SDNY 1990) (allowing aiding and abetting breach of fiduciary duty claim against attorney because he reaped legal fees for twenty-eight years in representation of trustee). In most instances, however, the receipt of normal legal fees in this circumstance would not constitute a personal financial interest in the matter. Although not an element in proving aiding and abetting the breach of a fiduciary duty, certainly these are circumstances to consider in gauging a lawyer's alleged knowing participation and substantial assistance.

Although in some instances actual knowledge may be required, constructive knowledge will often suffice. Constructive knowledge is adequate when the aider and abettor has maintained a long-term or in-depth relationship with the fiduciary.

In accordance with these principles, we hold that to establish a cause of action for aiding or assisting in the breach of a fiduciary duty, a plaintiff must prove that (1) the fiduciary breached an obligation to plaintiff; (2) defendant substantially assisted the fiduciary in the achievement of the breach; (3) defendant knew that the fiduciary's conduct constituted a breach of duty; and (4) damages were sustained as a result of the breach.

Glover recounts that shortly after incorporation, Dahl told him that the two investors, Pederson and Shepard, had decided not to proceed and that the business would be solely controlled by Dahl as a proprietorship. Because no shares were issued, Glover took the position that the company had no official existence. But we think that what Glover actually knew and what he should have known are questions of credibility. After all, Glover notarized Pederson's and Shepard's signatures on corporate documents without having them in his presence. If he did not know his client was in the midst of a swindle, he certainly knew Dahl had several questionable investment schemes in the past, leaving unhappy investors in his wake. Thus his decision to notarize these signatures may or may not have been an altogether innocuous act. Perhaps if Glover had met with Pederson and Shepard at that time, instead of simply notarizing their signatures unseen, and heard their expectations, he could have disabused them of any misunderstanding or encouraged them to

seek independent legal advice. Pederson and Shepard allege that this was part of a pattern in which Glover allowed Dahl to use his legal services as a means to allow Dahl to misappropriate investor funds. The creation of a corporation with the assistance of an attorney gave a patina of authenticity to Dahl's otherwise rogue activities. Moreover, Glover listed himself as registered agent for the company. Pederson and Shepard claim that they began investing more heavily once they learned the company had been incorporated and an attorney was onboard. They say that they felt reassured upon incorporation that the business would proceed with all the formalities required of corporations.

Four months after the business was incorporated, Glover received a "gift" of office furniture from Dahl, bought with the company credit card. Glover claimed he did not know how the furniture was paid for. Accepting such a "gift" from a client like Dahl, who Glover knew had longstanding financial problems, raises a question of constructive knowledge and exposes the problem of improper, personal financial gain in assisting Dahl.

We think it also significant that Glover assisted Dahl in selling assets that were obtained with investor funds in the corporation. In a meeting with the investors and their lawyer, Glover was present when Dahl assured the investors that upon the sale, they would be receiving their money back. The next month, with Glover's help, the company's assets were sold to a Wisconsin business. Dahl and Glover had taken the position that Chem-Age Industries, Inc., was not a corporation but a proprietorship owned solely by Dahl. Yet Glover helped to arrange the sale of Chem-Age assets through another entity: "Byron Dahl d/b/a BMD Associates, a South Dakota sole proprietorship." Glover later testified that he did not know the relationship between BMD and Chem-Age.

Although Glover may not have taken any active role in defrauding the investor-directors and may not have owed any direct fiduciary duty to them, Dahl did owe such a duty, and a material question of fact exists on whether Glover substantially assisted Dahl in breaching that duty. It may be that Glover, as much as Pederson and Shepard, was duped by

Dahl's conniving business dealings, but that is for a jury to decide.

F. CONCLUSION

... Because there are genuine issues of material fact, we reverse and remand for trial the claims of conversion and aiding and abetting the breach of fiduciary duty, and if the jury concludes that Glover was in fact representing the corporation, then the jury must also decide the company's claims of malpractice and breach of fiduciary duty.

■ Lawyers and Other Professionals: *Duties to Nonclients*

It seems axiomatic that professionals, especially lawyers, should be accountable only to their clients. The most obvious example is the often-repeated statement that lawyers owe no duties to adverse parties.[1] Yet *Greycas* and *Glover* indicate that lawyers can be held liable to nonclients. In this note we examine the various legal theories that make third-party liability a threat for modern professionals.

Consider first the tremendous scope of potential liability to third persons faced by professionals in modern society. Although courts continue to disagree about the extent of a professional's accountability to a third party, in the past century a substantial number of cases have found that such a duty exists for lawyers as well as other professionals.[2] Liability for physical harm extends to design professionals such as architects and engineers, whose negligent design causes a later structural collapse.[3] Physicians or pharmacists who negligently fail to warn a patient about the dangers of a disorder or a medication's side effects also may be held accountable to persons injured by their patients' medically affected behavior.[4] Liability for economic harm applies most often to

---

1. *E.g.,* Jeckle v. Crotty, 85 P.3d 931 (Wash. App. 2004); James v. The Chase Manhattan Bank, 173 F. Supp. 2d 544, 550 (N.D. Miss. 2001).
2. Jay M. Feinman, *Professional Liability to Third Parties* (2d ed., ABA Tort Trial and Ins. Prac. Sec. 2007).
3. Courts have long applied the rule of MacPherson v. Buick, 111 N.E. 1050 (N.Y. 1916), which abrogated the privity requirement in personal injury cases brought against design professionals whose negligence causes injury to third persons. Donald M. Zupanec, *Architect's Liability for Personal Injury or Death Allegedly Caused by Improper or Defective Plans or Design*, 97 A.L.R.3d 455 (1980); Francis M. Dougherty, *Personal Injury Liability of Civil Engineer for Negligence in Highway or Bridge Construction or Maintenance*, 43 A.L.R.4th 911 (1986).
4. *See* Gregory G. Sarno, *Liability of Physician, for Injury to or Death of Third Party, Due to Failure to Disclose Driving-Related Impediment*, 43 A.L.R.4th 153 (1986). A few courts have limited the scope of the duty to situations where the patient causes harm immediately following a medical treatment, *e.g.,* Lester v. Hall, 970 P.2d 590 (N.M. 1998) (physician who failed to warn patient of side effects of medication not liable to third party injured five days later).

accountants and lawyers whose negligence causes harm to persons who rely on their work or who are injured by the professional's negligent provision of services to a client.[5]

Consistent Professional and Public Duties

Courts recognize duties to nonclients only when doing so will foster the client's intent and not harm the professional-client relationship. Clients and patients should receive frank advice untainted by lawyer or physician concerns about liability to others. But at the same time, lawyers and other professionals cannot escape generally applicable law that creates responsibility to nonclients, as well as the growing number of occasions when failing to fulfill a client obligation coincides with harm to third parties as well.

Intentional Torts The easiest cases involve intentional torts, where most courts find duties to nonclients because professionals are subject to generally applicable law.[6] *Greycas* and *Glover* illustrate that lawyers and other professionals who commit fraud[7] or conversion[8] do not escape liability simply because they did so in the act of providing services to a client.[9] Judge Posner cites well-established law in *Greycas* that extends a professional's liability to all third persons who reasonably rely on fraudulent (intentionally false) statements.[10]

Negligence—Financial Harm *Greycas* and *Glover* also find lawyers liable for economic harm on a negligence theory. Here, the courts generally agree that liability to a third party should attach only if the duty imposed is consistent with the professional responsibility owed a client. For lawyers, this duty has been extended to nonclients in four circumstances.[11]

---

5. *See* Christine M. Guerci, *Liability of Independent Accountant to Investors or Shareholders*, 48 A.L.R.5th 389 (1997); Joan Teshima, *Attorney's Liability, to One Other Than Immediate Client, for Negligence in Connection with Legal Duties*, 61 A.L.R.4th 615 (1988).
6. RLGL §56, Comment b.
7. *E.g.,* Hartford Accident & Indemn. Co. v. Sullivan, 846 F.2d 377 (7th Cir. 1988), *cert. denied,* 490 U.S. 1089 (1989) (lawyer liable for fraud in helping client obtain fraudulent bank loan); Bonvire v. Wampler, 779 F.2d 1011 (4th Cir. 1985) (lawyer who knowingly misrepresented client's honesty and experience liable for fraud); Fire Ins. Exch. v. Bell, 643 N.E.2d 310 (Ind. 1994) (lawyer who misrepresented policy limits liable for fraud); St. Paul Fire and Marine Ins. Co. v. Touche Ross & Co., 507 N.W.2d 275 (Neb. 1993) (cause of action stated by third parties against accountants for fraud).
8. *E.g.,* ERA Realty Co. v. RBS Props., 586 N.Y.S.2d 831 (App. Div. 1992) (lawyer who used invalid legal process to acquire funds liable for conversion).
9. *See also* Givens v. Mullikin, 75 S.W.3d 383 (Tenn. 2002) (cause of action stated against lawyer for abuse of process for barraging opposing party with subpoenas, interrogatories, and a deposition seeking information that had already been turned over); Bevan v. Fix, 42 P.3d 1013 (Wyo. 2002) (cause of action stated by child who witnessed lawyer physically abuse his mother/client); Mack v. Soung, 25 Cal. Rptr. 2d 830 (Cal. App. 2000) (cause of action stated by children of elder patient against patient's physician who covered up nursing home abuse and abandoned patient when her condition became critical); Raine v. Drasin, 621 S.W.2d 895 (Ky. 1981) (lawyer liable for malicious prosecution for joining two physicians in malpractice case after reviewing records that clearly showed they had treated patient only after his injury had occurred).
10. *Restatement (Second) of Torts* §531; Ultramares Corp. v. Touche, Niven & Co., 174 N.E. 441 (N.Y. 1931).
11. RLGL §51(1) lists a fifth category of nonclients, prospective clients, which is actually an example of an implied client-lawyer relationship. *See also* RLGL §§14, 15.

Invitation to Rely   Nonclients who do not wish to hire a lawyer may nevertheless be invited by a lawyer or the lawyer's client to reasonably rely on the lawyer's services. As in *Greycas*, the client typically benefits from this invitation, often in the circumstance of providing a third party with an opinion. Note that had Proud competently completed a UCC search, he would have discovered that his client had lied to him about the absence of liens on the farm property. His duty to his client then would have required him to inform the client of that fact, as well as the fact that he would have to disclose those liens if he wrote the letter to the lender. His client then could have decided whether it would be better to send the letter or drop the matter. Either way, the lawyer would have succeeded in satisfying his ethical obligation to the client and would not have committed any tort toward the third party.[12]

Negligent Misrepresentation   *Greycas* also illustrates that nonclient liability can be based on either a malpractice or negligent misrepresentation theory. Often, liability for negligent (but not intentional) misrepresentation occurs when a lawyer completes a task, such as a UCC search, but negligently examines the wrong files or database. In that case, the lawyer would not have deliberately lied about a material fact, but his legal opinion (that no liens existed on the property) would have been based on a failure to exercise reasonable care in obtaining the information.[13]

   Today, some jurisdictions continue to require privity for malpractice or "general" liability, but are willing to extend liability to third persons in negligent misrepresentation cases.[14] They reason that professionals have no duty to warn third persons, but when they undertake a duty to speak, they must do so with care.[15] Initially, this duty extended beyond those in privity of contract with the professional only if the misrepresentation was made intentionally or recklessly.[16] Some jurisdictions have completely replaced the privity rule with one that

---

12. MR 2.3; RLGL §95. See, e.g., Banco Popular N. Am. v. Gandi, 876 A.2d 253 (N.J. 2005) (bank has cause of action for negligence against borrower's lawyer when bank relied on lawyer's opinion letter); Dean Foods Co. v. Pappathanasi, 2004 Mass. Super. LEXIS 571 (lawyers who opined that no litigation was pending against their client liable for negligent misrepresentation for failing to disclose pending grand jury subpoena).

13. *Restatement (Second) of Torts* §552; RLGL §51(2)(b). Although some courts also allow recovery for innocent misrepresentations in some business contexts, most refuse to extend the concept of innocent misrepresentation to lawyers who are sued by nonclients, because the misrepresentations have not been made in a transaction between the parties as required by *Restatement (Second) of Torts* §552C. E.g., Garcia v. Rodey, Dickason, Sloan, Akin & Robb, 750 P.2d 118 (N.M. 1988); Pasternak v. Sagittarius Recording Co., 617 F. Supp. 1514 (E.D. Mich. 1985), *aff'd*, 816 F.2d 681 (6th Cir. 1987).

14. *See, e.g.*, Bily v. Arthur Young & Co., 834 P.2d 745 (Cal. 1992) (accountants not liable to third parties for negligence in preparing an audit report, but may be liable for negligent misrepresentation to nonclients who are specifically intended beneficiaries of the audit report); Orshoski v. Krieger, 2001 Ohio App. LEXIS 5018 (prospective buyers who relied on negligent misrepresentations of lawyer for developer concerning subdivision's restrictive covenants could sue for negligent misrepresentation, but not for legal malpractice).

15. *E.g.*, Rubin v. Schottenstein, Zox & Dunn, 143 F.3d 263 (6th Cir. 1998) (en banc) (lawyer who represented seller in a securities transaction assumes a duty to provide complete and non-misleading information with respect to subjects on which he undertakes to speak under 17 C.F.R. §240.10b-5).

16. Ultramares Corp. v. Touche, Niven & Co., *supra* note 10.

depends solely on foreseeability,[17] while others have adopted the limited fore-seeability rule of the *Restatement (Second) of Torts* §552, which restricts liability to "a limited group of persons for whose benefit and guidance" the professional "intends to supply the information."[18]

Third-Party Beneficiaries   *Greycas* further demonstrates that most courts extend the client-lawyer relationship to third-party beneficiaries, those the client intends to benefit in documents created by the lawyer for the client. For lawyers, the earliest cases involved situations in which a client sought the lawyer's help to make a third party the beneficiary of a will or trust. Here, courts found that the client's intent to benefit a third person created a duty of care by the client's lawyer to that third person as well. This meant that breach of a duty of care to the client, such as negligent drafting of the document, which later caused frustration of the testator's intent, created a cause of action by the intended beneficiary against the testator's or settlor's lawyer.[19]

On the other hand, where the parties are potential adversaries or incidental rather than intended beneficiaries, courts have refused to apply the third-party beneficiary doctrine.[20] For example, many courts refuse to impose duties on an executor's lawyer to the estate beneficiaries, reasoning that the latter are not intended beneficiaries and their interests may conflict with those of the executor.[21] Similarly, children cannot pursue malpractice actions against their parent's lawyers for negligence in obtaining a divorce.[22]

Representing Fiduciaries   The facts in *Glover* do not support any of these rationales, because the plaintiff individuals were not perspective clients, were never personally invited to rely on Glover, were not lied to, and were, at most incidental, but not intended, beneficiaries of the lawyer's work. But the court does base its decision on the last duty to nonclients: to refrain from aiding and abetting a client's breach of fiduciary duty. When lawyers represent fiduciaries, such as executors, trustees, guardians, partners, or corporate officers, they know that their clients owe fiduciary duties of loyalty, disclosure, and honesty to the beneficiaries of their work. Lawyers become liable for the client's breach of fiduciary duty when they know about the client's breach and give substantial

---

17. *E.g.*, Molecular Tech. Corp. v. Valentine, 925 F.2d 910 (6th Cir. 1991).
18. *See, e.g.*, Walpert, Smullian & Blumenthal, P.C. v. Katz, 762 A.2d 582 (Md. 2000) (accountant malpractice); RLGL §51.
19. *E.g.*, RLGL §51(3); Guardianship of Karan, 38 P.3d 396 (Wash. App. 2002) (minor child has cause of action against mother's lawyer who set up child's trust to allow pilfering of the estate); Lucas v. Hamm, 364 P.2d 685 (Cal. 1961) (intended beneficiaries of a will could recover from lawyer whose negligence in drafting document caused them to lose their testamentary rights).
20. *See, e.g.*, Capitol Indem. Corp. v. Fleming, 58 P.3d 965 (Ariz. App. 2002) (surety who posted bond for an estate's conservator incidental, not intended beneficiary of services provided by conservator's lawyer); Bovee v. Gravel, 811 A.2d 137 (Vt. 2002) (bank shareholders were not beneficiaries of law firm's representation of bank); MacMillan v. Scheffy, 787 A.2d 867 (N.H. 2001) (buyers in real estate transaction unable to prove that seller's lawyer, who drafted the deed, intended to benefit them; mere fact they were grantees under the deed was not enough).
21. *See, e.g.*, Est. of Albanese v. Lolio, 923 A.2d 325 (N.J. App. 2007); Jensen v. Crandall, 1997 Me. Super. LEXIS 72; Trask v. Butler, 872 P.2d 1080 (Wash. 1994); Neal v. Baker, 551 N.E.2d 704 (Ill. App. 1990).
22. Connely v. McColloch, 83 P.3d 457 (Wyo. 2004).

assistance not just to the client, but to the client's breach. Substantial assistance requires something more than providing routine professional services.[23] Some courts articulate this as requiring that the professional's acts must fall outside the scope of any legitimate employment.[24] Others require wrongful intent, bad faith, or active participation in the fiduciary's breach.[25] However articulated, the requisite substantial assistance can be found in lawyer self-interest, breach of a statutory duty, or knowledge of serious misconduct such as a crime or fraud by the client.[26]

The result in *Glover* rests on perhaps three of the conditions that transform routine assistance into active participation. First, Glover committed a crime by notarizing the plaintiffs' signatures outside of their presence. Those signatures provided the legal basis for the corporation's existence, the plaintiff's monetary investment, and eventual receipt of corporate credit. Glover's self-interest is also evident in his acceptance of the desk he deemed a "gift" from his client, knowing that his client had substantial personal financial problems. Glover also represented Dahl for 20 years, and presumably benefited from legal fees during that time. Although receipt of normal fees does not indicate substantial assistance, long-term receipt combined with knowledge of the fiduciary's breach might.

Finally, aiding and abetting a breach of fiduciary duty requires knowledge, both that the client owes fiduciary duties (something obvious to Glover) and, more difficult to prove, that the lawyer knew about the client's breach. Here, the long-term relationship with Dahl created constructive knowledge based on Dahl's past questionable schemes. The court also found it significant that Glover assisted Dahl in selling corporate assets obtained with investor funds when he knew his client had assured the shareholders that any sale would result in the return of their money. Yet Glover arranged the sale as though Dahl were a sole proprietor, claiming he did not understand the relationship between that business entity and the corporation he also helped to create.

Inconsistent Professional and Public Duties

The most difficult situations occur where creating a duty to a third party appears to conflict directly with a professional obligation, such as confidentiality or loyalty to the client. Here, courts generally decline to impose liability, except

---

23. Reynolds v. Schrock, 142 P.3d 1062 (Or. 2006) (lawyer who provided client advice to revoke her consent to settlement agreement provided legal services within the scope of the lawyer-client relationship and did not provide substantial assistance); Witzman v. Lerhman, Lehrman & Flom, 601 N.W.2d 179 (Minn. 1999) (accountant who provided routine services did not provide substantial assistance).
24. Reynolds v. Schrock, *supra* note 23.
25. Cacciola v. Nellhaus, 733 N.E.2d 133 (Mass. App. 2000) (lawyer for family partnership who represented one partner in a transaction that conflicted with duty to the partnership); Fassihi v. Sommers, Schwartz, Silver, Schwartz & Tyler, P.C., 309 N.W.2d 645 (Mich. App. 1981) (lawyer for close corporation with two 50 percent shareholders who represented one shareholder in ousting the other from the corporation).
26. Weingarten v. Warren, 753 F. Supp. 491 (S.D.N.Y. 1990) (active assistance by trustee's lawyer of trustee's conversion); Morales v. Field, DeGoff, Huppert & MacGowan, 160 Cal. Rptr. 239 (1979) (failure of trustee's lawyer to disclose conflict to beneficiaries of trust); Fickett v. Super. Ct., 558 P.2d 988 (Ariz. App. 1976) (lawyer for guardian knew or should have known of guardian's misappropriation of estate assets).

where they find an important public policy in a statute or professional code. The most famous case that imposed liability despite harm to the professional-client relationship was Tarasoff v. Regents of the University of California,[27] where the court imposed a duty on counseling professionals to warn identifiable victims of a patient's serious threat of harm.[28] The court found that such a duty arises when the therapist determines, or under applicable professional standards should determine, the dangerous threat to another, adopting essentially a malpractice standard.

The *Tarasoff* court cited several cases that relied on state statutes to create a physician's duty to warn a patient's caregivers about the contagious nature of the patient's disease.[29] Similar cases involve the duty to warn about HIV status,[30] and the duty to warn state agencies about child abuse.[31] The presence of statutes designed to protect the public from harm also helps explain the imposition of third-party liability on lawyers and accountants in securities cases.[32]

---

27. 551 P.2d 334 (Cal. 1976).
28. *See also* Cal. Civ. Code §43.92 (2006), which restricts the duty to warn to situations where the patient has communicated "a serious threat of physical violence against a reasonably identifiable victim or victims."
29. Wojcik v. Aluminum Co. of Am., 18 Misc. 2d 740 (N.Y. Sup. Ct. 1959); Jones v. Stanko, 160 N.E. 456 (Ohio 1928); Davis v. Rodman, 227 S.W. 612 (Ark. 1921); Skillings v. Allen, 173 N.W. 663 (Minn. 1919). *See* Tracy A. Bateman, *Liability of Doctor or Other Health Practitioner to Third Party Contracting Contagious Disease from Doctor's Patient*, 3 A.L.R.5th 370 (1992). *See also* Krejci v. Akron Pediatric Neurology, Inc., 511 N.E.2d 129 (Ohio App. 1987) (basing a physician's duty to a third party to use reasonable care in certifying the driving ability of a patient with epilepsy on state statute).
30. *E.g.,* Doe v. Roe, 599 N.Y.S.2d 350 (App. Div. 1993) (cause of action stated against a physician who disclosed HIV infection in violation of AIDS confidentiality statute); Doe v. Marselle, 675 A.2d 835 (Conn. 1996) (physician's unauthorized disclosure was "willful" with the meaning of the AIDS confidentiality statute); Tex. Dept. of Health v. Doe, 994 S.W.2d 890 (Tex. App. 1999) (Health Dept. not immune from suit for violating AIDS confidentiality statute). *Cf.,* Doe v. High-Tech Institute, Inc., 972 P.2d 1060 (Colo. App. 1998) (disclosure of HIV status required by AIDS statute based on blood test not authorized by AIDS statute states a cause of action for public disclosure of private facts).
31. Some states require "any person" to report, *e.g.,* Fla. Stat. §39.201 (2007); others require specific reporters, such as teachers, physicians, and counselors to report, *e.g.,* Cal. Penal Code §11165.7 (2007), Mass. Ann. Laws, ch. 119, §51A (2003). A few statutes designate lawyers as mandated reporters and waive the lawyer-client privilege in some or all circumstances, *e.g.,* Tex. Fam. Code §261.101[0] (2007); Ohio Rev. Code §2151.421 (2007). Most courts agree that a clear statutory duty is required to create tort liability. *See, e.g.,* Landeros v. Flood, 551 P.2d 389 (Cal. 1976) (physician who breached statutory duty to report child abuse may be liable to the child); Wilson v. Darr, 553 N.W.2d 579 (Iowa 1996) (priest who knew and did not report child abuse not liable to abused child because not a "mandatory reporter" under state statute); Kimberly S.M. v. Bradford C. Sch., 649 N.Y.S.2d 588 (App. Div. 1996) (cause of action stated against a teacher who breached statutory duty to report child abuse).
32. *See, e.g.,* Jill E. Fisch, *The Scope of Private Securities Litigation: In Search of Liability Standards for Private Defendants*, 99 Colum. L. Rev. 1293 (1999); James D. Cox, *Just Deserts for Accountants and Attorneys After Bank of Denver*, 38 Ariz. L. Rev. 519 (1996); Richard J. Link, *Persons Liable for False Registration Statement Under §11 of Securities Act of 1933*, 114 A.L.R. Fed. 551 (1993); F.S. Tinio, *Who Is an "Insider" Within the Meaning of §10(b) of the Securities Exchange Act of 1943—and SEC Rule 10b-5 Promulgated Thereunder—Making Unlawful Corporate Insider's Nondisclosure of Information to Seller or Purchaser of Corporation's Stock*, 2 A.L.R. Fed. 274 (1969).

The Relevance of Professional Codes

No applicable statute existed in *Tarasoff*, but the court did cite the relevant professional code, the Principles of Medical Ethics of the American Medical Association, which at the time provided: "A physician may not reveal the confidence entrusted to him in the course of medical attendance . . . [u]nless he is required to do so by law or unless it becomes necessary in order to protect the welfare of the individual or of the community."[33] Relying on this professional code was akin to the court's malpractice rationale; it meant that the court's rule corresponded exactly with the professional custom.

To date, the only case to address this issue for lawyers held that a duty would only exist if the lawyer "believed beyond a reasonable doubt" that the client would harm an identifiable person, a holding that suggests that the answer turns on the certainty of the lawyer's belief.[34] The Restatement of the Law Governing Lawyers, however, does not endorse any *Tarasoff*-like duty against lawyers who fail to warn about a dangerous client. Focusing on *Tarasoff*'s reliance on professional codes, it points out that lawyers may, but are not required to, disclose threats of serious bodily harm or death.[35] It therefore concludes that lawyers are not, "solely by reason of such action or inaction, subject to professional discipline, liable for damages to the lawyer's client or any third person."[36] Because disclosure conflicts with the lawyer's "customary role of protecting client interests," the comments point out that "critical facts may be unclear, emotions may be high, and little time may be available" for lawyers to decide whether to warn.[37]

Of course, lawyers do differ significantly from mental health professionals in their specific training to diagnose dangerous behavior.[38] A California case subsequent to *Tarasoff* does seem to find this professional training important. In Nally v. Grace Community Church of the Valley,[39] the court refused to impose any duty of care to prevent a suicide on a nontherapist clergy counselor who was neither licensed nor professionally trained as a medical expert. While the court based its decision in part on the defendant's lack of training, it also emphasized that the state legislature specifically left the religious counselor's activity unregulated.

---

33. Tarasoff v. Regents of the U. of Cal., *supra* note 27, at 347.
34. Hawkins v. King County, *infra* p. 198. *See also* St. v. Hansen, 862 P.2d 117, 118 (Wash. 1993) (lawyers "have a duty to warn of true threats to harm a judge made by a client or a third party when the attorney has a reasonable belief that such threats are real"). Of course, a lawyer whose client authorizes the disclosure acts on his or her client's behalf in warning. *See, e.g.,* In re Gonnella, 570 A.2d 53 (N.J. Super. L. Div. 1989) (public defender's warning to prosecutor after his client told him to warn co-counsel to resign and threatened co-counsel with harm if he did not comply); People v. Fentress, 103 Misc. 2d 179 (Dutchess Cty. Ct. N.Y. 1980) (lawyer's call to the police about client's crime not "tainted evidence" because call authorized by his client).
35. RLGL §66(1) and (2). *See also* ABA, *Standards for Criminal Justice: Prosecution Function and Defense Function*, §4-3.7(d) (3d ed. 1993).
36. RLGL §66(3).
37. *Id.*, Comment g.
38. The psychological professions argue that they are notoriously unable to achieve much accuracy in their predictions. *See* Alan A. Stone, *The* Tarasoff *Decisions: Suing Psychotherapists to Safeguard Society*, 90 Harv. L. Rev. 358 (1976).
39. 763 P.2d 948 (Cal. 1988).

Lawyers fall right in the middle between unlicensed clergy and licensed mental health professionals. Although lawyers share with clergy a lack of formal psychological training, unlike clergy, lawyers are licensed, heavily regulated by the state, and subject to professional codes that allow, but usually do not require disclosure. The *Tarasoff* court spoke of our society as "crowded," "computerized," "risk infected," and "interdependent," and stated that "we can hardly tolerate the further exposure to danger that would result from a concealed knowledge of the therapist that his patient was lethal."[40] Should this mean that a lawyer, like a therapist, has a duty to warn foreseeable victims targeted by a client? Perhaps the most that can be said for the moment is that no case has yet imposed liability on a lawyer for failure to warn. Further, precisely because lawyers are not trained to recognize dangerous characteristics, the potential cases in which a court might impose such an obligation on lawyers are considerably fewer than those that might involve mental health workers.[41] On the other hand, mandatory disclosure provisions in some professional codes (or relevant expert testimony) might create the basis for liability in an extreme case.[42]

We can conclude that courts create duties to nonclients when the professional's duty to the client is consistent with finding a duty to a third party. When duty to a nonclient would compromise the professional relationship or conflicts with a duty to the client, courts impose duties only when some clear public policy justifies the imposition of such a duty. Statutes can create such duties, as can duties imposed where a professional code or expert testimony requires or recognizes it as well.

---

40. Tarasoff v. Regents of the U. of Cal., *supra* note 27, at 347.
41. One recent study finds that lawyers themselves are increasingly the target of such violence, citing examples from domestic, employment, and criminal law. Stephen Kelson, *Violence Against Lawyers: The Increasingly Attacked Profession,* 10 B.U. Pub. Int. L.J. 260 (2001).
42. Sarah Buel & Margaret Drew, *Do Ask and Do Tell: Rethinking the Lawyer's Duty to Warn in Domestic Violence Cases,* 75 U. Cin. L. Rev. 447 (2006).

Chapter 6

Confidentiality

"I'm sorry—I never discuss my clients with their mothers."

A. Introduction

This chapter addresses another basic fiduciary duty: confidentiality. We begin by examining the scope of the professional duty and proceed in the next chapter to consider exceptions to the obligation. Throughout, we refer to both the fiduciary duty of confidentiality, which is found in the lawyer codes and the law of agency, as well as the obligation of confidentiality imposed in litigation by the evidentiary attorney-client privilege and work product doctrine. These bodies of law parallel each other, as the chart below demonstrates.

CLIENT CONFIDENTIALITY

	Evidentiary Protections	Ethical/Fiduciary Duty
Source of Law	Statute; Common Law of Evidence	Agency Law; MR 1.6, 1.8(b), 1.9, 1.18; C.P.R. Canon 4
Definition	A/C Privilege: Communications between privileged persons in confidence for the purpose of obtaining or providing legal assistance. RLGL §§68-77; WP Immunity: Material prepared by a lawyer for a client in anticipation of litigation. RLGL §§87-89; FRCP 26(b)(3)	MR 1.6(a): Information relating to the representation of a client; DR 4-101 (A): Confidences and Secrets; RLGL §59: Confidential Client Information
Client Consent	Waiver: RLGL §§78-81; 91-92	Client consent, express, or implied: MR 1.6(a), 1.13(c), 1.14(c); RLGL §§61-62

Exceptions		
Physical Harm	Future and continuing crime or fraud: RLGL §82	Future serious bodily harm (crime): MR 1.6(b)(1); RLGL §66
Financial Harm/ Client Crime or Fraud	Future and continuing crime or fraud: RLGL §§82, 93	Future crime, prevent, rectify, mitigate substantial financial loss: MR 1.6(b)(2)(3); RLGL §67
Seeking Advice	None	MR 1.6(b)(4)
Lawyer Self-Defense and Compensation	Lawyer self-protection: RLGL §83	Lawyer self-defense: MR 1.6(b)(5); RLGL §§64, 65
Required by Law or Court Order	Invoking the privilege: RLGL §86	Required by law or court order: MR 1.6(b)(6); RLGL §63

In considering the law governing confidentiality, it is instructive to begin by examining the origins of and justifications for the professional obligation.

The recognition of confidentiality as a core professional obligation arose first in cases applying the attorney-client privilege, which Wigmore dates to the seventeenth century.[1] In the twentieth century, the idea that lawyers were

---

1. Geoffrey C. Hazard, Jr., *An Historical Perspective on the Attorney-Client Privilege*, 66 Cal. L. Rev. 1061, 1069-1070 (1978).

forbidden from disclosing client confidences created the basis for the recognition in agency law that confidentiality is an integral part of the fiduciary duty of loyalty that lawyer-agents owe to client-principals.[2] About 100 years ago, both the attorney-client privilege and the agency duty of confidentiality were incorporated into lawyer codes as the obligation not to divulge confidences and secrets of a client.[3]

Throughout this legal development, client-lawyer confidentiality has been justified by both a consequential utilitarian rationale as well as a rights or duty-based deontological rationale. The utilitarian view usually concludes that confidentiality promotes the greatest good for the greatest number because it is essential to making the legal system work. The deontological view holds that confidentiality promotes respect for human autonomy by guaranteeing trust and privacy in the client-lawyer relationship.

Utilitarians focus on consequences and argue that to do their job, lawyers need complete and accurate facts, about what has already occurred and what the client contemplates doing. Lacking these facts, the lawyer may either apply the wrong law or give incorrect legal advice, or both, which in turn will reduce public confidence in the legal system and in lawyers.[4] Others disagree, arguing that confidentiality actually harms society and the legal system. Jeremy Bentham, for example, argued that the attorney-client privilege should be abolished, because it obscured the truth from the courts and allowed those with something to hide to get away with unlawful behavior.[5]

Immanual Kant argued that deontological justifications, which rest on categorical imperatives or fundamental rights, should provide the yardstick for moral accountability. According to this notion, confidentiality obligations are essential to the purpose of the legal system, which exists to protect individual rights, such as the right to contract, own property, or due process. These rights, which respect persons by protecting individual liberty and promoting respect for human autonomy, easily can become vulnerable to infringement by powerful majoritarian interests of the government or others. Law and the legal system provide the means to ensure that such infringements are prevented or redressed.

Confidentiality promotes both the individual rights of citizens and the trust that is central to a client-lawyer relationship. It is a fundamental ethical value, just as loyalty and honesty are integral to a trusting relationship. Privacy also promotes the individual rights of citizens by giving them personal space to plan and define their own meaning in life. The government should not be able to infringe on that private space when it is used to promote that individual's

---

2. The First Restatement of Agency included the prohibition against using or disclosing confidential information with other duties of loyalty. *Restatement (First) of Agency* §395 (1933).
3. ABA Canons of Professional Ethics, Canon 6 (1908) provided: "The obligation to represent the client with undivided fidelity and not to divulge his secrets or confidences forbids also the subsequent acceptance of retainers or employment from others in matters adversely affecting any interest of the client with respect to which confidence has been reposed."
4. *See* Deborah L. Rhode & Geoffrey C. Hazard, Jr., *Professional Responsibility and Regulation* 64 (Found. Press 2002).
5. Jeremy Bentham, *Rationale of Judicial Evidence*, Vol. V, Book IX, Chap. 5, at 324 (1827). It is important to note that Bentham wrote at a time when no privilege against self-incrimination existed, so he reasoned that getting the facts from the mouth of the lawyer was no different from getting them from the mouth of the defendant. *Id.*

autonomous sense of self. A lawyer's obligation not to share the information further protects the client's own defined sphere of privacy, which can become especially important when government compulsion seeks to invade it.

The cases and other materials in this chapter and the next illustrate how both of these justifications inform professional obligations of confidentiality as well as exceptions to the doctrine.

B. Fiduciary Duty

Problems

6-1. May Martyn & Fox include in a firm website the names of clients they have represented, the results in their litigation matters, and the size and type of transactions they have handled? What if everything disclosed is a matter of public record, on file at the courthouse or the SEC?

6-2. Martyn & Fox represents Disney as undisclosed principal for the purpose of purchasing property to develop a new theme park. May Fox purchase stock in Disney? May Fox purchase adjacent land?

6-3. Small Co. asks Martyn & Fox to bring a huge fraud and RICO claim against Magna Co. Martyn & Fox currently represents Big Bank in a $600 million loan to Magna that is scheduled to close next Tuesday. What can we tell Big Bank?

Consider: **Model Rules 1.4, 1.6, 1.8(b), 1.18**
           Model Code DR 4-101
           RLGL §§15, 20, 59, 60

Matter of Anonymous
654 N.E.2d 1128 (Ind. 1995)

PER CURIAM.

The respondent has been charged by the Disciplinary Commission in a verified complaint for disciplinary action with violating Rules 1.6(a), 1.8(b), and 1.16(a)(1) of the Rules of Professional Conduct for Attorneys at Law. . . .

As stipulated by the parties, the respondent was contacted by an individual (the "mother") in April or May of 1994 about representing her in seeking a child support arrearage due to her from the father ("father") of her minor child. She supplied the respondent with records concerning

her support action and her income. Also included in these documents was information regarding the father, including the fact that he was going to receive a substantial inheritance, his salary, his place of employment, and his address.

In the course of reviewing the documents supplied by the mother, the respondent discovered that on July 17, 1992, a judgment had been entered against the mother and father, making them jointly liable for almost $4,500 of medical and hospital debt resulting from the birth of their child. The judgment was in favor of the local county welfare department. The respondent was, at all times relevant to this proceeding, the attorney under contract to represent the local county welfare department.

The respondent contacted the mother to determine if the medical debt owed to the welfare department had been paid by either her or the father. It had not. The respondent then informed the mother that he would be unable to represent her in the case because of a conflict of interest, then forwarded her documents, at her request, to another attorney. Thereafter, the respondent received approval from the local county welfare department to file a collection suit against the father, which he did on April 26, 1994. Later, the father's counsel joined the mother as a party defendant in the collection suit. The respondent ultimately obtained a summary judgment against the mother and the father. The respondent did not withdraw from the case after the mother was joined as a party defendant.

We find that, by revealing information relating to the representation of the mother without her consent, the respondent violated Ind. Professional Conduct Rule 1.6(a). By using that information to her disadvantage without her consent, he violated Prof. Cond. R. 1.8(b). By failing to withdraw as counsel for the local welfare department during the collection suit against the mother when such representation violated the Rules of Professional Conduct, the respondent violated Prof. Cond. R. 1.16(a)(1).

The respondent and the Commission agree that several factors mitigate the severity of his misconduct. They agree that the information gained by the respondent about the mother's case was readily available from public sources and not confidential in nature. The respondent declined to represent the mother after he learned of her outstanding debt owed to the county welfare department, and advised her to seek other counsel. He did not at any time request that she sign an employment agreement, seek a retainer fee, or otherwise charge her. We see no evidence of selfish motive on the respondent's part.

The respondent's use of information gained during consultations with the mother represents misuse of information entrusted to him in his capacity as a lawyer. Such conduct not only threatens harm to the individuals involved, but also erodes the integrity of the profession. At the same time, we note that the respondent appears to have had no sinister motives. For these reasons, we accept the agreed sanction of a private reprimand. . . .

Perez v. Kirk & Carrigan
822 S.W.2d 261 (Tex. App. 1991)

DORSEY, J. . . .

The present suit arises from a school bus accident on September 21, 1989, in Alton, Texas. Ruben Perez was employed by Valley Coca-Cola Bottling Company as a truck driver. On the morning of the accident, Perez attempted to stop his truck at a stop sign along his route, but the truck's brakes failed to stop the truck, which collided with the school bus. The loaded bus was knocked into a pond and 21 children died. Perez suffered injuries from the collision and was taken to a local hospital to be treated.

The day after the accident, Kirk & Carrigan, lawyers who had been hired to represent Valley Coca-Cola Bottling Company, visited Perez in the hospital for the purpose of taking his statement. Perez claims that the lawyers told him that they were his lawyers too and that anything he told them would be kept confidential.[1] With this understanding, Perez gave them a sworn statement concerning the accident.[2] However, after taking Perez' statement, Kirk & Carrigan had no further contact with him. Instead, Kirk & Carrigan made arrangements for criminal defense attorney Joseph Connors to represent

Perez. Connors was paid by National Union Fire Insurance Company which covered both Valley Coca-Cola and Perez for liability in connection with the accident.

Some time after Connors began representing Perez, Kirk & Carrigan, without telling either Perez or Connors, turned Perez' statement over to the Hidalgo County District Attorney's Office. Kirk & Carrigan contend that Perez' statement was provided in a good faith attempt to fully comply with a request of the district attorney's office and under threat of subpoena if they did not voluntarily comply. Partly on the basis of this statement, the district attorney was able to obtain a grand jury indictment of Perez for involuntary manslaughter for his actions in connection with the accident.[3] . . .

---

1. The summary judgment affidavits offered by Perez show the following with regard to Kirk & Carrigan's representations to him at the time they took Perez' statement:

    Ruben Perez—"Kirk told me that they were lawyers hired by Valley Coca Cola, that they were my lawyers too, and that whatever I told them would be kept confidential. I trusted what these lawyers told me and I answered their questions."

    Israel Perez (Ruben's father)—"Before beginning the questions, Kirk told Ruben that they were his lawyers, that they were going to help him, and that what they . . . learned from Ruben would be kept a secret."

    Joe Perez (Ruben's uncle)—"Before Ruben gave his statement, to Kirk, Kirk told Ruben that they (the lawyers) represented Valley Coca Cola, that they were Ruben's lawyers too, and that they did not want anyone else to come in the room and to talk to Ruben. Kirk then told Ruben 'I know you are in pain, but we need to ask you these questions. Your mind would be fresh to tell us what happened. This will be kept confidential. We will get you a copy of it tomorrow. We will not give anyone a copy. It is between you and us.' Kirk and Carrigan did not say that they represented only Valley Coca Cola."

2. Among other things, Perez generally stated that he had a previous accident while driving a Coke truck in 1987 for which he was given a citation, that he had a speeding violation in 1988, that he had not filled out a daily checklist to show that he had checked the brakes on the morning of the accident, that he had never before experienced problems with the brakes on his truck and that they were working just before the accident, that he tried to apply the brakes to stop the truck, but that the brakes for the trailer were not working at all to stop the truck (the truck had two sets of brakes: the ones for the cab worked; the ones for the trailer did not and the greater weight of the trailer had the effect of pushing the entire truck, even though the cab brakes were working), that Perez did not have enough time to apply the emergency brakes, and that there was nothing the managers or supervisors at Valley Coca-Cola could have done to prevent the accident.

3. By his summary judgment affidavit offered in support of Perez, Joseph Connors stated that, in his professional opinion as a board certified criminal law specialist, if he had known that the statement had been provided and had been able to have Perez explain his lack of training or knowledge about the brake system to the grand jury, Perez would not have been indicted for manslaughter. Ruben Perez also stated in his affidavit that Valley Coca-Cola Bottling Company had not given him any instruction in brake inspection, maintenance, or use in an emergency situation.

... Perez asserted numerous causes of action against Kirk & Carrigan for breach of fiduciary duty, negligent and intentional infliction of emotional distress, violation of the Texas Deceptive Trade Practices Act and conspiracy to violate article 21.21 of the Texas Insurance Code. ...

With regard to Perez' cause of action for breach of the fiduciary duty of good faith and fair dealing, Kirk and Carrigan contend that no attorney-client relationship existed and no fiduciary duty arose, because Perez never sought legal advice from them.

An agreement to form an attorney-client relationship may be implied from the conduct of the parties. Moreover, the relationship does not depend upon the payment of a fee, but may exist as a result of rendering services gratuitously.[4]

In the present case, viewing the summary judgment evidence in the light most favorable to Perez, Kirk & Carrigan told him that, in addition to representing Valley Coca-Cola, they were also Perez' lawyers and that they were going to help him. Perez did not challenge this assertion, and he cooperated with the lawyers in giving his statement to them, even though he did not offer, nor was he asked, to pay the lawyers' fees. We hold that this was sufficient to imply the creation of an attorney-client relationship at the time Perez gave his statement to Kirk & Carrigan.

The existence of this relationship encouraged Perez to trust Kirk & Carrigan and gave rise to a corresponding duty on the part of the attorneys not to violate this position of trust. Accordingly, the relation between attorney and client is highly fiduciary in nature, and their dealings with each other are subject to the same scrutiny as a transaction between trustee and beneficiary. Specifically, the relationship between attorney and client has been described as one of *uberrima fides*, which means, "most abundant good faith," requiring absolute and perfect candor, openness and honesty, and the absence of any concealment or deception. In addition, because of the openness and candor within this relationship, certain communications between attorney and client are privileged from disclosure in either civil or criminal proceedings under the provisions of Tex. R. Civ. Evid. 503 and Tex. R. Crim. Evid. 503, respectively.[5]

There is evidence that Kirk & Carrigan represented to Perez that his statement would be kept confidential. Later, however, without telling either Perez or his subsequently-retained criminal defense attorney, Kirk & Carrigan voluntarily disclosed Perez' statement to the district attorney. Perez asserts in the present suit that this course of conduct amounted, among other things, to a breach of fiduciary duty.

---

4. An attorney's fiduciary responsibilities may arise even during preliminary consultations regarding the attorney's possible retention if the attorney enters into discussion of the client's legal problems with a view toward undertaking representation.

5. Disclosure of confidential communications by an attorney, whether privileged or not under the rules of evidence, is generally prohibited by the disciplinary rules governing attorneys' conduct in Texas. See Supreme Court of Texas, Rules Governing the State Bar of Texas art. X, §9 (Disc. R. of Prof. Conduct) Rule 1.05. In addition, the general rule is that confidential information received during the course of any fiduciary relationship may not be used or disclosed to the detriment of the one from whom the information is obtained. Numed, Inc. v. McNutt, 724 S.W.2d 432, 434 (Tex. App.—Fort Worth 1987, no writ) (former employee is obligated not to use or divulge employer's trade secrets).

Kirk & Carrigan seek to avoid this claim of breach, on the ground that the attorney-client privilege did not apply to the present statement, because unnecessary third parties were present at the time it was given. However, whether or not the Rule 503 attorney-client privilege extended to Perez' statement, Kirk & Carrigan initially obtained the statement from Perez on the understanding that it would be kept confidential. Thus, regardless of whether from an evidentiary standpoint the privilege attached, Kirk & Carrigan breached their fiduciary duty to Perez either by wrongfully disclosing a privileged statement or by wrongfully representing that an unprivileged statement would be kept confidential. Either characterization shows a clear lack of honesty toward, and a deception of, Perez by his own attorneys regarding the degree of confidentiality with which they intended to treat the statement. . . .

In addition, however, even assuming a breach of fiduciary duty, Kirk & Carrigan also contend that summary judgment may be sustained on the ground that Perez could show no damages resulting from the breach. Kirk & Carrigan contend that their dissemination of Perez' statement could not have caused him any damages in the way of emotional distress, because the statement merely revealed Perez' own version of what happened. We do not agree. Mental anguish consists of the emotional response of the plaintiff caused by the tortfeasor's conduct. It includes, among other things, the mental sensation of pain resulting from public humiliation.

Regardless of the fact that Perez himself made the present statement, he did not necessarily intend it to be a public response as Kirk & Carrigan contend, but only a private and confidential discussion with his attorneys. Perez alleged that the publicity caused by his indictment, resulting from the revelation of the statement to the district attorney in breach of that confidentiality, caused him to suffer emotional distress and mental anguish. We hold that Perez has made a valid claim for such damages. . . .

■ Lawyers' Roles:
The Directive Lawyer and Fiduciary Duty

Viewed from the client's perspective, the lawyers in *Perez* breached all five basic fiduciary duties that lawyers owe clients. They ignored Mr. Perez's right to control the goals of the representation by failing to clarify his choice about the use of his statement. They ignored basic obligations to communicate by failing to obtain Mr. Perez's informed consent about key issues that surfaced during the representation. They acted incompetently by failing to recognize their own clear legal obligations to Mr. Perez. They violated Mr. Perez's confidentiality by disclosing his confidences to the prosecutor without his consent. And they disregarded conflict of interest by favoring another client's interests over Mr. Perez's, and by pursuing their own interests at Mr. Perez's expense.

All of this caused incalculable damage to Mr. Perez, who was 25 years old when the accident occurred, and was just beginning to realize his life-long ambition to be a truck driver like his father. The accident killed 21 of the 81 children on the bus, who drowned in a water-filled pit after the truck driven by

Mr. Perez pushed it off the road. Following the accident, Mr. Perez spent three-and-one-half years awaiting trial on the criminal charges in a self-imposed bedroom prison, never leaving his house.[1] The jury trial on the criminal charges acquitted Mr. Perez on all 21 counts after only 4 hours of deliberation.[2]

The behavior of Mr. Perez's lawyers indicates that they somehow inexplicably misconstrued their role in representing their client, thinking that they owed him none of the fiduciary duties they had assumed, even though they had promised Mr. Perez to fulfill all of them. They appear to have acted as directors, who imposed their own private judgment about the matter on a trusting, unsuspecting client. They perceived themselves as professional authorities in charge of directing a relationship, rather than agents with fiduciary duties subject to their client's instructions. Judge John Noonan calls this mindset "underidentification with a client."[3]

Fiduciary Duties

Agency law long has recognized the problem of generalized expertise: the tendency of experts to transfer their professional knowledge and expertise to a general control over all decisions and aspects of the relationship. Professionals easily can assume that professional competence equates with the ability to know what is best for clients. To ensure that the client's moral values control the agency relationship, lawyer agents owe client principals the 5 Cs to steer lawyers away from benefiting someone other than the client. These fiduciary duties also protect clients from lawyers who might intentionally or even inadvertently take advantage of the trust and power reposed in them.

Mr. Perez's lawyers' first, and most obvious breach of fiduciary duty was their failure to defer to their client's right to control the goals of the representation. Second, at several key points, their breach of the fiduciary duty of communication deprived Mr. Perez of the right to make these critical decisions.[4] In their first meeting with Mr. Perez, there is no indication that the lawyers disclosed that certain conflicts of interest might develop, which could require them to withdraw from representing either Mr. Perez, or Valley Coca-Cola or both. After they discovered that conflicts might exist, it is also not clear whether they told Mr. Perez that they no longer represented him, or why. And they obviously did not seek Mr. Perez's consent to disclosing his statement to the prosecutor, something that his subsequent lawyer claimed could have avoided 21 criminal indictments.

---

1. Maggie Rivas, *Truck Driver Says He Spent Years After Bus Crash Doing Penance; He Went into Self-Imposed Exile at Home as Punishment*, Dallas Morning News, at 1A (May 7, 1993).
2. Maggie Rivas, *Trucker Absolved of Bus Deaths; '89 Alton Tragedy Killed 21 Students*, Dallas Morning News, at 1A (May 6, 1993). Mr. Perez continues to suffer from brain injuries he received in the accident that reduced his intellectual capacity to that of a fifth-grader and he is permanently unable to work. *A Tragedy Remembered*, Dallas Morning News, at 17A (Sept. 21, 1999).
3. John T. Noonan Jr., *The Lawyer Who Overidentifies with his Client*, 76 Notre Dame L. Rev. 827, 833 (2001). *See also* David Luban, *Making Sense of Moral Meltdowns*, in Susan D. Carle, ed., *Lawyers' Ethics and the Pursuit of Social Justice: A Critical Reader*, 355 (NYU Press 2005) (characterizing the "chronic source of moral difficulty" for defense lawyers as whether assisting their "guilty" client's best interest requires hiding the truth).
4. RLGL §20; *Restatement (Second) of Agency* §381 (1958).

Mr. Perez's lawyers may have ignored their fiduciary obligations simply because they did not know about or understand them. If so, they breached a third duty, the fiduciary duty of competence.[5] If they mistakenly believed that they had the prerogative to disclose client information without consent or consultation, they either had never heard of, or had never understood the meaning of, either their own professional code provisions or case law that imposed these fiduciary duties.[6]

Fourth, these lawyers blatantly violated their duty of confidentiality.[7] They offered to represent Mr. Perez, promised him confidentiality, obtained his statement about the accident, and then turned it over to a hostile third party, the prosecutor, without their client's consent. The court makes the point that the lawyers' promise both to represent Mr. Perez's interests and to keep his confidences encouraged him to confide in the lawyers.

Mr. Perez's lawyers appeared to understand confidentiality (because they promised it), but they apparently did not know the long-term duration of this obligation under the professional rules. Perhaps they simply did not understand that their initial promise of confidentiality to Mr. Perez legally included both "privileged" communications, as well as an obligation not to use or reveal information relating to the representation without his consent.[8] If so, they acted incompetently by failing to preserve the privilege, either by not asking Mr. Perez's relatives to step outside during the interview, or by clarifying that the relatives' presence was necessary to effectuate his communication.[9] They apparently ignored the fact that this fiduciary obligation continues without limit after the client-lawyer relationship ends as well.[10] They also seemed to be oblivious to Model Rule 1.9, which prohibits not only use or disclosure of a former client's confidential information, but also any *potential* use or disclosure of former client confidences. It does this by prohibiting any representation of a subsequent client in the same or substantially related matter without the consent of the former client.[11] Together, these provisions meant that after the representation ceased, Mr. Perez's lawyers were prohibited both from using or disclosing his confidences and, unless Mr. Perez consented, from continuing their representation of Valley Coca-Cola. Yet, apparently no such consent was sought.

---

5. RLGL §§48-50; *Restatement (Second) of Agency* §379 (1958); MR 1.1.
6. The Texas equivalent of Model Rule 1.9 was adopted Oct. 17, 1989, about one month after the accident, and became effective Jan. 1, 1990. Tex. Govt. Code Ann. T.2, Subt. G, App. A, Art. 10, §9, R. 1.09 (2001). The comments to the rule indicate it was based on prior case law, including a case decided about six months before the accident where the Texas Supreme Court mandated that this rule be applied to all former client representations. *See* NCNB Tex. Bank v. Coker, 765 S.W.2d 398 (Tex. 1989).
7. RLGL §60; *Restatement (Second) of Agency* §§395-396 (1958); MR 1.6, 1.8(b), 1.9(a).
8. MR 1.6(a), 1.8(b).
9. RLGL §70 Comment f (allowing confidential agents if "the person's participation is reasonably necessary to facilitate the client's communication with the lawyer . . . and the client reasonably believes that the person will hold the communication in confidence").
10. MR 1.9(c); RLGL §60(1)(a) (prohibiting use or disclosure that would "adversely affect a material interest of the client" "during or after the representation of a client").
11. MR 1.9(a) and (b).

Why did these lawyers make such an obvious mistake? One answer might be found in their failure to properly understand their fifth fiduciary duty: conflicts of interest resolution.[12] Mr. Perez's lawyers initially were hired by an insurance company to represent two insureds, Valley Coca-Cola and Mr. Perez. Prior to representing Mr. Perez, they no doubt believed that the interests of both clients were consistent, that is, that the accident was not the fault of either client. In his statement, however, Mr. Perez admitted to several possible violations of company policy, such as a prior speeding violation, and his failure to check the truck's brakes the day of the accident. Mr. Perez's lawyers then appeared to realize that they had a conflict of interest: protecting the interests of one client (Valley Coca-Cola) might require that they take action contrary to the interest of their other client (Perez). This may explain why they "had no further contact with him" and made arrangements for another lawyer to defend Mr. Perez's interests. Yet their errors also indicate confusion about their duties following the conclusion of the joint representation. They allowed their continuing loyalty to Valley Coca-Cola to combine with their own interest in staying in the matter, which simply may have blinded them to their competing, continuing confidentiality duty to Mr. Perez.

The Problem with Directive Behavior

Judge Noonan recalls a strikingly similar joint client incident that became the focus of future Justice Louis Brandeis' Senate confirmation hearings.[13] Brandeis recommended that a client assign his business assets for the benefit of creditors. He did not tell the client that this assignment constituted an act of bankruptcy, or that Brandeis' law firm represented one of the creditors. Five days later, Brandeis, representing the creditor, instituted involuntary bankruptcy proceedings against the client. Brandeis later claimed that he had been "counsel to the situation," not counsel to the clients. Compare Judge Noonan's characterization of Brandeis's conduct with the acts of the lawyers in *Perez*.

> Underidentification is here, no doubt, carried to the point of caricature. The lawyer does not remember that he took the client as a client. The lawyer does not give the client the most elementary advice about the consequences of the act the lawyer is advising him to perform. The lawyer represents another client and, acting for that client, puts his unremembered client into bankruptcy. At the heart of the situation is the lawyer's desire to abstract himself from the needs and pressures of a particular individual in order to go on and straighten out a mess. In some other world, law could be practiced in that fashion. It is not the way law has been generally practiced in ours.[14]

Perhaps Mr. Perez's lawyers believed that they too were hired "to straighten out a mess," or to direct or implement their own view of social retribution. If so, they made all the mistakes that Noonan attributes to Brandeis. Mr. Perez's

---

12. RLGL §121; *Restatement (Second) of Agency* §387 (1958); MR 1.7.
13. Judge Noonan points out that this episode was far from typical, but was the "most damaging episode" that Brandeis's enemies could cull from a distinguished 30-year career in law practice. Noonan, *supra* note 3, at 829.
14. *Id.* at 833.

lawyers recognized the legal significance of his failure to check the brakes, just as Brandeis knew the legal significance of the assignment for the benefit of creditors. They then transformed themselves into agents for their other client, Valley Coca-Cola, just as Brandeis became the advocate for his other creditor-client. Mr. Perez's lawyers gave his confidential statement to the prosecutor's office, just as Brandeis used his client's confidences against him to force a bankruptcy proceeding. Brandeis and Mr. Perez's lawyers became lawyers for the situation, rather than the client. Each apparently assumed that his private judgment about the matter could dominate, even at the direct expense of his fiduciary duties. Conveniently sacrificing one client's goals to the lawyers' view of the greater good also happened to dovetail neatly with the lawyers' own interests in continuing to represent another client.

The Cure for Directive Behavior

Lawyers who abstract themselves from clients in this manner ignore fiduciary duties and often assume the role of an authority who knows best and directs the relationship. Like Brandeis, they act as judges when they are called on to advise and advocate. The law has long recognized fiduciary duty as the cure for this misguided private judgment. The power clients bestow on lawyers to handle matters enables lawyers to manipulate the representations for their own or another's benefit. Fiduciary duties curb this power by guarding against both intentional and unintentional exploitation by agents. For lawyers, each client is entitled to the right to choose which legal options to pursue and to be consulted about how to pursue them.

Directive behavior is most endemic and least justified in situations like Mr. Perez's, when lawyers represent individual clients unfamiliar with the law who are often facing litigation concerning past events. Professors Freedman and Smith focus on advocacy in litigation as the primary circumstance justifying zealous advocacy. Here, where clients are most vulnerable, lawyers should be most diligent in guarding against preempting their client's moral judgments.[15] This advice would have helped to avoid the harm foisted on Mr. Perez and Brandeis's client.

In the end, Mr. Perez settled his lawsuit against his former lawyers for an undisclosed amount. He also reached a settlement of $462,619 against Valley Coca-Cola, which paid over $133 million in overall settlements to those injured in the tragedy, largely because of its failure to properly maintain the truck's brakes.[16] The result in *Perez* is consistent with the result in *Busch, Machado, dePape, Togstad,* and *Roe:* Lawyers, regardless of their intent, will be subject to professional discipline and liable for tort damages when they breach fiduciary duties. On the other hand, lawyers who learn and incorporate into their practice the 5 Cs should not fall prey to professional discipline or subject themselves to the civil

---

15. Outside of litigation, Freedman and Smith argue that lawyers should view the advice they give about contracts and wills "with an adversary's eye" as well. Freedman & Smith, p. 4 *supra.*
16. The company that manufactured the bus also paid $23 million to accident victims due to improperly designed hatches that did not allow the children to escape as water filled the bus. *Truck Driver Settles Suit from Crash that Killed 21 Schoolchildren in '89,* Dallas Morning News, at 29A (May 26, 1994).

relief afforded to clients whose lawyers betray them. They also will move toward respecting client interests, and begin to think of themselves as collaborators in representing clients, rather than as authorities or judges who know best.

C. Evidentiary Protections: Attorney-Client Privilege and *Work Product Immunity*

Problems

6-4. At Client's request, Fox returns goods stolen by Client to the police. Can Fox be forced to testify about the identity of Client?

6-5. Martyn interviews 25 maintenance workers to determine how our client is disposing of used oil. Can Martyn be forced to testify about those conversations?

6-6. In a privileged conversation Client tells Martyn where he was on the night in question. Can Client now be compelled to testify as to his whereabouts?

6-7. Can Martyn be forced to testify about a conversation she had alone with an investment banker to understand what was required for our corporate client to pursue a merger?

Consider:
RLGL §§68-77, 87-89
FRCP 26(b)(3)

Hughes v. Meade
453 S.W.2d 538 (Ky. 1970)

CLAY, Commissioner.

This is an original proceeding for a writ of prohibition against the Honorable N. Mitchell Meade, Judge of the Fayette Circuit Court. Petitioner, an attorney, seeks to restrain the respondent from enforcing a contempt ruling entered against him because of his refusal to answer a question as a witness in a criminal trial. Petitioner was not a party to, nor did he represent anyone as an attorney in such proceeding.

The proceeding in which he was called as a witness was the trial of one Williams on a criminal charge involving the theft of an IBM typewriter. Petitioner had participated in the return of an IBM typewriter to

the Lexington Police Department. His testimony with respect thereto, and so much thereof as is pertinent to the question presented, is as follows:

Q "Would you tell the jury the circumstances and how you happened to deliver that typewriter?

A "Well, a certain party called me and employed me because of, first of all, my relationship with the Lexington Police Department, which is very good, and I do entirely criminal law and know all of the policemen and members of the Police Department, and asked me if I could get some property returned without getting me involved in it.

Q "Without getting who involved—
you or him?

A "Without getting me involved. . . . "So I called Morris
Carter, who was then either
assistant chief or a major. I
know Morris well, and I asked
him, I said, 'Morris, are you all
interested in getting some stolen
property back?' And he said 'Yes
we are,' and he said, 'What is
it?' I said 'I don't know, I have
no idea,' and I said, 'Morris, I
don't want to get involved in
this thing, I don't want to be
called as a witness, all I want to
do is get this taken care of.' He
said, 'All right, how is it going to
be delivered?' And I said, 'Well,
I'm watching the cartoons.' It
was Saturday morning, and I
said, 'Somebody is going to
leave it on my front porch,' and
the shades were down and I
heard a car come up and left,
and I called Morris back and I
said 'Morris, it's out here,' and
he said, 'Okay I'll send somebody out to get it,'. . . . (Officer
Sparks arrived and a taped box
was opened disclosing a typewriter.) . . .

Q "You say that the certain party
called you and employed you to
do what you have just described
and said you did, is that correct?

A "Yes, sir.

Q "Was this the extent of your employment?

A "Yes, sir.

Q "Have you been paid for that
service?

A "Yes, sir.

Q "And I'll ask you now if you will
tell us the name of the individual
who employed you?

A "I refuse to answer."

Petitioner was found in contempt of
court for failure to identify the person
who had called him. It is his contention that this information was a privileged communication under KRS
421.210(4), and the trial court improperly sought to compel him to disclose it. That subsection of the statute
provides (insofar as pertinent):

"No attorney shall testify concerning a *communication* made to
him, *in his professional character*, by
his client, or his advice thereon
without the client's consent;. . . ."
(Emphasis added.)

This statutory provision generally
conforms to the common law policy
and principle of attorney-client privilege (developed since 1800) and it is
generally recognized in the United
States. See 8 Wigmore, Evidence
§2291 (McNaughton rev. 1961). This
same author thus phrases the principle:

"(1) Where legal advice of any
kind is sought (2) from a professional
legal adviser in his capacity as such,
(3) the communications relating to
that purpose, (4) made in confidence
(5) by the client, (6) are at his instance permanently protected (7)
from disclosure by himself or by the
legal adviser, (8) except the protection be waived." . . .

. . . On the other hand, . . . [a]s
said in 97 C.J.S. Witnesses §280,
page 793:

"Neither is there any privilege as
to communications with reference
to a matter in which the attorney
acts, not in his professional capacity, but merely as an agent or attorney in fact, or in which the
attorney acts merely as a depositary
or as a trustee, particularly where
he has instructions to deliver the
instrument deposited to a third
person, or abstracter of titles."

Returning to the facts of this case, it is the opinion of the majority of the court that whether or not a bona fide attorney-client relationship existed between the petitioner and the undisclosed person, the principal transaction involved, i.e., the delivery of stolen property to the police department, was not an act in the professional capacity of petitioner nor was it the rendition of a legal service. He was acting as an agent or conduit for the delivery of property which was completely unrelated to legal representation. While repose of confidence in an attorney is something much to be desired, to use him as a shield to conceal transactions involving stolen property is beyond the scope of his professional duty and beyond the scope of the privilege.

Dean v. Dean

607 So. 2d 494 (Fla. App. 1992)

FARMER, J.

The issue raised here is whether the attorney-client privilege can be used to prevent the disclosure of the identity of a person who had previously consulted an attorney regarding the return of stolen property belonging to one of the parties in a civil case. . . .

The facts are unusual, to say the least. During the pendency of the Deans' dissolution of marriage case, the husband's place of business was allegedly burgled, resulting in the loss of two duffel bags containing various personal items belonging to husband's daughter, and from $35,000 to $40,000 in cash. Sometime after the theft, an unidentified person telephoned Krischer at his office. He related the conversation as follows:

I received a telephone call from an individual who knew that I was an attorney that was involved in the Baltes[1] matter and the individual asked me for advice with regard to returning property. I advised this person on the telephone that the experience that I have had in the State Attorney's office was that the best avenue was to turn the property over to an attorney and let the attorney bring it to the State Attorney's office or to the law enforcement. . . .

Krischer met twice and had one telephone conversation with this person. Nearly six weeks after the second meeting, the two duffel bags containing only the daughter's personal property were delivered to Krischer's office by someone who told his receptionist that he "would know what they are." No cash was included with the returned items. Krischer then delivered the bags to the police, telling them that they "may have some connection with" husband.

In a twist of irony, these events came to light through Krischer's former secretary, who had also by then become a client of husband's lawyer. Soon after, husband's lawyer served Krischer with a subpoena for a deposition, seeking the identity of Krischer's contact. Kri-

---

1. This refers to a widely publicized case in which a hit-and-run driver consulted Krischer for advice and, afterwards, Krischer asserted the attorney-client privilege when asked to disclose the name of the driver. The fact that the person consulting Krischer in this case referred to the widely publicized case when Krischer kept the identity of his contact confidential might reasonably be taken as evidencing the contact's strong interest in confidentiality.

scher asserted the privilege at the deposition. Husband then moved to compel the testimony. After a hearing, the trial court granted the motion. . . . Krischer's testimony makes plain the intent of his client. . . .

> "The individual called—I can expedite this if I can state a couple of things, judge. I had obviously been through this previously in another case. I was well aware of what was needed to be established in order to protect this client. I inquired of this client if that individual knew I was an attorney. That individual indicated that they did. I inquired if they were seeking legal advice. They indicated that they did. They discussed a legal problem with me. I gave them legal advice.
>
> A condition precedent to this person discussing the legal problem with me was that I not divulge their identity. . . ."

The trial judge . . . [relied on] Hughes v. Meade, 452 S.W.2d 538 (Ky. 1970). . . .

[W]e conclude that the trial court has misinterpreted the privilege and the policies underlying it. . . . It is indisputable that his contact . . . consulted Krischer as an attorney. It is indisputable that the client sought legal advice about a specific matter. It is indisputable that the specific matter concerned a crime that had already been committed, not a planned or future act which might be a crime. And it is indisputable that the client insisted on confidence.

The focus, as we have seen from the common law development of the privilege and our own Florida Evidence Code section 90.502 definition of "client," is on the perspective of the person seeking out the lawyer, not on what the lawyer does after the consultation. As we have also seen, it has long been understood that the representation of a client in a court or legal proceeding is not indispensable for the invocation of the privilege. That Krischer's client sought him out for purely legal advice was enough. Legal advice, after all, is by itself a legal service. It is not necessary to the existence of the privilege that the lawyer render some additional service connected with the legal advice. Nor, as we know, is it even necessary that the lawyer appear in court or contemplate some pending or future legal proceeding.

And even if it were, the engagement of an attorney to effect the return of stolen property should certainly qualify. Surely there is a public purpose served by getting stolen property in the hands of the police authorities, even if the identity of the thief is not thereby revealed. Here the consultation resulted in exactly that. Krischer advised his client to turn over the property to the state attorney or the police. A lawyer's advice can be expected to result in the return of the property if the confidentiality of the consultation is insured.

. . . [T]he mere fact that the consulted attorney acts as a "conduit" for the return of stolen property does not support the conclusion that the attorney has engaged in unprotected consultation with the person seeking the advice.[7] A legal service has been rendered just as surely as when the lawyer represents the accused thief in a criminal trial. . . .

---

7. In contrast, the attorney in Hughes testified that he had been contacted only to deliver stolen property to the police. His contact reached out for him, not because he was a lawyer, but instead because he was a good friend of many members of the police force. Unlike Krischer here, he gave no legal advice. His services amounted to a phone call informing the police that, if they were interested in the return of stolen property, they could pick it up on the attorney's front porch. Not surprisingly, the court determined that this attorney rendered no legal service, and therefore could not invoke the attorney-client privilege.

Upjohn Co. v. United States

449 U.S. 383 (1981)

Justice REHNQUIST delivered the opinion of the Court. . . .

Petitioner Upjohn Co. manufactures and sells pharmaceuticals here and abroad. In January 1976 independent accountants conducting an audit of one of Upjohn's foreign subsidiaries discovered that the subsidiary made payments to or for the benefit of foreign government officials in order to secure government business. The accountants so informed petitioner Mr. Gerard Thomas, Upjohn's Vice President, Secretary, and General Counsel. Thomas is a member of the Michigan and New York Bars, and has been Upjohn's General Counsel for 20 years. He consulted with outside counsel and R. T. Parfet, Jr., Upjohn's Chairman of the Board. It was decided that the company would conduct an internal investigation of what were termed "questionable payments." As part of this investigation the attorneys prepared a letter containing a questionnaire which was sent to "All Foreign General and Area Managers" over the Chairman's signature. The letter began by noting recent disclosures that several American companies made "possibly illegal" payments to foreign government officials and emphasized that the management needed full information concerning any such payments made by Upjohn. The letter indicated that the Chairman had asked Thomas, identified as "the company's General Counsel," "to conduct an investigation for the purpose of determining the nature and magnitude of any payments made by the Upjohn Company or any of its subsidiaries to any employee or official of a foreign government." The questionnaire sought detailed information concerning such payments. . . .

On March 26, 1976, the company voluntarily submitted a preliminary report to the Securities and Exchange Commission on Form 8-K disclosing certain questionable payments. . . . A copy of the report was simultaneously submitted to the Internal Revenue Service, which immediately began an investigation to determine the tax consequences of the payments. Special agents conducting the investigation were given lists by Upjohn of all those interviewed and all who had responded to the questionnaire . . . [but an IRS demand for the questionnaires themselves was opposed by Upjohn on the ground of privilege and work product]. . . .

Federal Rule of Evidence 501 provides that "the privilege of a witness . . . shall be governed by the principles of the common law as they may be interpreted by the courts of the United States in light of reason and experience." The attorney-client privilege is the oldest of the privileges for confidential communications known to the common law. Its purpose is to encourage full and frank communication between attorneys and their clients and thereby promote broader public interests in the observance of law and administration of justice. The privilege recognizes that sound legal advice or advocacy serves public ends and that such advice or advocacy depends upon the lawyer's being fully informed by the client. . . .

The Court of Appeals, however, considered the application of the privilege in the corporate context to present a "different problem," since the client was an inanimate entity and "only the senior management, guiding and integrating the several operations, . . . can be said to possess an identity analogous to the corporation as a whole." . . .

Such a view, we think, overlooks the fact that the privilege exists to protect not only the giving of professional advice to those who can act on it but also the giving of information to the lawyer to enable him to give sound and informed advice. . . .

In the case of the individual client the provider of information and the person who acts on the lawyer's advice are one and the same. In the corporate context, however, it will frequently be employees beyond the control group as defined by the court below—"officers and agents . . . responsible for directing [the company's] actions in response to legal advice"—who will possess the information needed by the corporation's lawyers. Middle-level—and indeed lower-level—employees can, by actions within the scope of their employment, embroil the corporation in serious legal difficulties, and it is only natural that these employees would have the relevant information needed by corporate counsel if he is adequately to advise the client with respect to such actual or potential difficulties. . . .

The control group test adopted by the court below thus frustrates the very purpose of the privilege by discouraging the communication of relevant information by employees of the client to attorneys seeking to render legal advice to the client corporation. . . .

The narrow scope given the attorney-client privilege by the court below not only makes it difficult for corporate attorneys to formulate sound advice when their client is faced with a specific legal problem but also threatens to limit the valuable efforts of corporate counsel to ensure their client's compliance with the law. In light of the vast and complicated array of regulatory legislation confronting the modern corporation, corporations, unlike most individuals, "constantly go to lawyers to find out how to obey the law". . . . But if the purpose of the attorney-client privilege is to be served, the attorney and client must be able to predict with some degree of certainty whether particular discussions will be protected. An uncertain privilege, or one which purports to be certain but results in widely varying applications by the courts, is little better than no privilege at all. The very terms of the test adopted by the court below suggest the unpredictability of its application. The test restricts the availability of the privilege to those officers who play a "substantial role" in deciding and directing a corporation's legal response. . . .

The communications at issue were made by Upjohn employees to counsel for Upjohn acting as such, at the direction of corporate superiors in order to secure legal advice from counsel. . . . Information, not available from upper-echelon management, was needed to supply a basis for legal advice concerning compliance with securities and tax laws, foreign laws, currency regulations, duties to shareholders, and potential litigation in each of these areas. The communications concerned matters within the scope of the employees' corporate duties, and the employees themselves were sufficiently aware that they were being questioned in order that the corporation could obtain legal advice. The questionnaire identified Thomas as "the company's General Counsel" and referred in its opening sentence to the possible illegality of payments such as the ones on which information was sought. A statement of policy accompanying the questionnaire clearly indicated the legal implications of the investigation. . . . It began "Upjohn will comply with all laws and regulations," and stated that commissions or payments "will not be used as a subterfuge for bribes or illegal payments" and that all payments must be "proper and legal." . . . This statement was issued to Upjohn employees worldwide, so that even those interviewees not receiving a questionnaire were aware of the legal implications of the interviews. Pursuant to explicit instructions from the Chairman of the Board, the communications were considered "highly confidential" when made, and have been kept confidential by the company. Consistent with the underlying purposes of the attorney-client privilege, these communications must be protected against compelled disclosure.

The Court of Appeals declined to extend the attorney-client privilege beyond the limits of the control group test for fear that doing so would entail severe burdens on discovery and create a broad "zone of silence" over corporate affairs. Application of the attorney-client privilege to communications such as those involved here, however, puts the adversary in no worse position than if the communications had never taken place. The privilege only protects disclosure of communications; it does not protect disclosure of the underlying facts by those who communicated with the attorney:

> [The] protection of the privilege extends only to communications and not to facts. A fact is one thing and a communication concerning that fact is an entirely different thing. The client cannot be compelled to answer the question, "What did you say or write to the attorney?" but may not refuse to disclose any relevant fact within his knowledge merely because he incorporated a statement of such fact into his communication to his attorney.

Here the Government was free to question the employees who communicated with Thomas and outside counsel. Upjohn has provided the IRS with a list of such employees, and the IRS has already interviewed some 25 of them. While it would probably be more convenient for the Government to secure the results of petitioner's internal investigation by simply subpoenaing the questionnaires and notes taken by petitioner's attorneys, such considerations of convenience do not overcome the policies served by the attorney-client privilege. . . .

. . . To the extent that the material subject to the summons is not protected by the attorney-client privilege as disclosing communications between an employee and counsel, we must reach the ruling by the Court of Appeals that the work-product doctrine does not apply to summonses.

. . . This doctrine was announced by the Court over 30 years ago in Hickman v. Taylor, 329 U.S. 495 (1947). In that case the Court rejected "an attempt, without purported necessity or justification, to secure written statements, private memoranda and personal recollections prepared or formed by an adverse party's counsel in the course of his legal duties." The Court noted that "it is essential that a lawyer work with a certain degree of privacy" and reasoned that if discovery of the material sought were permitted "much of what is now put down in writing would remain unwritten. An attorney's thoughts, heretofore inviolate, would not be his own. Inefficiency, unfairness and sharp practices would inevitably develop in the giving of legal advice and in the preparation of cases for trial. The effect on the legal profession would be demoralizing. And the interests of the clients and the cause of justice would be poorly served." . . .

. . . While conceding the applicability of the work-product doctrine, the Government asserts that it has made a sufficient showing of necessity to overcome its protections. . . .

The Government stresses that interviewees are scattered across the globe and that Upjohn has forbidden its employees to answer questions it considers irrelevant. The above-quoted language from *Hickman*, however, did not apply to "oral statements made by witnesses . . . whether presently in the form of [the attorney's] mental impressions or memoranda." As to such material the Court did "not

believe that any showing of necessity can be made under the circumstances of this case so as to justify production. If there should be a rare situation justifying production of these matters, petitioner's case is not of that type." Forcing an attorney to disclose notes and memoranda of witnesses' oral statements is particularly disfavored because it tends to reveal the attorney's mental processes.[8] . . .

The notes and memoranda sought by the Government here, however, are work product based on oral statements. If they reveal communications, they are, in this case, protected by the attorney-client privilege. To the extent they do not reveal communications, they reveal the attorneys' mental processes in evaluating the communications. As [FRCP] 26 and *Hickman* make clear, such work product cannot be disclosed simply on a showing of substantial need and inability to obtain the equivalent without undue hardship.

While we are not prepared at this juncture to say that such material is always protected by the work-product rule, we think a far stronger showing of necessity and unavailability by other means than was made by the Government or applied by the Magistrate in this case would be necessary to compel disclosure.

---

8. Thomas described his notes of the interviews as containing "what I considered to be the important questions, the substance of the responses to them, my beliefs as to the importance of these, my beliefs as to how they related to the inquiry, my thoughts as to how they related to other questions. In some instances they might even suggest other questions that I would have to ask or things that I needed to find elsewhere." . . .

▮ Lawyers and Clients:
Representing Organizations

Lawyers who provide legal services to organizations face unique ethical issues because their clients are legal fictions: entities, abstractions, or amalgams of individual interests. These legal fictions range in size from large corporations and government agencies, to small partnerships and professional and family companies. Because organizations are so pervasive, nearly every lawyer will represent one sometime in his or her legal career. In fact, at least half of all lawyers in practice represent organizations on a regular basis, either as outside counsel or inside employees.[1]

Upjohn illustrates how lawyers who represent client-organizations must consult with a wide range of individuals who are agents of the organization: employees, officers, members, directors, trustees, agents, shareholders, and the like. Each agent is a constituent of the whole, who speaks for the organization through a different role and with a distinctive view of the organization's interests, often filtered through a personal lens.

The result in *Upjohn,* upholding and defining the scope of the attorney-client and work product privileges for organizations, also demonstrates that courts have tailored specialized legal rules to fit to an entity setting. These court decisions have produced some clarity for the organization's lawyer, but determining the proper standards for identifying the entity client and affording the entity client the 5 Cs are obligations that continue to perplex the best lawyers and judges.

The Clients

Model Rule 1.13(a) adopts the entity theory for all organizations, including governments;[2] Indian tribes;[3] publicly held, professional, and closely held corporations; general and limited partnerships;[4] limited liability companies and partnerships; nonprofits; and unincorporated associations such as trade groups, condominium associations, and some unions. The entity concept assumes that an organization has a distinct legal personality apart from any individual constituent or aggregate of individual constituents within the whole. It is borrowed from corporate law, which recognizes corporations as distinct legal persons that can contract, sue, and be sued in their own right, and incur liability apart from that of its owners.

---

1. About 61,000 lawyers (approximately 10 percent of the practicing bar) serve as inside counsel to about 21,000 profit and nonprofit private sector corporations. Assn. of Corp. Counsel, *ACC 2006 Census of In-house Counsel.* Available at *http://www.acc.com/public/surveys/censussummary.pdf.,* last visited July 23, 2007; Susan Hackett, *Inside Out: An Examination of Demographic Trends in the In-House Profession,* 44 Ariz. L. Rev. 609 (2002). *See also* Deborah A. Demott, *The Discrete Roles of General Counsel,* 74 Fordham L. Rev. 955 (2005).
2. We deal with government lawyers in a subsequent note. *See* Lawyers and Clients: Governments, *infra* p. 388.
3. *See* David I. Gold, *I Know You're the Government's Lawyer, But Are You My Lawyer Too? An Exploration of the Federal-Native American Trust Relationship and Conflicts of Interest,* 19 Buff. Pub. Int. L.J. 1 (2000/2001).
4. ABA Formal Op. 91-361 (lawyer who represents a partnership represents the entity not the individual partners).

Applied to legal representation, the entity theory means that the organization's lawyer represents and has a client-lawyer relationship with the entity only, not with any constituent or group of constituents within the organization. It further recognizes that the organization must act through its "duly authorized constituents," that these constituents are not clients, and that these constituents (and the lawyer) easily can misconstrue the lawyer's role.[5]

Misunderstanding who the lawyer represents is more likely to occur in small organizations where management and ownership are merged in the same constituents. For example, in closely held corporations and small partnerships, many lawyers deal with just one person or a small group of individuals, who manage and own the business.[6] But the problem arises in even the largest of Fortune 500 companies in part because the constituents are the people the lawyer deals with and often are referred to as "clients." The confusion is further compounded when an organization's lawyer provides individual legal services to corporate officers and employees. In all of these circumstances, lawyers must clarify whether they represent the organization, the individual constituents, or both. Restatement §14, Comment f provides that in the absence of such a clarification, the reasonable expectations of the individual constituent, not the lawyer, will prevail.

Lack of clarity about client identity begins before an organization is established and has ramifications outside, as well as inside, the entity. The lawyer asked by an individual or group of individuals to establish an organization must first recognize whether the organizers are individual clients. A few jurisdictions allow lawyers and individuals to agree that the eventual entity is the only client, applying a kind of retroactive entity theory to the initial establishment of organizations.[7] According to this view, the lawyer who sets up an organization represents only the organization and not the individuals establishing it, provided the lawyer makes this fact clear from the beginning of the matter.

Representing organizations also can create "lateral dimension" problems, that is, a lawyer for one organization may be a lawyer for an affiliated company simply because one organization owns or controls another.[8] Comment [34] to Model Rule 1.7 and the Restatement §122, Comment d reject both an "all affiliates" and "no affiliates" approach[9] in favor of a three-factor analysis: (1) whether the nonclient is significantly controlled by the client, (2) whether financial loss or benefit to the nonclient will have a direct impact on the client, and (3) whether confidential information of the nonclient will be disclosed.[10]

---

5. William H. Simon, *Whom (Or What) Does the Organization's Lawyer Represent?: An Anatomy of Intraclient Conflict*, 91 Cal. L. Rev. 57 (2003).
6. Darian M. Ibrahim, *Solving the Everyday Problem of Client Identity in the Context of Closely Held Businesses*, 56 Ala. L. Rev. 181 (2004).
7. *See* Jesse v. Danforth, 485 N.W.2d 63 (Wis. 1992) (physicians who retain a law firm to organize a medical corporation were not individual clients where attorney's involvement with the physicians was directly related to the corporation and the medical corporation was eventually incorporated because the entity rule applied retroactively); St. Bar of Ariz. Op. 02-06.
8. Charles W. Wolfram, *Corporate-Family Conflicts*, 2 J. Inst. Stud. Leg. Eth. 295 (1999). Wolfram points out that financial statements required by federal securities law require information about "affliates." *Id.* at 304 n.30.
9. *Id.* at 328-331.
10. *See also* ABA Formal Op. 95-390, a decision from which one of the authors continues to dissent.

The 5 Cs

Control Once an organization is created, organizational lawyers must understand who controls decision making for the entity. The organization's organic rules should identify this authority, and if they do not, the lawyer must make sure that any ambiguity is addressed by properly authorized groups or individuals. Failure to do so can mean that the lawyer's work is not properly authorized or, worse, that the lawyer assists a constituent's breach of fiduciary duty to the organization. For example, lawyers who represent unincorporated associations might need to clarify whether the law that governs a specific client deprives group members with whom the lawyer deals of authority to represent others in the group.[11]

As with individual clients, lawyers should accept and abide by decisions made by constituents of organizational clients that the lawyer may believe unwise, as long as the lawyer has exercised independent professional judgment and rendered candid advice about the matter.[12] Lawyers are not required to, and in fact, should not second-guess business judgments made by an organization's agents, but must identify legal obligations of the client and, when clear violations arise, must not capitulate to a constituent's decision, and must communicate with other constituents, pursuing the matter further.

Communication Model Rule 1.13(b) makes plain that a lawyer who knows that an agent or constituent is violating a legal obligation of the organization must not remain silent and, if necessary, must pursue the matter beyond that person or group to a higher authority in the organization, including the highest authority that can act on the matter. This means that the organization's lawyer must first communicate to the appropriate constituent that a clear violation of law has or is occurring. If the constituent does not agree, referral of the matter for an independent legal opinion can help clarify the seriousness of the violation. If this confirms the lawyer's opinion but does not change the constituent's decision, then the lawyer must urge reassessment, by taking clear violations of law up the authority ladder, all the way to the highest authority that can act for the organization, for example, the board of directors of a corporation. Continuing crimes or frauds require the lawyer to withdraw, and to notify the highest authority of the reason for the withdrawal.[13]

Competence Identifying an organizational client requires understanding the law that regulates the entity. Advising such a client often requires specialized legal knowledge and skill. For example, although individual persons can appear pro se in litigation, most organizations cannot be represented by nonlawyer

---

11. *E.g.*, FRCP 17(b), which allows an unincorporated association to sue and be sued in its common name whether or not recognized as a separate entity under state law.
12. William T. Allen, *Corporate Governance and a Business Lawyer's Duty of Independence*, 38 Suffolk U. L. Rev. 1 (2004).
13. MR 1.2(d), 1.13(e).

constituents.[14] Similarly, although FRCP 17(b) allows unincorporated associations to sue and be sued in their common names, federal diversity of citizenship jurisdiction requires the association's capacity to sue or be sued be determined by state law.[15] Lawyers for organizations also must be able to advise small business owners under what circumstances the corporate veil might be pierced,[16] and advise constituents about their fiduciary duties to the organization.[17]

Beyond the body of law that regulates the organization's structure itself, lawyers for business organizations often need basic accounting knowledge to properly advise clients.[18] Organizational lawyers also must respond to increased legal regulation of business practice itself, as well as its globalization; in other words, be prepared to meet the organization's need for understanding foreign as well as domestic law.[19] Given this complex body of legal regulation, lawyers who represent organizations must know how to recognize their own lack of expertise and when to ask outside or inside counsel for assistance. Failing to do so can violate a duty of care to both the organization as well as to constituents who reasonably rely on the lawyer's legal advice.

Confidentiality While *Upjohn* makes clear that organizations are entitled to testimonial privileges, and Model Rule 1.13 combined with 1.6 extends confidentiality to entities, it is not always easy to understand or explain the precise scope of that obligation to clients and constituents. Of course, lawyers must communicate with constituent-agents who speak to the organization's lawyer for the purpose of receiving legal advice. But these agents easily can assume that they are speaking to "their" lawyer. This explains why a lawyer's assurance of confidentiality or privilege should include a clarification that confidentiality extends to the organization, not to any individuals within it, and that what individual constituents tell the lawyer may very likely be reported to others within the organization.[20]

The 2003 amendments to Model Rule 1.13 arose in the wake of the Enron scandal and include a grant of special discretion to an organization's lawyer to disclose confidential information outside of the organization in addition to

---

14. United States v. W. Processing Co., 734 F. Supp. 930 (W.D. Wash. 1990) (the only proper representative for a corporation or partnership is a licensed lawyer regardless of the unlicensed agent's close association with the entity); In re Global Constr. & Supply Co., 126 B.R. 573 (E.D. Mo. 1991) (bankruptcy petition filed by corporate president null and void, even where corporation later retained a lawyer to represent it).
15. Charles Alan Wright, Arthur R. Miller & Mary Kay Kane, *Federal Practice and Procedure Civ.* 2d §1861 (West 2007).
16. Kurt A. Strasser, *Piercing the Veil in Corporate Groups*, 37 Conn. L. Rev. 637 (2005).
17. *E.g.*, American Law Institute, *Principles of the Law of Nonprofit Organizations* §300 (Tentative Draft No. 1, Mar. 19, 2007); Larry E. Ribstein, *Are Partners Fiduciaries?*, 2005 Ill. L. Rev. 209.
18. Lawrence A. Cunningham, *Sharing Accounting's Burden: Business Lawyers in Enron's Dark Shadows*, 57 Bus. Law. 1421 (2002).
19. Milton C. Regan, Jr., *Professional Responsibility and the Corporate Lawyer*, 13 Geo. J. Leg. Ethics 197 (2000).
20. *E.g.*, Westinghouse Elec. Corp. v. Kerr-McGee Corp., 580 F.2d 1311 (7th Cir. 1978), *cert. denied*, 439 U.S. 955 (1978) (law firm that represented trade association and received confidential information from member of trade association disqualified from subsequent representation against member).

exceptions already found in Model Rule 1.6.[21] Model Rule 1.13(c) allows, but does not require, an organization's lawyer to disclose information the lawyer reasonably believes necessary to prevent substantial injury to the organization, if the lawyer's efforts in pursuing a matter up the organizational ladder have failed to prevent the organization's clear violation of law.[22] This exception does not encompass lawyers who have been hired to investigate or defend a company against allegations of past wrongdoing. But it does allow a lawyer who investigates, finds a clear legal violation, and unsuccessfully takes the matter up the organizational ladder to disclose when the board refuses to take remedial action that the lawyer reasonably believes is necessary to prevent substantial injury to the organization.

Dealing with an organization's confidentiality becomes doubly difficult in situations such as *Upjohn*, where lawyers are inquiring into possible wrongdoing in an organization, often pursuant to an ongoing or threatened governmental investigation. To clarify the situation, the lawyer speaking to an individual employee should make clear that the conversation is privileged and confidential, but that the privilege belongs to the organization, not the individual. Thus the company, through its duly authorized constituents, can waive the privilege, perhaps in response to a governmental demand for cooperation, and the information provided by the employee in the company's waived material could later be used by the government to provide the basis for an individual indictment.

Given this danger, lawyers who conduct corporate investigations where potential criminal liability exists read Model Rules 1.13(f) and 4.3 as requiring some kind of "Miranda" warning or explanation to employees to prevent any misunderstanding of the lawyer's role. The warning should include:

1. Identification of the lawyer, the client, and the matter;
2. Identification of the client organization's expectations (cooperate and tell the truth);
3. A basic explanation of confidentiality: that anything the employee tells the lawyer is confidential outside of the organization, but not within it, and the organization has the right to decide when to disclose to outsiders in litigation or otherwise;
4. An explanation that the lawyer does not (or does?) represent the employee; and
5. An explanation that the employee may retain separate counsel (including if available, the right of the employee to such counsel at the employer's expense).[23]

21. Lawrence A. Hamermesh, *The ABA Task Force on Corporate Responsibility and the 2003 Changes to the Model Rules of Professional Conduct*, 17 Geo. J. Leg. Ethics 35 (2003).
22. Richard W. Painter, *Toward a Market for Lawyer Disclosure Services: In Search of Optimal Whistleblowing Rules*, 63 Geo. Wash. L. Rev. 221 (1995).
23. *See* Nancy J. Moore, *Conflicts of Interest of In-House Counsel: Issues Emerging from the Expanding Role of the Attorney-Employee*, 39 S. Tex. L. Rev. 497 (1998); Sarah Helene Duggin, *Internal Corporate Investigations: Legal Ethics, Professionalism and the Employee Interview*, 2003 Colum. Bus. L. Rev. 859.

The federal government has precipitated the development of these corporate Miranda warnings by promulgating a series of internal Justice Department policies that allow consideration of an organization's willingness to waive the privilege as a factor in preventing criminal indictment of the organization.[24] Because indictment means sure business failure in many situations, organizations see no alternative to waiving the privilege, which means turning over all records of inside investigations by corporate counsel. Both employees and organizations oppose these governmental tactics, but as long as they persist, the organization and its employees are potentially adverse to each other. That, of course, triggers Model Rule 1.13(f)'s affirmative obligation to clarify, and where the employee is not represented, Model Rule 4.3's requirement of reasonable efforts to avoid misunderstanding, including the advice to seek independent counsel.[25]

Conflict of Interest Resolution   These obligations to explain both the identity of the client and the organization's, rather than the constituent's, right to confidentiality are triggered by the fact that the interests of employee and employer may conflict. In an internal investigation of wrongdoing, for example, the lawyer hopes not to find any, but when she does, the organization may be best served by distancing itself and perhaps disciplining the "rogue" employees. Since organizations only work through agents who may not always pursue the company's interests, the potential for conflict between agent and organization permeates the representation. This explains why the lawyer must travel up the organizational ladder in communicating competently with the client. It also explains why an organization's lawyers have affirmative obligations to clarify misunderstandings.

Model Rule 1.13(g) does allow the organization's lawyer to represent constituents as well, subject of course to the same loyalty obligations imposed by Model Rule 1.7, which we will take up in the Chapters 8 and 9. *Perez* offers a good example of such an initial joint representation.[26] Note that when Mr. Perez admitted failing to check the truck brakes on the morning of the accident (as required by company policy), the lawyers realized that his interests directly conflicted with those of his employer. This required the lawyers to withdraw

---

24. The most recent iteration is the McNulty Memo. Available at *http://www.usdoj.gov/dag/speeches/2006/mcnulty_memo.pdf*. Last visited July 23, 2007.
25. United States v. Stein (*Stein IV*), 495 F. Supp. 2d 390, 427-428 (S.D.N.Y. 2007) (in promulgating Thompson Memorandum, DOJ "deliberately or callously prevented many of these defendants from obtaining funds for their defense that they lawfully would have had absent the government's interference . . . thereby foreclose[ing them] from presenting the defenses they wished to present and, in some cases, even depriv[ing] them of counsel of their choice. . . . The responsibility for the dismissal of this indictment as to thirteen defendants lies with the government."); United States v. Stein (*Stein II*), 440 F. Supp. 2d 315 (S.D.N.Y. 2006) (corporate employer's economic pressure on employees under Thompson memorandum justified suppression of employees' statements that would not otherwise have been made absent government coercion); United States v. Stein, 435 F. Supp. 2d 330 (S.D.N.Y. 2006) (*Stein I*) (government violated employee's Fifth and Sixth Amendment rights by causing corporate employer, under threat of indictment, to apply economic pressure on employees to make full disclosure to the government or face firing and loss of corporate payment of legal fees).
26. *Perez v. Kirk & Carrigan, supra* p. 165; Lawyers' Roles: The Directive Lawyer and Fiduciary Duty, *supra* p. 168.

from further representation of Mr. Perez. *Perez* illustrates that whenever this occurs, another conflict develops: The organization's lawyer has a Model Rule 1.4 obligation to share the co-clients' information. At the same time the lawyer must protect the confidentiality of each joint client.

Of course, the clients can consent to subsequent disclosure of information. Increasingly, this issue is raised at the onset of a joint employee-employer representation if the employer seeks an advanced waiver of conflict of interest document, in which the parties agree that if the lawyer must withdraw from representing one party, the lawyer may continue to represent the other (usually the employer).[27] *Perez* illustrates the difficulty of proceeding without obtaining such a waiver, either before or after the joint representation proceeds. It also teaches that even when granted initially, such a waiver will not be adequate without a full understanding of the confidentiality obligations of the lawyer between the joint clients.[28] The clients could decide to disclose everything to each other, or not to disclose anything shared in individual confidence with the lawyer, as occurred in *Perez*. We will explore these issues further in Chapter 9.[29]

Lawyers for organizations must respond to another kind of conflict as well. They must recognize dual roles, which involve both legal advice and business judgment, such as general counsel-vice president or lawyer and board member of the entity.[30] For example, the lawyer acting as lawyer will cloak the representation in privilege; the lawyer acting as business decision maker will not.[31]

The Bounds of the Law

The in-house counsel lawyer-employee has only one client, the organization, and all financial rewards are provided by that same client, which can make it very difficult to remain objective in the face of client demands.[32]

Modern organizations operate in a heavily regulated climate. This means that their lawyers must be especially sensitive to two massive bodies of law: the criminal law and the law of fraud, both of which we explore in greater detail in the next chapter.[33] Whenever a client crime or fraud occurs, the Model Rules create lawyer obligations to clients and third parties. Organizational lawyers must understand these legal limits not only to give competent legal advice to their clients, but also to assess their own conduct under the applicable lawyer code.

---

27. Pa. Bar Assn. Op. 2006-200 (lawyers who contemplate representing both employer and employee should provide complete and objective disclosure of the risks and advantages of joint representation, reach an understanding about confidential information, and obtain written informed consent to the joint representation).

28. *E.g.*, ABA Formal Op. 05-436 (Informed Consent to Future Conflicts of Interest).

29. *See* Problem 9-5 and *A. v. B.*, p. 355.

30. ABA Sect. of Litig., *The Lawyer-Director: Implications for Independence: Report of the Task Force on the Independent Lawyer* (1998); Susanna M. Kim, *Dual Identities and Dueling Obligations: Preserving Independence in Corporate Representation*, 68 Tenn. L. Rev. 179 (2001).

31. *See* Nancy J. Moore, *Conflicts of Interest of In-House Counsel: Issues Emerging from the Expanding Role of the Attorney-Employee*, 39 S. Tex. L. Rev. 497 (1998).

32. Deborah L. Rhode & Paul D. Paton, *Lawyers, Ethics, and Enron*, in Nancy B. Rapoport & Bala G. Dharan, eds., *Enron: Corporate Fiascos and Their Implications*, 641 (Foundation 2004).

33. *See* The Bounds of the Law: Client Fraud, *infra* p. 237; The Bounds of the Law: Criminal Conduct, *infra* p. 254.

Beyond professional discipline, other specialized legal requirements also shape the life of modern lawyers in some organizations. One example is the Sarbanes-Oxley Act, which parallels and makes more specific the 2003 amendments to Model Rule 1.13 for lawyers who represent public companies.[34] Both the statute and accompanying regulations require lawyers for public companies "to report evidence of a material violation of securities law" to those within the corporate family. A lawyer's duty under this law is triggered by a "reasonable belief" that a material violation of securities law or breach of fiduciary by a corporate constituent has occurred or is about to occur. When that happens, the lawyer has a duty to report the violation up the corporate ladder to the CEO and eventually to the board of directors if appropriate action has not been taken. Lawyers who violate these regulations face SEC disbarment, that is, they would lose their ability to prepare documents or otherwise appear before the SEC.[35]

Although the scope of reportable violations in this law seems to parallel Model Rule 1.13's "violation of law" language, the "reasonable belief" reporting threshold in Sarbanes-Oxley is triggered by more conduct than Model Rule 1.13(b)'s knowledge standard. Sarbanes also parallels Model Rule 1.13(d)'s discretionary disclosure provision by allowing lawyers to inform the SEC of material violations to prevent or rectify them. These regulations apply to both inside and outside counsel who represent the public company in any matter, and provide for slightly different reporting procedures for subordinate and supervisory lawyers, a parallel to Model Rules 5.1 and 5.2.[36]

Conclusion

The ethical obligations of lawyers who represent organizations are complicated by the nature of organizations themselves. Legal fictions operate through agents, and agents may misunderstand their own role in the organization, the lawyer's role in representing the organization, or the organization's obligations to employees and third parties and vice versa. Lawyers can work their way through this thicket by remembering to identify their clients, clarifying this identity to their client's constituents when necessary, and providing the 5 Cs to the organizations they represent. They also need to be aware of specialized laws that create additional or particularized bounds to their representation of certain organizational clients.

D. Express or Implied Authority / Waiver

Of course, clients can decide for themselves whether to allow the use or disclosure of confidential information. Utilitarians note that the legal system

---

34. Karl. A. Groskaufmanis, *Climbing "Up the Ladder": Corporate Counsel and the SEC's Reporting Requirement for Lawyers*, 89 Cornell L. Rev. 511 (2004).
35. Lewis D. Lowenfels, Alan R. Bromberg & Michael J. Sullivan, *Attorneys as Gatekeepers: SEC Actions Against Lawyers in the Age of Sarbanes-Oxley*, 37 U. Tol. L. Rev. 877 (2006).
36. Roger C. Cramton, George M. Cohen & Susan P. Koniak, *Legal and Ethical Duties of Lawyers After Sarbanes-Oxley*, 49 Vill. L. Rev. 725 (2004); Thomas D. Morgan, *Sarbanes-Oxley: A Complication, Not a Contribution, in the Effort to Improve Corporate Lawyers' Professional Conduct*, 17 Geo. J. Leg. Ethics 1 (2003).

requires information to function, and therefore clients who wish to take advantage of the system's protections or allowances must agree as a condition of using the system to supply it with some information. Deontologists characterize client consent as the client's autonomous authorization to disclosure or use of the information. Agency law rests on such a consensual foundation, and protects extensions of autonomy by granting individuals the opportunity to act through others.

Problems

6-8. Martyn recommends that Martyn & Fox add the following clause to all personal injury retainer agreements. Should Fox agree?

"Client agrees to allow Martyn & Fox discretion to disclose any information relating to the representation whenever Martyn & Fox determines such action will promote the best interests of Client."

6-9. What may (must) Fox do if Client, in the course of estate planning, tells Fox that she is terminally ill and plans on taking a lethal dose of medication as soon as she signs the documents?

6-10 Can Martyn & Fox turn over notes of 25 interviews with maintenance workers to the Justice Department as part of a settlement on behalf of our corporate client?

6-11. Can Fox testify to privileged communications with old CEO of our client, if new CEO of our corporate client directs him to do so?

6-12. Martyn & Fox are ready to try the High Energy Case against Arthur Touche and five former High Energy directors. Fox's secretary hands him a thick fax with a cover page that says: "To all Defense Counsel. Privileged and Confidential. Summary of Decision Quest's Jury Profile." What should Fox do? What if the fax reveals misconduct by the other side? What if the same document is sent to us in a plain brown envelope with a note "Knew you'd find this interesting"?

Consider: Model Rules 1.0(e), 1.6, 1.13 (c). 1.14, 4.4(b)
Model Code DR 4-101(C)(1)
RLGL §§19, 24, 61-62, 78-81, 86, 91-92

In re Pressly

628 A.2d 927 (Vt. 1993)

PER CURIAM.

Respondent Thomas Pressly appeals from a decision of the Professional Conduct Board recommending a public reprimand as discipline for his misconduct in violating Disciplinary Rule (DR) 4-101 (B)(1) ("a lawyer shall not knowingly . . . reveal a confidence or secret of his client"). DR 1-102(A)(1); ("a lawyer shall not violate a disciplinary rule." . . . We affirm and impose the recommended sanction.

In 1989, respondent, a member of the Vermont bar since 1975, represented complainant in connection with relief from abuse and divorce proceedings. Complainant informed respondent that her husband had a history [of] alcoholism, battering, and abuse. After a hearing at which she was represented by respondent, complainant was granted a temporary order requiring her husband to refrain from abusing her, and, by stipulation of the parties, temporary custody of the couple's two children with supervised visitation by the father. About a month later, respondent filed a divorce complaint on his client's behalf. The parties negotiated an agreement under which complainant would retain temporary custody of the children and her husband would be allowed unsupervised visitation. Complainant, on respondent's advice, reluctantly agreed to the visitation provision.

At that time, complainant told respondent that she was being harassed by her husband, that his alcoholism was a continuing problem, and that she wanted the children's visits with their father to be supervised. Respondent advised her, however, that there were insufficient legal grounds to require supervised visits. Complainant continued to press respondent to help her prevent her husband from continuing unsupervised visitation, but no motion was filed seeking supervised visitation.

Near the end of August 1989, complainant told respondent her suspicions, based on consultation with a counselor, that her nine-year-old daughter had been sexually abused by the father. According to the counselor, a "yellow flag" went up when she observed several symptoms of abuse. Complainant told respondent her suspicions, the basis for them, and her plan to arrange for a doctor's appointment for the daughter, which she thought might provide needed evidence against the father. She asked that respondent not discuss her suspicions or plans with her husband's lawyer.

In response to opposing counsel's question as to why the wife continued to request supervised visitation and whether sexual abuse was an issue in the case, respondent, notwithstanding his client's request, revealed to him the suspicions of sexual abuse. Respondent then asked the husband's lawyer not to communicate this information to the husband.* The next day, opposing counsel wrote respondent stating, "I mentioned to [my client] the representation [your client] had made to you about their daughter making statements to her counselor about sexual abuse. . . . [They] are totally unfounded and he views them to be a blatant attempt on the part of [your client] to manufacture evidence to keep him away from his children."

Complainant confronted her attorney about the disclosure, and was told by respondent that he provided the information in response to questions from opposing counsel. She

---

* Complainant's testimony indicated that she directed her attorney not to disclose anything about sexual abuse to the husband. No mention was made of the opposing counsel. Although respondent points out this distinction as being contrary to the findings, we fail to understand its significance. The only ethical way respondent could communicate about the case was through the husband's lawyer. DR 7-104(A)(1) (lawyer not to communicate directly with adverse party). Respondent could not reasonably expect husband's counsel to keep the wife's confidences unrevealed. Respondent acknowledged that if he had been given similar information by opposing counsel, he would have disclosed it to his client, notwithstanding a request not to do so.

discharged respondent and retained new counsel. After the disclosure, complainant perceived that her husband became increasingly uncooperative, which heightened her sense of fear and anxiety and created emotional distress.

The report of the panel appointed to hear the wife's complaint was adopted verbatim by the Board, which agreed that respondent had violated Disciplinary Rule 4-101 of the Code of Professional Responsibility. In approving a public reprimand, the Board agreed that respondent, although he did not intend to harm his client, knew the disclosure he made was confidential. . . .

Whatever mental state we ascribe to respondent's conduct, he should have known not to disclose his client's confidence. He testified before the panel that he knew the information was to be held in confidence, but felt that when pressured as to why his client wanted supervised visitation, informing opposing counsel was best. When asked whether he had thought of ending the conversation with counsel by stating that an attorney-client privilege precluded him from revealing anything further, he stated "If I say that, I think I'm letting the cat out of the bag also." He understood that he should not have revealed what his client had requested him to hold in confidence. . . .

The Board gave respondent the benefit of the doubt on whether he knew that his disclosure to opposing counsel would cause his client anguish or jeopardize her case. If respondent did not actually know that his conduct would injure his client— his conduct being negligent because of his good intention (good faith) in making the disclosure—he still knew

that his conduct violated a confidence. . . .

The Board found that complainant suffered "emotional distress" as a result of the disclosure, which "heightened her level of fear and anxiety. . . ." As the Board discussed, Complainant was shocked by this news. She had relied upon respondent to protect the confidentiality of this information. She felt that Respondent had betrayed her trust. . . .

Respondent's conduct was injurious to his client to the extent that his actions caused her emotional distress. We do not find, however, that the disclosure had an adverse impact on the pending litigation although there was a potential for such injury. . . .

We adhere to the Board's recommendation. Respondent's infraction violated a core component of the attorney-client relationship, of which he, as an attorney in practice in this state for approximately sixteen years at the time of the infraction, should have been well aware. Respondent does not contend, nor does the record reflect, that his disclosure was intended or necessary to protect the child. His hope that opposing counsel would not disclose the information to the husband demonstrates naiveté, rather than any intent to simply disregard his client's confidence. Consequently, we agree with the Board that a suspension would be too harsh. On the other hand, a private admonition would unduly depreciate the violation.

The decision of the Professional Conduct Board is affirmed and its recommendation for discipline is approved. Thomas Pressly is publicly reprimanded for violation of DR 4-101(B)(1) of the Code of Professional Responsibility by knowingly revealing a confidence of his client.

United States v. Citgo Petroleum Corporation

2007 U.S. Dist. LEXIS 27986 (S.D. Tex.)

JOHN D. RAINEY, United States District Judge. . . .

FACTUAL BACKGROUND

Citgo became the subject of a criminal environmental investigation by the Department of Justice and the federal grand jury in early 2003. The investigation centered around Citgo's alleged mismanagement of its benzene waste operations at its Corpus Christi refinery in violation of the Clean Air Act. In response to several grand jury subpoenas *duces tecum* issued to Citgo, it produced thousands of documents, including privileged documents.

Citgo first learned of the inadvertently disclosed documents on December 15, 2005 when the Government subpoenaed Citgo's Senior Counsel claiming Citgo had waived its privilege. The Government provided Citgo's counsel at the time, Terence Lynam, with the documents upon which it based its waiver argument. In response, Lynam wrote a detailed letter on December 28, 2005 explaining that the documents either were not privileged or were inadvertently disclosed and requested their return. The Government refused. Citgo filed its motion to compel the return of the documents on March 1, 2007. . . .

DISCUSSION

The attorney-client privilege prevents disclosure of confidential communications between an attorney and client made while seeking or rendering legal services. Upjohn Co. v. United States, 449 U.S. 383, 389,

(1981). Its purpose is to encourage full and frank communication between attorneys and their clients, thereby promoting broader public interests in the observance of law and administration of justice. The privilege applies equally when the client is a corporation. The party asserting the attorney-client privilege must prove that the confidentiality of the communications ha[s] been preserved; otherwise, the client "forfeits" his claim to the privilege. Disclosure of attorney-client communications to a third party who lacks a common legal interest generally waives the attorney-client privilege.

In determining whether an inadvertent disclosure waives the attorney-client privilege, courts must consider the circumstances surrounding the disclosure on a case-by-case basis. Alldread v. City of Grenada, 988 F.2d 1425, 1434 (5th Cir. 1993). The court should consider several factors, none of which are dispositive: (1) the reasonableness of precautions taken to prevent disclosure; (2) the amount of time taken to remedy the error; (3) the scope of the discovery; (4) the extent of the disclosure; and (5) the overriding issue of fairness.

The work product protection can also be waived. The work-product doctrine protects documents prepared in anticipation of litigation, including a "lawyer's research, analysis of legal theories, mental impressions, notes, and memoranda of witnesses' statements." Hickman v. Taylor, 329 U.S. 495 (1947). For a document to be prepared in "anticipation of litigation," litigation does not necessarily have to be imminent, but "the primary motivating purpose behind the creation of the document [must be] to aid in possible future litigation." Excluded from work product protection are "materials assembled in the ordinary course of business or pursuant to public requirements unrelated to litigation." Fed. R. Civ. P. 26(b)(3).

"[B]ecause the work product privilege looks to the vitality of the adversary system rather than simply seeking to preserve confidentiality, it is not automatically waived by the disclosure to a third party." Waiver of work product protection only results if the work product is disclosed to an adversary. To waive work product protection, the disclosure must be inconsistent with maintaining the secrecy of an attorney's trial preparation.

The issue presented to this Court is whether Citgo's inadvertent disclosure of privileged documents warrants a full subject matter waiver of its privilege as it relates to Citgo's compliance with benzene regulations. The Government claims Citgo waived its work product and attorney-client privileges relating to "all information on the issue of benzene waste management" by producing several documents containing privileged information. Citgo argues a full subject matter waiver is inappropriate because only four documents out of thousands were inadvertently produced pursuant to the grand jury subpoenas. Citgo requests the return of the four privileged documents and argues that the Government has mischaracterized several of the documents it claims are privileged and therefore cannot base its waiver argument on those documents. Specifically, Citgo asserts that many of the

documents cited by the Government were not privileged because they were related to the audits and compliance activities Citgo created in the ordinary course of business. Citgo also posits further reasons why the Government's waiver argument should fail, namely that it waited almost two years after the disclosure of the privileged documents before asserting waiver, and it violated its ethical obligations by failing to notify Citgo promptly once it discovered the privileged nature of the documents.

The positions of the parties on the status of the privileged nature of these documents presents almost a reversal of roles from the usual privilege disputes. The burden of demonstrating whether a document is privileged is placed on the holder of the privilege. However, in this case, the Government is asserting the privilege for several documents where Citgo disclaims privilege. Of course, the Government takes this position in order to bolster its waiver argument. Because of this unique situation, the Court will not discuss the privileged nature of all the documents cited by the Government, but will only address the four inadvertently produced documents. Both parties have effectively agreed that at least portions of the inadvertently disclosed documents are privileged. The following four documents are the inadvertently disclosed privileged documents:

(1) Handwritten notes. Notes of meeting between outside counsel, Susan Harris, and Citgo's environmental office on October 1, 1999. Citgo maintains that these notes were inadvertently disclosed and are privileged because they refer to communications with Susan Harris, which should have been redacted.

(2) Attorney Questions. Typewritten questions prepared by Susan Harris for a meeting with senior management titled "Citgo Benzene Waste NESHAPS Issues". The document also includes some handwritten notations. Citgo denies that the handwritten notes are privileged.

(3) Sidley Memo. An environmental management systems review conducted by Sidley & Austin. The document was on Sidley & Austin letterhead and was solicited by Citgo in order to respond to the Texas Natural Resources Conservation Commission's Notice of Enforcement.

(4) A near verbatim copy of the Sidley Memo contained in an undated draft of its 2001 HS&E Excellence Review report.

A. Waiver of Privilege

The Court must consider the *Alldread* factors to determine first if Citgo's inadvertent disclosures constitute a waiver of privilege. Evidence of multiple disclosures on multiple occasions leads the Court to believe that Citgo did not take reasonable precautions to prevent disclosure. This factor weighs against Citgo. While Citgo maintains that it thoroughly reviewed the documents before producing them, several facts surrounding the disclosures demonstrate that Citgo did not take reasonable precautions to preserve the confidentiality of the documents. First, Terence Lynam, Citgo's counsel during the grand jury investigation explained in his affidavit that it was Citgo's practice to label documents related to internal environmental audits "privileged"—whether they were privileged or not—because the legal department provided assistance

with the audits. This practice of "mislabeling" documents likely led to the inadvertent disclosure in this case. Although Citgo disclaims the importance of the privilege labels, marking a document "privileged" indicates that the document is worthy of close scrutiny. The failure of Citgo to carefully review these documents labeled "privilege" supports the finding that Citgo did not act reasonably to prevent disclosure. Further, each document produced in response to the grand jury subpoenas was Bates stamped. Presumably, these documents were subjected to some form of review, but obviously the steps taken were not adequate to prevent the privileged documents from being disclosed. Citgo, under the direction of current counsel, also reproduced the same documents on a disk to the Government during discovery. Before copying the disk for the Government, Citgo had another opportunity to withhold the documents they claimed were privileged. Moreover, allowing not one, but two versions of the Sidley Memo to be disclosed evidences the carelessness on Citgo's part in properly preserving its privilege. The multiple disclosures, by different law firms, at different times, before and after the Government's claim of waiver demonstrates the lack of reasonable efforts expended by Citgo to protect the confidentiality of these documents.

The amount of time taken to remedy the error also does not weigh in favor of Citgo. The first inadvertent disclosure occurred around July, 2003 during the grand jury investigation. Had the Government not presented its waiver argument in December, 2005, Citgo would have never known it inadvertently disclosed the documents. Citgo did promptly request the return of the documents at that point in December, 2005. However, despite the Government's repeated refusals to return the documents, it still took Citgo over a year to seek relief from the Court. Citgo's failure to take steps to effectuate the return of the documents until March, 2007 dooms its late attempt to assert the privilege.

Next, there is no question that the scope of the discovery was voluminous. There have been thousands, and perhaps hundreds of thousands, documents produced in this case. Citgo's "lost in the shuffle" argument would have greater weight had it not twice disclosed the privilege documents in different forms at different times. And while thousands of documents were produced, the number of documents produced that were labeled "privileged" was far less. A Government investigator estimated that of 27 file drawers of documents retained by the Government in this case from Citgo, only one and a half file drawers contained documents labeled "privileged." The Court does not discount that the overall scope of discovery was voluminous in this case, but when considering only those documents labeled "privileged," the extent of the disclosure is far more significant than Citgo would like to lead this Court to believe.

Finally, the overriding issue of fairness does not save Citgo from waiver. Citgo argues a waiver should not be found in this case because the Government violated its ethical duties when it did not timely notify Citgo that it had potentially privileged documents. Citgo also claims the Government's waiver argument is untimely because it waited for almost two years after the documents were disclosed to seek a waiver. While the

Court does not believe the Government handled its obligations with the utmost timeliness and candor, the Court cannot ignore the fact that Citgo failed to preserve its privilege. It was Citgo's burden to maintain the confidentiality of the privilege documents, and in that respect it failed. The Goverment's behavior will not exonerate Citgo's failures. Further, the essential function of the privilege, which is to protect a client's confidence, has been lost, leaving the privilege with no legitimate function to perform. After considering the *Alldread* factors, the Court finds that Citgo has waived its privilege by inadvertently disclosing privileged material to the Government. The Court will not relieve Citgo of the consequences of their carelessness because "the circumstances surrounding the disclosure do not clearly demonstrate that continued protection is warranted."

B. Scope of Waiver

Generally, the "disclosure of any significant portion of a confidential communication waives the privilege as to the whole." Nguyen v. Excel Corp., 197 F.3d 200, 208 (5th Cir. 1999); United States v. El Paso, 682 F.2d 530, 540 (5th Cir. 1982). This general principle has applied to circumstances in which the holder of the privilege voluntarily discusses privileged communications with a third party or selectively discloses privileged information for its tactical benefit. For example, in *Nguyen,* the executives (i.e. the holder of the privilege) voluntarily testified about attorney-client communications and the legal research undertaken by their attorneys in order to advance its defense that it had a good faith belief in the legality of its practices in a Fair Labor Standards Act suit. The Fifth Circuit held the defendant employer, through its executives, had waived its attorney-client privilege by selectively disclosing portions of privileged communications. Similarly, in *El Paso,* the Fifth Circuit found that the taxpayer corporation had waived its attorney client privilege relating to a tax pool analysis by disclosing that information to accountants, despite the fact that the attorneys and accountants worked in conjunction on the tax returns. In both cases, the Court found that the disclosing party had waived its privilege as to the whole subject matter of the communication. Thus, a broad subject matter waiver is often justified on the grounds that such waiver is warranted if the holder of the privilege relies on the advice of counsel as part of its defense or claim, or selectively discloses portions of privileged communications in their own self-interest, or by some other means intentionally waives privilege.

The primary distinction between this case and the cases permitting broad subject matter waiver is the inadvertent nature of Citgo's disclosure. Overall the treatment of the inadvertent and scope of waiver issues should be analyzed in terms of fairness and the "principal concern is selective use of privileged material to garble the truth, which mandates giving the opponent access to related privileged material to set the record straight. Citgo was not attempting to make strategic use of this information and has gained no tactical advantage by disclosing this privileged information. In those contexts where privileged information is selectively disclosed for strategic reasons or as part of a claim or defense, it absolutely would prejudice the opposing party to not have full access to all the privileged communications on the same subject. However, the Government in this case will suffer no prejudice by only having access to the specific documents disclosed. The Court believes this ruling strikes the appropriate balance between condemning Citgo's carelessness with respect to preserving the confidentiality of these specific documents and upholding the important and valued policies underlying the attorney-client privilege. Therefore, the Court finds the inadvertent disclosure of the four privileged documents does not waive the privilege with respect to the entire subject matter of the representation, i.e. all issues related to benzene waste management.

Chapter 7

Confidentiality Exceptions

Exceptions to confidentiality have coexisted with the obligation since its inception. If the rationales that support the obligation of confidentiality in the first place make sense, then the same policies should justify exceptions to the duty. In other words, if preserving confidentiality promotes efficient functioning of the legal system, an exception can be justified to restore or promote effective operation of the system of justice. Similarly, if preserving client confidences is deemed important to promote trust or privacy in the client-lawyer relationship, exceptions can be justified where preserving client confidences in fact create a breach of trust or foster misuse of the relationship to violate legal norms.

A. Physical Harm

Confidentiality seems less important when another human imperative such as life itself is at stake. Here, a utilitarian would argue that lawyers guarantee confidentiality in part to encourage clients to blow off steam, which affords lawyers an opportunity to counsel clients to abstain from vigilante justice. Occasionally this goal fails, either because the lawyer cannot talk the client out of dangerous behavior, or because the client describes the behavior of someone with whom the lawyer has no relationship. In that situation, the lawyer is justified in disclosing client confidences to promote the greater good of preserving human life and preventing injurious behavior. John Stuart Mill, for example, argued that "[a]s soon as any part of a person's conduct affects prejudicially the interests of others, society has jurisdiction over it."[1] The deontologist would argue that a client who wishes to use the relationship with her lawyer to harm someone else is misusing a trusting relationship and therefore forfeits the client's right to trust or privacy.

---

1. John Stuart Mill, *On Liberty*, Chap. IV (1859).

Problems

7-1. May (must) Martyn & Fox disclose that Husband just stomped out of Fox's office, screaming "I'm going to kill her rather than give her the Cape Cod house"? What if Dad tells Fox that's what Son just told him in a phone call, not ten minutes ago? What if Fox calls the police, and then is subpoenaed to testify at a grand jury proceeding considering whether to indict Son?

7-2. May (must) Martyn & Fox disclose that our client just discovered arsenic drums in back of the plant it bought last year? What if our client has owned the plant for 50 years?

7-3. May (must) Martyn & Fox, as lawyers for defendants, disclose that our physician's examination of plaintiff reveals that plaintiff has a life threatening aneurysm, a condition not uncovered by plaintiff's own physician?

7-4. May (must) Martyn & Fox disclose or testify that our client has committed a crime for which another person is now serving time? What if the innocent person is on death row?

Consider: Model Rule 1.6(b)(1)
Model Code DR 4-101(C)(3)
RLGL §§66, 77, 82

Hawkins v. King County

602 P.2d 361 (Wash. App. 1979)

SWANSON, A.C.J.

Michael Hawkins, acting through his guardian ad litem, and his mother Frances M. Hawkins, appeal from a summary judgment dismissing attorney Richard Sanders from an action sounding in tort. Appellants contend Sanders, court appointed defense attorney for Michael Hawkins, was negligent and committed malpractice by failing to divulge information regarding his client's mental state at a bail hearing. We find no error and affirm.

On July 1, 1975, Michael Hawkins was booked for possession of marijuana. Following his court appointment as Hawkins' defense counsel on July 3, 1975, Richard Sanders conferred with Hawkins for about 45

minutes, at which time Hawkins expressed the desire to be released from jail.

Also on July 3, 1975, Sanders talked with Palmer Smith, an attorney employed by Hawkins' mother Frances Hawkins, to assist in having Hawkins either hospitalized or civilly committed. Smith told Sanders then, and reiterated by letter, that Hawkins was mentally ill and dangerous. On July 8, 1975, Dr. Elwood Jones, a psychiatrist, telephoned and wrote Sanders and averred Hawkins was mentally ill and of danger to himself and others and should not be released from custody. Sanders represented that he intended to comply with his client's request for freedom.

On July 9, 1975, a district judge released Hawkins on a personal surety bond. At the bail hearing, Sanders did not volunteer any information regarding Hawkins' alleged illness or dangerousness, nor were any questions in that vein directed to him either by the judge or the prosecutor. Smith, Jones, and Mrs. Hawkins were informed of Hawkins' release, and all parties later met on two occasions in a counseling environment.

On July 17, 1975, about 8 days after his release, Michael Hawkins assaulted his mother and attempted suicide by jumping off a bridge, causing injuries resulting in the amputation of both legs. The Hawkinses commenced an action for damages against King County, the State of Washington, Community Psychiatric Clinic, Inc., and one of its employees on August 16, 1976, and amended the suit on November 30, 1977, to name Sanders a party defendant. Sanders filed a motion to dismiss for failure to state a claim. On June 16, 1978, the trial court granted Sanders' motion. . . .

On appeal, the Hawkinses essentially present two arguments: First, that by his failure at the bail hearing to disclose the information he possessed regarding Michael Hawkins' mental state, defense counsel Sanders subjected himself to liability for malpractice, as court rules and the Code of Professional Responsibility mandate such disclosure on ethical and legal grounds. Second, that by the same omission Sanders negligently violated a common-law duty to warn foreseeable victims of an individual he knew to be potentially dangerous to himself and others. See Tarasoff v. Regents of Univ. of Cal., 551 P.2d 334 (Cal. 1976).

Sanders asserts the Hawkinses have failed to demonstrate that he breached any duty owed to them. . . .

[The court examines the court rules that govern bail hearings and finds that they do not require a defense lawyer to disclose "information damaging to his client's expressed desire to be released from custody."]

We believe that the duty of counsel to be loyal to his client and to represent zealously his client's interests overrides the nebulous and unsupported theory that our rules and ethical code mandate disclosure of information which counsel considers detrimental to his client's stated interest. Because disclosure is not "required by law," appellants' theory of liability on the basis of ethical or court rule violations fails for lack of substance.

Turning then to the Hawkinses' theory of a common-law duty to warn or disclose, we note common-law support for the precept that attorneys must, upon learning that a client plans an assault or other violent crime, warn foreseeable victims. See Tarasoff v. Regents of Univ. of Cal., supra. . . . The difficulty lies in framing a rule that will balance properly "the public interest and safety from violent attack" against the public interest in securing proper resolution of legal disputes without compromising a defendant's right to a loyal and zealous defense. We are persuaded by the position advanced by amicus "that the obligation to warn, when confidentiality would be compromised to the client's detriment, must be permissive at most, unless it appears beyond a reasonable doubt that the client has formed a firm intention to inflict serious personal injuries on an unknowing third person."

Because appellants rely to a great extent upon *Tarasoff* in arguing a common-law duty to disclose, we will demonstrate that the *Tarasoff* decision is inapposite even though the facts are equally atypical and tragic. Tatiana Tarasoff was killed by one Prosenjit Poddar. The victim's parents alleged that 2 months earlier Poddar confided his intention to kill Tatiana to a defendant, Dr. Moore, a psychologist employed by the University of California. After a brief detention of Poddar by the police at Moore's request, Poddar was released pursuant to order of Dr. Moore's superior. No one warned Tatiana of her peril. The plaintiffs claimed the defendant psychologists had a duty to warn foreseeable victims. Defendants denied owing any duty of reasonable care to Tatiana. . . . The Supreme Court of California concluded that the complaint could be amended to state a cause of action against the psychologists by asserting that they had or should have determined Poddar presented a serious danger to Tatiana, pursuant to the standards of their profession, but had failed to exercise reasonable care for her safety.

In *Tarasoff*, the defendant psychologists had first-hand knowledge of Poddar's homicidal intention and knew it to be directed towards Tatiana Tarasoff, who was wholly unaware of her danger. The knowledge of the defendants in *Tarasoff* was gained from statements made to them in the course of treatment and not from statements transmitted by others. Further, the California court in *Tarasoff* did not establish a new duty to warn, but only held that psychologists must exercise such reasonable skill, knowledge, and care possessed and exercised by members of their profession under similar circumstances.

In the instant case, Michael Hawkins' potential victims, his mother and sister, knew he might be dangerous and that he had been released from confinement, contrary to Tatiana Tarasoff's ignorance of any risk of harm. Thus, no duty befell Sanders to warn Frances Hawkins of a risk of which she was already fully cognizant. Further, it must not be overlooked that Sanders received no information that Hawkins planned to assault anyone, only that he was mentally ill and likely to be dangerous to himself and others. That Sanders received no information directly from Michael Hawkins is the final distinction between the two cases.

The common-law duty to volunteer information about a client to a court considering pretrial release must be limited to situations where information gained convinces counsel that his client intends to commit a crime or inflict injury upon unknowing third persons. Such a duty cannot be extended to the facts before us. . . .

Purcell v. District Attorney for the Suffolk District
676 N.E.2d 436 (Mass. 1997)

WILKINS, C.J.

On June 21, 1994, Joseph Tyree, who had received a court order to vacate his apartment in the Allston section of Boston, consulted the plaintiff, Jeffrey W. Purcell, an attorney employed by Greater Boston Legal Services, which provides representation to low income individuals in civil matters. Tyree had recently been discharged as a maintenance man at the apartment building in which his apartment was located. On the day that Tyree consulted Purcell, Purcell decided, after extensive deliberation, that he should advise appropriate authorities that Tyree might engage in conduct harmful to others. He told a Boston police lieutenant that Tyree had made threats to burn the apartment building.

The next day, constables, accompanied by Boston police officers, went to evict Tyree. At the apartment building, they found incendiary materials, containers of gasoline, and several bottles with wicks attached. Smoke detectors had been disconnected, and gasoline had been poured on a hallway floor. Tyree was arrested and later indicted for attempted arson of a building.

In August, 1995, the district attorney for the Suffolk district subpoenaed Purcell to testify concerning the conversation Purcell had had with Tyree on June 21, 1994. A Superior Court judge granted Purcell's motion to quash the subpoena. The trial ended in a mistrial because the jury were unable to reach a verdict.

The Commonwealth decided to try Tyree again and once more sought Purcell's testimony. Another Superior Court judge concluded that Tyree's statements to Purcell were not protected by the attorney-client privilege, denied Purcell's motion to quash an anticipated subpoena, and ordered Purcell to testify. . . .

There is no question before this court, directly or indirectly, concerning the ethical propriety of Purcell's disclosure to the police that Tyree might engage in conduct that would be harmful to others. As bar counsel agreed in a memorandum submitted to the single justice, this court's disciplinary rules regulating the practice of law authorized Purcell to reveal to the police "the intention of his client to commit a crime and the information necessary to prevent the crime." S.J.C. Rule 3:07, Canon 4, DR 4-101(C)(3).[1] The fact that the disciplinary code permitted Purcell to make the disclosure tells us nothing about the admissibility of the information that Purcell disclosed. . . .

The attorney-client privilege is founded on the necessity that a client be free to reveal information to an attorney, without fear of its disclosure, in order to obtain informed legal advice. It is a principle of long standing. The debate here is whether Tyree is entitled to the protection of the attorney-client privilege in the circumstances.

The district attorney announces the issue in his brief to be whether a crime-fraud exception to the testimonial privilege applies in this case. He asserts that, even if Tyree's communication with Purcell was made as part of his consultation concerning the eviction proceeding, Tyree's

---

1. The same conclusion would be reached under Rule 1.6(b)(1) of the Proposed Mass. R. of Prof. Conduct, now pending before the Justices. Under rule 1.6(b)(1), as now proposed, a lawyer may reveal confidential information relating to a client "to prevent the commission of a criminal or fraudulent act that the lawyer reasonably believes is likely to result in death or substantial bodily harm, or in substantial injury to the financial interests or property of another." Unlike DR 4-101 (C)(3), which allows disclosure of a client's intention to commit any crime, disclosure of a client's intention to commit a crime is permissible under proposed rule 1.6(b)(1) only as to crimes threatening substantial consequences, and disclosure is permitted based on an attorney's reasonable belief of the likely existence of the threat rather than, as is the case under DR 4-101(C) (3), a known intention of the client to commit a crime.

communication concerning his contemplated criminal conduct is not protected by the privilege. . . .

We . . . accept the general principle of a crime-fraud exception. The Proposed Massachusetts Rules of Evidence adequately define the crime-fraud exception to the lawyer-client privilege set forth in rule 502 (d)(1) as follows: "If the services of the lawyer were sought or obtained to enable or aid anyone to commit or plan to commit what the client knew or reasonably should have known to be a crime or fraud." . . . The applicability of the exception, like the existence of the privilege, is a question of fact for the judge.

The district attorney rightly grants that he, as the opponent of the application of the testimonial privilege, has the burden of showing that the exception applies. . . . We conclude that facts supporting the applicability of the crime-fraud exception must be proved by a preponderance of the evidence. However, on a showing of a factual basis adequate to support a reasonable belief that an in camera review of the evidence may establish that the exception applies, the judge has discretion to conduct such an in camera review. Once the judge sees the confidential information, the burden of proof normally will be unimportant.

In this case, in deciding whether to conduct a discretionary in camera review of the substance of the conversation concerning arson between Tyree and Purcell, the judge would have evidence tending to show that Tyree discussed a future crime with Purcell and that thereafter Tyree actively prepared to commit that crime. Without this evidence, the crime of arson would appear to have no apparent connection with Tyree's eviction proceeding and Purcell's re-

presentation of Tyree. With this evidence, however, a request that a judge inquire in camera into the circumstances of Tyree's apparent threat to burn the apartment building would not be a call for a "fishing expedition," and a judge might be justified in conducting such an inquiry. The evidence in this case, however, was not sufficient to warrant the judge's finding that Tyree consulted Purcell for the purpose of obtaining advice in furtherance of a crime. Therefore, the order denying the motion to quash because the crime-fraud exception applied cannot be upheld.

There is a consideration in this case that does not appear in other cases that we have seen concerning the attorney-client privilege. The testimony that the prosecution seeks from Purcell is available only because Purcell reflectively made a disclosure, relying on this court's disciplinary rule which permitted him to do so. Purcell was under no ethical duty to disclose Tyree's intention to commit a crime. He did so to protect the lives and property of others, a purpose that underlies a lawyer's discretionary right stated in the disciplinary rule. The limited facts in the record strongly suggest that Purcell's disclosures to the police served the beneficial public purpose on which the disciplinary rule was based.

We must be cautious in permitting the use of client communications that a lawyer has revealed only because of a threat to others. Lawyers will be reluctant to come forward if they know that the information that they disclose may lead to adverse consequences to their clients. A practice of the use of such disclosures might prompt a lawyer to warn a client in advance that the disclosure of certain information may not be held confidential, thereby chilling free discourse between lawyer and client and reducing the prospect that the lawyer will learn of a serious threat to the well-being of others. To best promote the purposes of the attorney-client privilege, the crime-fraud exception should apply only if the communication seeks assistance in or furtherance of future criminal conduct. When the opponent of the privilege argues that the communication itself may show that the exception applies and seeks its disclosure in camera, the judge, in the exercise of discretion on the question whether to have an in camera proceeding, should consider if the public interest is served by disclosure, even in camera, of a communication whose existence is known only because the lawyer acted against his client's interests under the authority of a disciplinary rule. The facts of each situation must be considered.

It might seem that this opinion is in a posture to conclude by stating that the order denying the motion to quash any subpoena to testify is vacated and the matter is to be remanded for further proceedings concerning the application of the crime-fraud exception. However, the district attorney's brief appears to abandon its earlier concession that all communications between Tyree and Purcell should be treated as protected by the attorney-client privilege unless the crime-fraud exception applies. The question whether the attorney-client privilege is involved at all will be open on remand. We, therefore, discuss the issue.

The attorney-client privilege applies only when the client's communication was for the purpose of facilitating the rendition of legal services. The burden of proving that the attorney-client privilege applies to a communication rests on the party asserting the privilege. The motion judge did not pass on the question whether the attorney-client privilege applied to the communication at all but rather went directly to the issue of the crime-fraud exception, although not using that phrase.

A statement of an intention to commit a crime made in the course of seeking legal advice is protected by the privilege, unless the crime-fraud exception applies. That exception applies only if the client or prospective client seeks advice or assistance in furtherance of criminal conduct. It is agreed that Tyree consulted Purcell concerning his impending eviction. Purcell is a member of the bar, and Tyree either was or sought to become Purcell's client. The serious question concerning the application of the privilege is whether Tyree informed Purcell of the fact of his intention to commit arson for the purpose of receiving legal advice or assistance in furtherance of criminal conduct. Purcell's presentation of the circumstances in which Tyree's statements were made is likely to be the only evidence presented.

This is not a case in which our traditional view that testimonial privileges should be construed strictly should be applied. A strict construction of the privilege that would leave a gap between the circumstances in which the crime-fraud exception applies and the circumstances in which a communication is protected by the attorney-client privilege would make no sense. The attorney-client privilege "is founded upon the necessity, in the interest and administration of justice, of the aid of persons having knowledge of the law and skilled in its practice, which assistance can only be safely and readily availed of when free from the consequences or the apprehension of disclosure." Unless the crime-fraud exception applies, the attorney-client privilege should apply to communications concerning possible future, as well as past, criminal conduct, because an informed lawyer may be able to dissuade the client from improper future conduct and, if not, under the ethical rules may elect in the public interest to make a limited disclosure of the client's threatened conduct.

A judgment should be entered in the county court ordering that the order denying the motion to quash any subpoena issued to Purcell to testify at Tyree's trial is vacated and that the matter is remanded for further proceedings consistent with this opinion. . . .

Spaulding v. Zimmerman
116 N.W.2d 704 (Minn. 1962)

THOMAS GALLAGHER, J.

Appeal from an order of the District Court of Douglas County vacating and setting aside a prior order of such court dated May 8, 1957, approving a settlement made on behalf of David Spaulding on March 5, 1957, at which time he was a minor of the age of 20 years; and in connection therewith, vacating and setting aside releases executed by him and his parents, a stipulation of dismissal, an order for dismissal with prejudice, and a judgment entered pursuant thereto.

The prior action was brought against defendants by Theodore Spaulding, as father and natural guardian of David Spaulding, for injuries sustained by David in an automobile accident, arising out of a collision which occurred August 24, 1956, between an automobile driven by John Zimmerman, in which David was a passenger, and one owned by John Ledermann and driven by Florian Ledermann.

On appeal defendants contend that the court was without jurisdiction to vacate the settlement solely because their counsel then possessed information, unknown to plaintiff herein, that at the time he was suffering from an aorta aneurysm which may have resulted from the accident, because (1) no mutual mistake of fact was involved; (2) no duty rested upon them to disclose information to plaintiff which they could assume had been disclosed to him by his own physicians; (3) insurance limitations as well as physical injuries formed the basis for the settlement; and (4) plaintiff's motion to vacate the order for settlement and to set aside the releases was barred by the limitations provided in Rule 60.02 of Rules of Civil Procedure.[1]

---

1. Rule 60.02 of Rules of Civ. Proc. provides in part: "On motion . . . the court may relieve a party . . . from a final . . . order, or proceeding for the following reasons: (1) Mistake, inadvertence, surprise, or excusable neglect; (2) newly discovered evidence which by due diligence could not have been discovered in time to move for a new trial under Rule 59.03; (3) fraud (whether . . . intrinsic or extrinsic), misrepresentation, or other misconduct of an adverse party; . . . or (6) any other reason justifying relief from the operation of the judgment. The motion shall be made within a reasonable time, and for reasons (1), (2), and (3) not more than one year after the judgment, order, or proceeding was entered or taken. . . . This rule does not limit the power of a court to entertain an independent action to relieve a party from a judgment, order, or proceeding, . . . or to set aside a judgment for fraud upon the court."

After the accident, David's injuries were diagnosed by his family physician, Dr. James H. Cain, as a severe crushing injury of the chest with multiple rib fractures; a severe cerebral concussion, probably with petechial hemorrhages of the brain; and bilateral fractures of the clavicles. At Dr. Cain's suggestion, on January 3, 1957, David was examined by Dr. John F. Pohl, an orthopedic specialist, who made X-ray studies of his chest. Dr. Pohl's detailed report of this examination included the following:

" . . . The lung fields are clear. The heart and aorta are normal."

Nothing in such report indicated the aorta aneurysm with which David was then suffering. On March 1, 1957, at the suggestion of Dr. Pohl, David was examined from a neurological viewpoint by Dr. Paul S. Blake, and in the report of this examination there was no finding of the aorta aneurysm.

In the meantime, on February 22, 1957, at defendants' request, David was examined by Dr. Hewitt Hannah, a neurologist. On February 26, 1957, the latter reported to Messrs. Field, Arvesen & Donoho, attorneys for defendant John Zimmerman, as follows:

"The one feature of the case which bothers me more than any other part of the case is the fact that this boy of 20 years of age has an aneurysm, which means a dilatation of the aorta and the arch of the aorta. Whether this came out of this accident I cannot say with any degree of certainty and I have discussed it with the Roentgenologist and a couple of Internists. . . . Of course an aneurysm or dilatation of the aorta in a boy of this age is a serious matter as far as his life. This aneurysm may dilate further and it might rupture with further dilatation and this would cause his death.

"It would be interesting also to know whether the X-ray of his lungs, taken immediately following the accident, shows this dilatation or not. If it was not present immediately following the accident and is now present, then we could be sure that it came out of the accident."

Prior to the negotiations for settlement, the contents of the above report were made known to counsel for defendants Florian and John Ledermann.

The case was called for trial on March 4, 1957, at which time the respective parties and their counsel possessed such information as to David's physical condition as was revealed to them by their respective medical examiners as above described. It is thus apparent that neither David nor his father, the nominal plaintiff in the prior action, was then aware that David was suffering the aorta aneurysm but on the contrary believed that he was recovering from the injuries sustained in the accident.

On the following day an agreement for settlement was reached wherein, in consideration of the payment of $6,500, David and his father agreed to settle in full for all claims arising out of the accident.

Richard S. Roberts, counsel for David, thereafter presented to the court a petition for approval of the settlement, wherein David's injuries were described as:

" . . . severe crushing of the chest, with multiple rib fractures, severe cerebral concussion, with petechial hemorrhages of the brain, bilateral fractures of the clavicles."

Attached to the petition were affidavits of David's physicians, Drs. James H. Cain and Paul S. Blake, wherein they set forth the same diagnoses they had made upon completion of their respective examinations of David as above described. At no time was there information disclosed to the court that David was then suffering from an aorta aneurysm which may have been the result of the accident. Based upon the petition for settlement and such affidavits of Drs. Cain and Blake, the court on May 8, 1957, made its order approving the settlement.

Early in 1959, David was required by the army reserve, of which he was a member, to have a physical checkup. For this, he again engaged the services of Dr. Cain. In this checkup, the latter discovered the aorta aneurysm. He then reexamined the X rays which had been taken shortly after the accident and at this time discovered that they disclosed the beginning of the process which produced the aneurysm. He promptly sent David to Dr. Jerome Grismer for an examination and opinion. The latter confirmed the finding of the aorta aneurysm and recommended immediate surgery therefor. This was performed by him at Mount Sinai Hospital in Minneapolis on March 10, 1959.

Shortly thereafter, David, having attained his majority, instituted the present action for additional damages due to the more serious injuries including the aorta aneurysm which he alleges proximately resulted from the accident. . . . In a memorandum made a part of the order vacating the settlement, the court stated:

> "The facts material to a determination of the motion are without substantial dispute. . . ."

" . . . the Court finds that although the aneurysm now existing is causally related to the accident, such finding is for the purpose of the motions only and is based solely upon the opinion expressed by Dr. Cain (Exhibit 'F'), which, so far as the Court can find from the numerous affidavits and statements of fact by counsel, stands without dispute.

"The mistake concerning the existence of the aneurysm was not mutual. For reasons which do not appear, plaintiff's doctor failed to ascertain its existence. By reason of the failure of plaintiff's counsel to use available rules of discovery, plaintiff's doctor and all his representatives did not learn that defendants and their agents knew of its existence and possible serious consequences. Except for the character of the concealment in the light of plaintiff's minority, the Court would, I believe, be justified in denying plaintiff's motion to vacate, leaving him to whatever questionable remedy he may have against his doctor and against his lawyer. . . .

"There is no doubt of the good faith of both defendants' counsel. There is no doubt that during the course of the negotiations, when the parties were in an adversary relationship, no rule required or duty rested upon defendants or their representatives to disclose this knowledge. However, once the agreement to settle was reached, it is difficult to characterize the parties' relationship as adverse. At this point all parties were interested in securing Court approval. . . .

"When the adversary nature of the negotiations concluded in a settlement, the procedure took on the posture of a joint application to the Court, at least so far as the facts upon which the Court could and must approve settlement is concerned. It is here that the true nature of the concealment appears, and defendants' failure to act affirmatively, after having been given a copy of the application for approval, can only be defendants' decision to take a calculated risk that the settlement would be final. . . .

"To hold that the concealment was not of such character as to result in an unconscionable advantage over plaintiff's ignorance or mistake, would be to penalize innocence and incompetence and reward less than full performance of an officer of the Court's duty to make full disclosure to the Court when applying for approval in minor settlement proceedings."

1. The principles applicable to the court's authority to vacate settlements made on behalf of minors and approved by it appear well established. With reference thereto, we have held that the court in its discretion may vacate such a settlement, even though it is not induced by fraud or bad faith, where it is shown that in the accident the minor sustained separate and distinct injuries which were not known or considered by the court at the time settlement was approved, and even though the releases furnished therein purported to cover both known and unknown injuries resulting from the accident. The court may vacate such a settlement for mistake even though the mistake was not mutual in the sense that both parties were similarly mistaken as to the nature and extent of the minor's injuries, but where it is shown that one of the parties had additional knowledge with respect thereto and was aware that neither the court nor the adversary party possessed such knowledge when the settlement was approved.

2. From the foregoing it is clear that in the instant case the court did not abuse its discretion in setting aside the settlement which it had approved on plaintiff's behalf while he was still a minor. It is undisputed that neither he nor his counsel nor his medical attendants were aware that at the time settlement was made he was suffering from an aorta aneurysm which may have resulted from the accident. The seriousness of this disability is indicated by Dr. Hannah's report indicating the imminent danger of death therefrom. This was known by counsel for both defendants but was not disclosed to the court at the time it was petitioned to approve the settlement. While no canon of ethics or legal obligation may have required them to inform plaintiff or his counsel with respect thereto, or to advise the court therein, it did become obvious to them at the time that the settlement then made did not contemplate or take into consideration the disability described. This fact opened the way for the court to later exercise its discretion in vacating the settlement and under the circumstances described we cannot say that there was any abuse of discretion on the part of the court in so doing under Rule 60.02(6) of Rules of Civil Procedure. . . . Affirmed.

Swidler & Berlin v. United States
524 U.S. 399 (1998)

Chief Justice REHNQUIST delivered the opinion of the Court.

Petitioner, an attorney, made notes of an initial interview with a client shortly before the client's death. The Government, represented by the Office of Independent Counsel, now seeks his notes for use in a criminal investigation. We hold that the notes are protected by the attorney-client privilege.

This dispute arises out of an investigation conducted by the Office of the Independent Counsel into whether various individuals made false statements, obstructed justice, or committed other crimes during investigations of the 1993 dismissal of employees from the White House Travel Office. Vincent W. Foster, Jr., was Deputy White House Counsel when the firings occurred. In July, 1993, Foster met with petitioner James Hamilton, an attorney at petitioner Swidler & Berlin, to seek legal representation concerning possible congressional or other investigations of the firings. During a 2-hour meeting, Hamilton took three pages of handwritten notes. One of the first entries in the notes is the word "Privileged." Nine days later, Foster committed suicide. . . .

The Independent Counsel argues that the attorney-client privilege should not prevent disclosure of confidential communications where the client has died and the information is relevant to a criminal proceeding. There is some authority for this position. One state appellate court, Cohen v. Jenkintown Cab Co., 357 A.2d 689 (Pa. Super. 1976), and the Court of Appeals below have held the privilege may be subject to posthumous exceptions in certain circumstances. In *Cohen*, a civil case, the court recognized that the privilege generally survives death, but concluded that it could make an exception where the interest of justice was compelling and the interest of the client in preserving the confidence was insignificant.

But other than these two decisions, cases addressing the existence of the privilege after death—most

involving the testamentary exception —uniformly presume the privilege survives, even if they do not so hold. . . .

The Independent Counsel . . . argues that the exception reflects a policy judgment that the interest in settling estates outweighs any posthumous interest in confidentiality. He then reasons by analogy that in criminal proceedings, the interest in determining whether a crime has been committed should trump client confidentiality, particularly since the financial interests of the estate are not at stake.

But the Independent Counsel's interpretation simply does not square with the caselaw's implicit acceptance of the privilege's survival and with the treatment of testamentary disclosure as an "exception" or an implied "waiver." And the premise of his analogy is incorrect, since cases consistently recognize that the rationale for the testamentary exception is that it furthers the client's intent. There is no reason to suppose as a general matter that grand jury testimony about confidential communications furthers the client's intent.

Commentators on the law also recognize that the general rule is that the attorney-client privilege continues after death. Undoubtedly, as the Independent Counsel emphasizes, various commentators have criticized this rule, urging that the privilege should be abrogated after the client's death where extreme injustice would result, as long as disclosure would not seriously undermine the privilege by deterring client communication. See, e.g., C. Mueller & L. Kirkpatrick, 2 *Federal Evidence* §199, at 380-381 (2d ed. 1994); *Restatement (Third) of the Law Governing Lawyers* §[77], Comment

d. But even these critics clearly recognize that established law supports the continuation of the privilege and that a contrary rule would be a modification of the common law.

Despite the scholarly criticism, we think there are weighty reasons that counsel in favor of posthumous application. Knowing that communications will remain confidential even after death encourages the client to communicate fully and frankly with counsel. While the fear of disclosure, and the consequent withholding of information from counsel, may be reduced if disclosure is limited to posthumous disclosure in a criminal context, it seems unreasonable to assume that it vanishes altogether. Clients may be concerned about reputation, civil liability, or possible harm to friends or family. Posthumous disclosure of such communications may be as feared as disclosure during the client's lifetime.

The Independent Counsel suggests, however, that his proposed exception would have little to no effect on the client's willingness to confide in his attorney. He reasons that only clients intending to perjure themselves will be chilled by a rule of disclosure after death, as opposed to truthful clients or those asserting their Fifth Amendment privilege. This is because for the latter group, communications disclosed by the attorney after the client's death purportedly will reveal only information that the client himself would have revealed if alive. . . .

The contention that the attorney is being required to disclose only what the client could have been required to disclose is at odds with the basis for the privilege even during the client's lifetime. In related cases, we have said that the loss of evidence admittedly caused by the privilege is justified in part by the fact that without the privilege, the client may not have made such communications in the first place. This is true of disclosure before and after the client's death. Without assurance of the privilege's posthumous application, the client may very well not have made disclosures to his attorney at all, so the loss of evidence is more apparent than real. In the case at hand, it seems quite plausible that Foster, perhaps already contemplating suicide, may not have sought legal advice from Hamilton if he had not been assured the conversation was privileged.

The Independent Counsel additionally suggests that his proposed exception would have minimal impact if confined to criminal cases, or, as the Court of Appeals suggests, if it is limited to information of substantial importance to a particular criminal case. . . . However, there is no case authority for the proposition that the privilege applies differently in criminal and civil cases. . . . In any event, a client may not know at the time he discloses information to his attorney whether it will later be relevant to a civil or a criminal matter, let alone whether it will be of substantial importance. Balancing *ex post* the importance of the information against client interests, even limited to criminal cases, introduces substantial uncertainty into the privilege's application. For just that reason, we have rejected use of a balancing test in defining the contours of the privilege. *See Upjohn,* 449 U.S. at 393.

In a similar vein, the Independent Counsel argues that existing exceptions to the privilege, such as the crime-fraud exception and the testamentary exception, make the impact of one more exception marginal. However, these exceptions do not demonstrate that the impact of a posthumous exception would be insignificant, and there is little empirical evidence on this point.[4] The established exceptions are consistent with the purposes of the privilege, while a posthumous exception in criminal cases appears at odds with the goals of encouraging full and frank communication and of protecting the client's interests. A "no harm in one more exception" rationale could contribute to the general erosion of the privilege, without reference to common law principles or "reason and experience."

It has been generally, if not universally, accepted, for well over a century, that the attorney-client privilege survives the death of the client in a case such as this. While the arguments against the survival of the privilege are by no means frivolous, they are based in large part on speculation—thoughtful speculation, but speculation nonetheless—as to whether posthumous termination of the privilege would diminish a client's willingness to confide in an attorney. In an area where empirical information would be useful, it is scant and inconclusive.

. . . Interpreted in the light of reason and experience, that body of law requires that the attorney client privilege prevent disclosure of the notes at issue in this case. The judgment of the Court of Appeals is Reversed.

Dissent: Justice O'CONNOR, with whom Justice SCALIA and Justice THOMAS join, dissenting.

Although the attorney-client privilege ordinarily will survive the death of the client, I do not agree with the Court that it inevitably precludes disclosure of a deceased client's communications in criminal proceedings. In my view, a criminal defendant's right to exculpatory evidence or a compelling law enforcement need for information may, where the testimony is not available from other sources, override a client's posthumous interest in confidentiality. . . .

I agree that a deceased client may retain a personal, reputational, and economic interest in confidentiality. But, after death, the potential that disclosure will harm the client's interests has been greatly diminished, and the risk that the client will be held criminally liable has abated altogether. . . . The privilege does not "protect[ ] disclosure of the underlying facts by those who communicated

---

4. Empirical evidence on the privilege is limited. Three studies do not reach firm conclusions on whether limiting the privilege would discourage full and frank communication. Alexander, *The Corporate Attorney Client Privilege: A Study of the Participants*, 63 St. John's L. Rev. 191 (1989); Zacharias, *Rethinking Confidentiality*, 74 Iowa L. Rev. 352 (1989); Comment, *Functional Overlap Between the Lawyer and Other Professionals: Its Implications for the Privileged Communications Doctrine*, 71 Yale L.J. 1226 (1962). These articles note that clients are often uninformed or mistaken about the privilege, but suggest that a substantial number of clients and attorneys think the privilege encourages candor. Two of the articles conclude that a substantial number of clients and attorneys think the privilege enhances open communication, Alexander, *supra*, at 244-246, 261, and that the absence of a privilege would be detrimental to such communication, Comment, 71 Yale L.J., *supra*, at 1236. The third article suggests instead that while the privilege is perceived as important to open communication, limited exceptions to the privilege might not discourage such communication, Zacharias, *supra*, at 382, 386. Similarly, relatively few court decisions discuss the impact of the privilege's application after death. This may reflect the general assumption that the privilege survives—if attorneys were required as a matter of practice to testify or provide notes in criminal proceedings, cases discussing that practice would surely exist.

with the attorney," *Upjohn, supra*, at 395, and were the client living, prosecutors could grant immunity and compel the relevant testimony. After a client's death, however, if the privilege precludes an attorney from testifying in the client's stead, a complete "loss of crucial information" will often result.

. . . Extreme injustice may occur, for example, where a criminal defendant seeks disclosure of a deceased client's confession to the offense. See State v. Macumber, 544 P.2d 1084, 1086 (Ariz. 1976). . . . Indeed, even petitioner acknowledges that an exception may be appropriate where the constitutional rights of a criminal defendant are at stake. An exception may likewise be warranted in the face of a compelling law enforcement need for the information. . . .

. . . The American Law Institute, moreover, has recently recommended withholding the privilege when the communication "bears on a litigated issue of pivotal significance" and has suggested that courts "balance the interest in confidentiality against any exceptional need for the communication." *Restatement (Third) of the Law Governing Lawyers* §[77], Comment d.

Where the exoneration of an innocent criminal defendant or a compelling law enforcement interest is at stake, the harm of precluding critical evidence that is unavailable by any other means outweighs the potential disincentive to forthright communication. In my view, the cost of silence warrants a narrow exception to the rule that the attorney-client privilege survives the death of the client. . . . Accordingly, I would affirm the judgment of the Court of Appeals. . . .

■ The Bounds of the Law: *Court Orders*

Courts order all kinds of conduct in order to carry out their duties.[1] *Hughes, Dean*, and *Upjohn* in Chapter 6, and *Purcell* and *Swidler & Berlin* in this chapter illustrate this legal limit on the conduct of both lawyers and clients. Each of these cases recognized a court's inherent power to order disclosures consistent with the confines of the attorney-client privilege. In Chapter 3, *Bothwell* discussed the inherent power of a court to order a lawyer to provide uncompensated representation.[2] Lawyers must be aware of the importance of these court orders to avoid both contempt sanctions and professional discipline.[3]

---

1. *See* RLGL §105.
2. We will see further illustrations of inherent court power in the notes in The Law Governing Lawyers: Losing a Client by Disqualification or Injunction, *infra* p. 289, and in several cases in Chapters 3 and 12.
3. *E.g.*, Stark County Bar Assn. v. Ake, 855 N.E.2d 1206 (Ohio 2006) (lawyer who violated several court orders during his own divorce, suspended for six months); In re Shearin, 765 A.2d 930 (Del. 2000) (lawyer who, inter alia, violated court order enjoining her from interfering with the quiet title, operation, use, enjoyment, and governance of a church property suspended for three years); Herschfeld v. Super. Ct., 908 P.2d 22 (Ariz. 1995) (lawyer who continued to verbally assault a party opponent after being admonished to stop by the judge convicted of criminal contempt); In re Anonymous, No. 34 D.B. 93, 32 Pa. D. & C. 4th 23 (1995) (lawyer who violated a protective order barring him from contact with woman and her child held in contempt and disciplined); In re Belue, 766 P.2d 206 (Mont. 1988) (lawyer who violated federal judge's order to release property from attachment suspended from practice for three months and censured).

The Model Rules

The Model Rules of Professional Conduct recognize the power of court orders in several key provisions. Most prominent are Model Rule 1.6(b)(6), which allows lawyers to disclose confidential information where required by a court order, and Model Rule 3.4(c), which states the lawyer's basic obligation to obey the rules of tribunals, including court orders.

These provisions recognize and integrate the legal limit of a court order into the requirement of a professional obligation. They also presume that lawyers have a clear fiduciary and procedural obligation to properly raise and protect client interests.[4]

For example, lawyers have an obligation to assert the attorney-client privilege on the client's behalf whenever a nonfrivolous claim against disclosure or limitation of the scope of disclosure can be made.[5] Failure to do so could result in legally effective waiver of the privilege by the lawyer, who a court will later characterize as acting with apparent authority as the client's agent.[6] Any harm that results from such a nonconsensual disclosure could then subject the lawyer to claims of malpractice or breach of fiduciary duty.[7]

The Contempt Power

Once a court has declared that confidential information is not privileged, the lawyer either must comply with the court order to disclose, or appeal the court's decision.[8] The clients and lawyers in *Hughes, Upjohn, Swidler & Berlin,* and *Purcell* elected to raise claims about the privilege on appeal. Except for *Hughes,* the lawyers were successful in convincing appellate courts that the information was privileged, which resulted in reversal of the lower court's order to disclose or remand for further factual findings about the matter.

The lawyer in *Hughes* did not succeed on appeal, which meant that any further failure to disclose his client's identity would result in the enforcement of the trial court's contempt order. Judges use contempt sanctions to coerce or punish a lawyer or litigant. Civil contempt occurs when a judge orders fines or imprisonment to accrue until the person in contempt complies with the court order.[9] Criminal contempt punishes refusal to comply and requires elaborate

---

4. In an extreme case, a court may dismiss an action for failure to comply with a court order. *See* Washington v. Alaimo, 934 F. Supp. 1395 (S.D. Ga. 1996) (plaintiff's failure to respond to a show-cause order regarding Rule 11 sanctions after plaintiff was warned that failing to respond would cause dismissal resulted in dismissal with prejudice).

5. MR 1.6, Comment [13]; RLGL §86; ABA Formal Op. 94-385.

6. RLGL §77.

7. RLGL §63, Comment b.

8. RLGL §105, Comment d. If a court rules during "routine discovery," the court order may not be immediately appealable. *See, e.g.,* United States ex rel. Pogue v. Diabetes Treatment Ctrs. of Am. Inc., 444 F.3d 462 (6th Cir. 2006).

9. Courts also can sanction lawyers who use obstructive tactics to assist clients in violating court orders. *See, e.g.,* Guardianship of Melissa W., 18 Cal. Rptr. 2d 42 (Cal. App. 2002) (lawyer who helped clients evade custody order caused dismissal of client's appeal, and also was sanctioned $13,004 for opposing party's attorney's fees, and referred to the bar for further investigation).

procedural guarantees, similar to those in criminal trials.[10] Occasionally, a lawyer will risk contempt by violating a court order for the express purpose of challenging its validity, scope, or meaning.[11] Usually this is done only if no other procedural avenue of appeal is open to the client.[12] In situations where procedural rules provide for appeal, however, lawyers have been both held in contempt and disciplined for failing to obey the court order or properly challenging it.[13]

While court orders legally limit a lawyer's advocacy on behalf of a client, their availability also offers lawyers the opportunity to challenge otherwise unassailable legal rules. For example, Model Rules 3.5(b) and (c) prohibit communication with jurors, unless authorized by law or a court order. Similarly, the prohibition in Model Rule 4.2 against communication with a represented person recognizes the exception of "law or a court order." Thus, lawyers with nonfrivolous legal reasons to seek communication with jurors or represented persons may seek court approval in order to protect themselves against both contempt and disciplinary action.

Court Orders and Client Advocacy

The lawyers in the cases discussed in this note understood that court orders, combined with a court's contempt power, could limit their duties to a client. At the same time, they vigorously advocated (often successfully) for legal recognition of their client's interests within and up to this limit of the law.

B. Financial Harm

No one disputes that lawyers cannot counsel or assist a client crime or fraud. Specific exceptions to client confidentiality that allow disclosure to prevent, rectify or mitigate financial harm caused by a client, however, continue to generate substantial disagreement among lawyers and the public, including the

---

10. Intl. Union, UMWA v. Bagwell, 512 U.S. 821 (1994). Criminal contempt proceeding requires proof beyond a reasonable doubt, a special prosecutor, and a jury trial for any imprisonment beyond six months. Fleming James, Jr., Geoffrey C. Hazard, Jr. & John Leubsdorf, *Civil Procedure* §5.14 (5th ed., Found. 2001). *See, e.g.,* Downey v. Clauder, 30 F.3d 681 (6th Cir. 1994) (criminal contempt citation reversed because lawyer not given adequate notice of the charges against him and did not willfully disobey court order).

11. RLGL §94, Comment e. Such a claim may be raised about the scope of the attorney-client privilege, the work product doctrine, or other evidentiary claims, such as irrelevancy or hearsay. *Id.* at §63, Comment b.

12. *E.g.,* Maness v. Meyers, 419 U.S. 449 (1975) (lawyer who advised a client to refuse to obey a court order to testify in order to trigger immediate appellate review of the issue and to protect the client's Fifth Amendment rights could not be punished where procedural rules provided no other means to test the validity of the trial court's ruling and the lawyer believed in good faith that disclosure of the information tended to incriminate the client).

13. *E.g.,* Britt v. State, 2007 Ga. LEXIS 847 (lawyers who refused to proceed with court ordered hearing properly held in criminal contempt, even if court order was erroneous. Remedy for erroneous court order was appeal, not disobedience); Fla. Bar v. Gersten, 707 So. 2d 711 (Fla. 1998) (lawyer who refused to obey a court order that required him to give a sworn statement suspended); Disc. Action Against Giberson, 581 N.W.2d 351 (Minn. 1998) (lawyer who refused to pay court-ordered child support indefinitely suspended).

authors of this book. Yet, perhaps because the human willingness to lie can cause serious harm, confidentiality exceptions have long been recognized when clients seek to use lawyers to promote fraudulent activity.

Utilitarians recognize that efficient operation of both a market economy and a democratic government requires honesty. If everyone could use lawyers to promote their own illegal deception, the market system, many aspects of government, and the legal system itself would lose the confidence of its citizens. To prevent this erosion in confidence, some lawyers argue that they should be able to disclose activities of clients that seek to use the lawyer's services to perpetrate a fraud when the greater good would be promoted by disclosure. Others maintain that confidentiality remains an essential incentive for clients to disclose their plans to lawyers, who then are in the best position to dissuade clients from engaging in fraudulent activity. Focusing on trust and privacy, the deontologist would agree that clients should be encouraged to facilitate their plans through the client-lawyer relationship. They would add, however, that when the client seeks to use the relationship to violate another categorical imperative such as honesty, then the client's right to confidentiality has been lost. If the lawyer's services unwittingly have been used to further that fraud, the lawyer's duty of reparation for her own acts also could justify disclosure.

Problems

7-5. May Martyn tell the other side that our client "won't possibly pay more than $500,000" when she has recommended that our client settle the case quickly or face far more extensive liability? How about if Martyn tells the other side that she "isn't authorized to settle for more than $500,000," when she has settlement authority of $5,000,000?

7-6. Martyn & Fox, representing Seller, mistakenly told Buyer's lawyer that the property is zoned commercial. What happens if when we discover the mistake we don't correct it, the deal closes, and Buyer then discovers the correct zoning?

7-7. What may (must) Martyn & Fox do if at a celebration dinner the night before the initial public offering the CEO tells us, "I sure am glad we didn't have to disclose that threatened patent infringement suit"? What if it's the CFO and he tells us, "I sure am glad the auditors didn't insist we footnote the $65 million in off-balance sheet financing we cleverly arranged"? May we withdraw? Will client have a claim against us if we do? What if we learn these things a week after the IPO?

7-8. Martyn admonished Client about the importance of fully disclosing all assets on a bankruptcy filing. Client failed to do so and was indicted for bankruptcy fraud. Can Martyn be forced to testify about the original warning?

Consider: Model Rules 1.0(d), 1.2(d), 1.6(b)(2) and (3), 1.13, 1.16, 2.1, 4.1, 8.4(c)
Model Code DR 4-101(C)(2) and (3), DR 7-102(A) and (B)
RLGL §§67, 82, 93, 98

Lawrence J. Fox
Legal Tender: A Lawyer's Guide to Handling Professional Dilemmas
157-166 (ABA 1995)
The Opinion Letter

Forty years ago they were in the third grade at Highlands School. George was the new kid on the block, Lonnie the veteran from kindergarten. They met in the playground before school, quickly learned they both loved baseball (even the hapless Philadelphia A's), and soon found themselves as rival pick-up team captains. How many times they had used that elaborate ritual of alternately grabbing the baseball bat to determine who would choose first.

George's family's move to the suburbs five years later did not separate the boys for long, as Lonnie's folks followed them to Claymont one year later. There they found themselves teammates on the Claymont High School baseball team (Class B Delaware High School champions in 1959), sharing both the visits to colleges and the springtime anxiety as they awaited the results of the torturous college admissions process. When both lads were accepted at Syracuse, the fact that Lonnie had also been admitted to his original first choice, Trinity College, was quickly ignored as the friends deliciously contemplated spending four more years together—two hundred miles from home. Visions of intercollegiate athletics, fraternity memberships, new friendships, and football weekends soon became reality; Lonnie and George thrived despite the harsh winters of upstate New York.

College was a total success, launching the new graduates into their first period of separation in nearly ten years; George went off to Villanova Law School and Lonnie to the business school at Northwestern. They had often discussed their differing interests into the night over coffee and even, it had to be admitted, over more than a few Genessee beers, jokingly suggesting that Lonnie might some day become George's biggest client. But this was no more than a joke designed to ease the pain of their going down different paths since, at the time, George envisioned himself as Assistant District Attorney in New Castle County, prosecuting the clients of Perry Mason.

Nonetheless, twenty years later, with George firmly established at the Wilmington office of the prestigious, old-line Philadelphia firm, Caldwell & Moore—practicing corporate law no less—Lonnie, who had risen to president and chief operating officer of the Mercury Maintenance Company, was presented with his first opportunity to send business George's way. Mercury, whose growth had been spectacular, found itself in need of major new financing. Its old law firm had recently forced the retirement of Mercury's original lawyer and board member, Lewis Stern. Thus Lonnie felt free to steer this important matter to George.

During the interim they had remained friends. Both moved to Greenville as they each rose up their respective ladders. Their children were friends, baseball had given way to golf (now played regularly at Wilmington Country Club), and the two couples socialized at every opportunity. But this was the first time they had actually worked together.

At Lonnie's initial visit, he explained the plan to George. Mercury had a series of long-term contracts to replace streetlights and traffic controls for municipalities throughout the Delaware Valley. Because of its reputation for high-quality, prompt, and low-cost service, Mercury had signed multi-year contracts with over two hundred boroughs, townships, three of the five major counties surrounding Philadelphia, and, of course, the City of Wilmington. In discussions with Integrity Bank it had become clear that these contracts were Mercury's biggest asset. Based on the cash flow stability they represented, the bank was prepared to lend significant sums to Mercury. Lonnie had negotiated the broad outline of a deal in which Mercury would receive a $5 million loan to be drawn down in equal installments quarterly across four years, permitting Mercury, as it expanded its operations into New Jersey, to purchase the additional trucks and cherry pickers that were critical to its delivery of service. He called on George to document the transaction, represent Mercury, and provide Integrity with any routine legal opinions it required.

"Protect us as best you can," Lonnie implored George, "but none of your aggressive stuff—we need this money and you know how cussedly independent these banks can be."

"You can count on me, Lonnie. I want your board to be proud of your selection of lawyers, even though I know the real reason you hired me is to make up for your stealing my Mickey Mantle rookie card. That's something that you should feel guilty about. Do you know what that would be worth today?"

"Your mom would've thrown it out with your old Lionel trains anyway," Lonnie replied.

George returned to the office, called up his friend Vince Almond at Integrity to inquire who would be "lawyering" this transaction for the bank, learned that Vince himself would be working on it, and made a date with Vince to meet within a week to discuss the matter.

The loan processing could not have been easier. The bank officials were so impressed with Mercury's success that many of the issues typically raised did not need to be addressed. Similarly, the documentation went smoothly, and George's firm was only asked to provide opinion letters on the corporate authority of Mercury to enter into the loan transaction and the enforceability of the long-term contracts, including the effect of the penalty clauses, if any of Mercury's customers attempted to terminate them early. Neither legal question was difficult, and George confidently and, if truth be told, proudly delivered each opinion—printed on crisp ivory Caldwell & Moore letterhead—to Vince at closing. This was the final step prior to the delivery of the first $300,000-plus installment to Mercury. New equipment would soon be on its way, and George could only think that his good friend Lonnie might be well on his way to being CEO of a major public corporation, now that Mercury had this assured flow of capital.

A celebratory dinner at the Hotel duPont brought the old friends, their spouses, and a few key colleagues together for one of those events where the fact that the wine bill actually exceeded the cost of the food only seemed embarrassing the next morning. The repeated toasts to all involved only confirmed what high hopes everyone present shared as they dined among the Winterthur reproductions.

It was just one year later that George got the call from Lonnie. George immediately could tell something was wrong. There was a tension in Lonnie's voice, a hesitancy in his approach, and no desire for small talk. Rather, Lonnie asked George if they could meet right away at the club. George knew this was important, but his idle speculation as to why they had to meet immediately did not include anything close to the story that unfolded.

Lonnie's face was drawn, his normally neatly combed auburn hair, now just flecked with grey, appeared a little disheveled, and he sat poised at the edge of his highback club chair, as he began his tale.

"George, it's just terrible. I don't even know what to say. We just had a meeting with the folks from Arthur Andersen, our auditors. They have uncovered a massive fraud. We don't even know how big it is. Seems our best sales representative, Arnold Plinger, has been systematically bribing township officials to get these contracts—not just to get them, but to have the contracts include a five-year term when the governing body has only authorized two or three. He even did it with New Castle County! All those contracts we thought were for five years paid Arnold a commission based on five years. Now it turns out some expire as soon as December of this year."

"How many are there?" George interrupted more to ease his anxiety than to learn any information.

"We don't know. At least twenty. Maybe more, many more. Arnold isn't cooperating. His psychiatrist has put him on sedatives and ordered him not to talk to anyone. But he has hired a lawyer, on our advice. We only know from contacting a few officials who, of course, had not admitted the bribes but have stated that their versions of the contract are only for two years or, at most, three years. Arnold had over one hundred customers, so who knows?"

"Well," George observed, silently thanking his lucky stars he had not opined on the genuineness of the contracts, "we must act in a forthright manner. Tell the bank. After all, they are about to give you guys another $300,000 in a few weeks, if I'm not mistaken. Based on our firm's opinion that those five-year contracts are enforceable according to their terms. We can't let that happen."

"We can't do that," replied Lonnie. "That's why I wanted to meet with you today. I remember way back when, how you told me that everything a client told you you had to keep confidential. I even remember you and I having a major fight over that case of the lawyer who knew his client had killed those kids in upstate New York. I said he had to tell the victims' families. You said it was unethical to do so."

"That was different," said George, realizing he was shouting. "That client wasn't the lawyer's best friend. The lawyer hadn't given an opinion to anyone."

"That's what Lewis Stern said you would say."

"When did you talk to him?" George inquired, not hiding his annoyance.

"We had a special board meeting yesterday to discuss all of this. One of the board members invited Lewis to join us—said we needed someone who knew the company better than you, someone who wouldn't panic. The board decided that Mercury had no choice but to keep this under wraps. If we tell the bank, they'll never lend us another dime and they'll demand repayment of what they've already paid. Without that $300,000 per quarter, we'd probably have to file a chapter proceeding. We've already spent that money, y'know. Anyway, Lewis told us that we should tell you what had happened so that you would understand why we were consulting him."

"Caldwell & Moore will have to resign if you go forward like this."

"He told us you would say that, too, and he agreed you would have to resign. In fact, he thought that was best. But he also told us you would not be able to tell anyone about our little problems with Arnold."

"But the bank is relying on my opinion. Certainly I can call them up and tell them they shouldn't continue to do so."

"Not according to Lewis. He says you lawyers call these 'noisy withdrawals.' The rules don't permit them when the fraud's complete."

"But you're taking down more money from the bank."

"That may be so. Otherwise, our company will die and your best friend Lonnie will be sleeping in your garage. But we aren't requiring any further services from you. In fact, you've withdrawn. But I must warn you, as Lewis instructed me, we better not hear another peep out of Caldwell & Moore . . . especially if you ever want to see any of the $100,000 we still owe you."

"You're being impossible. I better talk to Lewis myself. I'll be back to you shortly. Maybe all of this will seem less explosive with the passage of a few days. But those kind of threats will get you nowhere, Lonnie. If our friendship means anything, you'll not repeat such outrageous statements," George intoned, now almost unable to control his mixture of anger and shock.

George returned to his office and, after consulting with his most trusted colleague, Henry Gill, the conscience of Caldwell & Moore, it was agreed that he would make a personal call on Lewis the very next day. It was a meeting George did not look forward to at all. Lewis Stern was a giant at the bar. A member of the American College of Trial Lawyers, he had served for years as chairman of the Ethics Committee of the Delaware Bar Association, of which he had also been president. Jousting with Lewis on the issue of confidentiality was, at best, a formidable task.

The meeting began pleasantly enough. Lewis's office was spacious and encrusted with the memorabilia from a career of service to clients, charities, and the bar. Lewis greeted him warmly, an approach George found both welcoming and intimidating: he knew Lewis was planning to charm him into acquiescence.

"This is all very sad stuff, George. It's terrible that your friend, Lonnie, and the others at Mercury have been so injured by Arnold's unfortunate conduct. Now all we can do is make sure this doesn't snowball into a total disaster. I am sure you agree with Lonnie and the others that, despite the fact that these contracts are for a shorter time than we thought, Mercury is likely to obtain renewals of contracts because of its reputation for speedy, low-cost service."

"But not once they find out about the bribes," George rejoined. "At that point, Mercury may not be eligible even to bid on the renewals."

"That's true if you go blabbing about. But the way this is structured," Lewis continued, "no one has to find out—as long as you recognize your professional responsibility not to violate Model Rule 1.6."

"Violate Rule 1.6. I should say not. As you know all too well, because you led the opposition to the change, I am totally free to disclose this information to prevent, mitigate or rectify a client fraud in which the lawyer's services have been used."

"I know. I know. Damn ABA panicked in the face of threats from the SEC, and gave into those who would turn lawyers into cops, letting them arrest their own clients, of all things. But at least they didn't require you to disclose. It's only permissive. So you still have a chance to demonstrate your loyalty to your old friend, I mean your former friend."

George leaped at the opening Lewis had left him. "You know it isn't that easy. Our firm told the bank that these contracts were enforceable in accordance with their terms when, in fact, we didn't even have the version of the contracts with the correct number of years in front of us."

"Exactly my point," Lewis interrupted. "If you give discretion to lawyers to breach confidentiality then when lawyers are faced with difficult choices they will put their own interests ahead of their clients."

"Back then I agreed with you," George responded. "I'm not so sure now that I've been betrayed by Arnold Plinger."

"You've been betrayed! I should say not." Lewis was shaking now. "Your client has been betrayed by Arnold, and now is about to be betrayed by you. You can choose and you better choose non-disclosure." Lewis was pulling out all the stops.

"Lewis, you might be right if I had discretion. And under Rule 1.6 it appears I do. But not when you read Rule 4.1. That rule requires me to disclose to prevent assisting a client fraud. I have no choice but to disclose."

"But you are not aiding and abetting a fraud. This fraud already took place. I do not see how anything your firm does from this day forward will assist your former client in committing a fraud. Caldwell & Moore will be asked to do *nothing* having anything to do with the financial transactions—the loan, its extension, or its repayment. All of *that* will now be undertaken by others. Your firm will be completely shielded from all contact with any transaction. The only hint of Caldwell & Moore's existence in those ongoing transactions (whatever they may be) is your once-issued opinion. It simply is not necessary for you to do anything other than withdraw."

George listened carefully. The argument seemed too pat. Where was the place where the rabbit went into the hat? Then it struck him: "Lewis, I admire you greatly and your advocacy skills have never been greater. But frankly, you are wrong. This is a mandatory disclosure situation under Model Rule 4.1. That's why I must let the bank know they can't rely on my opinion."

"You're wrong again," Lewis replied. "The mandatory disclosure provisions of Model Rule 4.1 come into play only if the 1.6 exceptions allow disclosure, and disclosure is only allowed 'where reasonably necessary' to prevent a fraud that is 'reasonably certain to result in substantial financial injury' to the bank. The operative words here are 'reasonably necessary' and 'reasonably certain.' Here disclosure is not 'reasonably necessary' because your work is complete and therefore you are not assisting in a fraud. It's also not 'reasonably certain' that the bank will be harmed, because Lonnie and Mercury will find a way to get out of this mess."

"I can't believe you are telling me this. It's pure sophistry, Lewis. Your reading of 'reasonably' is far too narrow. Surely, one can assist a person in the future through work that was completed in the past. The fact that the work is completed renders the assistance no more or less helpful, or actionable, I might add, than if it were taking place at the same time as the client's conduct. It's also reasonably certain that the bank will lose its money. If you were the bank, wouldn't you want to know?"

But Lewis remained indomitable. "What you are saying is that by hiding behind an overly broad interpretation of 1.6(b), you can conjure up an obligation to contact the bank, and withdraw your opinion, and destroy your client. But the truth is all your clever argumentation about aiding and abetting cannot obscure the fact that Rule 1.6 gives you complete discretion whether to disclose. So when you do disclose, know that no one will celebrate George's observance of the rules. No, they will recognize a lawyer who breached his confidentiality commitment to his client because he put his own interests first. George, simply withdraw and give Lonnie one last chance to save his company, your once treasured client."

"If you would only persuade *your* client to do the right thing," George replied, "we wouldn't be in this pickle. And if I thought just withdrawing would accomplish the purpose, I would do that. But here I know that our silent withdrawal won't do anything. It's not like the bank is calling us up each week to find out if we are still representing Mercury. Under these special circumstances, we simply have no choice."

Now Lewis stood, pressing his palms on his mammoth desk as he leaned forward for emphasis. "You're right about no choice. But you're wrong about the result. You have no business disclosing Arnold's indiscretions to the bank. And if you do so, I can assure you that Caldwell & Moore will find itself the subject of a malpractice suit for the damages flowing from the bank's cutting off the credit and calling the loan. If you do anything other than withdraw, it will be a very sad day for all of us. Think about it, son. Think of Lonnie; think of your firm; think of your fine reputation. I know you'll do the right thing."

Stunned, George slowly rose from the chair and, without a word or a gesture, shuffled out of Lewis's office, his legs heavy and wooden, his hands clammy, his forehead beaded with sweat, and his psyche a battlefield of conflicting emotions—remorse, anger, regret, dismay. How difficult it was to be a lawyer, an ethical lawyer, the conscientious lawyer he always wanted to be.

In re American Continental Corporation/Lincoln Savings & Loan Securities Litigation

794 F. Supp. 1424 (D. Ariz. 1992)

BILBY, District Judge. . . .

V. RULINGS PERTINENT TO INDIVIDUAL DEFENDANTS

D. Jones, Day, Reavis & Pogue

Jones Day . . . focuses its summary judgment motion on an individual opinion letter given in connection with a 1986 registration statement. Jones Day claims this opinion letter was neither false, nor was it written in an expert capacity. Jones Day generally claims that it has not engaged in conduct for which it could be held liable because lawyers are obligated to keep their clients' confidence and to act in ways that do not discourage their clients from undergoing regulator compliance reviews.

1. The Record

The record reveals the following facts concerning Jones Day's involvement with ACC and Keating.

Prior to joining Jones Day, defendant William Schilling was director of the FHLBB Office of Examinations and Supervision. In that capacity, he was directly involved in the supervision of Lincoln Savings. During the summer of 1985, he wrote at least one memorandum and concurred in another, expressing serious regulatory concerns about numerous aspects of Lincoln's operations. For example, he wrote:

> [U]nder new management, Lincoln has engaged in several serious regulatory violations. Some of these violations, such as the overvaluation of real estate and failure to comply with Memorandum R-4l(b), are the same type of violations that have lead to some of the worst failures in FSLIC's history.

Later in 1985, Schilling was hired by Jones Day to augment its expertise in thrift representation. On January 31, 1986, Schilling and Jones Day's Ron Kneipper flew to Phoenix to solicit ACC's business. ACC retained Jones Day to perform "a major internal audit of Lincoln's FHLBB compliance and a major project to help Lincoln deal with the FHLBB's direct investment regulations."

During the regulatory compliance audit, which Jones Day understood to be a pre-FHLBB examination compliance review, the law firm found multiple regulatory violations. There is evidence that Jones Day knew that Lincoln had backdated files, destroyed appraisals, removed appraisals from files, told appraisers not to issue written reports when their oral valuations were too low, and violated affiliated transaction regulations. Jones Day found that Lincoln did no loan underwriting and no post-closure loan followup to ensure that Lincoln's interests were being protected. Jones Day learned Lincoln had multiple "loans" which were, in fact, joint ventures which violated FHLBB regulations, made real estate loans in violation of regulations, and backdated corporate resolutions which were not signed by corporate officers and did not reflect actual meetings. There is evidence that Jones Day may have tacitly consented to removal of harmful documents from Lincoln files. For example, one handwritten notation on a memorandum memorializing Jones Day's advice not to remove documents from files reads, "If something *is* devastating, consider it individually." (Emphasis in original.)

There is evidence that Jones Day instructed ACC in how to rectify deficiencies so that they would not be apparent to FHLBB examiners. Jones Day attorneys, including Schilling, testified that they told ACC/Lincoln personnel to provide the Jones Day-generated "to do" lists only to the attorneys responsible for rectifying the deficiencies, and to destroy the lists so that FHLB-SF would not find them in the files. For the same reason, Jones Day's regulatory compliance reports to ACC/Lincoln were oral. Jones Day paralegals testified that responsibilities for carrying out the "to do" lists were divided among Jones Day and ACC staff. Jones Day continued this work into the summer of 1986.

The evidence indicates that Jones Day may have been aware that ACC/

Lincoln did not follow its compliance advice with respect to ongoing activities. There are material questions of fact concerning the procedures Jones Day used—if any—to ascertain whether their compliance advice was being heeded. The testimony suggests that Jones Day partners knew ACC/Lincoln personnel were preparing loan underwriting summaries contemporaneously with Jones Day's regulatory compliance review, even though the loan transactions had already been closed. Moreover, the evidence reveals that Jones Day attorneys participated in creating corporate resolutions to ratify forged and backdated corporate records.

On April 23, 1986, Jones Day partner Fohrman wrote:

> I received Neal Millard's memo on ACC. In looking at the long list of people involved, it occurred to me that there will be times when individuals may be called upon to render legal services that might require the issuance of opinion letters from Jones, Day. As we all know, we now possess information that could affect the way we write our opinion letters and our actual ability to give a particular opinion may be severely restricted. However, this large list of individuals may not be aware of knowledge that is held by Messrs. Fein and Schilling. I would suggest that a follow up memo be issued by Ron Fein indicating that any work involving ACC which requires the issuance of opinions, must be cleared by Ron. . . .

Also in April 1986, ACC's Jim Grogan wrote to Jones Day's Kneipper, soliciting a strategy to "sunset" the FHLBB direct investment regulation. Jones Day subsequently made multiple Freedom of Information Act requests to FHLBB in furtherance of a direct investment rule strategy, for which Lincoln was billed. In a

September 12, 1986 telephone conversation, Grogan allegedly told Kneipper: "Comment letters were great success FHLBB picked it up 'hook, line and sinker' . . . Charlie wants to do again. . . ."

The record indicates that the concept of selling ACC debentures in Lincoln savings branches may have originated at an April 9, 1986 real estate syndicate seminar given by Jones Day Defendant Ron Fein. There is evidence that Fein may have contributed to the detailed bond sales program outline, attending to details such as explaining how the sales would work, and insuring that the marketing table was far enough from the teller windows to distinguish between ACC and Lincoln Savings employees. The evidence indicates that Jones Day reviewed the debenture registration statement and prospectus, which is corroborated by Jones Day's billing records. As a result, in January 1987, ACC was able to assure the California Department of Savings & Loan that:

> The process of structuring the bond sales program was reviewed by Kaye, Scholer and Jones Day to assure compliance not only with securities laws and regulations, but also with banking and FSLIC laws and regulations.

Moreover, there is evidence which suggests that political contributions were made on behalf of ACC, in exchange for ACC's consent that Jones Day could "bill liberally." On June 23, 1986, Kneipper memorialized a phone conversation:

> (1) 1:15 p.m. Ron Kessler—in past, firm has given $amt. to PAC, has premium billed, & PAC contri. to candidate; concern that we're an out of state law firm and that a $# in excess of $5,000.00 would look like an

unusual move; Barnett and Kessler have done before; question re whether and how we can get some busi. from GOV. for this.

(2) 3:40 p.m. Jim Grogan

Ten tickets at $1,000.00 equals $10,000.00

Barr wants limits of $5,000.00/ contribution.

Agreed that we could bill liberally in future in recognition of this.

At deposition, Kneipper testified that his note—"agreed could bill liberally in recognition for this,"—"is what it appears to be." Jones Day set up an Arizona Political Action Committee ("PAC") specifically for the purpose of making a contribution to an Arizona gubernatorial candidate. The PAC was opened on September 4, 1986 and closed in December, 1986, after the contribution was made.

In June 1986, Jones Day solicited additional work from ACC. Jones Day attorney Caulkins wrote, in part:

Rick Kneipper reports that ACC is very explicit that it does not care how

much its legal services cost, as long as it gets the best. He states that Keating gave him an unsolicited $250,000 retainer to start the thrift work, and sent another similar check also unsolicited in two weeks. On the down side, he reports that he has never encountered a more demanding and difficult client, . . .

It appears to Rick and to me that American Continental is made for us and we for them.

On October 28, 1986, Jones Day provided an opinion letter, required by Item 601(b) of SEC regulation S-K, for inclusion in an ACC bond registration statement. Jones Day's opinion letter stated that the indenture was a valid and binding obligation under California law.

2. Section 10(b), RICO, and Common Law Fraud

Jones Day seeks summary judgment on Plaintiffs' claims under Section 10(b),[a] RICO,[b] and common law fraud.[c]

---

a. [A] primary violation of Section 10(b) and Rule 10b-5 entails: (1) a scheme or artifice to defraud; (2) an affirmative misrepresentation or omission of a fact necessary to make other statements not misleading; or (3) a course of business which operates as a fraud or deceit. In addition, the act or omission must be made or conducted "in connection with" the purchase or sale of securities, with resultant damage to plaintiffs. Proof of scienter is a requisite to any 10b-5 action. The United States Supreme Court has defined scienter as "a mental state embracing intent to deceive, manipulate, or defraud." Ernst & Ernst v. Hochfelder, 425 U.S. 185 (1976). In Hollinger v. Titan Capital Corp., 914 F.2d 1564 (9th Cir. 1990), cert. denied, 499 U.S. 975 (1991), the Ninth Circuit adopted a standard for the minimal culpable mindset, referred to hereinafter by this court as "reckless scienter."

b. RICO, 18 U.S.C. §1962(c), provides: It shall be unlawful for any person employed by or associated with any enterprise engaged in, or the activities of which affect, interstate or foreign commerce, to conduct or participate, directly or indirectly, in the conduct of such enterprise's affairs through a pattern of racketeering activity or collection of unlawful debt. RICO also provides that it is unlawful for any person to conspire to violate subsection (c). "Racketeering activity" is defined as any act indictable under various provisions of Title 18, including . . . mail fraud, . . . wire fraud, and securities fraud under Title 11. . . ."

c. Under California common law, an action for fraud and deceit requires proof of: (1) a false representation; (2) knowledge of the falsity; (3) an intent to induce reliance; (4) actual and reasonable reliance; and (5) resulting damage to the plaintiff. Secondary liability, or aiding and abetting, . . . requires proof of knowledge of the primary violation, which may be inferred from the circumstances, and substantial assistance, which may be in the form of encouragement or advice. . . . The aider and abetter's conduct must be a substantial factor in causing the plaintiff's harm.

Jones Day contends that it may not be held liable for counseling its client. The line between maintaining a client's confidence and violating the securities law is brighter than Jones Day suggests, however. Attorneys must inform a client in a clear and direct manner when its conduct violates the law. If the client continues the objectionable activity, the lawyer must withdraw "if the representation will result in violation of the rules of professional conduct or other law." Ethical Rule 1.16 ("ER"). Under such circumstances, an attorney's ethical responsibilities do not conflict with the securities laws. An attorney may not continue to provide services to corporate clients when the attorney knows the client is engaged in a course of conduct designed to deceive others, and where it is obvious that the attorney's compliant legal services may be a substantial factor in permitting the deceit to continue.

The record raises material questions about whether Jones Day knew of ACC/Lincoln's fraud, but nevertheless provided hands-on assistance in hiding loan file deficiencies from the regulators, offered detailed advice about setting up the bond sales program, carried out a lobbying strategy with respect to the direct investment rule, made political contributions on ACC's behalf, reviewed SEC registration statements and prospectuses, and lent its name to a misleading legal opinion. This evidence raises material questions concerning... RICO, AZRAC,[d] common law fraud and deceit, and violations of Cal. Corp. Code §§25401 and 25504.1.[e]

3. Section 11 Liability...

b. Expert Status

Jones Day further contends that it cannot be held liable under Section 11 because it did not issue an "expert" opinion. Section 11 applies to misleading statements made by one "whose profession gives authority to statements made by him."[f] Jones Day concedes that its October 28, 1986 opinion letter was required by SEC Regulation S-K, which provides in part:

> (5) Opinion Re Legality—(i) An opinion of counsel as to the legality of the securities being registered, indicating whether they will, when sold, be legally issued, fully paid and non-assessable, and, if debt securities, whether they will be binding obligations of the registrant.

The court holds that an attorney who provides a legal opinion used in connection with an SEC registration statement is an expert within the meaning of Section 11.

---

d. AZRAC, A.R.S. §13-2312, applies to state sales of securities and generally parallels Rule 10b-5.
e. These sections impose liability on any corporate director, officer, employee, or agent who publishes a prospectus, report, financial statement or other public document which is false in any material respect.... Proof of reliance is unnecessary.
f. 15 U.S.C. §77l. This section provides that every person who acquires a security burdened by an untrue statement or omission of material fact may sue: (1) every person who signed the registration statement; (2) every director and officer of the offerer; (3) "every accountant, engineer, appraiser, or any person whose profession gives authority to a statement made by him, who has with his consent been named as having prepared or certified" any part of a registration statement or any report or valuation used in connection with it; and/or (4) every underwriter with respect to such security. 15 U.S.C. §77k.

4. Breach of Fiduciary Duty to Lincoln . . .

An attorney who represents a corporation has a duty to act in the corporation's best interest when confronted by adverse interests of directors, officers, or corporate affiliates. It is not a defense that corporate representation often involves the distinct interests of affiliated entities. Attorneys are bound to act when those interests conflict. There are genuine questions as to whether Jones Day should have sought independent representation for Lincoln.

Moreover, where a law firm believes the management of a corporate client is committing serious regulatory violations, the firm has an obligation to actively discuss the violative conduct, urge cessation of the activity, and withdraw from representation where the firm's legal services may contribute to the continuation of such conduct. Jones Day contends that it would have been futile to act on these fiduciary obligations because those controlling ACC/Lincoln would not have responded. Client wrongdoing, however, cannot negate an attorney's fiduciary duty. Moreover, the evidence reveals that attorney advice influenced ACC/Lincoln's conduct in a variety of ways. Accordingly, summary judgment as to this claim is denied.

5. Professional Negligence Claims

Jones Day issued an opinion letter that was included with ACC's 1986 shelf registration statement. California authority provides that independent public accountants have a duty to those who are foreseeably injured from representations made in connection with publicly held corporations. While this duty does not extend to confidential advice which an attorney gives to its clients, it would apply where an attorney issues an SEC opinion letter to the public. Roberts v. Ball, Hunt, Hart, Brown & Baerwitz, 128 Cal. Rptr. 901 (Cal. App. 1976).

Accordingly, a question of fact remains as to whether the . . . Plaintiffs who purchased bonds issued pursuant to the November, 1986 shelf registration and amendments, were injured by the Jones Day opinion letter.

■ Lawyers' Roles:
The Instrumental Lawyer and the Bounds of the Law

Viewed from a public perspective after the massive costs of the fraud were known, the Jones Day lawyers in *ACC*, like Mr. Perez's lawyers, appear to have misconstrued their role in the representation. Indeed, two years before Judge Bilby's decision in *ACC*, Judge Stanley Sporkin upheld the federal receivership of Lincoln Savings & Loan, concluding his opinion with these observations:

> There are other unanswered questions presented by this case. Keating testified that he was so bent on doing the "right thing" that he surrounded himself with literally scores of accountants and lawyers to make sure all the transactions were legal. The questions that must be asked are:
>
> > Where were these professionals, a number of whom are now asserting their rights under the Fifth Amendment, when these clearly improper transactions were being consummated?

Why didn't any of them speak up or disassociate themselves from the transactions? Where also were the outside accountants and attorneys when these transactions were effectuated?[1]

ACC involves serious allegations against lawyers who appear to have over-identified with a client and illustrates what can happen when lawyers fail to maintain the distance critical to evaluating a client's conduct. The ACC lawyers seemed to have lacked a healthy skepticism that may have helped them avoid entanglement in their client's wrongdoing, and allowed themselves, wittingly or unwittingly, to be used as instruments and technicians of inappropriate conduct by a client. Perhaps they experienced the business lawyers' "chronic source of moral difficulty," where assisting a client's business goal of gaining a competitive advantage required the lawyers to skate too close to the edge of the law, putting other people's money at risk.[2] Lawyers who continue to advocate for such a client unwittingly, negligently, or knowingly can become an instrument of wrongdoing or an accessory to corrupt and dishonest conduct. The behavior of the ACC lawyers suggests that they may have seen the law as a malleable means to pursue a client's objectives, rather than as a set of rules with some clear boundaries that should have shaped both their client's and their own behavior.

The Bounds of the Law

The fiduciary relationship between principal-client and agent-lawyer is subject to one significant limitation: Neither may violate the limits or bounds of the law.[3] Both principal and agent remain responsible for the consequences of their own conduct. Agency law recognizes principal and agent as distinct, autonomous legal persons, and anticipates that they will behave accordingly.[4]

Lawyers can be put in a position of real conflict when it comes to abiding by client instructions. On one hand, fiduciary duty admonishes lawyers to do everything they can to help fulfill the client's goals of the representation, goals that are to be determined by the client. On the other, clients can make decisions that the lawyer believes reflect bad judgment, or worse, that suggest to the lawyer that the client might be engaging in conduct that could run afoul of the law and subject the client to liability. When lawyers place too much weight on the former proposition—simply being instruments and unquestioningly abiding their client's instructions—they disserve the client by failing to share their independent view of the merits of the course of action and they open their clients to potential liability.[5] ACC illustrates that lawyers who are willfully blind to their client's

---

1. Lincoln Savings & Loan Assn. v. Wall, 743 F. Supp. 901, 919-920 (D.D.C. 1990).
2. *See* David Luban, *Making Sense of Moral Meltdowns*, in Susan D. Carle, ed., *Lawyers' Ethics and the Pursuit of Social Justice: A Critical Reader* 355 (NYU Press 2005).
3. RLGL §23; *Restatement (Third) of Agency* §1.01, Comment f(1) (Tentative Draft No. 2, 2001).
4. *Id.* at Comment c.
5. Charles Keating was convicted of 90 federal and state counts of fraud, racketeering, and conspiracy. He served less than five years of a twelve and one-half year sentence and was released after two appellate courts found legal error in his convictions. Adam Zagorin, *Charlie's an Angel? Charles Keating, Demon of the $500 Billion S&L Fiasco, Is Now Innocent, Sort Of*, Time 36 (Feb. 3, 1997).

actual goals also disserve themselves, by exposing themselves and their law firms to significant liability.

It is important to realize that lawyers can be subjected to allegations of assisting client misconduct in at least three different circumstances. In the first, lawyers, like those in *Chen*, unwittingly or innocently participate in the client's fraud by providing legal advice to a client who, unbeknownst to the lawyer, is using it to break the law. In the second, lawyers act negligently by failing to identify or act upon red flags, which, with the benefit of 20-20 hindsight, will be characterized as clear warnings that the client was engaged in wrongful conduct. The third, and most serious, involves lawyers who act recklessly or intentionally by blindly ignoring clear warning signs, or worse, purposefully assisting a client to violate the law. Everyone recognizes the last as a clear example of lawyer misconduct. But the middle example can get lawyers in almost as much trouble, and the first, unwitting involvement, requires immediate response at the point the lawyer discovers the client's unlawful activity. In all of these circumstances, the lawyer who fails to keep the proper distance and overidentifies with the client is the lawyer who is most likely to ignore the warning signs.

What Happened in *ACC*?

In *ACC*, Charles Keating, Jr., first hired Jones Day, after he and his general counsel met with William Schilling and Rick Kneipper.[6] Schilling, a Jones Day partner, had recently stepped down from his job as director of the Federal Home Loan Bank Board, where he had supervised and participated in an investigation that found serious regulatory concerns about Keating's Lincoln Savings & Loan. Schilling's prior "personal and substantial involvement" meant that he could not personally represent ACC after he left the government and that his new law firm could represent ACC only if Schilling had no involvement in the matter.[7] Yet, Schilling testified that he not only solicited ACC's business, but he also personally performed legal services for ACC (the "to do" lists).[8]

Second, the law firm's first legal service for ACC, a major internal audit of Lincoln's compliance with federal regulations, uncovered multiple regulatory violations. Judge Bilby correctly summarized the professional codes on this subject. Lawyers in this situation must begin by telling their client "in a clear and direct manner when its conduct violates the law." If the client's violations

---

6. Rita Henley Jensen, *Lawyers Share the Blame for the Savings and Loan Scandal*, 95 Bus. & Socy. Rev. 54, 56 (1995). Keating controlled both Lincoln Savings & Loan and American Continental Corporation (ACC), which was a wholly owned subsidiary of Lincoln.

7. *See* MR 1.11(b), which requires that the former government lawyer be "screened from any participation in the matter and apportioned no part of the fee therefrom." *See also* 18 U.S.C. §207 (2006), the federal government's conflict of interest statute, which prohibits former governmental employees from communicating or appearing before their former agencies within certain time periods in any matters in which they participated personally and substantially while in government service. If Schilling confined his representation of ACC to advising them, and avoided contact on their behalf with the FHLBB, he complied with this statute.

8. The government refused to settle the case unless the settlement included Schilling's agreement not to work on any additional banking matters. John H. Cushman, Jr., *Despite Big Settlement, Firm Feels Little Pinch*, N.Y. Times, at B10 (Apr. 23, 1993).

are continuing rather than past, and the lawyer knows about them, the lawyers are required to withdraw to avoid violating Model Rule 1.2(d).[9] ACC's lawyers seemed to be instinctively aware of this requirement, because, one of them (Ronald Fein) testified he warned ACC's inside counsel that ACC's conduct would have to stop and was assured that it would not recur. He also told ACC that if the regulatory violations continued, Jones Day would have to withdraw. At that point, its initial work on regulatory compliance "wound down."[10]

Third, just two days after this warning, Fein himself solicited ACC's securities business, and Jones Day was hired for that purpose.[11] One of the statements made in securities documents Jones Day prepared for ACC was, "Lincoln Savings complies with the rules and regulations promulgated by the FHLBB (Federal Home Loan Bank Board) and the California Department of Savings and Loan regarding appraisals. . . ."[12] If the firm knew this language was incorrect, Jones Day not only "lent its name to misleading legal opinions"[13] in violation of Model Rule 1.2(d), but also engaged in deceit itself in violation of Model Rules 4.1(a) and 8.4(c). If this occurred, Jones Day crossed the line from counseling a client about the limits of the law to assisting a client in violating it.

The memo written by Jones Day partner Neal Millard appears to have anticipated this problem: " . . . we now possess information that could affect the way we write our opinion letters. . . ." Millard's memo appears to "remedy" this problem by assigning opinion letter responsibilities to those within the firm who lacked first-hand knowledge of ACC's regulatory violations. Of course, this advice ignores the basic agency rule that attributes the knowledge of one agent to those in the rest of the firm. In other words, there was no way any lawyer at Jones Day could write opinion letters certifying ACC's compliance with banking regulations if some in the firm knew that such compliance was not a reality.

Fourth, note that the cause of action for breach of fiduciary duty in *ACC* was instituted by constituents of the client itself: the shareholders who now claimed that Jones Day should not have obeyed Keating when he was in fact acting contrary to the best interests of both Lincoln and ACC. Here, the court's response anticipates recent specific amendments to Model Rule 1.13 and the Sarbanes-Oxley Act of 2002.[14] Lawyers who believe that constituents of entity clients are acting against its best interests should seek outside opinions and refer the matter to a higher authority within the organization. If that does not stop the wrongdoing, the lawyer should resign.[15] Model Rule 1.13 today also instructs lawyers who reasonably believe it necessary to prevent substantial injury to

---

9. Today, MR 1.13(d) and Comment [4] clarify this distinction as well. *See also* The Bounds of the Law: Client Fraud, *infra* p. 237 .
10. Rita Henley Jensen, *Lawyers Share the Blame for the Savings and Loan Scandal*, 95 Bus. & Socy. Rev. 54 (Sept. 22, 1995).
11. *Id.*
12. *Id.* at 59.
13. *ACC, supra* p. 220.
14. 15 U.S.C. §7245 (2006); 17 C.F.R. §§205.1-205.7 (2007); 68 Fed. Reg. 6296 (Feb. 6, 2003).
15. MR 1.13, Comment [4]. Comment [6] provides that a lawyer in such a situation also "may" resign and mirrors the *ACC* court's conclusion that withdrawal is mandatory where the ongoing conduct is criminal or fraudulent and the lawyer knows about it. *See* MR 1.2(d).

the organization to disclose information outside the organization to prevent, stop, or rectify the wrongdoing.[16]

ACC illustrates that this reality about the many faces of corporate identity often has grave consequences for lawyers when an entity fails. At that point, a successor in interest, such as a trustee in bankruptcy (or the receiver in ACC) reassesses the entity's best interests, with a view toward maximizing the funds available to creditors or other stakeholders. In such cases, corporate officials like Keating, who may have violated legal regulations, often blame the professionals they say they relied upon and organizations or their successors waive the attorney-client privilege, resulting in the disclosure and adverse use of documents and conversations the lawyer thought would never see the light of day. The lawyer who acted instrumentally may in fact have agreed to the course of action, knowing it was risky, but believing all along that the corporate officials' course of conduct would succeed on behalf of the entity. When that fails, the legal advice will be very carefully scrutinized by a successor in interest of the now failed enterprise.

The Problem with Instrumental Behavior

ACC demonstrates that no lawyer or law firm is invulnerable to serious allegations of complicity in client misconduct. In retrospect, what is so amazing about this case is that very well educated and talented lawyers could appear to be duped by a clever and self-serving client. ACC offers one clue to how they might have lost their way when it quotes an ambiguous, but troubling, Jones Day memo from its lawyer, Hugh Caulkins, written after Jones Day solicited additional business from Keating.

> ACC is very explicit that it does not care how much its legal services cost, as long as it gets the best. . . . On the down side, he reports that he has never encountered a more demanding and difficult client. . . . It appears to Rick and to me that American Continental is made for us and we for them.

In fact, Jones Day solicited Keating's business at a time when its managing partner, Richard W. Pogue, was "pushing the Los Angeles branch to break into the lucrative business of advising banks and other financial institutions."[17] In the year before this, Pogue had overseen a firm merger that transformed Jones Day from a five-office, 330-lawyer firm to the country's second-largest firm with nearly 600 lawyers. Perhaps a powerful client saw an economic opportunity in this situation to make the law firm a tool of his will.

It is also possible that overidentification with a client may have been caused by non-monetary considerations. Lincoln Savings & Loan did business in a highly regulated, competitive environment. Its CEO appears to have been a flamboyant man, accustomed to taking risks.[18] It is conceivable that Jones Day

---

16. MR 1.13(c)(2).
17. Jensen, *supra* note 6, at 55.
18. For an account of Keating's view of the matter, *see* Michael Binstein & Charles Bowden, *Trust Me: Charles Keating and the Missing Billions* (Random House 1993).

lawyers, like several public figures,[19] identified with or admired this powerful man and his entrepreneurial abilities.[20] Whatever their motivations, the role assumed by these lawyers apparently enabled Keating to turn them into instruments of his wrongful conduct. The law firm appears not only to have allowed but also to have invited Keating and ACC to treat them instrumentally. In the process, the firm apparently lost some of its ability to evaluate objectively its client's conduct, and, as a result, was implicated in ACC's wrongdoing.

In the end, Jones Day billed ACC about $1.2 million for its services,[21] an amount that pales in relation to the $24 million for which it eventually settled the private claims of the stockholders against the firm. The government claims went to trial, but just after jury selection, the law firm settled these claims for an additional $51 million. At a press conference on the day of the settlement, Pogue denied wrongdoing by the firm but concluded after watching jury selection that the jury would never understand the firm's complex defense.[22]

All told, Jones Day settled the public and private claims against the firm for $75 million. Jones Day's new managing partner said that the settlement would not have a "significant financial impact" on the firm even though $19.5 million of the settlement was uninsured.[23] The firm also claimed it was "infected" by its association with Keating and released a statement that characterized its services to Lincoln as "limited" and "performed competently and in accord with applicable standards of professional conduct."[24]

The Cure for Instrumental Behavior

Professor Rhode warns that this kind of instrumental behavior is especially dangerous and misplaced in representing entities rather than individuals, and in counseling clients rather than litigating on their behalf. When a powerful enterprise rather than an autonomous individual's interests are at stake, the rights-based justification for role-differentiated behavior has much less legitimacy. When lawyers counsel clients, Rhode points out that lawyers deal with ongoing and future behavior, which provides an opportunity and obligation to prevent, rather than justify, massive social and personal harm.[25] ACC illustrates how an initial litigation-minded advocacy (appropriate perhaps for defending the entity against bank regulators) may have infected subsequent transactional service as well. Thinking

---

19. The "Keating Five," was the derogatory moniker placed on five United States Senators (Alan Cranston, Dennis DeConcini, John Glenn, Donald Riegle, and John McCain) whose careers were nearly ruined by their close association to Keating. *See* Richard L. Berke, *Cranston Rebuked by Ethics Panel*, N.Y. Times, at A1 (Nov. 20, 1991).
20. This is the way Judge Noonan describes the transformation of another influential lawyer, Hoyt Moore, whose representation of Bethlehem Steel led him to bribe a federal judge to secure his client's goals. John T. Noonan, Jr., *The Lawyer Who Overidentifies with His Client*, 76 Notre Dame L. Rev. 827, 840-841 (2001).
21. Jensen, *supra* note 6, at 57.
22. *Id.* at 59.
23. Henry J. Reske, *Firm Agrees to Record S & L Settlement: Shifting Standards Require Lawyers to Disclose More to Regulatory Agencies*, 79 ABA J. 16 (July 1993). The law firm that represented Lincoln on regulatory matters after Jones Day finally withdrew, Kaye, Scholer, Fierman Nays & Handler, also settled with both private investors ($21 million) and the government ($41 million). Stephen Labaton, *Law Firm Will Pay a $41 Million Fine in Savings Lawsuit*, N.Y. Times, at A1 (Mar. 9, 1992).
24. Reske, *supra* note 23.
25. *See supra* pp. 8-10.

about how to protect the client against legal sanctions may have erased practical wisdom about legal limits on future activity.

In retrospect, one might argue that a lack of moral integrity on the part of lawyers prevents them from recognizing these dangers before they materialize.[26] While it is no doubt true that lawyers need to listen to their own moral intuition, it also appears to be the case that personal conscience can be significantly affected by implicit but often unexpressed values in social milieus, including the moral world of both clients and law firms.[27]

Lawyers can recognize these dangers by setting up a kind of early warning system, which prompts them to assess both risky practice environments and the strength of their own counterintuitions. Risk can stem from the client's world as well as the lawyer's practice environment. ACC may indicate the typical client and law firm risk: a place where everyday activity involved significant risk-taking in businesses that were heavily regulated by law. These risks can be exacerbated by clients or law firms who engage in generally dishonest strategies, such as blaming or shifting loss to others, or worse, covering up misconduct or bad results.[28] Lawyers who practice in such environments can prevent dilution of their own moral intuitions by creating baselines for themselves that might warn about changes in the lawyer's personal judgments. Professor Luban suggests you create your own, such as: "I will never backdate a document," "paper a deal I don't understand," or "do something I cannot explain to my (grandmother, father, or significant other)."[29] He also recommends noticing when you begin to blame others for your conduct, and suggests that self-doubt, rather than hubris, best fosters a lawyer's best chance to recognize a limit on his or her client's or own behavior.[30] All of this advice is also subsumed in the mandate of Model Rule 1.2(d): Lawyers must recognize clear legal limits to a client's behavior, inform the client, and be willing to withdraw from the representation when the client will not cease and desist.

United States v. Chen
99 F.3d 1495 (9th Cir. 1996), cert. denied, 520 U.S. 1167 (1997)

KLEINFELD, Circuit Judge:

This case deals with the scope of the crime-fraud exception to the attorney-client privilege, where the attorney is innocent of any wrongdoing or guilty knowledge.

FACTS

Mr. Chen and his wife own Sunrider Corporation and operate TF Chen Products, Inc., a subsidiary of Sunrider. The companies manufacture health food and skin care

---

26. See, e.g., Stephen L. Pepper, *Counseling at the Limits of the Law: An Exercise in the Jurisprudence and Ethics of Lawyering*, 104 Yale L.J. 1545 (1995).
27. See Milton C. Regan, Jr., *Moral Intuitions and Organizational Culture*, 51 St. Louis U. L.J. 941 (2007).
28. Luban, *supra* note 2 at 364. For an example of a Wall Street lawyer who was convicted of perjury and bankruptcy fraud for conduct that occurred during a client's business reorganization, *see* Milton C. Regan, Jr., *Eat What You Kill: The Fall of a Wall Street Lawyer* (U. Mich. 2004).
29. Luban, *supra* note 2 at 369.
30. *Id.*

products and import from Taiwan, Hong Kong, Japan, and other countries. The importation tariffs the companies pay depend on the price they declare they paid for the goods. Undervaluation may result in administrative, civil, and criminal penalties. A statutory procedure allows an importer to mitigate or avoid penalties by filing a disclosure statement before the Customs Service learns of the undervaluation independently. *See* U.S.C. §1592(c)(4).

Of course an importer also pays taxes on profits. The higher the cost of goods sold, then, other things being equal, the lower the level of income taxes. Thus, an importer saves money on tariffs to the extent the goods are cheap, but pays more in income tax. Conversely, the company saves money on taxes, but pays higher tariffs, to the extent its cost of goods is higher.

The Customs duties on the higher values are much less than the additional taxes which would be due based on the true values. Thus an importer can come out ahead by overpaying tariffs and underpaying income taxes, by overstating the cost of the goods imported.

Mr. and Mrs. Chen and Sunrider were indicted for conspiracy, tax evasion, and other crimes. The indictment alleged that Mr. and Mrs. Chen imported their inventory and paid tariffs based on the true invoiced price. Then Mr. Chen's sister, Jau Hwa, the comptroller of Sunrider, would prepare entirely fictional invoices on blank forms from Sunrider's Hong Kong affiliate, owned largely by the Chens and operated by Mrs. Chen's brother. The fake invoices purported to charge much higher prices for the goods. The fake invoices were then given to Sunrider's

accountants to prepare trial balances, which were themselves given to Sunrider's tax preparers. Thus, tariffs would be paid on the true lower price of the goods, but taxes would be paid as though the goods had cost much more than they really did. Mr. Chen periodically instructed Jau Hwa to wire excess money to the Hong Kong affiliate's bank accounts, to maintain the fiction that Sunrider's payments were based on the fake invoices, not the real ones. Mr. and Mrs. Chen would subsequently recover the excess with the connivance of Mrs. Chen's brother. The government alleges that the Chens skimmed almost $90 million this way.

According to the indictment, the Chens eventually became concerned that IRS and Customs enforcement agents might communicate on their case and discover the difference in the claimed cost of their inventory. To protect themselves, they caused a disclosure to be made to Customs, purporting to acknowledge that they had understated their cost of goods imported. In the disclosure, they stated that the true cost of the goods was what they had reflected in their tax returns. Thus, the original Customs declarations were true, but the correcting disclosure was actually not a disclosure at all, but a fraud, intended to shield their tax evasion scheme. This scheme is entirely theoretical at this point, because nothing has yet been proven.

Mr. Chen's attorneys, Stein, Shostak, Shostak & O'Hara, filed a prior disclosure pursuant to 19 U.S.C. §1592(c)(4) and section 162.74 of the Customs regulations stating that a review gave rise to the discovery that "certain charges relating to the imported products may not have been properly included in the entered value." A check for over $381,000 was enclosed with the disclosure. The law firm said that more money would be paid as more data were assembled revealing underpayments.

Jau Hwa eventually left Sunrider. She then gave the government materials she had taken from Sunrider's files, and gave a customs agent her account of events on which the indictment is based. The Customs agent filed an affidavit saying that according to Jau Hwa, "Marjorie Shostak [Sunrider's lawyer] proposed that Sunrider should file a disclosure with Customs." Though this affidavit does not say in so many words that Ms. Shostak knew that the disclosure would be false, and intended to hide a tax evasion scheme, the Assistant United States Attorney argued that the differences between the initial and supplemental invoices was "substantial enough to put any reasonable professional on notice that this was, in all likelihood, a fraudulent scheme."

Joseph P. Cox had worked on the Sunrider matter for the Stein, Shostak firm; James D. Wilets was in-house Sunrider counsel. Both were subpoenaed before the Grand Jury. The Chens and Sunrider moved to quash these two subpoenas based on their attorney-client privilege. . . .

Ms. Shostak filed a declaration that her firm was employed to avoid litigation by bringing Sunrider into compliance with the Customs laws, by voluntarily disclosing supplemental payments already reported to the IRS . . . She explained in detail the nature of the transactions and why her firm "saw nothing to suggest that a prior disclosure would further some alleged tax evasion scheme." She stated plainly that neither she nor any attorney to her knowledge had engaged in

the conduct alleged by Jau Hwa, done anything to mislead Customs, or had any knowledge of or participation in any fraud on the government. Mr. Wilets and Mr. Cox also filed affidavits explaining what services they had performed on behalf of the Chens and Sunrider, stating that to the best of their knowledge neither they, the accountants, the Ernst & Young Customs group assisting with the prior disclosure, nor anyone else involved, including the Chens, had ever intended to further any tax evasion scheme or known about such a scheme. General counsel for Sunrider, Cynthia Muldrow, filed an affidavit establishing that no one had authorized Jau Hwa to take any documents with her when she left the corporation, or to disclose any attorney-client information to anyone outside Sunrider.

After considering all the evidence, the district judge . . . found "the attorneys are not involved in the involved crime," because there was not even a "prima facie case that these attorneys in any way participated in or joined the alleged criminal conspiracy." . . . The judge nevertheless denied the Chens' motions to quash the Grand Jury subpoenas, "provided the questioning is confined to matters concerning the disclosures which TFCP/Sunrider made to United States Customs in 1989-1990." The district judge expressly found a prima facie case establishing reasonable cause to believe that the Chens and Sunrider had used their lawyers to make false statements, albeit not known to the lawyers to be false, to the Customs Service. . . .

ANALYSIS . . .

The attorney-client privilege is essential to preservation of liberty against a powerful government. People need lawyers to guide them through thickets of complex government requirements, and, to get useful advice, they have to be able to talk to their lawyers candidly without fear that what they say to their own lawyers will be transmitted to the government.

Much of what lawyers actually do for a living consists of helping their clients comply with the law. Clients unwittingly engage in conduct subject to civil and even criminal penalties. This valuable social service of counseling clients and bringing them into compliance with the law cannot be performed effectively if clients are scared to tell their lawyers what they are doing, for fear that their lawyers will be turned into government informants. . . .

It is a truism that while the attorney-client privilege stands firm for client's revelations of past conduct, it cannot be used to shield ongoing or intended future criminal conduct. United States v. Zolin, 491 U.S. 554, 563 (1989). That principle is easily applied when a lawyer is retained to defend a client in a criminal prosecution or civil litigation relating to an entirely completed course of conduct. But it is difficult to apply when the lawyer's role is more in the nature of business planning or counseling or bringing the client into compliance for past wrongs, as opposed to simply defending the client against a charge relating to past wrongs. The act of bringing a client into compliance with the law ordinarily and properly engages the lawyer in an effort to assure the client is sanctioned no more harshly than the law requires. Because of the delicacy and importance of the attorney-client privilege in the counseling relationship, both

the district court's task and ours are especially difficult when the United States Attorney insists upon using a person's own lawyer against him.

The government argues without citation that "where attorneys are involved in business decision-making, or, as Cox and Wilets acted here, as spokespersons for a company, they are clearly not acting as 'professional legal advisors.'" The government argues that this proposition takes the lawyers' planning for correcting understated customs declarations out of the privilege.

The lawyers in this case were "spokespersons" only in the sense that, as lawyers, they communicated their clients' positions to the government agencies dealing with their clients. They were not engaged in a public relations business separate from their law firm, as the government's term "spokespersons" may imply. For a lawyer to tell a judge, jury, or administrative agency, his client's position and the basis for it, that is, to be his client's spokesman, is a traditional and central attorney's function as an advocate. The communications between lawyer to perform this function are privileged. . . .

That a person is a lawyer does not, ipso facto, make all communications with that person privileged. The privilege applies only when legal advice is sought "from a professional legal advisor in his capacity as such." . . . For example, where a counterfeiter hired a man who was a lawyer to buy printing equipment for him, no privilege could be asserted because the lawyer was merely a "business agent" and not a "legal advisor." United States v. Huberts, 637 F.2d 630, 640 (9th Cir. 1980). . . .

If a person hires a lawyer for advice, there is a rebuttable presumption that the lawyer is hired "as such" to give "legal advice," whether the subject of the advice is criminal or civil, business, tort, domestic relations, or anything else. But the presumption is rebutted when the facts show that the lawyer was "employed without reference to his knowledge and discretion in the law." . . . That the lawyers were "involved in business decision-making," as the government puts it, is irrelevant. What matters is whether the lawyer was employed with or without "reference to his knowledge and discretion in the law," to give the advice. In this case, the attorneys were employed for their legal knowledge, to bring their clients into compliance with the law in the least burdensome way possible (so far as the lawyers knew). Their communications with their client were therefore within the scope of the attorney-client privilege.

Appellants correctly argue that Jau Hwa, a past employee of Sunrider Corporation, lacked authority to waive the corporation's attorney-client privilege. . . . "The power to waive the corporate attorney-client privilege rests with the corporation's management and is normally exercised by its officers and directors." Commodity Futures Trading Commn. v. Weintraub, 471 U.S. 343, 348 (1985). "When control of a corporation passes to new management, the authority to assert and waive the corporation's attorney-client privilege passes as well." *Id.* at 349. It follows a fortiori that since a corporate employee cannot waive the corporation's privilege, that same individual as an ex-employee cannot do so. An employee must generally keep an employer's confidences. *See Restatement (Second) of Agency* §395 (1958). The uncontradicted evidence in the record established that Jau Hwa never was given any authority to waive the attorney-client privilege. Thus, Jau Hwa's disclosures of attorney-client communications could not and did not waive the privilege.

Appellants next argue that the government improperly submitted Jau Hwa's affidavit and Agent Diciurcio's affidavit, thereby disclosing to the judge material protected by the attorney-client privilege, before the court decided that such a disclosure should be made. They are correct. The Supreme Court established in *Zolin* that the parties seeking to strip attorney-client communications of their privilege under the crime-fraud exception must satisfy the court with some showing prior to judicial in camera review of the privileged material. . . .

. . . Thus there are two steps. First the government must satisfy the judge that there is "a factual basis adequate to support a good faith belief by a reasonable person that in camera review of the materials may reveal evidence to establish the claim that the crime-fraud exception applies," and then if the judge decides this question in favor of the government, the otherwise privileged material may be submitted for in camera examination. *Id.* The government cannot show the otherwise privileged material to the judge unless and until the judge has made this preliminary judgment. . . .

In the case at bar, the United States Attorney submitted Jau Hwa's disclosures of attorney-client communications, and Diciurcio's affidavit telling more about her disclosures, without first making a prima facie showing and obtaining the court's permission. This was incorrect under *Zolin.* . . .

What is left of the case is whether the government's showing, without Jau Hwa's disclosures, was adequate to invoke the crime-fraud exception. It was. "To invoke the crime-fraud exception successfully, the government has the burden of making a prima facie showing that the communications were in furtherance of an intended or present illegality and that there is some relationship between the communications and the illegality." . . . The test for invoking the crime-fraud exception to the attorney-client privilege is whether there is "reasonable cause to believe that the attorney's services were utilized in furtherance of the ongoing unlawful scheme." Reasonable cause is more than suspicion but less than a preponderance of evidence. The government must submit "evidence that if believed by the jury would establish the elements of an ongoing violation."

In this case, there was reasonable cause to believe that the Chens and Sunrider were using attorneys' services to conceal income tax fraud. The government submitted copies of blank presigned invoices from Sunrider's supplier, which would facilitate the kind of fraud claimed by the government. The portions of Jau Hwa's affidavit other than her disclosures of attorney-client communications, tended to show, if true, that the company was claiming a low value of goods purchased for Customs' purposes, a high value for income tax purposes, and was proposing to make a fraudulent corrective disclosure to Customs in order to evade income taxes. The evidence, excluding the improperly submitted disclosures of attorney-client communications, further gave reasonable cause to believe that the Chens were using their lawyers to help prepare the paperwork for this fraudulent scheme, and using their prestige in the customs bar to hide it.

The district judge found that the lawyers in this case were innocent of any wrongful intent, and had no knowledge that their services were being used to trick the Customs' Service or the IRS. But the lawyers' innocence does not preserve the attorney-client privilege against the crime-fraud exception. The privilege is the client's, so "it is the client's knowledge and intentions that are of paramount concern to the application of the crime-fraud exception; the attorney need know nothing about the client's ongoing or planned illicit activity for the exception to apply. It is therefore irrelevant . . . that [the lawyers] may have been in the dark." . . .

CONCLUSION

The prosecution should have followed the two-step submission procedure in *Zolin*, and did not. But that error was harmless, because the judge disregarded the incorrectly submitted attorney-client communications. The attorneys' lack of any guilty knowledge did not matter, because the privilege was the client's, and the client's misconduct sufficed to lose it, despite the lawyers' innocence of wrongdoing. The properly submitted materials established reasonable cause to believe that the Chens and Sunrider were using their lawyers as part of an ongoing scheme to evade taxes, so the district judge was within his discretion in allowing the government to compel disclosures under the crime-fraud exception.

■ The Bounds of the Law:
Client Fraud

In a previous note about lawyer dishonesty, we saw that lawyers are subject to the law of fraud and misrepresentation and need to understand this law in all its permutations to avoid suffering a number of adverse consequences.[1] *American Continental Corporation (ACC)* indicates that the law of fraud also plays a significant role in the advice lawyers give to clients. *Chen* further illustrates that a client's fraudulent intent may create an exception to a testimonial privilege, even if the lawyer is unaware of the fraud.

Some of the most notorious corporate frauds of the past 50 years have raised similar questions about the lawyer's role in advising clients. Commenting on his late nineteenth-century law practice, former Secretary of State and ABA President Elihu Root is often quoted as saying "half of the practice of a decent lawyer consists in telling would-be clients that they are damned fools and should stop."[2] This note examines the way the criminal and civil law of fraud and the lawyer codes instruct lawyers when they must identify, respond, and extricate themselves from client fraud.

The vast scope of the modern law of fraud reflects its equally frequent and widespread occurrence.[3] The lawyer's advice can play a central role in avoiding the massive personal and social costs of criminal and fraudulent activity, both to a client and to the others such as shareholders and employees of corporations and family members of individuals. Proper legal advice also may prevent injury to the economic system itself. Fraudulent practices can undercut competition, raise the price of goods, and cause loss of confidence in the market system. Potential economic actors may refrain from market transactions if they do not trust its mechanisms. This chilling effect further impedes the market and can damage social ties, many of which also depend upon trust.[4]

The Model Rules

The Model Rules of Professional Conduct include five provisions, Model Rules 1.2(d), 1.13, 1.16, 3.3, and 4.1(b), that require lawyers to recognize and respond to client fraud. Model Rule 1.2(d) prohibits lawyers from counseling or assisting clients in conduct the lawyer knows to be criminal or fraudulent.

---

1. *See* The Bounds of the Law: Lawyer Dishonesty, Fraud, Deceit, and Misrepresentation, *supra* p. 139.
2. Phillip C. Jessup, *Elihu Root* Vol. 1, 133 (Dodd, Mead & Co., 1938). Root was noted for his vigorous advocacy of powerful (and occasionally corrupt) individual and corporate clients, including Boss Tweed. Fred Zacharias, *Lawyers as Gatekeepers*, 41 San Diego L. Rev. 1387, 1389-1390 (2004).
3. Overall statistics concerning fraud are not available in the United States, but a comparison of several studies indicates that fraud crimes account for ten times the loss that more conventional crimes (such as burglary, robbery, and auto theft) cause. Brenda L. Nightingale, *The Law of Fraud and Related Offences* 1-24.1 (Carswell 2000). One example is the failure of Lincoln Savings & Loan, which cost taxpayers at least $2.5 billion. *Bad Day at Jones Day; A Record Payment Gets the Law Firm off the Hook in the S&L Debacle*, Time 23 (May 3, 1993). Canadian statistics for the year 1999 indicate that over one-quarter of all criminal prosecutions were for fraud related crimes. Nightingale, *supra* at 1-21.
4. Nightingale, *supra* note 3, at 1-24.2 to 1-25.

Lawyers who represent organizations also are given discretion to disclose violations of law to those outside the entity by Model Rule 1.13, but "only if and to the extent the lawyer reasonably believes necessary to prevent substantial injury to the organization."[5] Model Rule 1.16 requires lawyers to withdraw from representing clients when the "representation will result in violation of the rules of professional conduct" (such as Model Rule 1.2(d)), and allows withdrawal when "the client persists in a course of action involving the lawyer's services that the lawyer reasonably believes is criminal or fraudulent." Model Rules 3.3 and 4.1(b) further require lawyers to disclose information where necessary to avoid knowingly assisting a criminal or fraudulent act by a client on a tribunal or third person.[6]

Ethics opinions over the past 20 years illustrate that lawyers more than occasionally need guidance understanding these provisions. For example, lawyers have sought advice from ethics committees concerning a client's fraud on a bank,[7] an insurance company,[8] courts,[9] the INS,[10] and opposing parties.[11] Lawyers also have needed advice when a client was threatening or has committed bankruptcy fraud,[12] tax fraud,[13] welfare fraud,[14] and workers' compensation fraud.[15]

The Lawyer's Knowledge

Note that Model Rules 1.2(d), 1.13, 3.3, and 4.1 all hinge on the lawyer's knowledge of the client's activity (knowledge that it constitutes a fraud or crime is not required).[16] A lawyer has no duty to withdraw to avoid assisting client fraud under Rule 1.2(d) unless the lawyer "knows" about the client's conduct.[17]

---

5. MR 1.13(c)(2).
6. The duty to disclose to third persons in MR 4.1(b) (client frauds on third persons) is subject to MR 1.6 with respect to confidentiality, but the duty in MR 3.3(b) (frauds on tribunals) is not. As we have seen in a previous note about lawyer dishonesty, MR 8.4(c) also prohibits lawyers themselves from engaging "in conduct involving dishonesty, fraud, deceit or misrepresentation."
7. ABA Formal Op. 93-375, 92-366; Conn. Informal Op. 93-8.
8. Pa. Bar Assn. Op. 98-27; Pa. Bar Assn. Op. 98-5; Pa. Bar Assn. Op. 91-22; R.I. Op. 93-1.
9. S.D. Op. 2001-2.
10. D.C. Op. 296 (2000); Maryland Op. 99-17; Va. LEO 1687 (1996).
11. Fla. Op. 00-2; N.J. Op. 710 (2006); Pa. Op. 2003-04; Utah Op. 06-04.
12. *E.g.,* Conn. Informal Op. 96-5; Texas Op. 480 (1993); Va. LEO 1643 (1995).
13. ABA Informal Op. 1490 (1982); ABA Informal Op. 1470 (1981).
14. Pa. Bar. Assn. Op. 91-39 (1992).
15. Ala. Op. RO-94-08; Pa. Bar Assn. Op. 97-21.
16. *E.g.,* Mahoning County Bar Assn. v. Sinclair, 822 N.E.2d 360 (Ohio 2004) (lawyer indefinitely suspended for preparing a quitclaim deed for client to client's daughter at time lawyer knew of tax judgments against client and knew client was trying to hide assets from creditors but did not sign as the document's preparer because he felt "uncomfortable" with the transaction and suspected it might be a fraudulent conveyance); In re Headlee, 756 N.E.2d 969 (Ind. 2001) (lawyer who learned after filing suit to recover client's medical expenses that client had medical bills discharged in bankruptcy but did not inform the court or the defendant assisted client's fraud and was suspended for 24 months).
17. MR 1.0(f) defines knowledge as "actual knowledge of the fact in question, which may be inferred from the circumstances," a definition that seems to include willful blindness as well as actual subjective knowledge. *E.g.,* In re Wahlder, 728 So. 2d 837 (La. 1999) (lawyer who permitted his client to place the signature of client's wife on a settlement document and witnessed the signature when he knew wife did not personally sign the document violated MR 4.1(a) and 8.4(a) and (d)); In re

If the client refrains from or stops the wrongful activity after the lawyer learns of it, the lawyer will not have assisted or counseled it. However, if a prospective client expresses an intent to undertake the conduct, the lawyer will have to decline the representation to avoid violating Rule 1.2(d).

The knowledge requirement raises the question whether a lawyer who suspects but does not know of client wrongdoing should investigate further. On the one hand, not investigating seems an easy way to avoid triggering these rules. On the other, not investigating risks later allegations of complicity, incompetent representation, and a lost opportunity for the lawyer to counsel the client in some manner that would avoid a crime or a fraud.[18] For example, the lawyer may be able to structure a transaction in an alternate way, or additional facts may create the basis for a new claim or defense in litigation. Further, the law that governs some tasks lawyers undertake for clients requires "due diligence"; that is, a competent investigation into the facts surrounding the transaction. Failure to meet these obligations or to explore alternatives for clients could result in discipline and civil and criminal liability.[19]

Beyond competence, anyone who contemplates questionable future behavior, including lawyers and clients, faces the problem of "hindsight bias," a cognitive distortion that causes humans to believe that the fact that a past event (like fraud) has occurred must have meant the event could have been anticipated.[20] Lawyers should anticipate that hindsight bias is especially likely to occur in situations where they have some warning of wrongdoing and then encourage a client to push the law to its limits.[21] Finally, discovery of a client's ongoing or contemplated crime or fraud may mean that a lawyer loses a client's business, but it also affords the lawyer an opportunity to extricate herself from the client misconduct before it results in massive liability.[22]

The Duty to Withdraw

When the lawyer learns of the client's intent to begin or continue the wrongful conduct after the representation has commenced, withdrawal from the representation is mandated by Model Rule 1.16(a), because continuing to represent the client in the matter will result in a violation of Model Rule 1.2(d). If the

---

Disbarment Proc., 184 A. 59 (Pa. 1936) (lawyer disbarred for knowingly participating in a numbers racket by agreeing in advance to regularly represent the organized criminals and their henchmen).
18. *E.g.,* Janet Fairchild, *Legal Malpractice for Advising Client to Commit a Crime or Unlawful Act,* 51 A.L.R.4th 1227 (1987).
19. *E.g.,* United States v. Benjamin, 328 F.2d 854 (2d Cir. 1964) (criminal prosecution of lawyers and accountants for aiding clients in mail and securities fraud).
20. *See* Jeffrey J. Rachlinski, *A Positive Psychological Theory of Judging in Hindsight,* 65 U. Chi. L. Rev. 571 (1998).
21. *See, e.g.,* FDIC v. O'Melveny & Myers, 969 F.2d 744 (9th Cir. 1992), *rev'd and remanded on other grounds,* 512 U.S. 79 (1994), *reaff'd on remand,* 61 F.3d 17 (9th Cir. 1995) (receiver of a failed financial institution stated a cause of action against the institution's lawyer assigned to the receiver by investors for not questioning auditors and a law firm that resigned just before the firm assisted the client in a private real estate syndication); FDIC v. Clark, 978 F.2d 1541 (10th Cir. 1992) (jury verdict against failed financial institution's outside counsel upheld for negligence in failing to investigate or inform the bank directors of claims of fraud made against the bank's president in a civil suit).
22. *See* Lawyer's Roles: The Instrumental Lawyer and the Bounds of the Law, *supra* p. 225, for details of the financial consequences of Jones Day's representation of ACC.

lawyer does not "know," but only "reasonably believes" that the client's course of action is criminal or fraudulent, then the lawyer may, but is not required, to withdraw under Model Rule 1.16(b)(2).

Disclosure

Withdrawing from a representation that involves the lawyer in a client's crime or fraud may not exhaust the lawyer's obligations. Model Rules 1.13, 3.3, and 4.1 raise the question of whether the lawyer also must disclose some or all of the facts to avoid or remedy the client's fraud. With respect to frauds on tribunals, Model Rule 3.3(b) makes clear that even if the lawyer withdraws, the lawyer also must disclose if that step is necessary to avoid assisting the client's criminal or fraudulent act. Outside of tribunals, Model Rule 4.1(b) conditions the duty to disclose on the exceptions in Model Rule 1.6 regarding disclosing confidential information. Model Rule 1.13, however, specifically grants the lawyer for an entity discretion to disclose violations of law regardless of Model Rule 1.6 exceptions where "the lawyer reasonably believes [this is] necessary to prevent substantial injury to the organization."[23]

The question of whether a lawyer should be able to disclose a client's fraud has been the subject of unrelenting debate for over a quarter century. Rules permitting or requiring a lawyer to disclose information to prevent or rectify a client fraud were adopted where the fraud was perpetrated on a tribunal (Model Rule 3.3), but initially failed to be adopted where the fraud occurred outside the presence of a tribunal (Model Rules 1.6 and 4.1). A 1981 compromise resulted in the so-called noisy withdrawal provision added to the comments in Model Rule 1.6:

> After withdrawal the lawyer is required to refrain from making disclosure of the client's confidences, except as otherwise permitted in Rule 1.6. Neither this Rule nor Rule 1.8(b) nor Rule 1.16(a) prevents the lawyer from giving notice of the fact of withdrawal, and the lawyer may also withdraw or disaffirm any opinion, document, affirmation or the like.[24]

Disagreement about these provisions resurfaced when the American Law Institute adopted the Restatement of the Law Governing Lawyers in 2000, and again when the ABA debated the Revised Model Rules in the summers of 2001 and 2003. The Restatement debate resulted in the adoption of §67, which allows lawyers to use or disclose client information to prevent, rectify, or mitigate substantial financial loss. In 2003, following Enron and other corporate disasters, the ABA reversed course, abandoning "noisy withdrawal" for the current explicit exceptions in Model Rules 1.6(b)(2) and (3), which allow disclosure to prevent, mitigate, or rectify client acts that constitute a crime or fraud and are "reasonably certain to result in substantial injury to the financial interest or property of another and in furtherance of which the client has used or is using the lawyer's services."

---

23. MR 1.13(c)(2). This language reflects ABA amendments adopted in August 2003.
24. MR 1.6, Comment [15] (1983).

The Policy Debate

As jurisdictions consider their own version of the Model Rules, debate over these provisions continues. Today, jurisdictions agree on three rules and disagree about a fourth. They agree that lawyers cannot knowingly counsel or assist criminal or fraudulent client activity (Model Rule 1.2(d)), that lawyers must withdraw to avoid doing so when clients refuse to stop (Model Rule 1.16(a), and that lawyers have duties to tribunals, which may require disclosure of client confidences when fraud has occurred (Model Rule 3.3). Jurisdictions disagree, however, on the lawyer's obligations outside of tribunals when the client contemplates or commits fraud (Model Rules 1.6 (b)(2) and (3), 1.13 (c), and 4.1(b)).

Lawyers and jurisdictions that oppose disclosures designed to allow lawyers to warn of or rectify client fraud make several arguments. First, they maintain that fewer exceptions to confidentiality create more opportunity for lawyers to encourage full and frank communication with clients and therefore enhance the ability of lawyers to give legal advice to avoid or mitigate wrongful conduct. Second, they argue that "fraud" is always difficult to identify at the time it occurs, and easier to recognize after the fact. Any exception to confidentiality tied to client fraud therefore increases the likelihood that tort liability will be extended to lawyers who did not warn or rectify. This in turn will force lawyers to practice law defensively, erring on the side of disclosure and undermining client trust. Third, they maintain that exceptions to save human life recognize a competing value of "unique importance," where no remedy will suffice to prevent the harm.[25] Client fraud, on the other hand, usually results in monetary loss, for which clients not their lawyers are properly responsible. Finally, they argue that when client fraud does occur, the lawyer's withdrawal from the matter is sufficient to extricate the lawyer from the client's wrongdoing.[26]

Lawyers and jurisdictions that support client fraud exceptions to confidentiality address the same issues, but disagree on the result. They concede the possibility that clients might be less willing to confide in lawyers, but maintain that clients who misuse the client-lawyer relationship are not entitled to absolute confidentiality.[27] Further, they argue that the ability of the lawyer to encourage the client to act lawfully will be enhanced by a discretionary disclosure provision. With respect to the threat of civil liability, they note that civil liability already exists in some cases (as it did in *ACC*), but it should not be expanded, and to clarify this point, added §67(4) to the Restatement. This section provides that any exercise of discretion under this exception does not create grounds for discipline or liability. Finally, they argue that an exception to confidentiality dependant on the client use of the lawyer's services to perpetrate the fraud actually allows lawyers to extricate themselves from the client's acts before they

---

25. Freedman & Smith, *Understanding Lawyers' Ethics* 152 (3d ed., Lexis-Nexis 2004).
26. *Legislative History of the Model Rules of Professional Conduct: Their Development in the ABA House of Delegates* 48-49 (ABA 1987).
27. RLGL §67, Comment b. Professor Burt argues that the mistrust that pervades the client-lawyer relationship might actually be addressed and alleviated by more discretionary disclosure exceptions because they would force honest exploration of the basis for the mistrust. *See* Robert A. Burt, *Conflict and Trust Between Attorney and Client*, 69 Geo. L.J. 1015 (1981).

otherwise might be able to respond under the self-defense exception in Model Rule 1.6. Disclosing client misconduct when they withdraw from the representation also avoids the fiction of limited disclosure by notification and disavowal allowed by "noisy withdrawal."

Client Fraud and Client Advocacy

Whatever their view of the appropriate answers to these issues, lawyers do agree on several key points: First, you must be competent. This means that you must know the relevant facts and law that govern your representation of a client, including whether the activity constitutes a crime or fraud. Second, you must clearly communicate these findings to your client so that activity can be avoided or stopped. Third, if you have been retained to defend a client's wrongful activity that is completely ended and not continuing, you are not assisting or counseling it. Fourth, if a client seeks to use your services to assist in future or ongoing criminal or fraudulent activity, failure to withdraw will subject you to professional discipline as well as potential civil and criminal liability. Fifth, if you represent an entity, you have special obligations to address serious legal violations with others beyond your immediate supervisor, going to higher authorities, such as corporate boards, for reconsideration.[28] Finally, you need to know your jurisdiction's exceptions to confidentiality to determine whether you also have discretion or an obligation to warn third persons.

C. Seeking Advice and Self-Defense

When an accusation of misconduct against a lawyer has occurred, utilitarians would argue that the need for information to produce a just outcome allows lawyers the freedom to disclose the information necessary to defend themselves. Lawyers also are justified in seeking advice about their own conduct or in making an affirmative claim for fees, at least as long as the client has violated a legal obligation that should be redressed. The deontologist would defend the lawyer's right to seek advice and to respond to an accusation on the grounds that the lawyer deserves a chance to explain her conduct, especially when unjustly accused. Similarly, the lawyer who has provided legal services to a client deserves to be paid for those services because the client has promised to do so and promises should be kept. In all of these situations, the personal interest of the lawyer often is corralled by protective orders or limitations on the permissible scope of disclosure.

Problems

7-9. Martyn & Fox is dealing with several difficult clients.

   (a) Client A threatens to sue Martyn & Fox for malpractice in a real estate transaction. Fox wants to threaten back, telling client we will tell his wife about Client's illegitimate child. How should Martyn respond?

---

28. MR 1.13. For public corporations, this obligation also stems from the Sarbanes-Oxley Act, 15 U.S.C. §7245 (2006); 17 C.F.R. §§205.1-205.7 (2007), 68 Fed. Reg. 6296 (Feb. 6, 2003).

(b) Martyn & Fox want to sue to collect a fee. Can they disclose how difficult and irresponsible Client B was? How Client B repeatedly lied to the other side in negotiations?

(c) Martyn & Fox represented Client C on a loan from Big Bank. Now Martyn & Fox is being sued by Big Bank, which is claiming "aiding and abetting" a fraud. What, if anything, may Martyn & Fox reveal?

7-10. Client fired Martyn & Fox after Martyn accused Client of fraudulent conduct in connection with certain lease transactions in which Martyn & Fox could not confirm the existence of the underlying equipment. Lawyer A, successor counsel, calls Fox to find out why such a fine firm was terminated. "Were there any disagreements?" Lawyer A asks.

7-11. Lawyer B, from another law firm, consults Martyn & Fox in her representation of Apex. She is worried that the CEO of Apex is lying to her and she wants another lawyer to hear all the details for a reality check. Can we help her?

Consider: **Model Rule 1.6(b)(4) and (5)**
Model Code DR 4-101(C)(4)
RLGL §§64, 65, 83

Meyerhofer v. Empire Fire & Marine Insurance Co.

497 F.2d 1190 (2d Cir. 1974), cert. denied, 419 U.S. 998 (1974)

MOORE, Circuit Judge:

This is an appeal by . . . plaintiffs, and their counsel, from an order of the United States District Court for the Southern District of New York . . . (a) dismissing without prejudice plaintiffs' action against defendants, (b) enjoining and disqualifying plaintiffs' counsel, Bernson, Hoeniger, Freitag & Abbey, and Stuart Charles Goldberg from acting as attorneys for plaintiffs in this action or in any future action against defendant Empire Fire and Marine Insurance Company (Empire) involving the same transactions, occurrences, events, allegations, facts or issues, and (c) enjoining Bernson, Hoeniger, Freitag & Abbey and Stuart Charles Goldberg from disclosing confidential information regarding Empire to others. Intervenor Stuart

Charles Goldberg also appeals from said order.

The full import of the problems and issues presented on this appeal cannot be appreciated and analyzed without an initial statement of the facts out of which they arise.

Empire Fire and Marine Insurance Company on May 31, 1972, made a public offering of 500,000 shares of its stock, pursuant to a registration statement filed with the Securities and Exchange Commission (SEC) on March 28, 1972. The stock was offered at $16 a share. Empire's attorney on the issue was the firm of Sitomer, Sitomer & Porges. Stuart Charles Goldberg was an attorney in the firm and had done some work on the issue.

Plaintiff Meyerhofer, on or about January 11, 1973, purchased 100 shares of Empire stock at $17 a share. He alleges that as of June 5, 1973, the market price of his stock was only $7 a share—hence, he has sustained an unrealized loss of $1,000. . . . Plaintiff Federman, on or about May 31, 1972, purchased 200 shares at $16 a share, 100 of which he sold for $1,363, sustaining a loss of some $237 on the stock sold and an unrealized loss of $900 on the stock retained.

On May 2, 1973, plaintiffs, represented by the firm of Bernson, Hoeniger, Freitag & Abbey (the Bernson firm), on behalf of themselves and all other purchasers of Empire common stock, brought this action alleging that the registration statement and the prospectus under which the Empire stock had been issued were materially false and misleading. Thereafter, an amended complaint, dated June 5, 1973, was served. The legal theories in both were identical, namely, violations of various sections of the Securities Act of 1933, the Securities Exchange Act of 1934, Rule 10b-5, and common law negligence, fraud and deceit. Damages for all members of the class or rescission were alternatively sought.

The lawsuit was apparently inspired by a Form 10-K which Empire filed with the SEC on or about April 12, 1973. This Form revealed that "The Registration Statement under the Securities Act of 1933 with respect to the public offering of the 500,000 shares of Common Stock did not disclose the proposed $200,000 payment to the law firm as well as certain other features of the compensation arrangements between the Company [Empire] and such law firm [defendant Sitomer, Sitomer, and Porges]." Later that month Empire disseminated to its shareholders

a proxy statement and annual report making similar disclosures.

The defendants named were Empire, officers and directors of Empire, the Sitomer firm and its three partners, A. L. Sitomer, S. J. Sitomer and R. E. Porges, Faulkner, Dawkins & Sullivan Securities Corp., the managing underwriter, Stuart Charles Goldberg, originally alleged to have been a partner of the Sitomer firm, and certain selling stockholders of Empire shares.

On May 2, 1973, the complaint was served on the Sitomer defendants and Faulkner. No service was made on Goldberg who was then no longer associated with the Sitomer firm. However, he was advised by telephone that he had made a defendant. Goldberg inquired of the Bernson firm as to the nature of the charges against him and was informed generally as to the substance of the complaint and in particular the lack of disclosure of the finder's fee arrangement. Thus informed, Goldberg requested an opportunity to prove his non-involvement in any such arrangement and his lack of knowledge thereof. At this stage there was unfolded the series of events which ultimately resulted in the motion and order thereon now before us on appeal.

Goldberg, after his graduation from Law School in 1966, had rather specialized experience in the securities field and had published various books and treatises on related subjects. He became associated with the Sitomer firm in November 1971. While there Goldberg worked on phases of various registration statements including Empire, although another associate was responsible for the Empire registration statement and prospectus. However, Goldberg expressed concern over what he regarded as excessive fees, the non-disclosure or inadequate disclosure thereof, and the extent to which they might include a "finder's fee," both as to Empire and other issues.

The Empire registration became effective on May 31, 1972. The excessive fee question had not been put to rest in Goldberg's mind because in middle January 1973 it arose in connection with another registration (referred to as "Glacier"). Goldberg had worked on Glacier. Little purpose will be served by detailing the events during the critical period January 18 to 22, 1973, in which Goldberg and the Sitomer partners were debating the fee disclosure problem. In summary, Goldberg insisted on a full and complete disclosure of fees in the Empire and Glacier offerings. The Sitomer partners apparently disagreed and Goldberg resigned from the firm on January 22, 1973.

On January 22, 1973, Goldberg appeared before the SEC and placed before it information subsequently embodied in his affidavit dated January 26, 1973, which becomes crucial to the issues now to be considered.

Some three months later, upon being informed that he was to be included as a defendant in the impending action, Goldberg asked the Bernson firm for an opportunity to demonstrate that he had been unaware of the finder's fee arrangement which, he said, Empire and the Sitomer firm had concealed from him all along. Goldberg met with members of the Bernson firm on at least two occasions. After consulting his own attorney, as well as William P. Sullivan, Special Counsel with the Securities and Exchange Commis-sion, Division of Enforcement, Goldberg gave plaintiffs' counsel a copy of the January 26th affidavit which he had authored more than three months earlier. He hoped that it would verify his nonparticipation in the finder's fee omission and convince the Bernson firm that he should not be a defendant. The Bernson firm was satisfied with Goldberg's explanations and, upon their motion, granted by the court, he was dropped as a defendant. After receiving Goldberg's affidavit, the Bernson firm amended plaintiffs' complaint. The amendments added more specific facts but did not change the theory or substance of the original complaint.

By motion dated June 7, 1973, the remaining defendants moved "pursuant to Canons 4 and 9 of the Code of Professional Responsibility, the Disciplinary Rules and Ethical Considerations applicable thereto, and the supervisory power of this Court" for the order of disqualification now on appeal.

By memorandum decision and order, the District Court ordered that the Bernson firm and Goldberg be barred from acting as counsel or participating with counsel for plaintiffs in this or any future action against Empire involving the transactions placed in issue in this lawsuit and from disclosing confidential information to others.

. . . The basis for the Court's decision is the premise that Goldberg had obtained confidential information from his client Empire which, in breach of relevant ethical canons, he revealed to plaintiffs' attorneys in their suit against Empire. . . .

There is no proof—not even a suggestion—that Goldberg had revealed any information, confidential or otherwise, that might have caused the instigation of the suit. To the contrary, it was not until after the suit was commenced that Goldberg learned that he was in jeopardy. The District Court recognized that the complaint had been based on Empire's—not Goldberg's—disclosures, but concluded because of this that Goldberg was under no further obligation "to reveal the information or to discuss the matter with plaintiffs' counsel."

Despite the breadth of paragraphs EC4-4 and DR4-101 (B), DR4-101(C) recognizes that a lawyer may reveal confidences or secrets necessary to defend himself against "an accusation of wrongful conduct." This is exactly what Goldberg had to face when, in their original complaint, plaintiffs named him as a defendant who wilfully violated the securities laws.

The charge, of knowing participation in the filing of a false and misleading registration statement, was a serious one. The complaint alleged violation of criminal statutes and civil liability computable at over four million dollars. The cost in money of simply defending such an action might be very substantial. The damage to his professional reputation which might be occasioned by the mere pendency of such a charge was an even greater cause for concern.

Under these circumstances Goldberg had the right to make an appropriate disclosure with respect to his role in the public offering. Concomitantly, he had the right to support his version of the facts with suitable evidence.

The problem arises from the fact that the method Goldberg used to accomplish this was to deliver to Mr. Abbey, a member of the Bernson firm, the thirty page

affidavit, accompanied by sixteen exhibits, which he had submitted to the SEC. This document not only went into extensive detail concerning Goldberg's efforts to cause the Sitomer firm to rectify the nondisclosure with respect to Empire but even more extensive detail concerning how these efforts had been precipitated by counsel for the underwriters having come upon evidence showing that a similar nondisclosure was contemplated with respect to Glacier and their insistence that full corrective measures should be taken. Although Goldberg's description reflected seriously on his employer, the Sitomer firm and, also, in at least some degree, on Glacier, he was clearly in a situation of some urgency. Moreover, before he turned over the affidavit, he consulted both his own attorney and a distinguished practitioner of securities law, and he and Abbey made a joint telephone call to Mr. Sullivan of the SEC. Moreover, it is not clear that, in the context of this case, Canon 4 applies to anything except information gained from Empire. Finally, because of Goldberg's apparent intimacy with the offering, the most effective way for him to substantiate his story was for him to disclose the SEC affidavit. It was the fact that he had written such an affidavit at an earlier date which demonstrated that his story was not simply fabricated in response to plaintiffs' complaint. . . .

The burden of the District Court's order did not fall most harshly on Goldberg; rather its greatest impact has been felt by Bernson, Hoeniger, Freitag & Abbey, plaintiffs' counsel, which was disqualified from participation in the case. The District Court based its holding, not on the fact that the Bernson firm showed bad faith when it received Goldberg's affidavit, but rather on the fact that it was involved in a tainted association with Goldberg because his disclosures to them inadvertently violated Canons 4 and 9 of the Code of Professional Responsibility. Because there are no violations of either of these Canons in this case, we can find no basis to hold that the relationship between Goldberg and the Bernson firm was tainted. The District Court was apparently unpersuaded by appellees' salvo of innuendo to the effect that Goldberg "struck a deal" with the Bernson firm or tried to do more than prove his innocence to them. Since its relationship with Goldberg was not tainted by violations of the Code of Professional Responsibility, there appears to be no warrant for its disqualification from participation in either this or similar actions. A fortiori there was no sound basis for disqualifying plaintiffs or dismissing the complaint.

Order dismissing action without prejudice and enjoining Bernson, Hoeniger, Freitag & Abbey from acting as counsel for plaintiffs herein reversed. . . . To the extent that the orders appealed from prohibit Goldberg from acting as a party or as an attorney for a party in any action arising out of the facts herein alleged, or from disclosing material information except on discovery or at trial, they are affirmed.

D. Compliance with Law or Court Order: Physical Evidence

Legal obligations such as court orders, statutes or procedural rules often require the disclosure of confidential client information. Creating an exception to client confidentiality when other law requires or allows such disclosure promotes the policy of that other law. At the same time, allowing other legal obligations to trump client-lawyer confidentiality may compromise a central justification for confidentiality, especially if the purpose of the other law does not mirror another pre-existing exception already justified by the underlying rationales for the protection.

Utilitarians may argue about the precise line to draw in creating an efficient and fair legal system, but probably would agree that court orders and procedural rules should be obeyed in order to promote the proper functioning of the courts. Some statutes, such as child and elder abuse disclosure provisions, also could be justified if their purpose is to protect human welfare and prevent harm. Similar arguments could be made about the law of fraud. Insofar as it prevents unfair use of the market or the legal system, a lawyer could be justified in disclosing client confidences in order to comply with the criminal or civil law of fraud. A deontologist would agree that court rules or laws designed to protect basic human freedoms are important. When a client seeks to infringe such an obligation, the client's conduct is blameworthy, which creates a valid reason for the lawyer to prevent such a misuse of others.

Problems

7-12. What, if any, obligation to disclose does Martyn have if her client tells her where he hid the stolen money? What if he hands her the key to the safe deposit box where the money is? Can Martyn give it back? If she keeps the key, can she be forced to testify that her client gave it to her?

7-13. May (must) Fox disclose that his client killed two children and Fox knows where the bodies are buried? Does it matter if the parents still hope the children are alive, and the town has been conducting a massive search for two weeks?

Consider: Model Rules 1.6(b)(6), 3.4(a), 8.4(b)
          Model Code DR 1-102(A)(3), 4-101(C)(2), 7-109(A)
          RLGL §§63, 86, 119

People v. Belge
372 N.Y.S.2d 798 (S. Ct. 1975), affirmed, 359 N.E.2d 377 (N.Y. 1976)

ORMAND N. GALE, J.

In the summer of 1973 Robert F. Garrow, Jr., stood charged in Hamilton County with the crime of murder. The defendant was assigned two attorneys, Frank H. Armani and Francis R. Belge. A defense of insanity had been interposed by counsel for Mr. Garrow. During the course of the discussions between Garrow and his two counsel, three other murders were admitted by Garrow, one being in Onondaga County. On or about September of 1973 Mr. Belge conducted his own investigation based upon what his client had told him and with the assistance of a friend the location of the body of Alicia Hauck was found in Oakwood Cemetery in Syracuse. Mr. Belge personally inspected the body and was satisfied, presumably, that this was the Alicia Hauck that his client had told him that he murdered.

This discovery was not disclosed to the authorities, but became public during the trial of Mr. Garrow in June of 1974, when to affirmatively establish the defense of insanity, these three other murders were brought before the jury by the defense in the Hamilton County trial.

Public indignation reached the fever pitch, . . . [and] the District Attorney of Onondaga County caused the Grand Jury of Onondaga County, then sitting, to conduct a thorough investigation. As a result of this investigation Frank Armani was no-billed by the Grand Jury but Indictment No. 75-55 was returned as against Francis R. Belge, Esq., accusing him of having violated subdivision 1 of section 4200 of the Public Health Law, which, in essence, requires that a decent burial be accorded the dead, and section 4143 of the Public Health Law, which, in essence, requires anyone knowing of the death of a person without medical attendance, to report the same to the proper authorities. Defense counsel moves for a dismissal of the indictment on the grounds that a confidential, privileged communication existed between him and Mr. Garrow, which should excuse the attorney from making full disclosure to the authorities. . . .

The effectiveness of counsel is only as great as the confidentiality of its client-attorney relationship. If the lawyer cannot get all the facts about the case, he can only give his client half of a defense. This, of necessity, involves the client telling his attorney everything remotely connected with the crime.

Apparently, in the instant case, after analyzing all the evidence, and after hearing of the bizarre episodes in the life of their client, they decided that the only possibility of salvation was in a defense of insanity. For the client to disclose not only everything about this particular crime but also everything about other crimes which might have a bearing upon his defense, requires the strictest confidence in, and on the part of, the attorney.

When the facts of the other homicides became public, as a result of the defendant's testimony to substantiate his claim of insanity, "Members of the public were shocked at the apparent callousness of these lawyers, whose conduct was seen as typifying the unhealthy lack of concern of most lawyers with the public interest and with simple decency." A hue and cry went up from the press and other news media suggesting that the attorneys should be found guilty of such crimes as obstruction of justice or becoming an accomplice after the fact. From a layman's standpoint, this certainly was a logical conclusion. However, the Constitution of the United States of America attempts to preserve the dignity of the individual and to do that guarantees him the services of an attorney who will bring to the Bar and to the Bench every conceivable protection from the inroads of the State against such rights as are vested in the Constitution for one accused of crime. Among those substantial constitutional rights is that a defendant does not have to incriminate himself. His attorneys were bound to uphold that concept and maintain

what has been called a sacred trust of confidentiality.

The following language from the brief of the amicus curiae further points up the statements just made: "The client's Fifth Amendment rights cannot be violated by his attorney. . . . Garrow, although constitutionally privileged against a requirement of compulsory disclosure, was free to make such a revelation if he chose to do so. Attorney Belge was affirmatively required to withhold disclosure. The criminal defendant's self-incrimination rights become completely nugatory if compulsory disclosure can be exacted through his attorney."

. . . In the case at bar we must weigh the importance of the general privilege of confidentiality in the performance of the defendant's duties as an attorney, against the inroads of such a privilege on the fair administration of criminal justice as well as the heart tearing that went on in the victim's family by reason of their uncertainty as to the whereabouts of Alicia Hauck. In this type situation the court must balance the rights of the individual against the rights of society as a whole. There is no question but Attorney Belge's failure to bring to the attention of the authorities the whereabouts of Alicia Hauck when he first verified it, prevented bringing Garrow to the immediate bar of justice for this particular murder. This was in a sense, obstruction of justice. This duty, I am sure, loomed large in the mind of Attorney Belge. However, against this was the Fifth Amendment right of his client, Garrow, not to incriminate himself. If the Grand Jury had returned an indictment charging Mr. Belge with obstruction of justice under a proper statute, the work of this court would have been much more difficult than it is.

There must always be a conflict between the obstruction of the administration of criminal justice and the preservation of the right against self-incrimination which permeates the mind of the attorney as the alter ego of his client. But that is not the situation before this court. We have the Fifth Amendment right, derived from the Constitution, on the one hand, as against the trivia of a pseudo-criminal statute on the other, which has seldom been brought into play. Clearly the latter is completely out of focus when placed alongside the client-attorney privilege. . . .

It is the decision of this court that Francis R. Belge conducted himself as an officer of the court with all the zeal at his command to protect the constitutional rights of his client. Both on the grounds of a privileged communication and in the interests of justice the indictment is dismissed.

New York Penal Law (2007)

§205.50. Hindering prosecution; definition of term

. . . [A] person "renders criminal assistance" when, with intent to prevent, hinder or delay the discovery or apprehension of, or the lodging of a criminal charge against, a person who he knows or believes has committed a crime or is being sought by law enforcement officials for the commission of a crime, or with intent to assist a person in profiting or benefiting from the commission of a crime, he:

1. Harbors or conceals such person; or
2. Warns such person of impending discovery or apprehension; or
3. Provides such person with money, transportation, weapon, disguise or other means of avoiding discovery or apprehension; or
4. Prevents or obstructs, by means of force, intimidation or deception, anyone from performing an act which might aid in the discovery or apprehension of such person or in the lodging of a criminal charge against him; or
5. Suppresses, by any act of concealment, alteration or destruction, any physical evidence which might aid in the discovery or apprehension of such person or in the lodging of a criminal charge against him; or
6. Aids such person to protect or expeditiously profit from an advantage derived from such crime.
   (L 1965, c 1030)

E. Compliance with Law or Court Order: Practice Before a Tribunal

Problems

7-14. If Martyn & Fox's client lies to an IRS agent during an audit, do we have any obligation to correct the record? Does it matter whether we were present? Whether the lie came as a surprise?

7-15.   What should Martyn tell a judge who asks Martyn to reveal her client's bottom line?

7-16.   If Martyn & Fox's client lies about her name in a criminal case, what should we do?

7-17.   If Martyn & Fox's client dies of natural causes while the client's personal injury action is pending, can we settle the case before the other side finds out? What if our client dies as a result of the injury inflicted by the alleged tortfeasor?

7-18.   May (must) Martyn & Fox disclose the presence just outside the courtroom of a witness we know the other side has been trying to subpoena for weeks?

7-19.   May (must) Martyn & Fox disclose an error by the court (e.g., our client has no prior convictions) that we played no role in causing to occur?

7-20.   Martyn is preparing an appellate brief, which argues that the trial court properly dismissed an indictment against her client because the court correctly construed a criminal statute narrowly so as to exclude her client's conduct. Martyn finds only one reported decision citing the statute, a ten-year-old state supreme court case that upheld the statute's constitutionality. The prosecutor's brief does not mention this case, and Martyn doesn't like the case's dicta, which might suggest a broader statutory meaning. Should Martyn cite the case?

7-21.   Prior to trial, Fox discusses with Client whether he has ever smoked marijuana. Client asks what that has to do with the matter, and Fox tells him: "Nothing, but I am worried the other side just might ask that question." Client admits he smokes marijuana from time to time. At trial, opposing counsel asks Client whether he has ever smoked marijuana, and he immediately responds "no." Does Fox have any obligation to correct the record? Can we settle the case before the lie is disclosed? What if the same thing happened during Client's deposition?

7-22.   How does Martyn & Fox deal with our criminal defendant client who insists on testifying and insists on lying? What if we know in advance? What if it happens as a surprise? Does it matter that we are convinced our client is innocent?

Consider: Model Rules 1.0(m), 1.2(d), 1.6(b)(6), 3.3, 3.4, 3.9, 4.1, 8.4(c) and (d)
Model Code DR 4-101(C)(2), DR 7-102(A) and (B), DR 7-106(B)
Model Code of Judicial Conduct, Rule 2.9 (A)(4)
RLGL §§63, 98, 111, 120

People v. Casey
948 P.2d 1014 (Colo. 1997)

PER CURIAM.

A hearing panel of the supreme court grievance committee approved the findings and the recommendation

of a hearing board that the respondent in this lawyer discipline case be suspended for forty-five days from the practice of law and be ordered to take and pass the Multi-State

Professional Responsibility Examination (MPRE). The respondent has excepted to the recommendation as too severe. We disagree, and we accept the recommendation of the hearing panel and hearing board.

I.

The respondent was licensed to practice law in Colorado in 1989. . . .

In December 1994, S.R., a teenager, and her mother, met with the senior partner at the law firm where the respondent was an associate. In August 1994, S.R. attended a party held in the home of third parties. The police were called and they cited several persons at the party with trespassing and underage drinking. S.R. gave the police a driver's license in her possession that had been issued to her friend, S.J. A criminal summons charging trespass was issued to S.R. in the name of her friend, S.J. Since she was not aware of the summons in her name, S.J. failed to attend the first court hearing and a bench warrant was issued in her name. S.R., posing as S.J., later appeared to reset the matter. S.R. was arrested, jailed, and later released under the name of S.J.

After being assigned the case by the senior partner, the respondent wrote to the Colorado Springs City Attorney's Office, and advised the City Attorney, falsely, that he represented S.J., when he actually represented S.R. He requested and obtained discovery using S.J.'s name. He also notified the court clerk of his entry of appearance in the S.J. case. The senior partner "consulted and advised" the respondent, but the hearing board did not make findings as to when this occurred or as to the details of the conversation.

On February 14, 1995, the respondent appeared at a pretrial conference scheduled for S.J. His client, S.R., waited outside during the hearing. Although he spoke with an assistant city attorney about the case, the respondent did not reveal his client's true identity. The assistant city attorney agreed to dismiss the S.J. matter. The respondent presented the city's motion to dismiss the case and the court entered an order of dismissal on February 14, 1995.

Prior to the pretrial conference, S.J. called the respondent about the case. The respondent told her that he intended to get the trespassing charge dismissed, but that S.J. would then have to petition on her own to get the criminal record sealed. He also told S.J. the date and time of the pretrial hearing.

After the case was dismissed, the respondent met with his client and her mother, and S.J. and her stepfather. S.J. was upset that the respondent had spoken with the assistant city attorney outside of S.J.'s presence and she wanted to know if her name had been cleared. The respondent took S.J. and her stepfather outside, and explained that the trespassing charge had been dismissed and that his client would pay the court costs. The respondent admitted that S.J. would nevertheless have a criminal record and that she would have to petition the court to have her criminal record sealed. S.J.'s stepfather subsequently called his lawyer who reported the events to the district attorney.

The respondent stipulated that the foregoing conduct violated Colo. RPC 1.2(d) (counseling a client to engage, or assisting a client, in conduct that the lawyer knows is criminal or fraudulent)[1]; Colo. RPC 3.3(a)(1) (knowingly making a false statement of material fact or law to a tribunal); Colo. RPC 3.3(a)(2) (failing to disclose a material fact to a tribunal when disclosure is necessary to avoid assisting a criminal or fraudulent act by the client); Colo. RPC 8.4(c) (engaging in conduct involving dishonesty, fraud, deceit or misrepresentation); Colo. RPC 8.4(d) (engaging in conduct prejudicial to the administration of justice). . . .

II . . .

The respondent portrays his situation as involving a close question between the loyalty he owed his client, and his duty to the court. He apparently seeks to invoke the status of a "subordinate lawyer," as addressed in Colo. RPC 5.2. . . .

However, . . . the respondent admits to having violated [Colo. RPC 3.3]. . . . Colo. RPC 3.3(a)(2) applies because of his initial appearance before the court in which he represented, falsely, that he was appearing on behalf of the named defendant, S.J. At the pretrial conference he presented the motion to dismiss to the court resulting in the case being dismissed. The respondent had the duty to disclose to the court that his client was impersonating S.J. in the criminal proceedings.

Further, Colo. RPC 3.3(b) clearly resolves the respondent's claimed dilemma in that it provides that the duty to be truthful to the court applies even if to do so requires disclosure of otherwise confidential information. It is not "arguable" that the respondent's duty to his client prevented him from fulfilling his duty to be truthful to the court. The protection afforded by Colo. RPC 5.2(b) for a subordinate who acts in accordance with a supervisory lawyer's direction is not available to the respondent. However, . . . a good-faith, but unsuccessful, attempt to bring an ethical problem to a superior's attention to receive guidance may be a mitigating factor. . . .

While we have determined that Colo. RPC 5.2(b) does not entitle the respondent to immunity, an attempt to obtain guidance from a senior partner and a failure of a senior partner to suggest a reasonable and ethical course of conduct for the respondent could be a factor to be considered in mitigation. . . . Here, the board's finding that the senior partner "consulted and advised" the respondent, without detail about the advice, if any, given is inadequate to allow us to conclude that the consultation is a mitigation factor.

---

1. Section 18-5-113, 6 C.R.S. (1997), provides in part:

18-5-113. Criminal impersonation. (1) A person commits criminal impersonation if he knowingly assumes a false or fictitious identity or capacity, and in such identity or capacity he:

(d) Does an act which if done by the person falsely impersonated, might subject such person to an action or special proceeding, civil or criminal, or to liability, charge, forfeiture, or penalty; or

(e) Does any other act with intent to unlawfully gain a benefit for himself or another or to injure or defraud another.

(2) Criminal impersonation is a class 6 felony.

▓ The Bounds of the Law:
Criminal Conduct

In two previous notes,[1] we addressed the law of fraud and saw that lawyers have no special immunity from that law, either in representing clients or in their own personal conduct outside of law practice. In this chapter, two cases, *Belge* and *Casey*, illustrate several ways that the equally vast scope of the criminal law imposes significant limitations on a lawyer's behavior.[2]

The Model Rules

Appellate decisions regarding lawyer discipline reveal that courts impose severe sanctions on lawyers who commit crimes. Lawyers must be aware of the contours of the criminal law both to avoid committing crimes themselves (as in *Belge*) and to avoid counseling or assisting client crimes (as in *Casey*). When either of these dangers arise, Model Rules 8.4(b) and 1.2(d) become relevant. Model Rule 8.4(b) regulates lawyers who commit crimes. When a client engages in or plans conduct that constitutes a crime, Model Rule 1.2(d) comes into play.

Belge's conduct implies recognition of a significant legal limit on his own action created by New York's obstruction of justice statute. Belge observed, but did not alter, conceal, or destroy the physical evidence of his client's crime. Note that the court says its work would have been much more difficult if the grand jury had indicted Belge for obstruction of justice, presumably because in that case the lawyer's conduct would have moved beyond merely protecting confidentiality to an active criminal cover-up of a client crime.[3] To understand this point, imagine what would have occurred if, when Belge discovered the bodies, he dug a deep hole and buried them in order to protect his client. His conduct then would have violated the New York obstruction of justice statute, because he would have intended to prevent discovery of the physical evidence and would have done so by an act of concealment.

Lawyer Crimes

If Belge had violated the obstruction of justice statute, he also would have been subject to professional discipline for violation of Model Rule 8.4(b), which prohibits lawyers from committing crimes "that reflect adversely on the lawyer's honesty, trustworthiness or fitness as a lawyer in other respects." Several aspects of this rule have been extensively litigated.

First, it has been argued that lawyers who commit crimes do not respect the law and therefore should not be allowed to continue to practice. However, not

---

1. The Bounds of the Law: Lawyer Dishonesty, Fraud, Deceit, and Misrepresentation, *supra* p. 139; The Bounds of the Law: Client Fraud, *supra* p. 237.
2. Although an exact count of criminal prohibitions probably is impossible, one author estimates about 3,600 federal and 985 state crimes in her jurisdiction (Arizona). Susan A. Ehrlich, *The Increasing Federalization of Crime*, 32 Ariz. St. L.J. 825, 826 (2000). *See also* ABA Task Force on the Federalization of Criminal Law, *The Federalization of Criminal Law* (ABA 1998), App. C, which lists over 3,000 federal crimes.
3. *See* Bruce A. Green, *The Criminal Regulation of Lawyers*, 67 Fordham L. Rev. 327 (1998).

all crimes fall within the prohibition of this rule.[4] Consider, for example, whether Belge should have been disciplined if he had been convicted of failing to provide decent burial of the dead. If every misdemeanor (including traffic offenses) qualified, most of us would be in trouble. On the other hand, professional code provisions and courts hold that most serious crimes (often defined to include most felonies) do reflect on the lawyer's ability to practice law.

Some criminal conduct is so serious and so related to character traits necessary to practice law that courts discipline lawyers involved regardless of whether the conduct constitutes a misdemeanor or felony.[5] Crimes involving dishonesty or lack of trustworthiness, such as fraud and theft, clearly fit this category.[6] The same is true of offenses that involve violence, or serious interference with the administration of justice, such as obstruction of justice or bribery.[7] Courts also agree that domestic violence constitutes a ground for professional discipline, not only because of the violent acts involved, but also because the lawyer cannot be trusted with vulnerable or defenseless persons.[8] For similar reasons, courts find sexual misconduct that exploits another

---

4. The Model Code of Professional Responsibility DR 1-102(A)(3) attempted to convey this idea by referring to "illegal conduct involving moral turpitude." That term proved too vague, but the cases under that provision gradually came to convey the idea that the crime must be related to a fitness to practice law. *See* Charles W. Wolfram, *Modern Legal Ethics* §3.3 (West 1986).

5. Rule 19 of the ABA Model R. for Lawyer Disc. Enforcement (1999) defines "serious crime" to include, generally, any felonies or lesser crimes that reflect adversely on the lawyer's fitness to practice and specifically, those that involve "interference with the administration of justice, false swearing, misrepresentation, fraud, deceit, bribery, extortion, misappropriation, theft, or an attempt, conspiracy or solicitation of another to commit a 'serious crime.'"

6. *E.g.*, Atty. Grievance Commn. v. Bereano, 744 A.2d 35 (Md. 2000) (lawyer convicted of mail fraud based on violations of state election fundraising laws disbarred regardless of lack of potential for direct personal gain); In re Mmahat, 736 So. 2d 1285 (La. 1999) (lawyer convicted of felony misapplication of bank funds in a scheme to avoid detection of the bank's insolvency disbarred); In re Moore, 691 A.2d 1151 (D.C. 1997) (lawyer convicted of a misdemeanor for willful failure to file tax returns suspended for three years); Wilson v. Neal, 964 S.W.2d 199 (Ark. 1998), *aff'd*, 16 S.W.3d 228 (Ark. 2000) (lawyer who pleaded guilty to misdemeanors of knowingly disposing of soybeans and rice that were mortgaged and pledged to the Farmers Home Administration and knowingly taking money from a Department of Agriculture bank account and using it for unapproved purposes suspended for five years). *See also* Milton C. Regan, *Eat What You Kill: The Fall of a Wall Street Lawyer* (U. Mich. 2004) (detailing the bankruptcy fraud and perjury convictions and subsequent disbarment of John Gellene); In re Gellene, 182 F.3d 578 (7th Cir. 1999); In re Gellene, 709 A.2d 196 (N.J. 1998).

7. In re Convery, 765 A.2d 724 (N.J. 2001) (lawyer who pled guilty to a federal misdemeanor of promising employment in return for political activity, due to his attempts to get zoning variances for a client, suspended for six months); In re Floyd, 527 S.E.2d 357 (S.C. 2000) (lawyer who stole an automobile, robbed bank, and shot a teller disbarred); Fla. Bar v. Simmons, 581 So. 2d 154 (Fla. 1991) (lawyer involved in potential jury tampering suspended for one year); Disc. Proc. Against Curran, 801 P.2d 962 (Wash. 1990) (lawyer convicted of vehicular homicide of two clients, whom he attempted to drive home after several drinks at lunch, suspended for six months); In re Ettinger, 538 N.E.2d 1152 (Ill. 1989) (lawyer who bribed a police officer disbarred).

8. *E.g.*, Atty. Grievance Commn. v. Painter, 739 A.2d 24 (Md. 1999) (lawyer guilty of repeated domestic violence of wife and child disbarred); Iowa S. Ct. Bd. of Prof. Ethics & Conduct v. Polson, 569 N.W.2d 612 (Iowa 1997) (lawyer guilty of domestic abuse suspended from practice two years); In re Magid, 655 A.2d 916 (N.J. 1995) (lawyer convicted of simple assault, based on isolated incident of domestic violence with girlfriend, publicly reprimanded); In re Walker, 597 N.E.2d 1271, *modified*, 601 N.E.2d 327 (Ind. 1992) (lawyer who assaulted female companion he had previously represented in a divorce and her nine-year-old daughter suspended from practice for 60 days).

indicative of a lack of trustworthiness.[9] On the other hand, Model Rule 8.4, Comment [2] excludes "some matters of personal morality, such as adultery and comparable offenses" that also may be criminal but do not necessarily indicate that the lawyer is incompetent, dishonest, or untrustworthy.[10]

Second, as long as the evidence in a disciplinary proceeding shows that the lawyer committed the requisite criminal act, professional discipline can occur whether or not that lawyer was convicted or even charged with a crime.[11] Professional discipline has even occurred in cases where a jury has acquitted the lawyer,[12] and where the lawyer was later pardoned for the crime.[13] At the same time, a conviction is conclusive evidence that a lawyer committed the crime.[14]

Third, the cases make clear that the criminal conduct need not involve client representation. Criminal acts such as fraud, negligent homicide, and failing to render assistance to children injured in a hit and run accident have resulted in successful disciplinary action.[15] Fourth, serious criminal conduct may indicate an immediate risk to clients or the public. For this reason, many states allow for immediate interim suspension of a lawyer following the conviction of a serious crime or a felony.[16] The lawyer remains entitled to a disciplinary hearing at a later date that might provide evidence of mitigation of the sanction.

---

9. *E.g.,* In re Boudreau, 815 So. 2d 76 (La. 2002) (lawyer pleaded guilty to possession of child pornography disbarred); Atty. Grievance Commn. v. Thompson, 786 A.2d 763 (Md. 2001) (lawyer who pled guilty to stalking a teenage boy suspended indefinitely); In re Parrott, 480 S.E.2d 722 (S.C. 1997) (lawyer convicted of simple assault for pulling down a woman's bathing suit at a beach suspended). Sexual behavior with clients also may fall into this category. *See* Lawyers and Other Professionals: Sexual Relationships with Clients, *infra* p. 311.
10. *See, e.g.,* In re Nuss, 67 P.3d 386 (Or. 2003) (lawyer convicted of misdemeanor crime of harassment for intentionally reaching into another's car and offensively touching the victim's shoulder not subject to discipline). Some of the most difficult cases concern lawyers who commit alcohol or drug crimes. *See, e.g.,* In re Lock, 54 S.W.3d 305 (Tex. 2001) (lawyer's guilty plea to possession of a controlled substance (cocaine), a third degree felony, should not subject lawyer to compulsory discipline, but rather to standard disciplinary procedure where mitigating factors can be considered).
11. In re Treinen, 131 P.3d 1282 (N.M. 2006) (lawyer placed on supervised probation under conditional discharge after pleading no contest to a misdemeanor count of battery against a household member committed a criminal act and was subject to discipline; any legislative attempt to limit to grounds for professional discipline would be unconstitutional violation of separation of powers).
12. *E.g.,* In re Segal, 719 N.E.2d 480 (Mass. 1999) (lawyer acquitted of making false statements to a federally insured bank later suspended for two years for the same conduct); People v. Odom, 941 P.2d 919 (Colo. 1997) (lawyer who committed the felony of concealing property to avoid seizure, but who was never charged with the crime, disbarred).
13. In re Abrams, 689 A.2d 6 (D.C. 1997) (en banc) (lawyer who received presidential pardon after pleading guilty to testifying falsely to Congress publicly censured for dishonesty, deceit, and misrepresentation).
14. RLGL §5, Comment g.
15. *E.g.,* In re Capone, 689 A.2d 128 (N.J. 1997) (lawyer who committed mail fraud by making a false statement on loan application suspended for two years); In re Brown, 674 So. 2d 243 (La. 1996) (lawyer convicted of negligent homicide disbarred); Tate v. St. Bar, 920 S.W.2d 727 (Tex. Crim. App. 1996) (lawyer who fled the scene and failed to stop and render assistance to three injured children disbarred).
16. *E.g.,* N.Y. Jud. Law §90(4) (McKinney 2003) (interim suspension for "serious crimes" and for failure to file income tax returns); Ohio Gov. Bar R. V §5 (2003) (interim suspension for felonies and default of child support orders).

Client Crimes

Unlike Belge, Casey seemed oblivious to the fact that criminal law placed legal limits on his representation of a client. He was either unaware of Colorado's criminal impersonation statute, or unaware of its application in his client's case. *Casey* illustrates that lawyers must not only avoid criminal acts themselves, but also must understand the criminal law to give competent legal advice to clients. Model Rule 1.2(d) prohibits lawyers from knowingly assisting or counseling client crimes or frauds.[17] Courts focus on whether the lawyer knew about the client's conduct; ignorance that the client's conduct was a crime is no defense.[18]

This rule first requires that lawyers understand what their clients are doing. Failing to garner all of the relevant facts opens lawyers to allegations of incompetence for failing to provide clients with crucial legal advice. Second, Model Rule 1.2(d) requires that a lawyer properly identify the legal characterization of his client's conduct. For example, the moment Casey learned that his client had given the police an assumed name, he also learned that she had committed a crime. At that point, Casey should have told his client about the legal significance of her conduct and advised her to correct the record, that is to cease committing the crime. His incompetence eventually led him to facilitate a client felony (criminal impersonation) that was much more serious than the original misdemeanor charge (trespass).

A lawyer who fails to identify his client's crime also can fail to properly categorize the criminal activity as past, continuing, or future. The crime of Casey's client did not end when she gave someone else's driver's license to the police. She continued her criminal conduct by using the assumed identity in court records and in negotiations with the prosecutor. Casey's failure to understand that his client was engaged in a continuing crime prevented him from recognizing that Model Rule 1.2(d) had been triggered. Failing to appreciate his client's continuing crime further meant that his appearance on behalf of a client with an assumed name assisted her crime. It also meant that he lied to the court.

Accessorial Liability

One issue *Casey* did not discuss was whether the lawyer's conduct went far enough to constitute a violation of Model Rule 8.4(b) as well as 1.2(d). Although Casey did not violate the criminal impersonation statute directly, he may have been guilty of accessorial liability—that is, he may have been an accomplice to his client's crime.

Typical accomplice statutes prohibit intentional "aiding," "abetting," "advising," "assisting," "counseling," or "encouraging" the criminal act of

---

17. We discussed the application of this rule to fraud in The Bounds of the Law: Client Fraud, *supra* p. 237.
18. *E.g.*, Fla. Bar v. Brown, 790 So. 2d 1081 (Fla. 2001) (lawyer who, at client's request, solicited campaign contribution checks from subordinate lawyers, delivered them to client, and premium billed client for reimbursement suspended for 90 days for violating Rule 1.2(d) despite his apparent lack of knowledge that client's conduct was criminal); In re Bloom, 745 P.2d 61 (Cal. 1987) (lawyer unsuccessfully argued that he thought helping a client transport plastic explosives to Libya was not unlawful).

another.[19] Model Rule 1.2(d) loosely incorporates these principles of accessorial liability.[20] The knowledge requirement in Model Rule 1.2(d) roughly parallels the *mens rea* of the crime of accomplice liability[21] and the "counsels or assists" language in the rule tracks the *actus reus* commonly required by most accomplice statutes. Thus, a lawyer like Casey who facilitates a client crime may be disciplined not only for violating Model Rule 1.2(d), but also for violating Model Rule 8.4(b) if that lawyer has acted as a criminal accomplice.

Lawyers who intend to commit a serious crime (*mens rea*) and agree to aid the client in committing it (*actus reus*)[22] also can become entangled in client crimes as co-conspirators. In many situations, an accomplice is also a co-conspirator.[23] Unlike accomplice liability, however, conspiracy to commit a crime constitutes a separate crime, even if the underlying crime itself is never completed.[24] The lawyer need not actually aid, abet, or assist, as long as she purposely promotes the criminal act and agrees with the others that one of them will commit it.[25] Conspiracy liability also can occur where lawyers claim mere incompetence, that they simply failed to recognize client criminal conduct. Where there is evidence showing that the lawyer assisted the client's crime and the lawyer "deliberately closed his eyes to facts he had a duty to see,"[26] courts have been willing to imply the knowledge or recklessness necessary to make the lawyer liable as an accessory as well as subject to professional discipline. In other words, lawyers who ignore what most lawyers would not ignore can become co-conspirators. Of course, like accomplices, lawyer co-conspirators also have been subject to professional discipline for violating Model Rule 8.4(b).[27]

The Criminal Law and Client Advocacy

Together, *Belge* and *Casey* illustrate the operation of the professional rules involving lawyer and client criminal conduct. Lawyers who commit crimes themselves, or who assist or counsel clients in committing crimes, may not only be indicted and convicted, but they may also lose their license to practice law. As

---

19. Wayne R. LaFave, *Criminal Law* §6.7 (3d ed., West 2000); Model Penal Code §2.06.

20. Other specific examples include MR 3.3(a)(3) (knowing presentation of false testimony), 3.4(a) (unlawfully obstructing access to evidence), and 3.4(b) (falsifying evidence, assisting others in falsifying evidence). Geoffrey C. Hazard, Jr. & W. William Hodes, *The Law of Lawyering* §5.12 (3d ed., Aspen Law & Business 2002).

21. The Model Penal Code requires that an accomplice have the "purpose" or conscious desire to facilitate the commission of the offense. Model Penal Code §2.06(3)(a). *See, e.g.,* In re DeRose, 55 P.3d 126 (Colo. 2002) (lawyer who pled guilty to aiding and abetting a client's illegal structure of financial transactions to evade reporting requirements disbarred).

22. Arnold H. Loewy, *Criminal Law in a Nutshell* 260 (3d ed., West 2000).

23. *See, e.g.,* Joshua Dressler, *Understanding Criminal Law* 487 (3d ed., Lexis-Nexis 2001).

24. Ellen S. Podgor & Jerold H. Israel, *White Collar Crime in a Nutshell* 40 (2d ed., West 1997).

25. Model Penal Code §5.03. The federal conspiracy statute, 18 U.S.C. §371 (2006), prohibits conspiracies to commit any offense against the United States or to defraud the United States. A number of federal criminal statutes also include conspiracy provisions. For a list of representative provisions, *see* Podgor & Israel, *supra* note 24, at 37.

26. United States v. Benjamin, 328 F.2d 854 (2d Cir. 1964) (conviction of lawyer for conspiracy to commit securities fraud).

27. *E.g.,* In re Lee, 755 A.2d 1034 (D.C. App. 2000) (lawyer convicted of conspiracy with client to launder money disbarred); In re Petition of Anderson, 851 S.W.2d 408 (Ark. 1993) (lawyer convicted of conspiracy with client to possess cocaine with intent to distribute failed to gain readmission to the bar).

federal and state criminal codes grow to address ever-widening areas of conduct, lawyers in all kinds of practice need to be able to identify and respond to applicable criminal limitations on their client's conduct as well as their own.

In re Forrest

730 A.2d 340 (N.J. 1999)

PER CURIAM. . . .

I

In 1984, respondent was admitted to the New Jersey bar. At the time the ethics complaint was filed, respondent practiced with the law firm of Lieberman & Ryan in Somerville. In March 1993, Robert and Mary Ann Fennimore, husband and wife, retained Lieberman & Ryan to represent them in a personal injury action resulting from a car accident in which the Fennimores' car had been hit by another vehicle. The Fennimores, both of whom were in the car at the time of the accident, sought to recover from the driver of the other car. Mr. Fennimore claimed that as a result of the accident he suffered a rotator cuff tear, limitation of movement in his right ring finger, limitation of strength in his left shoulder, chronic cervical strain, and headaches. He further claimed that all of his injuries were "permanent. . . ."

On April 5, 1993, Lieberman & Ryan filed a complaint against the driver of the other car on behalf of the Fennimores. Respondent was assigned to work on the Fennimores' file.

Mr. Fennimore died sometime between April 1993 and December 1993, for reasons unrelated to the car accident . . . Mrs. Fennimore notified respondent of her husband's death.

In December 1993, respondent, knowing of Mr. Fennimore's death, served unsigned answers to interrogatories, entitled "Plaintiff Robert A. Fennimore's Answers to Defendant's . . . Interrogatories," on his adversary, Christopher Walls, Esq. Neither the answers nor the cover letter indicated that Mr. Fennimore had died.

On June 8, 1994, respondent and Mrs. Fennimore appeared at an arbitration proceeding apparently conducted pursuant to Rule 4:21A (mandating arbitration in automobile negligence actions with amount in controversy less than $15,000 and other personal injury actions with amount in controversy less than $20,000). Before the proceeding, respondent advised Mrs. Fennimore that when she testified she should not voluntarily reveal her husband's death. When the arbitrator inquired about Mr. Fennimore's absence, respondent replied that Mr. Fennimore was "unavailable." The arbitrator awarded $17,500 to Mrs. Fennimore and $6000 to Mr. Fennimore. At no time before, during, or after the arbitration proceeding did respondent or Mrs. Fennimore inform the arbitrator that Mr. Fennimore had died.

After the arbitration, respondent contacted Walls to discuss a possible settlement. Again, respondent did not inform Walls of Mr. Fennimore's death.

From January to August 1994, Walls propounded several requests on respondent to produce Mr. Fennimore for a medical examination, but respondent did not reply to those requests. Consequently, Walls filed a motion with the trial court to compel Mr. Fennimore to appear for a medical examination. Respondent did not oppose or otherwise reply to the motion, and the court entered an order on September 9, 1994, that directed Mr. Fennimore to submit to a medical examination on October 4, 1994. After the order was entered, respondent did not disclose Mr. Fennimore's death but nevertheless contacted Walls to further discuss settlement. Only when Mr. Fennimore failed to appear for the court-ordered medical examination did respondent inform Walls of Mr. Fennimore's death.

The DEC [District Ethics Committee] found respondent's conduct in handling the Fennimore matter to be unethical and concluded that respondent violated . . . RPC 3.3(a)(5) (failure to disclose material fact to tribunal), RPC 3.4(a) (obstructing party's access to evidence of potential evidentiary value), and RPC 8.4(c) (engaging in conduct involving dishonesty, fraud, deceit or misrepresentation). . . .

. . . Respondent admits that he acted imprudently when he failed to disclose Mr. Fennimore's death to the court, the arbitrator, and opposing counsel. Respondent argues, however, that certain circumstances mitigate his conduct. Specifically, respondent contends that he acted out of a desire to enhance the recovery for his clients and always had his clients' best interests in mind; that he made no misrepresentations throughout the Fennimore matter but merely withheld certain information, a negotiation technique he describes as "bluffing" and "puffing"; and that he did not knowingly or intentionally violate the Rules of Professional Conduct. Respondent has expressed regret for his misguided conduct in failing to disclose Mr. Fennimore's death.

II

A

The failure to disclose a material fact to a tribunal is an ethical violation under RPC 3.3(a)(5). Respondent violated that rule when he failed to inform the trial court that opposing counsel's motion to compel Mr. Fennimore to appear for a doctor's examination was moot.

We find guidance in Virzi v. Grand Trunk Warehouse & Cold Storage Co., 571 F. Supp. 507, 512 (E.D. Mich. 1983), in which the court held that, under [Rule 3.3], plaintiff's attorney had an affirmative duty to disclose the fact of his client's death to the court and his adversary. The attorney in *Virzi*, after learning of his client's death, appeared before the court at a pretrial conference and entered into a settlement agreement without notifying the court or opposing counsel of plaintiff's death. In setting aside the settlement, the court held that "by not informing the court of plaintiff's death, . . . plaintiff's attorney led this court to enter an order of a settlement for a non-existent party." Acknowledging that an attorney has an affirmative duty to zealously represent a client's interests, the court noted that an attorney "also owes an affirmative duty of candor and frankness to the court and opposing counsel when such a major event as the death of the plaintiff has taken place." *See also* Toledo Bar Assn. v. Fell, 364 N.E.2d 872, 873 (Ohio 1977) (imposing indefinite suspension from practice of law on Workmen's Compensation attorney who "understood that it had been the long established practice . . . to deny any claim for permanent-total disability benefits upon notice of the death of the claimant, [and] deliberately withheld information concerning his client's death prior to the hearing on the motion concerning the claim"); American Bar Association, Formal Opinion No. 95-397 (1995) (advising that, when client dies in midst of settlement negotiations, lawyer has duty to inform court and opposing counsel of death in first communication to either); In re Jeffers, 1994 WL 715918 (Cal. Review Dept. of State Bar Court Dec. 16, 1994) (imposing two-year probation on attorney who failed to inform court of client's death and represented to court during settlement discussions that he could not communicate with client because "client's brain was not functioning"). . . .

In addition, respondent violated RPC 3.3(a)(5) when he withheld the fact of Mr. Fennimore's death from the arbitrator. The fact that the violation occurred before an arbitrator as opposed to a court does not render the rule inapplicable. Arbitration is "a substitution . . . of another tribunal for the tribunal provided by the ordinary processes of law." . . .

We view respondent's proffer to the arbitrator that Mr. Fennimore was "unavailable" for the arbitration hearing as nothing less than a concealment of the material fact that Mr. Fennimore was deceased. Unquestionably, the arbitrator would have been compelled to consider Mr. Fennimore's death in determining the amount of any monetary award. Additionally, we note that the cause of action originally filed on behalf of Mr. Fennimore—an automobile negligence/personal injury

action—would have been transformed into a survivor's action upon Mr. Fennimore's death. See N.J.S.A. 2A:15-3. To withhold information about Mr. Fennimore's death from the arbitrator effectively prevented the arbitrator from properly discharging his responsibilities under the court rules.

B

As did the DEC and the DRB, we find that respondent obstructed opposing counsel's access to potentially valuable evidence, in violation of RPC 3.4(a), by failing to inform opposing counsel that Mr. Fennimore was deceased. Respondent deliberately misled his adversary by serving answers to interrogatories propounded on Mr. Fennimore without disclosing that his client was deceased. Respondent exacerbated that deception by attempting to negotiate a settlement of the claim although his adversary remained uninformed of Mr. Fennimore's death. As the court observed in *Virzi*, *supra*, the attorney

> did not make a false statement regarding the death of plaintiff. He was never placed in a position to do so because during the . . . settlement negotiations defendants' attorney never thought to ask if plaintiff was still alive. Instead, in hopes of inducing settlement, [he] chose not to disclose plaintiff's death. . . . But the fact of plaintiff's death . . . would have had a significant bearing on defendants' willingness to settle.

We also find that respondent engaged in conduct involving dishonesty, deceit, and misrepresentation, in violation of RPC 8.4(c). Respondent misrepresented to the arbitrator the reasons for Mr. Fennimore's absence at the arbitration proceeding, encouraged Mrs. Fennimore to withhold from the arbitrator the fact of her husband's death, and misled opposing counsel throughout the discovery and negotiation process.

III

The principal goal of disciplinary proceedings is to foster and preserve public confidence in the bar, and to protect the public from an attorney who does not meet the high standards of professional responsibility. . . .

Attorneys must "possess a certain set of traits—honesty and truthfulness, trustworthiness and reliability, and a professional commitment to the judicial process and the administration of justice." . . .

A misrepresentation to a tribunal "is a most serious breach of ethics because it affects directly the administration of justice." . . . Accordingly, we have recognized that "the destructive potential of such conduct to the justice system warrants stern sanctions." . . .

In the instant matter, respondent concealed a material fact from the court and arbitrator. That concealment was compounded by respondent's misrepresenting to the arbitrator the reasons for Mr. Fennimore's absence at the hearing, encouraging Mrs. Fennimore to evade questions about her husband's death, and obstructing Walls's access to the

fact of Mr. Fennimore's death. Respondent's misconduct extended far beyond adversarial tactics that might constitute acceptable "puffing" or "bluffing." Respondent's nondisclosure of Mr. Fennimore's death deceived both his adversary and the arbitrator about a fact that was crucial to the fair and proper resolution of the litigation.

. . . Respondent's conduct was not an isolated incident but occurred over a period of at least nine months. Respondent engaged in a continuing course of dishonesty, deceit, and misrepresentation. Respondent's deception of his adversary and the arbitrator is inexcusable, and the contention that it occurred because of a sincere but misguided attempt to obtain a permissible tactical advantage in a lawsuit strains our credibility. Misrepresentation of a material fact to an adversary or a tribunal in the name of "zealous representation" never has been nor ever will be a permissible litigation tactic.

We believe that respondent now understands the gravity of his misdeeds. Nonetheless, respondent's ethical transgressions are serious, and he must be sanctioned accordingly. We conclude that respondent should be suspended from the practice of law for six months. Respondent is also ordered to reimburse the Disciplinary Oversight Committee for appropriate administrative costs.

Matter of Hendrix
986 F.2d 195 (7th Cir. 1993)

POSNER, Circuit Judge.

This appeal concerns the effect of a discharge in bankruptcy on litigation against the debtor's liability insurer outside of bankruptcy. In re Shondel,

950 F.2d 1301 (7th Cir. 1991), decided well before the appeal briefs were filed yet cited by neither party, dooms the appeal, but we shall not stop with that observation, as there are a few new wrinkles in this case.

On April 6, 1990, an automobile driven by Daniel Hendrix injured Sara Page. Hendrix had liability insurance, but, . . . he and his wife . . . declared bankruptcy under Chapter 7 of the Bankruptcy Code on June 5, 1990. On July 13, Hendrix added to the list of creditors that he had filed in the bankruptcy court the Pages, who at some time . . . between April 6 and July 13 had filed a personal injury suit against Hendrix in an Indiana state court. The Pages, despite being listed and receiving notice, did not file a claim in the bankruptcy proceeding. On September 12, 1990, the bankruptcy court granted Hendrix a discharge from his debts to the listed creditors. . . .

. . . [T]he Pages filed a motion to reopen the bankruptcy proceeding. The motion asked the bankruptcy judge to modify Hendrix's discharge so that they could ask the Indiana state court to reopen their suit for the purpose of proceeding against Hendrix's insurer. The bankruptcy judge granted the relief sought on September 23, 1991, the district judge affirmed, and Hendrix—which is to say Atlanta Casualty Company, for Hendrix has no interest in the matter, his discharge being secure, unmodified, and unchallenged, as far as any effort by the Pages to collect a judgment against him arising from the accident is concerned—appeals. . . .

The discharge had by virtue of 11 U.S.C. §524(a)(2) the force of an injunction against a suit by any holders of listed debts (such as the Pages) to collect those debts from Hendrix. But as to whether such an injunction extends to a suit only nominally against the debtor because the only relief sought is against his insurer, the cases are pretty nearly unanimous that it does not. In re

Shondel, *supra*, 950 F.2d at 1306-09; Green v. Welsh, 956 F.2d 30 (2d Cir. 1992); In re Jet Florida Systems, Inc., 883 F.2d 970 (11th Cir. 1989) (per curiam); In re Western Real Estate Fund, Inc., 922 F.2d 592, 601 n.7 (10th Cir. 1990) (per curiam); 3 Collier on Bankruptcy ¶524.01 at pp. 524-16 to 524-17 (Lawrence P. King ed., 15th ed. 1991); *see also* In re Fernstrom Storage & Van Co., 938 F.2d 731, 733-34 (7th Cir. 1991); *contra*, In re White Motor Credit, 761 F.2d 270, 274-75 (6th Cir. 1985). . . . If this is right, the discharge did not in fact prevent the Pages from proceeding in state court against Hendrix, provided they were seeking only the proceeds of his insurance policy. . . .

We recur in closing to the parties' failure to cite *Shondel*. Although the cases are not identical, this appeal could not succeed unless we overruled *Shondel*. Needless to say, the appellant failed to make any argument for overruling *Shondel*, for it failed even to cite the case. This omission by the Atlanta Casualty Company (the real appellant) disturbs us because insurance companies are sophisticated enterprises in legal matters, *Shondel* was an insurance case, and the law firm that handled this appeal for Atlanta is located in this circuit. The Pages' lawyer, a solo practitioner in a nonmetropolitan area, is less seriously at fault for having failed to discover *Shondel*—and anyway his failure could not have been a case of concealing adverse authority, because *Shondel* supported his position. At all events, by appealing in the face of dispositive contrary authority without making arguments for overruling it, Atlanta Casualty filed a frivolous appeal.

This conclusion may seem questionable because, given the intrinsic difficulty of the issues presented by the appeal, and the fact that *Shondel* is the only case on point, the appellant, although it would still have lost, would not have risked sanctions had it urged us to overrule *Shondel*. But that is true in a great many cases in which sanctions are imposed under Fed. R. App. P. 38 for filing a frivolous appeal. The court does not ask whether the appeal might have been nonfrivolous if presented differently, with arguments and authorities to which the appellant in fact never alluded. If the appeal is blocked by authorities that the appellant ignored, the appellant is sanctioned without inquiry into whether the authorities if acknowledged might have been contested.

There is a further point. Although as we noted in Thompson v. Duke, 940 F.2d 192, 196 n.2 (7th Cir. 1991), the circuits are divided (and we have not taken sides) on whether a failure to acknowledge binding adverse precedent violates Fed. R. Civ. P. 11, if Atlanta Casualty's counsel knowingly concealed dispositive adverse authority it engaged in professional misconduct. ABA Model Rules of Professional Conduct Rule 3.3(a)(3) (1983). The inference would arise that it had filed the appeal for purposes of delay, which would be an abuse of process and thus provide an additional basis for imposition of sanctions under Fed. R. App. P. 38 ("damages for delay"). A frivolous suit or appeal corresponds, at least approximately, to the tort of malicious prosecution, that is, groundless litigation; a suit or appeal that is not necessarily groundless but was filed for an improper purpose, such as delay, corresponds to—indeed is an instance of—abuse of process. Both, we hold, are sanctionable under Rule 38. We direct Atlanta Casualty's counsel to submit within 14 days a statement as to why it or its client, or both, should not be sanctioned under Rule 38 for failing to cite the *Shondel* case to us.

We are not quite done. Rule 46(c) of the appellate rules authorizes us to discipline lawyers who practice before us. In deciding whether a lawyer has engaged in conduct sanctionable under that rule, we have looked not only to the rules of professional conduct but also to Rule 11 of the civil rules, which makes it sanctionable misconduct for a lawyer to sign a pleading or other paper, including a brief, if he has failed to make a reasonable inquiry into whether his position "is well grounded in fact and is warranted by existing law or a good faith argument for the extension, modification, or reversal of existing law." Reasonable inquiry would have turned up *Shondel*. The lawyer who signed Atlanta Casualty's briefs in this court is therefore directed to submit a statement within 14 days as to why he should not be sanctioned under Rule 46(c)....

United States v. Shaffer Equipment Co.

11 F.3d 450 (4th Cir. 1993)

NIEMEYER, Circuit Judge:

In an action brought by the United States Environmental Protection Agency ("EPA") under the Comprehensive Environmental Response, Compensation, and Liability Act ("CERCLA"), 42 U.S.C. §9601 et seq., to recover over $5 million in costs incurred in cleaning up a hazardous waste site in Minden, West Virginia, the district court found that the government's attorneys deliberately and in bad faith breached their duty of candor owed to the court during the course of proceedings. The court found that Robert E. Caron, the EPA's on-scene coordinator for the cleanup, had misrepresented his academic achievements and credentials in this and in other cases and that the government's attorneys wrongfully obstructed the defendants' efforts to root out the discrepancies and failed to reveal them once they learned of them.[1] . . . .

On appeal, the government contends that the district court adopted an overly broad interpretation of the applicable rules of lawyer conduct and abused its discretion in imposing the most severe sanction by dismissing the action. . . .

I . . .

When the defendants first scheduled the deposition of Caron for September 12, 1991, an EPA assistant regional counsel, Charles Hayden, reviewed Caron's academic credentials. Caron was unable to produce his college diploma (allegedly because his mother failed to mail it to him), but he stated that he had received an undergraduate degree from Rutgers University in 1978 and had taken courses at Drexel University, Trenton State College, and Brookdale Community College. . . .

On the morning of September 12, prior to the deposition, Hayden learned that Caron had not formally received a degree from Rutgers and so advised J. Jared Snyder, a Department of Justice attorney representing the government at the deposition. At the deposition, however, Caron testified, in the presence of Snyder, that he had completed all of the requirements for a degree at Rutgers and that the only reason he had not received his diploma was a question of paperwork. Caron also testified that he had continued taking courses at Drexel for a masters degree. He stated that his bachelors degree work was in environmental science and that his masters degree work was in organic chemistry.

When the deposition was resumed about two months later, on November 27, 1991, Caron was shown a copy of a professional resume on which he had claimed to have received a B.S. degree in environmental science from Rutgers and an M.S. degree in organic chemistry from Drexel. At that point, Snyder directed the witness not to answer any questions about the resume, claiming that the inquiry was not relevant, despite defense counsel's assertion that Caron's credibility was at issue. When counsel for the defendants suggested that the parties obtain a court ruling, Snyder took a recess from the deposition . . . called his superior at the Department of Justice, William A. Hutchins, who called his superior, Bruce Gelber, who called the Deputy Regional Counsel of the EPA, Michael Vaccaro. Following the various calls, Hutchins eventually called Snyder back and instructed him to advise Caron of the option to refuse giving further testimony until Caron

---

1. Caron later resigned from the EPA and pled guilty to the criminal charge of making material false declarations in violation of 18 U.S.C. §1623.

obtained his own attorney. In addition, Hutchins advised Snyder to permit Caron to answer if Caron so elected and to place any objections on the record. When the deposition resumed, Snyder followed Hutchins' instructions, but he continued to maintain that the questioning was irrelevant . . . Defense counsel agreed not to proceed on the issue of Caron's credentials further because, as the court found, counsel concluded that to do so would create the appearance of taking advantage of Caron by questioning him without his having first consulted an attorney.

Two days after the deposition, Snyder researched the question of whether Caron's credibility was relevant to the litigation and concluded that it was relevant as a matter of law. Snyder nonetheless did not supplement the government's response to an earlier interrogatory directed to Caron's credentials (to which the government had objected on the basis of irrelevance) and did not withdraw the relevancy objection to the discovery, despite his conclusion that the inquiry was relevant under current law. . . .

On December 19, 1991, after Vaccaro told the EPA Office of the Inspector General about "the Caron problem," the Inspector General began a criminal investigation. . . .

Hutchins learned in December, during the course of his own investigation, that of the Superfund sites on which Caron had worked six were in litigation. Hutchins then instructed the government attorneys on each of those six cases that the government was not to rely on Caron's testimony. Hutchins also directed the attorneys not to disclose the existence of any investigation because to do so might prejudice the investigation and might also violate Caron's privacy rights.

As the attorney on this case, Snyder received Hutchins' instructions and followed them. Thus, in December 1991, when Snyder prepared the government's motion for summary judgment, he did not cite any testimony from Caron, nor did he include any affidavits executed by Caron. But Snyder did base the summary judgment motion on the administrative record compiled under Caron's direction as the On-Scene Coordinator during the cleanup. The district court found that "Caron [had] played a significant role in the preparation of documents contained in the administrative record."

On January 7, 1992, the defendants, in an effort to learn more facts about Caron's qualifications and credentials, subpoenaed records from the various colleges identified by Caron during his deposition. When Snyder learned of this, he telephoned counsel for the defendants to object because the subpoena was served after December 31, 1991, the discovery cutoff date. Snyder followed up with a letter requesting that the subpoena be withdrawn and that the documents be returned to the various institutions. Drexel University later reported that it had no record of Caron's attendance there, and Snyder was so advised by defense counsel. In response, Snyder wrote a letter of thanks dated January 17, 1992, stating that "we are looking into the matter and will let you know if Mr. Caron's testimony requires correction." While Snyder had also intended, in that letter, to disclose the existence of the criminal investigation and had so drafted the letter, Hutchins and Gelber directed him to delete the reference, and Snyder followed the instruction.

On January 17, 1992, Snyder filed the government's motion for summary judgment which he had started preparing in December. He made no mention of the EPA investigation, the criminal investigation, or the misstatements or misrepresentations of Caron's credentials.

Still attempting to discover the extent of the Caron problem after the government filed its summary judgment motion, defense counsel discovered in late January 1992, through independent means, that Caron had testified falsely in another case. Defense counsel decided to bring this evidence to the attention of the Assistant United States Attorney on the case who, following consultation with Snyder and Hutchins, then advised the court for the first time in a letter dated January 31, 1992, of the Caron problem and requested a stay.

Based on these facts, the district court concluded that Snyder and Hutchins violated their general duty of candor to the court as well as the particular duties imposed by West Virginia Rule of Professional Conduct 3.3 (describing the lawyer's duty of candor toward the tribunal) and Federal Rule of Civil Procedure 26(e)(2) (obliging counsel to supplement discovery requests). . . .

. . . Stating that the only sanction appropriate to address the violation was dismissal, the [district] court dismissed the action under its inherent powers and awarded the defendants their attorney's fees incurred in responding to the government's misconduct, under the Equal Access to Justice Act, 28 U.S.C. §2412.

This appeal followed.

II . . .

Our adversary system for the resolution of disputes rests on the unshakable foundation that truth is the object of the system's process which is designed for the purpose of dispensing justice. However, because no one has an exclusive insight into truth, the process depends on the adversarial presentation of evidence, precedent and custom, and argument to reasoned conclusion—all directed with unwavering effort to what, in good faith, is believed to be true on matters material to the disposition. Even the slightest accommodation of deceit or lack of candor in any material respect quickly erodes the validity of the process. As soon as the process falters in that respect, the people are then justified in abandoning support for the system in favor of one where honestly is preeminent.

. . . [I]t is important to reaffirm . . . the principle that lawyers, who serve as officers of the court, have the first line task of assuring the integrity of the process. Each lawyer undoubtedly has an important duty of confidentiality to his client and must surely advocate his client's position vigorously, but only if it is truth which the client seeks to advance. . . . [W]e recognize that the lawyer's duties to maintain the confidences of client and advocate vigorously are trumped ultimately by a duty to guard against the corruption that justice will be dispensed on an act of deceit.

While Rule 3.3 articulates the duty of candor to the tribunal as a necessary protection of the decision-making process, and Rule 3.4 articulates an analogous duty to opposing lawyers, neither of these rules . . .

displaces the broader general duty of candor and good faith required to protect the integrity of the entire judicial process. . . .

. . . For example, in Tiverton Board of License Commissioners v. Pastore, 469 U.S. 238 (1985), counsel failed to apprise the Supreme Court that during the appeal process, one of the respondents, a liquor store challenging the admission of evidence at a Rhode Island liquor license revocation proceeding, had gone out of business, rendering the case moot. Rebuking counsel for failing to comply with a duty of candor broader than Rule 3.3, the Supreme Court stated, "It is appropriate to remind counsel that they have a *continuing duty to inform the Court* of any development *which may conceivably affect the outcome' of the litigation.*" . . .

Even limiting our consideration to the provisions of Rule 3.3 which, the government argues, define a lawyer's duty of candor more restrictively, we are nevertheless satisfied that the district court was justified in finding that the government's attorneys breached their duty of candor under that rule. . . .

Addressing first the "actual knowledge" requirement of Rule 3.3, the government contends that, while it may have had suspicions about Caron's misstatements, it did not fully appreciate their falsity until the investigation was completed. While it is true that a mere suspicion of perjury by a client does not carry with it the obligation to reveal that suspicion to the court under Rule 3.3, the government's attorneys in this case cannot find shelter behind any such doubt. Caron admitted to Snyder as early as September 1991 that he did not have a college de-

gree. By December 1991, when an EPA investigation was under way and EPA regional counsel had referred the matter to the Office of Inspector General, the lawyers for the United States had actual knowledge of the discrepancy in Caron's sworn testimony in which he said, on the one hand, that he had no college degree and, on the other, that he had both a bachelor of science degree and a masters degree. At that time, the government's lawyers also had had conversations with Rutgers University which confirmed that no degree had been issued, were aware of misrepresentations on Caron's employment application, and actually possessed a copy of Caron's fraudulent resume. Against this evidence, the government's claim to have held only a suspicion rings hollow.

We move to the government's principal argument under Rule 3.3, that the information which Caron falsified in his credentials was not material to the proceeding. First of all, we find the sincerity of the position undermined because Snyder, the Justice Department attorney in this case, reached the exact opposite conclusion during the course of his independent research in November 1991. . . .

The issue before the district court in this case was whether the defendants are liable to the EPA for costs incurred in cleaning up a hazardous waste site. To establish its case, the government must demonstrate that the release or the threatened release of hazardous wastes caused the EPA to incur "response costs." One method for challenging the appropriateness of the response costs is for the defendant to demonstrate that the methods of cleaning up are not consistent with the National Contingency Plan established by CERCLA. Procedurally, the government relies on the administrative record developed during the clean-up, and the defendant bears the burden of demonstrating that this reliance is arbitrary and capricious. Because this method for establishing its case relies on the administrative record and not testimony, the government argues that Caron's credibility and credentials are not material. . . .

The administrative record in this case is large, consisting of volumes of bills, communications, and authorizations developed primarily from on-site activity. The person placed in overall charge of the site was Robert Caron. While Caron's decisions were subject to approval by superiors, as On-Scene Coordinator he made most of the decisions and, when he sought the approval of superiors, his recommendations were adopted in virtually all of the cases. It was Caron who recommended and obtained approval for the solvent extraction method, side-stepping the traditional method of physically removing the contaminated soil. As it turned out, the pilot process proved unsatisfactory and the traditional method of removing the soil was ultimately utilized. However, the experimental process was abandoned only after over $1 million in costs were incurred, which the EPA now seeks to impose on the defendants. While Caron's role in this litigation relates primarily to supporting response selection, he also had a major role in approving project-related expenditures. Thus, Caron's credentials, capability and credibility are relevant to the examination of the administrative record in this case.

Even where review of a case is confined to the evidence contained in the administrative record, the Supreme Court has concluded that evidence of bad faith or improper behavior by an administrative agency's official in compiling that record justifies inquiry beyond the record compiled. The fact that the government's agent in charge of monitoring expenses and selecting responses filed fraudulent documents with the federal government and perjured himself repeatedly in connection with his federal employment is, we think, of primary relevance to an examination of the integrity and reliability of the administrative record.

It is obviously difficult to assess the impact that Caron's fraud may have had on the development of the record, particularly on the selection of the solvent extraction method, an issue hotly debated by the parties. Would Caron have been given the responsibility for initiating a pilot program if his credentials had not been misrepresented to the EPA in his employment application? Would his recommendations have carried the same weight on review by superiors? To what extent are the defendants saddled in this case with decisions in the administrative record tainted by questions of competence and integrity? . . . Given the great possibility that Caron's deception affected administrative decisions in this case and disguised a weakness in his capabilities, we cannot agree with the government that the sole relevance of the "Caron problem" is with regard to impeachment of Caron's testimony. That approach is too narrow. Moreover, the significance of impeaching the principal EPA witness, who was largely responsible for developing the record, renders impeachment information material. . . .

Once we find the government's attorneys had actual knowledge of Caron's deception and that the deception was material under Rule 3.3, we move to a review of whether Caron's conduct amounted to a fraudulent act of the EPA. . . . Caron's perjury in an attempt to cover up his earlier deception was certainly a fraudulent act. Since Caron was involved in the case as an important agent of the EPA and his misrepresentation was made in the course of his employment with the EPA with the effect of disguising a weakness in the EPA's case, his action is fairly characterized as an act of the EPA.

Distilling the district court's findings, this case reduces to an effort by an important EPA witness to cover up or minimize his long history of fraud. The government's attorneys compounded the problem by obstructing the defendants' efforts to uncover this perjury and in failing themselves to reveal it. When the government's attorneys filed a motion for summary judgment dependent on the administrative record made by Caron and requested a favorable resolution of the case prior to a full documentation of the perjury, these attorneys overstepped the bounds of zealous advocacy, exposing themselves and their employer to sanctions. While this violation was effectively brought to light by opposing counsel, this was not done until after the expenditure of significant time and money.

III

Due to the very nature of the court as an institution, it must and does have an inherent power to impose order, respect, decorum, silence, and compliance with lawful mandates. This power is organic, without need of a statute or rule for its definition, and it is necessary to the exercise of all other powers. Because the inherent power is not regulated by Congress or the people and is particularly subject to abuse, it must be exercised with the greatest restraint and caution, and then only to the extent necessary. . . .

In this case, the government proposed to the district court a lesser sanction to be imposed if a breach of the duty of candor were to be found. It suggested (1) opening for de novo review the administrative record with respect to the selection of the solvent extraction method; (2) allowing discovery by defendants on the EPA's selection of the solvent extraction method; and (3) allowing discovery on any and all matters involving Caron. The district court rejected this offer as a "rather slight sanction." . . .

In doing so, we believe that the district court did not adequately address the broad policies of deciding the case on the merits where the orderly administration of justice and the integrity of the process have not been permanently frustrated, and of exercising the necessary restraint when dismissal is based on the inherent power. Thus, we reverse its dismissal order. We are confident that the district court's objective of punishing the wrongdoers, deterring similar future conduct, and compensating the defendant can be achieved by a sanction, short of dismissal, tailored more directly to those goals.

The occasion to consider the disciplining of members of the bar is not a happy one, and the district court's response was understandably stern. We are in full agreement with the district court's expressed concern, and we repeat that our adversary system depends on a most jealous safeguarding of truth and candor. But we also observe that through an outright dismissal, the defendants receive the benefit of a total release from their obligations under the environmental protection laws. This would provide the defendants relief far beyond the harm caused by the government attorneys' improper conduct and would frustrate the resolution on the merits of a case which itself has strong policy implications. . . .

Without suggesting a sanction which is appropriate, we point out that in considering the proper role of the administrative record in this case and the respective burdens of proof, the district court may deny the government the benefit of any portion of the record or the right to claim any expense, which may have been tainted by Caron's misconduct, even if it becomes impossible to assess accurately the extent of that taint. Because of the government's misconduct, the benefit of any doubt must be resolved in the defendants' favor. . . .

Accordingly, we affirm the district court's finding that a breach of ethical conduct occurred, but we vacate the judgment of the district court dismissing the case and remand for the imposition of a sanction short of outright dismissal. Since an award of attorney's fees may be part of the district court's overall calculus in selecting a sanction after further proceedings, we leave for later review, if necessary, any question on whether attorney's fees were appropriately awarded.* . . .

Wisconsin v. McDowell

681 N.W.2d 500 (Wis. 2004)

ANN WALSH BRADLEY, J. . . .

This case discusses the important issue of how criminal defense attorneys should deal with the prospect of client perjury. Specifically, it addresses under what circumstances counsel has knowledge of the perjury sufficient to trigger a requirement that a client testify in the unaided narrative rather than the usual question and answer format.[2] . . .

---

* On remand, the district court ordered lawyers Hutchins and Snyder to pay personal sanctions of $2,000 each and prohibited them from seeking reimbursement from the government. It also accepted a consent decree, which it deemed necessary because of Mr. Caron's misconduct in the case and the government's inability to rely on his testimony. Finally, it vacated its initial award of attorney's fees to the defendants to enhance the value of the consent decree to the government. U.S. v. Shaffer Equipment Co., 158 F.R.D. 80 (S.D. W. Va. 1994).

2. Commentators have described the narrative format as follows:

The narrative approach allows the lawyer to put the client on the stand and allow him to tell his story in a free narrative manner. While this occurs, the lawyer does not engage in the testimony; she asks no questions of the client and presents no corroborating evidence. The client is allowed to present his testimony to the court without help from the attorney. In his closing argument, the attorney does not and cannot rely on any of the client's false testimony.

I

On April 21, 1997, an 18-year-old woman was sexually assaulted near a building at 4720 West Burleigh Street, Milwaukee. She had exited a bus and was followed by two men with guns. The men rushed her and forced her off the street. With guns to her head, they robbed her, fondled her, and repeatedly assaulted her sexually, penetrating her orally and vaginally by both penis and gun barrel. After the assaults, the victim spat ejaculate.

Although the victim could not identify her attackers, the State built its case based on evidence collected from her body, her clothing, and the scene. Police recovered a sample of the victim's saliva mixed with semen containing McDowell's DNA. They also recovered evidence containing the DNA of the second man, who eventually pled guilty.

McDowell was appointed counsel from the State Public Defender's Office. . . .

On the third day of trial, after the State had rested, defense counsel expressed reservations to the court about his ability to effectively proceed as counsel. Although not specific, he implied that his concerns related to the possibility that McDowell would testify untruthfully. The court advised counsel that he had two options: (1) he could recommend to McDowell that he not testify if his intended account was untrue or so outrageous that a trier of fact would hold it against him; or (2) take the "middle ground" by calling McDowell to testify in narrative form.

While the court acknowledged a third option in counsel's motion to withdraw, it rejected that request because the resulting mistrial would affect "not only the rights of [McDowell] but the rights of all the other people" involved in the nearly completed jury trial. The court further reasoned that allowing counsel to withdraw would not necessarily accomplish anything since McDowell's next attorney would likely face the same ethical dilemma.

After a short break in which defense counsel conferred with McDowell, he informed the court that his client would be testifying truthfully. . . .

The court accepted counsel's decision. However, it warned him that "should something change," he should immediately advise the court and then proceed in the narrative form of questioning.

Defense counsel subsequently gave his opening statement. He told the jury that McDowell would testify that he never assaulted the victim and that the area where the crime took place was behind the building where his father lived. Counsel further explained that McDowell had been in the area the night before the assault, had oral sex with his girlfriend, Sunshine, and had ejaculated, which would account for the semen being found at the scene.

After completing his opening statement, defense counsel called McDowell to the witness stand. Shortly after McDowell took the stand, counsel received a note from the public defender's office. Defense counsel began his examination in the conventional question and answer format and asked three questions about McDowell's age and residence. He then stated, "Mr. McDowell, I want you to look at this jury and tell this jury about the events of April 20 and April 21 of 1997. Take your time and speak loudly and clearly please." . . .

... The defendant responded with the following narrative answer:

> On April 20, 1997, I was by my father's house at 4720 West Burleigh. Later on in the afternoon I had company. My girlfriend came over sometime in the afternoon. We watched TV. We got movies and ate, joked around, played around. And as the evening went through we continued to watch movies, and I asked my father could I go to the gas station. He told me to take out the garbage before I went to the gas station so me and my girlfriend was cuddled up and I continued to ask did she want to go out in the back with me. And she first continued to tell me no, but afterward she told me yes. So I asked my father can I go to the gas station. He told me to take out the garbage.
>
> Instead of me taking out the garbage, me and Sunshine, my girlfriend, had just went out the door to go to the gas station. That is where we were at. At the gas station we had two sodas and returned back to my father's apartment, 4720, but then we didn't go inside the apartment. We went outside around the back. While we was in the back we was fooling around and had oral sex in the back, and then by the time we had oral sex, after we were through and everything like that, my father ended up coming out in the back bringing out the garbage and caught me and my girlfriend fooling around back there and got yelling and screaming at me and my girlfriend telling us to go in the house. As we went to the house he told my girlfriend to call her mother, and he continued to yell and fuss and everything at us. . . .

In his closing statement, defense counsel commented at length on the nature of DNA evidence. He then asked, "Where would you expect to find DNA material of yours? In your house? . . . Where else would you expect to find your DNA material but around where you in fact live or work or someplace that you frequent?" Counsel observed, "There is an expectation that you could find evidence of Mr. McDowell being related and associated with 4720 West Burleigh."

After the case was submitted to the jury, defense counsel provided an account of the off-the-record sidebar that had occurred when he shifted from question and answer to narrative form. . . . He explained:

> Subsequent to the initial decision to go ahead and do a question and answer with regards to Mr. [McDowell's] testimony, I did in fact receive an opinion back from Attorney Bill Tyroller [sic], who is both an appellate attorney as well as legal counsel for the agency, advising me that I should go with narrative. I did in fact advise Mr. Derryle McDowell that that is the way we would be proceeding, and we had already discussed what the narrative entailed prior to, as a result of prior discussions, so he was familiar with what it was that I was advising him that we were going to do in terms of his testimony. So that was the result of me making a switch from question and answer to the narrative. . . .

Ultimately, the jury found McDowell guilty of all counts [and] he was sentenced to 40 years in prison. . . .

At the *Machner*[5] hearing, defense counsel testified that he initially believed that McDowell and his girlfriend, Sunshine, had not engaged in

---

5. Under State v. Machner, 285 N.W.2d 905 (Ct. App. 1979), a hearing may be held when a criminal defendant's trial counsel is challenged for allegedly providing ineffective assistance. At the hearing, trial counsel testifies as to his or her reasoning on challenged action or inaction.

any sexual activity behind the building the night before the assaults based on his pretrial discussion with them. He noted inconsistencies between their accounts.[6] Moreover, he explained that McDowell had introduced the oral-sex-the-night-before theory of defense only after learning that any scientific challenge to the DNA evidence would be useless. Counsel ultimately decided not to call Sunshine as a witness.

In addition, defense counsel testified that McDowell had asked, "[']What if Sunshine and I get together and we say . . . ,[']" and had told him, "[']I'll say what I need [to] say to help myself out and if I have to say something untruthful I'll say that. I need to help myself out.[']". Counsel said that he warned McDowell that he might have to testify in the narrative. In that situation, he advised McDowell to testify to everything he wanted the jury to hear because it would be his only opportunity.

Finally, defense counsel elaborated on the events leading to McDowell's actual testimony. He explained that he had intended to proceed in the question and answer format, as McDowell had eventually informed him that he was going to tell the truth. However, counsel acknowledged that his plan later changed when he received a note from the public defender's office, urging him to shift to the narrative. The note said, "Tyroler says go with a narrative. Tell that to the client. It must be narrative." Accordingly, defense counsel converted to the narrative form. He conceded, however, that he did so without either advising McDowell of the change beforehand or having concluded that McDowell intended to lie.

McDowell, meanwhile, testified at the hearing that he never told defense counsel he was going to testify untruthfully. He maintained that he was of the impression that counsel was going to employ the traditional question and answer format, not the narrative. Furthermore, McDowell stated that he had never testified before a jury before and was nervous and confused. He insisted that had he been asked, he would have testified that the night before the assaults Sunshine performed oral sex on him, that he was not wearing a condom, that he ejaculated at the scene, and that he never committed the crimes. . . .

II

This case presents an opportunity to address how criminal defense attorneys should deal with the prospect of client perjury. The issue is raised in the context of the first argument in this case: ineffective assistance of counsel.

A claim of ineffective assistance of counsel invokes the analysis set forth in Strickland v. Washington, 466 U.S. 668 (1984). To find success, a defendant must demonstrate both (1) that counsel's representation was deficient; and (2) that this deficiency was prejudicial. . . .

---

6. . . . [D]efense counsel testified that Sunshine's statements regarding the location of their alleged oral sex conflicted with the physical evidence, specifically the location of the semen recovered from the crime scene.

III

... In Nix v. Whiteside, 475 U.S. 157, 173 (1986) [the United States Supreme Court] observed that "whatever the scope of a constitutional right to testify, it is elementary that such a right does not extend to testifying falsely." The Court further recognized that, "although counsel must take all reasonable lawful means to attain the objectives of the client, counsel is precluded from taking steps or in any way assisting the client in presenting false evidence or otherwise violating the law." However, *Nix* provided no guidance in determining when attorneys had sufficient basis to conclude that their clients intend to commit perjury. . . . [9]

... [W]e determine that an attorney may not substitute narrative questioning for the traditional question and answer format unless counsel knows that the client intends to testify falsely. Absent the most extraordinary circumstances, such knowledge must be based on the client's expressed admission of intent to testify untruthfully. While we recognize that the defendant's admission need not be phrased in "magic words," it must be unambiguous and directly made to the attorney. . . .

On those occasions when a defendant informs counsel of the intention to testify falsely, the attorney's first duty shall be "to attempt to dissuade the client from the unlawful course of conduct." *Nix*, 475 U.S. at 169. As the court of appeals noted, "we do not dismiss the persuasive power of counsel to do so on ethical, legal, and moral grounds." Moreover, we recognize counsel's ability to be persuasive on pragmatic grounds. "By explaining what may be the evidentiary weakness of the false account, counsel can describe the likely consequences that, obviously, the defendant does not desire."

In addition, we emphasize that an attorney should seriously consider moving to withdraw from the case. As noted by *Nix*, withdrawal "deprives the defendant of neither his right to counsel nor the right to testify truthfully."

If, however, the motion to withdraw is denied and the defendant insists in committing perjury, we conclude that counsel should proceed with the narrative form, advising the defendant beforehand of what that would entail. While far from perfect, we recognize that the narrative represents the best of several imperfect options.[17] . . .

Finally, we agree with the court of appeals that attorneys must also inform opposing counsel and the circuit court of the change of ques-

---

9. Commentators and courts in other jurisdictions have set forth a myriad of standards for determining when an attorney "knows" his or her client intends to testify falsely. These include: "good cause to believe" a client intends to testify falsely; "compelling support" for concluding that the client will commit perjury; "knowledge beyond a reasonable doubt," "a firm factual basis," "a good faith determination," and "actual knowledge." *See generally*, Commonwealth v. Mitchell, 781 N.E.2d 1237, 1246-47 (Mass. 2003).

17. These imperfect options include conducting a separate hearing on the potential perjury, refusing to call the client to the stand, and fully cooperating with the defendant. . . . Despite [the] skepticism [expressed in *Nix*, 145 U.S. at 163 n.6], the narrative has continued to enjoy widespread use and acceptance in criminal trials. *See, e.g.,* Shockley v. State, 565 A.2d 1373 (Del. 1989); Com. v. Jermyn, 620 A.2d 1128 (Pa. 1993); State v. Layton, 432 S.E.2d 740 (W. Va. 1993); State v. Waggoner, 864 P.2d 162 (Idaho Ct. App. 1993); Reynolds v. State, 625 N.E.2d 1319 (Ind. Ct. App. 1993).

tioning style prior to use of the narrative. Courts, in turn, shall be required to examine both counsel and the defendant and make a record of the following: "(1) the basis for counsel's conclusion that the defendant intends to testify falsely; (2) the defendant's understanding of the right to testify, notwithstanding the intent to testify falsely; and (3) the defendant's, and counsel's, understanding of the nature and limitations of the narrative questioning that will result."

IV . . .

We turn next to McDowell's claim that he was afforded ineffective assistance of trial counsel. . . .

Here, McDowell contends that his trial counsel's actions were deficient in that he had no reason that justified a switch from the question and answer format to the narrative format. McDowell notes that defense counsel specifically told the court that his client would testify truthfully. Moreover, McDowell observes that counsel did not change his mind regarding the presentation of the testimony until he was given the "Tyroler note." That note, McDowell reminds us, instructed counsel to "inform the client," which he did not do. . . .

We agree with the parties that defense counsel's performance was deficient in this case. Although we are sympathetic to counsel's dilemma, we determine that his actions ultimately fell "outside the wide range of professionally competent assistance" in two respects. First, he shifted to narrative questioning without advising his client beforehand. Second, he used narrative questioning despite believing that his client intended to testify truthfully.

Accordingly, we address next whether defense counsel's deficiency prejudiced McDowell. Under *Strickland*, . . . "the defendant must show that there is a reasonable probability that, but for counsel's unprofessional errors, the result of the proceeding would have been different." . . .

. . . Like the court of appeals, we "readily acknowledge that McDowell's testimony could have been enhanced and clarified through counsel's questioning." It is true that McDowell's narrative account did not specify that Sunshine had performed oral sex on him, that he was not wearing a condom, or that he had ejaculated on the ground behind the building the day before the assaults. It is also true that McDowell did not actually deny that he had committed the assaults.

However, upon consideration of the totality of the evidence before the trier of fact, we are satisfied that McDowell suffered no actual prejudice in this case. When called upon to testify in the narrative form, McDowell produced an account of his actions during the period in question. That testimony included the date ("April 20, 1997"), activity ("fooling around and had oral sex in the back"), and location ("4720 West Burleigh") that were critical to his "oral-sex-the-night-before" theory of defense. Such information, bracketed by defense counsel's opening statement and closing argument, provided a sufficient basis for the jury to reason its way to an acquittal if it so chose. Indeed, the question submitted by the jury indicates that McDowell's defense was on the mind of the jurors.

Our conclusion that McDowell suffered no prejudice is further supported by "two even more powerful reasons: his defense was preposterous, and the State's evidence was overwhelming." The court of appeals cogently explains:

> ... McDowell's defense depended not only on the jury's acceptance of his oral-sex-the-night-before account, but also on the extraordinary coincidence of the victim's semen-filled saliva landing on the exact location of his ejaculate. It was not just that McDowell's DNA was discovered at the scene, but that his semen was mixed with the victim's saliva. . . .

VI

In the case before us, we conclude that [although] defense counsel's performance was deficient . . . McDowell suffered no prejudice under the facts of this case. . . .

PATIENCE D. ROGGENSACK, J. (*concurring*). While I agree with the majority opinion's conclusion to affirm the judgment, I write separately because I would hold that: (1) counsel has knowledge that his or her client intends to testify falsely when his or her belief is based on objective uncontradicted facts. . . .

B. Knowledge of Intent to Testify Falsely

The State asks us to conclude that sufficient knowledge may be based on facts obtained from sources other than a defendant's admission, and to apply "firm factual basis" as the necessary quantum of proof for those facts. It cites *Mitchell, supra,* as supportive of its position. . . .

. . . I would require knowledge based upon objective, uncontradicted facts as that which is sufficient to show a defendant's intent to present perjured testimony. This standard recognizes that an attorney may have knowledge that his client is about to lie, without the client directly admitting that to counsel. It also strikes a proper balance between the truth-seeking function of a trial and a defendant's right to present a vigorous defense. In my view, applying the majority's standard will result in more perjured testimony than would a standard based on knowledge obtained from objective, uncontradicted facts, and it will place ethical defense attorneys in the position of having to assist with direct examinations of clients whom counsel know are not testifying truthfully.

That standard could include, of course, a statement by the client that he or she intended to relate facts that are not true. It could also be satisfied by objective facts such as McDowell's explanation of how his semen came to be mixed with the victim's saliva at the crime scene. . . . McDowell's testimony cannot be true because if it were, there would be DNA from three persons in the sample the police had examined: DNA from the victim, DNA from her assailant and DNA from McDowell. However, the specimen contained DNA from only two sources: the victim and McDowell. In my view, that is sufficient objective, uncontradicted facts such that when McDowell began to relate what supposedly occurred with his girlfriend, defense counsel had a sufficient quantum of proof to have "knowledge" that McDowell was about to commit perjury.

C. Deficient Performance . . .

In *Nix*, the defendant, Whiteside, was charged with murder. When Whiteside's attorney began representing him, he obtained a statement from

Whiteside that he had stabbed the victim as the victim "was pulling a pistol from underneath the pillow on the bed." However, upon further investigation by counsel, Whiteside explained that he had not really seen a gun; no gun was found on the premises; and no one who was present at the time of the stabbing had seen a gun.

Shortly before trial, Whiteside, for the first time, told counsel that he had seen "something metallic" in the victim's hand. When asked about what he meant, Whiteside responded, "In Howard Cook's case there was a gun. If I don't say I saw a gun, I'm dead." Trial counsel explained to Whiteside that such testimony would be perjury and that he would not assist him in providing perjured testimony. Trial counsel also informed Whiteside that if he insisted on testifying that he saw "something metallic" in the victim's hand, trial counsel would advise the court that in his view Whiteside was going to commit perjury and that counsel would probably be permitted to impeach that testimony before the jury.

Based on counsel's statements, Whiteside testified truthfully and did not say he saw "something metallic" in the victim's hand. Whiteside said that the reason he stabbed the victim was because he was afraid he was going to be shot when he thought the victim was reaching for a gun, thereby raising the issue of self-defense. Testimony also came in that the victim had been seen with a sawed-off shotgun on other occasions and that the police search of the apartment could have been careless and missed a weapon.

. . . The Supreme Court concluded that, "Although counsel must take all reasonable lawful means to attain the objectives of the client, counsel is precluded from taking steps or in any

way assisting the client in presenting false evidence or otherwise violating the law." The Supreme Court emphasized that lawyers have a dual ethical obligation: an obligation to the client for zealous advocacy within the bounds of the law and an obligation to the system of justice as a whole as an officer of the court. . . .

In my view, under the standards set in *Nix*, McDowell's trial counsel did not render deficient performance when he switched to a narrative format for the presentation of McDowell's testimony. Trial counsel had objective, uncontradicted facts sufficient to have knowledge that when McDowell began testifying about what he and his girlfriend did that he was about to commit perjury. . . .

D. Passive Toleration of Perjury . . .

[In *Nix*], the United States Supreme Court rejected the approach of the majority in the case before us, e.g., that a lawyer should explain to the client how to do narrative testimony; call the client to the stand and passively facilitate perjured testimony. The Court in *Nix* also pointed out that this approach in treating a client's intent to present perjured testimony has been rejected by . . . the Model Rules of Professional Conduct. . . .

Accordingly, I would conclude that counsel should follow the example of trial counsel in *Nix* who, by explaining to Whiteside that counsel would not tolerate perjured testimony and that if necessary he would disclose Whiteside's perjury to the court or withdraw, persuaded Whiteside to testify truthfully. In so doing, Whiteside maintained his right to testify and counsel was not put in the position of suborning perjury.

Lawyers' Roles:
Zealous Representation Within the Bounds of the Law

Several of the cases in this chapter and the last provide dramatic examples of lawyers who underidentified or overidentified with clients. Those who apparently underidentified with clients, like the lawyers in *Perez, Anonymous,* and *Pressly,* breached fiduciary duties. The other extreme involved lawyers who apparently overidentified, like the lawyers in *ACC,* and, as a result, were implicated in their client's violations of law. The lawyers in *Casey, Forrest,* and *Shaffer Equipment* also fell into this trap and, as a result, facilitated a client crime (*Casey*) and a fraud on the court (*Forrest* and *Shaffer Equipment*).

The vast majority of lawyers, like most of those in the cases in the last two chapters, avoid these extremes by representing their clients zealously within the bounds of the law.[1] These lawyers refrain from directive behavior by fulfilling their fiduciary duties and providing zealous representation. At the same time, these lawyers avoid instrumentalism by maintaining the professional objectivity necessary to provide their clients with good legal advice. They are able to recognize definitive legal norms but remain willing to challenge them openly when significant rights of a client are at stake. This is what Judge Noonan calls the "right relation . . . struck most of the time."[2] It is a relation of collaborator, "wise counselor,"[3] or translator, rather than parent or puppet.

Lawyers as Collaborators

Consider first the lawyers in *Upjohn* and *Swidler & Berlin.* In both cases, they promised confidentiality, used it to generate trust and gain the facts necessary to advise their clients, and then claimed the attorney-client privilege when these facts were sought. In both cases, the Supreme Court thought that the availability of the privilege facilitated the work of the lawyer and protected the client.

Consider second the lawyers in *Hawkins* and *Purcell.* Each learned facts about a client that indicated a risk of harm to third persons. Hawkins' lawyer did not disclose, either to the court or to others; Purcell's did. Yet both acted appropriately.

In *Hawkins,* the Washington court points out that the lawyer's disclosure of danger was not required, since those persons already knew about the potential for dangerous behavior by the client. Further, Hawkins's lawyer did not misrepresent any facts at the bail hearing, and he had no duty to disclose additional facts unless asked. In short, Hawkins's lawyer pursued his client's interests zealously (by seeking his release on bail) within the bounds of the law (by steering clear of fraud on the court and maintaining confidentiality). You may have less sympathy for the lawyer's failure to prevent his client's suicide attempt,

---

1. This phrase closely parallels the language in both Canon 31 of the 1908 Canons of Ethics, the title of Canon 7 of the 1969 Code of Professional Responsibility ("A Lawyer Should Represent a Client Zealously Within the Bounds of the Law") and ¶9 of the Preamble to the Model Rules of Professional Conduct.
2. John T. Noonan, Jr., *The Lawyer Who Overidentifies with His Client,* 76 Notre Dame L. Rev. 827, 840 (2001).
3. Lon L. Fuller & John D. Randall, *Professional Responsibility: Report of the Joint Conference,* 44 ABA J. 1159, 1161 (1958).

but even here, the lawyer acted within the bounds of the law, imperfect though those bounds may have been. As the court indicates, the lawyer's ability to disclose client confidences reached only to future criminal conduct.[4] Since suicide is not a crime, the only justification for the discretionary disclosure would have been the client's threat to a third party.[5] In any case, it is understandable why Hawkins's lawyer did not disclose. The client was charged with a nonviolent crime and had expressed a desire to be released on bail. All of the information about the client's potential danger came from third parties who did not want him released from custody. Hawkins's lawyer sided with his client, and even accompanied him to two counseling sessions with all of these parties.

Purcell, on the other hand, listened to very credible threats of harm from his own client and realized that the third parties who were likely to be harmed by his client's behavior could not protect themselves. He then exercised his discretion to warn authorities to prevent the harm. But when a court later sought his testimony in order to convict his former client, he protected his client's confidentiality by appropriately asserting the privilege on his client's behalf. The Massachusetts court points out that he too acted within the bounds of the law and zealously protected his client's interests. Further, the result in *Purcell* gives lawyers an incentive to prevent serious harm when efforts to dissuade their clients from harmful conduct prove unsuccessful. Lawyers can act to save lives and at the same time avoid betraying their client's confidence in a subsequent proceeding.

Similarly, the lawyers in *Belge* steered clear of obstructing justice by merely observing rather than actively concealing the buried bodies they discovered. The information was disclosed only after their client blurted it out on the stand. The court holds that their apparent violation of a misdemeanor statute had to give way to the client's Fifth Amendment right. These lawyers not only observed the limits of the law, they also zealously advocated their client's interests throughout the proceeding, by preparing a legally recognized defense (insanity) justified by the facts.

The Collaborative Model

All of these lawyers acted as collaborators with their clients. They did not control or manipulate their clients and observed all of the fiduciary duties the law demands. They acted competently and loyally, communicated with their clients, enabled them to make decisions about the matter, and kept their confidences. At the same time, they did not shirk from clear explanations to clients when the latters' conduct approached legally unacceptable boundaries. When necessary, these lawyers refused to act instrumentally, and told their clients why. They were empathetic, but offered objective advice. They identified with their clients

---

4. DR 4-101(C)(3), which allowed lawyers to reveal "the intention of his client to commit a crime and the information necessary to prevent the crime," governed the case.
5. This gap in the rule has been closed by MR 1.6(b)(1), which allows lawyers to disclose information relating to the representation "to prevent reasonably certain death or substantial bodily harm." MR 1.14(c) also classifies these disclosures as impliedly authorized under 1.6(a) if made for the purpose of taking protective action when a client suffers from diminished capacity and is at risk of substantial physical harm.

enough to do a good job, but did not become tools of their client's wrongdoing. When they disagreed with the clients' proposed conduct, they respected the clients enough to remonstrate with the clients about the propriety of the clients' conduct. When legal competence demanded that they draw a line between their clients' behavior and their own, they did so.

Professor James Boyd White invokes another metaphor for this collaborative model, the metaphor of lawyers as translators. He develops this concept by considering the lawyer's role in representing clients in divorce or dissolution of marriage.[6] He speaks of an empirical study of client-lawyer interactions in divorce cases, which concluded that the clients consistently complained that their lawyers disregarded what the clients told them, especially when they related "who did what to whom."[7] While it is true that good divorce lawyers need to learn about personal as well as legal dimensions of their clients' situations, Professor White offers an alternative explanation for the clients' critical assessment of their lawyers: Good divorce lawyers understand they have a social role that cannot be reduced simply to meeting all of their clients' wishes. The law of marriage dissolution teaches these lawyers that their clients will have to plan realistically for the future, both in economic and relational terms. These lawyers know that they will in turn have to educate their clients and divert them from their desire to express anger and frustration to resolving the future problems they inevitably must face. One of the objectives of good divorce lawyers is to get their clients to "give up the fight, and the claims of right and wrong by which they carry it on" and to move in that direction earlier than they otherwise might.[8] Similar accounts can be given for almost every kind of law practice. Each client-lawyer relationship brings with it the opportunity to translate the client's desires and moral values into legal categories. It also affords a lawyer the opportunity to gain new insight into the impact of the legal system on a client.[9] The client brings a desire to accomplish an objective, which the lawyer must listen to with care. Lawyers advocate for the client, but also advocate to the client, teaching the client about competing moral values or public policy choices the law has embodied to protect the interests of others.[10] For example, the lawyer who assists a client in a securities transaction understands that securities law requires certain disclosures to achieve some fairness in market transactions. The same lawyer understands her client's desire to raise money. Both can be met with some effort and collaboration through compromise, though not perhaps in the way the client or the lawyer originally envisioned.

Ultimately, lawyers, like other professionals, listen to clients' stories, translate these client narratives into legal language, and translate law and legal policy back to their clients in order to offer guidance. In most cases, lawyers can help clients achieve their legal goal. In some instances, they must inform clients

---

6. James Boyd White, *Translation as a Mode of Thought*, 77 Cornell L. Rev. 1388 (1992).
7. Austin Sarat & William L. F. Felstiner, *Law and Social Relations: Vocabularies of Motive in Lawyer/Client Interaction*, 22 Law & Socy. Rev. 737, 742 (1988).
8. White, *supra* note 6, at 1395.
9. Clark D. Cunningham, *The Lawyer as Translator, Representation as Text: Towards an Ethnography of Legal Discourse*, 77 Cornell L. Rev. 1298 (1992).
10. William F. May, *Beleaguered Rulers: The Public Obligation of the Professional* 80 (Westminster John Knox 2001).

that certain actions cannot be taken or even that certain goals cannot be realized. In each case, they are not only translating the clients' desires to the legal system and back again, but they are also acting as private lawmakers, who both influence and are influenced by the law and legal system they function in. To do this well, lawyers must respect each client's moral autonomy, but also help each client understand the moral values and public policy choices embedded in the law itself. The best lawyers also respect their own moral integrity and are willing to deliberate and, if necessary, argue with clients about their goals and interests.

Chapter 8

Conflicts of Interest: Clients, Lawyers, and Third Persons

"If it pleases the Court, Your Honor, I'd like to
quit the defense and join the prosecution."

A. Introduction

This chapter and the next explore another core fiduciary duty, loyalty, which can be traced back several centuries in the law of agency. Loyalty imposes an obligation on lawyers to avoid harm to clients by recognizing and responding to any influences (conflicts of interest) that may interfere with the lawyer's obligation to act in the client's best interests. In the last two chapters, we saw that the obligation to maintain client confidences constitutes one facet of the loyalty obligation. This chapter and the next focus on the principal feature of loyalty: the need to recognize and respond to conflicts of interest created by the lawyer's own interest, the interest of a third person, or the interest of another current or former client of the lawyer or law firm.

We begin this chapter as by identifying the kinds of conflicts the law governing lawyers regulates. We next turn to consider an additional remedy commonly sought to ameliorate conflicts of interest: judicial disqualification. Both this chapter and the next then address the various categories of conflicts of interest that lawyers face. Throughout this material, we find it helpful to address conflicts of interest by following the four-step analysis outlined below.

Conflicts of Interest

1. Identify the client(s)

2. Determine whether a conflict of interest exists. Six categories:

A. Personal Interests of a Lawyer:

General Rule:	1.7	
Specific Rules:	1.8(a)	Business transactions w/clients
	1.8(b)	Use of client information
	1.8(c)	Client gifts to lawyer
	1.8(d)	Literary rights
	1.8(e)	Financial assistance to client
	1.8(h)	Limitation of liability to client
	1.8(i)	Proprietary interest in litigation
	1.8(j)	Lawyer/client sexual relationship
	3.7	Lawyer as witness

B. Interests of Another Current Client:

General Rule: 1.7
Specific Rules: 1.8(g), 1.13(g)

C. Interests of a Third Person:

General Rule: 1.7
Specific Rules: 1.8(f), 5.4(c), 1.13(a)

D. Interests of a Former Client:

General Rule: 1.9

E. **Government Lawyers:**

General Rule: 1.11
Specific Rule: 1.12

F. **Imputed Conflicts:**

General Rule: 1.10
Specific Rules: 1.8(k), 1.11, 1.12

3. Decide whether the conflict is consentable.

4. If it is, consult with affected clients and obtain informed consent. (Writing preferred or required.)

Problem

8-1. CEO of Megacorp asks Martyn & Fox to draft a deed transferring vacant land owned by Mega to CEO. "It's just a liability for Mega," CEO explains. What should Martyn & Fox do?

Consider: **Model Rules 1.7, 1.13, 1.18**
          Model Code DR 5-105
          RLGL §§14, 96, 131

Maritrans GP Inc. v. Pepper, Hamilton & Scheetz
602 A.2d 1277 (Pa. 1992)

PAPADAKOS, J. . . .

Maritrans is a Philadelphia-based public company in the business of transporting petroleum products along the East and Gulf coasts of the United States by tug and barge. Maritrans competes in the marine transportation business with other tug and/or barge companies, including a number of companies based in New York. Pepper is an old and established Philadelphia law firm. Pepper and Messina represented Maritrans or its predecessor companies in the broadest range of labor relations matters for well over a decade. In addition, Pepper represented Maritrans in a complex public offering of securities, a private offering of

$115 million in debt, a conveyance of all assets, and a negotiation and implementation of a working capital line of credit. Over the course of the representation, Pepper was paid approximately $1 million for its labor representation of Maritrans and, in the last year of the representation, approximately $1 million for its corporate and securities representation of Maritrans.

During the course of their labor representation of Maritrans, Pepper and Messina became "intimately familiar with Maritrans' operations" and "gained detailed financial and business information, including Maritrans' financial goals and projections, labor cost/savings, crew costs and operating costs." This information was discussed with Pepper's labor attorneys, and particularly with Messina, for the purpose of developing Maritrans' labor goals and strategies. In addition, during the course of preparing Maritrans' public offering, Pepper was furnished with substantial confidential commercial information in Maritrans' possession—financial and otherwise—including projected labor costs, projected debt coverage and projected revenues through the year 1994, and projected rates through the year 1990. Pepper and Messina, during the course of their decade-long representation of Maritrans, came to know the complete inner-workings of the company along with Maritrans' long-term objectives, and competitive strategies in a number of areas including the area of labor costs, a particularly sensitive area in terms of effective competition. In furtherance of its ultimate goal of obtaining more business than does its competition, including the New York-based companies, Maritrans analyzed each of its competitors with Pepper and Messina. These analyses included an evaluation of each competitor's strengths and weaknesses, and of how Maritrans deals with its competitors.

Armed with this information, Pepper and Messina subsequently undertook to represent several of Maritrans' New York-based competitors. Indeed, Pepper and Messina undertook to represent the New York companies in their labor negotiations, albeit with a different union, during which the New York companies sought wage and benefit reductions in order to compete more effectively with, i.e., to win business away from, Maritrans.

In September, 1987, Maritrans learned from sources outside of Pepper that Pepper and Messina were representing four of its New York-based competitors in their labor relations matters. Maritrans objected to these representations, and voiced those objections to many Pepper attorneys, including Mr. Messina. Pepper and Messina took the position that this was a "business conflict," not a "legal conflict," and that they had no fiduciary or ethical duty to Maritrans that would prohibit these representations.

To prevent Pepper and Messina from taking on the representation of any other competitors, especially its largest competitor, Bouchard Transportation Company, Maritrans agreed to an arrangement proposed by Pepper whereby Pepper would continue as Maritrans' counsel but would not represent any more than the four New York companies it was then already representing. In addition, Messina—the Pepper attorney with the most knowledge about Maritrans—was to act not as counsel for Maritrans but, rather, as counsel for the New York companies, while two other Pepper labor attorneys would act as counsel for Maritrans; the attorneys on one side of this "Chinese Wall" would not discuss their respective representation with the attorneys on the other side. Maritrans represented that it agreed to this arrangement because it believed that this was the only way to keep Pepper and Messina from representing yet more of its competitors, especially Bouchard.

Unbeknownst to Maritrans, however, Messina then "parked" Bouchard and another of the competitors, Eklof, with Mr. Vincent Pentima, a labor attorney then at another law firm, at the same time that Messina was negotiating with

Pentima for Pentima's admission into the partnership at Pepper. Moreover, notwithstanding Pepper's specific agreement not to represent these other companies, Messina for all intents and purposes was representing Bouchard and Eklof, as he was conducting joint negotiating sessions for those companies and his other four New York clients. On November 5, 1987, Maritrans executives discussed with Pepper attorneys, inter alia, Maritrans' plans and strategies of an aggressive nature in the event of a strike against the New York companies. Less than one month later, on December 2, 1987, Pepper terminated its representation of Maritrans in all matters. Later that month, on December 23, 1987, Pepper undertook the representation of the New York companies. Then, on January 4, 1988, Mr. Pentima joined Pepper as a partner and brought with him, as clients, Bouchard and Eklof. In February, 1988, Maritrans filed a complaint in the trial court against Pepper and Messina.

Discovery procedures produced evidence as follows: (i) testimony by principals of the New York companies to the effect that the type of information that Pepper and Messina possess about Maritrans is of the type considered to be confidential commercial information in the industry and that they would not reveal that information about their companies to their competitors; (ii) testimony by principals of the New York companies that they were desirous of obtaining Maritrans' confidential commercial information; (iii) testimony by principals of the New York companies that labor costs are the one item that make or break a company's competitive posture; (iv) an affidavit from the United States Department of Labor attesting that, contrary to defendant Messina's sworn testimony at the first preliminary hearing in February, 1988, Maritrans' labor contracts are not on file with the Department of Labor and thus not available under the Freedom of Information Act; and other information as well. . . .

The public's trust in the legal profession undoubtedly would be undermined if this Court does not correct the Superior Court's failure to recognize the common law foundation for the principle that an attorney's representation of a subsequent client whose interests are materially adverse to a former client in a matter substantially related to matters in which he represented the former client constitutes an impermissible conflict of interest actionable at law. The Superior Court's decision is diametrically opposed to law established by the courts of this Commonwealth and throughout the United States which have imposed civil liability on attorneys for breaches of their fiduciary duties by engaging in conflicts of interest, notwithstanding the existence of professional rules under which the attorneys also could be disciplined.

I. ACTIONABILITY AND INDEPENDENT FIDUCIARY DUTY AT COMMON LAW OF AVOIDING CONFLICTS OF INTEREST—INJUNCTIVE RELIEF . . .

Activity is actionable if it constitutes breach of a duty imposed by statute or by common law. Our common law imposes on attorneys the status of fiduciaries vis à vis their clients; that is, attorneys are bound, at law, to perform their fiduciary duties properly. Failure to so perform gives rise to a cause of action. It is "actionable." Threatened failure to so perform gives rise to a request for injunctive relief to prevent the breach of duty.

At common law, an attorney owes a fiduciary duty to his client; such duty demands undivided loyalty and prohibits the attorney from engaging in conflicts of interest, and breach of such duty is actionable. As stated by the United States Supreme Court in 1850:

> There are few of the business relations of life involving a higher trust and confidence than those of attorney and client or, generally speaking, one more honorably and faithfully discharged; few more anxiously guarded by the law, or governed by sterner principles of morality and justice; and it is the duty of the court to administer them in a corresponding spirit, and to be watchful and industrious, to see that confidence thus reposed shall not be used to the detriment or prejudice of the rights of the party bestowing it. Stockton v. Ford, 52 U.S. at 247. . . .

Adherence to those fiduciary duties ensures that clients will feel secure that everything they discuss with counsel will be kept in confidence. . . .

II. AN ATTORNEY'S COMMON LAW DUTY IS INDEPENDENT OF THE ETHICS RULES . . .

Long before the [professional codes] were adopted, the common law recognized that a lawyer could not undertake a representation adverse to a former client in a matter "substantially related" to that in which the lawyer previously had served the client. . . .

As regards misuse of a former client's confidences, the disciplinary rules derive from the lawyer's common law duties, not the other way around.

III. SCOPE OF DUTIES AT COMMON LAW

. . . Attorneys have always been held civilly liable for engaging in conduct violative of their fiduciary duties to clients, despite the existence of professional rules under which the attorneys could also have been disciplined.

Courts throughout the country have ordered the disgorgement of fees paid or the forfeiture of fees owed to attorneys who have breached their fiduciary duties to their clients by engaging in impermissible conflicts of interests. . . .

Courts have also allowed civil actions for damages for an attorney's breach of his fiduciary duties by engaging in conflicts of interest.

Courts throughout the United States have not hesitated to impose civil sanctions upon attorneys who breach their fiduciary duties to their clients, which sanctions have been imposed separately and apart from professional discipline. . . .

IV. EQUITY

Injunctive relief will lie where there is no adequate remedy at law. The purpose of a preliminary injunction is to preserve the status quo as it exists or previously existed before the acts complained of, thereby preventing irreparable injury or gross injustice. A preliminary injunction should issue only where there is urgent necessity to avoid injury which cannot be compensated for by damages. . . .

Pepper and Messina argue that a preliminary injunction was an abuse of discretion where it restrains them from representing a former client's competitors, in order to supply the former client with a "sense of security" that they will not reveal confidences to those competitors where there has been no revelation or threat of revelations up to that point. We disagree. Whether a fiduciary can later represent competitors or whether a law firm can later represent competitors of its former client is a matter that must be decided from case to case and depends on a number of factors. One factor is the extent to which the fiduciary was involved in its former client's affairs. The greater the involvement, the greater the danger that confidences (where such exist) will be revealed. Here, Pepper and Messina's involvement was extensive as was their knowledge of sensitive information provided to them by Maritrans. We do not wish to establish a blanket rule that a law firm may not later represent the economic competitor of a former client in matters in which the former client is not also a party to a law suit. But situations may well exist where the danger of revelation of the confidences of a former client is so great that injunctive relief is warranted. This is one of those situations. There is a substantial relationship here between Pepper and Messina's former representation of Maritrans and their current representation of Maritrans' competitors such that the injunctive relief granted here was justified. It might be theoretically possible to argue that Pepper and Messina should merely be enjoined from revealing the confidential material they have acquired from Maritrans but such an injunction would be difficult, if not impossible, to administer. . . . As fiduciaries, Pepper and Messina can be fully enjoined from representing Maritrans' competitors as that would create too great a danger that Maritrans' confidential relationship with Pepper and Messina would be breached.

Here, the trial court did not commit an abuse of discretion. On these facts, it was perfectly reasonable to conclude that Maritrans' competitive position could be irreparably injured if Pepper and Messina continued to represent their competitors and that Maritrans' remedy at law, that is their right to later seek damages, would be difficult if not impossible to sustain because of difficult problems of proof, particularly problems related to piercing what would later become a confidential relationship between their competitors and those competitors' attorneys (Pepper and Messina). . . . In short, equitable principles establish that injunctive relief here was just and proper. Damages might later be obtained for breach of fiduciary duties and a confidential relationship, but that remedy would be inadequate to correct the harm that could be prevented by injunctive relief, at least until the court could examine the case in greater detail. . . .

▪ The Law Governing Lawyers:
Losing a Client by Disqualification or Injunction

We have seen examples of multiple remedies throughout these materials. *Maritrans* identifies multiple remedies that the law of agency has made available to clients whose lawyers breach fiduciary duties of loyalty or confidentiality. When conflicts of interest have caused harm, clients can bring a malpractice or breach of fiduciary duty claim,[1] seek fee forfeiture,[2] and pursue professional discipline when a violation of the relevant professional code occurs.[3] In egregious cases, lawyers have been held criminally accountable as well.[4]

In the past half century, however, courts have examined most conflicts of interest in the context of motions to disqualify lawyers.[5] Often these cases present circumstances like those in *Maritrans,* where harm is threatened but has not yet occurred. *Maritrans* teaches us that clients or former clients can seek injunctive relief to prevent the representation of other clients in transactional representations outside of court. It also makes clear that the breach of a fiduciary duty by one lawyer vicariously disqualifies the entire law firm. Clients, former clients, and other judicial participants can seek similar relief through a disqualification motion in a matter pending before a court.[6]

Injunctive Relief

With respect to the equitable remedy of injunctive relief, the *Maritrans* court first makes clear that breaches of statute or common law qualify as actionable activity. Since lawyers are fiduciaries, and fiduciaries owe duties of loyalty and confidentiality, it follows that agency remedies for breach of fiduciary duty should be available. Injunctive relief is such a remedy, but should only be granted when "there is urgent necessity to avoid injury" and no adequate legal remedy exists. The facts in *Maritrans* presented just such a case, because Maritrans should not have been forced to wait until damage occurred to stop its former law firm from using its secrets for the benefit of its competitors. To rule otherwise might require Maritrans to lose all or part of the company's business before claiming a remedy.[7]

Disqualification

Injunctive relief is related to the most common remedy for conflicts of interest: court-ordered disqualification of lawyers. Like injunctive relief, disqualification prevents a lawyer or former lawyer (and that lawyer's current law firm) from representing another client. When granted, disqualification can prevent harm to clients or former clients by ensuring that the case will be presented without

---

1. Recall dePape v. Trinity Health Systems, Inc., *supra* p. 88, and Perez v. Kirk & Carrigan, *supra* p. 165.
2. *See* The Law Governing Lawyers: Loss of Fee or Other Benefits, *infra* p. 339.
3. *See, e.g.,* St. ex rel. Neb. St. Bar Assn. v. Frank, 631 N.W.2d 485 (Neb. 2001) (lawyer who simultaneously represented an insurance company in litigation and another client in a claim against the insurance company publicly reprimanded).
4. *See, e.g.,* United States v. Bronson, 658 F.2d 920 (2d Cir. 1981) (mail fraud conviction based on lawyer's conflict of interest).
5. Richard E. Flamm, *Lawyer Disqualification: Conflicts of Interest and Other Bases* (Banks Jordan 2003).
6. *See, e.g.,* Franklin v. Callum, 782 A.2d 884 (N.H. 2001) (both parties granted disqualification of the other side's lawyer on different legal theories).
7. Of course, if damages had already been caused by the firm's conflict of interest, then Maritrans could seek a remedy at law for the past harm in addition to an equitable remedy to prevent future damage.

conflicting loyalties or improper use of confidential information.[8] For example, if Pepper Hamilton had attempted to represent one of Maritrans' competitors against Maritrans in litigation, Maritrans could have asked the court to disqualify its former law firm as a means to prevent the firm's use of its secrets against it in subsequent litigation. We first encountered this remedy in *Meyerhofer* in Chapter 7, and we will see repeated consideration of disqualification as a remedy in the cases in the next chapter.

Disqualification motions originated over a century ago as requests for court orders.[9] They are addressed to the inherent power of judges designed to regulate the course of proceedings, through court orders and other relief.[10] Such motions usually are addressed to trial courts, but may be raised in any court where a conflict occurs.[11] The motion to disqualify may be made by the lawyer's client, former client, or any other party to the litigation.[12] Trial judges also are empowered to raise such an issue *sua sponte*.[13] Although a few courts initially thought they had no such power, litigation over the past 50 years has left no doubt that courts can, and should, disqualify lawyers when their conduct threatens the fairness of a judicial proceeding.[14]

While disqualification provides relief from real or serious threats of breaches of loyalty or confidentiality, unlike other remedies, it imposes costs on other parties to a proceeding. When a lawyer is disqualified, the time schedule of a proceeding often must be adjusted to allow the client who has lost a lawyer time to retain new counsel. When the motion to disqualify comes from opposing counsel or the court, clients can be deprived of their chosen lawyers without their consent. For these reasons, courts recognize that motions to disqualify can be used to tactical advantage by opposing parties in litigation. Courts have responded to this potential for misuse of the court's power in three ways.

First, courts are careful to scrutinize the facts and law offered in support of disqualification motions. Second, courts increasingly use the doctrines of laches, estoppel, or waiver to deny motions to disqualify when they have not been

---

8. RLGL §6, Comment i.

9. The first case was Gauden v. Ga., 11 Ga. 47 (1852). *See* Kenneth L. Penegar, *The Loss of Innocence: A Brief History of Law Firm Disqualification in the Courts*, 8 Geo. J. Leg. Ethics 831, 832 (1995).

10. RLGL §6, Comment i. *See also* The Bounds of the Law: Court Orders, *supra* p. 211.

11. *See, e.g.,* Williams v. St., 805 A.2d 880 (Del. 2002) (appellate counsel disqualified for positional conflict of interest). Appellate courts review disqualification decisions of trial courts using an abuse of discretion standard. *See, e.g.,* People ex rel. Dept. of Corporations v. Speedee Oil Change Sys., Inc., 980 P.2d 371, 378 (Cal. 1999).

12. Ronald E. Mallen & Jeffrey Smith, *Legal Malpractice* §16.15 (2007 ed.).

13. This may be especially likely to occur in criminal cases, where judges assume special responsibility for the fairness of the proceeding. *E.g.,* Fed. R. Crim. P. 44(c) (federal district courts required to inquire into any proposed joint representation); Cuyler v. Sullivan, 446 U.S. 335 (1980) (trial judge has important role in assuring fairness of trial of joint defendants).

14. *E.g.,* Ennis v. Ennis, 276 N.W.2d 341, 348 (Wis. App. 1979). Administrative law judges also exercise this power in appropriate circumstances. *See, e.g.,* Prof. Reactor Operator Socy. v. United States NRC, 939 F.2d 1047 (D.C. Cir. 1991) (Administrative Procedure Act's right to counsel guarantee requires concrete evidence that counsel's presence would impede its investigation in order to exclude a lawyer from representing a subpoenaed witness); SEC v. Csapo, 533 F.2d 7 (D.C. Cir. 1976) (same standard required for similar SEC rule granting agency authority to disqualify lawyers); In re Scioto Broadcaster, 5 FCC Rcd. 5158 (1990) (FCC review board and Commission will intervene only in cases of clear conflicts of interest).

made on a timely basis.[15] Third, orders granting or denying disqualification usually are not appealable until a final judgment on the merits.[16] This means that where disqualification is denied, the targeted lawyer may continue the representation, but the other side can raise the issue on appeal. On the other hand, if the motion is granted, the client represented by the now disqualified lawyer is forced to find new counsel.[17] If that client settles or wins the case, the disqualified lawyer has no independent right to appeal. Only if the client loses the case can the issue be raised on appeal.

The Relevance of Lawyer Codes

In assessing whether a lawyer should be disqualified, courts begin with the relevant conflict of interest rules in the relevant professional code or case law.[18] If lawyer code rules have been violated, disqualification commonly follows, because, as *Maritrans* teaches, the applicable professional rules derive from the lawyer's common law duties. A few courts impose an additional requirement, explicitly limiting disqualification to breaches of the relevant lawyer code conflict of interest provisions that would "taint" the trial.[19] Perhaps because it has faced the greatest number of disqualification motions, the Second Circuit adopts this "restrained approach" to disqualification motions, both to promote judicial economy and because it prefers "disciplinary machinery" for "less serious allegations of ethical impropriety."[20] More typical is the Fifth Circuit, which explicitly rejects this "hands-off approach," finding that "a motion to disqualify counsel is the proper method for a party-litigant to bring the issues of conflict of interest or breach of ethical duties to the attention of the court."[21]

Where the lawyer code rules have been violated, the Fifth Circuit approach makes sense because the lawyer should have recognized the conflict and responded by withdrawing from the representation that created it.[22] Granting a disqualification motion simply requires the lawyer to do what she already should have done—move to withdraw under Model Rule 1.16(a)—in order to avoid a violation of the professional code.[23]

15. *See, e.g.,* Universal City Studios, Inc. v. Reimerdes, 98 F. Supp. 2d 449 (S.D.N.Y. 2000).

16. In the federal courts, an order granting or denying disqualification cannot be appealed until a final judgment on the merits has been reached. Richardson-Merrell Inc. v. Koller, 472 U.S. 424 (1985); Flanagan v. United States, 465 U.S. 259 (1984); Firestone Tire & Rubber v. Risjord, 449 U.S. 368 (1981). State courts are split on this issue. *See* David B. Harrison, *Appealability of State Court's Order Granting or Denying Motion to Disqualify Attorney,* 5 A.L.R.4th 1251 (1981).

17. Successor counsel will usually be allowed to use the disqualified lawyer's work product if it does not contain impermissible client confidential information. RLGL §6, Comment i; In re George, 28 S.W.3d 511 (Tex. 2000) (identifying various approaches to making the determination whether the work product contains confidential information).

18. In some situations such as bankruptcy, statutory provisions impose additional conflict of interest standards. *See, e.g.,* In re Leslie Fay Cos., 175 B.R. 525 (Bankr. S.D.N.Y. 1994).

19. Armstrong v. McAlpin, 625 F.2d 433 (2d Cir. 1980), *vacated on other grounds,* 449 U.S. 1106 (1981).

20. *See* The European Community v. RJR Nabisco, Inc., 134 F. Supp. 2d 297, 303 (E.D.N.Y. 2001) (reviewing Second Circuit decisions).

21. *See* In re Am. Airlines, Inc., 972 F.2d 605, 611 (5th Cir. 1992).

22. *See, e.g.,* Schlumberger Tech., Inc. v. Wiley, 113 F. 3d 1553, 1561 (11th Cir. 1997).

23. *See, e.g.,* Williams v. St., 805 A.2d 880 (Del. 2002) (trial counsel's motion to withdraw as appellate counsel granted due to a conflict created by previous Supreme Court argument).

A more difficult situation is presented when a potential or threatened violation of the rules appears in a case. Then, courts look to seriousness of the potential violation and the likelihood that it will affect the fairness of the matter before the court. Relief will be denied unless the possibility of an injury to a party or the fairness of the proceeding can be shown.[24]

Although disqualification motions are the most common remedy sought by clients and former clients to redress conflicts of interest, *Maritrans* illustrates that other remedies, including civil damages, fee forfeiture, dismissal of a claim or defense, and professional discipline, also exist.[25] The potential for each of these remedies will be explored throughout the materials in this chapter and the next. Each remedy has its own legal requirements, and multiple remedies may exist for the same breach of fiduciary duty. One thing is certain: lawyers today have to worry about more than malpractice suits and professional discipline. They also realize that injunctive relief or disqualification may be granted to an opposing party, involuntarily depriving them of the opportunity to represent a client, as well as exposing them to potential liability and loss of compensation.

B. Client and Lawyer Interests

Problems

8-2. Should Martyn agree to accept one-third of the shares of stock issued in a new business start-up in lieu of an hourly fee? Should she agree to serve on the new company's board of directors?

8-3. Should Martyn & Fox insert a clause in all of its estate planning documents that appoints a Martyn & Fox lawyer as the fiduciary (executor, administrator, or personal representative) of an estate or trustee of a trust? When Martyn & Fox lawyers act as fiduciary or trustee, may they hire Martyn & Fox as counsel for the trust or estate?

8-4. Should Martyn & Fox provide free legal services to a criminal defendant who agrees to grant it the movie rights to his story?

8-5. Our client, in order to survive financially, is warned she'll have to settle her case early and for too little. Should Martyn & Fox pay her living expenses through trial?

8-6. Martyn & Fox failed to file a client's case within the appropriate statute of limitations. Should Martyn sit down with the client,

---

24. *See, e.g.,* United States v. Kitchin, 592 F.2d 900, 903 (5th Cir.), *cert. denied,* 444 U.S. 843 (1979) (lawyer may be disqualified "only where there is a reasonable possibility that some specifically identifiable ethical impropriety actually occurred, and, in light of the interests underlying the standards of ethics, the social need for ethical practice outweighs the party's right to counsel of his choice"); Bd. of Educ. v. Nyquist, 590 F.2d 1241, 1246 (2d Cir. 1979) (conflict must "taint the trial"); In re Infotechnology, Inc., 582 A.2d 215, 216 (Del. 1990) (conflict must "adversely affect . . . the fair and effective administration of justice").
25. *See* RLGL §6. In fact, Pepper Hamilton settled with Maritrans for $3 million following the Pennsylvania Supreme Court decision, an amount slightly less than its legal fees in the matter. *See* James L. Kelly, *Lawyers Crossing Lines: Nine Stories* 79 (Carolina Academic Press 2001).

confess her error, and offer to pay the entire amount of the underlying claims?

8-7. Martyn & Fox represents Acme Corp. in contested litigation against Zenon Inc. Can a senior associate assume a major role in the case when he is married to the lead lawyer for Zenon?

8-8. Client tells Martyn & Fox that he is strapped for cash and cannot afford our requested retainer in a divorce case. Can Martyn & Fox have Client sign a promissory note secured by a mortgage on the family home in lieu of the retainer?

8-9. Martyn & Fox represents Big Bank in a wide variety of matters. A colleague tells Fox at lunch: "Did you hear the latest? Sarah Snyder [an associate at Martyn & Fox] is dating the General Counsel of Big Bank."

Consider: Model Rules 1.4, 1.7, 1.8, 1.10
Model Code DR 4-101(B), 5-101, 5-104, and 6-102
Cal. Rules 3-120, 3-320, 4-210; D.C. Rule 1.8(d); N.Y. Rule DR 5-111
RLGL §§6, 36, 54, 126, 127

Monco v. Janus

583 N.E.2d 575 (Ill. App. 1991)

Justice BUCKLEY delivered the opinion of the court:

In February 1987, plaintiff Dean Monco (Monco) petitioned to dissolve on the grounds of deadlock JISCO-NI Enterprises, Inc. (Jisconi), an Illinois corporation, owned 50% each by Monco and defendant Ronald Janus (Janus). Jisconi's sole asset is its ownership of patent rights to an invention which Monco and Janus had assigned to Jisconi. Janus counter-claimed against Monco seeking to vacate the assignment and to compel Monco to turn over the Jisconi shares he owned on the grounds that the invention was Janus' idea, that Monco was Janus' personal attorney, and that the assignment and Monco's stock ownership in Jisconi were the result of Monco's undue influence and breach of fiduciary duty to Janus....

On October 4, 1989, the circuit court of Cook County dismissed Janus' counterclaim holding that, while an attorney-client relationship existed and a breach of fiduciary duty had occurred, Janus knowingly ratified his dealings with Monco....

... The record shows that Janus is a college graduate, a certified teacher, and the sole proprietor of his own landscaping business for over 17 years. Monco is an attorney admitted to practice in Illinois and before the United States Patent and Trademark Office. Monco is also a shareholder in a Chicago law firm.

Prior to the transaction in question, Janus and Monco had been social acquaintances since 1970. In 1981 and 1984, Janus contacted Monco to discuss possible patentable ideas. These ideas were not pursued. In the spring of 1985, Monco engaged Janus to perform landscaping services for his home. On Memorial Day weekend, while performing such services, Janus sat down with Monco at Monco's kitchen table and drew a sketch of an idea for a beverage container to be worn around the neck of the user. The contents of the conversation which next transpired is disputed by the parties and nothing in writing exists to verify either party's version of the agreement.

Janus testified that after Monco told him that his idea was fantastic, Janus asked Monco if he was interested in pursuing the idea together. Janus told Monco that Monco could help him with the idea and share in any profits. Janus testified that he and Monco agreed to share expenses equally and that Monco would provide business contacts and free legal services to the venture. Janus denied that Monco told him to obtain independent legal advice and denied that he and Monco were "50/50" partners.

Monco testified that Janus specifically asked him to go into business and offered Monco a 50% interest in the venture. Monco accepted Janus' offer and the two shook hands. Monco testified they discussed various matters, including licensing the patent to a manufacturing concern, from which they would receive royalties, versus assigning the patent to a separate corporation owned by them equally, which would avoid personal liability but would require business capital and marketing. Monco testified that he specifically advised Janus to obtain outside counsel to make sure that Janus' interests were represented. Janus agreed. Monco's wife, who was present for much of the conversation, corroborated Monco's testimony.

Significantly, at the kitchen table meeting, or any time thereafter, Monco admitted that he never advised Janus that if Janus were to assign the patent to a jointly-owned corporation, Janus would lose exclu-

sive control over the patent in the event of corporate dissolution. In such situation, Janus and Monco as co-owners of the patent would have equal rights to market the patent without accounting to the other for profits. Monco also testified that he did not inform Janus of the option of licensing the patent to Jisconi as opposed to a full assignment. Monco explained that Janus was not his client and that anything less than a full assignment to a jointly-owned company would be inconsistent with their agreement to be "50/50" partners.

In the summer months following the "kitchen table" meeting, Janus and Monco communicated by telephone and letter and exchanged ideas on numerous matters involving the beverage container, including what entity would be best for liability and tax purposes. Ultimately, the parties agreed to incorporate and name the entity using the first names of their children. Monco also suggested and conducted a "prior art" search to determine if Janus' idea was patentable. Based on the results of this search, Monco concluded and Janus agreed that a patent application was appropriate.

On September 19, 1985, Janus and Monco met with Mark Fine, an attorney and friend of Monco, about incorporating Jisconi. Fine prepared draft articles of incorporation and testified that Monco and Janus told him that they were equal partners in the new business; Fine heard nothing during this conversation to indicate to him that Monco and Janus were anything other than business partners. Fine also testified that he advised Janus to obtain independent counsel to prepare a buy/sell and shareholders' agreement in order to protect Janus' interests. Janus' recollection about this meeting conflicted with Fine's. Janus denied ever discussing anything regarding specific ownership interests, and he could not remember Fine's advice to obtain independent counsel.

After the meeting with Fine, Janus asked Monco to prepare the incorporation papers. Monco was reluctant to prepare these papers because he did not practice corporate law. However, using Fine's draft, Monco prepared the papers and forwarded them to Janus for his review and signature. Janus admitted that Monco told him to have his own counsel review the papers but Janus never did. Janus testified that he considered Monco his attorney and thought that Monco would assure that Janus' interests were protected. Jisconi was incorporated on October 2, 1985.

Following the incorporation of Jisconi, Monco prepared the initial patent application for the beverage container. The application, related documents, and the assignment of the patent to Jisconi were forwarded to Janus for his review. Monco testified that he again told Janus to have his own counsel review the documents, but Janus denied ever receiving this advice. On October 28, 1985, without the aid of independent counsel, Janus executed the parent patent application and an initial assignment. Monco filed the parent patent application and related documents on November 12, 1985. . . .

On July 30, 1986, Monco wrote Janus and addressed several subjects, including a proposed shareholders' agreement which Monco had previously drafted and . . . also stated that, as he had told Janus on several occasions since forming Jisconi, Janus should obtain independent

counsel to review the agreement as well as other matters connected with Jisconi. This was the first time in writing that Monco advised Janus to obtain independent counsel. Neither Janus nor Anthony Vaccarello, an attorney retained shortly thereafter by Janus, raised any concerns about the statements in the letter. . . .

On August 5, 1986, Vaccarello wrote Monco and identified himself as Janus' counsel regarding the proposed shareholders' agreement. In this letter, Vaccarello requested certain corporate documents, including any pre-incorporation agreements, shareholders' meeting minutes and certificates, and directors' resolutions and minutes.

On August 9, 1986, without Vaccarello's presence, Monco and Janus met at Monco's office to sign numerous corporate documents including the documents that Vaccarello requested. In particular, Janus and Monco executed a shareholders' resolution setting forth their original agreement that they each would assign all patent rights to Jisconi; that Monco would prepare the patent applications; and that Monco and Janus would equally share the expenses of the business. Monco and Janus also executed share certificates showing each to own 500 shares of Jisconi stock and meeting minutes of the first shareholders' meeting formally designating themselves as Jisconi's sole directors. Monco and Janus dated these documents as of November 1, 1985, to conform the written record to their agreement as of the time of incorporation. Janus gave the executed documents to Vaccarello; neither Janus or Vaccarello objected to the documents at any time thereafter.

Beginning in late summer, Janus began to voice objections to Monco. . . . These differences soon led to a total breakdown in the parties' relationship. In early September, a meeting was held between Monco and Janus and their respective counsel in an attempt to resolve the deadlock. The meeting was only partially successful. However, despite the parties' differences, on September 29, 1986, Janus executed an application for a design patent and another assignment of all patent rights to Jisconi. Neither Janus, . . . or Vaccarello objected.

In December 1986, Janus arranged a meeting with Monco in an attempt to resolve the deadlock. . . . The parties remained deadlocked.

Monco initiated this lawsuit by filing his petition to dissolve Jisconi in February 1987. Janus counterclaimed in June 1987 alleging undue influence, overreaching and Monco's failure to inform Janus that, upon Jisconi's dissolution, each party could get 100% of the non-exclusive rights to market the patent and keep profits without accounting to the other. Janus alleged that he did not know this legal consequence, as it was a peculiarity of the patent laws, and requested as relief that the assignment to Jisconi be vacated, that Monco's 50% interest in Jisconi be forfeited as an excessive fee, and that damages be awarded.

In July 1988, Monco filed a motion for summary judgment on Janus' counterclaim . . . [where he] claimed that he was acting as Janus' business partner and not as his attorney. . . .

The first issue we address is whether a client's subsequent conduct can cure an attorney-client transaction which is the product of the attorney's undue influence. This is an issue of first impression in Illinois.

Transactions between attorneys and clients are closely scrutinized. When an attorney engages in a transaction with a client and is benefited thereby, a presumption arises that the transaction proceeded from undue influence. Once a presumption is raised, the burden shifts to the attorney to come forward with evidence that the transaction was fair, equitable and just and that the benefit did not proceed from undue influence. Because a strong presumption of undue influence arises when an attorney engages in a transaction with a client and is benefited thereby, courts require clear and convincing evidence to rebut this presumption. . . . Some of the factors the courts deem persuasive in determining whether the presumption of undue influence has been overcome include a showing by the attorney (1) that he or she made a full and frank disclosure of all relevant information; (2) that adequate consideration was given; and (3) that the client had independent advice before completing the transaction. (McFail v. Braden, 166 N.E.2d 46, 52 (Ill. 1960)). Once the presumption has been rebutted, the burden of production and persuasion is again on the client to show undue influence.

Initially, we agree with the circuit court that an attorney-client relationship existed between Monco and Janus. The evidence supports that Monco was acting as the attorney for Jisconi as well as for both himself and Janus. While the evidence also shows that Monco and Janus were business partners, Monco's role as Janus' partner does not foreclose the conclusion that Monco was also Janus' personal attorney.

We also agree with the circuit court that Monco entered into a beneficial business transaction with Janus. Accordingly, under relevant supreme court precedent, Monco was required to prove by clear and convincing evidence the three *McFail* factors. We agree that Monco failed to meet his burden.

Under the first factor, it cannot be readily disputed that Monco failed to give Janus a "full and frank disclosure of all relevant information" prior to Janus making the first assignment of all his rights in the patent to Jisconi. Monco admitted at trial that he did not learn of the effect of Jisconi's dissolution under the patent laws until shortly before he filed his petition for dissolution in February 1987. Thus, there is no way Monco could have timely given Janus the required information.

Under the second factor, Monco did not present clear and convincing evidence to show that he gave adequate consideration to support the 50% ownership interest in Jisconi he received. Admittedly, Monco was the "brains" behind taking the appropriate measures to assure that Janus' idea became patented and that the idea was marketed profitably. In this regard, Monco spent, as he testified, hundreds of hours of his own time working on Jisconi matters. While Monco worked on Jisconi at a time when he was fully compensated by his firm, Monco testified that his work on Jisconi prevented him from billing firm clients which in turn contributed to a lower yearly salary. Aside from the legal and non-legal time Monco contributed towards Jisconi, the record shows that Monco contributed over $13,000 in capital contributions. These expenses were never reimbursed by Jisconi. More-

over, Monco fronted Janus' one-half of the expenses from time to time when Janus became unable to pay his share.

Notwithstanding the above consideration contributed by Monco, we agree that it was not clear and convincing evidence of adequate consideration. Monco's 50% interest gave him an equal voice in Jisconi affairs. If Janus and Monco disagreed, Monco's interest gave him the ability to deadlock Jisconi's affairs and potentially hold Janus hostage. It must be remembered that this extreme leverage was given to Monco at a time when an attorney-client relationship existed. More importantly, the beverage container idea originated with Janus. Even in Monco's opinion, the idea had great money-making potential. We agree that Monco's labor and capital contributions were not adequate consideration to support the benefits which Monco could ultimately reap.

As for the third factor, the record shows that Janus did not have independent counsel before executing the first assignment. According to Janus, at this stage of their relationship, Monco was his personal attorney and was looking out for his interests. Although Monco advised Janus to have independent counsel to look over his work, this advice was insufficient. Janus' trust in Monco was great. The two had been personal acquaintances since 1970, and Janus had consulted Monco on two prior occasions regarding other patentable ideas. In light of Janus' extreme trust in Monco, Monco's suggestion that Janus have someone look over his work was insufficient to satisfy Monco's obligation to assure that Janus had independent counsel before executing the assignment.

As the foregoing analysis shows, we agree that Monco failed to rebut the presumption of undue influence. Accordingly, we next focus on Monco's affirmative defense of ratification. . . .

The fact that attorney-client transactions are voidable and not void supports our conclusion that in certain situations, a client's post-transaction conduct can properly amount to an affirmance of that transaction notwithstanding that it is the product of the attorney's undue influence. To hold otherwise would, in our opinion, unsettle attorney-client transactions despite an attorney's reasonable reliance that the transaction was a "done deal." Moreover, to hold otherwise would contradict settled principles of traditional contracts and trusts law relating to ratification. . . .

. . . During its analysis, the circuit court initially concluded that Monco had failed to present clear and convincing evidence as to any of the three *McFail* factors. In its ratification analysis, the circuit court . . . conclude[d] that Janus' ratification occurred with the benefit of independent counsel and full knowledge of the effect the patent laws had on an assignment of a patent to a jointly owned corporation which later dissolved.

Our disagreement with the circuit court's ratification analysis is that the court failed to address for the second time whether the Monco-Janus transaction was fair. . . . As we have stated, the fairness of the transaction is a separate and indispensable inquiry to a ratification analysis of an attorney-client transaction. Because we conclude that the Monco-Janus transaction is unfair, we hold that the affirmative defense of ratification is unavailable to Monco.

As previously discussed, Monco did not present clear and convincing evidence that he gave adequate consideration to support the 50% interest he received in the patent. Monco has not directly appealed this finding and, in any event, it is supported by the manifest weight of the evidence. Even when all of the benefits Monco conferred are taken together, we believe they are out of all proportion to the 50% interest he received and the corresponding rights associated with a shareholder holding such interest. Accordingly, for these reasons, the circuit court erred in dismissing Janus' counterclaim. . . .

The unfairness of the transaction, and this court's duty to set it aside, is made even more clear in light of the Code of Professional Responsibility, [which] this court has found . . . a relevant consideration in malpractice actions between attorney and client. . . .

Here, the initial assignment of Janus' patent rights to Jisconi and Monco's 50% interest therein allowed Monco to deadlock Jisconi. At the same time as the assignment, Janus expected Monco to exercise professional judgment on his behalf. Monco's representation of Janus and his ownership interest in Jisconi cannot be reconciled, as Monco's position in this case makes apparent. Janus was never informed on these matters, nor for that matter, of his right to expect under the Canons Monco's zealous representation of his interests and Monco's exercise of independent professional judgment on his behalf.

In summary, we conclude that the circuit court erred in dismissing Janus amended counterclaim. . . .

Lawrence J. Fox

Legal Tender: A Lawyer's Guide to Handling Professional Dilemmas

85-96 (ABA 1995)

It Wasn't the Money

It wasn't the money. He was sure it wasn't the money. Though, if he were honest (heaven knew this was no time not to be honest), that part pleased him, too. But there really had been other factors that had prompted him far more than the money. Peter could remember, as if it had just happened, the sense of pride he felt when he received the telephone call from Edward Frazier, the CEO of Hanscom Industries.

Peter met Ed when Peter was a third-year associate at Caldwell & Moore. Ed, at the time, had just been promoted to Sector Manager in the Life Sciences Division of Hanscom, Caldwell & Moore's third-largest client. Life Sciences was planning a joint venture with a Norwegian pharmaceutical firm, and Ed and he had put together their respective teams to conduct the due diligence, negotiate, and then document the transaction. They had worked literally around the clock, made two trips to Oslo together, and become fast friends.

This first business connection was followed by many others as each of them moved up the ladder at their respective places of employment. Ed was the first non-Caldwell & Moore person to call Peter to congratulate him when he made partner. It was not two years later that Ed became a corporate vice president, the level one had to achieve in order to be awarded the much-sought-after Hanscom Industry stock options under a plan that Peter had established for Hanscom with the help of one of his tax department colleagues.

At the time of the call, Peter had tried to remember how many "deals" he had undertaken for Hanscom—five or six, at least. But nothing had been more significant in his work for Hanscom than when Old Man Taylor had come to Peter in 1984 and told Peter he would, henceforth, be in charge of the Hanscom client relationship for Caldwell & Moore. Taylor had placed his hand on Peter's shoulder, looked him in the eye, and emphasized to Peter how the Hanscom–Caldwell & Moore relationship went back 70 years. It was now Peter's to preserve for the next generation of his firm's lawyers.

From that point forward, Peter had become both the point person to receive calls from key personnel at Hanscom and the distributor within Caldwell & Moore of the treasured Hanscom work assignments. Being assigned Hanscom matters was a sure sign to associates that their work was viewed as meeting Caldwell & Moore's rather exalted standards.

In early 1987, Ed Frazier had been elected CEO of Hanscom, and only six months after that, Peter reluctantly accepted the chairmanship of his firm. How ironic his ascendancy to this new position had seemed in light of his many talks with Ed in which Peter lorded over Ed how lucky Peter was to work in an enterprise whose management was shared among all 55 or 60 partners, a principle that elicited a high level of skepticism from Ed. Indeed, Ed had offered his view that, at some point, Caldwell & Moore just wouldn't be able to function in the old way, a thought Peter had dismissed out-of-hand at the time.

In any event, when Peter received the call from Ed, he attached no special significance to it. They talked at least once a month, often on business matters (though at that point each seemed to be presiding more than they were working). But this call was different. "Peter," he started, "The board of directors of Hanscom just met in executive session out here in Hatboro. We had some really tough personnel decisions to make, as you probably know. Your partner Carol really helped us. But that's not why I'm calling. Carol's got that covered, as you would expect. What we want to know, Peter, is whether you would go on the Hanscom board of directors?"

Peter immediately interrupted, "You don't need me on your board. I attend the meetings when you need a lawyer and I send my colleagues when you need someone who really knows the law."

"You're right enough about that," responded Ed, "but we don't want you to join our board as a lawyer. We value your judgment and, frankly, when we searched for a replacement for Reg Stevens, everyone agreed you were the best choice. You know us, you used to know the law and, heaven knows, you're independent, too independent if you ask me."

"Well," Peter gathered himself together, "I am deeply flattered by the offer. I would very much like to do it for you, Ed. Caldwell & Moore, however, has an elaborate policy governing these directorships." Turning to a more delicate subject, Peter continued, "I don't want you to think this is an issue, but what are the director fees, Ed? Under our rules I would get to keep the fees. But I'll have to report them to my compensation committee."

"We pay our directors $50,000 per year, $5,000 per board or committee meeting. You get some stock options, too."

"I guess my partner John Mangas knows what your D & O coverage is. I hope you don't still have that Union American policy. My partners will want to know you have real insurance," Peter responded, thinking at the time that extra money might finance the little Porsche he had been admiring.

But it certainly wasn't just the money. He had been honored that the Hanscom board valued his judgment. He had considered how going on the board would cement the relationship between Caldwell & Moore and this valued client. Those poaching competitor law firms, particularly the New York lawyers selling their expertise as if the Philadelphians were country bumpkins, might back off once they knew Peter was sitting in the inner sanctum.

But these arguments in favor did not forestall considerable discussion when he breathlessly shared with his fellow partners his good news. His partners were hardly enthusiastically endorsing his acceptance of this offer.

There were certain arguments that were stated openly. Hanscom's stock had been particularly volatile over the years. Caldwell & Moore earned giant fees defending two 10b-5 actions when announcements of negative news had caused the share price to drop. Hanscom engaged in risky lines of business—pharmaceuticals, chain saws. The company was a defendant in Superfund litigation. The reasons that made Hanscom a fascinating client hardly commended it as a company on whose board one would willingly serve.

Then there were the arguments that went unspoken, contained in simply a glance or an avoidance in the halls. Peter could feel the resentment, the sense that he was being too uppity, that the last thing he needed with his exalted partnership share was more income.

In the end, the executive committee had approved his going on the board. The approval meeting went more smoothly than he had expected; whatever else could be said, securing the Hanscom Industries client relationship was a priority. These perilous times cried out for preserving existing clients at almost any cost.

It was only minutes later that Peter called Ed. "Caldwell & Moore is thrilled that you asked me to join," he lied. Then, compensating for his unprincipled characterization of the firm's deliberative process, he reminded Ed that he really didn't think it was important that they nominate him, hoping nonetheless that Ed would stick to his resolve.

Peter soon became a regular in the boardroom. Being a director was a genuine high. Peter got to rub elbows with a cluster of prominent fellow Philadelphians—the CEO of First Philadelphia Trust, the Provost of the University, and the head of the local NAACP chapter.

The seat on the board also more than fulfilled his firm's expectations that it would cement the Hanscom-Caldwell & Moore relationship. Since all major corporate transactions showed up on the board agenda at an early stage, it became psychologically impossible for discussion not to proceed on the assumption that Peter's firm would handle each.

Financially, Peter could hardly believe how well his directorship turned out. The $50,000 not only funded the Porsche, but also gave him a chance to make a substantial contribution to his old prep school. More important, his stock options to purchase 10,000 shares of Hanscom had yielded him a six-figure paper profit. Lawyers in their practice certainly had no way of accumulating capital without creating billable hours; yet this nest egg had been created without a single time sheet entry!

Finally, he enjoyed the challenge of deciding the matters that came to the board. Peter particularly loved the opportunity his board membership gave him to pretend he was a businessman, yes, even an entrepreneur, rather than a staid lawyer who was always telling his business clients why they could not do something.

Maybe he would be forced to acknowledge it was the money. But that thought only increased his pain as he tried to sort out the events that prompted this reminiscence. He never imagined he would find himself at such a juncture of crisis. The thought that at least a few of his partners would now view this as a just reward for his hubris in becoming a director also acted as an irritant.

Peter recalled that he had been as enthusiastic as anyone with the proposal that Hanscom sell limited-partnership interests in their various resort hotels. The idea of splitting away the expected appreciation in the underlying real estate—appreciation that would get lost in the basic evaluations by the market of the price of Hanscom stock—provided an excellent way for Hanscom to secure a much-needed capital infusion to finance expansion of its other lines of business. It also had the not-undelightful side benefit that all of the resources of Caldwell & Moore's excellent business department would have to be mustered to bring the offering to fruition. The icing on the cake, if you will, was the opportunity this offering provided Peter and his partners to buy these limited-partnership interests at a discount (they had to pay no commission to the underwriters, a fact duly disclosed in the offering material).

The year of the offering turned out to be a banner year for everyone: Hanscom ended up raising $115 million (to be received across five years); Caldwell & Moore broke firm revenue and profits per partner records; Peter had his highest billings ever.

The board meeting of May 21 was held in the usual location, Aronomink Country Club, away from the neurosis that gripped the headquarters every time these monthly meetings occurred. The agenda gave no hint of what was to come.

It was only when Edward moved to the head of the table that Peter noticed the strain in his face. Edward began, "I think, with your indulgence, I will omit the usual preliminaries. We have a matter to address that is so important I think we will need all the time we have scheduled.

"There is no point in beating about the bush. I received a call yesterday from our local U.S. Attorney, Bill Allan. Bill told me that a grand jury has been investigating M.A.I. Appraisal Company and its president, Marvin Hammer. You will recall that M.A.I. appraised our resort properties in Martha's Vineyard, the two in Maine, Padre Island, the Berkshires, and Cape May in connection with the limited-partnership offering. Bill tells me he has uncovered substantial evidence that M.A.I. received bribes."

"Bribes!" shrieked Jay Harris, the university Provost. "Who could have given him bribes?"

"That's the real problem. Bill tells me it was our own CFO, George Sandel; he even knew the amounts."

"But how could that happen?" Peter numbly asked.

"Well, George, as we all recognize, is in charge of our accounting function. Apparently, he was able to code the payments in such a way that they were lumped in with our commission payments to travel agencies."

"But, why would George do such a thing? He's our most conservative executive. My God, he still wears a pocket liner!" interjected another director.

"I was as incredulous as all of you. It appears George got nervous that the appraisals wouldn't come in high enough. Only George really appreciated how much we needed the cash. So he decided to ensure our success by offering a little extra to Marvin."

"I hate to ask—as if it mattered—but . . . how much?" stuttered Peter.

"Bill claims he's documented $100,000; it may be more," replied Ed.

"No," said Peter, betraying his rising annoyance, "I mean how much did he overstate the appraised amounts?"

"We really don't know. In fact, we don't know whether they were over-appraised or not. All we know at this point is that Marvin received an extra fee. For all we know, the appraisals are the same as they would have been."

"Spoken like a true lawyer," Peter observed wryly.

"How can we ever replace George?" asked the Provost.

"That's the least of our problems," Ed answered. "Bill sounded like he thought we at Hanscom had hired Marvin because he could be bought. Some snide remarks about M.A.I. meaning 'made as instructed.'"

"Well," Peter began, carefully choosing his words, "wearing my lawyer hat, I can tell you we have one immediate problem. The next annual payments from the limited partners are due June 1. We have to tell them about this before that date."

"Tell them!" bellowed Ed. "We can't tell them. If we don't receive that money on June 1, we'll have no cash to pay Chemical Bank our quarterly interest."

"But you can't have our investors making payments when they don't know about these phony appraisals. Our prospectus made all kinds of representations. . . ."

Ed instantly cut him off. "I should never have let you and your partners buy into that deal. Now all you can think of is saving the partners their money."

"You're missing the point," Peter started.

"I am missing nothing of the kind. We don't even know if the appraisals were wrong. They seemed fair to all of us. I was surprised how high Padre Island came in but . . . " Ed trailed off.

"No, the point is that we raised all that money from investors without telling them our appraiser was receiving bribes . . . from us. The prospectus, the Caldwell & Moore prospectus, omitted a material fact."

"Peter, for all we know that was a harmless error. Now you just sound like a lawyer trying to cover his butt. If the appraisals would have been the same anyway, what difference does it make? There's nothing material about a $100,000 expense in a $115 million transaction."

"There is if it involves fraud. Ed, we better think about how we're going to inform our investors," declared Peter, trying to lower the decibel level.

"Peter, you are a director of this company. You must act in the best interests of the company. And I'm telling you the best interests of Hanscom Industries are to publicize nothing. It is *not* to worry about Caldwell & Moore or our investors. In fact, Peter, if you think your firm can't handle the investigation I propose we undertake, I know three law firms that would be glad to help Hanscom out of this difficulty without compromising their loyalty to us."

Peter was stunned. His old friend Ed had never spoken to him in this way. But the predicament was real enough. He could not sort out the issues as they seemed to turn him upside down like ferocious ocean waves the day after a storm.

Hanscom needed the money, and if the payment were not received, a Chapter XI filing was not unlikely. But the liability to the investors if the prospectus contained an omission was clear. And that liability could run to Caldwell & Moore—his firm had drafted virtually every line of the Registration Statement. Letting the investors make yet one more annual payment after all this was known was the type of fact the plaintiffs' class action bar drooled for.

But what if Ed was right? Did they really have to disclose a harmless error? And what of his partners who would be paying over $800,000 of the June 1 payment? What would they say? Worse, what would his wife say when she heard this investment was in jeopardy, she who had urged him to buy zero-coupon bonds with this money, money earmarked for the kids' college education? She would be *ruthless*.

The rest of the meeting passed as a blur. He was sure he had supported Ed's resolution that a special committee of the board conduct an investigation. He was equally certain that he had agreed Caldwell & Moore would be glad to act as counsel to the committee, since he was now convinced that it was in everyone's interest that the matter be investigated before any action were taken. But did he actually make a speech that it was in the best interests of the investors that the circumstances surrounding the appraisals not be disclosed to them? He wasn't positive, but his cotton-filled cranial cavity suggested such a thought as he found himself talking with his trusted counselor and partner, Harry Gill.

"You won't believe what's happened" were his opening words, as he sought counsel as he had so many times in the past from Harry, everyone's first refuge when the pressure became too much. Harry was smart, he was nonjudgmental, and he could be trusted. After Peter recounted the events at Aronomink, even admitting that he might have said a few foolish things in the panic that he was about to lose his directorship, the firm's biggest client, and his investment as a limited partner, Harry looked heavenward, pressed his fingers to his forehead, and spun his chair around, looking for the longest time out his window, saying nothing. The silence was as palpable as in a Friends meeting, as meaningful as an eloquent speech, telling Peter in no uncertain terms that he had reached some pinnacle in challenging Harry. It was every bit as bad as when a physician told you that he had never seen such a condition before, precisely what you didn't want to hear. And now, sitting behind Harry's back, Harry's silence was exactly what Peter didn't want to hear. Answer me, he thought. Tell me there's a solution.

Finally, Harry slowly turned to face Peter, his voice choked with emotion as he began, "Peter, I don't know what to say. You know I didn't want you to take the directorship. I was even more upset when you and the rest of our partners bought into the resort deal. So I don't want you to think this is an 'I told you so.' But the real problem for me, Peter, and the reason I've taken so long staring out the window at Billy Penn, is that I don't think I can advise you on this. I'm a partner at Caldwell & Moore. Our client is Hanscom Industries. The questions you're asking me go to your role as a director, to Hanscom's duties to its investors, some of whom are my partners. The conflicts of interest diagram like the path of the cueball in three-corner billiards. And that doesn't include the interests of Caldwell & Moore; the firm will very likely end up a defendant in a 10b-5 action, an action whose centerpiece is going to be your board membership and our partners' purchasing of these investment interests."

"I feel sick that I would be forced to even say these words to you. But frankly, the best advice I can give you right now is to call up Alan over at White & Mager. If he has no conflicts, maybe you can gain counsel from him, counsel that would preserve whatever confidentiality you will need, counsel who will represent only you. You better just hope that the Union American policy comes through."

Peter was aghast. In the space of two hours he had been attacked by two of his closest friends. He couldn't consult his own partner. He had to start worrying about liability and insurance and defense.

Of course, as usual, Harry was right. But that fact gave him no comfort. As he rose from the chair, he searched helplessly for the right words. Tears welled up as he avoided eye contact with Harry. He mumbled a hapless thank you and slowly, oh so slowly, left the room, knowing he would be forced to admit it was the money.

In re Halverson

998 P.2d 833 (Wash. 2000)

En Banc. . . .

IRELAND, J. . . .

Lowell K. Halverson has been a member of the WSBA in private practice since 1968, concentrating on family law for the last 20 years. He has lectured and published extensively in this area. From 1990-91, Halverson served as president of the WSBA.

Although Halverson has been married to his wife, Diane, since 1964, he admits that since the early 1970s he has had consensual sexual relationships with six different female clients. Five of these clients retained Halverson as their attorney before the sexual relationship began. The most recent of these relationships was with Lisa Wickersham, the grievant in this action. Halverson first met Wickersham in 1989 when Wickersham accompanied a friend to Halverson's office. At this point, Wickersham was married to an attorney, Neil Sarles.

During this office visit, Halverson gave Wickersham and her friend a personality questionnaire that he regularly used with clients; he also asked Wickersham if she might like to work in his office on a special project involving artwork. Following this meeting, Wickersham worked at Halverson's office for a few months until early in 1990.

Wickersham retained Halverson as her attorney in May 1991, at which time Halverson administered another personality questionnaire. . . . Halverson filed a dissolution petition on her behalf in June 1991, and Wickersham moved out of her husband's house in early July.

Later in July while at Halverson's office, Wickersham confided to him that she was "attracted to [her] attorney." . . . Shortly thereafter, following a successful court appearance, Halverson took Wickersham on a tour of photographs displayed at the Rainier Club in Seattle. According to Halverson, while on the tour, Wickersham suggested that they get a room, but Wickersham denies this occurred.

Both agree, however, that after the tour they went to a restaurant on the waterfront where they expressed a mutual attraction and discussed Halverson's "ground rules" for a potential relationship: Halverson's wife could not find out about the affair

and there could be no bonding between Halverson and Wickersham's young daughter. According to Halverson, he explained to Wickersham that a potential relationship between them would not be of any significance to the pending divorce action if these "ground rules" were followed. Wickersham herself recognized the need for them to be discreet because of Halverson's high profile as president of the WSBA.

Halverson, however, did not advise Wickersham of the possible ramifications if the relationship were to become known. For example he did not tell her that, if Sarles were to discover the relationship, he would most likely become less willing to compromise in the divorce proceeding and that this would increase the complexity and cost of the dissolution and could impact the custody determination. Neither did Halverson advise Wickersham that either his wife's or Sarle's discovery of the affair could lead to his withdrawal as her attorney. . . .

. . . For the next six months, Wickersham and Halverson maintained a sexual relationship seeing each other whenever they could.

On January 1, 1992, Halverson's wife discovered the affair. Within a few days, Halverson withdrew as Wickersham's attorney because he felt that he had lost his objectivity and could no longer keep his roles separate, particularly in view of his wife's position as his office manager.

Halverson temporarily moved out of his home and continued his personal relationship with Wickersham for several weeks. In mid-February, however, Halverson told Wickersham that he was returning to his wife.

Meanwhile, Halverson provided Wickersham with the names of

several other attorneys who could take over her case. Although Wickersham wanted Halverson to continue as her attorney, he refused, and Wickersham, thus, hired another attorney, Eric Watness, to complete her dissolution. Halverson transferred the balance of Wickersham's account to Watness and wrote off her outstanding bill to him. There is no evidence that Halverson at any time revealed any client confidences or otherwise used information obtained from Wickersham. . . .

. . . Watness represented Wickersham until September 1992, when her case settled and a decree of dissolution was entered. Overall, Watness felt Wickersham received a "fair outcome" in her case.

A year later in October 1993, Wickersham complained to the WSBA about Halverson's conduct and, in 1994, filed a civil lawsuit. Wickersham's civil suit against Halverson settled in 1995 by sealed agreement for a substantial sum and with no admission of liability. Wickersham's former husband subsequently sued Wickersham and received one-half of the settlement.

The WSBA filed a formal complaint against Halverson in February 1997. Following proceedings in December 1997 and February 1998, the hearing officer issued findings of fact and conclusions of law and recommended a sanction consisting of six months' suspension and two years' probation with the conditions that Halverson disclose to female clients the purpose of his discipline and continue treatment with his mental health physician. . . .

Halverson challenges several of the Board's factual findings. . . .

. . . [T]he record is clear that Wickersham depended upon Halverson regarding temporary living arrangements, custody of her daughter, and a favorable property division in her dissolution action.

As to the power imbalance, an experienced family law practitioner testified to the inherent power imbalance in a dissolution attorney-client relationship. In addition, Dr. Laura Brown, a psychologist who studies sexual relationships between clients and professionals, testified that Halverson's administration of personality tests to Wickersham "added a more psychological aura to what he was doing" and, therefore increased "the risk of harm because the power differential was greater." According to Dr. Brown, Halverson's status as Wickersham's former employer further contributed to a power differential.

. . . [T]he testimony that Wickersham received a "fair outcome" in her dissolution proceeding does not undermine the substantial testimony from mental health professionals that as a result of Halverson's conduct, Wickersham suffered personal harm in the form of depression and anxiety. In addition, Wickersham's relationship with Halverson had an adverse impact upon her relationship with her former husband. In the years following the divorce, Wickersham described the relationship as "brutally adversarial; abusive and emotionally and financially difficult." Further, after her relationship with Halverson, Wickersham was unable to trust her new attorney. . . .

. . . Halverson's admission to sexual relationships with five prior clients clearly supports the finding that he knew or should have known the risks of such relationships, particularly because one of these relationships resulted in a fee dispute where the client threatened to disclose the details of the relationship to Halverson's wife unless Halverson wrote off his bill.

Further, Halverson's book, *Divorce in Washington: A Humane Approach*,[5] discouraged those involved in a dissolution from getting involved in a new sexual relationship. A section in the Washington *Family Law Deskbook* of which Halverson was editor and chief,[6] and the written materials for a Continuing Legal Education course at which Halverson spoke, both discussed the potential adverse ramifications of an attorney-client sexual relationship, as did three prominent family law attorneys who testified.

Where the evidence conflicted as to the potential effect of the Wickersham/Halverson affair upon Wickersham's dissolution proceeding, the hearing officer was entitled to credit the testimony of those experts who testified that the affair increased the legal risks to Wickersham. . . .

II. LEGAL CONCLUSIONS. . . .

A. Violation of RPC 1.7(b) . . . — Duty to Avoid Conflicts of Interest

"RPC 1.7(b) generally prevents a lawyer from representing a client if that representation will be materially limited by the lawyer's own interests unless the lawyer reasonably believes the representation will not be affected and the client consents in writing." . . . Halverson concedes no written consent was obtained, but argues that this was merely a technical violation of the rule. We disagree.

It was not objectively reasonable for Halverson to believe that the re-

presentation would not be adversely affected by the sexual relationship, nor did Halverson disclose to Wickersham the risks involved or the material implications of the sexual relationship upon the dissolution proceeding. Consequently, Halverson's failure to obtain written consent was more than a mere technical violation of the rule.

Halverson should have known that discovery of the affair could worsen the relationship between Wickersham and Sarles and, thus, unnecessarily complicate the dissolution proceeding. Further, Halverson should have known that the affair could impact the custody determination of Wickersham's daughter. Finally, Halverson should have known that discovery of the affair by his wife might lead to his withdrawal as Wickersham's attorney. Thus, Halverson's subjective belief that the relationship would not adversely affect the representation was not objectively reasonable.

In any event, Halverson did not disclose any of these risks to Wickersham before commencing the relationship. Rather, the "ground rules" discussed at the start of the relationship focused primarily on Halverson's own interests: keeping the relationship secret from his wife and avoiding any emotional bonding with Wickersham's daughter. Under these circumstances, the Board properly affirmed the hearing officer's conclusion that Halverson violated RPC 1.7(b).

B. Violation of RPC 1.4(b)—Duty to Communicate

Pursuant to RPC 1.4(b), "A lawyer shall explain a matter to the extent

---

5. Lowell K. Halverson & John W. Kydd, *Divorce in Washington: A Humane Approach* (1985).
6. Wash. St. Bar Assn., *Family Law Deskbook* §3.9 (1989).

reasonably necessary to permit the client to make informed decisions regarding the representation." We agree with the Board that the same failures to disclose supporting the conclusion that Halverson violated RPC 1.7(b) also support the conclusion that he violated RPC 1.4(b).

C. Violation of RPC 2.1—Duty to Exercise Independent Professional Judgment

"In representing a client, a lawyer shall exercise independent professional judgment and render candid advice. In rendering advice, a lawyer may refer not only to law but to other considerations such as moral, economic, social and political factors, that may be relevant to the client's situation." RPC 2.1.

As recently noted by the Court of Appeals in a criminal case where the defendant claimed ineffective assistance of counsel, a lawyer who "commences a sexual relationship with the client during the course of the representation . . . creates significant but needless risks that emotions arising from the relationship will impair . . . his or her ability to 'exercise independent professional judgment' . . . " Although we do not adopt a per se rule that a lawyer who commences a sexual relationship with a client always fails to exercise independent professional judgment, we find that under the circumstances here Halverson violated RPC 2.1.

Halverson did not exercise independent professional judgment when he failed to (1) advise Wickersham of the potential ramifications the affair might have on the dissolution or his ability to represent her; (2) advise Wickersham of his published profes-

sional opinion that persons involved in a dissolution should be discouraged from getting involved in a new sexual relationship; and (3) take precautions to avoid pregnancy or discuss with Wickersham the consequences of such event. Thus, we affirm the Board's conclusion that Halverson violated RPC 2.1. . . .

III. SANCTION . . .

Under the circumstances here, we are persuaded that a six-month suspension is inadequate to maintain public confidence in the integrity of the legal profession and deter others from such conduct. As a frequent lecturer and extensive publisher in the family law area, and as the past president of the WSBA, other attorneys as well as the public looked to Halverson for advice. His book demonstrates not only that he knew of the serious psychological and legal risks entering into a new sexual relationship presented to a dissolution client but that he specifically advised others against it. Yet, Halverson knowingly carried on his affair with Wickersham while he was president of the WSBA.

His practice of using personality questionnaires increased his clients' perceptions of him as a personal counselor or quasi-therapist and engendered their trust. Yet, Halverson violated the trust Wickersham placed in him by taking advantage of her status as his dissolution client for his own sexual gratification.

What seems most lacking in the Board's sanction determination is the fact that Halverson engaged in a pattern of misconduct. By his own admission, he has engaged in a sexual relationship with six clients. We find the contradiction between Halverson's published professional advice and status in the legal community, and his personal conduct particularly damaging to the integrity of the legal profession. . . .

CONCLUSION . . .

We increase the recommended term of suspension from six months to one year to adequately serve the purposes of attorney discipline.

SANDERS, J. (concurring in part, dissenting in part)— . . .

By upholding certain challenged findings of fact, the majority demonstrates its paternalistic perception of female dissolution clients. The majority opines "Wickersham depended upon Halverson," and claims a "power imbalance" Halverson allegedly exercised in his representation of female dissolution clients. . . . However these conclusions are neither supported by the facts of this case nor based on human experience. . . .

Viewing female dissolution clients as "victims" who need the support, assistance and guidance of their powerful male attorneys is degrading because it undermines women's right of independent self-determination. Moreover it does not accurately portray the dynamics of an attorney-client relationship.[1] Rather it is the client who has the power to choose her attorney from the multitude of attorneys competing to gain her

business. It is the client who has the power to determine the objectives of the representation and whether to accept or reject an offer of settlement. It is the client who has the power to terminate the services of her lawyer for any reason or no reason at all. It is the client who has the power to sue an attorney if he fails to adequately represent her wishes—a power successfully exercised by Halverson's client here.[2] And it was this client who chose to initiate and enter a consensual sexual relationship with her attorney.

While rules governing attorney-client sex appear to control male sexuality—by disciplining attorneys who engage in the sexual relationships, the vast majority of whom are male—they indirectly control female sexuality by denying self-determination to female clients who desire a dual relationship with an attorney.

Thus, characterizing Halverson's client as a defenseless victim subject to the overwhelming power of her attorney is inaccurate, not supported by the record, and inconsistent with the legal entitlements of all concerned.

The majority also improperly focuses on the emotional harm which purportedly befell Halverson's client as a result of their affair. "As a result of Halverson's conduct, Wickersham suffered personal harm in the form of depression and anxiety." . . . While this may be true,

---

1. Counsel for the WSBA perpetuates this outdated stereotype, arguing: "Mr. Halverson was a very prominent, successful, powerful lawyer, a President of the Bar Association. Ms. Wickersham was a much younger, a woman without a college degree, with a young child, who was intimidated by her attorney husband, and who was terrified of losing custody of her baby daughter. . . ."
2. Not only did Halverson settle his client's civil suit for an undisclosed "substantial sum" of money, Halverson provided his client with over $13,000 of free legal work—described by Wickersham's second attorney as work of "excellent" quality—which greatly aided Halverson's client in obtaining a good outcome. . . .

broken hearts and personal dis-
appointments are not the proper
subjects of an attorney discipline
proceeding which must focus on
state licensure requirements. . . .

. . . As previously discussed, Halverson advised his client against any
sexual relationship, explained that a
relationship with him would be improper, and instructed her to tell the
truth if asked about their relationship. More fundamentally, there is no
showing his advice regarding the
substance of the litigation was un-
sound. . . .

CONCLUSION

No one disputes that Lowell Halverson acted wrongly, foolishly, and
hurtfully when he entered into a
sexual relationship with Lisa Wickersham. It was a grievous wrong and
grievously has Halverson answered
for it. . . . Although Halverson's conduct arguably violated RPC 1.7(b), it
did not violate RPC 1.4(b) or RPC
2.1. And as both the hearing officer
and the majority acknowledge Halverson "should have known" better,
the appropriate sanction under these
circumstances is a reprimand.

■ Lawyers and Other Professionals:
Sexual Relationships with Clients

Halverson is typical of a growing number of cases that discipline lawyers for
engaging in sexual relationships with clients. The fact that Halverson settled a
civil suit brought by the same client "for a substantial sum" indicates that
lawyers can be subject to civil liability as well as professional discipline for such
conduct. During the past decade, the number of civil, criminal, and professional
disciplinary actions brought against a myriad of professionals for sexual misconduct has grown exponentially.[1] The rise in the number of claims against
clergy, counselors, dentists, lawyers, mental health professionals, nurses, and
physicians indicates both that victims are more likely to complain, and that
many professionals do not appreciate, and therefore take advantage of, the
vulnerability of their clients.[2]

Power, Vulnerability, and Transference

Fiduciary duties are imposed on professionals in trusting relationships. Clients
repose trust in a professional, empowering that person to act solely on the
client's behalf. The professional's power derives not only from that trust, but
also from an inherent inequality that arises from the professional's superior
knowledge and skill. The client's vulnerability stems partly just from the need for
professional assistance, and is exacerbated by the sharing of confidential information. Often, a significant event has caused a loss of control that renders
that person vulnerable. A client who seeks a divorce, who must file for a

---

1. *See* Steven B. Bisbing, Linda Mabus Jorgenson & Pamela K. Sutherland, *Sexual Abuse by
Professionals: A Legal Guide* (Michie 1995).
2. Detailed statistics are hard to find, but one Illinois study of lawyers documents 50 complaints in
1989 alone, calling the problem a "systematic, unchanging and consistent trend." ABA Formal
Op. 92-364.

bankruptcy, or who has been indicted, injured, or lost a job faces circumstances that have caused a loss of control in some aspect of his or her life. Further, in order to get professional help, clients must entrust confidential information to professionals, which increases both the professional's power to help and the potential for the professional to misuse the information. In many client-professional relationships, these power differentials can be exacerbated by the emotional stress of the legal process itself.

The majority opinion in *Halverson* credits the expert testimony of a lawyer and a psychologist, who agreed that Halverson further exploited his client's trust by administering personality tests, which further increased trust and intimacy, and also added to the risk of harm to the client in the relationship. This testimony reflects the training of mental health professionals to expect and understand a phenomenon common to all human relationships known as "transference." Literally, transference means that one person unconsciously assigns or transfers onto another the feelings or attributes associated with some third person.[3] Persons can transfer negative or positive feelings, and often these feelings involve strong reactions about the underlying legal matter or relationship about which the client or patient seeks advice. The knowledge, experience, power, and social class of most professionals, combined with the client's need for relief and dependence on the professional to get it, may lead the client unconsciously to project positive feelings or wishes onto that person that reflect the client's own needs. When this occurs, powerful emotions, including love and sexual fantasies, can follow.[4]

Psychotherapists are trained to expect transference as a normal and therapeutically helpful part of the counseling they provide.[5] They also are trained to recognize "countertransference," or the professional's own emotional reactions to the patient or client, that reflect the professional's personal needs.[6] Professionals who are untrained to recognize either phenomenon may assume that a client's expression of personal interest can be taken at face value, yet it actually expresses another need. Professionals also may fail to understand that a client's trust in this circumstance makes undue influence nearly impossible to avoid. About a decade ago, the American Medical Association concluded that both transference and countertransference were common and powerful enough to make any sexual contact with a patient ethically inexcusable.[7]

When Halverson responded to his client's initial expression of sexual attraction by establishing the "ground rules" for the relationship, he reflected either his unawareness of his client's transference, his own willingness to take

---

3. Andrew S. Watson, *Psychiatry for Lawyers* 2-3 (Intl. Us. 1978).
4. *See, e.g.,* Joel Friedman & Marcia Mobilia Boumil, *Betrayal of Trust: Sex and Power in Professional Relationships* 21 (Praeger 1995).
5. Transference offers insight into the way the client relates to other significant people. *Id.* at 22.
6. The concepts of transference and countertransference were first introduced into the law in a civil case where a patient successfully complained that her psychiatrist committed malpractice by engaging in a sexual relationship with her during the course of her therapy. *See* Zipkin v. Freeman, 436 S.W.2d 753 (Mo. 1969).
7. Am. Med. Assn., Council on Ethical and Judicial Affairs, *Sexual Misconduct in the Practice of Medicine,* 266 JAMA 2741, 2742 (1991).

advantage of it, or both. His response also signals his own countertransference, or projection of his own needs, which were powerful enough to cause him to ignore his own advice to other lawyers and clients to avoid lawyer-client sexual relationships.[8] Both the majority and the dissenting opinions conclude that Halverson's conduct was "a grievous wrong," and as a result, he was properly subject to professional discipline as well as a civil suit for damages. These same remedies are available to victims of sexual misconduct caused by other professionals. In some cases, professionals also may be held criminally accountable, even when the client or patient "consents" or initiates the contact.

Criminal Accountability

In 1975, Masters and Johnson addressed the American Psychiatric Association and recommended that "sexual seduction of patients . . . regardless of whether the seduction was initiated by the patient or the therapist," should result not just in a civil complaint, but also in an indictment for rape.[9] In cases of egregious exploitation of professional power, such as rendering patients helpless with medication, some professionals have been convicted of rape.[10] In many cases, however, the consent element of a rape statute creates problems for prosecutors who are able to establish exploitation, but have difficulty countering a defense raised by facts that show a client who appeared to "consent."

Today, nearly two dozen jurisdictions provide that counseling professionals who intentionally establish sexual contact during a professional relationship are guilty of criminal conduct.[11] Typical statutes prohibit "sexual exploitation,"[12] or "sexual misconduct,"[13] by mental health and counseling professionals of their clients or patients during the time the professional service was rendered.[14] All of these provisions provide for criminal accountability, regardless of the consent of the victim, on the theory that any consent in such a relationship is coerced or the product of undue influence.[15]

Lawyers are not currently included in sexual exploitation criminal statutes that eliminate consent as a defense. This means that lawyers can be held

---

8. At the very least, his repeated sexual misconduct with clients suggests that he had developed a number of irrational justifications for his conduct. *See* Gene G. Abel & Candice A. Osborn, *Cognitive-Behavioral Treatment of Sexual Misconduct*, in Joseph D. Bloom, Carol C. Nadelson & Malkah T. Notman, eds., *Physician Sexual Misconduct* 188, 230 (Am. Psychiatric Press 1999).
9. Bisbing et al., *supra* note 1, at 833.
10. *Id.* at 835.
11. *Id.* at §4-7, citing statutes in Ariz., Cal., Colo., Conn., D.C., Fla., Ga., Iowa, Me., Mich., Minn., N.H., N.M., N.D., Ohio, R.I., S.D., Tex., Utah, Wis., and Wyo. In addition to counseling professionals, these provisions also may include teachers, coaches, physicians, nurses, and clergy.
12. *E.g.*, Wis. Stat. §940.22 (2007).
13. *E.g.*, Fla. Stat. §491.0112 (2007).
14. Constitutional challenges to these provisions based on vagueness have not met with success. *See, e.g.*, St. v. McKeeth, 38 P.3d 1275 (Idaho 2001); Ferguson v. St., 824 P.2d 803 (Colo. 1992); St. v. Jenkins, 326 N.W.2d 67 (N.D. 1982).
15. A study of the Wisconsin experience with such a statute concludes that, although two thirds of the confirmed cases of sexual misconduct were prosecuted under the generally applicable sexual assault statute, the specific sexual exploitation statute probably has had a deterrent effect. Andrew W. Kane, *The Effects of Criminalization of Sexual Misconduct by Therapist: Report of a Survey in Wisconsin*, in John C. Gonsiorek, ed., *Breach of Trust: Sexual Exploitation by Health Care Professionals and Clergy* 317, 333 (Sage 1995).

criminally accountable only under a typical sexual assault law, where proof of the victim's lack of consent may be required as an element of the crime.[16] Some have argued that lawyers should be subject to such provisions, because disciplinary actions do not provide enough relief to injured clients.[17] Others point out that lawyers, unlike psychotherapists, are not trained to recognize transference-like reactions and do not always represent dependent, vulnerable clients.[18]

Civil Remedies

Clients who have been victimized by sexual misconduct during a professional relationship have used several legal theories to seek tort damages. Some claim battery, arguing that any consent to the contact was fraudulently obtained. Others seek damages for professional malpractice, alleging both harm due to incompetent professional services and emotional distress damages. Most successful have been suits for breach of fiduciary duty, which, in essence, allege a kind of constructive fraud that coerced or unduly influenced the client or patient to enter into a sexual relationship with the professional.[19]

Fraud and battery provide relief in situations where the professional has intentionally misrepresented a material fact concerning the sexual relationship.[20] The tort of the intentional infliction of emotional distress has provided relief where a professional refuses or delays professional services as a means of coercing a sexual relationship with a client or patient.[21]

Clients who sue for malpractice are required to prove breach of the standard of care using expert testimony, as well as causation and damage. In sexual

---

16. Most of these statutes do make consent irrelevant where a mental illness or deficiency causes the victim to be temporarily or permanently incapable of appraising the assaulter's conduct. *E.g.,* Tex. Penal Code §22.011(b)(4) (2007); Wis. Stat. §940.225(2)(C) (2007). Even then, the state has the burden of proof to show that the victim was incapable of appraising the conduct. Further, if such an allegation were made, the defendant probably would be entitled to a psychiatric examination of the client. *See, e.g.,* Jonas v. St., 773 P.2d 960 (Alaska App. 1989).

17. *See, e.g.,* William D. Langford, Jr., *Criminalizing Attorney-Client Sexual Relations: Toward Substantive Enforcement,* 73 Tex. L. Rev. 1223, 1239 (1995).

18. *See, e.g.,* Friedman & Boumil, *supra* note 4, at 6, 94-97.

19. *See, e.g.,* Walter v. Stewart, 67 P.3d 1042 (Utah App. 2003). When complaints allege negligence or malpractice, they trigger the duty to defend in professional liability policies. However, the same policies specifically exclude intentional acts, such as battery and fraud. Insurers typically are required to provide a defense when both are pleaded. In such cases, the insurer reserves the right to claim later that no duty to indemnify the defendant exists because sexual misconduct is not a covered occurrence. *See, e.g.,* St. Paul Fire & Marine Ins. Co. v. Engelmann, 639 N.W.2d 192 (S.D. 2002).

20. *See, e.g.,* DiLeo v. Nugent, 592 A.2d 1126 (Md. Ct. Spec. App. 1991) (therapist told patient that drugs and sexual intercourse with him were part of his treatment); Barbara A. v. John G., 193 Cal. Rptr. 422 (Cal. App. 1983) (lawyer who told client he "couldn't possibly get anyone pregnant," liable for battery and fraud after client suffered a tubal pregnancy which rendered her sterile).

21. *See, e.g.,* Corbett v. Morgenstern, 934 F. Supp. 680 (E.D. Pa. 1996) (psychologist's 12-year sexual relationship with patient sufficient to allow claim for both intentional and negligent infliction of emotional distress); Figueiredo-Torres v. Nichel, 584 A.2d 69 (Md. 1991) (husband entitled to damages for intentional infliction of emotional distress against marriage counselor who engaged in sexual relationship with his wife and encouraged her to leave husband); McDaniel v. Gile, 230 Cal. Rptr. 242 (Cal. App. 1991) (lawyer whose sexual advances were refused by client stopped working on the client's case and gave her incorrect advice about her legal rights).

misconduct cases, the expert testimony requirement created a significant hurdle for plaintiffs until a clear professional custom emerged. Proving the need for further counseling or other professional services demonstrates causation and damages.[22] Malpractice actions also have proven useful when a professional has a sexual relationship with the spouse of the client or patient.[23]

To clarify the common law, several states have enacted statutes that provide a civil cause of action for sexual exploitation, including damages against various named counseling professionals.[24] These statutes eliminate the need for expert testimony, providing for damages if sexual contact occurred during the time the patient received counseling, regardless of that person's consent.

The same result has been reached when clients allege breach of fiduciary duty against professionals who misuse confidential information to establish sexual contact.[25] In cases against counseling professionals that allege breach of fiduciary duty without any specific showing of misuse of confidences, some courts refuse to find a fiduciary relationship in the absence of a trust relationship concerning property.[26] Others disagree, reasoning that a counselor's position of trust allows him or her to manipulate a patient's emotions.[27]

Lawyers obviously owe fiduciary duties, but in cases that allege sexual misconduct, some courts have narrowly construed them. For example, some cases have restricted a lawyer's fiduciary duty to the lawyer's "legal representation," and concluded that no cause of action could be stated absent proof that the client's underlying legal action was somehow compromised.[28] Other cases disagree, upholding damages for emotional distress alone if the lawyer has reason to know that a breach of fiduciary duty was likely to cause it.[29]

---

22. *See, e.g.,* Zipkin v. Freeman, *supra* note 6 (negligent mishandling of transference reaction). Employers have been found vicariously liable in malpractice cases as well. *See, e.g.,* Simmons v. United States, 805 F.2d 1363 (9th Cir. 1986) (government liable for $150,000 judgment based on negligence of a social worker in Indian Health Service in handling patient's transference); Russell G. Donaldson, *Liability of Hospital or Clinic for Sexual Relationships with Patients by Staff Physicians, Psychologists, and Other Healers,* 45 A.L.R.4th 289 (1986).

23. *See, e.g.,* Rowe v. Bennett, 514 A.2d 802 (Me. 1985) (psychotherapist); Mazza v. Huffaker, 300 S.E.2d 833 (N.C. App. 1983) (psychiatrist). *But see* Kahlig v. Boyd, 980 S.W.2d 685 (Tex. App. 1998) (lawyer).

24. *See* Bisbing et al., *supra* note 1, at §4-7, citing statutes in Cal., Colo., Ill., Minn., N.H., N.C., Tex., and Wis.

25. *See, e.g.,* Tante v. Herring, 453 S.E.2d 686 (Ga. 1994) (lawyer who misused confidential information about the client's mental and emotional condition to convince her to engage in sex with him liable to both client and her husband, no expert testimony required). The lawyer was suspended from practice for 18 months for the same conduct. In re Tante, 453 S.E.2d 688 (Ga. 1994).

26. *See, e.g.,* Gray v. Ward, 929 S.W.2d 774 (Mo. App. 1996).

27. *See, e.g.,* Horak v. Biris, 474 N.E.2d 13 (Ill. App. 1985) (social worker); Norberg v. Wynrib, 92 D.L.R. 449 (Cal. 1992) (dentist); F.G. v. MacDonell, 696 A.2d 697 (N.J. 1997) (clergy counselor).

28. Suppressed v. Suppressed, 565 N.E.2d 101 (Ill. App. 1990) *rev. denied,* 571 N.E.2d 156 (1991). The court admitted that a claim for battery or intentional infliction of emotional distress might be possible, but it was not pleaded, probably because it was barred by the statute of limitations. *Id. See also* Kling v. Landry, 686 N.E.2d 33 (Ill. App. 1997) (dismissing breach of fiduciary duty but upholding battery cause of action). *But see* Gaspard v. Beadle, 36 S.W.3d 229 (Tex. App. 2001) (lawyer's sexual relationship with a client, while socially inappropriate, was not outrageous as a matter of law).

29. *See, e.g.,* Walter v. Stewart, 67 P.3d 1042 (Utah App. 2003); Doe v. Roe, 681 N.E.2d 640 (Ill. App. 1997).

Professional Discipline

Mental health professionals were the first to address the issue of sexual misconduct with patients or clients in their professional codes. Today, nearly every counseling profession's code includes an absolute prohibition on sexual relationships with current clients or patients.[30] Many professions extend this ban to former clients or patients for a period of time after the professional relationship ends as well.[31] Some courts have interpreted more general professional code provisions that prohibit client exploitation to include such a ban.[32] Some of these prohibitions have been added to state licensing statutes.[33]

Lawyers have taken longer to respond. *Halverson* illustrates the approach found in some jurisdictions, where general professional code provisions are applied to lawyer sexual misconduct.[34] In these cases, lawyers have been disciplined for violating conflict of interest and communication rules, as well as those that prohibit criminal conduct and fraud.[35] Applying general lawyer code

---

30. *See* Am. College of Phys., *Ethics Manual* (Sexual Contact between Physician and Patient) (1998), in Rena A. Gorlin, *Codes of Professional Responsibility: Ethics Standards in Business, Health and Law* 318 (BNA 1999); Am. Counseling Assn., *Code of Ethics and Standards of Practice*, Section A.7 (Sexual Intimacies with Clients) (1997), in Gorlin, *supra* at 422; Am. Psych. Assn., *Principles of Medical Ethics with Annotations Especially Applicable to Psychiatry* §§2-1, 4-14 (1998), in Gorlin, *supra*, at 455, 457; Am. Psychol. Assn., *Ethical Principles of Psychologists and Code of Conduct*, Standard 4.05 (1992), in Gorlin *supra*, at 478; Clinical Social Work Fedn., *Code of Ethics* §II(3)(b) (1997), in Gorlin, *supra*, at 519; Natl. Assn. of Soc. Workers, *Code of Ethics* §1.09 (1996), in Gorlin, *supra* at 537.
31. *See, e.g.*, Am. College of Phys., *supra* note 30 ("Sexual involvement between physicians and former patients raises concern."); Am. Counseling Assn., *supra* note 30 (two-year bar after counseling relationship terminates, after two years, counselors "have the responsibility to thoroughly examine and document that such relations did not have an exploitative nature"); Am. Med. Assn., *supra* note 7 ("Sexual or romantic relationships with former patients are unethical if the physician uses or exploits trust, knowledge, emotions, or influence derived from the previous professional relationship."); Am. Psych. Assn., *supra* note 30 ("Sexual activity with a current or former client is unethical."); Am. Psychol. Assn., *supra* note 30, at §4.07 (two-year bar after treatment terminates, after two years only in the "most unusual circumstances" and psychologist "bears the burden of demonstrating that there has been no exploitation"); Clinical Social Work Fedn., *supra* note 30 (no romantic or sexual contact with either current or former clients); *see also* Gladieux v. Ohio St. Med. Bd., 728 N.E.2d 459 (Ohio App. 1999) (disciplining physician for sexual relationships with mothers of pediatric patients).
32. *See* Am. Med. Assn., *supra* note 7; Gorlin, *supra* note 30, at 401; Am. Chiropractic Assn., Ethics Committee, *Sexual Intimacies with a Patient* (1992-3), *id.* at 278; Budde v. Mich. Dept. of Consumer & Indus. Services, 2001 Mich. App. LEXIS 2564 (social worker's license revoked on basis of expert testimony); Heinecke v. Dept. of Com., 810 P.2d 459 (Utah 1991) (nurse's license revoked for having sexual relationship with a mentally ill client that culminated in the client's pregnancy).
33. Bisbing, *supra* note 1, at §4-7.
34. ABA Formal Op. 92-364, *supra* note 2 (opining that sexual relationships during the course of representation raise a significant risk of impairment to the lawyer's representation, which could involve violations of competence (MR 1.1), confidentiality (MR 1.6 and 1.8(b)), loyalty (MR 1.7 and 3.7), or prevent the lawyer from exercising independent judgment (MR 2.1).
35. *See, e.g.*, Disc. Counsel v. Krieger, 843 N.E.2d 765 (Ohio 2006) (public defender's extended sexual relationship with client constitutes dishonest, deceitful conduct and unwarranted conflict of interest); In re Tsoutsouris, 748 N.E.2d 856 (Ind. 2001) (sexual relationship with client violates Rule 1.7(b)); People v. Riddle, 1999 Colo. Discipl. 88 (lawyer who became sexually involved with client who was also a lawyer violated Rules 1.7(b) and 1.16(a)); In re Berg, 955 P.2d 1240 (Kan. 1998) (lawyer who engaged in sexual relations with several divorce clients disbarred for violating MR. 1.7(b), 1.8(b), 2.1, 3.7, and 8.4(d)); In re Rinella, 677 N.E.2d 909 (Ill. 1997) (sexual relationships with several clients constitutes conduct prejudicial to the administration of justice and overreaching). *See also* Gregory G. Sarno, Jr., *Sexual Misconduct as Ground for Disciplining Attorney or Judge*, 43 A.L.R.4th 1062 (1986).

provisions to sexual relationships with clients assumes that they are appropriate in some circumstances as long as a lawyer obtains a client's informed consent to legitimate the relationship.[36]

California was the first jurisdiction to recognize that such an approach neither clearly warns lawyers about sexual misconduct nor protects clients by deterring it. To "ensure that a lawyer acts in the best interest of his or her client,"[37] the California Supreme Court in 1992 enacted the first specific lawyer code provision, which prohibits coercive or exploitive sexual relationships with clients.[38] Since then, most jurisdictions (including Washington following *Halverson*) have enacted partial or total bans on sexual relationships with clients.[39]

Most of these professional code provisions mirror Model Rule 1.8(j), which flatly bans all sexual relations with clients that did not precede the professional relationship.[40] Enactment of such a provision means that a lawyer must choose between providing legal services and pursuing a personal sexual relationship.[41] The comment points out that the client-lawyer relationship "is almost always unequal" and that a sexual relationship violates "the lawyer's basic ethical obligation not to use the trust of the client to the client's disadvantage."[42] This means that an absolute prohibition applies "regardless of whether the relationship is consensual and regardless of the absence of prejudice to the client," "because of the significant danger of harm to client interests and because the client's own emotional involvement renders it unlikely that the client could give adequate informed consent."[43] When the client is an organization, the rule applies to representatives of entity clients who regularly consult with the lawyer.[44] Unlike other parts of Model Rule 1.8, this conflict is personal, and therefore another lawyer in the law firm may carry out the representation, subject, of course, to other general conflict of interest provisions.[45]

---

36. *Halverson* illustrates that some jurisdictions also require a written document. *See* Practice Pointers: Written Consents to Conflicts of Interest, *infra* p. 360.

37. Cal. Bus. & Prof. Code §6106.8 (1992).

38. Cal. R. Prof. Conduct 3-120 (2007). *See also* Ariz. R. Prof. Conduct 1.8(j) (2007); Del. R. Prof. Conduct 1.8(j) (2000); Fla. R. Prof. Conduct 4-8.4(i) (2007); Iowa R. Prof. Conduct 1.8(j) (2007); Minn. R. Prof. Conduct 1.8(1) (2005); N.C. R. Prof. Conduct 1.19 (2003); N.Y. DR 5-111 (b) (2007); Or. R. Prof. Conduct 1.8(j) (2006); S.D. R. Prof. Conduct 1.8(j) (2004); Utah R. Prof. Conduct 8.4(g) (2007); W. Va. R. Prof. Conduct 8.4(g) (2005); Wis. S. Ct. R. 20:1.8(j) (2007). *See, e.g.,* Fla. Bar v. Bryant, 813 S.2d 38 (Fla. 2002) (lawyer who exchanged sex with exotic dancer client for legal representation violated Rule 8.4(i), which prohibits "sexual conduct with a client that exploits the lawyer-client relationship").

39. *E.g.,* Wash. R. Prof. Conduct 1.8(j) (2006). New York has adopted a hybrid rule that prohibits sexual relationships between lawyers and clients in "domestic relations" matters, and creates an anti-exploitive rule for all other client-lawyer relationships. N.Y. DR 5-111(b)(3) (2007).

40. While lawyers may represent spouses, any conflicts that may occur remain subject to MR 1.7.

41. *See, e.g.,* Musick v. Musick, 453 S.E.2d 361 (W. Va. 1994) (lawyer who engaged in sexual relationship with client disqualified from further representation on motion of opposing party).

42. MR 1.8, Comment [17].

43. *Id.*

44. *Id.,* Comment [19]. *See also* Cal. R. Prof. Conduct, *supra* note 38, and Iowa, Minn., Or., Utah, and Wis. R. of Prof. Conduct, *supra* note 38, which include certain representatives of organizational clients.

45. MR 1.8(k), 1.10(a).

The Future

Halverson illustrates that professional discipline certainly is possible under current general professional code provisions. But the approach lacks clear notice to lawyers and more certain deterrence to protect clients. This explains why a specific provision, such as Model Rule 1.8(j) has been seen as both necessary and preferable in most jurisdictions. To date, the majority of states that have enacted a specific rule have chosen an absolute prohibition because of both its clarity and ease of administration. The dissent in *Halverson* represents the other point of view: Not all clients of lawyers are vulnerable and dependent.[46]

While an anti-exploitive rule may be fairer to lawyers (and according to the dissent in *Halverson,* also to clients), such a rule requires the lawyer who is emotionally involved with a client to make a determination whether his or her own conduct involves coercion, intimidation, or undue influence. If the client later files a disciplinary complaint, such a rule also shifts the burden of proving coercion or other exploitive factors to disciplinary counsel. Other professions have not been willing to let professionals exercise their own judgment in a circumstance where the risk of transference, countertransference, and undue influence is so high.

The analogy to the complete bans in the counseling professions may not be completely helpful, however, if the reason for those prohibitions stem from the belief that virtually every counseling relationship involves some degree of transference and opportunity for undue influence. Nearly every lawyer can imagine some client-lawyer relationships where transference, even if it occurs, does not subject the client or the lawyer to undue influence.[47] Legal rules about business transactions with clients such as *Monco* recognize this, presuming undue influence in every situation, but shifting the burden of proof to the lawyer to justify the fairness of the transaction. Of course, such a rule would require the lawyer to obtain an extensive informed consent, probably in writing. The difficulty of imagining what such a document would contain perhaps explains why Halverson did not think to draft one, and has led others to call for the clarity of an absolute prohibition.

Specific professional rules about lawyer sexual misconduct may have other impacts as well. Such a prohibition acknowledges "that the professional relationship is inextricably bound up with the personal feelings of the individuals involved."[48] At the same time, proof that a lawyer violated a professional code provision will be admissible, but not determinative, of whether that lawyer should be liable in a civil action. Even without such a professional code provision, most courts are adopting the view that a sexual relationship with a client constitutes a breach of fiduciary duty. The lesson of this chapter is that such a breach leads to many potential remedies, including damages, fee forfeiture, and disqualification.

---

46. *See, e.g.,* Linda Fitts Mischler, *Reconciling Rapture, Representation, and Responsibility: An Argument Against Per Se Bans on Attorney-Client Sex,* 10 Geo. J. Leg. Ethics 209 (1996).
47. *See, e.g.,* Lawrence J. Fox, *When It Comes to Sex With Clients, Whom Do You Trust: Nanny or the ABA?* 19 GP Solo 36 (Oct./Nov. 2002).
48. Anthony E. Davis & Judith Grimaldi, *Sexual Confusion: Attorney-Client Sex and the Need for a Clear Ethical Rule,* 7 Notre Dame J.L. Ethics & Pub. Policy 57, 98 (1993).

C. Client and Third-Person Interests

Problems

8-10. Fox is an estate lawyer. One day he receives a visit from an individual who says: "I need some help for Dad. It is too hard for Dad to travel downtown these days. He needs to change his will to make sure his grandchildren's education is paid for." What should Fox do?

8-11. Martyn & Fox is hired by Insurance Company to represent several of its insureds.

(a) Who is our client?

(b) Can Insurance Company tell Martyn & Fox: how many depositions to take? Whether and when to hire an expert witness? What motions to file? To send bills to an outside auditing company for review?

(c) In the course of investigating our first case, Fox comes across a confidential medical file that shows the insured was told by his physician to stop driving because of his Parkinson's disease. The insured's policy includes standard language that excludes coverage for drivers who have certain medical conditions. What should Fox do with this information?

(d) The plaintiff's complaint in our second case demands $300,000 in damages resulting from an auto accident. Plaintiff offers to settle the case for the policy limits of $100,000 but Insurance Company tells Martyn "We'd rather pay you to litigate this case than settle with that malingerer." What should Martyn do?

(e) In our third case, the insured is a physician accused of medical malpractice. Plaintiff offers to settle well within policy limits, and Insurance Company agrees, but the physician refuses saying, "Settling this case will destroy my professional reputation." What should Fox do?

Consider: Model Rules 1.7, 1.8(f), 1.14, 5.4(c)
        Model Code DR 5-105, 5-107
        RLGL §134

Paradigm Insurance Co. v. The Langerman Law Offices, P.A.

24 P.3d 593 (Ariz. 2001)

En Banc. . . .

FELDMAN, J.

The ultimate question in this case is whether an attorney may be held liable to an insurer, which assigned him to represent an insured, when the attorney's negligence damages only the insurer. . . .

Paradigm issued an insurance policy covering Dr. Benjamin A. Vanderwerf for medical malpractice liability. Vanderwerf, Medical Director of Samaritan Transplant Service, a division of Samaritan Health Service

(Samaritan), and another doctor were sued by Renee Taylor, who alleged that Vanderwerf committed malpractice by injuring her during a catheter removal procedure. Taylor included Samaritan as a defendant, alleging that at the time of the negligent act, Vanderwerf was acting as Samaritan's agent or employee. . . .

. . . In due course, Paradigm assigned defense of Taylor's claims to Langerman. Langerman undertook the assignment, with Vanderwerf evidently acquiescing, and appeared in the action as Vanderwerf's counsel. During the course of representation, Langerman advised Paradigm that it believed there was no viable theory of liability against Samaritan. Langerman, however, failed to investigate whether Vanderwerf was covered by Samaritan's liability insurance and, thus, was unable to advise Paradigm whether the defense could be tendered to Samaritan.

After a time, . . . Paradigm terminated Langerman's representation in Taylor and retained new counsel for Vanderwerf.

Vanderwerf's new lawyer discovered that Samaritan had liability coverage through Samaritan Insurance Funding (SIF) that not only covered Vanderwerf for Taylor's claim but probably operated as the primary coverage for the claim. . . . Accordingly, new counsel tendered the claim to SIF, which rejected it on the grounds that the tender was untimely.

Taylor v. Vanderwerf was eventually settled for an amount within Paradigm's policy limits. Thus, Vanderwerf was not injured by Langerman's failure to make a timely tender to SIF. However, Paradigm, compelled to act as Vanderwerf's primary carrier, was forced to settle Taylor's claim with its own funds and without being able to look to SIF for contribution or indemnification.

Langerman then presented Paradigm with its statement for legal services. Paradigm refused to pay, claiming Langerman had been negligent both in failing to advise it of SIF's exposure as the primary carrier and by not promptly tendering the defense. When Langerman sued for fees, Paradigm counterclaimed for damages. . . .

DISCUSSION

A. Whether an express agreement is necessary to form an attorney-client relationship

Langerman argues that, before an attorney-client relationship can form between an insurer and the counsel it retains to represent an insured, express mutual consent must be reached among all of the respective parties. We disagree. The law has never required that the attorney-client relationship must be initiated by some sort of express agreement, oral or written. Quite to the contrary, the current rule is described as follows:

> A relationship of client and lawyer arises when: (1) a person manifests to a lawyer the person's intent that the lawyer provide legal services for the person; and . . . (a) the lawyer manifests to the person consent to do so. *Restatement (Third) of The Law Governing Lawyers* §14.

Indeed, comment c to section 14 indicates that either intent or acquiescence may establish the relationship. . . .

B. Potential and actual conflicts of interest with the insurer as client

Langerman contends that absent the consent of the insured, a lawyer assigned by an insurer to represent the insured forms an attorney-client relationship only with the insured and never with the insurer. Any contrary conclusion, asserts Langerman, inherently creates a strong potential conflict of interest for the attorney, weakens his "undivided allegiance" to the insured, and creates "situations rife with opportunities for mistrust and second guessing." Langerman's concern over conflicts of interest between attorney, insurer, and insured is not unfounded. This case presents the typical situation found when defense is provided by a liability insurer: as part of the insurer's obligation to provide for the insured's defense, the policy grants the insurer the right to control that defense—which includes the power to select the lawyer that will defend the claim. But the fact that the lawyer is chosen, assigned, and paid by the insurer for the purpose of representing the insured does not automatically create an attorney-client relationship between the insurer and lawyer. . . .

Thus, because the insured has given the insurer control of the defense as part of the agreement for indemnity, the assigned lawyer more or less automatically becomes the attorney for the insured. But does the assigned lawyer automatically also become the attorney for the insurer in every case? . . . Langerman . . . argu[es] that even in the absence of actual conflict between the insured and insurer, there is always a great potential for it. . . .

. . . There can be no doubt that actual conflicts between insured and insurer are quite common and that the potential for conflict is present in every case. Conflicts may arise over the existence of coverage, the manner in which the case is to be defended, the information to be shared, the desirability of settling at a particular figure or the need to settle at all, and an array of other factors applicable to the circumstances of a particular case. This is especially true in cases involving medical malpractice claims.[1] We have recognized such tensions, holding . . . that when a conflict actually arises, and not simply when it potentially exists, the lawyer's duty is exclusively owed to the insured and not the insurer. Because a lawyer is expressly assigned to represent the insured, the lawyer's primary obligation is to the insured, and the lawyer must exercise independent professional judgment on behalf of the insured. Thus, a lawyer cannot allow an insurer to interfere with the lawyer's independent professional judgment, even though, in general, the lawyer's representation of the insured is directed by the insurer.

. . . We have, in fact, previously held that an attorney assigned to represent an insured cannot supply the insurer with information that either may be or actually is detrimental to the insured's interests. . . . Where a substantial danger of harming the client does not exist, there is no actual conflict of interest—only the potential of a future conflict. . . .

---

1. For instance, in the ordinary case in which liability is probable, even if somewhat questionable, it would almost always be in the interest of the insurer to make a reasonable settlement offer within policy limits. However, such a settlement might not be in the insured's interest and he or she may prefer to take a chance at trial because any settlement payment will require reporting that physician to the National Practitioner Data Bank, thus potentially affecting the physician's ability to obtain hospital privileges or malpractice insurance in the future.

We agree with Langerman that the potential for conflict between insurer and insured exists in every case; but we note that the interests of insurer and insured frequently coincide. For instance, both insurer and insured often share a common interest in developing and presenting a strong defense to a claim that they believe to be unfounded as to liability, damages, or both. Usually insured and insurer have a joint interest in finding additional coverage from another carrier. Thus, by serving the insured's interests the lawyer can also serve the insurer's, and if no question arises regarding the existence and adequacy of coverage, the potential for conflict may never become substantial. In such cases, we see no reason why the lawyer cannot represent both insurer and insured; but in the unique situation in which the lawyer actually represents two clients, he must give primary allegiance to one (the insured) to whom the other (the insurer) owes a duty of providing not only protection, but of doing so fairly and in good faith.

Perhaps recognizing this, the court of appeals determined that the "majority rule" was "in the absence of a conflict, the attorney has two clients, the insurer and the insured." We believe the court of appeals' characterization of the majority rule is too absolute. A host of potential problems are created by holding that, as a matter of law, a lawyer hired by the insurer to represent an insured always accepts the responsibilities of

dual representation until a conflict actually arises—thus always automatically forming an attorney-client relationship with both the insurer and insured. There are many cases in which the potential for conflict is strong enough to implicate ER 1.7 . . . from the very beginning. Think, for example, of a claim with questionable liability against an insured covered by limits much lower than the amount of damages. The potential for conflict is quite substantial unless and until the insurer has committed itself to offering or waiving the policy limits. Thus we do not endorse the view that the lawyer automatically represents both insurer and insured until the conflict actually arises.[3] . . .

C. Duty to a nonclient . . .

If a lawyer's liability to the insurer depends entirely on the existence of an attorney-client relationship and for some reason the insurer is not a client,[6] then the lawyer has no duty to the insurer that hired him, assigned the case to him, and pays his fees. There are many problems with that result: if that lawyer's negligence damages the insurer only, the negligent lawyer fortuitously escapes liability. Or if the lawyer's negligence injures both insurer and insured in a case in which the insured is the only client but refuses to proceed against the lawyer, the insurer is helpless and has no remedy. Such unjust results are not just bad policy but unneces-

---

3. To forestall confusion among the bar, we hasten to point out that even when the insurer is not the lawyer's client, it certainly is the insured's agent to prepare and handle the defense. Thus, for instance, communications between the nonclient insurer and the lawyer would generally be entitled to the same degree of confidentiality—as long as the general requirements for privilege are met—as those between the insured client and the lawyer.

6. When, for instance, the insured does not consent to a dual relationship, the potential for conflict is great, or the conflict is real.

sary. The Restatement holds the view that a lawyer may, in certain circumstances, owe a duty to a nonclient. [The court quotes RLGL §51(3).]

Comment g to this section advises:

[A] lawyer designated by an insurer to defend an insured owes a duty of care to the insurer with respect to matters as to which the interests of the insurer and insured are not in conflict, whether or not the insurer is held to be a co-client of the lawyer.

In addition, comment f to Restatement section 14 states:

Because and to the extent that the insurer is directly concerned in the matter financially, the insurer should be accorded standing to assert a claim for appropriate relief from the lawyer for financial loss proximately caused by professional negligence or other wrongful act of the lawyer.

. . . Arizona's courts have long recognized situations in which a professional is under a duty of care to nonclients. In Fickett v. Superior Court, for example, the attorney representing a guardian of an estate was accused of negligence by the ward in failing to discover that the guardian had dissipated the estate by misappropriation, conversion, and improper investing. 558 P.2d 988, 89 (Ariz. 1976). . . . The court of appeals [held] that one could not say, as a matter of law, that the guardian's attorney owed no duty to the ward. . . .

In Napier v. Bertram we recognized that, although the "general rule is that a professional owes no duty to a non-client unless special circumstances require otherwise," there are "special circumstances" where we have "imposed liability on a professional to the extent that a foreseeable and specific third party is injured by

the professional's actions." 954 P.2d 1389 (Ariz. 1998). . . . [T]hese circumstances are found in a myriad of contexts. See, e.g., Lombardo v. Albu, 14 P.3d 288 (Ariz. 2000) (purchaser's real estate agent has duty to disclose purchaser's financial difficulties to seller); Hamman v. County of Maricopa, 775 P.2d 1122, 1127-28 (Ariz. 1989) (psychiatrist has duty to exercise reasonable care to protect foreseeable victim of patient); Mur-Ray Mgmt. Corp. v. Founders Title Co., 819 P.2d 1003, 1008-09 (Ariz. App. 1991) (imposing duty of reasonable care for escrow agent's representations to third persons). The "common thread [that] exists between" such cases is that "there was a foreseeable risk of harm to a foreseeable nonclient whose protection depended on the actor's conduct."

But Langerman argues that Paradigm need not have depended on it, as every insurer has both the freedom and financial ability to hire separate counsel to protect the insurer's own interests. This, of course, must be done in cases in which a conflict exists or is imminent, but we certainly need not impose such an expense on every insurer in every case just to provide the insurer with protection against malpractice by the lawyer it has chosen to handle the defense. When the interests of insurer and insured coincide, as they often do, it makes neither economic nor practical sense for an insurer to hire another attorney to monitor the actions and decisions of the attorney assigned to an insured. More important, we believe that a special relationship exists between the insurer and the counsel it assigns to represent its insured. The insurer is "in some way dependent upon" the lawyer it hires on behalf of its insureds. For instance, the insurer depends on the lawyer to represent the insured zealously so as to honor its contractual agreement to provide the defense when liability allegations are leveled at the insured. In addition, the insurer depends on the lawyer to thwart claims of liability and, in the event liability is found, to minimize the damages it must pay. Thus, the lawyer's duties to the insured are often discharged for the full or partial benefit of the nonclient. *See Fickett,* 558 P.2d at 990. We reject Langerman's attempt to distinguish the present case from our cases that recognize that a professional has a duty to third parties who are foreseeably injured by the lawyer's negligent actions.

CONCLUSION

. . . [B]ased on a long line of precedent, when an insurer assigns an attorney to represent an insured, the lawyer has a duty to the insurer arising from the understanding that the lawyer's services are ordinarily intended to benefit both insurer and insured when their interests coincide. This duty exists even if the insurer is a nonclient. We hold again today that a lawyer has a duty, and therefore may be liable for negligent breach, to a nonclient under the conditions set forth in previous case law and the Restatement. . . .

The record does not allow us, however, to determine whether, as a matter of law, Langerman actually breached its duty to Paradigm in this case. Thus, our holding does not determine whether the applicable standard of conduct would have required Langerman to investigate the existence of a different primary insurer or advise Paradigm to tender the defense to that other insurer. Although we have decided that an attorney-client relationship is not a prerequisite to Paradigm's maintaining a tort action against Langerman for its alleged negligence, whether Langerman actually breached its duty to Paradigm or caused damage is left for the trial court to decide on remand. Under the circumstances of this case, suffice it to say that absent any conflict or significant risk of conflict that compelled Langerman to act as it did, Langerman had a duty to Paradigm—regardless of whether Paradigm was a client. . . .

▨ Lawyers and Clients:
Insurance Defense

Lawyers who provide insurance defense representation live in a triangular world, caught between the routine demands of insurers, who select the lawyers who will receive large groups of cases, and the individual insureds, whose interests may depart from those of the insurer. As a consequence, lawyers in this kind of practice often face pressure from either insured or insurer, or both, to shape, and in some cases cramp, the bounds of fiduciary duty owed clients.

Most of the problems created by insurance defense practice originate in the insurance contract itself. Typical liability policies promise to "defend" when a covered person is sued for a covered event, and to "indemnify" that person up to an insured amount. They also provide that the insured agrees to "cooperate" in the defense of the matter, and usually delegate authority to the insurer "to make such investigation, negotiation, and settlement of any claim or suit as it deems expedient."

These contract provisions can create a conflict between the interests of insured and insurer, for example, when the insured insists on the insurer's duty to defend and the insurer stands on its right to control settlement. Insurance law addresses any such conflict by construing the contract language against the insurer-drafter. Courts read the insurance contract to promote more consistent obligations—for example, to both defend and settle with due consideration for the insured's interests. By requiring due regard for the insured's interests, this insurance law also indirectly supports defense lawyers' obligations to their client-insureds.

The Clients

When an insurer hires a lawyer or law firm to defend an insured, all jurisdictions agree that the lawyer represents the insured.[1] Providing a "defense" necessarily includes providing a lawyer, complete with the 5 Cs. Jurisdictions do not agree about whether the lawyer also represents the insurer. Many characterize insurance defense as a one-client/third-party payer situation.[2] Lawyers have only one client, the insured, and must comply with Model Rules 1.8(f) and 5.4(c) by resisting pressure from insurers that might interfere with the lawyer's independent professional judgment. Other jurisdictions, as in *Paradigm,* adopt a joint-client approach, meaning that the defense lawyer represents both the insured and the insurer,[3] and is subject to the rigors of Model Rule 1.7 with respect to each client.[4] Some courts do not specify, but instead require lawyers to clarify the matter in each representation.[5]

Each of these constructs solves some problems and creates others. Consider, for example, the following three issues that may be resolved differently depending upon which view a jurisdiction has adopted:

First, who can sue for incompetence? *Paradigm* indicates that, at least where the harm was caused to the insurer but not the insured, some jurisdictions find the insurer need not be a client to seek malpractice relief.[6] Some jurisdictions invoke the equitable subrogation doctrine to reach the same result. Others allow the insurer to sue only if it is properly a second client of the lawyer, a situation that necessitates adequate attention to waivers of conflicts of interest by the insured.[7]

---

1. MR 1.8(f) and Comment [11], 5.4(c); RLGL §134, Comment f.
2. *Id.; see also* In re R. of Prof. Conduct, 2 P.3d 806 (Mont. 2000). *See* Thomas D. Morgan, *What Insurance Scholars Should Know About Professional Responsibility,* 4 Conn. Ins. L.J. 1 (1997-1998).
3. MR 1.7.
4. Stephen Pepper, *Applying the Fundamentals of Lawyers' Ethics to Insurance Defense Practice,* 4 Conn. Ins. L.J. 27 (1997); Charles Silver & Kent Syverud, *The Professional Responsibilities of Insurance Defense Lawyers,* 45 Duke L.J. 255 (1995).
5. *E.g.,* Amend. to R. Regulating the Fla. Bar; In re R. of Prof. Conduct, 838 So. 2d 1140 (Fla. 2003) (adopting new R. Prof. Conduct 4-1.7(e), that requires lawyers to ascertain whether they represent only the insured or both the insured and insurer in insurance defense).
6. *See also* St. & County Mut. Fire Ins. Co. v. Young, 490 F. Supp.2d 741 (N.D. W. Va. 2007).
7. *E.g.,* Pine Is. Farmers Coop v. Erstad & Riemer, P.A., 649 N.W.2d 444 (Minn. 2002) (in the absence of a conflict of interest between the insured and the insurer, the insurer can become a co-client of defense counsel if defense counsel consults with the insured, explains the implications of dual representation and the advantages and risks involved, and the insured gives its express consent to the dual representation); *see also* Zenith Ins. Co v. Cozen O'Connor, 55 Cal. Rptr. 3d 998 (Cal. App. 2007) (lawyer hired by insurance company to defend claim owed no duty to reinsurance carrier).

Similarly, vicarious liability claims against the insurer will turn on the insurer's right to control the details of the lawyer's conduct.[8]

Second, who can invoke and waive the attorney-client and work-product privileges? If both insured and insurer are clients, the co-client privilege[9] protects matters of common interest against third persons, but not between the co-clients. Note 3 in *Paradigm* points to the same result even if the insurer is not a client so long as the insurer acts as agent of the insured for purposes of preparing the defense.[10]

Third, can insurers use inside counsel-employees to represent insureds? Some courts have allowed such a practice,[11] on the grounds that a lawyer/employee owes the same loyalty to the client whether employed directly by the insured or retained as an independent contractor.[12] Others have specifically prohibited it,[13] on the grounds that an insurer/employer would be able to assert so much pressure on its employee/counsel that insurers would interfere with the exercise of counsel's professional judgment.[14]

Overall, it may not matter which of these characterizations a jurisdiction has adopted, because when conflicts develop, two-client courts such as *Paradigm* typically assert that the insured becomes the primary client. Similarly, third-party payment/one-client courts often find reason to grant insurers some rights, such as in finding that the insurer is the agent of the insured for purposes of the attorney-client or work-product privilege, or by invoking the doctrine of equitable subrogation to allow a malpractice suit by the insurer against the defense lawyer.

Regardless of the characterization that is adopted, the insurance defense lawyer must remain focused on the interests of the insured, despite the reality that the insurer is a repeat player in the world of law firm finance. Neither Rule 1.7 nor Rule 1.8(f) allows lawyers to behave in any other way.[15]

The 5 Cs

Control The typical insurance policy's delegation of the right to control settlement decisions to the insurer creates the potential for a direct conflict

---

8. St. Farm Mut. Auto. Ins. Co. v. Traver, 980 S.W.2d 625 (Tex. 1998) (insurer does not have the right, comparable to that of a client, to control defense lawyer). *But see* Givens v. Mullikin, 75 S.W.3d 383 (Tenn. 2002) (insurer may be vicariously liable for abuse of process by independent contractor defense counsel it selected where insurer knowingly authorized or directed the acts in question).
9. RLGL §75.
10. Palmer by Diacon v. Farmers Ins. Exch., 861 P.2d 895 (Mont. 1993) (in bad faith cases, the insured is entitled to the entire claim file, but where the insurer denies any coverage, the lawyers represented only the insurer, and, therefore, the files were privileged against the insured).
11. *E.g.,* In re Youngblood, 895 S.W.2d 322 (Tenn. 1995).
12. *See* Charles Silver, *The Future Structure and Regulation of Law Practice: When Should Government Regulate Lawyer-Client Relationships?*, 44 Ariz. L. Rev. 787 (2002).
13. *E.g.,* Am. Ins. Assn. v. Ky. Bar Assn., 917 S.W.2d 568 (Ky. 1996) (a lawyer cannot agree to do all of an insurer's defense work for a set fee because it would violate MR 1.7(b) and 1.8(f)).
14. Aviva Abramovsky, *The Enterprise Model of Managing Conflicts of Interest in the Tripartite Insurance Defense Relationship*, 27 Cardozo L. Rev. 193 (2005).
15. ABA Formal Op. 01-421.

between insured and insurer whenever the two do not agree about the response to a settlement offer. The lawyer for the insured should realize that the policy language granting the insured the right to a "defense" includes a lawyer who owes an ordinary fiduciary duty of obedience, as required by Model Rule 1.2(a). On the other hand, when the policy cedes the decision to settle to the insurer, the same lawyer cannot escape the reality that the insurer controls the decisions and holds the purse strings.

In all situations, the lawyer's representation of the insured continues to be governed by the lawyer's ethical obligations, including the obligation to relay each settlement offer to the insured and to relay each insured's response to the insurer.[16] Any conflict in the decision to settle requires disclosure to the insured, and if serious enough, may create affirmative duties of good faith imposed by insurance law on the insurer.[17] Usually, this will put pressure on the insurer to settle in a manner consistent with the best interests of the insured.

The right to settle has been especially contentious in professional liability cases. *Paradigm* points to medical malpractice defense, where an actual conflict can develop if an insurer wishes to settle a matter rather than pay the cost of litigating it, but an insured demands a full defense, complete with expensive expert witnesses, perhaps because his or her professional reputation may be at stake. Some professional insurance policies solve this conflict by specifically assigning the right to decide whether and when to settle to the insured. Courts construe ambiguous policies to achieve the same result.[18] Policies that specifically reserve the right to settle to the insurer are subject to the law of bad faith.[19] But in that situation, the insured who disagrees has another option: to release the insurer of its obligations under the policy and defend the action at the insured's own expense. The lawyer's failure to advise the insured of this option creates liability, as does the failure to follow the insured's instruction not to settle.[20]

Communication Model Rule 1.4 applies to a number of recurring circumstances in insurance defense practice. Initially, Rules 1.7 and 1.8(f) require the lawyer to inform the insured that the insurer is a third-party payer or joint client, and explain that certain conflicts might develop during the course of the representation. A few jurisdictions have created required disclosure statements

---

16. MR 1.2(a); RLGL §134, Comment f. *See also* Kent D. Syverud, *The Duty to Settle*, 76 Va. L. Rev. 1113 (1990).

17. Betts v. Allstate Ins. Co., 201 Cal. Rptr. 528 (Cal. App. 1984) (insurer and defense counsel jointly and severally liable for excess verdict, emotional distress, and punitive damages for failing to settle within policy limits where liability was clear).

18. Saucedo v. Winger, 915 P.2d 129 (Kan. App. 1996) (insurance policy that did not specifically give insurer the right to settle without insured physician's consent was ambiguous and interpreted to mean that insurer could not settle without insured's consent).

19. Feliberty v. Damon, 527 N.E.2d 261 (N.Y. 1988) (malpractice insurer not liable for settling malpractice case without physician's consent where policy gave insurer the specific right to settle without the insured's consent).

20. Rogers v. Robson, Masters, Ryan, Brumund & Belom, 392 N.E.2d 1365 (Ill. App. 1979), *aff'd*, 407 N.E.2d 47 (Ill. 1980) (failure to inform insured of settlement offer and option of releasing insurer from its contractual obligations and defending suit at insured's own expense creates malpractice liability for damages caused by lack of disclosure).

regarding an insured client's rights and have mandated that each insured receive such a statement at the beginning of each representation.[21] Typical required disclosures run the gamut of the 5 Cs, including the lawyer's obligation to keep the client informed, to provide competent service including the insured's right to control the representation when the interests of the insured and insurer conflict, to maintain confidentiality, and to identify and respond to conflicts of interest.[22]

Competence The insured client has no incentive to seek anything other than a Lexus defense. The insurer, however, tends to look at these matters on a macro basis, and therefore includes defense costs among its highest costs of doing business. Insurers may attempt to limit their costs by relying on insurance policy language that cedes substantial control of the representation to the insurer. Decisions about fees and strategy extending to matters such as staffing, motion practice, and the need for expert witnesses, all can be second-guessed, often by nonlawyer auditors.[23] At the very least, insureds are entitled to know when insurers refuse to pay for a service the defense lawyer deems necessary for the insured's defense.[24]

Billing audits are another example of the guerilla war between insurance companies and defense counsel, with insurers insisting on these audits of defense fee billings, usually performed by independent contractors paid by contingent fees. Here, the contingent fee paid to third-party, nonlawyer auditors creates an incentive to quibble with each hour billed, and causes additional pressure on defense counsel to cut down on expenditures. Courts generally do not prohibit such practices,[25] but do construe Rule 1.6 to require explicit consent by insureds to the confidential disclosures necessitated by such audits.[26]

This conflict about the cost necessary to provide competent representation has led to literally dozens of bar association opinions that often condemn insurers' interference with retained counsel.[27] Many of these opinions hold that lawyers may not ethically comply with any insurer's requirement of prior approval before undertaking research, depositions, or retaining expert witnesses.[28] The Restatement does allow for some outside direction but only if it is reasonable in scope, does not create interference with the lawyer's independent professional judgment, and the client consents.[29] This means that so long as a

---

21. *E.g.*, Fla. R. Prof. Conduct 4-1.8 (j) (2007); Ohio R. Prof. Conduct 1.8(f) (2007).
22. *Id.*
23. *E.g.*, Glenn K. Jackson, Inc. v. Roe, 273 F.3d 1192 (9th Cir. 2001) (auditor that found errors in law firm's billings to insurer, which resulted in insurer firing law firm, owed no duty of care to law firm and could not be liable for fraud because the law firm presented no evidence of reasonable reliance; but auditor may be liable for libel or slander if law firm can show reckless disregard of the truth).
24. Fla. R. Prof. Conduct 1.8(j).
25. *E.g.*, Bronx Leg. Servs. v. Leg. Serv. Corp., 64 Fed. Appx. 310 (2d Cir. 2003) (LSC authorized by law to audit operations and therefore may require groups that receive federal funding to disclose client names and the nature of the representation to government).
26. In re R. of Prof. Conduct, 2 P.3d 806 (Mont. 2000) (detailed descriptions of professional services can only be provided to third-party auditors after first obtaining contemporaneous fully informed consent of insureds); Ohio R. Prof. Conduct 1.8(f) (2007).
27. ABA Formal Op. 01-421 cites these state opinions.
28. *Id.*
29. RLGL §134(2).

defense lawyer reasonably believes that forgoing a deposition, motion, or an expert will not violate his or her duty of competent representation, he or she may comply, but only if the insured consents.[30]

A defense lawyer who does not reasonably believe that cost cutting will allow for competent representation may well worry about malpractice liability. *Wolpaw* illustrates that such a worry is justified. *Paradigm* demonstrates the potential for such an action by the insurer, whether or not a client. The issue of incompetence has also been raised in the context of wrongful discharge actions filed by former inside counsels, who claimed they were fired because they unsuccessfully attempted to resist pressure to reduce necessary litigation costs.[31]

Confidentiality One-client/third-party payer courts rely on Model Rule 1.8(f), which makes clear that the lawyer who represents the insured cannot share an insured's confidential information without consent. Courts that find a defense lawyer represents two clients face the same conflict between the lawyer's duty to inform one client under Model Rule 1.4 and the lawyer's duty to maintain confidentiality to the other client under Model Rule 1.6. Recall that the court in *A. v. B.* justified disclosure in such a joint client situation only on the basis of an explicit exception in its state version of Model Rule 1.6. When no such exception exists, the lawyer who discloses will be liable for breach of fiduciary duty, as were the lawyers in *Perez* who made this mistake in a similar joint client context.

Confidentiality issues also occur when a lawyer discovers facts suggesting that coverage is at issue, such as facts that tend to establish that the insured's conduct was intentional rather than negligent. Most two-client courts require separate counsel for the insured when this occurs. Some jurisdictions allow the insurer to bring a separate declaratory judgment action to determine the issue of coverage, but the insurer cannot use any information relating to the underlying representation of the insured to raise or litigate the issue. Lawyers who learn such information that compromises coverage will have to withdraw from representing the insurer, and will not be able to disclose the insured's confidences or otherwise provide reasons why they are withdrawing.

Lawyers who disclose such information without obtaining the insured's express informed consent will be subject to malpractice or breach of fiduciary liability if the insured is injured by disclosure to the insurer.[32] Further, the insurer will be estopped to deny the policy coverage if this information is used to promote a policy defense before the underlying case is properly defended.[33] An

30. *Id.*, ill. 5.
31. *E.g.*, Lewis v. Nationwide Mut. Ins. Co., 2003 U.S. Dist. LEXIS 5126 (D. Conn. 2003) (lawyer who worked as inside counsel for an insurer to defend its insureds stated cause of action for wrongful discharge and intentional infliction of emotional distress when he was demoted and fired for refusing to permit the insurer to interfere with his independent professional judgment); Spratley v. St. Farm Mut. Auto. Ins. Co., 78 P.3d 603 (Utah 2003) (lawyers who quit their jobs as in-house counsel for insurer claiming that insurer required them to violate ethical duties to insureds could disclose matters relating to their representation of the insurer as long as disclosures were reasonably necessary).
32. *See, e.g.*, Perez v. Kirk & Carrigan, *supra* p. 165.
33. Employers Cas. Co. v. Tilley, 496 S.W.2d 552 (Tex. 1973) (insurer estopped to deny coverage because it attempted to use insured's statements obtained by lawyer hired by insurer to defend insured).

insurer also might be liable for bad faith if it refuses to settle the case due to the leaked policy defense.[34]

Conflict of Interest Resolution   Using an insured's confidences to create a policy defense constitutes one of at least four situations courts have characterized as actual conflicts of interest that require defense lawyers to represent one client only, the insured. *Paradigm* identifies several other actual conflicts that require defense counsel to shift allegiance exclusively to the insured, and if necessary, notify the insurer to retain its own counsel in the matter. In one-client/third-party payer jurisdictions, these same conflicts require special attention to prevent interference with the lawyer's independent professional judgment.

The second actual conflict occurs when multiple claims are alleged against an insured, some of which may involve conduct that the insurer asserts is not covered by the insurance policy. Here, courts hold that the duty to defend extends beyond the duty to indemnify, which means that the insurer must provide an adequate defense against the allegedly uncovered conduct. Courts have developed two approaches to this issue. Some require defense under a "reservation of rights," which means that the insurer can reserve its right to claim any policy exclusion later, but must provide a conflict-free defense in the meantime. Others allow a declaratory judgment action to be filed by the insurer before any trial on the merits to determine coverage and the obligation to defend.

Providing an adequate defense under a reservation of rights requires defense counsel to ignore the interests of the insurer, and focus exclusively on the interests of the insured. For example, a complaint that alleges both intentional and negligent misconduct usually creates an actual conflict between insured, who desires insurance coverage of any liability, and insurer, which prefers a finding of intentional tort that will release it from its contractual obligations. The insurer is entitled to hire its own counsel in the matter, but the lawyer retained to provide the insured's defense must be guided solely by the insured's best interests.[35] Once again, insurance law provides that failure to send a reservation of rights letter or provide independent counsel to an insured estops the insurer from later denying coverage.[36]

The third actual conflict occurs when an insured is sued for an amount in excess of policy limits.[37] When this occurs, insurance law imposes an obligation on the insurer to act in good faith in responding to settlement offers. Where

---

34. Parsons v. Contl. Natl. Am. Group, 550 P.2d 94 (Ariz. 1976) (insurer estopped from denying coverage under its policy when its denial was based on confidential information obtained from insured's lawyer, and insurer's refusal to settle within policy limits after it learned of the policy defense constituted bad faith, resulting in an obligation to pay all of the underlying judgment, which was twice the policy limit).

35. For a case involving sexual misconduct by a physician where the court found that the lawyer offered a "splendid" defense under a reservation of rights, *see* St. Paul Fire and Marine Ins. Co. v. Engelmann, 639 N.W.2d 192 (S.D. 2002).

36. Beckwith Mach. Co. v. Travelers Indem. Co., 638 F. Supp. 1179 (W.D. Pa. 1986) (where the failure to send a reservation of rights letter or file a declaratory judgment action estopped the insurer from denying coverage and created liability for bad faith and breach of contract).

37. *See* Shaya B. Pacific, LLC v. Wilson, Elser, Moskowitz, Edelman & Dicker, LLP, 38 A.D.3d 34 (N.Y. App. 2006) (law firm hired to defend an insured may have a duty to investigate issue of excess coverage by another insurer).

there is a reasonable probability that the insured will be found liable for an excess judgment, the insurer must take the insured's interests into account.[38] This means that the insurer must have an objective legal basis to justify its refusal to settle. If a lawyer representing the insured alone would advise litigating genuine issues of liability or damages, failure to settle within policy limits may have a reasonable basis; if a lawyer representing the insured alone would recommend settlement, and the insured would settle, failure to settle within policy limits constitutes bad faith.[39]

Wolpaw illustrates another variation of this circumstance: multiple insureds facing excess damage claims. Recall that the court there required separate counsel for each insured to guarantee each his or her right to a conflict-free defense. *Wolpaw* also indicates that failure to recognize this conflict can create insurer liability for bad faith refusal to settle, including the full amount of any eventual judgment against the insured. Lawyers faced with insurers who refuse to settle within policy limits or provide independent counsel must remind insurers about this potential for bad-faith liability.[40]

Insurance Law

In most jurisdictions, insurance law facilitates the work of defense lawyers by creating additional incentives for insurers to abide by their obligation to provide a "defense" free of unwarranted interference in the client-lawyer relationship. Lawyers who represent insurers must explain this law to provide competent representation. Similarly, lawyers who represent insureds need to understand insurance law ramifications to inform and protect their clients.

We have seen, for example, that insurance law created the tort of bad faith, designed to encourage reasonable settlements in the best interests of insureds. Insurance law also includes the remedy of estoppel to prevent the insurer from unfairly relying on a policy defense. Similarly, courts find that conflicts created by the duty to defend and policy limitations necessitate a reservation of rights letter when some claims are made outside of policy coverage. These letters promote a fair response to conflicts by notifying insureds about the contractual limits of their policies, thereby allowing them to seek additional counsel for the uncovered conduct. Insurer's obligations to defend under a reservation of rights also require lawyers to provide a defense for covered events focused on the insured's interests alone.

---

38. ABA Formal Op. 96-403.
39. Behn v. Legion Ins. Co., 173 F. Supp. 2d 105 (D. Mass. 2001) (insurer acted reasonably in refusing to settle medical malpractice case where expert witness opined that defendant psychiatrist complied with the standard of care, facts indicated comparative fault of plaintiff, and insured refused consent to settle).
40. Haddick ex rel. Griffith v. Valor Ins., 763 N.E.2d 299 (Ill. 2001) (cause of action for bad faith refusal to settle found where liability conceded, medical expenses were in excess of policy limits, and insurer did not offer to settle for policy limits until one year after settlement demand initially made).

Conclusion

Understanding the ethical obligations of insurance defense counsel begins with identifying the insured as the primary or sole client of the lawyer. Once this has been done, four conclusions quickly follow:

1. Defense lawyers owe insureds all of the 5 Cs, meaning that they cannot allow insurers to interfere in the exercise of their independent professional judgment. Lawyers who breach any of the 5 Cs will be accountable to insured. Insurers harmed by incompetence also may be able to obtain relief.
2. Insurers may exert some control over fees and strategy, but cannot impose prior approval requirements on defense counsel. Lawyers can agree to direction that is reasonable in scope, but must inform insureds about insurer's imposed limitations and obtain informed consent to any disclosures to the insurer.
3. Arrangements with defense counsel that offer insurers more opportunity to control fees and strategy, such as flat fees or inside counsel status, are prohibited in some jurisdictions to prevent interference with independent professional judgment.
4. Insurers may have contractual control over settlement decisions, but insurance law and the ethical responsibilities of defense counsel impose obligations of good faith on both in communicating and responding to settlement offers.

When any conflict over confidentiality, coverage, settlement, or control develops, defense lawyers who understand that the insured is their primary or only client will view that matter through the correct lens of the insured's best interests. They will communicate relevant facts and options, insist on competent defense of the insured's case, keep the insured's confidences, and identify and respond to conflicts of interest. When a conflict is identified, defense lawyers will notify their client(s) about the source and nature of the conflict and determine how counsel without such a conflict would proceed. Insurance law usually assists defense lawyers in fully understanding their obligations, because it provides additional incentives for insurers to meet their contractual obligations.

Chapter 9

Conflicts of Interest: Multiple Clients

A. Current Clients

1. Aggregate Settlements

Problem

9-1. An automobile accident resulted in the death of Wife and serious injuries to Daughter and Grandmother. Martyn & Fox undertook the representation of Daughter and Grandmother, as well as the estate of Wife. Defendant's insurer offers policy limits of $1,000,000 to settle all claims. Should Martyn & Fox accept the offer?

Consider: Model Rule 1.8(g)
Model Code DR 5-106
RLGL §§6, 37

Burrow v. Arce
997 S.W.2d 229 (Tex. 1999)

Justice HECHT delivered the opinion of the Court.

The principal question in this case is whether an attorney who breaches his fiduciary duty to his client may be required to forfeit all or part of his fee, irrespective of whether the breach caused the client actual damages. Like the court of appeals, we answer in the affirmative and conclude that the amount of the fee

to be forfeited is a question for the court, not a jury. . . .

I

Explosions at a Phillips 66 chemical plant in 1989 killed twenty-three workers and injured hundreds of others, spawning a number of wrongful death and personal injury lawsuits. One suit on behalf of some 126 plaintiffs was filed by five attorneys, David Burrow, Walter

Umphrey, John E. Williams, Jr., F. Kenneth Bailey, Jr., and Wayne Reaud, and their law firm, Umphrey, Burrow, Reaud, Williams & Bailey. The case settled for something close to $190 million, out of which the attorneys received a contingent fee of more than $60 million.

Forty-nine of these plaintiffs then filed this suit against their attorneys in the Phillips accident case alleging professional misconduct and demanding forfeiture of all fees the attorneys received. More specifically, plaintiffs alleged that the attorneys, in violation of rules governing their professional conduct, solicited business through a lay intermediary, failed to fully investigate and assess individual claims, failed to communicate offers received and demands made, entered into an aggregate settlement with Phillips of all plaintiffs' claims without plaintiffs' authority or approval, agreed to limit their law practice by not representing others involved in the same incident, and intimidated and coerced their clients into accepting the settlement. Plaintiffs asserted causes of action for breach of fiduciary duty, fraud, violations of the Deceptive Trade Practices—Consumer Protection Act, . . . negligence, and breach of contract. The attorneys have denied any misconduct and plaintiffs' claim for fee forfeiture.

The parties paint strikingly different pictures of the events leading to this suit:

The plaintiffs contend: In the Phillips accident suit, the defendant attorneys signed up plaintiffs en masse to contingent fee contracts, often contacting plaintiffs through a union steward. In many instances the contingent fee percentage in the contract was left blank and 33-1/3% was later inserted despite oral promises that a fee of only 25% would be charged. The attorneys settled all the claims in the aggregate and allocated dollar figures to the plaintiffs without regard to individual conditions and damages. No plaintiff was allowed to meet with an attorney for more than about twenty minutes, and any plaintiff who expressed reservations about the settlement was threatened by the attorney with being afforded no recovery at all.

The defendant attorneys contend: No aggregate settlement or any other alleged wrongdoing occurred, but regardless of whether it did or not, all their clients in the Phillips accident suit received a fair settlement for their injuries, but some were disgruntled by rumors of settlements paid co-workers represented by different attorneys in other suits. After the litigation was concluded, a Kansas lawyer invited the attorneys' former clients to a meeting, where he offered to represent them in a suit against the attorneys for a fee per claim of $2,000 and one-third of any recovery. Enticed by the prospect of further recovery with minimal risk, plaintiffs agreed to join this suit, the purpose of which is merely to extort more money from their former attorneys.

These factual disputes were not resolved in the district court. Instead, the court granted summary judgment for the defendant attorneys on the grounds that the settlement of plaintiffs' claims in the Phillips accident suit was fair and reasonable, plaintiffs had therefore suffered no actual damages as a result of any misconduct by the attorneys, and absent actual damages plaintiffs were not entitled to a forfeiture of any of the attorneys' fees. . . .

The Clients contend that the Attorneys' serious breaches of fiduciary duty require full forfeiture of all their fees, irrespective of whether the breaches caused actual damages, but if not, that a determination of the amount of any lesser forfeiture should be made by a jury rather than the court. The Clients also contend that their lack of actual damages has not been established as a matter of law. The Attorneys argue that no fee forfeiture can be ordered absent proof that the Clients sustained actual damages, but even if it could, no forfeiture should be ordered for the misconduct the Clients allege. . . .

II

At the outset we consider whether the Attorneys have established as a matter of law that the Clients have suffered no actual damages as a result of any misconduct by the Attorneys. . . .

. . . [W]e conclude that the Attorneys failed to establish as a matter of law that the Clients did not suffer actual damages, and thus the Attorneys were not entitled to summary judgment dismissing the Clients' claims on that basis.

III

The Attorneys nevertheless argue that the Clients have not alleged grounds that would entitle them to forfeiture of any of the Attorneys' fees. . . . The Clients counter that whether they sustained actual damages or not, the Attorneys, for breach of their fiduciary duty, should be required to forfeit all fees received, or alternatively, a portion of those fees as may be determined by a jury.

These arguments thus raise four issues: (a) are actual damages a prerequisite to fee forfeiture? (b) is fee forfeiture automatic and entire for all misconduct? (c) if not, is the amount of fee forfeiture a question of fact for a jury or one of law for the court? and (d) would the Clients' allegations, if true, entitle them to forfeiture of any or all of the Attorneys' fees? We address each issue in turn.

A

To determine whether actual damages are a prerequisite to forfeiture of an attorney's fee, we look to the jurisprudential underpinnings of the equitable remedy of forfeiture. The parties agree that as a rule a person who renders service to another in a relationship of trust may be denied compensation for his service if he breaches that trust. Section 243 of the Restatement (Second) of Trusts states the rule for trustees: "If the trustee commits a breach of trust, the court may in its discretion deny him all compensation or allow him a reduced compensation or allow him full compensation." Similarly, section 469 of the Restatement (Second) of Agency provides:

> An agent is entitled to no compensation for conduct which is disobedient or which is a breach of his duty of loyalty; if such conduct constitutes a willful and deliberate breach of his contract of service, he is not entitled to compensation even for properly performed services for which no compensation is apportioned.

Citing these two sections, section [37] of the . . . Restatement (Third) of The Law Governing Lawyers applies the same rule to lawyers, who stand in a relation of trust and agency toward their clients. Section [37] states in part: "A lawyer engaging in clear and serious violation of duty to a client may be required to forfeit some or all of the lawyer's compensation for the matter."

Though the historical origins of the remedy of forfeiture of an agent's compensation are obscure, the reasons for the remedy are apparent. The rule is founded both on principle and pragmatics. In principle, a person who agrees to perform compensable services in a relationship of trust and violates that relationship breaches the agreement, express or implied, on which the right to compensation is based. The person is not entitled to be paid when he has not provided the loyalty bargained for and promised. . . . Pragmatically, the possibility of forfeiture of compensation discourages an agent from taking personal advantage of his position of trust in every situation no matter the circumstances, whether the principal may be injured or not. The remedy of forfeiture removes any incentive for an agent to stray from his duty of loyalty based on the possibility that the principal will be unharmed or may have difficulty proving the existence or amount of damages. In other words, as comment b to section [37] of the . . . Restatement (Third) of The Law Governing Lawyers states, "forfeiture is also a deterrent."

To limit forfeiture of compensation to instances in which the principal sustains actual damages would conflict with both justifications for the rule. It is the agent's disloyalty, not any resulting harm, that violates the fiduciary relationship and thus impairs the basis for compensation. An agent's compensation is not only for specific results but also for loyalty. Removing the disincentive of forfeiture except when harm results

would prompt an agent to attempt to calculate whether particular conduct, though disloyal to the principal, might nevertheless be harmless to the principal and profitable to the agent. The main purpose of forfeiture is not to compensate an injured principal, even though it may have that effect. Rather, the central purpose of the equitable remedy of forfeiture is to protect relationships of trust by discouraging agents' disloyalty. . . .

The Attorneys nevertheless argue that forfeiture of an attorney's fee without a showing of actual damages encourages breach-of-fiduciary claims by clients to extort a renegotiation of legal fees after representation has been concluded, allowing them to obtain a windfall. The Attorneys warn that such opportunistic claims could impair the finality desired in litigation settlements by leaving open the possibility that the parties, having resolved their differences, can then assert claims against their counsel to obtain more than they could by settlement of the initial litigation. The Attorneys urge that a bright-line rule making actual damages a prerequisite to fee forfeiture is necessary to prevent misuse of the remedy. We disagree. Fee forfeiture for attorney misconduct is not a windfall to the client. An attorney's compensation is for loyalty as well as services, and his failure to provide either impairs his right to compensation. While a client's motives may be opportunistic and his claims meritless, the better protection is not a prerequisite of actual damages but the trial court's discretion to refuse to afford claimants who are seeking to take unfair advantage of their former attorneys the equitable remedy of forfeiture. Nothing in the caselaw in Texas or elsewhere suggests that opportunistically motivated litigation to forfeit an agent's fee has ever been a serious problem. . . .

We therefore conclude that a client need not prove actual damages in order to obtain forfeiture of an attorney's fee for the attorney's breach of fiduciary duty to the client.

B

The Clients argue that an attorney who commits a serious breach of fiduciary duty to a client must automatically forfeit all compensation to the client. . . .

. . . [T]o require an agent to forfeit all compensation for every breach of fiduciary duty, or even every serious breach, would deprive the remedy of its equitable nature and would disserve its purpose of protecting relationships of trust. A helpful analogy, the parties agree, is a constructive trust, of which we have observed:

> Constructive trusts, being remedial in character, have the very broad function of redressing wrong or unjust enrichment in keeping with basic principles of equity and justice. . . . Moreover, there is no unyielding formula to which a court of equity is bound in decreeing a constructive trust, since the equity of the transaction will shape the measure of relief granted.

Like a constructive trust, the remedy of forfeiture must fit the circumstances presented. It would be inequitable for an agent who had performed extensive services faithfully to be denied all compensation for some slight, inadvertent misconduct that left the principal unharmed, and the threat of so drastic a result would unnecessarily and perhaps detrimentally burden the agent's exercise of judgment in conducting the principal's affairs.

The . . . Restatement (Third) of The Law Governing Lawyers rejects a rigid approach to attorney fee forfeiture. Section [37]states:

> A lawyer engaging in clear and serious violation of duty to a client may be required to forfeit some or all of the lawyer's compensation for the matter. In determining whether and to what extent forfeiture is appropriate, relevant considerations include the gravity and timing of the violation, its wilfulness, its effect on the value of the lawyer's work for the client, any other threatened or actual harm to the client, and the adequacy of other remedies.

The remedy is restricted to "clear and serious" violations of duty. Comment d to section [37] explains: "A violation is clear if a reasonable lawyer, knowing the relevant facts and law reasonably accessible to the lawyer, would have known that the conduct was wrongful." The factors for assessing the seriousness of a violation, and hence "whether and to what extent forfeiture is appropriate," are set out in the rule. . . . Comment a states: "A lawyer is not entitled to be paid for services rendered in violation of the lawyer's duty to a client, or for services needed to alleviate the consequences of the lawyer's misconduct." And comment e observes: "Ordinarily, forfeiture extends to all fees for the matter for which the lawyer was retained. . . ." But comment e adds: "Sometimes forfeiture for the entire matter is inappropriate, for example when a lawyer performed valuable services before the misconduct began, and the misconduct was not so grave as to require forfeiture of the fee for all services." And comment b expands on the necessity for exercising discretion in applying the remedy:

> Forfeiture of fees, however, is not justified in each instance in which a

lawyer violates a legal duty, nor is total forfeiture always appropriate. Some violations are inadvertent or do not significantly harm the client. Some can be adequately dealt with by the remedies described in Comment a or by a partial forfeiture (see Comment e). Denying the lawyer all compensation would sometimes be an excessive sanction, giving a windfall to a client. The remedy of this Section should hence be applied with discretion. . . .

Section [37] sets out considerations similar to those for trustees in applying the remedy of fee forfeiture to attorneys. . . . The several factors embrace broad considerations which must be weighed together and not mechanically applied. For example, the "wilfulness" factor requires consideration of the attorney's culpability generally; it does not simply limit forfeiture to situations in which the attorney's breach of duty was intentional. The adequacy-of-other-remedies factor does not preclude forfeiture when a client can be fully compensated by damages. Even though the main purpose of the remedy is not to compensate the client, if other remedies do not afford the client full compensation for his damages, forfeiture may be considered for that purpose.

To the factors listed in section [37] we add another that must be given great weight in applying the remedy of fee forfeiture: the public interest in maintaining the integrity of attorney-client relationships. . . . The Attorneys' argument that relief for attorney misconduct should be limited to compensating the client for any injury suffered ignores the main purpose of the remedy. . . .

Accordingly, we conclude that whether an attorney must forfeit any or all of his fee for a breach of fidu-

ciary duty to his client must be determined by applying the rule as stated in section [37] of the proposed Restatement (Third) of The Law Governing Lawyers and the factors we have identified to the individual circumstances of each case.

C

The parties agree that the determination whether to afford the remedy of forfeiture must be made by the court. The Clients argue, however, that they are entitled to have the amount of the forfeiture set by a jury. The Attorneys argue, and the court of appeals held, that the amount of any forfeiture is also an issue to be decided by the court.

Forfeiture of an agent's compensation, we have already explained, is an equitable remedy similar to a constructive trust. As a general rule, a jury "does not determine the expediency, necessity, or propriety of equitable relief." Consistent with the rule, whether a constructive trust should be imposed must be determined by a court based on the equity of the circumstances. However, when contested fact issues must be resolved before equitable relief can be determined, a party is entitled to have that resolution made by a jury.

These same principles apply in deciding whether to forfeit all or part of an agent's compensation. Thus, for example, a dispute concerning an agent's culpability—whether he acted intentionally, with gross negligence, recklessly, or negligently, or was merely inadvertent—may present issues for a jury, as may disputes about the value of the agent's services and the existence and amount of any harm to the principal. But factors like the adequacy of other remedies and the public interest in protecting the integrity of the attorney-client relationship, as well as the weighing of all other relevant considerations, present legal policy issues well beyond the jury's province of judging credibility and resolving factual disputes. The ultimate decision on the amount of any fee forfeiture must be made by the court. . . .

Thus, when forfeiture of an attorney's fee is claimed, a trial court must determine from the parties whether factual disputes exist that must be decided by a jury before the court can determine whether a clear and serious violation of duty has occurred, whether forfeiture is appropriate, and if so, whether all or only part of the attorney's fee should be forfeited. Such factual disputes may include, without limitation, whether or when the misconduct complained of oc-curred, the attorney's mental state at the time, and the existence or extent of any harm to the client. If the relevant facts are undisputed, these issues may, of course, be determined by the court as a matter of law. Once any necessary factual disputes have been resolved, the court must determine, based on the factors we have set out, whether the attorney's conduct was a clear and serious breach of duty to his client and whether any of the attorney's compensation should be forfeited, and if so, what amount. Most importantly, in making these determinations the court must consider whether forfeiture is necessary to satisfy the public's interest in protecting the attorney-client relationship. The court's decision whether to forfeit any or all of an attorney's fee is subject to review on appeal as any other legal issue. . . .

▨ The Law Governing Lawyers: *Loss of Fee or Other Benefits*

In *Burrow,* the Supreme Court of Texas explains the jurisprudential underpinnings of another equitable remedy for breach of fiduciary duty: fee forfeiture. In *Monco,* the Illinois Appellate court granted a similar remedy: rescission of a transaction with a client, with concomitant loss of benefits to the lawyer. Both courts also cite lawyer code provisions that restate basic fiduciary duties. In this note, we examine some of the details of these well-established remedies.

Loss of Contractual Benefits

Lawyer-agents who breach duties of obedience, loyalty, or confidentiality lose their entitlement to fees or other contractual rights because they have violated a basic fiduciary duty essential to the contract. In refusing to enforce such contracts, *Monco* illustrates that agency rules, such as a presumption of undue influence, require close scrutiny of business transactions between lawyers and clients in order to give lawyers incentives to preserve fiduciary duties. Similarly, the *Burrow* court typifies the view that the fee forfeiture remedy should be provided both for breaches of fiduciary duty to a particular client, and also to deter similar conduct in other cases.

Either or both of these remedies can arise as an issue when a lawyer sues a client to obtain a contractual benefit, such as an unpaid fee, or other benefit, such as Monco's petition to dissolve the corporation. *Burrow* points out that clients can seek such remedies on their own as well. If the fee has already been paid, or the contractual benefit has already occurred, the client can seek return of the benefit through other equitable remedies, such as a constructive trust or fee forfeiture.[1] One example involves civil actions to order lawyers or other agents to account for, return, or hold in constructive trust specific property acquired because of the improper use of confidential information.[2] Lawyers who breach fiduciary duties also may be ordered to disgorge profits to the client.[3]

Fee Forfeiture

Although *Burrow* represents a contemporary example of the usefulness of fee forfeiture, the remedy itself, like the constructive trust, is quite old. In a bankruptcy case, Judge Learned Hand traced the lawyer's duty not to represent opposing interests back three centuries, and found that the usual consequence of doing so had been that the lawyer was "debarred from receiving any fee from either, no matter how successful his labors."[4] *Burrow* represents the well-settled view that the forfeiture follows from breach of the contract, does not require proof of other damages, and may overlap with other legal remedies.

We have already seen examples of legal relief available to clients who can prove that a lawyer's breach of fiduciary duty caused them harm. For example, Dr. dePape was able to show that his lawyers' failure to inform him about legal options caused him $278,760 in lost income and emotional distress. Similarly, Mr. Perez was able to state a claim for emotional distress damages due to his lawyers' breach of confidentiality. Both of these clients could have sought fee forfeiture as well, but neither did, probably because third parties paid the fees in their cases.[5]

Further, liability insurance would certainly cover a damage award, but rarely will be available to pay a fee forfeiture award. The Minnesota Supreme Court has analogized fee forfeiture to cases about punitive damages and concluded that the availability of insurance to cover a lawyer's individual breach of fiduciary duty was contrary to public policy, but coverage for a law firm's vicarious responsibility was not.[6] This means that an insurer will be required to pay the fee forfeiture award on behalf of a law firm, but the law firm can seek indemnity against the errant lawyer who breached a fiduciary duty to the client.[7]

---

1. When a client seeks a forfeiture of fees already paid, courts sometimes refer to the remedy as "fee disgorgement."
2. RLGL §6, Comments d and e.
3. *See, e.g.,* In re Est. of Mark F. Corriea, 719 A.2d 1234 (D.C. App. 1998) (the court found that the disgorgement of profits was insurable as damages, unless the insurer could justify refusal of coverage by proving that the lawyer intended to deceive the client in not disclosing his conflict of interest).
4. Silbiger v. Prudence Bonds Corp., 180 F.2d 917, 920 (2d Cir. 1950) (citing cases). *See also* Woods v. City Natl. Bank & Trust Co. of Chic., 312 U.S. 262 (1941).
5. Mr. Janus also paid no fee to Monco, so he had no fee forfeiture to seek.
6. Perl v. St. Paul Fire & Marine Ins. Co., 345 N.W.2d 209 (Minn. 1984).
7. *Id.* at 216-217.

Clear and Serious Violations

Although clients do not have to prove causation or actual damages to be entitled to fee forfeiture, they do have to prove a clear and serious violation of a duty owed the client. Breaches of the core agency duties of obedience, disclosure, confidentiality, and loyalty usually qualify, although the source of the duty can be civil law (for example, legal malpractice) or criminal law (for example, fraud) as well.[8] Most common are violations of conflicts of interest obligations, such as representing a client's wife in a divorce,[9] failing to disclose that the law firm employed the opposing party's adjuster,[10] or pressuring a client to change a fee contract,[11] all of which evidence clear disloyalty. Settling a client's case without consent also qualifies.[12]

Burrow adopts the Restatement factors to determine whether the breach constituted a clear and serious violation. The first factor, whether the violation was "clear," is determined by an objective standard: whether "a reasonable lawyer, knowing the relevant facts and law reasonably accessible to the lawyer, would have known that the conduct was wrongful."[13] For example, Model Rule 1.8(g)'s regulation of aggregate settlements means that breach of the rule by the lawyers in Burrow would constitute a "clear" violation whether or not they knew such a rule existed. The second factor, whether the violation was "serious," can be demonstrated in a number of ways. Some courts hold that a serious breach of duty can be shown only if the client was harmed.[14] Burrow represents the modern view, that harm is not necessary as long as the breach of a duty is otherwise clear and serious, such as a representation under a conflict of interest.[15] Isolated, inadvertent breaches, such as the failure to explain fully the terms of a settlement when the trial judge in fact explained them to the client, do not rise to the level of a clear and serious breach.[16]

Multiple breaches in the same case are much more likely to qualify as "serious." For example, in a Texas case following Burrow, a law firm succeeded in getting a client a $56 million divorce settlement, even though she had signed a prenuptial agreement that limited her to about $12 million.[17] Along the way, the firm charged an unjustified contingent fee and changed the fee contract after

---

8. RLGL §37, Comment c.
9. Jeffry v. Pounds, 136 Cal. Rptr. 373 (Cal. App. 1977).
10. Rice v. Perl, 320 N.W.2d 407 (Minn. 1982).
11. Searcy, Denney, Scarola, Barnhart & Shipley, P.A. v. Scheller, 629 So. 2d 947 (Fla. App. 1993).
12. Francisco v. Foret, 2002 Tex. App. LEXIS 2610.
13. RLGL §37, Comment d. See, e.g., Hardison v. Weinshel, 450 F. Supp. 721 (E.D. Wis. 1978) (lawyer who withdrew from case shortly before trial because he mistakenly believed client would not prevail forfeits all fee).
14. See, e.g., Sealed Party v. Sealed Party, 2006 U.S. Dist. LEXIS 28392; Frank v. Bloom, 634 F.2d 1245 (10th Cir. 1980); Crawford v. Logan, 656 S.W.2d 360 (Tenn. 1983); Burk v. Burzynski, 672 P.2d 419 (Wyo. 1983).
15. See, e.g., Hendry v. Pelland, 73 F.3d 397 (D.C. Cir. 1996) (lawyers represented property owners with conflicting interests); In re Eastern Sugar Antitrust Litig., 697 F.2d 524 (3d Cir. 1982) (law firm failed to disclose merger negotiations with opposing party's firm); Jackson v. Griffith, 421 So. 2d 677 (Fla. App. 1982) (lawyer coerced client to sign fee contract).
16. Hoover v. Larkin, 2001 Tex. App. LEXIS 6313.
17. Angela Ward, *Arce Jeopardizes Family Lawyers' Fee; Jury Awards 6.3 Million Verdict for Breach of Fiduciary Duty*, Texas Lawyer 16 (Nov. 15, 1999).

the representation was underway, all the while knowing that the client's "alcohol and prescription drug problem impaired her ability to agree to the amount of attorney fees."[18] One of the lawyers pursued a romantic relationship with the client that included his acceptance of expensive gifts and use of her charge card. When the client disputed some of the fee, the lawyers failed to keep the disputed portion in a trust account until the dispute was resolved. The court concluded that the serious breaches of duty to the client "did not affect the value of their legal work but would have if the underlying case had not settled," and ordered forfeiture of the $3 million fee.[19]

Total or Partial Forfeiture

When the client has shown a clear and serious breach, *Burrow* relies on the Restatement of the Law Governing Lawyers for the proposition that, normally, fee forfeiture will be total.[20] The court eschews an absolute rule of total forfeiture in all cases, recognizing that other courts have imposed partial fee forfeiture when the misconduct can be separated in time from other valuable services the lawyer has performed. The court cites other factors as well, including the willfulness of the violation, its effect on the client, and the adequacy of other remedies. It then adds a final factor to be given great weight: "the public interest in maintaining the integrity of attorney-client relationships." The court avoids, however, the question of burden of proof. The most logical view seems to be that the client must show the clear and serious breach, at which point total forfeiture is presumed. The burden of proof then shifts to the lawyer to justify less than full forfeiture, by establishing the value of the service rendered apart from the breach.[21] Such an approach parallels the reasoning in *Monco*, where the court presumed undue influence because of the lawyer's self dealing and then shifted the burden of proof to the lawyer to establish that the transaction was indeed reasonable and fair.

How might these factors play out on remand in *Burrow*? First, note that the aggregate settlement rule that the law firm allegedly breached is a long-standing rule that protects each client's right to individualized fiduciary duties. If the rule were violated, it is possible that the court could impose total fee forfeiture regardless of the lack of demonstrable harm to the clients. However, it is also possible that the law firm provided valuable services to each client up until the point of settlement. Suppose, for example, that the firm vigorously developed the liability issues in the case and worked up the damage claims of each client individually. It is conceivable that this work prompted the settlement negotiations, which would not have otherwise occurred. At that point, the breach of the aggregate settlement rule, while still a serious matter, might be viewed as less of a breach of all duties owed during the total representation. On the other hand, if the law firm did little of this work and the defendant conceded liability, the breach appears nearly total.

---

18. Piro v. Sarofim, 80 S.W.3d 717 (Tex. App. 2002).
19. *Id.* The court also upheld the trial judge's finding that the $6 million verdict, half for compensatory damages and half for fee forfeiture, was made in the alternative, but it added that "the trial court could have rendered judgment against the lawyers on both awards without creating a double recovery." *Id.* at 21.
20. RLGL §37, Comment e.
21. *See* RLGL §42(2).

Thus, where the breach of fiduciary duty permeates the entire relationship, the grounds for total fee forfeiture are found. This explains why so many of the full forfeiture cases involve conflicts of interest, which tainted the entire representation. On the other hand, where the conflict arises during the representation, the lawyer may be reimbursed for services provided before he should have responded to the conflict.[22] Since so much is unknown and disputed in *Burrow*, the court properly remands for additional development of the facts.

Statutory Fee Forfeiture

Fee forfeiture can occur pursuant to statute as well. Most prominent are criminal statutes that provide for forfeiture of the fruits of criminal activity, including lawyer's fees.[23] Of course, lawyers who know that their clients are paying them with the fruits of the crime also risk other criminal penalties, such as aiding and abetting the crime or receiving stolen property.[24] Forfeiture statutes provide for civil forfeiture of the client's funds traceable to criminal activity, on the theory that they passed to the government at the time of the crime.[25] The government can seize all assets of a defendant at the point of indictment on a showing of probable cause to believe that the assets will ultimately be found to be subject to forfeiture.[26] If the criminal case determines that the assets are the proceeds of the crime, they are permanently forfeited to the government. The statute exempts a "bona fide purchaser for value" of property otherwise subject to forfeiture.[27]

The Supreme Court has held that these statutes are intended to reach lawyer's fees, as well as other assets of the defendant, and that using this statutory power to freeze cash paid to a lawyer does not violate a client's rights.[28] The Court was not persuaded by the argument that this meant that some defendants would be deprived of counsel of their choice. The majority pointed out that the Sixth Amendment guaranteed them a lawyer, but gave them no constitutional right "to spend another person's money" for such services. Publicly appointed counsel would suffice if no untainted sources of money could be found to retain private counsel.[29] The practical reality created by these cases is that a lawyer retained by a defendant where such a statute applies takes a risk of nonpayment. Courts also have held that lawyers must essentially audit the source of the client's money in order to ensure payment.[30]

---

22. *E.g.*, Hill v. Douglas, 271 So. 2d 1 (Fla. 1971) (lawyer did not forfeit fee until he should have known he would be a witness).
23. *E.g.*, 21 U.S.C. §§848, 853 (2006).
24. *See* The Bounds of the Law: Criminal Conduct, *supra* p. 254.
25. *See* Geoffrey C. Hazard & W. William Hodes, *The Law of Lawyering* §9.32 (2002).
26. United States v. Monsanto, 924 F.2d 1186 (2d Cir. 1991) (en banc).
27. A "bona fide purchaser for value" is a person who "was reasonably without cause to believe that the property was subject to forfeiture" when he took the property. 21 U.S.C. §853(c) (2006).
28. Caplin & Drysdale v. United States, 491 U.S. 617 (1989); United States v. Monsanto, 491 U.S. 600 (1989).
29. *Caplin & Drysdale, supra* note 28, at 626.
30. *See, e.g.*, United States v. McCorkle, 321 F.3d 1292 (11th Cir. 2002) (burden of proof on lawyer F. Lee Bailey to identify the portion of the fee collected while he was a bona fide purchaser for value).

Overlapping Remedies

Courts have created different equitable remedies to fill gaps in legal relief. Occasionally, these remedies overlap, allowing a client to seek several in the same case. For example, *Burrow* leaves open the possibility of a breach of fiduciary duty tort damages in addition to fee forfeiture.[31] Courts also have ordered fee forfeiture as part of a disciplinary sanction.[32] A former client who succeeded in disqualifying his former lawyer from representing his wife in a divorce also was entitled to reversal of the trial court's order to pay his wife's attorney fees.[33] The client later filed a grievance as well, which resulted in a public reprimand of the lawyer.[34] In an analogous case claiming fee forfeiture under a federal statute, the court disqualified the law firm due to the defendant's statement that he wanted to plead guilty, but could not, because such a plea would jeopardize the $103,000 fee he had paid his lawyer. Following disqualification, the court also ordered fee forfeiture, including a state common law conversion action to recover the money the firm had already spent.[35]

One issue that commonly arises is whether a law firm that defends its own disqualification motion can charge its current client for the defense.[36] If the firm is disqualified, the client may have a partial or complete defense to the payment of legal fees.[37] Such a client also may seek disgorgement of a fee already paid.

Together, common law agency remedies of fee forfeiture and other loss of contractual benefits, as well as statutes that accomplish the same result, create minefields for unwary lawyers. You can avoid the common law remedies by honoring your fiduciary obligations, including duties of obedience, disclosure, confidentiality, and conflict of interest resolution.

2. Joint Representations

Problems

9-2. Husband and Wife ask Martyn & Fox to prepare the papers for their dissolution of marriage. May Martyn & Fox represent both spouses? Does it matter if they have already agreed to property division, child custody, and support obligations? What if Husband and Wife ask Martyn to mediate their disputes regarding these issues? If the mediation is successful, may Martyn represent both in drafting the legal papers necessary to effectuate the dissolution?

---

31. *See also Hendry, supra* note 15; *Piro, supra* note 18.
32. Fla. Bar v. Rodriguez, 959 So. 2d 150 (Fla. 2007) (lawyer suspended for two years and ordered to disgorge fee to client who was the victim of a conflict of interest); Fla. Bar v. St. Louis, 967 So. 2d 108 (Fla. 2007) (companion case, lawyer disbarred and ordered to disgorge fee).
33. Ennis v. Ennis, 276 N.W.2d 341 (Wis. 1979). *See also* Image Tech. Serv. v. Eastman Kodak Co., 136 F.3d 1354 (9th Cir. 1998) (former client not entitled to attorney fees under Clayton Act for work done by lawyer who was later disqualified).
34. In re Conway, 301 N.W.2d 253 (Wis. 1981).
35. United States v. Moffitt, Zwerling & Kemler, P.C., 83 F.3d 660 (4th Cir. 1996), *cert. denied*, 519 U.S. 1101 (1997).
36. Some clients in this position agree to defend the action but at the law firm's own expense. *See, e.g.*, Padco v. Kinney & Lange, 444 N.W.2d 889 (Minn. App. 1989).
37. *See, e.g.*, In re Bonneville Pacific Corp., 196 B.R. 868 (D. Utah 1996); Goldstein v. Lees, 120 Cal. Rptr. 253 (Cal. App. 1975).

9-3. Two defendants are charged with murder arising from a botched bank robbery that resulted in the killing of a customer. Can Martyn & Fox represent both defendants? What if only the "shooter" is eligible for the death penalty? Would it matter if Martyn represents one defendant and Fox represents the other?

9-4. Martyn & Fox is asked to represent driver-son and passenger-father in a lawsuit arising from an auto accident where the driver of the other car has been charged with speeding. Can we take on this case? What happens when Son tells Fox before his deposition "I had two drinks before I picked up Dad"?

9-5. Our long-time corporate brokerage client and two of its stockbrokers have been sued for violating insider-trading regulations. Can Martyn & Fox represent both the corporation and the stockbrokers?

9-6. Buyer and Seller of real estate come to Martyn & Fox to handle the deal. They have agreed on the price, date of closing, and identity of the property to be conveyed. Can Martyn & Fox undertake the engagement?

9-7. A long-time client of Martyn & Fox asks us to represent three partners in forming a new business: our long-time client, the money guy, and the new venture's CEO. May we?

9-8. A corporate client's CEO asks Martyn & Fox to represent his wife and him in drawing up new wills. Can we do so? What if the wife takes Martyn aside and tells her to draft a codicil that diverts a substantial part of her assets to a "friend"? What if later, during divorce proceedings, the wife calls Martyn & Fox to be refreshed as to husband's assets; may (must) Martyn & Fox share that information?

Consider: Model Rules 1.7, 1.8(b), 1.8(f), 1.10, 1.12, 1.13, 2.4
Model Code DR 5-105
RLGL §§75, 128, 129, 130, 131

ABA Formal Opinion 07-447
American Bar Association Standing Committee on Ethics and
Professional Responsibility

Ethical Considerations in Collaborative Law Practice

Before representing a client in a collaborative law process, a lawyer must advise the client of the benefits and risks of participation in the process. If the client has given his or her informed consent, the lawyer may represent the client in the collaborative law process. A lawyer who engages in collaborative resolution processes still is bound by the rules of professional conduct, including the duties of competence and diligence.[1]

In this opinion, we analyze the implications of the Model Rules on collaborative law practice.[2] Collaborative law is a type of alternative dispute resolution

---

1. This opinion is based on the Model Rules of Professional Conduct as amended by the ABA House of Delegates through February 2007. The laws, court rules, regulations, rules of professional conduct, and opinions promulgated in individual jurisdictions are controlling.
2. We do not discuss the ethical considerations that arise in connection with a lawyer's participation in a collaborative law group or organization. *See* Maryland Bar Ass'n Eth. Op. 2004-23 (2004) (discussing ethical propriety of "collaborative dispute resolution non-profit organization.").

in which the parties and their lawyers commit to work cooperatively to reach a settlement. It had its roots in, and shares many attributes of, the mediation process. Participants focus on the interests of both clients, gather sufficient information to insure that decisions are made with full knowledge, develop a full range of options, and then choose options that best meet the needs of the parties. The parties structure a mutually acceptable written resolution of all issues without court involvement. The product of the process is then submitted to the court as a final decree. The structure creates a problem-solving atmosphere with a focus on interest-based negotiation and client empowerment.

Since its creation in Minnesota in 1990, collaborative practice[5] has spread rapidly throughout the United States and into Canada, Australia, and Western Europe. Numerous established collaborative law organizations develop local practice protocols, train practitioners, reach out to the public, and build referral networks. On its website, the International Academy of Collaborative Professionals describes its mission as fostering professional excellence in conflict resolution by protecting the essentials of collaborative practice, expanding collaborative practice worldwide, and providing a central resource for education, networking, and standards of practice.

Although there are several models of collaborative practice, all of them share the same core elements that are set out in a contract between the clients and their lawyers (often referred to as a "four-way" agreement). In that agreement, the parties commit to negotiating a mutually acceptable settlement without court intervention, to engaging in open communication and information sharing, and to creating shared solutions that meet the needs of both clients. To ensure the commitment of the lawyers to the collaborative process, the four-way agreement also includes a requirement that, if the process breaks down, the lawyers will withdraw from representing their respective clients and will not handle any subsequent court proceedings.

Several state bar opinions have analyzed collaborative practice and, with one exception, have concluded that it is not inherently inconsistent with the Model Rules.[7] Most authorities treat collaborative law practice as a species of limited scope representation and discuss the duties of lawyers in those situations, including communication, competence, diligence, and confidentiality. However, even those opinions are guarded, and caution that collaborative practice carries with it a potential for significant ethical difficulties.

---

5. The terms "collaborative law," "collaborative process," and "collaborative resolution process" are used interchangeably with "collaborative practice." Although collaborative practice currently is utilized almost exclusively by family law practitioners, its concepts have been applied to employment, probate, construction, real property, and other civil law disputes where the parties are likely to have continuing relationships after the current conflict has been resolved.

7. Colorado Bar Ass'n Eth. Op. 115 (Feb. 24, 2007), is the only opinion to conclude that a non-consentable conflict arises in collaborative practice. Other state authorities analyze the disqualification obligation under Rules 1.2, 1.16, or 5.6. *See e.g.*, Kentucky Bar Ass'n Op. E-425 (June 2005), New Jersey Adv. Comm, on Prof'l Eth. Op. 699 (Dec. 12, 2005), North Carolina State Bar Ass'n 2002 Formal Eth. Op. 1 (Apr. 19, 2002), Pennsylvania Bar Ass'n Comm. on Legal Eth. & Prof'l Resp. Inf. Op. 2004-24 (May 11, 2004). Several states have special rules for collaborative law practice. *See, e.g.*, Cal. Fam §2013 (West 2007); N.C. Gen. Stat. §50-70 to 50-79 (2006); Tex. Fam. Code Ann. §§6.603 & 153.0072 (Vernon 2005).

As explained herein, we agree that collaborative law practice and the provisions of the four-way agreement represent a permissible limited scope representation under Model Rule 1.2, with the concomitant duties of competence, diligence, and communication. We reject the suggestion that collaborative law practice sets up a non-waivable conflict under Rule 1.7(a)(2).

Rule 1.2(c) permits a lawyer to limit the scope of a representation so long as the limitation is reasonable under the circumstances and the client gives informed consent. Nothing in the Rule or its Comment suggests that limiting a representation to a collaborative effort to reach a settlement is per se unreasonable. On the contrary, Comment [6] provides that "[a] limited representation may be appropriate because the client has limited objectives for the representation. In addition, the terms upon which representation is undertaken may exclude specific means that might otherwise be used to accomplish the client's objectives."

Obtaining the client's informed consent requires that the lawyer communicate adequate information and explanation about the material risks of and reasonably available alternatives to the limited representation.[9] The lawyer must provide adequate information about the rules or contractual terms governing the collaborative process, its advantages and disadvantages, and the alternatives. The lawyer also must assure that the client understands that, if the collaborative law procedure does not result in settlement of the dispute and litigation is the only recourse, the collaborative lawyer must withdraw and the parties must retain new lawyers to prepare the matter for trial.[10]

The [Colorado Bar] opinion that expressed the view that collaborative practice is impermissible did so on the theory that the "four-way agreement" creates a non-waivable conflict of interest under Rule 1.7(a)(2). We disagree with that result because we conclude that it turns on a faulty premise. As we stated earlier, the four-way agreement that is at the heart of collaborative practice includes the promise that both lawyers will withdraw from representing their respective clients if the collaboration fails and that they will not assist their clients in ensuing litigation. We do not disagree with the proposition that this contractual obligation to withdraw creates on the part of each lawyer a "responsibility to a third party" within the meaning of Rule 1.7(a)(2). We do disagree with the view that such a responsibility creates a conflict of interest under that Rule.

A conflict exists between a lawyer and her own client under Rule 1.7(a)(2) "if there is a significant risk that the representation [of the client] will be materially limited by the lawyer's responsibilities to . . . a third person or by a personal interest of the lawyer." A self-interest conflict can be resolved if the client gives informed consent, confirmed in writing,[12] but a lawyer may not seek the client's informed consent unless the lawyer "reasonably believes that [she] will be able to provide competent and diligent representation" to the client.[13]

---

9. Rule 1.0(c).
10. *See also* Rule 1.4(b), which requires that a lawyer "explain a matter to the extent reasonably necessary to permit the client to make informed decisions regarding the representation."
12. Rule 1.7(b)(4).
13. Rule 1.7(b)(1).

Responsibilities to third parties constitute conflicts with one's own client only if there is a significant risk that those responsibilities will materially limit the lawyer's representation of the client. It has been suggested that a lawyer's agreement to withdraw is essentially an agreement by the lawyer to impair her ability to represent the client.[14] We disagree, because we view participation in the collaborative process as a limited scope representation.

When a client has given informed consent to a representation limited to collaborative negotiation toward settlement, the lawyer's agreement to withdraw if the collaboration fails is not an agreement that impairs her ability to represent the client, but rather is consistent with the client's limited goals for the representation. A client's agreement to a limited scope representation does not exempt the lawyer from the duties of competence and diligence, notwithstanding that the contours of the requisite competence and diligence are limited in accordance with the overall scope of the representation. Thus, there is no basis to conclude that the lawyer's representation of the client will be materially limited by the lawyer's obligation to withdraw if settlement cannot be accomplished. In the absence of a significant risk of such a material limitation, no conflict arises between the lawyer and her client under Rule 1.7(a)(2). Stated differently, there is no foreclosing of alternatives, i.e., consideration and pursuit of litigation, otherwise available to the client because the client has specifically limited the scope of the lawyer's representation to the collaborative negotiation of a settlement.[16]

Wolpaw v. General Accident Insurance Co.

639 A.2d 338 (N.J. Super. 1994)

BRODY, P.J.A.D.

Defendant issued a homeowners' policy to Saranne Frew. Other members of Frew's household covered by the policy were plaintiff, who is Frew's sister, and plaintiff's son

Heath. All three were sued in a personal-injury action for their allegedly negligent conduct during the term of the policy. Defendant assigned the same firm of attorneys, third-party defendants Parker, McCay and Criscuolo, Esqs., to represent the three

---

14. Colorado Bar Ass'n Eth. Op.115, *supra* note 7 (practice of collaborative law violates Rule 1.7(b) of Colorado Rules of Professional Conduct insofar as a lawyer participating in the process enters into a contractual agreement with the opposing party requiring the lawyer to withdraw in the event that the process is unsuccessful).

16. *See* Lerner v. Laufer, 819 A.2d 471, 482 (N.J. Super. Ct. App. Div.), *cert. denied*, 827 A.2d 290 (N.J. 2003) (stating that "the law has never foreclosed the right of competent, informed citizens to resolve their own disputes in whatever way may suit them," court rejected malpractice claim against lawyer who used carefully drafted limited scope retainer agreement); Alaska Bar Ass'n Eth. Op. No. 93-1 (May 25, 1993) (lawyer may ethically limit scope of representation but must notify client clearly of limitations on representation and potential risks client is taking by not having full representation); Arizona State Bar Ass'n Eth. Op. 91-03 (Jan. 15, 1991) (lawyer may agree to represent client on limited basis as long as client consents after consultation and representation is not so limited in scope as to violate ethics rules); Colo. Bar Ass'n Ethics Comm. Formal Op. 101 (Jan. 17, 1998) (noting examples of "commonplace and traditional" arrangements under which clients ask their lawyers "to provide discrete legal services, rather than handle all aspects of the total project").

insureds even though their interests as defendants in that action were in conflict. Plaintiff brought this action to compel defendant to pay the substantial portion of the negligence-action judgment entered against her that exceeds the policy limit. We agree with the trial judge that defendant breached the policy by assigning a single firm of attorneys to represent insureds having conflicting interests. . . . Defendant's liability is limited to the portion of plaintiff's actual loss attributable to the breach.

On January 9, 1986, plaintiff's eleven-year-old son Heath accidently fired a BB from an air rifle that put out an eye of his playmate and neighbor Michael Heim. Plaintiff was divorced from Heath's father Ivan Wolpaw at the time and lived with Heath in the home of her sister Saranne Frew. Plaintiff, her sister and Heath were covered for the accident under a $50,000 homeowners' policy that defendant General Accident Insurance Company had issued to Frew. Michael and his parents brought an action for the ensuing damages against plaintiff, Heath, Frew, Ivan, the rifle's manufacturer, and the store where Ivan had purchased the rifle as a gift for his son. Defendant immediately deposited in court the $50,000 limit of its policy in offer of settlement. The Heims rejected the offer. A jury awarded the Heims damages totaling $502,000 after finding plaintiff 50% negligent, Ivan 30% negligent and Heath 20% negligent. The jury absolved the manufacturer and the store. The claims against Frew had been dismissed before trial on her motion for a partial summary judgment.

In this action, the trial judge held, on plaintiff's motion for summary judgment, that defendant had breached its policy by providing a single firm of at-

torneys to represent insureds having conflicting interests. . . .

A liability insurer that insures codefendants whose interests conflict with one another must retain separate and independent counsel for each insured or permit each insured to do so at the insurer's expense. That was the case here. The three insureds had the common interests of minimizing the amount of the Heims's judgment and maximizing the percentage of fault attributable to the other defendants. However, their interests in maximizing the percentage of the other insureds' fault and minimizing their own were clearly in conflict. For instance, it was in plaintiff's interest to argue that she adequately had secured the rifle from Heath's unattended use and had carefully instructed him in its safe use, which he negligently disregarded; on the other hand, it was in Heath's interest to argue that plaintiff negligently failed to secure the rifle, and that he was not negligent in view of his mother's negligence and his youth.

With the general abolition of parental immunity, and in the absence of sufficient liability insurance coverage, separate attorneys representing plaintiff and Heath might well have asserted cross-claims for contribution against the other's client. That was not done here. It was also in plaintiff's interest to assert a cross-claim against her sister and that she remain a codefendant to share the liability burden. Yet the single firm of attorneys, discharging its duty to her sister, not only did not file a cross-claim for contribution on plaintiff's behalf, but successfully moved to have Frew dismissed from the case. A trial is not necessary to determine the obvious. Defendant violated its contractual duty to provide plaintiff with counsel who were free of conflicting interests.

Where conflicting interests impose on a liability insurer the duty to provide multiple insureds with separate counsel, it may be that in a particular case the separate attorneys would manage the case the same way as one attorney representing all insureds. Even so, where there is the risk of a judgment that will exceed the policy limit, separate independent counsel for each insured must be employed to decide whether and how to act in light of the conflict.

A conflict that forms the basis of an insurer's breach, however, does not establish that compensatory damages are to be awarded against the insurer if the breach did not cause the insured an actual loss. . . .

Although it may not be certain that an injured party sustained damages from a breach, where the breach itself destroys the injured party's ability to prove damages with exactitude, the proof may be inexact. This tolerant approach has been applied to the proof of damages where, as here, a liability insurer breached its policy. . . .

. . . In such a case damages in a legal malpractice action can often be approximated by having the successor plaintiff's attorney recreate or create a defective or time-barred tort trial by conducting a "suit within a suit" in which the flawed attorney plays the role of the tort defendant. . . .

. . . Another option, which may be apposite in this case in light of the duality of defendants, the factor of role reversal, and the passage of time, is to proceed through the use of expert testimony as to what as a matter of reasonable probability would have transpired at the original trial. Such experts would testify, in light of their experience and expertise, concerning the outcome of the [malpractice case] if the case had been brought to trial as anticipated by [the attorney] and had been defended in the manner [the attorney] had initially planned. . . .

If the parties use experts to express opinions as to whether or as to how having separate counsel probably would have changed the Heim judgment, their opinions must be confined to changes in the allocation of fault among the three insureds. . . .

Thus, regardless of any reduction in the percentage share of plaintiff's fault, she would remain liable to the Heims for the full amount of their judgment unless but for defendant's breach the jury probably would have found that she was not at fault. Had plaintiff, if properly represented, been absolved of all fault then defendant would be liable to pay the whole judgment on her behalf—including the substantial excess over the policy limit. . . .

Anderson v. O'Brien

2005 Conn. Super. LEXIS 3365

CARMEN L. LOPEZ, Judge.

I. FACTS

. . . According to the allegations of the revised complaint, the plaintiff is an elderly, childless widow that was living alone in her home located in a desirable neighborhood of Guilford. Sometime in the year 2002, the O'Brien defendants (who are husband and wife) befriended her with the purpose of convincing her to sell them her home. The plaintiff had no desire to sell her home, as she had previously turned down offers to purchase her home by developers interested in developing a subdivision located to the west of the plaintiff's home. Her lack of desire to sell is evidenced by the fact that she never listed the property for sale.

The O'Briens continued in their efforts to buy the plaintiff's home and eventually included in their offer to purchase, an offer to build a cottage for the plaintiff on the property where she could live out her life and be treated as part of the family. The O'Briens agreed to assume all responsibility for the construction of the cottage. The O'Briens also arranged for their lawyer, the defendant Peter I. Manko, to represent the plaintiff in the real estate transaction.

On May 28, 2003, the plaintiff signed a real estate contract in which she agreed to sell the property to the O'Brien defendants. The contract called for a closing date of August 1, 2003. The contract was drafted by the defendant Manko. . . . On July 3, 2003, the O'Briens came to the plaintiff's home and told her they were picking her up to take her to the closing, which was scheduled for 5:00 that afternoon in Manko's office. The plaintiff was ill on that day and was not expecting to attend a closing.

When she arrived at Manko's office she inquired of both Manko and the O'Briens as to whether she should have her own attorney and she was reassured that Manko was a good lawyer and that he would take care of all of the parties, including the lender. According to the plaintiff, she did not read any of the closing documents that were placed before her,

nor were they read to her. Notwithstanding her concerns, she signed the documents. Although the contract contained a clause making reference to the plaintiff's right to remain on the property residing in the cottage, none of the closing documents referred to the plaintiff's life estate in the property.

The plaintiff further alleges that after the closing, the O'Briens changed their treatment of her. They were rude and cruel and kept all details of the construction of her cottage from her. She was constantly reminded that the property did not belong to her anymore but rather to the O'Briens. Although a structure was built for her, it was not a cottage, but rather a small barn like structure that could not accommodate her furnishings.

The plaintiff's revised complaint contains eleven counts. Counts one through six are against the O'Brien defendants and allege fraudulent representation, breach of contract and intentional or negligent infliction of emotional distress.

Counts seven through eleven are against the defendant Peter I. Manko. Count seven alleges legal malpractice, count eight alleges recklessness, count nine alleges fraudulent representation, count ten alleges that Manko violated [the Connecticut Unfair Trade Practices Act] (CUTPA) and count eleven alleges a breach of fiduciary duty by Manko. . . .

IV. DISCUSSION

A. The Eighth Count: Recklessness

In the eighth count of the complaint, entitled "Recklessness by the defendant Manko," the plaintiff restates the allegations contained in the seventh count, which is entitled

"Legal Malpractice by defendant Manko." According to the allegations of the seventh and eighth counts, the defendant Manko prepared a contract for the sale of the plaintiff's property to the O'Brien defendants. He prepared the contract on behalf of both the plaintiff and the O'Brien defendants. According to the allegations in the complaint, the representation of the plaintiff in this transaction created an attorney-client relationship between Manko and the plaintiff. As a result, Manko owed the plaintiff the duty to represent her with reasonable care and diligence.

The plaintiff also alleges, in this count, that Manko knew, or should have known, that the plaintiff, who was ill on the day of the closing, inquired about whether she should have separate counsel and was reassured that Manko could represent all of the parties. The closing of the sale of the plaintiff's property took place in Manko's office at about 5:00 in the afternoon, at least one month before the date specified in the contract. As a result, the plaintiff alleges that she was rushed into the closing.

Furthermore, the plaintiff alleges that Manko failed to inform the lender of her life estate thereby allowing the lender to have an interest in the property superior to hers. In addition, he did not prepare a deed subject to the plaintiff's life estate. As a result, the plaintiff's life estate was not recorded on the land records.

The plaintiff alleges that these facts state a claim for recklessness. Manko objects[,] stating that the facts as alleged merely support a claim for malpractice.

"While [courts] have attempted to draw definitional [distinctions] between the terms wilful, wanton or reckless, in practice the three terms

have been treated as meaning the same thing. . . . A wilful act is one done intentionally or with reckless disregard of the consequences of one's conduct."

After examining the alleged facts, and construing these facts in a light most favorable to the plaintiff, the court concludes that the plaintiff has pled a cause of action sounding in recklessness. The facts demonstrate that not only did Manko fail to exercise due care in the preparation of the legal documents on behalf of the plaintiff, but he also disregarded the consequences of his actions, as well as the rights of the plaintiff.

The allegations of the complaint go beyond asserting that an attorney's conduct fell below that of a reasonable attorney under the same circumstances. Here, the plaintiff, an elderly widow, was picked up at her home on the day of the closing by the buyers, who are clients of Manko. She did not know that the closing was to take place on that particular day since it was one month before the closing date that was designated in the contract. She was ill and it was late in the afternoon on the day of the closing. She questioned the appropriateness of proceeding with only one lawyer. The documents were not read to her before she signed them.

If these facts are proven at trial, they will establish something more than a failure to use the degree of care and skill which the ordinarily prudent attorney would use under similar circumstances. It will establish that this conduct took on the "aspect of highly unreasonable conduct, involving an extreme departure from ordinary care, in a situation where a high degree of danger is apparent. . . . It is at least clear . . . that such aggravated negligence must be more than any mere mistake resulting from inexperience, excitement, or confusion, and more than mere thoughtlessness or inadvertence, or simply inattention." . . .

B. The Tenth Count: CUTPA

In the tenth count, the plaintiff alleges the same facts as those alleged in counts seven and eight. In addition, in paragraph thirty of the tenth count, the plaintiff asserts that the "representation of seller, purchaser and mortgagee in the same real estate sales transaction impacts upon the entrepreneurial aspects of the practice of law."

As a result, Manko's conduct allegedly violates CUTPA/Connecticut Unfair Trade Practices Act, General Statutes §42-110a et seq.) in that it is (1) "unlawful, offends public policy as it has been established by . . . Rules of Professional Conduct, (2) immoral, unethical, oppressive or unscrupulous, or (3) causes substantial injury to consumers of legal services."

In the recent case of Anderson v. Schoenhorn 874 A.2d 798 (Conn. App. 2005) the Appellate court stated: "In general, CUTPA applies to attorney conduct, but only as to the entrepreneurial aspects of legal practice. . . . Professional negligence, or malpractice, does not fall under CUTPA. . . . Although many decisions made by attorneys eventually involve personal profit as a factor, but are not considered part of the entrepreneurial aspect of practicing law . . . the conduct of a law firm in obtaining business and negotiating fee contracts does fall within the ambit of entrepreneurial activities."

The facts in this case establish that the defendant Manko's conduct involves allegations which concern "obtaining business and negotiating fee contracts." This conduct must be tested against the "cigarette rule." "It is well settled that in determining whether a practice violates CUTPA we have adopted the criteria set out in the cigarette rule by the federal trade commission for determining when a practice is unfair: (1) Whether the practice, without necessarily having been previously considered unlawful, offends public policy as it has been established by statutes, the common law, or otherwise—in other words, it is within at least the penumbra of some common law, statutory, or other established concept of unfairness; (2) whether it is immoral, unethical, oppressive, or unscrupulous; (3) whether it causes substantial injury to consumers, [competitors or other businesspersons]. . . . All three criteria do not need to be satisfied to support a finding of unfairness. A practice may be unfair because of the degree to which it meets one of the criteria or because to a lesser extent it meets all three."

A careful review of the allegations contained in the tenth count in a manner most favorable to the plaintiff leads the court to conclude that the plaintiff has pled sufficient facts to state a cause of action under CUTPA.

If the facts as alleged are proven, the plaintiff will have established that Manko violated Rule 1.7 of the Rules of Professional Conduct. This in turn would satisfy the first prong of the cigarette rule which requires a determination of whether the practice offends public policy. In this court's opinion the Rules of Professional conduct are a judicially conceived public policy because "since October 1986, the conduct of attorneys has been regulated . . . by the Rules of Professional Conduct, which were approved by the judges of the Superior Court and which superseded the Code of Professional Responsibility."

Also, the Supreme Court has found clear statements of public policy in the Rules of Professional Conduct in other instances.

Regarding the second and third prongs of the cigarette rule, the court concludes that the allegations within the complaint, if proven, will establish that the conduct was unethical, (thereby satisfying the second prong) as well as a practice that caused substantial injury to consumers and to competitors alike.

C. The Eleventh Count: Breach of a Fiduciary Duty

Manko argues that the plaintiff has failed to allege sufficient facts to support a claim of a breach of a fiduciary duty. It is his position that the facts as alleged in the complaint do not implicate his honesty, loyalty or morality, which are the hallmarks of a fiduciary duty.

"Professional negligence alone, however, does not give rise automatically to a claim for breach of fiduciary duty. Although an attorney-client relationship imposes a fiduciary duty on the attorney; . . . not every instance of professional negligence results in a breach of that fiduciary duty. [A] fiduciary or confidential

relationship is characterized by a unique degree of trust and confidence between the parties, one of whom has superior knowledge, skill or expertise and is under a duty to represent the interests of the other. . . . Professional negligence implicates a duty of care, while breach of a fiduciary duty implicates a duty of loyalty and honesty."

The commentary to Rule 1.7 of the Rules of Professional Conduct states, in relevant part, that, "Loyalty is an essential element in the lawyer's relationship to a client." Here, the allegations include a claim that an elderly, and ill person was brought to Manko's office to sign a deed to her home. She was uncomfortable enough with the situation that she asked whether she should have her own attorney. Despite the plaintiff's expression of discomfort, Manko continued with the transaction, acting in the capacity of her attorney. He also presumably accepted the proceeds of the sale as her trustee.

As an attorney, Manko possessed a superior skill and expertise to those of the plaintiff. Pursuant to the Rules of Professional Conduct, he was under a duty of loyalty and trust to the plaintiff. The court concludes that the plaintiff has pled sufficient facts, as read in the light most favorable to the plaintiff, to support a claim of breach of a fiduciary duty.

Accordingly, the defendant's motion to strike counts eight, ten, and eleven of the plaintiff's revised complaint dated April 1, 2005, is hereby, denied.

A. v. B.

726 A.2d 924 (N.J. 1999)

POLLOCK, J.

This appeal presents the issue whether a law firm may disclose confidential information of one co-client to another co-client. Specifically, in this paternity action, the mother's former law firm, which contemporaneously represented the father and his wife in planning their estates, seeks to disclose the existence of the father's illegitimate child to the wife.

A law firm, Hill Wallack, . . . jointly represented the husband and wife in drafting wills in which they devised their respective estates to each other. The devises created the possibility that the other spouse's issue, whether legitimate or illegitimate, ultimately would acquire the decedent's property.

Unbeknown to Hill Wallack and the wife, the husband recently had fathered an illegitimate child. Before the execution of the wills, the child's mother retained Hill Wallack to institute this paternity action against the husband. Because of a clerical error, the firm's computer check did not reveal the conflict of interest inherent in its representation of the mother against the husband. On learning of the conflict, the firm withdrew from representation of the mother in the paternity action. Now, the firm wishes to disclose to the wife the fact that the husband has an illegitimate child. To prevent Hill Wallack from making that disclosure, the husband joined the firm as a third-party defendant in the paternity action. . . .

I . . .

In October 1997, the husband and wife retained Hill Wallack, a firm of approximately sixty lawyers, to assist them with planning their estates. On the commencement of the joint representation, the husband and wife each signed a letter captioned "Waiver of Conflict of Interest." In explaining the possible conflicts of interest, the letter recited that the effect of a testamentary transfer by one spouse to the other would permit the transferee to dispose of the property as he or she desired. The firm's letter also explained that information provided by one spouse could become available to the other. Although the letter did not contain an express waiver of the confidentiality of any such information, each spouse consented to and waived any conflicts arising from the firm's joint representation.

Unfortunately, the clerk who opened the firm's estate planning file misspelled the clients' surname. The misspelled name was entered in the computer program that the firm uses to discover possible conflicts of interest. The firm then prepared reciprocal wills and related documents with the names of the husband and wife correctly spelled.

In January 1998, before the husband and wife executed the estate planning documents, the mother coincidentally retained Hill Wallack to pursue a paternity claim against the husband. This time, when making its computer search for conflicts of interest, Hill Wallack spelled the husband's name correctly. Accordingly, the computer search did not reveal the existence of the firm's joint representation of the husband and wife. As a result, the estate planning department did not know that the family law department had instituted a paternity action for the mother. Similarly, the family law department did not know that the estate planning department was preparing estate plans for the husband and wife.

A lawyer from the firm's family law department wrote to the husband about the mother's paternity claim. The husband neither objected to the firm's representation of the mother nor alerted the firm to the conflict of interest. Instead, he retained Fox Rothschild to represent him in the paternity action. After initially denying paternity, he agreed to voluntary DNA testing, which revealed that he is the father. Negotiations over child support failed, and the mother instituted the present action.

After the mother filed the paternity action, the husband and wife executed their wills at the Hill Wallack office. The parties agree that in their wills, the husband and wife leave their respective residuary estates to each other. If the other spouse does not survive, the contingent beneficiaries are the testator's issue. The wife's will leaves her residuary estate to her husband, creating the possibility that her property ultimately may pass to his issue. Under N.J.S.A. 3C:1-2, :2-48, the term "issue" includes both legitimate and illegitimate children. When the wife executed her will, therefore, she did not know that the husband's illegitimate child ultimately may inherit her property.

The conflict of interest surfaced when Fox Rothschild, in response to Hill Wallack's request for disclosure of the husband's assets, informed the firm that it already possessed the requested information. Hill Wallack promptly informed the mother that it unknowingly was representing both the husband and the wife in an unrelated matter.

Hill Wallack immediately withdrew from representing the mother in the paternity action. It also instructed the estate planning department not to disclose any information about the husband's assets to the member of the firm who had been representing the mother. The firm then wrote to the husband stating that it believed it had an ethical obligation to disclose to the wife the existence, but not the identity, of his illegitimate child. Additionally, the firm stated that it was obligated to inform the wife "that her current estate plan may devise a portion of her assets through her spouse to that child." The firm suggested that the husband so inform his wife and stated that if he did not do so, it would. . . .

II

This appeal concerns the conflict between two fundamental obligations of lawyers: the duty of confidentiality, Rules of Professional Conduct (RPC) 1.6(a), and the duty to inform clients of material facts, RPC 1.4(b). The conflict arises from a law firm's joint representation of two clients whose interests initially were compatible, but now conflict.

Crucial to the attorney-client relationship is the attorney's obligation not to reveal confidential information learned in the course of representation. [The court cites Model Rule 1.6 (a).]

A lawyer's obligation to communicate to one client all information needed to make an informed decision qualifies the firm's duty to maintain the confidentiality of a co-client's information. [The Court cites Model Rule 1.4 (b).] In limited situations, moreover, an attorney is permitted or required to disclose confidential information. Hill Wallack argues that RPC 1.6 mandates, or at least permits, the firm to disclose to the wife the existence of the husband's illegitimate child. RPC 1.6(b) requires that a lawyer disclose "information relating to representation of a client" to the proper authorities if the lawyer "reasonably believes" that such disclosure is necessary to prevent the client "from committing a criminal, illegal or fraudulent act that the lawyer reasonably believes is likely to result in death or substantial bodily harm or substantial injury to the financial interest or property of another. . . ." Despite Hill Wallack's claim that RPC 1.6(b) applies, the facts do not justify mandatory disclosure. The possible inheritance of the wife's estate by the husband's illegitimate child is too remote to constitute "substantial injury to the financial interest or property of another" within the meaning of RPC 1.6(b).

By comparison, in limited circumstances RPC 1.6(c) permits a lawyer to disclose a confidential communication. RPC 1.6(c) permits, but does not require, a lawyer to reveal confidential information to the extent the lawyer reasonably believes necessary "to rectify the consequences of a client's criminal, illegal or fraudulent act in furtherance of which the lawyer's services had been used." Although RPC 1.6(c) does not define a "fraudulent act," the term takes on meaning from our construction of the word "fraud," found in the analogous

"crime or fraud" exception to the attorney-client privilege.

We likewise construe broadly the term "fraudulent act" within the meaning of RPC 1.6(c). So construed, the husband's deliberate omission of the existence of his illegitimate child constitutes a fraud on his wife. When discussing their respective estates with the firm, the husband and wife reasonably could expect that each would disclose information material to the distribution of their estates, including the existence of children who are contingent residuary beneficiaries. The husband breached that duty. Under the reciprocal wills, the existence of the husband's illegitimate child could affect the distribution of the wife's estate, if she predeceased him. Additionally, the husband's child support payments and other financial responsibilities owed to the illegitimate child could deplete that part of his estate that otherwise would pass to his wife.

In effect, the husband has used the law firm's services to defraud his wife in the preparation of her estate. . . .

Under RPC 1.6, the facts support disclosure to the wife. . . .

[T]he husband and wife signed letters captioned "Waiver of Conflict of Interest." These letters acknowledge that information provided by one client could become available to the other. The letters, however, stop short of explicitly authorizing the firm to disclose one spouse's confidential information to the other. Even in the absence of any such explicit authorization, the spirit of the letters supports the firm's decision to disclose to the wife the existence of the husband's illegitimate child.

Neither our research nor that of counsel has revealed a dispositive judicial decision from this or any other jurisdiction on the issue of disclosure of confidential information about one client to a co-client. Persuasive secondary authority, however, supports the conclusion that the firm may disclose to the wife the existence of the husband's child.

The . . . Restatement of The Law Governing Lawyers §[60] comment l ("the Restatement") suggests, for example, that if the attorney and the co-clients have reached a prior, explicit agreement concerning the sharing of confidential information, that agreement controls whether the attorney should disclose the confidential information of one co-client to another.

As the preceding authorities suggest, an attorney, on commencing joint representation of co-clients, should agree explicitly with the clients on the sharing of confidential information. In such a "disclosure agreement," the co-clients can agree that any confidential information concerning one co-client, whether obtained from a co-client himself or herself or from another source, will be shared with the other co-client. Similarly, the co-clients can agree that unilateral confidences or other confidential information will be kept confidential by the attorney. Such a prior agreement will clarify the expectations of the clients and the lawyer and diminish the need for future litigation.

In the absence of an agreement to share confidential information with co-clients, the Restatement reposes the resolution of the lawyer's competing duties within the lawyer's discretion:

> [T]he lawyer, after consideration of all relevant circumstances, has the . . . discretion to inform the affected

co-client of the specific communication if, in the lawyer's reasonable judgment, the immediacy and magnitude of the risk to the affected co-client outweigh the interest of the communicating client in continued secrecy. [Restatement (Third) The Law Governing Lawyers §[60], comment l.]

Additionally, the Restatement advises that the lawyer, when withdrawing from representation of the co-clients, may inform the affected co-client that the attorney has learned of information adversely affecting that client's interests that the communicating co-client refuses to permit the lawyer to disclose.

In the context of estate planning, the Restatement also suggests that a lawyer's disclosure of confidential information communicated by one spouse is appropriate only if the other spouse's failure to learn of the information would be materially detrimental to that other spouse or frustrate the spouse's intended testamentary arrangement. The Restatement provides two analogous illustrations in which a lawyer has been jointly retained by a husband and wife to prepare reciprocal wills. The first illustration states:

> Lawyer has been retained by Husband and Wife to prepare wills pursuant to an arrangement under which each spouse agrees to leave most of their property to the other. Shortly after the wills are executed, Husband (unknown to Wife) asks Lawyer to prepare an inter vivos trust for an illegitimate child whose existence Husband has kept secret from Wife for many years and about whom Husband had not previously informed Lawyer. Husband states that Wife would be distraught at learning of Husband's infidelity and of Husband's years of

silence and that disclosure of the information could destroy their marriage. Husband directs Lawyer not to inform Wife. The inter vivos trust that Husband proposes to create would not materially affect Wife's own estate plan or her expected receipt of property under Husband's will, because Husband proposes to use property designated in Husband's will for a personally favored charity. In view of the lack of material effect on Wife, Lawyer may assist Husband to establish and fund the inter vivos trust and refrain from disclosing Husband's information to Wife. . . .

The other illustration states:

Same facts as [the prior Illustration], except that Husband's proposed inter vivos trust would significantly deplete Husband's estate, to Wife's material detriment and in frustration of the Spouses' intended testamentary arrangements. If Husband will neither inform Wife nor permit Lawyer to do so, Lawyer must withdraw from representing both Husband and Wife. In the light of all relevant circumstances, Lawyer may exercise discretion whether to inform Wife either that circumstances, which Lawyer has been asked not to reveal, indicate that she should revoke her recent will or to inform Wife of some or all the details of the information that Husband has recently provided so that Wife may protect her interests. Alternatively, Lawyer may inform Wife only that Lawyer is withdrawing because Husband will not permit disclosure of information that Lawyer has learned from Husband. . . .

The Professional Ethics Committees of New York and Florida, however, have concluded that disclosure to a co-client is prohibited. N.Y. St. Bar Assn. Comm. on Prof. Ethics, Op. 555 (1984); Fla. St. Bar Assn. Comm. on Prof. Ethics, Op. 95-4 (1997).

The New York opinion addressed the following situation:

A and B formed a partnership and employed Lawyer L to represent them in connection with the partnership affairs. Subsequently, B, in a conversation with Lawyer L, advised Lawyer L that he was actively breaching the partnership agreement. B preceded this statement to Lawyer L with the statement that he proposed to tell Lawyer L something "in confidence." Lawyer L did not respond to that statement and did not understand that B intended to make a statement that would be of importance to A but that was to be kept confidential from A. Lawyer L had not, prior thereto, advised A or B that he could not receive from one communications regarding the subject of the joint representation that would be confidential from the other. B has subsequently declined to tell A what he has told Lawyer L.

In that situation, the New York Ethics Committee concluded that the lawyer may not disclose to the co-client the communicating client's statement. The Committee based its conclusion on the absence of prior consent by the clients to the sharing of all confidential communications and the fact that the client "specifically in advance designated his communication as confidential, and the lawyer did not demur."

The Florida Ethics Committee addressed a similar situation:

Lawyer has represented Husband and Wife for many years in a range of personal matters, including estate planning. Husband and Wife have substantial individual assets, and they also own substantial jointly-held property. Recently, Lawyer prepared new updated wills that Husband and Wife signed. Like their previous wills, their new wills primarily benefit the survivor of them for his or her life, with beneficial disposition at the death of the survivor being made equally to their children. . . .

Several months after the execution of the new wills, Husband confers separately with Lawyer. Husband reveals to Lawyer that he has just executed a codicil (prepared by another law firm) that makes substantial beneficial disposition to a woman with whom Husband has been having an extra-marital relationship.

Reasoning that the lawyer's duty of confidentiality takes precedence over the duty to communicate all relevant information to a client, the Florida Ethics Committee concluded that the lawyer did not have discretion to reveal the information. In support of that conclusion, the Florida committee reasoned that joint clients do not necessarily expect that everything relating to the joint representation communicated by one co-client will be shared with the other co-client.

In several material respects, however, the present appeal differs from the hypothetical cases considered by the New York and Florida committees. Most significantly, the New York and Florida disciplinary rules, unlike RPC 1.6, do not except disclosure needed "to rectify the consequences of a client's . . . fraudulent act in the furtherance of which the lawyer's services had been used." RPC 1.6(c). Second, Hill Wallack learned of the husband's paternity from a third party, not from the husband himself. Thus, the husband did not communicate anything to the law firm with the expectation that the communication would be kept confidential. Finally, the husband and wife, unlike the co-clients considered by the New York and Florida Committees, signed an agreement suggesting their intent to share all information with each other.

Because Hill Wallack wishes to make the disclosure, we need not reach the issue whether the lawyer's obligation to disclose is discretionary or mandatory. In conclusion, Hill Wallack may inform the wife of the existence of the husband's illegitimate child.

▪ Practice Pointers:
Written Consents to Conflicts of Interest

The lawyers involved in *A. v. B.* provided their clients with a written waiver of the conflicts of interest. Until recently, only three jurisdictions (California, Washington, and Wisconsin) required a written documentation of the client's informed consent to a conflict. In the last chapter, the Washington Supreme Court found that Halverson violated this rule by not obtaining a written waiver before embarking on a sexual relationship with his client. Today, Model Rules 1.7, 1.9, 1.10, 1.11, and 1.12 require that "each affected client gives informed consent, confirmed in writing."[1] Comment [20] to Rule 1.7 emphasizes that the writing is just part of the informed consent process:

> Such a writing may consist of a document executed by the client or one that the lawyer promptly records and transmits to the client following an oral consent. . . .
> The requirement of a writing does not supplant the need in most cases for the

---

1. Model Rule 1.7(b)(4). MR 1.8(a) and (g) further require that the client sign the writing.

lawyer to talk with the client, to explain the risks and advantages, if any, of representation burdened with a conflict of interest, as well as reasonably available alternatives, and to afford the client a reasonable opportunity to consider the risks and alternatives and to raise questions and concerns. Rather, the writing is required in order to impress upon clients the seriousness of the decision the client is being asked to make and to avoid disputes or ambiguities that might later occur in the absence of a writing.

The move to require written waivers parallels the evolution of other conflicts rules that have come to require written waivers, such as business deals with clients. Earlier versions of this rule, such as the one that governed the lawyer's conduct in *Monco v. Janus*, required informed consent of a client, but did not require a writing to memorialize either the lawyer's disclosures or the client's agreement. To prevent similar misunderstandings and to clarify that the burden is on the lawyer to obtain an informed consent, Model Rule 1.8(a) now includes a specific writing requirement.

The content of disclosure rules about business transactions with clients also has grown more specific over time because of repeated problems with old rules that did not offer clients enough information to assess the conflict realistically. Other recurring conflicts have generated similar attempts to articulate the information that clients need to control and monitor the representation. For example, some jurisdictions have adopted the ABA's model rule that requires lawyers to disclose in writing whether they carry malpractice insurance, a potential personal conflict of interest.[2] Florida and Ohio also have mandated that insurance defense lawyers present policyholders with written document entitled "Statement of Insured Client's Rights," intended to explain the conflicts of interest inherent in the three-way relationship between the insurer, the lawyer, and the policyholder.[3] The required statement addresses several important issues, including selection and direction of the lawyer, fees and costs, litigation guidelines, confidentiality, conflicts of interest, settlement, risk of judgment beyond policy limits, and how to report violations.

In most cases, however, a lawyer will be called on to draft an individualized consent to a conflict of interest. What should a written waiver look like? The Model Rule definition of "confirmed in writing"[4] does not require the client's signature or any specific language, but does require confirmation in a written document of "informed consent," or agreement of a client "after the lawyer has communicated adequate information and explanation about the material risks of and reasonably available alternatives to the proposed course of conduct."[5] If the writing is to reflect what actually occurred between lawyer and client, it should document the information the lawyer gave the client as well as the lawyer's explanation of risks and alternatives.[6]

---

2. *E.g.,* Alaska R. Prof. Conduct 1.4(c) (2007), N.H. R. Prof. Conduct 1.19 (2008), Ohio R. Prof. Conduct 1.4(c) (2007) S.D. R. Prof. Conduct 1.4(c) (2004).
3. *See* Amendments to R. Regulating the Fla. Bar, 820 So. 2d 210 (Fla. 2002) (Rule 1.8(j)); Ohio R. Prof. Conduct 1.8(f)(4) (2007).
4. MR 1.0(b).
5. MR 1.0(e).
6. *See* Lawyers and Other Professionals: Informed Consent, *supra* p. 80.

The lawyers in *A. v. B.* attempted to do just that. But the case illustrates how difficult it is for lawyers to foresee situations that will ripen into conflicts. The law firm in *A. v. B.* recognized that confidentiality might be an issue but failed to articulate an explicit authorization to disclose in the written retainer agreement. Ultimately, the court agreed that the waiver was not effective, because it did not adequately allow the clients to understand the material risks of the waiver or the alternatives to such an agreement. In retrospect, this might seem like a relatively easy case, because it involved a common kind of joint representation, where lawyers would have experience with typical conflicts that develop. Far more difficult are general, blanket, or open-ended advanced conflicts waivers that attempt to allow a law firm to represent future, unspecified, or undefined interests. Here, the lack of client understanding about material risks and alternatives will likely render any waiver ineffective.[7]

Taken together, the cases in this section illustrate that a written confirmation of informed consent should include at least three categories of information.

1. The material risks of the proposed course of conduct, including:
   - Conflicts created by the legal rights of the represented parties (such as the legal effect of one spouse's will on the other spouse's children);
   - Conflict created by the individual facts in each representation (such as the fact that one spouse has a child out of wedlock); and
   - Any prior or continuing relationship of the lawyer with either party.
2. The duty of confidentiality to clients, including:[8]
   - Full disclosure of all information shared by any client with the lawyer to all other clients; or
   - Limited disclosure of information shared by one client with the lawyer to the others; and
   - Explanation of the effect of the joint representation on the attorney-client privilege.[9]
3. Explanation about the advantages and disadvantages of the available alternatives to joint representation, including:
   - Representation by separate lawyers, or representation of one client alone;
   - Differences in the lawyer's role in individual and joint representations, such as the fact that joint representations will require each client to assume greater responsibility for making decisions than might be the case if a lawyer were to individually advocate on their behalf;[10]
   - The clients' rights to discharge the lawyer at any time;
   - Changes in the legal rights or individual situations of the clients that might require the lawyer to withdraw; and
   - An explanation of what will happen if the representation ends before the legal service is completed. Absent explicit and still effective consent to the contrary, the lawyer probably will be required to withdraw

---

7. MR 1.7, Comment [22].
8. *See* MR 1.7, Comment [31].
9. *See* MR 1.7, Comment [30].
10. *See* MR 1.7, Comment [32].

from both or all of the representations, causing additional expense and effort.[11]

Although drafting a conflicts waiver that canvasses all of this information may seem daunting, lawyers in jurisdictions like California indicate that the writing requirement benefits both clients and lawyers. Clients benefit because a written document provides the client with a continual specific reminder of the nature of the conflict, which allows the client to monitor and control the ongoing course of the lawyer's service. Lawyers benefit because articulating the nature of the conflict in writing prods them to be diligent in recognizing, articulating, and responding to conflicts and further gives them protection when a client decides to proceed with the representation. Think, for example, of how such a properly prepared writing would have reminded the clients in *Anderson v. O'Brien* or *A. v. B.* about the nature of the alternatives and risks if they had agreed to accept them.

Now recall *Halverson*. Can you envision the written informed consent the court said might legitimate some sexual relationships with clients? If not, the conflict probably is nonconsentable, as many jurisdictions (including Washington) have now concluded.[12] Attempting to draft a written waiver affords lawyers an opportunity to assess whether a conflict can be the subject of adequate informed consent. If the lawyers in *Halversen and Wolpaw* had attempted such an exercise, perhaps they (and their clients) would have been spared significant additional litigation.

3. Simultaneous Representation of Adversaries

Problems

9-9. Viacom and Disney are both competing for an open TV channel in New York.
   (a) Can Martyn represent Viacom while Fox represents Disney if each lawyer seeks his or her client's consent?
   (b) What if Martyn & Fox lawyers feel comfortable taking on the representation of both?
   (c) If Martyn & Fox already represents Viacom in another unrelated matter, can we take on representation of Disney?

9-10. Local Municipality filed a motion to disqualify Martyn & Fox, claiming that Martyn & Fox cannot represent a developer in an appeal from a zoning decision because we currently represent local Municipality on some tax collection matters. Martyn, who is handling the zoning appeal, distinctly recalls chatting with the City Solicitor and getting a waiver. Is Martyn & Fox safe?

9-11. Martyn & Fox has been retained by Magnum Industries to defend a products liability action. In-house counsel for Magnum tells Fox that the case is "routine," but she wants to know what to do about

---

11. *See* MR 1.7, Comment [29].
12. Wash. R. Prof. Conduct 1.8 (j) (2007).

the fact that plaintiff's counsel works for a law firm that regularly represents Forest Products, Inc., a wholly owned Magnum subsidiary. Does it make any difference whether Forest Products is a partially owned subsidiary?

Consider: Model Rules 1.7, Comment [34]; 1.10, 1.13
              Model Code DR 5-105
              RLGL §§97, 121, Comment d, 122, 128

Eastman Kodak Company v. Sony Corporation

2004 U.S. Dist. LEXIS 29883 (W.D.N.Y.)

JONATHAN W. FELDMAN, United States Magistrate Judge.

DECISION AND ORDER

Preliminary Statement

Sometimes a case will present an issue that requires a court to choose between the lesser of two unfair results. This is one of those cases.

Relevant Facts

Founded in Rochester, Eastman Kodak Company (hereinafter Kodak) is the area's largest private employer. Kodak's important and widespread presence in our community inevitably results in the company becoming involved in a myriad of court proceedings in both state and federal courts. These lawsuits run the gamut, from intellectual property cases, to contract actions, to employment discrimination claims. Woods Oviatt Gilman, LLP (hereinafter Woods Oviatt) is one of Rochester's oldest law firms and has an active litigation practice in both state and federal courts. Woods Oviatt's business model intentionally seeks to avoid having Kodak as a client. This business decision has obvious benefits to Woods Oviatt, as it allows the firm to attract and represent clients who may have interests adverse to Kodak, without offending conflict of interest rules associated with the practice of law. The instant dispute pays tribute to the difficult conflict problem created when an otherwise legitimate corporate acquisition by Kodak results in Kodak becoming an uninvited client of Woods Oviatt.

For several years, Woods Oviatt has represented Heidelberg Digital LLC (hereinafter Heidelberg).[1] Indeed, Heidelberg chose Woods Oviatt as their counsel because, among other things, the law firm could represent Heidelberg in its business dealings with Kodak. Among the many matters Woods Oviatt handled for Heidelberg were two employment discrimination lawsuits, one pending in this Court

---

1. Woods Oviatt began representing Heidelberg in 1999, shortly after the company was formed. Heidelberg came into existence when its parent company, Heidelberger Druckmaschinen AG ("Druckmaschinen"), acquired Kodak's black and white printing business. Since that time, Woods Oviatt has represented Heidelberg in a variety of matters, including a major construction financing project, an intellectual property dispute, an environmental matter, and employment discrimination cases.

(Jackson v. Heidelberg) and the other pending in New York State Supreme Court (McEwen v. Heidelberg). The Jackson case has proceeded through discovery and defendant's summary judgment motion is now pending before the Court. In McEwen, New York State Supreme Court Justice Evelyn Frazee has ordered the parties to complete all discovery by January 31, 2005 and file a note of issue by February 15, 2005. Both the Jackson and McEwen cases have been actively litigated by Woods Oviatt on behalf of Heidelberg for several years.

In May 1, 2004 Kodak acquired Heidelberg. There is no dispute that Woods Oviatt was aware of the Kodak-Heidelberg transaction before it occurred. On April 1, 2004, a month before the acquisition closed, Woods Oviatt attorney Andrew J. Ryan, Esq. submitted an affidavit in the Jackson case which confirmed the expectation that Kodak was going to purchase Heidelberg on May 1, 2004. . . . Woods Oviatt also performed legal work for Heidelberg in furtherance of the transaction, although the firm describes their involvement as "peripheral" and limited to "some minor housekeeping matters." In addition, during the pre-closing "due diligence" process, Woods Oviatt maintained Heidelberg's records at their office for Kodak representatives to review. Following Kodak's acquisition of Heidelberg, Woods Oviatt continued to act as defense counsel in the Jackson and McEwen cases and continued to bill for legal services rendered in those cases.[3]

In July 2004, William G. Bauer, a partner at Woods Oviatt, entered an appearance as local counsel in two separate cases currently pending in this Court. In both cases Kodak is the opposing litigant. One of the cases (Kodak v. Sony Corporation) is a patent infringement suit. The other (Employees Committed for Justice ("ECJ") v. Kodak) is a class action complaint alleging, *inter alia*, that "Kodak has engaged in an ongoing pattern and practice of discrimination against its African-American employees." According to Kodak, Ms. McEwen is a putative member of the potential class in the ECJ v. Kodak case.

After the May acquisition of Heidelberg, Kodak's legal department assumed responsibility for all litigation matters involving Heidelberg. In June or July 2004, W. Stephen Tierney, a partner in Woods Oviatt, called Joseph Leverone, an in-house attorney with Heidelberg, to ascertain "what role, if any, Heidelberg wanted [Woods Oviatt] to play in the pending discrimination cases going forward." Tierney did not receive a reply to his phone messages and on August 2, 2004, he sent an e-mail to Heidelberg asking whether "we should continue to work on the [litigation] files, now that [Kodak] has acquired [Heidelberg]."

A week later, on August 9, 2004, Gary Van Graafeiland, General Counsel and Senior Vice President of Kodak, wrote to James P. McElheny, the Managing Partner of Woods Oviatt, stating that Kodak had "recently learned" that Bauer was "representing

---

3. On August 16, 2004, Woods Oviatt filed a motion to withdraw from further representation of Heidelberg in the Jackson case. It has also, consistent with direction from Kodak and its own ethical obligations, continued to prosecute the summary judgment motion and filed Reply papers as recently as November 9, 2004.

clients with interests adverse to those of Kodak" in the ECJ v. Kodak and Sony v. Kodak cases. Because Kodak had acquired Heidelberg, and Woods Oviatt continued to represent Heidelberg in litigation, Van Graafeiland requested that "your firm [Woods Oviatt] remove this conflict of interest by withdrawing from the representation of the plaintiffs in the ECJ action and the defendants in the Sony action." By letter dated August 13, 2004, McElheny responded, asserting that "Heidelberg is our client" and therefore, Woods Oviatt does "not believe the Code of Professional Responsibility is implicated." However, in order to alleviate Kodak's ethical "concerns," McElheny informed Van Graafeiland that Woods Oviatt would withdraw from further representation of Heidelberg in the Jackson and McEwen cases.

By letter dated August 20, 2004, Van Graafeiland responded to McElheny's August 13, 2004 letter. Van Graafeiland rejected Woods Oviatt's request to withdraw from the Jackson and McEwen cases as "not acceptable" because it would cause "substantial prejudice to Heidelberg and Kodak, given the firm's long-term representations in those cases and the level of activity therein." The instant motions to disqualify Woods Oviatt from acting as local counsel in the Sony v. Kodak and ECJ v. Kodak cases followed.

Discussion

Is Kodak a Current Client of Woods Oviatt? The first issue to be addressed is whether Kodak's acquisition of Heidelberg transformed them into one and the same "client" for conflict purposes. Resolution of this initial issue is critical because if the two entities are to be treated as a single client, then under the Code of Professional Responsibility, Woods Oviatt's representation of ECJ and Sony as local counsel is *"prima facie* improper." Cinema 5, Ltd. v. Cinerama, Inc., 528 F.2d 1384, 1387 (2d Cir. 1976).

Determining the existence and nature of conflicts in the context of "corporate families" and the appropriate remedy upon the finding of a conflict can be a difficult and complicated undertaking. The relevant inquiry centers on whether the corporate relationship between the two corporate family members is "so close as to deem them a single entity for conflict of interest purposes." Discotrade Ltd. v. Wyeth-Ayerst International, Inc., 200 F. Supp. 2d 355, 358 (S.D.N.Y. 2002). See JPMorgan Chase Bank v. Liberty Mutual Insurance Co., 189 F. Supp. 2d 20, 21 (S.D.N.Y. 2002) (conflict found where, even though corporations may not be "alter egos" of one another, their relationship was "extremely close and interdependent, both financially and in terms of direction").

The evidence of a "close and interdependent relationship" between Kodak and Heidelberg is compelling here. The Kodak-Heidelberg transaction was neither a merger of equals, nor an attenuated corporate affiliation. Rather, Kodak essentially swallowed Heidelberg. Heidelberg is now wholly owned by Kodak. Heidelberg's "one person" Board of Directors is a Senior Vice President of Kodak. Three-fourths of Heidelberg's eight corporate officers are Kodak employees. After the acquisition, Heidelberg's technology system was integrated with Kodak's. Significantly, Heidelberg shares Kodak's legal department. Indeed, Kodak's

Legal Division has direct supervisory responsibility over both the McEwen and Jackson cases. *See* Hartford Accident and Indemnity Co. v. RJR Nabisco, Inc., 721 F. Supp. 534, 540 (S.D.N.Y. 1989) ("If the parent and subsidiary were in fact distinct and separate entities for representation purposes, then there would have been no need for the parent's general counsel to have retained this supervisory role."). Heidelberg is unquestionably intertwined with Kodak, both in terms of corporate ownership and business management.[6] Hence, for conflict purposes, Kodak and its wholly owned and operationally integrated subsidiary, Heidelberg, are the same client. *See* Stratagem Development Corp. v. Heron International N.V., 756 F. Supp. 789, 792 (S.D.N.Y. 1991) (where "the liabilities of a [wholly owned] subsidiary corporation directly affect the bottom line of the corporate parent," law firm could not simultaneously represent both in adverse actions).

Is There a Conflict? Because Kodak and Heidelberg's post-acquisition relationship constitutes a single client for conflict purposes, the applicable conflict analysis is the more exacting "*prima facie* conflict" standard. . . . "The more stringent alternative, known somewhat misleadingly as the '*per se*' rule, pertains to situations where a law firm undertakes to represent two adverse parties, both of which are 'clients in the traditional sense,' and the relationship between

the firm and the clients is continuing." University of Rochester, 2000 U.S. Dist. LEXIS 19030. The more stringent test is warranted because the propriety of the lawyer's conduct "must be measured not so much against the similarities in litigation, as against the duty of undivided loyalty which an attorney owes to each of his clients." *Cinema 5, Ltd.*, 528 F.2d at 1386. "Under the Code [of Professional Responsibility], the lawyer who would sue his own client, asserting in justification the lack of 'substantial relationship' between the litigation and the work he has undertaken to perform for that client, is leaning on a slender reed indeed."

Under the foregoing analysis, there is little doubt that a *prima facie* conflict exists here. By accepting employment as local counsel in the Sony v. Kodak and ECJ v. Kodak cases, Woods Oviatt essentially agreed to participate in two lawsuits in which an existing client (Kodak) is an adverse party. Because such concurrent representation could weaken Woods Oviatt's fiduciary and fundamental duty of undivided loyalty owed to Kodak, it is "*prima facie* improper." Moreover, the concurrent representation is *prima facie* improper, irrespective of any substantial relationship among or between the various state and federal cases.

Does the Conflict Require Disqualification? A finding that Woods Oviatt is simultaneously representing adverse parties does not end the disqualification analysis." . . . The

---

6. A review of Heidelberg's post-acquisition website (*http://www.nexpress.com*) only confirms the close family relationship of the two companies, as well as their integrated business operations and interests. The website describes NexPress as "a Kodak company headquartered in Rochester, New York." The company's web page "logo" includes the following description: "NexPress: A Kodak Company."

decision of whether to grant a motion to disqualify is within the discretion of the Court and the movant bears the burden of demonstrating that disqualification is warranted. However, once the doctrine of concurrent representation is held to apply, the burden of avoiding disqualification shifts to the lawyer to either (1) obtain consent from the client or (2) "show at the very least, that there will be no actual or apparent conflict in loyalties or diminution in the vigor of his representation."

Kodak obviously does not consent here, thus Woods Oviatt bears the burden of demonstrating that there will be no actual or apparent conflict in their duty of undivided loyalty owed to Kodak. Aside from proposing that Kodak should, in fairness, waive the conflict, the firm does not argue that it could realistically be Kodak's zealous advocate and champion in defending Kodak's wholly owned subsidiary against employment discrimination charges in federal court, while simultaneously representing a plaintiff suing Kodak on employment discrimination charges in the same federal court. . . . [I]t is difficult to imagine a clearer conflict of interest or an appearance of divided loyalties. And because the stricter "prima facie" test applies to concurrent representation situations, Woods Oviatt's defense of Kodak in the Heidelberg discrimination suits while at the same time defending Sony, Kodak's adversary in the patent case, is similarly problematic, even without factual or legal similarities in the two actions. Put simply, without Kodak's consent, it is ethically impermissible for Woods Oviatt to have a wholly owned and integrated subsidiary of Kodak as a client and simultaneously represent Kodak's adversaries in pending litigation in state and federal court. Case law clearly supports this conclusion.

What Is the Appropriate Remedy?
The foregoing is really a prelude to the crux of the present dispute—what client should Woods Oviatt be disqualified from representing? Kodak contends that given the advanced stages of the Jackson and McEwen litigation, Kodak would be severely prejudiced if Woods Oviatt were to withdraw from either case at this late date. Invoking the so-called "hot potato" principle, Kodak argues that the only ethically acceptable remedy is for the Court to disqualify Woods Oviatt from representing Sony and ECJ. Under the hot potato principle,

> an attorney cannot avoid disqualification under the *Cinema 5* rule merely by "firing" the disfavored client, dropping the client like a hot potato, and transforming a continuing relationship to a former relationship by way of client abandonment. Indeed, the offense inherent in taking on the conflicting representation is compounded by seeking to "fire" the client in pursuit of the attorney's interest in taking on a new, more attractive representation. If, as one judge has written, "the act of suing one's client is a 'dramatic form of disloyalty,'" what might be said of trying to drop the first client in an effort to free the attorney to pursue his or her self-interest in taking on a newer and more attractive professional engagement?

Universal City Studios, Inc. v. Reimerdes, 98 F. Supp. 2d 449, 453 (S.D.N.Y. 2000) *See* Stratagem Development Corp., 756 F. Supp. at 794 (absent consent, "a firm is to remain with the client in the already-existing litigation and seek new counsel to represent the other, not vice-versa").

Woods Oviatt counters that if Kodak's purchase of Heidelberg made

Kodak an uninvited client of their firm, the firm should be permitted to simply withdraw from the Jackson and McEwen cases and continue as local counsel for clients adverse to Kodak in the Kodak v. Sony and ECJ v. Kodak cases. Woods Oviatt points to its longstanding policy of not representing Kodak and argues that the conflict predicament the firm finds itself in was not due to any action on their part, but was created solely by Kodak purchasing their long-time client. Lawyers for Sony and ECJ also appeared before this Court and argued that their clients would be prejudiced if Woods Oviatt, and in particular William Bauer, Esq., were not able to be their local counsel. Based on the foregoing, Woods Oviatt urges the Court not to automatically apply the "hot potato rule". Instead, the firm advocates taking a more "flexible approach" to attorney disqualification where the conflict arises solely due to the business activities of the client. The rationale for the "flexible approach" to disqualification issues was described by the court in Gould, Inc. v. Mitsui Mining and Smelting Co., 738 F.Supp. 1121, 1126 (N.D. Ohio 1990):

> The explosion of merger activity by corporations during the past fifteen years, and the corresponding increase in the possibility that attorney conflicts of interest may arise unexpectedly, make it appropriate for a court to adopt a perspective about the disqualification of counsel in ongoing litigation that conforms to the problem. This means taking a less mechanical approach to the problem, balancing the various interests. The result is that the courts are less likely to order disqualification and more likely to use other, more tailored measures to protect the interests of the public and the parties.

In *Gould*, a conflict arose when several years after litigation had commenced, the defendant acquired a company that plaintiff's counsel represented in unrelated matters. The court held that although plaintiff's counsel ... represent[ed] conflicting interests, disqualification pursuant to the "hot potato" rule would not be mechanically applied, but rather would be subject to a balancing of competing factors. The relevant factors include: (1) prejudice to the parties, including whether confidential information has been conveyed, (2) costs and inconvenience to the party being required to obtain new counsel, (3) the complexity of the various litigations, and (4) the origin of the conflict. After analyzing the factors, the Court in *Gould* gave the law firm the right to choose which client it wanted to represent and which it wanted to drop. . . .

This court agrees that the "flexible approach" provides a far more practical framework to disqualification issues generated by mergers and acquisitions than the rigid "hot potato rule," but under either analytical model Woods Oviatt's continued representation of Sony or ECJ is ethically problematic. Indeed, most, if not all, of the *Gould* factors favor the disqualification position urged by Kodak.

First, there is no dispute that in purchasing Heidelberg, Kodak's labor department has assumed supervisory responsibility over both the McEwen and the Jackson cases. While Kodak does not refer to any specific confidential information that has been disclosed to Woods Oviatt since the acquisition, given the factual and legal overlap of McEwen and the allegations of race discrimination in ECJ, Kodak's concern is justified. For example, an internal Kodak study of wage and promotion disparity for African-American employees is relied upon by Woods Oviatt's clients in the ECJ complaint. The same Kodak document has been demanded by Woods Oviatt in their defense of Heidelberg in the McEwen action. Moreover, it appears (and is not disputed by Woods Oviatt) that Ms. McEwen is a potential class member in the ECJ v. Kodak case. Allowing Woods Oviatt to assume representation of Ms. McEwen as a member of a class suing Kodak for race discrimination, after having defended Kodak's wholly owned subsidiary on charges of race discrimination filed by Ms. McEwen in which she claims both Heidelberg and Kodak discriminated against her, clearly suggests conflicted loyalties and thus weighs against allowing Woods Oviatt's choice of clients.

The second and third *Gould* factors, the cost and inconvenience of obtaining new counsel in light of the complexity of the litigations involved, also tip in Kodak's favor. The prejudice to Kodak in having to find new counsel to assume the defense of Heidelberg in the Jackson and McEwen cases is not insignificant. In McEwen, Judge Frazee's scheduling order requires Woods Oviatt to complete all discovery by January 31, 2005 and file a note of issue two weeks thereafter. In Jackson, Woods Oviatt has filed and briefed a summary judgment motion now pending before this Court. Allowing Woods Oviatt to drop the Jackson and McEwen cases at this point and forcing Kodak to locate new counsel willing

and able to assume representation at crucial junctures in both these cases creates a real potential for prejudice to the client. Kodak complains that if Woods Oviatt is permitted to drop the Heidelberg cases, it may unduly delay the ongoing litigation and increase their legal fees as new counsel gets "up to speed" on each case. Finally, while the complexity of the Sony and ECJ cases would appear to be substantial, the gravity of this factor is offset by the fact that both the Sony and ECJ cases are in the very early stages of litigation and capable lead counsel for both clients would remain in the cases, even if Woods Oviatt were disqualified.

The final *Gould* factor is the origin of the conflict, that is, which party created the conflict? In *Gould*, as in this case, as a result of an acquisition, a law firm found itself representing a subsidiary in one litigated matter, while simultaneously suing the subsidiary's parent in an unrelated matter. In allowing the law firm to choose which client to continue to represent, the *Gould* court emphasized that the creation of the conflict was not due to any "affirmative act" of the law firm. Rather, the conflict spawned the moment the acquisition was consummated, as it was not until that point that the law firm represented conflicting interests.

Here, however, it was Woods Oviatt's decisions to act as local counsel for Sony and ECJ, decisions the firm made with full knowledge of Kodak's intent to acquire their client, Heidelberg, that created the relevant conflicts.[9] In sum, *Gould* is factually

---

9. Woods Oviatt refers the Court to two other clients (Marie Long and Canon U.S.A.) who have or had interests adverse to Kodak at the time of Kodak's acquisition of Heidelberg. Woods Oviatt argues that Kodak's position would require the firm to "abandon" these clients as well. However,

distinguishable from the instant case because here, Woods Oviatt accepted clients with interests adverse to Kodak after Kodak acquired the firm's existing client. Accordingly, the final *Gould* factor also weighs against Woods Oviatt's request to drop the Heidelberg cases and continue to represent Sony and ECJ.

The foregoing is not meant to suggest that Sony, ECJ, or even Woods Oviatt will not be prejudiced if Woods Oviatt is not allowed to choose Sony and ECJ as clients and terminate its defense of Heidelberg in the Jackson and McEwen cases. Woods Oviatt avers that "Kodak's real motive in bring[sic] this motion is to deny the plaintiffs in this [ECJ] case and the defendants in the Sony case access to Mr. Bauer's knowledge and experience." That accusation is one this Court takes very seriously, especially because "courts must guard against tactical use of motions to disqualify counsel." Indeed, during the hearing on the motion to disqualify, this Court inquired whether Kodak intended to discharge Woods Oviatt from the Jackson and McEwen cases should the Court grant its motions to disqualify Woods Oviatt from the ECJ and Sony cases. Kodak's lawyers repeatedly assured this Court that their motions to disqualify Woods Oviatt were not interposed for tactical reasons and that Kodak wanted Woods Oviatt to remain as counsel in order to complete the Jackson and McEwen litigations.

I accept counsels' representations as officers of this Court.

Nevertheless, and to be clear, while the "flexible approach" may require Woods Oviatt's disqualification from being local counsel for Sony and ECJ, the approach also mandates flexibility in allowing Woods Oviatt to resume their legitimate business model and avoid having Kodak or any Kodak "family member" as a client of the firm. Nothing in this decision is meant to link Woods Oviatt and Kodak together any longer than necessary to complete the two Heidelberg litigations. Once completed, any attempt by Kodak to use its new-found status as a "former client" of Woods Oviatt as a strategy to preclude the firm from welcoming clients with interests adverse to Kodak would be looked upon with skepticism, at least by this Court.

CONCLUSION

I began with observing that this case involved the Court having to choose a result that would inevitably involve some degree of unfairness to whichever clients Woods Oviatt would not be representing. In making the choice, "[a] delicate balance must be struck between two competing considerations: the prerogative of a party to proceed with counsel of its choice and the need to uphold ethical conduct in courts of law." After due consideration to the competing interests involved, I

Woods Oviatt's representation of Marie Long and Canon pre-dated the Kodak's acquisition of Heidelberg by a year, whereas their decision to enter an appearance as local counsel for ECJ and Sony occurred after the Heidelberg acquisition. This important distinction brings the Long and Canon situations closer to the facts of Gould, Inc. v. Mitsui Mining and Smelting Co., 738 F.Supp. 1121 (N.D. Ohio 1990). In any event, any potential conflict in the Long and Canon representations is not before this Court and Kodak here has specifically represented it will not waive the conflict with respect to Sony and ECJ cases.

conclude that: (1) for conflict purposes, Kodak and Kodak's wholly owned subsidiary, Heidelberg, are to be treated as a single client; (2) absent consent, Woods Oviatt may not simultaneously represent both Kodak and clients with litigation interests adverse to Kodak; and (3) application of the "flexible approach" to disqualification results in Woods Oviatt's disqualification from acting as local counsel to Sony and ECJ. Therefore, Kodak's motions to disqualify Woods Oviatt from representing Sony and ECJ in the instant cases are granted.

4. Positional Conflicts

Problem

9-12. General Amalgamated asks Martyn to assert that the fact that the lawyer of Amalgamated's adversary shared information with adversary's auditor regarding this litigation acted as a waiver of the attorney-client privilege for all of adversary's communications with its counsel. At the same time, Colossus asks Fox to defend its right not to turn over attorney-client privileged material to the lawyers who have instituted a class action against Colossus. The plaintiffs' lawyers are asserting that, since Colossus cooperated with SEC in its investigation of the same transactions by sharing with the SEC Martyn & Fox's investigation report, that cooperation waived the privilege as to the plaintiffs. Can Martyn & Fox make both arguments? Does it matter where the cases are pending?

Consider: Model Rule 1.7
Model Code DR 5-105
2LQL §128 Comment f

B. Former Clients

Problems

9-13. Three years ago, Martyn & Fox prepared tax returns for Wife's business. Husband now wants Martyn & Fox to represent him in a divorce. Can we? Does it matter if we prepared the tax returns ten years ago? What if we handled an employment discrimination claim for Wife's business?

9-14. Martyn was general counsel for Capital Hospital for ten years before joining Martyn & Fox.

(a) Can Martyn & Fox represent Small Hospital, a competitor of Capital, in lobbying the state legislature for changes in state Medicaid rates?

(b) Can Martyn & Fox advise Sunshine Hospital and rehab center in another county that there are no antitrust ramifications of potential expansion when Martyn advised Capital that a planned expansion would not be wise under the same law?

(c) Can Martyn & Fox represent plaintiff, who alleges medical malpractice that occurred while a patient at Capital Hospital?

9-15. Martyn & Fox received a call to defend a major accounting firm in a 10b-5 class action involving a dot.com company whose stock has precipitously dropped. The accounting firm sent Fox the pleadings and Fox met with them for three hours yesterday, explaining the firm's approach and the possible lines of defense the accounting firm might use. The firm promised to get back to Martyn & Fox next week. Today Martyn circulated a conflicts memo asking whether the firm could take on the representation of the defendant underwriter in the same matter. What should Fox do?

Consider: Model Rules 1.0(k), 1.9, 1.10, 1.18,
     Model Code DR 4-101, 5-105(D)
     RLGL §§15, 132

Mitchell v. Metropolitan Life Insurance Company
2002 U.S. Dist. LEXIS 4675 (S.D.N.Y.)

WILLIAM H. PAULEY III, District Judge:

Defendant Metropolitan Life Insurance Company ("MetLife") moves to disqualify Lieff, Cabraser, Heimann & Bernstein, LLP ("Lieff Cabraser"), one of the two law firms representing plaintiffs. MetLife seeks disqualification on the ground that Wendy R. Fleishman, now a Lieff Cabraser partner, defended MetLife in a number of lawsuits while employed by her former firm, Skadden, Arps, Slate, Meagher & Flom LLP ("Skadden"). For the reasons stated below, the motion is granted.

BACKGROUND

Plaintiffs, five current or former MetLife employees, assert individual and class claims of gender discrimination arising out of their employment within the MetLife Financial Services ("MLFS") division of the company. The MLFS division of MetLife, through its account representatives located nationwide, markets and sells the company's financial and insurance products. The complaint, filed on March 13, 2001, alleges that MetLife has engaged in a continuing policy and practice of gender discrimination in hiring, promotions, job assignments, compensation and other terms and privileges of employment. The complaint alleges that women are underrepresented in each level of MLFS and that the company maintains a gender-based "glass ceiling" by reserving for male employees the support and opportunities for advancing within MLFS. The complaint further alleges that the company engaged in retaliation in response to complaints of gender inequality. Plaintiffs bring this action pursuant to Title VII of the Civil Rights Act of 1964, 42 U.S.C. §2000e et seq., and New York State and City antidiscrimination statutes.

Two law firms presently represent plaintiffs, the Lieff Cabraser firm and Outten & Golden LLP. In January 2001, about two months prior to the filing of the complaint in this action, attorney Wendy Fleishman left her position as counsel with Skadden and joined Lieff Cabraser's New York office as a partner. Lieff Cabraser, a 54-lawyer firm based in San Francisco, California, employs approximately twelve attorneys in its New York office. At the time Fleishman was set to change firms, she informed a MetLife officer that the Lieff Cabraser firm had a matter against MetLife and requested a waiver of conflicts on account of her prior representation of the company. The MetLife officer was unable to locate any action brought against the company by Lieff Cabraser, presumably because the action had yet to be filed. No waiver was provided and Fleishman did not pursue the matter further.

Lieff Cabraser maintains that, upon Fleishman's arrival at the firm, it erected screening measures to ensure that confidential information regarding MetLife could not pass to any Lieff Cabraser employee. The record reflects, however, that Lieff Cabraser's conflicts attorney did not circulate any memorandum formally establishing screening procedures until March 9, 2001, some two months after Fleishman joined the firm.

Before her departure in January 2001, Fleishman had worked at Skadden since 1993 as counsel in its products liability department. In the fall of 1998, Skadden (together with another law firm) was selected as national coordinating counsel for sales practices related lawsuits brought against MetLife. In the sales practices lawsuits, Skadden defended MetLife against claims relating to the conduct of employees in the MLFS field force, the same group that employed the plaintiffs in this action. Fleishman was part of the team assembled by Skadden to defend those lawsuits. Prior to its retention as national coordinating counsel, Skadden represented MetLife in a number of matters where Fleishman also had senior-level involvement.

More specifically, the affidavits submitted on behalf of MetLife by its in-house and outside legal counsel reveal that from the fall of 1998 through her resignation from Skadden in January 2001, Fleishman devoted a substantial portion of her professional time to the defense of MetLife matters. Skadden's billing records from 1999 reflect that Fleishman spent over 1,800 client billable hours representing MetLife in almost fifty matters. In 2000, Fleishman accrued over 1,540 client billable hours representing the company in almost forty matters. In many of those matters, Fleishman, as a senior-level attorney, had the primary day-to-day responsibilities as lead outside counsel. . . .

From these facts, MetLife argues that Fleishman became intimately familiar with confidential MetLife policies and information that are substantially related to the subjects that are at issue in this employment discrimination lawsuit. Therefore, as MetLife contends, Fleishman is subject to a personal conflict of interest. . . . MetLife further contends that since Fleishman personally must be disqualified, this disqualification is imputed to the Lieff Cabraser firm. In this regard, MetLife submits that the screening procedures implemented by Lieff Cabraser are insufficient to insulate the firm from disqualification in this action.

In response, Lieff Cabraser argues that there is no substantial relationship between this employment discrimination action and the sales practices related litigations in which Fleishman represented MetLife. Still, in her affirmation submitted to the Court, Fleishman does not materially dispute the nature and extent of the information she gained in her prior representations of MetLife. . . .

DISCUSSION . . .

The Court of Appeals has cautioned that motions to disqualify counsel are not to be granted indiscriminately because they interfere with a party's right freely to choose counsel and may be interposed for tactical reasons. . . .

Under the restrained approach adopted by the Second Circuit, relief will be granted only when the facts concerning the lawyer's conduct poses a significant risk of trial taint. This risk is commonly encountered "where the attorney is at least potentially in a position to use privileged information concerning the other side through prior representation . . . , thus giving his present client an unfair advantage."

Ordinarily a lawyer may not knowingly reveal a confidence of his client or use that confidence if it would work to the client's disadvantage. [The Court cites NY DR 5-108, which is substantially similar to Model Rule 1.9(a).] The rule against successive representations "concerns itself with the unfair advantage that a lawyer can take of his former client in using adversely to that client information communicated in confidence in the course of the representation," such as "knowing what to ask for in discovery, which witnesses to seek to depose, what questions to ask them, what lines of attack to abandon and what lines to pursue, what settlements to accept and what offers to reject, and innumerable other uses". . . .

Disqualification of a lawyer or firm on the basis of a prior representation of an adverse party typically requires a showing of a substantial relationship between the subject matter of the prior representation and the issues in the present litigation. . . . After a thorough examination of the leading successive representation cases, Judge Leisure of this court articulated the relevant standard as follows: "if the facts giving rise to an issue which is material in both the former and the present litigations are as a practical matter the same, then there is a 'substantial relationship' between the representations for purposes of a disqualification." United States Football League v. National Football League, 605 F. Supp. 1448, 1459 (S.D.N.Y. 1985).

The substantial relationship test serves an important function. It permits a court to "assume that during the course of the former representation confidences were disclosed to the attorney bearing on the subject matter of the representation." As the Second Circuit has held, "a court should not require proof that an attorney actually had access to or received privileged information while representing the client in a prior case." To require such proof would "put the former client to the Hobson's choice of either having to disclose his privileged information in order to disqualify his former attorney or having to refrain from the disqualification motion altogether." All that must be shown is that the attorney whose disqualification is sought was likely to have access to relevant privileged information in the course of his prior representation of the client.

While admitting that Fleishman acquired "general background information" about MetLife, Lieff Cabraser contends that the nature and subject matter of client confidences revealed to Fleishman are insufficient to justify disqualification under the substantial relationship test. This Court disagrees.

Unlike the cases cited by Lieff Cabraser, this is not a case where a lawyer previously represented a client in a narrowly-defined, single-issue lawsuit or may have simply assisted a client in settlement discussions in a small number of cases. . . .

Rather, here, MetLife has demonstrated that Fleishman, as a result of her prolonged and extensive prior representations of the company, acquired or was privy to confidential institutional information about MetLife, its MLFS division and MLFS personnel and that this information is relevant to this pending action in which plaintiffs, on an institutional level, attack the company's employment policies and practices. Fleishman's role in defending MetLife in sales practices related litigation afforded her access to confidential information pertaining to how account representatives and managers within MLFS were hired, trained, supervised, compensated and disciplined; how general performance levels of MLFS employees and managers were evaluated and would be measured against their colleagues; and how MetLife's management and corporate legal department assess exposure to suits of this magnitude and approach litigating or settling such cases. Plainly, this knowledge is

substantially related to disputed factual issues material to the resolution of the present action.

For example, as already indicated, Fleishman would have become fully familiar with the process by which MLFS branch managers evaluated the conduct and performance of account representatives. In this case, plaintiffs contend that this process is entirely subjective and a principal cause of gender inequality of MetLife. . . .

There are further, more direct examples of substantial relationship. One of the named plaintiffs, Barbara LaChance, claimed in her amended charge of discrimination that she could not succeed as an account representative because, as a result of her gender, she received insufficient training and was denied opportunities to develop client and other business relationships. Certainly, with the benefit of confidential information acquired from MetLife about the extent and nature of training provided to account representatives, Fleishman would be positioned to offer strategies for challenging any non-discriminatory reasons proffered by MetLife to rebut those charges. . . .

Perhaps dispositive of the matter, Fleishman personally interviewed managers who had decision-making authority over certain named plaintiffs and who, at least in one documented instance, have been identified as potential witnesses. Fleishman would be privy to confidential information that could serve to challenge credibility, to prepare cross-examinations, and to otherwise contest their proffered justifications for the adverse employment decisions challenged by plaintiffs. Taken together, these circumstances establish a sufficiently close factual nexus between Fleishman's previous representations of MetLife and the matters fairly raised in the current employment discrimination action to pose a significant risk of trial taint to the disadvantage of MetLife. It is no surprise, then, that Fleishman sought a waiver of conflicts from MetLife on account of her prior representations in advance of joining the Lieff Cabraser firm.

Courts in this district have ordered disqualification in comparable contexts, such as where an attorney or law firm gained extensive or highly confidential knowledge about a client through a prior, broad-based representation and that knowledge pertained to a subsequent lawsuit to the disadvantage of the client. In United States Football League v. National Football League, 605 F. Supp. 1448 (S.D.N.Y. 1985), a newly formed football league and its members brought an antitrust action against an established football league and its members. . . . Judge Leisure determined that

> knowledge of a former client's financial and business background is not in itself a basis for disqualification if the client's background is not in issue in the later litigation.
>
> If, however, the litigation must deal with questions of the movant's market behavior, then the challenged attorney's knowledge of the business plans, economic organization, prospective market position and other such background information about the movant becomes relevant. This is particularly true in antitrust cases. The more wide-ranging the allegations of the complaint, the more likely it is that background legal work will be relevant to the instant litigation.

Lieff Cabraser is being overly formalistic in their approach to disqualification, as the relevant inquiry is not limited to whether there are common legal claims or theories between the representations, but extends to whether there are common factual issues that are material to the adjudication of the prior and current representations. . . .

Saliently, Lieff Cabraser's approach is undercut by the published writings of its expert, Professor Charles Wolfram, a prominent legal ethicist . . . :

> In that respect let me turn to the playbook problem. There have been cases suggesting that if you know something about the way the client's head works you know something that's relevant for purposes of applying the substantial relationship test. . . . Those cases that are [truly] cases of substantial relationship would be cases where what you probably learn about the client's inclination, the client's willingness to settle, the client's unwillingness ever to be deposed is both relevant and unknown to others in the second litigation. That is to say it's still a secret. It was a secret obviously when you obtained it but it's still a secret that others don't know it.

Charles W. Wolfram, The Vaporous And The Real In Former-Client Conflicts, 1 J. Inst. for Study of Legal Ethics 133, 138 (1996). As Lieff Cabraser conceded at oral argument, Fleishman was privy to highly privileged communications originating with MetLife's corporate law department regarding settlement strategies in class action litigations.

Accordingly, upon examination of the issues in Fleishman's prior representations of MetLife and in the present action, this Court is constrained to conclude that she suffers from a disabling conflict of interest under the rules of conduct. Client confidences are not so inert as to limit their usefulness to defined legal disciplines or practice areas. They are fungible, and once disclosed can be applied by an experienced lawyer in ways too numerous to anticipate at this stage of the proceeding. . . .

. . . Fleishman's personal conflict of interest [will] . . . be imputed to the Lieff Cabraser firm as well. Nothing presented by Lieff Cabraser persuades this Court that the screening measures implemented by the firm suffice to prevent its disqualification.

The Second Circuit has expressed consistent skepticism about screening as a remedy for conflicts of interest and declared that such procedures ultimately must be rejected if they are subject to doubt. Indeed, the New York Code of Professional Responsibility does not recognize the use of screening devices except in cases involving former government lawyers or judges, and recently the ABA House of Delegates voted to reject a proposal to permit screening to avoid disqualification. Courts have only approved screening procedures in the limited circumstances where a conflicted attorney possesses information unlikely to be material to the current action and has no contact with the department conducting the current litigation, which typically occurs only in the context of a large firm. Compare In re Del-Val Fin. Corp. Sec. Litig., 158 F.R.D. 270, 274-75 (S.D.N.Y. 1994) (imputed disqualification rebutted by screening procedures where conflicted attorney joined a 400-lawyer firm and was involved in the prior representation only in a peripheral manner) and Solow v. W.R. Grace & Co., 632 N.E.2d 437 (N.Y. 1994) (imputed disqualification rebutted because the conflicted attorneys transferred to a 350-plus lawyer firm,

their involvement in the prior representation had been negligible, and the principle attorneys responsible for the matter left the firm before the current representation) with Decora Inc. v. DW Wallcovering, Inc., 899 F. Supp. 132, 141 (S.D.N.Y. 1995) (implied disqualification not rebutted by screening procedures because conflicted attorney joined a small firm of 44 lawyers and did not work in a department separate from the one handling the current action) and Yaretsky v. Blum, 525 F. Supp. 24, 29-30 (S.D.N.Y. 1981) (implied disqualification not rebutted by screening procedures because conflicted attorney joined a firm with about 30 lawyers in its New York office and worked in the department handling the case). . . . In addition, to rebut the presumption, the screening measures must have been established from the first moment the conflicted attorney transferred to the firm or, at a minimum, when the firm first received actual notice of the conflict. *See* Marshall v. State of New York Div. of State Police, 952 F. Supp. 103, 111 (N.D.N.Y. 1997) ("a screening device implemented only after a disqualified lawyer has been with a firm will not provide adequate protection of confidences.

In this case, the screening measures put in place by Lieff Cabraser do not suffice to avoid disqualification. Fleishman had extensive exposure to relevant confidential information in the course of her representations of MetLife. Although Fleishman personally is not involved in prosecuting this action, she works in the 12-lawyer New York office of a relatively small firm. Two of the attorneys in the New York office are assigned to this case, and Fleishman is working directly with one of them on another significant class action suit. Given that Fleishman works in close proximity to attorneys responsible for this action, and regularly interacts with at least one of them, there exists a continuing danger that Fleishman may inadvertently transmit information gained through her prior representations of MetLife.

Parenthetically, Professor Wolfram's writings again impeach the position taken by Lieff Cabraser. In his treatise on legal ethics, Professor Wolfram observes:

> In the end there is little but the self-serving assurance of the screening-lawyer foxes that they will carefully guard the screened-lawyer chickens. Whether the screen is breached will be virtually impossible to ascertain from outside the firm. On the inside, lawyers whose interests would all be served by creating leaks in the screen and not revealing the leaks would not regularly be chosen as guardians by anyone truly interested in assuring that leaks do not occur. Charles W. Wolfram, Modern Legal Ethics §7.6.4, at 402 (West 1986).

Timing also militates against upholding the efficacy of the screening measures adopted by Lieff Cabraser. The record shows that the firm did not formally implement the screen until March 9, 2001, almost two months after Fleishman joined the firm and well after the time the firm had actual notice of the conflict. A screening device implemented only after a disqualified lawyer has joined the firm, in an instance where the firm knew of the problem at the time of her arrival, further diminishes the possibility that screening remedies the conflict present this case.

Under the circumstances arising in this case, the potential of inadvertent disclosure would lurk constantly in the background. As a result, this Court finds that the presumption of shared confidences has . . . not been rebutted. This Court notes that disqualification is unlikely to prejudice plaintiffs in any material way since MetLife interposed its motion at the outset of the litigation and plaintiffs can continue to be represented by the Outten firm. Thus, the Lieff Cabraser firm must be disqualified.

C. Imputed Conflicts

Problems

9-16. Martyn & Fox is in a ten-day countdown to trial when one of its associates darkens Fox's door to announce that she is leaving the firm on Friday. When Fox recovers from the shock of losing his right arm in the case on such short notice, the associate tells him that she will be joining the firm on the other side of the case, but not to worry—she'll be screened. What should Martyn & Fox do?

9-17. Martyn & Fox signs a joint defense agreement with a law firm representing a co-defendant of Martyn & Fox's client. Plaintiff succeeds in getting the other law firm disqualified because plaintiff is the other firm's former client. What happens to Martyn & Fox?

9-18. Martyn & Fox agrees to staff a hot line for the local legal services project every Tuesday. One Tuesday a Martyn & Fox associate received a phone call from an individual who has been the subject of predatory lending by The Dollar Store. Without seeing any documents, the associate gave the woman advice about possible remedies and only learned upon returning to the firm that Big Bank, Martyn & Fox's largest client, owns The Dollar Store. Is Martyn & Fox in trouble?

9-19. Martyn & Fox, representing Chrysler in a dispute with Renault, hires a Belgian lawyer who worked on the same matter for Renault five years ago. Under rules applicable to the Belgian lawyer, screening of a lateral lawyer is permitted to lift imputation; under the rules applicable to Martyn & Fox, no screening is permitted. Should Martyn & Fox be disqualified?

Consider: Model Rules 1.0(c), 1.0(K), 1.7, 1.9, 1.10, 6.5, 8.5
          Model Code DR 4-101, 5-105(D)
          RLGL §124

Lawrence J. Fox
Legal Tender: A Lawyer's Guide to Handling Professional Dilemmas
122-125 (ABA 1995)

My Lawyer Switched Sides; Don't Worry, There's a Screen

The litigation department breakfasts always seemed to be scheduled for the wrong day of the week. Just when the key deposition loomed with its 10:00 A.M. start, the chairman insisted everyone meet at 7:30 in the tired windowless conference room on 13, the one with the boring duck prints that were always askew. Obligations and self-interest overcame the need for last-minute deposition preparations. After all, associate reviews were just around the corner. She wondered, as she raced to be on time, why she had ever bothered to switch firms. It was true: they weren't all identical; they were just the same. They made you feel the same—tired and overworked—and the paycheck was delivered with the same heavy resentment. They made you feel the same anxiety that you would not meet the firm's billable hour "targets," the euphemism employed by the chair of each firm to describe her 2,200 hour quota. She had to find a better way, she thought, as she slumped resignedly into the well-worn conference room chair. How many hours had she spent in this room? In these meetings? Being bored?

Barely listening, she maintained her studied attentive pose, one she had mastered to get her through those interminable depositions. She would follow her usual rule: make an attempt at one cogent remark, but otherwise remain silent. Talking at meetings like this could only hurt her chances for partnership (as if she cared), and no one ever made partner because of her "performance" at departmental meetings. Wait, look alert, pick your moment, and then get out as soon as possible.

The conversation turned to privileged documents: something about whether you could withhold internal corporate memos in document discovery on the grounds of privilege when they were addressed to multiple executives as well as in-house general counsel. Her mind wandered back to the practice of one of her clients at the old firm. Suddenly sensing this anecdotal tidbit as "her" moment, she shared with the assembled group, "When I was at Bryans & Putnam, one of our clients, City Trust Company, had a bright line rule: so long as the document had counsel's name or initials on it anywhere—as writer, addressee, copied in or later sent the document—they deemed it privileged. It made it real easy to decide which documents to withhold."

Several minutes later, as the discussion rejected her formulation as far too broad, even unprofessional, it suddenly occurred to her. Of course! The firm had litigation against City Trust Company, she was "screened" from that litigation (she had prepared some early interrogatories for City Trust) and she had suddenly revealed a City Trust confidence to everyone. Panic replaced boredom; nausea gripped her. What should she do? What would her firm colleagues do? Was her career going up in smoke before her eyes? She had broken her trust; she hadn't intended to, she hadn't been thinking. It was just a passing remark. She rose shakily, mumbled an apology and hurried to the ladies' room.

Her mind raced back to her first thoughts about leaving her old firm. The head-hunter had called and indicated how easy it was to place a young associate practicing in Pennsylvania, one of the few states that provided for screening of private lawyers when they switched firms. It made looking for a job so much simpler. She did not have to worry about whether the possible new employers had cases against her old clients. If the headhunter found a firm that liked her, she could just accept the job without worrying about potential conflicts. If any were discovered, the Pennsylvania rules would simply require that she be screened from those matters.

She felt comfortable with that arrangement. She knew how she viewed client confidences—she would never share them. In fact, it gave her great pride to think of herself as a lawyer of integrity, one who could be trusted with confidential information. Indeed it was one of the things that drove her husband crazy—the way she always knew the best secrets weeks before he would hear about it at a cocktail party or read it in the newspaper. She even felt flattered when, after the two matters from which she had to be screened were identified, the chairman of her new firm's professional responsibility committee said to her that the firm was not going to take any elaborate measures to screen her because the firm had a long tradition of placing substantial trust in their associates.

But now! What could she do? Maybe she shouldn't do anything. If she talked to anyone at her new firm that would just emphasize the importance of her disclosure. Would her new firm then have to resign from handling the City Trust matters? One of them involved Pegasus Construction Company, her new firm's largest litigation client. And did she have to tell City Trust? Or anyone at Bryans & Putnam? So many questions! No one to turn to. She was spinning with concerns. It was too much to handle. She would leave early—it would be her first pre-8:00 P.M. departure in weeks—and maybe she could persuade her husband that dinner at the new Thai restaurant on South Street would be in order . . . she needed a chance to clear her head, to regroup.

The next day dawned early and bright—the kind of day that gave June such a good reputation. The dinner had been close to perfect, perhaps a tad too much wine. And while she hated to admit it, it may have been the wine that permitted her to see the situation clearly.

There was no doubting her mistake; she shouldn't have blurted out those remarks at the meeting the day before, but it was only after the dinner that she recalled how upset she had been originally when she learned that City Trust took this position on the privilege. She recalled with clarity how it had offended her at the time, how surprised she was that the partners at old Bryans & Putnam had so blithely accepted the client's notion of privilege. So was there really anything wrong with what she had said? If City Trust's position were defensible . . . maybe she had an obligation to tell someone, maybe her new firm would be obliged to resign. But since it was her view that City Trust was wrong, there really was no harm. If her colleagues who worked on City Trust matters at her new firm used her information to press a little harder for documents that City Trust withheld on the ground of privilege, it would be for the courts to decide who was right. And it wasn't like she had shared confidential facts about the case.

As she contemplated all of this, she couldn't really tell whether it was the weather, the Cabernet Sauvignon, or the chicken satay that had induced this new sense of calm; the problems of yesterday had been put to rest and, particularly pleasing, she had handled the entire matter herself. Off she went to work with a new lightness in her step, not unlike the way she felt the day she learned she had passed the bar exam. Maybe she would go for partner after all.

▓ Practice Pointers:
Implementing a Conflicts Control System

This chapter and the last illustrate the need to identify and properly respond to a wide variety of conflicts of interest. Model Rule 5.1 further requires lawyers with managerial authority in law firms to "make reasonable efforts to ensure that the firm has in effect measures giving reasonable assurance that all lawyers in the firm conform to the Rules of Professional Conduct." A law firm will not be able to identify or avoid conflicts unless it collects information that will reveal them. To this end, the firm needs to establish, maintain, and continually update a system of accurate information. As soon as this information reveals the presence of a potential conflict, the firm will be in a position to respond by understanding the nature of the conflict and the sources of legal regulation that govern it.

Establishing a Database

Current law regulates personal, concurrent, third-person, and former client conflicts and requires precise identification of the client, nature of the matter, and the lawyers who will work on the case. Model Rules 1.8(h), 1.10, 1.11, and 1.12 generally impute the conflict of one lawyer to others in the firm.[1] These aspects of the law governing lawyer conflicts of interest should shape similar

---

1. MR 1.10(a) exempts prohibitions "based on a personal interest of the prohibited lawyer" if the personal interest "does not present a significant risk of materially limiting the representation of the client by the remaining lawyers in the firm." Of course, a firm will not be able to evaluate whether a personal conflict of one of its lawyers materially limits the client's representation without knowing that it exists.

categories of information that are entered in the conflicts checking database of every law practice.

Personal Conflicts: Law Firm Lawyers   A separate entry should be made in the law firm lawyers database for each lawyer in the law firm, and each entry should include three distinct pieces of information:

- The name of each lawyer;
- A list of material interests (property, business, and financial) owned by that lawyer; and
- Substantial property, business, or financial interests of persons in that lawyer's household.

Concurrent and Third-Person Conflicts: Current Clients   Each entry for current clients should include at least four elements:

- Identification of each current client. Subsidiaries, parents, or other affiliates, and control persons (key officers and employees) of entity clients as well as all changes or variations in corporate or personal name;[2]
- A description of the subject matter of the client representation, including the identities (with changes when they occur) of actual and potential opposing parties;
- Any third persons or entities, such as insurers, who are paying for or are direct beneficiaries of the representation; and
- The names of law firm lawyers responsible for the matter.

Former Client Conflicts: Former Clients   Each entry for former clients should also include three elements:

- Accurate identification of the client, including subsidiaries, parents, or other affiliates and control persons of entity clients, as well as changes or variations in personal or corporate name;
- Subject matter of the representation, including the identities (with changes when relevant) of related and opposing parties; and
- The names of lawyers who were responsible for the matter.

Since former client conflicts can be generated not only by past law firm representation but also by the past employment of law firm personnel, it is essential to include the three elements listed above (client identification, subject matter, lawyers) for all of the following:

- All former clients of the firm;
- All former clients of lawyers joining the firm; and
- All former client matters of current law firm paralegals, secretaries, investigators, and related paraprofessionals.

---

2. Commercial services make this information available to law firms.

Maintaining the Database

Once the initial database has been established, new data should be added before any new client matter is opened by the firm, as well as at any time new personnel join the firm. Any information about changes in client identity, opposing parties, or lawyers working on the file should be entered on the day the change occurs or the firm becomes aware of it. Entries should be moved from the current client database to the former client database whenever the firm concludes its representation in a client matter, whether by withdrawal, completion, or client termination.

Identifying and Responding to Conflicts

Lawyers never should rely exclusively on either their memory or a law firm database for a conflicts check.[3] Instead, conflicts should be monitored by timely entries into the database, by timely use of the database to search for relevant matches, and by notification about new client matters through interoffice memoranda, which trigger the memory of all firm lawyers. These procedures help assure that information from each source is supplemented by the other.

A new client file should not be opened and no time should be billed to the client by the firm (absent an emergency) until at least four steps have been completed:

1. The prospective client's identifying information has been run through the law firm's database;
2. A written conflicts memo has been circulated throughout the firm;
3. The responsible lawyer has indicated in writing either that no matches were found, or if they were, that they indicate no conflict or a consentable conflict for which consent has been obtained; and
4. A neutral person has reviewed any information, matches, and any explanatory memoranda.

To accomplish these steps, the law firm should undertake all of the following tasks:

- Using both the law firm database and inter-office memos, search for any matches between prospective clients on the one hand and law firm lawyers, probable opponents and their lawyers, current clients, and former clients on the other;
- If any matches occur, does the client's interest potentially differ from an interest of any of the matches?
- If so, is the conflict consentable in the relevant jurisdiction?
- If so, are you free to disclose the requisite information to secure consent consistent with your duties of confidentiality?
- If so, seek informed consent of the client(s) in writing.

---

3. Recall *A. v. B., supra* p. 355, where a misspelled name in a database prevented the firm from discovering a blatant conflict.

- If not, you cannot represent both clients. However, if the conflict is a former-client conflict, does your jurisdiction recognize screens without the former client's consent?
- If screens for former-client conflicts are available, establish an adequate screening mechanism, and seek consent from the current client as well.
- If the firm withdraws from any representation, the entry for that client should be moved from the current-client list to the former-client list.

Establishing Effective Screens

Mitchell illustrates that, absent client consent, courts are skeptical about law firm screens.[4] But screens are established in many law firms, usually by client consent,[5] and occasionally where clients do not consent but where allowed by professional code,[6] or common law.[7] If allowed, all courts require that adequate and effective screens be timely and properly established and maintained, including proper notice to affected parties.[8]

Model Rule 1.0(k) defines "screened" as "isolation of a lawyer from any participation in a matter through the timely imposition of procedures within a firm that are reasonably adequate under the circumstances to protect information that the isolated lawyer is obligated to protect under these Rules or other law."[9] To meet this standard, law firm should:

---

4. The vast majority of jurisdictions reject involuntary screens absent client informed consent. *See, e.g.,* Towne Dev. of Chandler v. Super. Ct., 842 P.2d 1377 (Ariz. App. 1st Div. 1992). These courts apply the same rules to other law firm employees. *See, e.g.,* Zimmerman v. Mahaska Bottling Co., 19 P.3d 784 (Kan. 2001) (screen not allowed for secretary who overheard conversations about the same matter at former law firm); In re Am. Home Prods. Corp., 985 S.W.2d 68 (Tex. 1998) (disqualification ordered where law firm assigned legal assistant to work on the same case she had previously researched for the other side).

5. *E.g.,* MR 1.7, 1.8, and 1.9.

6. MR 1.11(b)-(c) (former government employees), 1.12(c) (former judges, arbitrators, and mediators), 1.18(d) (prospective clients).

7. *See, e.g.,* RLGL §124; Kala v. Aluminum Smelting & Refining Co., Inc., 688 N.E.2d 258 (Ohio 1998). Courts that generally approve of screens for lawyers also approve of them for other employees, such as secretaries and paralegals. *See, e.g.,* Green v. Toledo Hosp., 764 N.E.2d 979 (Ohio 2002). Courts do not allow screens in side-switching cases, *see, e.g.,* Natl. Union Fire Ins. Co. v. Alticor, 472 F.3d 436 (6th Cir. 2007); Lennartson v. Anoka-Hennepin Indep. Sch. Dist. No. 11, 662 N.W.2d 125 (Minn. 2003); Doe v. Perry Community Sch. Dist., 650 N.W.2d 594 (Iowa 2002); Clinard v. Blackwood, 46 S.W.3d 177 (Tenn. 2001); Commnw. v. Maricle, 10 S.W.3d 117 (Ky. 1999) (despite Rule 1.11, no screen allowed where lead counsel for the prosecution joined firm that represented defendant after negotiating employment for more than two months while the case was pending); Kassis v. Teacher's Ins. & Annuity Assn., 717 N.E.2d 674 (N.Y. 1999).

8. Several empirical studies indicate that lawyers often do not understand these requirements. Susan P. Shapiro, *Tangled Loyalties: Conflict of Interest in Legal Practice* 411-412 (U. Mich. Press 2002) (screens do not always meet the specifications found in ethics codes and case law and reinforce a double standard between clients with clout and one-time less powerful clients); Lee A. Pizzimenti, *Screen Verite: Do Rules About Ethical Screens Reflect the Truth About Real-Life Law Firm Practice?* 52 U. Miami L. Rev. 305 (1997) (the majority of firms take conflicts seriously, but that they "are hampered by flawed conflicts detection, flawed systems for maintaining screens and to some extent, an adversarial rather than fiduciary analysis of screen issues.").

9. MR 1.0(k).

- Establish the screen before the screened lawyer joins the firm, or if the lawyer is already in the firm, as soon as the conflict has been timely detected;
- Have the screened lawyer acknowledge in writing that he or she will not communicate with any firm lawyers about the matter;
- Notify all law firm personnel about the screen, indicating they may not communicate with the screened lawyer about the matter;
- Quarantine all law firm files about the screened matter. Electronic files should be available only with a proper password, and paper files should be kept in an area not available to the screened lawyer;
- Establish bookkeeping procedures that assure the screened lawyer does not share in the fee revenue from the case; and
- Promptly notify all clients, former clients, or other parties of the screen.[10]

Maintaining Effective Screens

Once screens are timely implemented and carefully established, they also must be maintained. Inadvertent or intentional breaches of screens must be reported to affected clients to prevent further sanctions. Recall, for example, the cost to the law firms in *Maritrans* and *ACC* that followed breaches of screens in those cases.[11] Further, whether by client consent, lawyer codes, or common law, screens can proliferate, and their proliferation in law firms can cause huge administrative difficulties.[12] Large law firms that have established consensual screens could find themselves with hundreds of them, each one generating the need to notify affected parties, segregate files, prevent communication, and preclude revenue sharing. Keeping track of these details requires a great deal of skill. This is why, once established, law firms should maintain screens by:

- Creating law firm mechanisms that periodically remind screened lawyers of their obligations and inquire about the maintenance of proper screening procedures, and
- Promptly notify the affected clients and former clients if the screen is breached.[13]

---

10. *Id.*, 1.11(b) (former government officers and employees), 1.12(c) (former judges, arbitrators, and mediators).

11. We do not mean that Pepper Hamilton disclosed or used confidential information against Maritrans; but recall that the court found that, notwithstanding Pepper's agreement, in the consent screen it established "for all intents and purposes" that it represented Bouchard, conduct that breached the screening agreement. Pepper Hamilton eventually settled with Maritrans for $3 million. *See* James L. Kelly, *Lawyers Crossing Lines: Nine Stories* 79 (Carolina Academic Press 2001). *See also* Lawyer's Roles: The Instrumental Lawyer and the Bounds of the Law, *supra* p. 225, discussing breach of a former government lawyers screen in *ACC*. Recall that Jones Day eventually settled the litigation relating to that representation for $75 million.

12. Susan R. Martyn, *Visions of the Eternal Law Firm: The Future of Law Firm Screens*, 45 S.C. L. Rev. 937 (1994).

13. *E.g.*, Spur Prod. Corp. v. Stoel Rives LLP, 153 P.3d 1158 (Idaho 2007) (valid malpractice claim presented by client for failure of law firm to inform client of breach in a screen, causing client to agree to settle the underlying litigation client would not otherwise have agreed to if it had known about screen breach); Steel v. Gen. Motors Corp., 912 F. Supp. 724 (D.N.J. 1995) (inadvertent breach in screen required disqualification). *See also* Prince Jefri Bolkiah v. KPMG, 2

Integrating a Conflicts Control System into Law Firm

Management Law firms should establish a committee or designate a partner with responsibility for implementing the conflicts control system. Once a committee or partner is identified as having responsibility for monitoring conflicts within the firm, all conflicts detection and avoidance practices should be made routine by written policies and procedures that require compliance by all law firm personnel. When potential conflicts are discovered, the partner or committee should have the authority to decide how to respond. Law firm policy should include the requirement that any member of a law firm ethics committee potentially involved in any conflict be disqualified from considering its resolution. The partner or committee in charge of conflicts should also make clear that deviations from the firm policy are serious concerns and will result in appropriate sanctions.[14]

Following these procedures will not prevent conflicts, but they will put you in a position to know about them and respond appropriately. Two things are certain. First, lawyers must know both the conflicts rules and the provisions about screening if they are to have any hope of convincing a client to consent to a screen or a court to accept an involuntary substitute. Second, the law governing lawyering makes clear that failure to discover a conflict is no defense to discipline, disqualification, fee forfeiture, or other client remedies.

D. Government Lawyers

Problems

9-20. Martyn & Fox recently hired Julia Davis, a lawyer who worked for the state attorney general's office for the past six years. Ms. Davis' first case in the AG's office was the successful defense of a race discrimination class action against the State Department of Taxation. In her last case, she served as lead counsel in negotiating a settlement in an antitrust suit on behalf of the State Department of Transportation against General Motors.

  (a) Can Martyn & Fox take on the representation of Paula Pearson who wishes to bring a race discrimination complaint against the State Department of Taxation based on events that occurred four years after Ms. Davis's defense of the Department?

  (b) Can Martyn & Fox take on the representation of Local Municipality against General Motors based on facts identical to the State Department of Transportation case?

9-21. Grayson, the senior partner at Martyn & Fox, has been mediating a dispute between Hydrogen Electric and Steel Company over electric rates for the year 2000. He finished facilitating the participants'

A.C. 222 (H.L. 1999) (disqualification required where lawyers in accounting firm disregarded screen in favor of team approach to pre-litigation services); Westinghouse Elec. Corp. v. Kerr-McGee Corp., 580 F.2d 1311 (7th Cir. 1978) (blatant breach of attempted screen in simultaneous representation case requires disqualification).

14. Elizabeth Chambliss & David B. Wilkins, *The Emerging Role of Ethics Advisors, General Counsel, and Other Compliance Specialists in Large Law Firms*, 44 Ariz. L. Rev. 559 (2002).

agreement last Tuesday. Now Martyn has been called by Steel Company to see if the firm will represent Steel Company against Hydrogen Electric for the year 2002 electric charges. May Martyn take the case?

Consider: Model Rules 1.11, 1.12, 2.4, 7.6
Model Code DR 9-101
RLGL §133

Lawyers and Clients: *Governments*

A substantial group of lawyers provide legal services to federal, state, and local government units in the widest variety of matters.[1] Model Rule 1.13, Comment [9] extends the rule's entity concept of organizations to governmental organizations, but cautions that issues related to client identity and fiduciary obligations may be shaped not only by the government lawyer's general and specific ethical obligations but also by the client-government's public obligations imposed by constitution, statute, regulation, or common law.

For example, the last problems regarding mediators and government lawyers required you to apply special conflict of interest rules found in Model Rules 1.11 and 1.12. In addition to these specific lawyer code provisions, lawyers who work for governmental units also are subject to federal and state statutes and regulations that govern their conduct. Comment [1] to Model Rule 1.11 expressly refers to this other law.[2]

The Clients

At various times, government lawyers have identified their client as an agency official, the agency itself, a branch of government, the government itself, or the people served by the government.[3] Government lawyers work within complex legal structures that authorize their own and their clients' work. Lawyers who work for government agencies typically view their client as the agency, with its policy articulated by the agency officer who has the power to decide a particular matter.[4] On the other hand, lawyers who work in a state attorney general office

---

1. The federal government currently employs about 28,500 lawyers, state governments about 34,750, and local governments about 49,000. The total of about 112,000 accounts for about 10 percent of all U.S. lawyers, and about 20 percent of all practicing lawyers. *See* Bureau of Labor Statistics, *Occupational Employment and Wages, May 2006.* Available at *http://www.bls.gov/oes/current/oes231011.htm.* Last visited July 23, 2007; ABA, *Lawyer Demographics* (2006). Available at *http://www.abanet.org/marketresearch/lawyer_demographics_2006.pdf.* Last visited July 23, 2007.
2. MR 1.12 generally parallels MR 1.11 and, together with the Code of Judicial Conduct, forms the primary source of rules that regulate the conduct of judges, arbitrators, and mediators. We explore issues of judicial ethics in Chapter 15.
3. Catherine J. Lanctot, *The Duty of Zealous Advocacy and the Ethics of the Federal Government Lawyer: The Three Hardest Questions,* 64 S. Cal. L. Rev. 951 (1991); Geoffrey P. Miller, *Government Lawyers' Ethics in a System of Checks and Balances,* 54 U. Chi. L. Rev. 1293, 1296 (1987).
4. *See* D.C. R. Prof. Conduct 1.6(k) (2007) ("The client of the government lawyer is the agency that employs the lawyer unless expressly provided to the contrary by applicable law, regulation, or order."). *See also* Jeffrey Rosenthal, *Who Is the Client of the Government Lawyer?* in Patricia E. Salkin, ed., *Ethical Standards in the Public Sector: A Guide for Government Lawyers, Clients, and Public Officials* 13 (ABA Sect. of St. and Local Gov. L. 1999).

or the U.S. Department of Justice may define their client as the state or federal government itself, where the public interest is articulated by the person or persons in the office with legitimate authority to direct government policy.[5] Government lawyers such as Judge Advocate General lawyers or public defenders also may be assigned to represent individuals.[6] Prosecutors, on the other hand, do not represent individuals, but are "ministers of justice"[7] who represent a sovereign government, which has an obligation to "govern impartially."[8]

The Restatement adopts a contextual approach, which eschews universal definitions of governmental clients and focuses instead on political and organizational responsibility of government officials, legal organizations within which government lawyers work, and the purpose for which one is identifying the client.[9]

Take for example the situation where agencies of the same government feud over governmental policy. Lawyers who work for those agencies typically view their client as the agency. But the client's identity can be further complicated in jurisdictions where the attorney general is charged by constitution or statute with the task of providing representation to each agency. There, legal regulation essentially requires that two lawyers in the same office represent each agency's point of view to the appropriate decision maker; or, in the alternative, special assistants outside the office may be required to remove control of the attorney general over the matter.[10]

The 5 Cs

Control and Communication   Like the organization's lawyer, the government lawyer must take direction from duly authorized constituents of the client. When a given constituent or group of constituents propose to engage in unlawful conduct, the lawyer must pursue the matter up the ladder of government

---

5. Jonathan R. Macey & Geoffrey P. Miller, *Reflections on Professional Responsibility in a Regulatory State*, 63 Geo. Wash. L. Rev. 1105 (1995).

6. *See* D.C. R. Prof. Conduct 1.6, Comment [39] (2007); D.C. Op. 313 (2002) (whether former Navy JAG lawyer may continue to represent same defendant in post-conviction proceeding in private practice); Kathleen Clark, *Government Lawyering: The Ethics of Representing Elected Representatives*, 61 Law & Contemp. Prob. 31 (1998). We deal with the special ethical dilemma of public defenders and JAG lawyers in Lawyers and Clients: Criminal Defense, *infra* p. 124.

7. MR 3.8, Comment [1].

8. Berger v. United States, 295 U.S. 78, 88 (1935). *See* Bruce A. Green & Fred C. Zacharias, *Prosecutorial Neutrality*, 2004 Wis. L. Rev. 837. This obligation to seek justice may be especially complex after conviction. *See* Fred C. Zacharias, *The Role of Prosecutors in Serving Justice After Convictions*, 58 Vand. L. Rev. 171 (2005). *See also* Freeport-McMoRan Oil & Gas Co. v. F.E.R.C., 962 F.2d 45 (D.C. Cir. 1992) (the principle in *Berger* applies equally to the government's civil lawyers, who should have dismissed an appeal when the issue became moot).

9. RLGL §97, Comment c.

10. *See, e.g.,* Granholm v. PSC Mich. Pub. Serv. Commn., 625 N.W.2d 16 (Mich. App. 2000) (when the Attorney General is a party to litigation against a state agency, which is entitled to representation by the attorney general's office, dual representation creates a conflict of interest that must be remedied by appointment of an independent special assistant attorney general for the State agency); EPA v. Pollution Control Bd., 372 N.E.2d 50 (Ill. 1977) (where attorney general is not an actual party, he may represent opposing state agencies in the dispute); Justin G. Davids, *State Attorneys General and the Client-Attorney Relationship: Establishing the Power to Sue State Officers*, 38 Colum. J.L. & Soc. Probs. 365 (2005).

authority.[11] For example, when lawyers and constituents disagree, lawyers for executive branch agencies can appeal a matter not only to the political or cabinet head of the agency, but all the way to the executive itself.[12] Lawyers for agencies empowered to make decisions independent of the executive would stop at the agency level.[13] When the disagreement cannot be resolved by such an appeal, the lawyer and constituents may end up asking a court to resolve it.[14]

Some government lawyers have the power to control and decide certain legal matters that ordinarily would be reposed only in the client.[15] For example, the client's authority to settle or decide whether to appeal a matter may be exercised by a government lawyer properly empowered by statute, constitution, or common law.[16] When a government lawyer has this responsibility, the lawyer essentially serves as trustee for the government, taking into consideration some version of the public interest in making the decision.[17]

Competence   Some government lawyers face the same huge caseloads that also plague lawyers for private clients.[18] In addition, they obviously must be aware of the often complex body of law that creates and regulates their clients. But they also must be diligent in recognizing special regulations that govern their own conduct, such as restrictions on accepting gifts or outside compensation, as well as personal financial interests.[19]

---

11. MR 1.13(b); RLGL §97, Comment f.

12. Peter L. Strauss, *Overseer, or "The Decider"? The President in Administrative Law*, Geo. Wash. L. Rev. (2007); Robert P. Lowry, *Who Is the Client of the Government Lawyer? An Analysis of the Wrong Question*, 37 Fed. B. J. 61 (1978).

13. Kathleen Clark, *Government Lawyers and Confidentiality Norms*, 85 Wash. U. L. Rev. (forthcoming 2008).

14. *See, e.g.*, Vaughn v. King, 167 F.3d 347 (7th Cir. 1999) (City of Gary Sanitary District had statutory power to hire independent outside counsel without mayor's signature); State ex rel. McGraw v. Burton, 569 S.E.2d 99 (W. Va. 2002) (Office of Attorney General may not be stripped of its inherent core functions, including: (1) playing a central role in providing day-to-day professional legal services to State officials and entities in and associated with the executive branch of government, (2) ensuring that the adoption of legal policy and positions by the State is made only after meaningful consideration of the potential effects of such policy on a full range of State entities and interest particularly before tribunals, but in light of long-established statutes, practice, and precedent, the State executive branch and related entities may in some circumstances employ and use non-employee lawyers); Salt Lake City Commn. v. Salt Lake City Atty., 985 P.2d 899, 907 (Utah 1999) (In the absence of any contradictory statutes, county attorney represents county as an entity, not individual commissioners, who are duly authorized agents of the County. Commissioners therefore have no power to hire outside counsel when they disagree with county attorney except when county attorney "refuses to act or is incapable of acting or is unavailable for some other reason." Disagreements about whether this exception has occurred may be settled by appeal to the Attorney General or by seeking a declaratory judgment from a court).

15. Model Rules, Scope ¶[18]; RLGL §97(1) and Comment g.

16. *See, e.g.*, 28 U.S.C. §§516, 519 (2007) (authorizing the Department of Justice to make and control most litigation decisions—this power varies considerably at the state level). *See* Justin G. Davids, *State Attorneys General and the Client-Attorney Relationship: Establishing the Power to Sue State Officers*, 38 Colum. J.L. & Soc. Probs. 365 (2005); William P. Marshall, *Break Up the Presidency? Governors, State Attorneys General, and Lessons from the Divided Executive*, 115 Yale L.J. 2246 (2006).

17. Clark, *supra* note 13.

18. *See, e.g.*, N.Y. St. Bar Op. 751 (2002) (a lawyer who represents a government agency may not undertake more matters than the lawyer can competently handle, but must accept a superior's resolution of the issue if it constitutes an arguable question of professional duty).

19. The U.S. Justice Department administers its regulations through its Office of Professional Responsibility, and issues annual reports about the sources and outcomes of its investigations. *See http://www.usdoj.gov/opr/annualreport2004.htm.* Last visited July 23, 2007.

For example, current federal government lawyers in all three branches of government are subject to the federal conflict of interest statutes, which limit the ability of all federal employees, including federal lawyers, to represent or receive compensation to represent private parties in a "particular matter" in which the United States is a party or has an interest.[20] Violations of these governmental ethics codes can result in administrative sanctions and criminal prosecution. Many governments administer these codes through an internal administrative process.

Prosecutors exercise substantial power in the criminal justice system. It is often said that they have the duty to seek justice rather than a professional obligation to win.[21] Model Rule 3.8 recognizes this obligation to fairly execute the criminal law by imposing disciplinary rules that reflect constitutional requirements; for example, the duty to provide exculpatory evidence to criminal defendants[22] or not to prosecute a case without probable cause.[23]

The American Bar Association, the National District Attorney's Association, and the United States Department of Justice all have promulgated guidelines that seek to promote this goal.[24] At the same time, unlike other lawyers, prosecutors have civil immunity for judicial actions,[25] which perhaps explains in part why misconduct in charging, plea bargaining, granting immunity, and suppression of evidence continue to occur.[26] On the other hand, the prosecutor's affirmative obligations to protect the constitutionally protected rights of

---

20. 18 U.S.C. §§203, 205 (2007). Members of Congress also are prohibited from practicing in the Court of Federal Claims or the Court of Appeals for the Federal Circuit. 18 U.S.C. §204. *See also* Kathleen Clark, *Do We Have Enough Ethics in Government Yet?: An Answer from Fiduciary Theory,* 1996 U. Ill L. Rev. 57.

21. MR 3.8, Comment [1]; ABA, *Standards for Criminal Justice: Prosecution Function and Defense Function,* 3-1.2(c) (3d ed. 1993). *See also* Bruce A. Green, *Why Should Prosecutors Seek Justice?,* 26 Fordham Urb. L.J. 607 (1999); H. Richard Uviller, *The Virtuous Prosecutor in Quest of an Ethical Standard: Guidance From the ABA,* 71 Mich. L. Rev. 1145 (1973).

22. MR 3.8(d) recognizes the constitutionally required rule of Brady v. Maryland, 373 U.S. 83 (1963). *See also* RLGL §97(4), which requires prosecutors and other government lawyers to "observe applicable restrictions imposed by law."

23. MR 3.3(a); RLGL §97(3).

24. ABA *Standards, supra* note 21; *National District Attorney's Association Prosecution Standards* (2d ed. 1991). Available at *http://www.ndaa.org/pdf/ndaa_natl_prosecution_standards.pdf,* last visited July 23, 2007; *United States Attorney's Manual,* Title 9-27.000 "Principles of Federal Prosecution" (January 2007). Available at *http://www.usdoj.gov/usao/eousa/foia_reading_room/usam/title9/27mcrm.htm,* last visited July 23, 2007.

25. Imbler v. Pachtman, 424 U.S. 409 (1976) (prosecutors who engage in quasi-judicial/advocacy roles such as bringing criminal prosecutions and presenting evidence in court or to a grand jury are absolutely immune from civil liability); Burns v. Reed, 500 U.S. 478 (1991) (prosecutors who engage in non-advocacy/investigative or administrative roles such as giving erroneous advice to police entitled to only qualified immunity for good-faith actions). Some courts apply a functional test to determine whether a prosecutor's act is administrative or judicial. *See, e.g.,* Mink v. Suthers, 482 F.3d 1244 (10th Cir. 2007) (prosecutor's review of a search warrant application administrative, not judicial).

26. *See* Bennett L. Gershman, *Prosecutorial Misconduct* (2d ed., West 2007). In a 2003 study of appellate decisions since 1970, the Center for Public Integrity found prosecutorial misconduct as a factor in dismissing or reversing criminal convictions or reducing criminal sentences in 2,012 cases, including courtroom and grand jury misconduct, mishandling of physical evidence, failure to disclose exculpatory evidence, tampering with witnesses, using false or misleading evidence, or engaging in harassing or biased behavior. *See* Steve Weinberg, *Breaking the Rules: Who Suffers When a Prosecutor Is Cited for Misconduct?* Available at *http://www.publicintergrity.org/pm/default. aspx?act=main.* Last visited July 23, 2007.

criminal defendants, such as the obligation to disclose exculpatory evidence, have been made part of Model Rule 3.8, which specifically governs prosecutors.[27] Although professional discipline is not common,[28] it does occur.[29] Beyond discipline, prosecutors obviously need to avoid conduct that results in reversals of criminal convictions.[30] Prosecutors also have been held liable under civil rights statutes for erroneous advice that violates a defendant's constitutional right.[31]

Confidentiality   Like all other lawyers, government lawyers are prohibited from both using confidential information to their client's disadvantage and from disclosing it without adequate informed consent.[32] In addition, the government's power gives its lawyers access to information about not only the government-client, but also about individuals outside of government. Government lawyers also must keep this "confidential governmental information" about individuals confidential because the government client itself has an obligation to keep such information secret.[33]

---

27. The McDade Amendment, 28 U.S.C. §530B (2007), explicitly makes federal DOJ lawyers and other law enforcement lawyers subject to the lawyer codes in the jurisdictions where they are admitted to practice law. *See also* Ramsey v. Bd. of Prof. Resp. of Tenn. Sup. Ct., 771 S.W.2d 116 (Tenn. 1989) (prosecutors subject to professional discipline despite state constitutional provision that prosecutors can be removed only by impeachment).

28. Fred C. Zacharias, *The Professional Discipline of Prosecutors*, 79 N.C. L. Rev. 721 (2001).

29. *See, e.g.,* Duff Wilson, *Prosecutor in Duke Case Is Suspended*, N.Y. Times A13 (June 20, 2007) (District Attorney Michael Nifong disbarred and suspended from office for failing to disclose exculpatory evidence and misleading a judge in a rape case); In re Stuart, 803 N.Y.S. 2d 577 (App. Div. 2006) (prosecutor who misrepresented location of critical witness to the court suspended for three years); In re Janklow, 709 N.W.2d 28 (S.D. 2006) (prosecutor convicted of reckless driving and second degree manslaughter suspended for 26 months); In re Peasley, 90 P.3d 764 (Ariz. 2004) (prosecutor who deliberately presented false testimony disbarred for violating Rule 3.3); Atty. Grievance Commn. v. Gansler, 835 A.2d 548 (Md. 2003) (prosecutor's extrajudicial comments violated Rule 3.6); In re Paulter, 47 P.3d 1175 (Colo. 2002) (prosecutor who impersonated a public defender when suspect asked to speak to a lawyer suspended for three months for violating Rules 4.3 and 8.3(c)); State v. Mucklow, 35 P.3d 527 (Colo. 2000) (prosecutor who failed to disclose exculpatory evidence publicly censured for violating Rule 3.8 (c)); In re Swarts, 30 P.3d 1011 (Kan. 2001) (prosecutor who engaged in ten different instances of misconduct evidencing lack of respect for individuals suspended from practice and forced to resign); In re Bonet, 29 P.3d 1242 (Wash. 2001) (prosecutor who offered co-defendant inducement not to testify in co-defendant's case disbarred for violating Rules 3.4(b), 8.4(b), and (d)); In re Howes, 940 P.2d 159 (N.M. 1997) (prosecutor who spoke to represented criminal defendant without permission publicly reprimanded for violating Rule 4.2); Massameno v. Statewide Grievance Comm., 663 A.2d 317 (Conn. 1995) (prosecutor who brought criminal action without probable cause violated Rule 3.8(a)).

30. Gershman, *supra* note 26, at 567-579. *See also* United States v. Stein, 495 F. Supp. 2d 390 (S.D.N.Y. 2007) (dismissing indictment against individual corporate officers because in promulgating Thompson Memorandum, DOJ "deliberately or callously prevented many of these corporate defendants from obtaining funds for their defense that they would have had absent the government's interference . . . thereby foreclos[ing them] from presenting the defenses they wished to present and in some cases, even depriv[ing] them of counsel of their choice").

31. *See, e.g.,* Buckley v. Fitzsimmons, 509 U.S. 259 (1993) (prosecutor who made false statements about criminal defendant to the media); Mitchell v. Forsyth, 472 U.S. 511 (1985) (attorney general who participated in illegal wiretapping); McSurely v. McClellan, 697 F.2d 309 (D.C. Cir. 1982) (prosecutor who prepared illegal search warrant and led illegal raid).

32. MR 1.6, 1.8(b); RLGL §§16(3), 97, Comment a.

33. MR 1.11(c).

Government lawyers who seek to disclose confidential information must be attuned to a careful identification of their client in order to obtain adequate informed consent. For example, a state attorney general was disciplined for disclosing to an environmental group an agency's potential change of position on landfill requirements. The agency had revealed this information to an opposing party in an individual case, but claimed that the subsequent AG's disclosure could have hamstrung its political ability to change course. The fact that the agency's disclosure might have constituted a privilege waiver,[34] or the fact that disclosure might have been required if a FOIA request had been made, were not defenses to the unauthorized disclosure.[35]

On the other hand, the government's ability to keep information confidential is also shaped by extensive legal regulation, which recognizes that transparency in many government functions is essential to maintaining the government's legitimacy. For example, federal and state whistleblowing statutes allow government employees to disclose government wrongdoing, and prohibit retaliation if they do so.[36] Extensive regulation of government information also requires disclosure of some information, such as agency structure and management, or open meeting acts, as well as Freedom of Information Acts (FOIA), which require disclosure of other information when requested. These provisions may increase the scope of permitted government lawyer disclosure, especially if the legislative branch requires such disclosure, which would trigger the "required by law" exception in Model Rule 1.6(b)(6).[37]

Model Rule 1.13(c) creates another ground for discretionary disclosure if a government client is engaged in a clear violation of law reasonably certain to result in substantial injury to the organization, and the lawyer has been unsuccessful in remedying it through appropriate channels. No crime or fraud need be involved, as long as the government's violation of law is related to the

---

34. The attorney-client privilege and work product doctrine extends to government clients, but courts pay careful attention to proper identification of the client in applying the privilege. RLGL §74. *See, e.g.,* In re Grand Jury Investigation, 399 F.3d 527 (2d Cir. 2005) (governor's office could invoke attorney-client privilege against United States in investigation of alleged bribery in the state); In re Lindsey, 158 F.3d 1263 (D.C. Cir. 1998) (information that Deputy White House Counsel learned when acting as intermediary between the President and his private counsel was protected by the President's personal attorney-client privilege but Deputy White House Counsel could not rely on "common interest" doctrine and the President's personal attorney-client privilege to withhold information about possible criminal misconduct obtained in conferring with the President and his private counsel on matters of overlapping concern to the President personally and in his official capacity); St. ex rel. Leslie v. Ohio Hous. Fin. Agency, 824 N.E.2d 990 (Ohio 2005). For a discussion of the meaning of a range of similar cases, *see* Patricia E. Salkin & Allyson Phillips, *Eliminating Political Maneuvering: A Light in the Tunnel for the Government Attorney-Client Privilege,* 39 Ind. L. Rev. 561 (2006).

35. Law. Disc. Bd. v. McGraw, 461 S.E.2d 850 (W. Va. 1995).

36. Robert T. Begg, *Whistleblower Law and Ethics,* in *Ethical Standards in the Public Sector: A Guide for Government Lawyers, Client, and Public Officials* at 136; James E. Moliterno, *The Federal Government Lawyer's Duty to Breach Confidentiality,* 14 Temp. Pol. & Civ. Rights L. Rev. 633 (2005); Jesselyn Radack, *The Government Attorney-Whistleblower and the Rule of Confidentiality: Compatible at Last,* 17 Geo. J. Leg. Ethics 125 (2003); Roger C. Cramden, *The Lawyer as Whistleblower: Confidentiality and the Government Lawyer,* 5 Geo. J. Leg. Ethics 291 (1991).

37. *See, e.g.,* Law. Disc. Bd. v. McGraw, *supra* note 35 (particular disclosure not allowed because it was not required by the state FOIA statute, as no request for the information had been made).

lawyer's representation.[38] This discretion rests on a lawyer's reasonable belief that substantial harm to the government will result, an estimation about which those in power may disagree. Nevertheless, assuming the lawyer has documented a clear violation of law, presumably substantial tort damages or patterns of illegal activity that would substantially undermine public trust may suffice.[39]

Conflict of Interest Resolution   Lawyers working for government clients are subject to both the general conflicts provision in Model Rule 1.7 and the former client conflict provision in Model Rule 1.9.[40] Lawyers currently working for the government and those who leave government service also are subject to the specialized conflicts provisions of Model Rule 1.11. Lawyers who leave government service are subject to a narrower former client disqualification based on whether the lawyer "participated personally and substantially" in a "matter,"[41] rather than the broader substantially related matter protection for private clients in Model Rule 1.9(a).[42] A few jurisdictions extend this prohibition to substantially related matters as well.[43]

Where a former government lawyer is disqualified, the Model Rule provides for either government agency consent or screening to remove the problem.[44]

---

38. MR 1.13, Comment [6].
39. *See, e.g.,* Christopher A. Britt, *The Commissioning Oath and the Ethical Obligation of Military Officers to Prevent Subordinates from Committing Acts of Torture,* 19 Geo. J. Leg. Ethics 551 (2006); Kathleen Clark, *Ethical Issues Raised by the OLC Torture Memorandum,* 1 J. Natl. Sec. L. & Policy 455 (2005).
40. MR 1.11(d). *See, e.g.,* City and Co. of San Francisco v. Cobra Solutions, Inc., 135 P.3d 20 (Cal. 2006) (city attorney who formerly represented technology company when in private practice in substantially related matter disqualified from subsequent representation and conflict imputed to the rest of the city attorney's office); Mass. Op. 2004-3 (a municipal Solicitor may ordinarily represent the municipality before its Zoning Board of Appeals even though the Solicitor represents the Zoning Board of Appeals in other matters, except when a conflict of interest or a personal relationship with Board members precludes such representation); N.Y. St. Bar Op. 773 (2004) (a lawyer who serves on a municipal board is prohibited from appearing before that board on behalf of a private client and lawyers who are "of counsel" to the lawyer's law firm are likewise disqualified); Mich. Op. RI-331 (2003) (a lawyer who serves as a member of a legislative body must decline representation of private clients in matters that require the exercise of the lawyer's duty to the public that are contrary to the private client's interests in the matter of the representation); Cal. Formal Op. 2001-156 (2002) (a city attorney's provision of legal advice on the same matter to constituent sub-entities and officials will not necessarily give rise to a conflict of interest even if the sub-entities and officials take contrary positions on the matter because the constituent sub-entities and officials of the city are normally not separate clients of the city attorney); Ark. Op. 2001-01 (a law firm with a member who is a part-time attorney for the city cannot bring a lawsuit against the city, even if the lawsuit is unrelated, unless both the city and the proposed civil litigant consent to and waive the conflict).
41. MR 1.11(a), (e); RLGL §133.
42. *E.g.,* Gatewood v. St., 880 A.2d 322 (Md. 2005) (prosecutor who represented defendant on substantially related matter not disqualified); D.C. Op. 315 (2002) (a former EPA lawyer who had no more than official responsibility or participation in litigation substantially related to the drafting status of proposed regulations may represent a private client in challenging the EPS's final rules); N.Y. St. Bar Op. 748 (2001) (a former prosecutor may represent criminal defendants investigated and prosecuted during the former prosecutor's tenure with a district attorney's office if he or she did not participate personally and substantially in the investigation or prosecution of the defendant, and where doing so violated neither the duty to represent the new client zealously nor the duty to protect the former client's confidences).
43. *See, e.g.,* D.C. R. Prof. Conduct 1.11(a) (2007); Jordan v. Philadelphia Hous. Auth., 337 F. Supp. 2d 666 (E.D. Pa. 2004).
44. MR 1.11(b); RLGL §124(3).

Screening also has been upheld in moves from one government office to another, such as from a public defender office to a prosecutor's office.[45]

The Bounds of the Law

Federal Regulation Beyond the lawyer codes, state and federal conflict of interest statutes regulate government lawyers during and after their government service. Officers and employees of the executive branch are subject to provisions concerning financial conflicts of interest.[46] Specific conflict of interest rules also apply to lawyers who serve as trustees in bankruptcy courts.[47] Several agencies add additional requirements that govern who can practice before that agency.[48] Some lawyers, such as special prosecutors, also are subject to particular agency regulations.[49] Former government employees are governed by the Ethics in Government Act, which contains several restrictions that are stricter than those found in the professional codes.[50] Violations of all of these provisions are felonies, punishable with fines and imprisonment for up to five years.[51] Courts have used the elements of these statutes as the basis for granting disqualification motions.[52] State disciplinary agencies also have relied on these provisions in cases of professional discipline.[53] Like Model Rule 1.11, these statutes governing government employees are sometimes referred to as "revolving door rules," a phrase that refers to the practice of lawyers moving back and forth between government service and private practice. The goal of both sets of rules is to prevent potential abuses, such as use of confidential governmental information or the risk that a lawyer might misuse a government position to benefit herself in later private practice. Most relevant is 18 U.S.C. §207, which contains three provisions that stringently regulate the conduct of former government lawyers.

The first provision permanently prohibits appearances and communications with any government agency, department, or court in particular matters where the person participated "personally and substantially" while a government employee.[54] The consent of the agency is not a defense (as it would be in Model

---

45. St. ex rel. Horn v. Ray, 138 S.W.3d 729 (Mo. App. 2002).
46. 18 U.S.C. §§208, 209 (2006).
47. 18 U.S.C. §154 (2006) imposes criminal liability on trustees and others for certain personal conflicts of interest. Lawyers hired by the trustee also are subject to 11 U.S.C. §327 (2006), which creates standards for disinterested representation. *See* Lawrence P. King, ed., *Collier on Bankruptcy* §§8.02, 8.03 (15th ed., Matthew Bender 2000).
48. *See, e.g.,* Practice Before the Internal Revenue Service, 31 C.F.R. §10.25 (2003) (Practice by Former Government Employees, Their Partners and Their Associates).
49. For a discussion of how these regulations impacted on the work of Kenneth Starr, *see* David Halperin, *Ethics Breakthrough or Ethics Breakdown? Kenneth Starr's Dual Roles as Private Practitioner and Public Prosecutor,* 15 Geo. J. Leg. Ethics 231 (2002).
50. 18 U.S.C. §207 (2006). *See* Thomas D. Morgan, *Appropriate Limits on Participation by a Former Agency Official in Matters Before an Agency,* 1980 Duke L.J. 1 (discussing the history of the Ethics in Government Act).
51. 18 U.S.C. §216 (2006).
52. *See, e.g.,* In re Rest. Dev. of P.R., Inc., 128 B.R. 498 (Bankr. D.P.R. 1991); Kessenich v. Commodity Futures Trading Commn., 684 F.2d 88 (D.C. Cir. 1982).
53. *See, e.g.,* Disc. Counsel v. Eilberg, 441 A.2d 1193 (Pa. 1982) (lawyer who violated 18 U.S.C. §203(a) suspended from practice for five years).
54. 18 U.S.C. §207(a)(1) (2006); D.C. Op. 297 (2000) (the Indian Self-Determination Act, 25 U.S.C. §450*i*(j), creates an exception to the restrictions in 18 U.S.C. §207(a) for former

Rule 1.11). As long as the former employee made the communication "with the intent to influence" the government on behalf of another person in a matter in which she formerly participated, the crime is complete. Thus, a lawyer who filed an amicus brief on behalf of a private client in a case she worked on as a government lawyer would violate the statute, but not Model Rule 1.11. Yet, a former government lawyer who counsels a client on a matter that the lawyer worked on at the government has violated Model Rule 1.11, but not 18 U.S.C. §207.[55]

The second provision creates a two-year restriction on communication or appearance with any governmental agency, court, or department on behalf of another party in connection with particular matters under that person's official responsibility before she left the government.[56] For example, a high-level employee of the Internal Revenue Service who retired and started a tax service violated this provision when he attended meetings with an IRS officer and three taxpayers whose tax collection had been his responsibility prior to retirement.[57]

The third provision creates a one-year prohibition on certain senior governmental personnel from appearing before or communicating with the governmental agency for which they worked.[58]

State Provisions The majority of states also have enacted ethics laws that restrict the practice of both current and former lawyers and other governmental employees.[59] State and municipal agencies also regulate the conduct of employees, including lawyers.[60] Like federal lawyers, state lawyers are subject to both these ethics statutes and the relevant professional code.[61] State provisions generally parallel those in the federal law and Model Rule 1.11. For example, many include bans on appearances or representation before the lawyer's former agency for a period of time.[62] Many states also bar representation in matters in

---

government employees retained by Indian Tribes, but Rule 1.6 protects the government's confidentiality).

55. A lawyer acting as an expert witness on behalf of the government may not violate the statute. 18 U.S.C. §207(j)(6) (2000); EEOC v. Exxon Corp., 202 F.3d 755 (5th Cir. 2000).

56. 18 U.S.C. §207(a)(2) (2006).

57. United States v. Coleman, 805 F.2d 474 (3d Cir. 1986).

58. 18 U.S.C. §207(c) (2006).

59. See, e.g., National Conference of State Legislators, The State of State Legislative Ethics: A Look at the Ethical Climate and Ethics Laws for State Legislators (Ctr. for Ethics in Govt. 2002); Rachel E. Boehm, Student Author, Caught in the Revolving Door: A State Lawyer's Guide to Post-Employment Restrictions, 15 Rev. Litig. 525, 532 n.26 (1996), citing statutes in 30 states.

60. See Mark Davies, Considering Ethics at the Local Government Level, in Ethical Standards in the Public Sector, supra note 36, at 127-155. These provisions generally have withstood constitutional attack. See, e.g., Ortiz v. Taxn. and Revenue Dept., 954 P.2d 109 (N.M. App. 1998) (statute prohibiting former public officers and employees from representing persons for pay before their former government agency employers is constitutional as applied to executive branch employees); Midboe v. Commn. on Ethics for Pub. Employees, 646 So. 2d 351 (La. 1994) (Code of Governmental Ethics for public servants was not unconstitutional as applied to lawyer because the legislature was not regulating law practice in general). Cf., Shaulis v. Pa. St. Ethics Commn., 833 A.2d 123 (Pa. 2003) (Public Official and Employee Ethics Act violated separation of powers because it specifically targeted lawyers who were former government employees).

61. See, e.g., P.J.S. v. Pa. St. Ethics Commn., 723 A.2d 174 (Pa. 1999) (lawyer who served as part-time city solicitor subject to both state ethics laws and state lawyer code).

62. See, e.g., Cal. Govt. Code §87406(d)(1) (2007) (one-year ban on acting as an attorney for any person before the agency that formerly employed the lawyer); N.Y. Pub. Off. Law §73(8)(a)(i)

which the former government lawyer participated personally and substantially.[63] A few jurisdictions regulate additional matters as well, such as prohibiting former government lawyers from accepting employment with entities that are subject to regulation by their former agency employer or with those that do business with the state.[64] State law also parallels federal law in targeting former employees of particular agencies or commissions.[65] Despite these similarities, each state has enacted its own special mix of prohibitions, often in response to a particular political embarrassment.[66]

Conclusion

All of this legal regulation demands careful attention, especially to several details that many of these rules share. First, each rule makes the role of the government employee relevant to its reach. Second, many of these rules also define the lawyer's role after leaving government service. Finally, each rule creates a distinctive penalty. Some create criminal penalties, others administrative remedies, such as loss of a government contract or benefit.[67] Federal and state governments have found these additional remedies necessary to curb specific abuses of the public trust. Courts also have used these provisions as a guide to other relief, such as disqualification. Wise government lawyers need to remain aware of both professional code provisions and other state and federal law to fully understand their obligations.

(2002) (two-year ban on appearing or practicing before state agency that formerly employed the person in any matter).

63. *See, e.g.,* Ark. Code §19-11-709(b)(1) (2007) (permanent disqualification); Ind. Code §4-2-6-11(c) (2007) (permanent disqualification).

64. Boehm, *supra* note 59, at 535.

65. *See, e.g.,* Ohio Rev. Code §102.03(2) (2007) (regulating practice of former commissioners and attorney examiners of the public utilities commission); Tex. Water Code §26.0283 (2002) (regulating assistance by former employees of the Texas Natural Resource Conservation Commission); Or. Rev. Stat. §244.045(2) (2001) (regulating former deputy and assistant attorneys general).

66. *See, e.g.,* Robert C. Newman, *New York's New Ethics Law: Turning the Tide on Corruption,* 16 Hofstra L. Rev. 319 (1988).

67. *E.g.,* Tex. Water Code, *supra* note 65, provides that the Texas Water Commission "shall deny an application . . . for a permit" if a former employee provides assistance to the applicant.

Chapter 10

Fees and Client Property

*"I'm certain I speak for the entire legal profession when
I say that the fee is reasonable and just."*

The materials in this chapter represent a very small sample of an enormous body of law that governs the fees lawyers can contract for and collect from their clients. Disputes over fees are common, and occur for at least three reasons. First, some lawyers do a good job of explaining the basis of the fee and keep more than adequate records of the time they have expended on the matter but nevertheless face clients who are unhappy with the lawyer or the result in their case, or are otherwise unwilling to pay for the representation. Second, some lawyers fail to explain their fee or their progress in the matter so that clients are unpleasantly taken by surprise when they later receive the bill. Third, some lawyers charge clients unreasonable fees, and a few do so fraudulently.

Although it may appear that lawyers are free to bargain with clients at arms length regarding fees before they enter into a client-lawyer relationship, notions of fiduciary duty in the law governing lawyers in fact limit the freedom of lawyers to contract for and collect fees. Fee agreements nearly always involve some degree of conflict of interest, because the lawyer's personal financial interest potentially conflicts with the client's interests in the representation. As we have seen in prior chapters, the remedy for a potential conflict in loyalty is consultation, communication, and informed consent. For fees, as for other conflicts, the greater the potential for conflict, the greater the legal regulation provided to control it.

The loyalty based conflict of interest rules discussed in the last two chapters apply only after a lawyer has agreed to represent a client. Model Rule 1.5 nevertheless imposes several fiduciary-like requirements in the context of pre-contractual fee negotiations, such as obligations to communicate the basis of the fee, limitations on the propriety of certain fee arrangements, and the general requirement that fees are subject to an objective standard of reasonableness. This chapter explores these obligations in the context of hourly, contingent, statutory, and flat fees, as well as the lawyer's correlative fiduciary obligation to handle client funds and property.

A. Hourly Fees

Problems

10-1. Martyn flies to San Francisco for a client that pays full hourly rates for travel. If during a six-hour flight, Martyn works on another client's matters for four hours, may she bill two clients a total of ten hours? What if the work on the plane was *pro bono*?

10-2. May Martyn & Fox charge clients $2/page for all incoming and outgoing faxes? What about billing clients $200/hour for contract lawyers whose agency charges us $150?

Consider: Model Rule 1.5
Model Code DR 2-106

ABA Formal Opinion 93-379
American Bar Association Standing Committee on Ethics and
Professional Responsibility

Billing for Professional Fees, Disbursements and Other Expenses

Consistent with the Model Rules of Professional Conduct, a lawyer must disclose to a client the basis on which the client is to be billed for both professional time and any other charges. Absent a contrary understanding, any invoice for professional services should fairly reflect the basis on which the client's charges have been determined. In matters where the client has agreed to have the fee determined with reference to the time expended by the lawyer, a lawyer may not bill more time than she actually spends on the matter, except to the extent that she rounds up to minimum time periods (such as one-quarter or one-tenth of an hour). . . .

It is a common perception that pressure on lawyers to bill a minimum number of hours and on law firms to maintain or improve profits may have led some lawyers to engage in problematic billing practices. These include charges to more than one client for the same work or the same hours, surcharges on services contracted with outside vendors, and charges beyond reasonable costs for in-house services like photocopying and computer searches. Moreover, the bases on which these charges are to be assessed often are not disclosed in advance or are disguised in cryptic invoices so that the client does not fully understand exactly what costs are being charged to him.

The Model Rules of Professional Conduct provide important principles applicable to the billing of clients, principles which, if followed, would ameliorate many of the problems noted above. The Committee has decided to address several practices that are the subject of frequent inquiry, with the goal of helping the profession adhere to its ethical obligations to its clients despite economic pressures.

The first set of practices involves billing more than one client for the same hours spent. In one illustrative situation, a lawyer finds it possible to schedule court appearances for three clients on the same day. He spends a total of four hours at the courthouse, the amount of time he would have spent on behalf of each client had it not been for the fortuitous circumstance that all three cases were scheduled on the same day. May he bill each of the three clients, who otherwise understand that they will be billed on the basis of time spent, for the four hours he spent on them collectively? In another scenario, a lawyer is flying cross-country to attend a deposition on behalf of one client, expending travel time she would ordinarily bill to that client. If she decides not to watch the movie or read her novel, but to work instead on drafting a motion for another client, may she charge both clients, each of whom agreed to hourly billing, for the time during which she was traveling on behalf of one and drafting a document on behalf of the other? A third situation involves research on a particular topic for one client that later turns out to be relevant to an inquiry from a second client. May the firm bill the second client, who agreed to be charged on the basis of time spent on his case, the same amount for the recycled work product that it charged the first client?

The second set of practices involve billing for expenses and disbursements, and is exemplified by the situation in which a firm contracts for the expert witness services of an economist at an hourly rate of $200. May the firm bill the client for the expert's time at the rate of $250 per hour? Similarly, may the firm add a surcharge to the cost of computer-assisted research if the per-minute total charged by the computer company does not include the cost of purchasing the computers or staffing their operation? . . .

Professional Obligations Regarding the Reasonableness of Fees

Implicit in the Model Rules and their antecedents is the notion that the attorney-client relationship is not necessarily one of equals, that it is built on trust, and that the client is encouraged to be dependent on the lawyer, who is dealing with matters of great moment to the client. The client should only be charged a reasonable fee for the legal services performed. Rule 1.5 explicitly addresses the reasonableness of legal fees. The rule deals not only with the determination of a reasonable hourly rate, but also with total cost to the client. The Comment to the rules states, for example, that "[a] lawyer should not exploit a fee arrangement based primarily on hourly charges by using wasteful procedures." The goal should be solely to compensate the lawyer fully for time reasonably expended, an approach that if followed will not take advantage of the client. . . .

The lawyer's conduct should be such as to promote the client's trust of the lawyer and of the legal profession. . . . An unreasonable limitation on the hours a lawyer may spend on a client should be avoided as a threat to the lawyer's ability to fulfill her obligation under Model Rule 1.1 to "provide competent representation to a client." . . .

On the other hand, the lawyer who has agreed to bill on the basis of hours expended does not fulfill her ethical duty if she bills the client for more time than she actually spent on the client's behalf. In addressing the hypotheticals regarding (a) simultaneous appearance on behalf of three clients, (b) the airplane flight on behalf of one client while working on another client's matters and (c) recycled work product, it is helpful to consider these questions, not from the perspective of what a client could be forced to pay, but rather from the perspective of what the lawyer actually earned. A lawyer who spends four hours of time on behalf of three clients has not earned twelve billable hours. A lawyer who flies for six hours for one client, while working for five hours on behalf of another, has not earned eleven billable hours. A lawyer who is able to reuse old work product has not re-earned the hours previously billed and compensated when the work product was first generated. Rather than looking to profit from the fortuity of coincidental scheduling, the desire to get work done rather than watch a movie, or the luck of being asked the identical question twice, the lawyer who has agreed to bill solely on the basis of time spent is obliged to pass the benefits of these economies on to the client. The practice of billing several clients for the same time or work product, since it results in the earning of an unreasonable fee, therefore is contrary to the mandate of . . . Model Rule 1.5.

Moreover, continuous toil on or over-staffing a project for the purpose of churning out hours is also not properly considered "earning" one's fees. One job of a lawyer is to expedite the legal process. Model Rule 3.2. . . . A lawyer should take as much time as is reasonably required to complete a project, and should certainly never be motivated by anything other than the best interests of the client when determining how to staff or how much time to spend on any particular project.

It goes without saying that a lawyer who has undertaken to bill on an hourly basis is never justified in charging a client for hours not actually expended. If a lawyer has agreed to charge the client on this basis and it turns out that the lawyer is particularly efficient in accomplishing a given result, it nonetheless will not be permissible to charge the client for more hours than were actually expended on the matter. When that basis for billing the client has been agreed to, the economies associated with the result must inure to the benefit of the client, not give rise to an opportunity to bill a client phantom hours. This is not to say that the lawyer who agreed to hourly compensation is not free, with full disclosure, to suggest additional compensation because of a particularly efficient or outstanding result, or because the lawyer was able to reuse prior work product on the client's behalf. The point here is that fee enhancement cannot be accomplished simply by presenting the client with a statement reflecting more billable hours than were actually expended. On the other hand, if a matter turns out to be more difficult to accomplish than first anticipated and more hours are required than were originally estimated, the lawyer is fully entitled (though not required) to bill those hours unless the client agreement turned the original estimate into a cap on the fees to be charged.

Charges Other than Professional Fees

In addition to charging clients fees for professional services, lawyers typically charge their clients for certain additional items which are often referred to variously as disbursements, out-of-pocket expenses or additional charges. . . . [W]e believe that the reasonableness standard explicitly applicable to fees under Rule 1.5(a) should be applicable to these charges as well. . . .

First, which items are properly subject to additional charges? Second, to what extent, if at all, may clients be charged for more than actual out-of-pocket disbursements? Third, on what basis may clients be charged for the provision of in-house services? . . .

A. General Overhead

When a client has engaged a lawyer to provide professional services for a fee (whether calculated on the basis of the number of hours expended, a flat fee, a contingent percentage of the amount recovered or otherwise) the client would be justifiably disturbed if the lawyer submitted a bill to the client which included, beyond the professional fee, additional charges for general office overhead. In the absence of disclosure to the client in advance of the engagement to the contrary, the client should reasonably expect that the lawyer's cost in maintaining a library, securing malpractice insurance, renting of office space, purchasing utilities and the like would be subsumed within the charges the lawyer is making for professional services.

B. *Disbursements*

At the beginning of the engagement lawyers typically tell their clients that they will be charged for disbursements. When that term is used clients justifiably should expect that the lawyer will be passing on to the client those actual payments of funds made by the lawyer on the client's behalf. Thus, if the lawyer hires a court stenographer to transcribe a deposition, the client can reasonably expect to be billed as a disbursement the amount the lawyer pays to the court reporting service. Similarly, if the lawyer flies to Los Angeles for the client, the client can reasonably expect to be billed as a disbursement the amount of the airfare, taxicabs, meals and hotel room.

It is the view of the Committee that, in the absence of disclosure to the contrary, it would be improper if the lawyer assessed a surcharge on these disbursements over and above the amount actually incurred unless the lawyer herself incurred additional expenses beyond the actual cost of the disbursement item. In the same regard, if a lawyer receives a discounted rate from a third party provider, it would be improper if she did not pass along the benefit of the discount to her client rather than charge the client the full rate and reserve the profit to herself. Clients quite properly could view these practices as an attempt to create additional undisclosed profit centers when the client had been told he would be billed for disbursements.

C. *In-House Provision of Services*

Perhaps the most difficult issue is the handling of charges to clients for the provision of in-house services . . . [such as] charges for photocopying, computer research, on-site meals, deliveries and other similar items. Like professional fees, it seems clear that lawyers may pass on reasonable charges for these services. Thus, in the view of the committee, the lawyer and the client may agree in advance that, for example, photocopying will be charged at $.15 per page, or messenger services will be provided at $5.00 per mile. However, the question arises what may be charged to the client, in the absence of a specific agreement to the contrary, when the client has simply been told that costs for these items will be charged to the client. We conclude that under those circumstances the lawyer is obliged to charge the client no more than the direct cost associated with the service (i.e., the actual cost of making a copy on the photocopy machine) plus a reasonable allocation of overhead expenses directly associated with the provision of the service (e.g., the salary of a photocopy machine operator).

. . . Any reasonable calculation of direct costs as well as any reasonable allocation of related overhead should pass ethical muster. On the other hand, in the absence of an agreement to the contrary, it is impermissible for a lawyer to create an additional source of profit for the law firm beyond that which is contained in the provision of professional services themselves. The lawyer's stock in trade is the sale of legal services, not photocopy paper, tuna fish sandwiches, computer time or messenger services.

Matter of Fordham
668 N.E.2d 816 (Mass. 1996)

O'CONNOR, J.

This is an appeal from the Board of Bar Overseers' (board's) dismissal of a petition for discipline filed by bar counsel against attorney Laurence S. Fordham . . .

We summarize the hearing committee's findings. On March 4, 1989, the Acton police department arrested Timothy, then twenty-one years old, and charged him with OUI, operating a motor vehicle after suspension, speeding, and operating an unregistered motor vehicle. At the time of the arrest, the police discovered a partially full quart of vodka in the vehicle. After failing a field sobriety test, Timothy was taken to the Acton police station where he submitted to two breathalyzer tests which registered .10 and .12 respectively.

Subsequent to Timothy's arraignment, he and his father, Laurence Clark (Clark) consulted with three lawyers, who offered to represent Timothy for fees between $3,000 and $10,000. Shortly after the arrest, Clark went to Fordham's home to service an alarm system which he had installed several years before. While there, Clark discussed Timothy's arrest with Fordham's wife who invited Clark to discuss the case with Fordham. Fordham then met with Clark and Timothy.

At this meeting, Timothy described the incidents leading to his arrest and the charges against him. Fordham, whom the hearing committee described as a "very experienced senior trial attorney with impressive credentials," told Clark and Timothy that he had never represented a client in a driving while under the influence case or in any criminal matter, and he had never tried a case in the District Court. The hearing committee found that "Fordham explained that although he lacked experience in this area, he was a knowledgeable and hard-working attorney and that he believed he could competently represent Timothy. Fordham described himself as efficient and economic in the use of [his] time. . . .

"Towards the end of the meeting, Fordham told the Clarks that he worked on [a] time charge basis and that he billed monthly . . . In other words, Fordham would calculate the amount of hours he and others in the firm worked on a matter each month and multiply it by the respective hourly rates. He also told the Clarks that he would engage others in his firm to prepare the case. Clark had indicated that he would pay Timothy's legal fees." After the meeting, Clark hired Fordham to represent Timothy.

According to the hearing committee's findings, Fordham filed four pretrial motions on Timothy's behalf, two of which were allowed. One motion, entitled "Motion in Limine to Suppress Results of Breathalyzer Tests," was based on the theory that, although two breathalyzer tests were exactly .02 apart, they were not "within" .02 of one another as the regulations require. The hearing committee characterized the motion and its rationale as "a creative, if not novel, approach to suppression of breathalyzer results." . . . [T]he trial, which was before a judge without jury, was held on October 10 and October 19, 1989. The judge found Timothy not guilty of driving while under the influence.

Fordham sent . . . bills to Clark . . . [that] totaled $50,022.25, reflecting 227 hours of billed time, 153 hours of which were expended by Fordham and seventy-four of which were his associates' time. Clark did not pay the first two bills when they became due and expressed to Fordham his concern about their amount. Clark paid Fordham $10,000 on June 20, 1989. At that time, Fordham assured Clark that most of the work had been completed "other than taking [the case] to trial." Clark did not make any subsequent payments. Fordham requested Clark to sign a promissory note evidencing his debt to Fordham and, on October 7, 1989, Clark did so. In the October 13, 1989, bill, Fordham added a charge of $5,000 as a "retroactive increase" in fees. On November 7, 1989, after the case was completed, Fordham sent Clark a bill for $15,000.

Bar counsel and Fordham have stipulated that all the work billed by Fordham was actually done and that Fordham and his associates spent the time they claim to have spent. They also have stipulated that Fordham acted conscientiously, diligently, and in good faith in representing Timothy and in his billing in this case.

. . . Although the hearing committee determined that Fordham "spent a large number of hours on [the] matter, in essence learning from scratch what others . . . already know," . . . [it] reasoned that even if the number of hours Fordham "spent [were] wholly out of proportion" to the number of hours that a lawyer with experience in the trying of OUI cases would require, the committee was not required to conclude that the fee based on time spent was "clearly excessive." It was enough, the hearing committee concluded, that Clark

instructed Fordham to pursue the case to trial, Fordham did so zealously and, as stipulated, Fordham spent the hours he billed in good faith and diligence. We disagree.

Four witnesses testified before the hearing committee as experts on OUI cases. One of the experts, testifying on behalf of bar counsel, opined that "the amount of time spent in this case is clearly excessive." He testified that there were no unusual circumstances in the OUI charge against Timothy and that it was a "standard operating under the influence case." The witness did agree that Fordham's argument for suppression of the breathalyzer test results, which was successful, was novel and would have justified additional time and labor. He also acknowledged that the acquittal was a good result; even with the suppression of the breathalyzer tests, he testified, the chances of an acquittal would have been "not likely at a bench trial." The witness estimated that it would have been necessary, for thorough preparation of the case including the novel breathalyzer suppression argument, to have billed twenty to thirty hours for preparation, not including trial time.

A second expert, testifying on behalf of bar counsel, expressed his belief that the issues presented in this case were not particularly difficult, nor novel, and that "the degree of skill required to defend a case such as this . . . was not that high." He did recognize, however, that the theory that Fordham utilized to suppress the breathalyzer tests was impressive and one of which he had previously never heard. Nonetheless, the witness concluded that "clearly there is no way that [he] could justify these kind of hours to do this kind of work." . . .

An expert called by Fordham testified that the facts of Timothy's case presented a challenge and that without the suppression of the breathalyzer test results it would have been "an almost impossible situation in terms of prevailing on the trier of fact." He further stated that, based on the particulars in Timothy's case, he believed that Fordham's hours were not excessive and, in fact, he, the witness, would have spent a comparable amount of time. The witness later admitted, however, that within the past five years, the OUI cases which he had brought to trial required no more than a total of forty billed hours, which encompassed all preparation and court appearances. He explained that, although he had not charged more than forty hours to prepare an OUI case, in comparison to Fordham's more than 200 expended hours, Fordham nonetheless had spent a reasonable number of hours on the case in light of the continuance and the subsequent need to reprepare, as well as the "very ingenious" breathalyzer suppression argument, and the Clarks' insistence on trial. In addition, the witness testified that, although the field sobriety test, breathalyzer tests, and the presence of a half-empty liquor bottle in the car placed Fordham at a serious disadvantage in being able to prevail on the OUI charge, those circumstances were not unusual and in fact agreed that they were "normal circumstances."

The fourth expert witness, called by Fordham, testified that she believed the case was "extremely tough" and that the breathalyzer suppression theory was novel. She testified that, although the time and labor consumed on the case was more than usual in defending an OUI charge,

the hours were not excessive. They were not excessive, she explained, because the case was particularly difficult due to the "stakes [and] the evidence." She conceded, however, that legal issues in defending OUI charges are "pretty standard" and that the issues presented in this case were not unusual. . . .

In considering whether a fee is "clearly excessive" within the meaning of S.J.C. Rule 3:07, DR 2-106(B), the first factor to be considered pursuant to that rule is "the novelty and difficulty of the questions involved, and the skill requisite to perform the legal service properly." That standard is similar to the familiar standard of reasonableness traditionally applied in civil fee disputes. Based on the testimony of the four experts, the number of hours devoted to Timothy's OUI case by Fordham and his associates was substantially in excess of the hours that a prudent experienced lawyer would have spent. According to the evidence, the number of hours spent was several times the amount of time any of the witnesses had ever spent on a similar case. We are not unmindful of the novel and successful motion to suppress the breathalyzer test results, but that effort cannot justify a $50,000 fee in a type of case in which the usual fee is less than one-third of that amount.

The board determined that "because [Fordham] had never tried an OUI case or appeared in the district court, [Fordham] spent over 200 hours preparing the case, in part to educate himself in the relevant substantive law and court procedures." Fordham's inexperience in criminal defense work and OUI cases in particular cannot justify the extraordinarily high fee. It cannot be that an inexperienced lawyer is entitled to charge three or four times as much as an experienced lawyer for the same service. A client "should not be expected to pay for the education of a lawyer when he spends excessive amounts of time on tasks which, with reasonable experience, become matters of routine." . . .

DR 2-106(B) provides that the third factor to be considered in ascertaining the reasonableness of the fee is its comparability to "the fee customarily charged in the locality for similar legal services." The hearing committee made no finding as to the comparability of Fordham's fee with the fees customarily charged in the locality for similar services. However, one of bar counsel's expert witnesses testified that he had never heard of a fee in excess of $15,000 to defend a first OUI charge, and the customary flat fee in an OUI case, including trial, "runs from $1,000 to $7,500." Bar counsel's other expert testified that he had never heard of a fee in excess of $10,000 for a bench trial. In his view, the customary charge for a case similar to Timothy's would vary between $1,500 and $5,000. One of Fordham's experts testified that she considered a $40,000 or $50,000 fee for defending an OUI charge "unusual and certainly higher by far than any I've ever seen before." The witness had never charged a fee of more than $3,500 for representing a client at a bench trial to defend a first offense OUI charge. She further testified that she believed an "average OUI in the bench session is two thousand [dollars] and sometimes less." . . .

Although finding that Fordham's fee was "much higher than the fee charged by many attorneys with more experience litigating driving under the influence cases," the hearing committee nevertheless determined that the fee charged by Fordham was not clearly excessive because Clark "went into the relationship with Fordham with open eyes," [and] Fordham's fee fell within a "safe harbor." . . .

The finding that Clark had entered into the fee agreement "with open eyes" was based on the finding that Clark hired Fordham after being fully apprised that he lacked any type of experience in defending an OUI charge and after interviewing other lawyers who were experts in defending OUI charges. . . . It is also significant, however, that the hearing committee found that "despite Fordham's disclaimers concerning his experience, Clark did not appear to have understood in any real sense the implications of choosing Fordham to represent Timothy. Fordham did not give Clark any estimate of the total expected fee or the number of $200 hours that would be required." The express finding of the hearing committee that Clark "did not appear to have understood in any real sense the implications of choosing Fordham to represent Timothy" directly militates against the finding that Clark entered into the agreement "with open eyes."

That brings us to the hearing committee's finding that Fordham's fee fell within a "safe harbor." The hearing committee reasoned that as long as an agreement existed between a client and an attorney to bill a reasonable rate multiplied by the number of hours actually worked, the attorney's fee was within a "safe harbor" and thus protected from a challenge that the fee was clearly excessive. . . .

The "safe harbor" formula would not be an appropriate rationale in this case because the amount of time Fordham spent to educate himself and represent Timothy was clearly excessive despite his good faith and diligence. Disciplinary Rule 2-106 (B)'s mandate that "[a] fee is clearly excessive when, after a review of the facts, a lawyer of ordinary prudence, experienced in the area of the law involved, would be left with a definite and firm conviction that the fee is substantially in excess of a reasonable fee," creates explicitly an objective standard by which attorneys' fees are to be judged. We are not persuaded by Fordham's argument that "unless it can be shown that the 'excessive' work for which the attorney has charged goes beyond mere matters of professional judgment and can be proven, either directly or by reasonable inference, to have involved dishonesty, bad faith or overreaching of the client, no case for discipline has been established." Disciplinary Rule 2-106 plainly does not require an inquiry into whether the clearly ex-

cessive fee was charged to the client under fraudulent circumstances, and we shall not write such a meaning into the disciplinary rule.

Finally, bar counsel challenges the hearing committee's finding that "if Clark objected to the numbers of hours being spent by Fordham, he could have spoken up with some force when he began receiving bills." Bar counsel notes, and we agree, that "the test as stated in the DR 2-106(A) is whether the fee 'charged' is clearly excessive, not whether the fee is accepted as valid or acquiesced in by the client." . . .

In charging a clearly excessive fee, Fordham departed substantially from the obligation of professional responsibility that he owed to his client. The ABA Model Standards for Imposing Lawyer Sanctions §7.3 (1992) endorses a public reprimand as the appropriate sanction for charging a clearly excessive fee. We deem such a sanction appropriate in this case. Accordingly, a judgment is to be entered in the county court imposing a public censure. . . .

Lawrence J. Fox

Raise the Bar: Real World Solutions for a Troubled Profession

15-29 (ABA 2007)

End billable hour goals . . . now

We are delighted you have selected Austen Dental Services for all your dental needs. We look forward to providing you with high quality cost effective services. Our team of talented young dentists are highly motivated to give you outstanding services not only by virtue of their professional commitment to you, but also because the very best of them will be offered partnership in our great organization. To that end, we are sure you will be pleased to learn that we will charge for our services on an hourly basis. To demonstrate their dedication, we require our young dentists to record at least 2,000 billable hours per year, with bonuses if the dentist should achieve benchmarks of hourly dedication beyond 2,000.

* * *

Hourly billing has been with the legal profession a very long time. The evolution from one line bills "for professional services" to billing on the basis of precise calculation of time began when clients, particularly those with in-house counsel, as well as insurance companies that hire lawyers to represent insureds, looked for greater accountability and precision in the way they were charged for lawyer services. What started as an innovation grudgingly accepted by law firms, soon became the gold standard, applied almost universally to this day, despite numerous objections and staunch advocates in favor of alternative billing methods.

From accepting hourly billing, it was not very long before the tracking of time became not only a basis for preparing invoices but also a welcomed, even celebrated, management tool. Raise the hourly rate $5 or $10 and the revenue went right to the bottom line. Get each lawyer to add one billable hour per month, per week or per day, and you achieved the same results. Review time accounting records and you could rank order not just associates, but all lawyers, in terms of their commitment to the enterprise. Lawyers went from being professionals evaluated on their excellence to being full time equivalent timekeepers ("FTE's") evaluated on the basis of numbers. Differences among lawyers' billable hours became the source of much grinding of teeth. If only Caldwell & Moore could move the fifth quintile of timekeepers up to the fourth, the firm's profits would soar. If every lawyer's hours were above average, the possibilities were unlimited. And what started as an effort at simply drawing comparisons, slowly evolved into a method of punishing, at first, associates whose billable hours were below average, and then, partners whose low billable hours translated into their being perceived as "unproductive." That perception may even have provided reason enough to urge these slackers, who had grown up and become members of the firm in a different era, to look elsewhere for future employment.

The next step in the march of the billable hour was the adoption by firms of billable hour goals—just like those describing so many affirmative action initiatives. And not, heaven forefend, to be confused with billable hour quotas or requirements. Just a gentle nudge directed at all lawyers that the firm had expectations. But it was not long before these goals became much more than that. Firms told their lawyers, especially the associates, that the firms would provide bonuses to those lawyers whose billable hour production exceeded certain thresholds, perhaps $25,000 for 2,000 hours, another $10,000 for the next 200 and so on, bonuses cascading without limit. It is these billable hour requirements, with both their attendant bonuses and the unspoken but inevitable negative effects of failing to meet the firm's expectations, that prompt this ethical rumination, addressing the question of whether what we are doing with billable hours violates principles of professional responsibility, if not the professional responsibility rules themselves.

Lawyers Are Good People

Let me start by observing that I firmly believe that most lawyers are honest in keeping track of their time and conscientious in undertaking tasks that are consistent with their clients' best interests. I do not believe the profession is engaged in wholesale fraud. But it does not require a finding of rampant criminal conduct to conclude that billable hour goals raise important ethical issues. Nor are the professional responsibility implications of billable hour quotas and bonuses the only reasons why law firms should cease this practice and cease it now.

The Conflict—Compounded

Though hourly billing is universally employed, and has many characteristics that recommend it, hourly billing certainly has one huge ethical deficit. The client has a very real interest in limiting the client's legal fees; the lawyers get rewarded, at least in the short run, for an increased number of hours. In short, hourly billing is a great incentive for the lawyer to undertake more tasks and to complete them more slowly, perhaps contrary to the interests of the client.

The imposition of specific goals, quotas or requirements for billable hours by law firms only heightens this conflict and, as the fictional disclosure in the preface to this article makes clear, they are hard to justify as serving any legitimate client interest. Simply ask yourself how you would feel if your dentist made that disclosure to you before you underwent painful root canal. While the pain the young dentist might be inclined to prolong to add to her hour total may be more stinging than any a lawyer can inflict, any incentive to inflict pain on clients by delaying resolution of their matters or increasing their fees is something our profession should stamp out, not encourage.

Distortions

Think about the distortions that are introduced by this system. The affected lawyers are always asking two questions: What are my hours? What goal can I achieve? As the year drags on the lawyer either falls behind the goal or realizes that yet a higher goal (and its resulting additional bonuses) is achievable. Either way the obsession with these statistics only grows. Assignments change, on the downside, from being opportunities for service to clients to way stations on the path to keeping one's job and, on the upside, to "earning" bonuses. These new job opportunities are not evaluated on the basis of the lawyer's interests or likely experiences (can I take a deposition? argue a motion? meet a client?) but on how many hours the matter will add to the associate's annual hour harvest.

Think also about the likely effect of this system on the recording of time. In the brave new world of lawyer time accounting, hours are measured in tenths (a mere six minutes), an absurd construct that was designed to avoid overcharging of clients by the earlier use of quarter hour billing. In fact, however, it has placed virtually every lawyer in America in a position in which he or she is guilty of multiple mini-frauds every day. If one really kept track of every hour every work day in six minute increments, that is, in fact, all one would have time to do. Stop watch or chess clock at the ready, lawyers probably could keep track of their time in tenths, but unless one were fortunate enough to be in a long deposition, on trial or at a closing, "keeping track of time," not substantive work, would be the task entry on the lawyer's billing sheets. And for the typical lawyer who waits until the end of the day to record time, accuracy to a tenth of an hour is an impossible assignment (was it twenty-four minutes or thirty?).

Given this reality—that when most lawyers put down their time they are doing so based on estimates—the question arises whether it is likely that the presence of billable hour punishments and rewards has any distortive effect on how these estimates are made. Do we suppose that estimates high and estimates low are essentially equivalent, making the use of estimates mere harmless error that comes out in the wash? Or do we think that the special incentives built into the system by billable hour rewards might, just might, encourage lawyers to estimate and record on the high side the number of six minute increments dedicated to any given task?

This distortive effect is undoubtedly compounded as the associate contemplates the day of reckoning: the end of the fiscal year. Am I close to the minimum requirement? To getting the next available bonus? If so, can I find some more work? Stretch out what I have? Or "borrow" work that I know I'll be doing next year? I'll just record extra time doing document review now and then do it for free come January.

Or what if I am already over and can't get close to the next higher goal? I'll work hard now, but not enter my time into the system. Then when January comes my "banked" November and December time will give me a big head start in 2007. Nothing wrong with that, both fictitious lawyers easily rationalize, as they game a system whose absurdities are manifest.

All of which says nothing about the unspeakable possibilities. Short on hours? Need a few to achieve the minimum requirement? The next highest goal? Who can really say all the research for this memorandum only required three hours? I'll just read a few more cases to make sure I've got it right. Or see if there are any law review articles on point. Or maybe I can draft a memorandum to the client. Write a few letters. Prepare a memo to the file documenting my work. I am just being careful, precise, conscientious, avoiding malpractice—all admirable goals worthy of nothing but high praise.

And then there is the most unspeakable effect of all. No one follows me around. No one really knows how much time I spent reviewing these documents in a lonely warehouse. Yet since I worked so efficiently isn't it fair to record an extra hour or two? No, not an even hour. How about 1.3 hours? Or that last memorandum took two point four hours but was worth so much more. What an insight I had! It's clearly worth, shall we say, 8.6? Or while I traveled for, and billed Client A, I was working on Client B's matters. Shouldn't they both pay for my six hour flight to L.A.? Twelve added billable hours credited to my account.

Yes, we hate to admit it, but even among the legal profession are those who would work extra slowly or record phantom hours, hours not dedicated to the client's matters, but hours nonetheless "earned," hours the lawyer is entitled to record to reflect the efficiency or excellence of the work that was performed, rationalizations that permit the surreptitious rewriting of a billable hours retainer agreement to include new qualitative terms that always result in an uptick in the bill, but that no one gets around to confirming with the client.

Bad Policy

Even if billable hours were scrupulously and honestly kept for only those tasks efficiently performed and essential to serving the best interests of the client, it still would be the wrong way to award bonuses to associates for a number of different reasons.

The purpose of having a billable hour requirement is to make sure every high paid associate is dedicated to hard work. Caldwell & Moore doesn't want to continue to employ those who don't "earn" their $125,000 per annum first year salary. And it is undoubtedly true that some associates may not actively seek out work, may leave early or arrive late, are never available when the legitimate demands of the practice require extraordinary efforts, even all-nighters and seven days per week commitment. Nor do I suggest for a moment that law firms may not design a program to ferret them out and either reform their conduct or terminate their employment.

But, because it fails to distinguish among very different situations, establishing a billable hour requirement is a ham-handed way of accomplishing this goal. While it is true Caldwell & Moore should want to reward hard work, lack of hours may not be the associate's fault. The ready, willing and able associate may be assigned to a department that does not generate the outsized tasks (interminable depositions or endless closings) that generate the high hours. Or by virtue of the assignment luck of the draw, the associate may not have been given the "opportunity" to spend hundreds of billable hours staring at a computer screen reviewing documents for attorney-client and attorney work product privilege. Or an associate may need to be on a reduced schedule to care for a child or an elderly parent or simply to maintain some balance in his or her life. Being put in this position by necessity or choice, it would be totally fair to conclude that the affected associate is not eligible for a billable hour bonus, but when that is the only basis on which associate bonuses are awarded, the firm has missed a chance to reward real talent for other meritorious accomplishments.

Put simply, looking at a chart of associate annual hours does provide a method of awarding bonuses with apparent precision, but its simplicity of application belies the fact that not all similar billable hour statistics reflect similar situations—or anything close to it. For that reason, it is critical that the firm embarked on such a billable hour reward and punishment enterprise must go behind the stark numbers on the computer printout to understand why the numbers are what they are, whether they reflect sloth or some failure on the part of the firm to provide sufficient work, allocate work fairly, or otherwise give the affected associate appropriate opportunities. A failure to take this nuanced approach, while surely reducing administrative time, breeds resentment among the associate corps, directed at both their "fortunate" colleagues pocketing the extra bonuses and the partners who use such a mechanical measure for allocating rewards.

The use of billable hour bonuses also only focuses on one narrow dimension of an associate's total performance. Think for a moment about the questionnaire we know Caldwell & Moore uses to evaluate associates. It certainly asks questions about the associate's ability to research and write, to be responsive, to deal with clients, to follow instructions, to accept increasing responsibility, to take the initiative and to succeed at myriad other activities. Yet when it comes to bonuses, Caldwell & Moore only rewards associates on the basis of billable hours. Where is the bonus for the brilliant brief, the riveting oral argument, the call the associate got directly from the client with new business for the firm, the imaginative idea that saved the client thousands of dollars? To make judgments like these certainly takes more familiarity with what associates are doing and how they are doing it than to look at the billable hour chart, but surely Caldwell & Moore owes its associates the awarding of bonuses (if any there shall be) on qualitative factors at least as much (I would say far more) as it does on raw billable hour totals. Far more important, Caldwell & Moore owes its clients the knowledge that when the client's law firm rewards its professionals for work done on behalf of the firm's clients, it values excellence, imagination, cost-savings, efficiencies and speed at least as much (again, I would say far more) as it values the accumulation of hour upon hour of professional services. In fact, should not clients be assured that if Caldwell & Moore is going to reward the achievement of billable hour thresholds, those rewards will only be granted if the hours are not just calculated but also evaluated for their necessity and competence?

Think for a moment, moreover, about what a billable hour reward and punishment system says about where the law firm's real values are. The hiring literature, the firm web-site, the summer associate presentations all may talk about a balanced life. Many firms have enshrined the work-life balance in their mission statement. But the true firm commitment to that concept is found, not in what the firm says, but in what it does. And what it does when it engraves its devotion to high billable hours in a billable hour reward and punishment system is to tell associates that the rhetoric of work-life balance is just so many eloquent but meaningless words. The real message—the one that counts—is that Caldwell & Moore is a sweat shop and the more you sweat the more you will be rewarded with bonuses now and with the fruits of the bonus-striving of associates later if you bill enough hours to become a partner.

Does It Count?

No. The answer to the question is no. Does [fill in the blank non-billable activity] count as billable hours for purposes of bonuses? That is the question out of every naïve associate's mouth. The sophisticated already know—whatever the activity, no matter how important to the health of the firm or the good of the poor—it doesn't really count. Hiring, pro bono, bar association work, writing an article, attending a CLE. Oh, sure, some firms pay lip service to permitting these hours dedicated to these frill endeavors to "count." But remember we are talking about billable hour goals. And that is because ever higher billable hours are what Caldwell & Moore is trying to achieve. So every time it agrees to "count" something that is not a billable hour as if it were, Caldwell & Moore might end up saying a given associate has met the minimum goal or even earned a bonus. But the firm does so with its collective fingers crossed, with more than a little reluctance, with a grudging admission that to do otherwise in public would be unseemly. Yet any associate who thinks these non-billable hours really count in the same way real billable, likely-to-yield-$200-or-more-dollars-per-hour, hours count was born yesterday. If it were otherwise, the firm would never have instituted such a unitary bonus system in the first place.

The Solution

In fact, all of these activities must count. In the long run, Caldwell & Moore will only succeed if its lawyers dedicate themselves with real quality time to hiring and retaining the very best talent, training the firm's lawyers to perform at the highest professional level, mentoring associates to become partners, developing a real diversity program that recruits, retains and promotes women and minorities. Moreover, the profession of law will only survive if lawyers— including Caldwell & Moore lawyers—dedicate themselves to pro bono, bar association work, continuing legal education and the greater civic good of the community.

But, instead of making these "non-productive" hours count in a billable hour bonus system, the entire rewards and punishments for billable hours method should be jettisoned in favor of a system of rewards and punishments that rewards excellence, innovation, imagination, savings for the client, pro bono dedication, bar association commitment, hiring, mentoring and training, diversity, and all of the other characteristics that yield a rich fulfilling professional life. Consider the following mythical memo:

TO: All Associates
FROM: Management Committee, Caldwell & Moore
RE: Compensation

The Managing Partners of Caldwell & Moore have spent the last year studying the way in which we compensate and provide bonuses to our associates. As a result, we are announcing effective as of the beginning of the firm's next fiscal year a new basis on which our associates will be rewarded for outstanding achievement.

Salaries

Effective July 1, 2006, our starting salary will be $135,000 for all full-time associates. Base salaries for associates in years two through six will increase by $10,000 and in years seven and eight by $15,000 each year.

Elimination of Billable Hour Bonuses

At the same time, we are eliminating any bonus system based solely on billable hours. We recognize that such a system is not only inconsistent with our commitment to our clients, but also both an unfair way of compensating associates and inconsistent with our desire to encourage some of the non-billable activities our firm and our profession must value.

This does not mean we do not expect hard work from our associates. Caldwell & Moore is a business in a competitive marketplace. We pay competitive salaries and expect every associate to be committed to earning such generous compensation. Indeed, bonuses will be awarded to those associates who make an extraordinary commitment in terms of time. It is simply that these bonuses in the future will not be tied automatically to the achievement of any given number of billable hours and will only be granted in light of a number of other factors described more fully below.

The Bonus System

Bonuses can be earned by all but first year associates. Bonuses will be rewarded at the sole discretion of the firm in amounts that will be significant, but without regard to any formula.

Professional Services

With respect to work for clients, associates may earn bonuses not only for the number of hours dedicated, but also for the quality of the work and imaginative ideas that advance the interests of our clients. To consider the latter, we will be asking partners to make an evaluation of each associate's hours in terms of efficiency, diligence, and necessity, and to nominate for bonuses those associates whose initiatives saved clients money or whose ideas enhanced clients' likelihood of achieving their goals.

Firm Activities

It is just as important for the firm to hire, retain and promote a talented, diverse associate corps. To that end, bonuses will be rewarded for recruiting, training and mentoring hours and initiatives in the same way as work on client matters. Similarly, service on the associates committee, if undertaken in a dedicated and effective way, may result in an award of a bonus to the associates involved.

Pro Bono

In the past, the firm "counted" so many hours of pro bono. Beyond that level, the associate had to seek a waiver for the hours to count. We know this misled some associates into believing that pro bono really did not count, discouraging them from undertaking pro bono engagements. It is Caldwell & Moore's policy to encourage and support pro bono endeavors. The firm would like to achieve 100 percent participation by all of its lawyers at a level of 50 hours per year within the next three years. Meanwhile, the firm recognizes that pro bono engagements do not come in 50-hour assignment blocks. Henceforth, once an associate undertakes an approved pro bono matter for the firm, it will be treated like any other firm matter. Associates will be expected to dedicate all necessary time and effort to the matter. And associates can expect that in the evaluation of their commitment and hard work, the firm will count all of their pro bono hours—so long as they meet the same criteria of necessity and competence as all other hours—toward the awarding of any bonuses. Our pro bono clients are not second-class citizens, and we do not want any associate to feel that our compensation system is inconsistent with that principle.

Bar Association and Other Civic Endeavors

Our lawyers' obligations do not end with commitment to clients—both paying and pro bono—and to the firm. Caldwell & Moore is a leader of the profession. We expect our lawyers to get involved in the organized bar by serving in leadership positions, writing articles and books, presenting at continuing legal education seminars. Similarly, our lawyers should serve as leaders of the larger community. School boards, houses of worship, charitable and arts organizations, and similar endeavors all will benefit from the leadership of Caldwell & Moore lawyers. You can expect to be evaluated on your participation in these activities and for bonuses for outstanding accomplishments in this area to be awarded in the same way as for other achievements.

Work-Life Balance

While Caldwell & Moore expects extra effort from all of its lawyers, we recognize that the number of hours a lawyer is able to devote to all of the activities listed above varies widely because of the necessity of fulfilling even more important personal obligations, such as child-rearing or other family obligations. We also recognize that some of you have made life-style choices that are inconsistent with 2,000 or more hours per year of professional time. Though those circumstances or choices may mean that you will not earn bonuses for your number of hours, Caldwell & Moore wants to emphasize that you will still be eligible for bonuses for the quality of your work, your imagination and skill, and for the other firm activities should your qualitative performance warrant it.

Business Generation

Though it is rare for associates to bring in significant business, any business generated by an associate will be evaluated in terms of the revenues generated and the quality of the work for possible bonus awards. Far more important, associates will be evaluated in terms of the foundation they are laying during their associate years for business generation thereafter. Is the associate dealing well with clients, making a name for herself in her field, writing articles, appearing in CLE's, taking leadership in young lawyer divisions of the various bar associations, joining civic and charitable organizations, developing a marketable specialty? Professional life is a long journey, but the first seven years of the trip set the course for all that follows. The associate who does this in an outstanding way can expect to be considered for bonuses based on how he or she starts his or her professional journey.

* * *

Having read the memorandum, the reader undoubtedly thinks I've been smoking a controlled substance. Admittedly, it is way too easy to craft such a memo when you do not have to consult eight other managing partners, a firm executive and chief financial officer or 135 partners. But it does seem to me that, though my offering does not reflect the perfect antidote to billable hour punishments and rewards, nor the perfect solution to so many other ills in the modern law firm, it could open a dialogue not only on how this memorandum to associates should read, but also how the modern American law firm must change to raise the bar to the level of professional commitment, professional responsibility and professional rewards the profession must offer, not just to associates, but to all lawyers.

Anticipating the Critics

This diatribe has already drawn considerable dissent. Perhaps it will draw more. I certainly welcome the dialogue. But permit me to answer in advance a few of my critics.

It has been asserted that my concern about the recording of billable hours is slanderous, that I am accusing the profession of wholesale fraud. That is certainly not my intent. But we also cannot blind ourselves to four things. First, there have been far too many documented cases of billable hour abuse. From the case of the celebrated Chicago law firm partner billing over 6,022 hours in one year,[2] to Lisa Lerman's catalogue of over-billing, expense padding and other criminal conduct by sixteen high profile lawyers at prestigious *American Lawyer 200* law firms,[3] to think our profession is pristine is to ignore the facts. Second, I am much more focused on the subtle effects that billable hour quotas and rewards create than I am on out-and-out fraud. To suggest that these effects are not likely is to assume lawyers are not human beings, when we know all too well that they are. Third, even if lawyers were perfect, it is impossible to think that we are carrying the right message to our firm colleagues—when we employ billable hour requirements and provide billable hour bonuses—about the importance we place on non-billable activities. Fourth, and most important, we are a profession that owes all these duties to our clients; they are our raison d'étre, and how must they feel if they know this is the basis on which lawyers working on their matters are rewarded? Consider again the mythical three-hour root canal procedure to capture the point.

It has also been argued that associates really want to be rewarded this way, they like the certainty of knowing that if they put in exactly 2,103 hours they will achieve the 2,000 bonus and the 2,100 extra bonus. This argument proves my point. While there is so much associates hate about our billable hour culture, of course they do like certainty. Everyone likes certainty. And knowing that I've got a lock on an extra $15,000 so long as I spend New Year's Eve in front of a CRT reviewing documents for privilege—guaranteeing compensation that will pay for far more than my midnight champagne makes me feel warm and fuzzy all over. But the certainty that arises from no more than the writing down of a pre-stipulated number of hours is not a desired result. Rather an associate should know that his or her lawyers' hours will be evaluated for quantity for sure, but also for quality, for innovation, for benefit to the client, and that the associate's non-billable hours will be evaluated too, and then—no certainty here—the associate may get a bonus if this overall review yields the conclusion that the associate is entitled to a bonus. Is it subjective? To be sure. But we are lawyers, producing legal work, running law firms, preserving a threatened profession,

---

2. "Chapman & Cutler Axes 17 Firm Staff," Chicago Daily Law Bulletin, March 22, 1995.
3. Lisa G. Lerman, "Blue-Chip Bilking: Regulation of Billing and Expense Fraud by Lawyers," 12 Geo. J. Ethics 205 (1999); *see* "Bill Padding Happens," Legal Times, Oct. 18, 2004.

and there is no way a lawyer's contribution to those goals should be evaluated in other than a qualitative, albeit subjective, way. Leave it to the production line employees installing windshields and rearview mirrors to get compensated by purely objective criteria.

Last I have been confronted by those who say that far too many firms operate this way to change things now. Indeed, I have been accused of systematically seeking to change virtually the whole big firm business model.

To this I plead guilty. My experience with the Raise the Bar Project has convinced me of two things. First, our problems are profound and deeply troubling. Any enterprise that loses 78% of its new hires in the first three years is in a state of crisis. Second, we must change the way we do business other than incrementally if we are going to turn the ship of state around. Half-measures will not work. Maybe this idea will not either. But in our search for solutions we will have to develop ideas that change in some dramatic way the manner in which we do business, that overcome the litany of problems—too long to repeat here—that started the Section of Litigation to declare, enough of decrying the current state of affairs, let us find solutions, the goal of the project and this article.

B. Contingent Fees

Problems

10-3.   Martyn & Fox entered into a one-third contingent fee agreement with Client, who has been seriously injured by Drunk Driver. Two weeks later, after we have spent about 10 hours on the case, Drunk Driver's insurer offered the policy limits of $150,000. Client threatens to file a disciplinary complaint unless we agree to reduce our fee to $5,000 ($500/hour). What should we do?

10-4.   Massachusetts hired Martyn & Fox to sue the tobacco companies at a time when the suit seemed hopeless. The fee agreement, signed for Massachusetts by the Attorney General, called for a 25 percent contingent fee. Two years later, as part of an overall settlement with 40 states, Massachusetts was awarded $8.3 billion. Should Martyn & Fox collect $2.075 billion?

10-5.   Martyn & Fox's client is sued for $10 million to be trebled as part of an alleged antitrust conspiracy among drug companies. May Martyn & Fox negotiate a fee agreement that would award the firm 25 percent of everything the client saves below $30 million?

10-6.   Martyn & Fox routinely refers medical malpractice actions to Hastie & Moore, in exchange for one-fourth of Hastie & Moore's 40 percent contingent fee. Fox just discovered that Hastie & Moore has not paid us our share after settling the last two cases we referred. What should we do?

Consider: Model Rule 1.5
           Model Code DR 2-106, 2-107

ABA Formal Opinion 94-389
American Bar Association Standing Committee on Ethics and
Professional Responsibility

Contingent Fees

A. Introduction . . .

In the opinion of the Committee, the charging of a contingent fee, in personal injury and in all other permissible types of litigation, as well as in numerous non-litigation matters, does not violate ethical standards as long as the fee is appropriate in the circumstances and reasonable in amount, and as long as the client has been fully advised of the availability of alternative fee arrangements. . . .

B. Contingent Fees Are Employed in Multiple Situations

It should be recognized at the outset that when we address contingent fees we are talking about a wide variety of situations. Contingent fees are no longer, if ever they were, limited to personal injury cases. Nor are contingent fees limited to suits involving tortious conduct. Contingent fees are now commonly offered to plaintiff-clients in collections, civil rights, securities and anti-trust class actions, real estate tax appeals and even patent litigation.

Nor is this compensation arrangement limited to plaintiffs. In this Committee's recent Formal Opinion 93-373, the Committee considered the ethical issues raised by the increasingly employed so-called "reverse contingent fees," in which defendants hire lawyers who will be compensated by an agreed upon percentage of the amount the client saves. The Committee concluded that as long as the fee arrangement reached between the lawyer and client realistically estimates the exposure of the defendant client, such a fee is consistent with the Model Rules.

Moreover, contingent fees are not limited to litigation practice. Fees in the mergers and acquisitions arena are often either partially or totally dependent on the consummation of a takeover or successful resistance of such a takeover. Additionally, fees on public offerings are often tied to whether the stocks or bonds come to market and to the amount generated in the offering. Banks are also hiring lawyers to handle loan transactions in which the fee for the bank's lawyers is dependent in whole or part on the consummation of the loan.

The use of contingent fees in these areas, for plaintiffs and defendants, impecunious and affluent alike, reflects the desire of clients to tie a lawyer's compensation to her performance and to give the lawyer incentives to improve returns to the client. The trend also may reflect a growing dissatisfaction with hourly rate billing. Because of the growing importance and widespread use of contingent fees, the Committee will first address in detail the factors that should be considered before a lawyer and client enter into such a fee arrangement, and then address the specific questions occasioning this opinion.

*C. The Decision by the Client to Enter Into a Contingent Fee
Agreement Must Be an Informed One*

Nothing in the Model Rules expressly prohibits a lawyer from entering into a contingent fee agreement with any client. Nevertheless, the lawyer must recognize that not all matters are appropriate for a contingent fee. For example, Model Rule 1.5(d) makes it clear that a contingent fee may never be agreed to, charged or collected in a criminal matter or divorce proceeding. More to the point, in Informal Opinion 86-1521 this Committee concluded that, "when there is any doubt whether a contingent fee is consistent with the client's best interest," and the client is able to pay a reasonable fixed fee, the lawyer "must offer the client the *opportunity* to engage counsel on a reasonable fixed fee basis before entering into a contingent fee arrangement." (Emphasis added.) . . .

In other words, regardless of whether the lawyer, the prospective client, or both, are initially inclined towards a contingent fee, the nature (and details) of the compensation arrangement should be fully discussed by the lawyer and client before any final agreement is reached.

The extent of the discussion, of course, will depend on whether it is the lawyer or the client who initiated the idea of proceeding with the contingent fee arrangement, the lawyer's prior dealings with the client (including whether there has been any prior contingent fee arrangement), and the experience and sophistication of the client with respect to litigation and other legal matters. Among the factors that should be considered and discussed are the following:

a. The likelihood of success;
b. The likely amount of recovery or savings, if the case is successful;
c. The possibility of an award of exemplary or multiple damages and how that will affect the fee;
d. The attitude and prior practices of the other side with respect to settlement;
e. The likelihood of, or any anticipated difficulties in, collecting any judgement;
f. The availability of alternative dispute resolution as a means of achieving an earlier conclusion to the matter;
g. The amount of time that is likely to be invested by the lawyer;
h. The likely amount of the fee if the matter is handled on a non-contingent basis;
i. The client's ability and willingness to pay a non-contingent fee;
j. The percentage of any recovery that the lawyer would receive as a contingent fee and whether that percentage will be fixed or on a sliding scale;
k. Whether the lawyer's fees would be recoverable by the client by reason of statute or common law rule;
l. Whether the jurisdiction in which the claim will be pursued has any rules or guidelines for contingent fees; and
m. How expenses of the litigation are to be handled. . . .

E. In a Case in Which Liability Is Clear and Some Recovery Is Certain, a Fee Based on a Percentage of the Recovery Can Be Ethically Proper . . .

... [E]ven in cases where there is no risk of non-recovery, and the lawyer and client are certain that liability is clear and will be conceded, a fee arrangement contingent on the amount recovered may nonetheless be reasonable. As the increasing popularity of reverse contingent fees demonstrates, for almost all cases there is a range of possible recoveries. Since the amount of the recovery will be largely determined by the lawyer's knowledge, skill, experience and time expended, both the defendant and the plaintiff may best be served by a contingency fee arrangement that ties the lawyer's fee to the amount recovered.

Also, an early settlement offer is often prompted by the defendant's recognition of the ability of the plaintiff's lawyer fairly and accurately to value the case and to proceed effectively through trial and appeals if necessary. There is no ethical reason why the lawyer is not entitled to an appropriate consideration for this value that his engagement has brought to the case, even though it results in an early resolution.

Given the foregoing, the Committee concludes that as a general proposition contingent fees are appropriate and ethical in situations where liability is certain and some recovery is likely.

That having been said, there may nonetheless be special situations in which a contingent fee may not be appropriate. For example, if in a particular instance a lawyer was reasonably confident that as soon as the case was filed the defendant would offer an amount that the client would accept, it might be that the only appropriate fee would be one based on the lawyer's time spent on the case since, from the information known to the lawyer, there was little risk of non-recovery and the lawyer's efforts would have brought little value to the client's recovery.[15] And even if, in such circumstances, after a full discussion, it were agreed between lawyer and client that a contingent fee was appropriate, the fee arrangement should recognize the likelihood of an early favorable result by providing for a significantly smaller percentage recovery if the anticipated offer is received and accepted than if the case must go forward through discovery, trial and appeal.[16] . . .

H. The Contingent Fee Arrangement Must Be Reasonable

In addition to the requirement that a fee be appropriate, Model Rule 1.5 requires that the fee, whether based on an hourly rate, a contingent percentage or some other basis, "shall be reasonable." . . .

---

15. Similar reasoning has led many courts to find that it is inappropriate to charge a contingent fee in cases involving first party insurance benefits where there is no risk of non-recovery and the lawyer merely submits the claim on behalf of the client. But courts have also found that contingent fees may be appropriate in these types of cases, if the lawyer performs additional services relating to the recovery by the client. *See* In re Doyle, 581 N.E.2d 669 (Ill. 1991).

16. A recognition of the amount of additional work required to take a case through trial and appeals is reflected by several states which cap percentage fees in certain types of cases but allow the percentage charged to rise after certain milestones, i.e., 25% if settled before trial, 33 1/2% if tried. *See* N.J. Ct. R. 1.27 (C)(f) (limiting fees in tort cases involving minors). States have also mandated differing percentages depending on the amount recovered. *See* N.Y. Jud. L. §474-A (McKinneys 1994 Supp.); Conn. Gen. St. Ann. §52-251(c) (1991). . . .

We stress that the lawyer should take all these factors into account in evaluating every case. *See* ABA Formal Opinion 329 (1972). For this reason, a lawyer who always charges the same percentage of recovery regardless of the particulars of a case should consider whether he is charging a fee that is, in an ethical context, a reasonable one. . . .

As with the question of appropriateness, the mere fact that liability may be clear and that some recovery is likely does not per se make any given contingent fee unreasonable. It is important to keep in mind that the reasonableness as well as the appropriateness of a fee arrangement necessarily must be judged at the time it is entered into. All contingent fee agreements carry certain risks: the risk that the case will require substantially more work than the lawyer anticipated; the risk that there will be no judgment, or only an unenforceable one; the risk of changes in the law; the risk that the client will dismiss the lawyer; and the risk that the client will require the lawyer to reject what the lawyer considers a good settlement or otherwise to continue the proceedings much further than in the lawyer's judgment they should be pursued. If a lawyer accepts a given risk—for example, the risk posed by the fact that the opposing party has a reputation for being intransigent in its approach to settlement—and offers a fee contract reflecting that risk, which is accepted by a fully informed client, the lawyer should not be required as a matter of ethics to give up the benefit of the agreement because the opposing party, to everyone's surprise, offers an early settlement that is acceptable to the client. . . . By the same token, a later development that increases the risk to the lawyer—for example, a statutorily imposed cap on liability, the loss of a summary judgment motion everyone expected to win, or the need to take three times the number of depositions originally anticipated—should not permit the lawyer to demand a new, more generous fee arrangement.[22]

I. The Percentage of a Contingent Fee May as an Ethical Matter Be Increased on the Basis of How Far the Lawyer Must Proceed in Prosecuting the Case

The Committee has also been asked whether it is ethical for a lawyer and client to enter into a fee agreement that provides for higher contingent fees after specific benchmarks, for example, 25% if the case settles within six months and 33% after trial. The higher contingent fee at advanced stages of the matter is meant to compensate the lawyer for the additional time and labor necessary in the case. As demonstrated in the factors set forth in Model Rule 1.5(a) set out above, the time and labor involved in a matter are among the reasonable bases for setting a fee. Therefore, it is the Committee's opinion that

---

22. *See, e.g.,* Chase v. Gilbert, 499 A.2d 1203 (D.C. 1985) (a lawyer cannot modify a fee agreement even if he ends up performing significantly more services than were contemplated when agreement was entered into). Because reasonableness is judged at the time the contract is entered into, there is nothing necessarily unethical about charging a contingent fee on the portion of any recovery that is equal to an early settlement offer. . . .

such a fee agreement is ethical as long as the overall fee is appropriate and reasonable. *See, e.g.*, Phila. Bar Assoc. Ethics Opinion 93-11 (approving such a fee arrangement).

J. *The Percentage of a Contingent Fee May Increase with the Amount of the Recovery*

Finally, the Committee has been asked whether it is ethical for a lawyer to enter into a fee agreement that provides for a higher percentage fee as the amount of the recovery goes up or the amount of the savings increases: for example, 15% on the first $100,000 recovered or saved, 20% on the next hundred thousand, and 25% on everything thereafter. Such an arrangement on its face runs contrary to what several states have mandated in terms of reducing the percentage recovery as the amount recovered rises. . . . Nonetheless, as a matter of ethics, the Committee is of the view that a percentage that increases with the amount of the recovery can be permissible. Model Rule 1.5(a) refers, in connection with the reasonableness of a fee, to "results obtained," and the "ability of the lawyer or lawyers performing the services" as factors that may be considered. Since a higher recovery would, by definition, reflect the first of these factors and, in all likelihood, reflect the other as well, the Committee is of the view that such a fee agreement is ethical, so long as the matter for which the fee is charged is appropriate and the amount of the fee is reasonable. Indeed, many would say that this form of contingent fee agreement more closely rewards the effort and ability the lawyer brings to the engagement than does a straight percentage fee arrangement, since everyone would agree that it is the last dollars, not the first dollars, of recovery that require the greatest effort and/or ability on the part of the lawyer. It may be that any lawyer would have been able to achieve a $100,000 verdict for a given plaintiff's injuries, but that only the most skilled would have been able to secure a $500,000 award plus an additional sum for exemplary damages. . . .

C. Flat Fees

Problems

10-7. Insurance company offers to hire Martyn & Fox to represent all of its insured physicians in medical malpractice cases for $250,000 per case. Can Martyn & Fox accept this arrangement?

10-8. Martyn & Fox agrees to defend Client's breach of contract action for a flat fee of $20,000. Six months later, Client fires us, saying, "I just like the lawyers down the block better," and demands a refund of $15,000. What should Martyn & Fox do?

Consider: Model Rules 1.5, 1.15
Model Code DR 2-106, 9-102
RLGL §40

In re Sather

3 P.3d 403 (Colo. 2000)

En Banc . . .

Justice BENDER delivered the Opinion of the Court.

I. INTRODUCTION

In this attorney regulation proceeding, we address the conduct of the attorney-respondent, Larry D. Sather, who spent and failed to place into a trust account $20,000 he received as a "non-refundable" advance fee for a civil case. Because Sather treated these funds as his own property before earning the fee, Sather's conduct violated Colo. RPC 1.15(a). Sather labeled the $20,000 fee "nonrefundable" even though he knew that the fee was subject to refund under certain circumstances, thereby violating Colo. RPC 8.4(c). After being discharged by his client, Sather failed to return all of the unearned portion of the $20,000 promptly, in violation of Colo. RPC 1.16(d). . . .

II. FACTS AND PROCEDURAL BACKGROUND

The hearing board found the following facts were established by clear and convincing evidence. Sather agreed to represent Franklin Perez in a lawsuit against the Colorado State Patrol and certain individual troopers. Perez alleged that the troopers violated his civil rights during a traffic stop on December 7, 1995. Almost a year after the stop, on November 15, 1996, Sather and Perez entered into a written agreement for legal services, captioned "Minimum Fee Contract." Sather drafted the agreement, the terms of which required Perez to pay Sather $20,000 plus costs to represent Perez in the case against the State Patrol. Sather testified that he had never charged this large an amount as a flat fee in a civil case.

The contract referred to the $20,000 alternatively as a "minimum fee," a "non-refundable fee," and a "flat fee." The contract stated that Perez understood his obligation to pay this fee "regardless of the number of hours attorneys devote to [his] legal matter" and that no portion of the fee would be refunded "regardless of the time or effort involved or the result obtained." The contract acknowledged Perez's right to discharge Sather as his attorney, but the contract informed Perez that in no circumstance would any of the funds paid be refunded:

> IN ALL EVENTS, NO REFUND SHALL BE MADE OF ANY PORTION OF THE MINIMUM FEE PAID, REGARDLESS OF THE AMOUNT OF TIME EXPENDED BY THE FIRM.
>
> The client has been advised that this is an agreed flat fee contract. The client acknowledges that the minimum flat fee is the agreed upon amount of $20,000, regardless of the time or effort involved or the result obtained.

Thus, the contract stipulated that Perez pay Sather $20,000 for his legal services; that he pay all legal costs incurred by Sather in the case; and that no funds would be refundable after Perez paid Sather the flat fee of $20,000.[3]

Perez paid Sather $5,000 of the minimum fee on November 17, 1996. He paid the remaining $15,000 on December 16th. Sather spent the $5,000 soon after receiving the money. Sather kept the second payment of $15,000 for approximately one month before spending these funds. Sather did not place any of these funds in his trust account before spending them. Sather testified that he spent Perez's $20,000 because he believed he earned the fees upon receipt. Sather stated that while he could not cite a specific rule for this opinion, he thought it was a common practice in the legal community to treat flat fees as being earned on receipt.

Less than a month after agreeing to represent Perez, on December 6, 1996, Sather filed suit in Denver District Court on behalf of Perez against the State Patrol and three troopers. In addition to claims for tort and civil rights injuries, the complaint included a claim for attorney's fees. The Attorney General's Office, which represented the State Patrol and three troopers, negotiated with Sather and offered Perez a $6,000 settlement, which Perez refused. Sather then requested an extension of time to respond to a pretrial motion, which the court granted.

On April 21, 1997, in a matter unrelated to the Perez case, this court suspended Sather from the practice of law for thirty days, effective May 21, 1997. See People v. Sather, 936 P.2d 576, 579 (Colo. 1997). As required, Sather notified Perez of his suspension and Perez responded on May 23, requesting an accounting of the hours Sather worked on his case. Perez requested that Sather provide the accounting by May 30, but Sather replied that he would be unable to provide this information until the third week of June. Thereafter, on June 4, 1997, Perez faxed Sather notice discharging him from his case because of the suspension.

Acting pro se, Perez received an extension of time to file a response to the State Patrol's motion after informing the court that he was seeking replacement counsel to handle the case. Then, on August 21, 1997, Perez wrote a letter to the Attorney General's Office, accepting the offer of $6,000 to settle all of his claims against the State Patrol and the troopers. . . .

Sather provided the accounting requested by Perez on June 27, 1997. Sather claimed that his fees, his paralegal assistant's fees, costs and expenses in Perez's case as of the date of discharge totaled $6,923.64. At that time, Sather acknowledged that he should refund $13,076.36, the balance of the $20,000 paid by Perez.

Despite acknowledging his duty to return the unearned $13,076.36 to Perez, Sather did not refund any money to Perez because at the time of discharge he had spent Perez's funds. On September 3, 1997—three months after Perez discharged him— Sather paid Perez $3,000. Sather paid the remaining $10,076.36 on November 2, 1997. The hearing board found that this delay prejudiced Perez because he did not

---

3. In contrast to the contract's language, Sather testified that he knew that the fees were subject to refund and that he "never treated the fees as non-refundable."

have access to his funds for almost five months.

At the time Sather and Perez entered into the flat fee agreement, Sather was involved in personal bankruptcy proceedings. Sather filed a Chapter 7 bankruptcy proceeding in U.S. Bankruptcy Court in March 1995, over a year before agreeing to represent Perez. Sather later converted this case to a Chapter 13 proceeding, and then attempted to reconvert the case to a Chapter 7 filing. At the time of the hearing, the bankruptcy case was still pending. During the representation, Sather never told Perez that he had declared bankruptcy. After discharging Sather, Perez hired an attorney to pursue a claim against Sather in the bankruptcy proceeding for a refund of the fees ($6,923.64) Sather charged for work on Perez's suit.

Much later, in June 1998, Perez and Sather agreed to an arbitration by the Colorado Bar Association concerning the amount of fees charged by Sather for his work. The arbitrator awarded Perez $2,100.00, which represented the cost to Perez to bring the arbitration action. The arbitrator did not award Perez any recovery of the fees Sather charged for work performed. Shortly before the hearing in this case, on November 17, 1998, Sather paid Perez the award. . . .

III. DISCUSSION . . .

A. Colo. RPC 1.15 Requires Segregation of Attorney and Client Property

. . . Colo. RPC 1.15(a) and (f) indicate that an attorney has an obligation to keep clients' funds separate from his own, and that advance fees remain the property of the client until such time as the fees are "earned."

The rule requiring that an attorney segregate funds advanced by the client from the attorney's own funds serves important interests. As a fiduciary to the client, one of an attorney's primary responsibilities is to safeguard the interests and property of the client over which the attorney has control. *See Restatement (Third) of the Law Governing Lawyers* §[44] cmt. (b). Requiring the attorney to segregate all client funds—including advance fees—from the attorney's own accounts unless and until the funds become the attorney's property protects the client's property from the attorney's creditors and from misuse by the attorney. Thus, Colo. RPC 1.15(a) and (f) further the attorney's fiduciary obligation to protect client property.

In addition to protecting client property, requiring an attorney to keep advance fees in trust until they are earned protects the client's right to discharge an attorney. Upon discharge, the attorney must return all unearned fees in a timely manner, even though the attorney may be entitled to quantum meruit recovery for the services that the attorney rendered and for costs incurred on behalf of the client.

If an attorney suggests to a client that any pre-paid or advance funds are "non-refundable" or constitute the attorney's property regardless of how much or how little work the attorney performs for the client, then the client may fear loss of the funds and may refrain from exercising his right to discharge the attorney. . . .

B. An Attorney Earns Fees by Conferring a Benefit on or Providing a Service for the Client

. . . When a client pays an attorney before the attorney provides legal services, the crucial issue becomes whether funds are "earned on receipt" and may be treated as the attorney's property, or whether the fees are unearned, in which case the funds must be segregated in a trust account under Colo. RPC 1.15. . . .

We hold that an attorney earns fees only by conferring a benefit on or performing a legal service for the client. Unless the attorney provides some benefit or service in exchange for the fee, the attorney has not earned any fees and, with a possible exception in very limited circumstances, the attorney cannot treat advance fees as her property.

Funds given by clients to attorneys as advance fees or retainers benefit attorneys and clients. Some forms of advance fees or retainers appropriately compensate an attorney when the fee is paid because the attorney makes commitments to the client that benefit the client immediately. Such an arrangement is termed a "general retainer" or "engagement retainer," and these retainers typically compensate an attorney for agreeing to take a case, which requires the attorney to commit his time to the client's case and causes the attorney to forego other potential employment opportunities as a result of time commitments or conflicts. Although an attorney usually earns an engagement retainer by agreeing to take the client's case, an attorney can also earn a fee charged as an engagement retainer by placing the client's work at the top of the attorney's priority list. Or the client may pay an engagement retainer merely to prevent the attorney from being available to represent an opposing party. In all of these instances, the attorney is providing some benefit to the client in exchange for the engagement retainer fee.

In contrast to engagement retainers, a client may advance funds— often referred to as "advance fees," "special retainers," "lump sum fees," or "flat fees"—to pay for specified legal services to be performed by the attorney and to cover future costs. We note that unless the fee agreement expressly states that a fee is an engagement retainer and explains how the fee is earned upon receipt, we will presume that any advance fee is a deposit from which an attorney will be paid for specified legal services.

Advance fees present an attractive option for both the client and the attorney. Like engagement retainers, advance fees allow clients to secure their choice of counsel. Additionally, some forms of advance fees, e.g., "lump sums" or "flat fees," benefit the client by establishing before representation the maximum amount of fees that the client must pay. . . . So long as the fees are reasonable, such arrangements do not violate ethical rules governing attorney fees.

Advance fees benefit the attorney because the attorney can secure payment for future legal services, eliminating the risk of non-payment after the attorney does the work. . . . Attorneys often deduct costs from advance payments as they incur the costs, similar to the manner in which they deduct their fees as they are earned. Advance fees represent an alternative method of obtaining legal assistance that accommodates legitimate needs of both clients and attorneys, and by this opinion we do not intend to discourage these fee arrangements provided the fee agreements comply with the ethical principles discussed in this case. . . .

C. "Non-refundable" Fees

Having discussed the ethical principle requiring that attorneys maintain in trust all advance fees until the attorney earns the fees, we address Sather's characterization of his fee as "nonrefundable." Because fees are always subject to refund under certain conditions, labeling a fee "non-refundable" misleads the client and may deter a client from exercising their rights to refunds of unearned fees under Colo. 1.16(d). Thus, we hold that attorneys cannot enter into "non-refundable" retainer or fee agreements. . . .

In the limited circumstances in which an attorney earns fees before performing any legal services (i.e., engagement retainers) or where an attorney and client agree that the attorney can treat advance fees as the attorney's property before the attorney earns the fees by supplying a benefit or performing a service, the fee agreement must clearly explain the basis for this arrangement and explain how the client's rights are protected by the arrangement. In either of these situations, however, an attorney's fees are always subject to refund if excessive or unearned, and an attorney cannot communicate otherwise to a client. . . .

IV. DISCIPLINE OF ATTORNEY-RESPONDENT SATHER . . .

. . . [W]e agree with the board's conclusion that Sather violated Colo.

RPC 1.16(d) by only partially repaying Perez's advance fee three months after being discharged and paying the balance of the refund five months after being discharged. . . . A discharged attorney must refund unearned fees in a timely fashion and failure to do so is a violation of Colo. RPC 1.16(d). Upon discharge, Sather acknowledged his obligation to return the unearned portion of the $20,000 to Perez, and Sather eventually returned the entire unearned amount of $13,076.36. Perez claimed that he was unable to retain alternate counsel because he did not have access to those funds after he discharged Sather, and the board concluded that his inability to use those funds caused harm to Perez. Because Sather only partially returned the unearned fees three months after being discharged and did not return the remainder of the unearned fees until five months after being discharged, we agree with the board that his conduct violated Colo. RPC 1.16(d).

We also agree with the board's determination that Sather violated Colo. 8.4(c) by materially misrepresenting to Perez the nature of the fee he paid. Colo. RPC 8.4(c) prohibits attorneys from engaging in conduct that involves "dishonesty, fraud, deceit, or misrepresentation." The fee agreement Sather drafted clearly expressed that the $20,000 was non-refundable, irrespective of the number of hours Sather spent on the case, and that "*In All Events, No Refund Shall Be Made Of Any Portion*" of the $20,000. (Emphasis in original.) Despite this strong language of the contract he drafted, Sather testified that he understood his ethical obligation to return any unearned portion of the fees in the event of discharge. We approve of the board's finding that Sather knowingly used misleading language to describe the fee arrangement and knowingly made a material misrepresentation to his client concerning the $20,000

advance fee. Thus, we accept the board's finding that Sather's conduct involved dishonesty, deceit, fraud and misrepresentation in violation of Colo. RPC 8.4(c). . . .

■ Practice Pointers:
Trust Fund Management

The Colorado Supreme Court disciplined Sather for failing to repay his client's advance fee after being discharged and materially misrepresenting the nature of the fee as "nonrefundable." Lawyers like Sather and those in *Malonis*, set out below, who are prematurely discharged without cause also may be forced to repay some or all of their client's previous payments.

Until the turn of the twentieth century, lawyers commonly commingled their client's funds with their own, and could have repaid these amounts from any account. Stock market crashes in both England and America led to a re-examination of professional accounting requirements, then to requirements that lawyers could not commingle client funds with lawyer operating accounts,[1] and eventually to specific regulations such as those in Model Rule 1.15, discussed in *Sather*. These provisions obviously are intended to protect client funds and property, but they also prohibit lawyers from using trust accounts to shield their own money from personal or business creditors.[2] In short, lawyers may not deposit their own funds in a client trust account (except to cover bank charges), nor may they deposit client funds, such as advance payment of fees and retainers, in their own business account. Lawyers also must notify clients and third parties whenever the lawyer receives property or funds to which the client or third party has an interest, promptly deliver the funds to the appropriate party, and provide an accounting of funds upon request.[3]

These rules mandate separation of client and lawyer funds, identification and safeguarding of other client property, complete and accurate recordkeeping, as well as the retention of any disputed fees or funds in the trust account,[4] and prompt distribution of all portions of the property not in dispute. Violating these provisions creates strict liability. *Sather* represents the view shared by nearly every jurisdiction: Knowing violations of rules that require segregation of client funds will result in severe discipline, even when client's interests are not oth-

---

1. ABA Canons of Prof. Ethics, Canon 11 Dealing with Trust Property (1908).
2. In re Valasquez, 507 A.2d 145 (D.C. 1986) (lawyer who deposited personal business funds in client trust account to avoid creditors disbarred in two jurisdictions).
3. St. ex rel. Okla. Bar Assn. v. Taylor, 71 P.3d 18 (Okla. 2003) (lawyer who failed to understand applicable law regarding distribution of client funds to third-party medical providers publicly reprimanded); In re Haar, 698 A.2d 412 (D.C. 1997) (lawyer who withdrew disputed legal fee from client's trust account negligently misappropriated funds despite lawyer's legal entitlement to the amount because client did not agree to the withdrawal); *cf.*, Rielgeman v. Krieg, 679 N.W.2d 857 (Wis. App. 2004), *rev. denied*, 684 N.W.2d 138 (2004) (lawyer who sent letter to client's medical provider promising to pay medical bill out of settlement proceeds personally liable for the bills because lawyer released all funds to client without protecting medical lien).
4. Model Rule 1.15(a) also applies to funds held for third parties. *See* Atty. Grievance Commn. v. Clark, 767 A.2d 865 (Md. 2001) (lawyer who repeatedly failed to pay state income withholding taxes violated Rule 1.15 by failing to remit money that belonged to the state).

erwise compromised.[5] Courts also agree that inadvertent commingling violates these rules, even if temporary and without harm to a client.[6]

Yet, in spite of these requirements, so many clients have been the victims of lawyers who have "borrowed" or stolen client funds that many jurisdictions have adopted additional specific rules that govern trust account management. By 1976, nearly every jurisdiction had created a client protection fund, financed by assessments on all lawyers, which reimburses clients who have been the victims of lawyer theft. In addition, some jurisdictions also require that lawyers keep specific records such as a ledger for each client showing the source of all funds deposited, the name and description of payees, and the amount of all deposits and payments,[7] and journals, which record receipts and disbursements from all law practice bank accounts.[8] Others require banks to notify disciplinary authorities of any overdrafts in a trust account.[9] A few even require audits of trust accounts.[10]

To meet the requirement of a separate account for client funds, most lawyers today establish an IOLTA or Interest on Lawyer Trust Account with a local bank. All client funds that cannot earn net interest are kept in this account, and the interest is paid to a central fund that is used to fund legal services for those unable to pay.[11] Local rules additionally may require that some client funds, such as those that are significant in size or held for a long period of time or those for trusts or estates, be kept in another separate account where the interest accrues to that client.

How do lawyers avoid inadvertent breach of these trust account obligations? First, just as law firms should not allow any one lawyer carte blanche in billing clients, law firms also should make at least two lawyers responsible for

---

5. *See, e.g.,* Douglas' Case, 809 A.2d 755 (N.H. 2002) (lawyer who improperly withdrew funds from client trust account in the "startlingly erroneous" belief that withdrawal was proper suspended from practice for six months); Atty. Grievance Commn. v. Hayes, 789 A.2d 119 (Md. 2002) (lawyer who operated practice for 30 years using only a trust account suspended for 90 days for commingling and misusing funds despite otherwise spotless record); In re Reynolds, 39 P.3d 136 (N.M. 2002) (neither lawyer's consent to discipline for misappropriating checks nor his cooperation with disciplinary authorities were sufficient to show that he was fit to be automatically reinstated).

6. Atty. Grievance Comm. v. Jeter, 778 A.2d 390 (Md. 2001) (inexperienced lawyer who failed to deposit client personal injury funds in trust account suspended for six months despite lawyer's remorse and lack of intent to defraud); In re Anonymous, 698 N.E.2d 808 (Ind. 1998) (lawyer who deposited earned fees and rent checks into client trust account and paid himself out of those funds privately reprimanded despite no improper use of client funds and no improper motive).

7. Ariz. S. Ct. R. 43(d)(2) (2007); Cal. R. Prof. Conduct 4-100(C) (2007); Colo. R. Prof. Conduct 1.15(j) (2007); Conn. R. Super. Ct. Gen. §2-24(b) (2007); Fla. Bar R. 5-1.2 (2006); Haw. R. Prof. Conduct 1.15(g) (2007); Ind. Admis. & Disc. R. 23, §29(a) (2007); Minn. R. Prof. Conduct 1.15 (h) (2005), *id.,* at App. 1; N.J. R. Prof. Conduct 1.15 (2006); N.J. R. Gen. Application 1:21-6(c) (2007); N.Y. Code Prof. Resp. DR 9-102(D) (2007); Ohio R. Prof. Conduct 1.15 (2007); R.I. R. Prof. Conduct 1.15 (2007); Vt. R. Prof. Conduct 1.15(e) (2007); Va. R. Prof. Conduct 1.15A(a) (2007).

8. Cal., Colo., Conn., Haw., Ind., Minn., N.J., N.Y., R.I., Va.

9. *See, e.g.,* Fla. Bar R. 5-1.2(c)(4) (2006); Ind. Admis. & Disc. R. 23, §29(b) (2007); Mass. R. Prof. Conduct 1.15(h) (2007).

10. *See, e.g.,* N.J. R. Gen. Application 1:21-6(h) (2007); Vt. R. Prof. Conduct 1.15A(b) (2007). For a compilation of the ABA Model Rules governing these subjects, *see* ABA, Model Rules for Client Protection (1999).

11. In Brown v. Leg. Found. of Wash., 123 S. Ct. 1406 (2003), the Supreme Court upheld the constitutionality of state IOLTA programs as long as client funds held in the accounts do not earn net interest for the client.

administration of law firm trust accounts.[12] Second, all trust accounts should adhere to certain fundamental rules designed to prevent inadvertent breaches. Jay Foonberg has written an entire book on the subject, and summarizes his advice in what he calls "The Ten Commandments of Good Trust Accounts."[13]

Rule 1: Have a trust account.

Rule 2: Never let anyone else sign your trust account.

Rule 3: Obtain and understand your IOLTA (Interest on Lawyers' Trust Account) rules.

Rule 4: Immediately notify the client every time something is added to the client's account balance and every time something is taken from the account balance.

Rule 5: Unearned fees and unexpended costs belong in the trust account until earned or spent.

Rule 6: Do not commingle your funds with the client funds in the trust account.

Rule 7: Be sure you understand the exact nature of the item deposited or credited to the trust account.

Rule 8: Reconcile the bank trust account monthly.

Rule 9: Reconcile and examine the individual client trust account balances monthly, and do not delay giving the clients their money.

Rule 10: Be alert to third party claims.

In addition, Foonberg recommends that all lawyers maintain specific records required by the ABA Model Rule on Financial Recordkeeping and a growing number of jurisdictions. Most important is a journal, which records all deposits, checks, dates, and amounts, and explains each item, and a client ledger, or running balance by client of all checks, disbursements, dates, amounts, and explanations. Lawyers and law firms also should keep all bank statements and records, and copies of each month's or quarter's reconciliation of the lawyer's accounts with the bank's statements.

Easy access to client funds continues to tempt lawyers. If history is any guide, you should expect increasing regulation of your bookkeeping practices to prevent further loss to clients.

D. Fees on Termination

Problem

10-9. Martyn & Fox agreed to take on Plaintiff's malpractice suit for a fixed fee of $30,000, plus a contingent fee equal to 50 percent of all amounts recovered in excess of $500,000. After Martyn & Fox spent

---

12. *See Reynolds, supra* note 5, at 142, where the court recommends allocation of responsibility to at least two lawyers within a law firm. *See also* In re Bailey, 821 A.2d 851 (Del. 2002) (managing partner of a law firm has enhanced duties to ensure the firm's obligation to comply with its recordkeeping obligations under the Rules of Prof. Conduct).

13. Jay G. Foonberg, *How to Start and Build a Law Practice* 491-496 (ABA L. Prac. Mgt. Sec. L. Student Div. 1999).

$100,000 on the matter, Plaintiff hired Caldwell & Moore, which settled the suit for $500,000. What fee is Martyn & Fox entitled to collect and from whom?

Consider: **Model Rule 1.5**
Model Code DR 2-106
RLGL §§40, 43

Malonis v. Harrington
816 N.E.2d 115 (Mass. 2004)

GREANEY, J.

We transferred this case here on our own motion to review a judgment entered in the Superior Court holding the defendant, Attorney Robert W. Harrington, liable to the plaintiff, Attorney George C. Malonis, for Malonis's reasonable attorney's fees and expenses. The fees and expenses were incurred by Malonis in his representation of Marc J. Loiselle, under a contingent fee agreement, in a personal injury action against Browning-Ferris Industries, Inc. (BFI). Loiselle discharged Malonis and retained Harrington, also under a contingent fee agreement, to represent him. Harrington settled the case with BFI and refused to pay Malonis's claim for attorney's fees and expenses. . . .

Loiselle suffered injuries on April 26, 1991, in a motor vehicle accident. The operator of the other vehicle was an employee of BFI. Within a few days of the accident, Loiselle retained Malonis to represent him in a personal injury action against BFI for a contingent fee of one-third the amount of any recovery received by Loiselle. Malonis secured a tape of the accident scene from the police; obtained Loiselle's medical bills and records; communicated with BFI (a self-insurer); obtained payment for Loiselle

of personal injury protection (PIP) benefits; and sent Loiselle's medical bills and records to BFI. In early 1993, BFI made a settlement offer of $7,500, which Loiselle rejected. Malonis then prepared and sent a G. L. c. 93A demand letter to BFI, to which BFI responded by extending a settlement offer of $30,000 (including the PIP benefits already paid). This offer also was rejected by Loiselle.

In June, 1993, Malonis filed a complaint in the Superior Court against BFI on Loiselle's behalf. Written discovery was exchanged, and Loiselle was deposed and underwent an independent medical examination. As the litigation continued, Loiselle still complained of back pain. In April, 1994, on Malonis's recommendation, Loiselle was examined by an orthopedic surgeon, who recommended disc surgery. Malonis forwarded the surgeon's report to BFI. As a consequence of receiving the report, BFI decided to increase its settlement offer to $57,500, although it did not communicate that offer to Malonis. Settlement discussions that continued between Malonis and BFI focused on figures in the $60,000-$80,000 range, but no agreement was reached.

On September 14, 1994, Loiselle discharged Malonis and engaged Harrington to represent him under a contingent fee agreement calling for one-third of the gross amount of the recovery. Harrington requested that Malonis forward his case file to him, and Malonis complied. On September 21, Malonis gave written notice to Loiselle, Harrington, and BFI, that he would seek to establish an attorney's lien, pursuant to G. L. c. 221, §50, on any recovery in the case. Between December 16, 1994, and March 27, 1995, Harrington sent Malonis four written requests for an itemized bill for his legal services performed for Loiselle with respect to the BFI case. On March 23, Loiselle himself sent Malonis a written demand "to submit a full and complete invoicing of your fees due you". . . .

In early April, Harrington completed a settlement with BFI for $57,500 (the figure that BFI had determined to offer the preceding year, but had not communicated to Malonis). Having received notice of Malonis's attorney's lien, and anticipating that Malonis expected to receive a portion of the settlement proceeds, counsel for BFI reminded Harrington of the issue of Malonis's payment. Harrington assured BFI's counsel that he "would take care of Mr. Malonis."

On April 4, BFI issued two checks: the first in the sum of $40,000, payable to Loiselle's wife, and the second in the sum of $17,500, payable to Harrington as attorney for Loiselle. Harrington subsequently paid the $40,000 to Loiselle's wife and retained the $17,500 as a legal fee. On April 4, the same day that the checks were issued, Malonis sent Harrington an itemized statement of his hours and costs, claiming $10,320 in hourly fees and $1,035.80 in costs, for a total of $11,355.80. Harrington viewed this amount as "ridiculous" and responded to a G. L.

c. 93A demand letter from Malonis with the words, "I will not tender one cent in settlement." Malonis offered to submit the dispute to fee arbitration, but Harrington refused. To date, Malonis has not been compensated for his legal services or expenses by either Loiselle or Harrington."

On July 31, Malonis filed a complaint in the Superior Court asserting claims against Loiselle, . . . and Harrington, with respect to his entitlement to payment for legal services performed for Loiselle in connection with the BFI case. . . . That judge then remanded the case to the District Court, where the case was tried against Harrington, on claims that (1) Harrington was unjustly enriched by failing to reimburse Malonis for his fees and costs out of his contingent fee; . . . and (3) Harrington had committed an unfair and deceptive practice in violation of G. L. c. 93A. The District Court judge concluded that Harrington was under no obligation to share any part of his fee with Malonis and awarded no damages. The Appellate Division affirmed the judgment.

Final judgment in favor of Harrington entered in the District Court on July 9, 2001, and, on Malonis's request, the case was retransferred to the Superior Court. . . . The judge concluded in a written memorandum of decision that Harrington was liable to Malonis and entered judgment accordingly. This appeal followed.

1. . . . The Superior Court judge determined that it was the shared "expectation" of all the affected parties that Malonis's attorney's fees and expenses would be paid by Harrington from his contingent fee. On the basis of that understanding, the judge concluded that Malonis was entitled to recovery from Harrington, on a

theory of quantum meruit, for the reasonable value of his efforts and contributions to the eventual recovery. We essentially agree with the judge's reasoning.

Loiselle was entirely within his rights to discharge Malonis. *See* Herbits v. Constitution Indem. Co., 181 N.E. 723 (Mass. 1932) (uniformly recognized that client has unquestioned right to discharge attorney, with or without cause). The discharge terminated Malonis's right to recover on the contingent fee contract.[6] Thereafter, Loiselle had an obligation to compensate Malonis for the fair and reasonable value of services and skills expended on Loiselle's behalf, on the theory of quantum meruit. The underlying basis for this legal obligation is derived from principles of equity and fairness, to prevent unjust enrichment of one party (the windfall of free legal services to the client) at the expense of another (the discharged attorney who expended time and resources for the client's benefit).

However, the record clearly establishes that, by the time settlement was reached with BFI, it was the reasonable expectation of all of the parties in this case that Harrington had assumed responsibility to pay Malonis. Loiselle, in his pro se answer to the complaint, stated that the case was settled "with the knowledge and understanding that Attorney Harrington was to see to [Malonis] at no cost to [Loiselle] whatsoever." BFI's counsel testified as to Harrington's specific assurance that he would "take care of" Malonis. His testimony on this matter is buttressed by letters to Harrington and Malonis reiterating his understanding that Harrington would pay Malonis out of his own $17,500 contingency fee. Malonis testified that, although at the time of his discharge he had no direct communications with Harrington or Loiselle on the matter of his payment, he assumed (based in part on past interaction with Harrington), that discussions with Harrington would follow if and when the case settled.[7] Finally, there is no question that Harrington himself understood that Malonis was entitled to payment, as shown by four written requests for an itemized bill for his legal services. Whatever his actual belief, Harrington's own words communicated to BFI's counsel an intention to pay Malonis a portion of his contingency fee. As noted by the judge, it is doubtful that BFI would have disbursed the settlement checks to Harrington without the latter's commitment to "take care of" Malonis."

Harrington is now obligated to compensate Malonis in quantum meruit for the value of his legal services. Given the expectations of the parties in this case, to conclude otherwise would allow Harrington to be

---

6. There is no claim, and no basis in the record to conclude, that the discharge was in bad faith. *See* Opert v. Mellios, 614 N.E.2d 996 (Mass. 1993), (recognizing that, after substantial performance, bad faith termination might permit attorney to recover under contingency fee contract).

7. . . . On principle, the fact that an attorney was retained on a contingency basis, which assumes that no fee will be owed unless the attorney's efforts secure an outcome favorable to the client, should have no bearing on a discharged attorney's right to recover in quantum meruit. As a practical matter, however, a client who discharges a lawyer before the conclusion of an unsuccessful claim may have received little or nothing of value and should not fairly be burdened with the obligation to pay his former counsel, over and above reasonable expenses and costs.

unjustly enriched, by permitting him to retain the entire fee, when he, admittedly, was not the major force in obtaining the settlement. . . .

We now consider the fair value of Malonis's quantum meruit recovery, mindful that "the question of what is fair and reasonable compensation for legal services rendered is one of fact for a trial judge to decide." The judge assessed the fees ($10,320) and expenses ($1,035.80) set forth in Malonis's invoice and, quite properly, accepted them as fair and reasonable. The record demonstrates that Malonis invested substantial time and funds in the case, and his efforts contributed materially to the resulting $57,500 settlement.[10] . . . BFI's counsel estimated that Malonis had performed fully eighty per cent of the pretrial work and the settlement negotiations at the time of his discharge, and Harrington does not contradict that estimate. . . .

2. We comment now on the broader question raised by the case. When a client discharges one attorney before settlement is reached and retains another on a contingent fee basis, who bears the cost of paying the discharged attorney the fair value of his legal services and expenses, the client or successor counsel?[11] Our resolution of this issue recognizes the highly fiduciary nature of the attorney-client relationship and duties on counsel imposed by the Massachusetts Rules of Professional Conduct. . . .

There is no question that a client must have absolute trust in the integrity, the judgment, and the ability of his or her attorney. When a client, for whatever reason, loses faith in his or her attorney, the client has the unqualified right to change lawyers. "But the right of a client so to do has not much value if the client is put at risk to pay the full contract price for services not rendered and to pay a second lawyer as well." The general rule in Massachusetts is that, on discharge, an attorney has no right to recover on the contingent fee contract, but, thereafter, the attorney may recover the reasonable value of his services on a theory of quantum meruit.

In withdrawing from a case, a discharged attorney must take all reasonable steps to protect the client's

---

10. The judge pointed out that Malonis's invoice, reconstructed from his copy of the BFI case file and not from contemporaneous time records, set forth more conservative estimates of time expended on various tasks than ordinarily might be reflected in an attorney's file.

11. The parties have suggested that courts elsewhere are divided on the answer. Our own reading of the cited cases reveals that other courts have resolved similar disputes much as we do today, by reference to governing rules of professional responsibility and application of equitable principles to the specific facts of each case. See, e.g., Saucier v. Hayes Dairy Prods., Inc., 373 So. 2d 102, 106 (La. 1979) (one contingency fee to be allocated among various attorneys involved in handling claim in question); Cohen v. Grainger, Tesoriero & Bell, 622 N.E.2d 28 (N.Y. 1993) (discharged attorney entitled to percentage of judgment recovered in separate action on same claim brought by successor counsel in United States District Court); Pryor v. Merten, 490 S.E.2d 590 (N.C. App. 1997) (discharged attorney may proceed against new attorney for rightful share of total attorney's fees). But see Adams v. Fisher, 390 So. 2d 1248, 1251 (Fla. Dist. Ct. App. 1980) (in absence of specific agreement, client must pay both discharged attorney for quantum meruit value of services and substituted attorney contingency fee in accordance with contract); Styer v. Hugo, 619 A.2d 347 (Pa. Super. 1993), aff'd, 637 A.2d 276 (Pa. 1994) (discharged attorney not entitled to portion of recovery from subsequent counsel, when record established no contribution by discharged attorney to ultimate settlement and no knowledge on part of subsequent counsel that former attorney expected payment).

interests, including surrendering papers and property to which the client is entitled, and discussing with the client the consequences of the discharge, including his or her expectation of being compensated for work performed. *See* Mass. R. Prof. C. 1.16 (c) and (d). To the extent that the discharge is followed by the retention of another attorney on a contingent fee basis, the successor attorney also should discuss this expectation with the client and make clear, by specific agreement, who will be responsible to pay former counsel's reasonable fee. *See* Mass. R. Prof. C. 1.4 (b), and 1.5. The agreement, no doubt, will depend on the circumstances of each case. In the words of the Superior Court judge, "if the case is an attractive one, successor counsel [may be] willing to commit to sharing his fee on some equitable basis with his predecessor; if he is not willing, the client may be able to find someone who is."

The significant point is that the matter should be resolved by express agreement with the client, based on a frank discussion of the matter, thus allowing an intelligent decision as to which course is in the client's best interests. Absent such express discussion, it is likely (as occurred here) that the client will simply assume that both lawyers will be paid out of the single contingency fee, and will fail to appreciate the potential that fee claims above that amount may be made. Protection of the client's interests—and the client's ability to make a reasoned decision with respect to any settlement offers— requires that this important subject be addressed with clarity and specificity. Any fees to the client ultimately charged by either attorney, of course, whether or not contingent on the outcome, must be reasonable. Mass. R. Prof. C. 1.5 (a). A client should never be made to pay twice. To avoid disputes in the future, we would advise successor counsel, before he or she receives the case, to confer with the client on the issue and to execute a written agreement unambiguously identifying the party responsible for payment of former counsel's reasonable attorney's fees and expenses.

This position is not cast in stone. We recognize some potential for a conflict of interest to arise when the burden of advising a client of the obligation to pay a former attorney, and the need to identify the source of payment, falls on the shoulders of the only alternate candidate, or when an attorney approaches settlement negotiations knowing that a portion of his fee (fixed or, as here, as yet undetermined) is owed to one no longer involved with the case. Attorneys in this situation should never lose awareness that, in matters of fees, attorneys "are fiduciaries who owe their clients greater duties than are owed under the general law of contracts." *Restatement (Third) of the Law Governing Lawyers* §[34] comment b. . . .

E. Statutory Fees

Problem

10-10. Martyn & Fox agrees to a one-third contingent fee contract with Client and spends 2,000 hours on Client's federal civil rights action alleging police brutality against Local Municipality, resulting in injunctive relief and a jury verdict of $21,000. What fee will Martyn & Fox receive? What if Local Municipality offers to settle for injunctive relief in exchange for Client's agreement not to seek statutory attorney fees?

Consider: Model Rule 1.5
Model Code DR 2-106
RLGL §38

Nilsen v. York County
400 F. Supp. 2d 266 (D. Me. 2005)

D. BROCK HORNBY, United States District Judge.

I. INTRODUCTION

This is an award of attorney fees and expenses, out of a $3.3 million class action settlement for arrestee strip searches at the York County Jail. . . .

II. PROCEDURAL BACKGROUND

Individuals processed at York County Jail ("Jail") filed a lawsuit under 42 U.S.C. §1983. They claimed that the Jail violated the Fourth Amendment by maintaining a policy of "strip searching" arrestees without individualized suspicion. After extensive discovery by the parties, I granted the plaintiffs' motion for class certification under Federal Rule of Civil Procedure 23(b)(3). Certification was appealed and affirmed. The parties then began discussions with a mediator. They subsequently filed a notice of voluntary settlement.

The settlement agreement requires York County to establish a common fund of $3.3 million in satisfaction of all its liabilities (including attorney fees). The fund is to be distributed to class members after deduction of costs and fees. The agreement also provides that the plaintiffs' lawyers will ask the Court to award attorney fees out of the fund, in the amount of 30% [$990,000], along with reimbursement for costs and expenses. Obviously the agreement does not and cannot dictate what amount I will actually award. . . .

(On the basis solely of hourly rates and hours spent, the lawyers estimated in June, 2005, that they would accrue somewhat less than $520,000 by the time everything is complete). . . ."

III. ANALYSIS

A. Attorney Fees

Under the Federal Rules of Civil Procedure, in a class action I may award "reasonable attorney fees and nontaxable costs authorized by law." Fed. R. Civ. P. 23(h). Had this lawsuit proceeded to a successful judgment for the plaintiffs, they could have recovered from the defendant York County reasonable attorney fees and costs under 42 U.S.C. §1988, on top of any damages they received. Instead, York County settled the lawsuit before trial for a lump sum of $3.3 million, covering all its liabilities, including attorney fees. That settlement amount reflects both the class members' compensable injuries *and* their statutory claim to attorney fees. . . . By the terminology of some of the caselaw, this settlement is a "common fund," and the common fund doctrine allows me to award attorney fees from it.

Making a fair fee award from a common fund in a class action settlement is a difficult determination for a judge. There are no adversarial presentations to test the fee claim, and our legal system does not ordinarily expect judges to behave as inquisitors, gathering testimony and collecting information on their own. Presented with an unopposed request, therefore, I depend upon my own analysis and secondary research—against a backdrop of popular dissatisfaction with large and highly publicized fees. *Third Circuit Task Force Report, Selection of Class Counsel,* 208 F.R.D. 340, 343-44 (2002). But the lawyers here are highly skilled and experienced civil rights attorneys. Their professional performance was exemplary; they represented the class members' interests zealously, achieving an excellent result for the class under the circumstances. For these reasons, they deserve a reasonable fee that duly recognizes their professional excellence and performance and provides an appropriate incentive for lawyers to take on future meritorious cases on behalf of a client class. At the same time, they do not deserve a windfall at the expense of the class and I do not want the size of the award to encourage frivolous litigation that benefits primarily lawyers.

In candor, I simply do not know the precise fee award that meets those concerns. I can only detail the process I have used.

(1) *Method: Lodestar or Percentage-of-Funds*

In the First Circuit, courts have discretion to award fees from a common fund "either on a percentage of the fund basis or by fashioning a lodestar." . . .

(2) *The Limited Role of the Lodestar*

As I have previously recognized, the "lodestar approach (reasonable hours spent times reasonable hourly rates, subject to a multiplier or discount for special circumstances, plus reasonable disbursements) can be a check or validation of the appropriateness of the percentage-of-funds fee, but is not required." Here, the lodestar figure is lower than the requested percentage fee, approximately $520,000 vs. $990,000. . . .

Under binding Supreme Court precedent, lodestar enhancements or multipliers in fee-shifting cases are almost completely unavailable, because many considerations that could lead to enhancement are contained within the lodestar itself. Penn. v. Del. Valley Citizens' Council for Clean Air, 478 U.S. 546, 566, (1986) ("The lodestar figure includes most, if not all, of the relevant factors constituting a 'reasonable attorneys' fee."). Outright prohibitions also exist. City of Burlington v. Dague, 505 U.S. 557, 567 (1992) (no enhancement for contingency or risk of litigation). The First Circuit is emphatic in rejecting multipliers to enhance the lodestar. In fact, since *Dague,* the First Circuit has never awarded a lodestar enhancement or multiplier. The unenhanced lodestar figure is strongly presumed to be the reasonable attorney fee that the losing defendant should pay in a fee-shifting case.

Do these constraints on multipliers apply when I am not making an award *against* a losing defendant, but instead determining the reasonable fee that the lawyers should recover from the plaintiff class's common fund settlement? I conclude that they do not.

First, it is well established that a defendant may settle, for a single lump sum, all outstanding claims in a fee-shifting case, including claims for attorney fees. Evans v. Jeff D., 475 U.S. 717, 731-32 (1986) (Congress intended fee awards to be part of civil rights plaintiff's "arsenal of remedies," and settlement including waiver of award is consistent with this goal).

Second, it is equally well established for nonclass actions that the statutory amount that a defendant is required to pay under fee-shifting principles does *not* limit the amount that the plaintiff must pay the plaintiff's lawyer. *Venegas*, 495 U.S. 82, 90 (1990) (fee-shifting statute "controls what the losing defendant must pay, not what the prevailing plaintiff must pay his lawyer"). The Supreme Court recently reaffirmed this principle in Gisbrecht v. Barnhart, 535 U.S. 789 (2002). There, it held that the plaintiff was bound to pay his lawyer the agreed-upon contingency fee of 25%, rather than the lower lodestar amount the district court assessed against the defendant under a fee-shifting statute.

These cases, read together, uncouple the fee analysis in determining an award *against* the losing defendant (the unenhanced lodestar) from the fee analysis for determining an award to the lawyer from the amount that he or she has recovered. . . . I conclude that the reasoning of these cases permits me to

award a percentage attorney fee (so long as it is reasonable) from a common fund in a class action settlement even if the fee effectively represents a multiplier of the lodestar amount.

(3) *The Reasonableness of the Requested Percentage*

In a class action, any fee I award must be reasonable. . . .

(a) Other Circuit Approaches. The majority of Circuits review percentage-of-funds fee awards by using multifactor tests in which the district court must examine and set forth findings on each factor. The Second Circuit requires analysis of six factors. The Sixth Circuit also uses six factors. The Third Circuit, both in caselaw and through its influential Task Force, requires seven.

Other circuits explicitly adopt the twelve factors of a seminal lodestar case, Johnson v. Georgia Highway Express, Inc., 488 F.2d 714, 717-19 (5th Cir. 1974) (adopting factors as "consistent with" the Model Code of Prof'l Responsibility). For example, the Fourth and Tenth Circuits mandate "pure" *Johnson* factors for percentage-of-funds fee awards. The Eleventh Circuit also mandates the *Johnson* factors, but adds still more factors, similar to those of the non-*Johnson* circuits.

It is easy to see that the multifactor tests largely overlap. Almost all include factors related to the lodestar amount (time and labor), the complexity and difficulty of the case, the quality of the lawyers or the representation (including skill, standing, and efficiency), the size of the fund (including the value of the benefit to the class), and the risk of nonpayment or contingency of the case.

Additionally, both the Third Circuit and the three *Johnson* circuits add comparison to other awards in similar cases, and the Third and Eleventh Circuits also look to whether there are objections. These, then, comprise the bulk of the factors used in the multifactor jurisdictions.

Three other circuits do not mandate specific multifactor tests. Instead, the Ninth Circuit uses a benchmark of 25%, from which deviation is permitted upon consideration of various case-specific factors. . . .

The Seventh Circuit determines reasonableness through a market-mimicking approach with the goal of awarding a fee that is the "market price for legal services, in light of the risk of nonpayment and the normal rate of compensation in the market" at the outset of the case. . . . This approach emulates the incentives of a private client-attorney relationship; the market price should take into account "the risk of nonpayment," "quality of performance," "the amount of work," and "the stakes of the case." For the Seventh Circuit, the key inquiry is what a private plaintiff would have negotiated with the lawyers, if they had bargained at arm's length at the outset of the case.

The Seventh Circuit approach presents special concerns in the context of class actions, of course, for generally no contract exists between lawyers and the class. After all, attorney fees in a class action require court, not client, approval. Thus, there is no readily apparent source of information about the market. That is the major criticism leveled at the Seventh Circuit approach: that for some fee-shifting class action claims, any "market" is simply illusory and speculative and that instead of any sort of privately negotiated fee, for many noncommercial cases the fee is set entirely by judicial reference to what is reasonable. While the Seventh Circuit has recognized that this is a legitimate concern, it retorts that a "consider-everything," factor-based method of setting fees "assures random and potentially perverse results," and that a "list of factors without a rule of decision is just a chopped salad." In re Synthroid Mktg. Litig., 264 F.3d 712, 719 (7th Cir. 2001).

(b) The Method I Shall Adopt in This Case. . . . The path of least resistance is to employ the multifactor approach to reasonableness. The majority of circuits use it and the fee-seeking lawyers have used it here. It will support virtually any percentage fee I award in a range from 16% to 33-1/3%.

But the preceding statement is the first and primary reason I reject the multifactor approach. It offers little predictability to either the awarding court, or the lawyers who seek fee awards. That is not a rule of law or even a principle. Instead, it allows uncabined discretion to the fee-awarding judge. A judge who likes lawyers and remembers the hazards of practice can be generous; a judge who cares more about public reaction or who never used contingent fees in practice can be stingy.[30] . . .

---

30. A district judge using the multifactor analysis has an instinctive notion, consciously or unconsciously, of what is an appropriate fee (a fee "Gestalt," as it were). The multifactor analysis merely supports the judge's instinctive view. And on review, appellate courts then take comfort from the weighing and juggling of the various considerations. But the factors do not produce a

The second reason I reject the multifactor approach is that some of the factors seem inconsistent with the reason for using a percentage-of-funds method in the first place, which is designed to create incentives for the lawyer to get the most recovery for the class by the most efficient manner (and penalize the lawyer who fails to do so). . . .

The third reason I reject the factor-based approaches is that they consume significant lawyer and judicial resources, a consideration that has led to the criticism (and in some quarters, the abandonment) of the lodestar method in favor of the percentage-of-funds method.

I believe that in setting a fee, a judge, consciously or unconsciously, necessarily compares what lawyers typically get paid for equivalent services—*i.e.*, the market price. . . . The Seventh Circuit appropriately makes this measure explicit, rather than a Gestalt lurking behind the multifactor review. Making the standard explicit, in turn, allows the lawyers or objectors to provide evidence to correct judicial misimpressions. . . .

The market-mimicking approach has its own shortcomings but it is better than the fuzzier alternatives.

Unfortunately, in this case I do not have direct data on the market price for civil rights class action lawyers, or for strip search class action cases inside or outside of Maine. To some degree, that is unavoidable for the reasons already described: the class action "market" is controlled by judges. That is why this is a market "mimicking" approach. But there should be contextual market information avail-

able, such as what lawyers charge as percentage fees for various types of litigation. . . .

(1) Standard Contingency Fees. First, I consider standard contingency fees and the limitations imposed upon them by statutes or regulations. Although there is considerable variation by type of case and by stage of litigation, one-third of the amount recovered is considered by most to be the general standard in personal injury litigation. . . .

Looking to other facets of contingent fee practice, I observe that Maine statutes limit the contingency fee in medical malpractice claims to what is ultimately a lower percentage. 24 M.R.S.A. §2961(1) (2000) (in medical malpractice actions, total contingent fee that may be contracted is 33.33% of first $100,000 of recovery, 25% of next $100,000, and 20% of any amount over $200,000). For the amount recovered here, the blended fee would be 20.6%. Maine also places declining limits on attorney fees in proceedings before the Workers Compensation Board. 39-A M.R.S.A. §325(4)(B) (2001) (if case tried to completion, fees may not exceed 30% of benefits accrued; for lump-sum settlements post-expenses, fees restricted to 10% of first $50,000, 9% through 6% of the next increments of $10,000, and 5% of any amount over $90,000). For the award requested here, the blended fee would be 5.1%. . . .

For certain claims, Federal statutes also limit the amount that a lawyer may collect from a client. *See generally* Gisbrecht v. Barnhart, 535 U.S. at 802-03 (2002) (collecting

---

result or even a substantive standard of reasonableness. At the very least, the market-mimicking approach is situated outside the judge's Gestalt, in a somewhat more objective realm.

representative statutes). For example, courts may approve contingency fees to a maximum of only 25% of past due benefits awarded to a successful plaintiff in Social Security proceedings. 42 U.S.C. §406(b) (2003). The Federal Tort Claims Act allows courts to approve contingency fees from the successful plaintiff's recovery to a maximum of 25% if the fund is created through judgment, or 20% if through settlement. 28 U.S.C. §2678; *see also* Veterans' Benefit Act, 38 U.S.C. §5904(d)(1) (1994) (20% of past due benefit). Several other federal statutes are less generous and allow a maximum of only 10% of the recovery to go toward attorney fees. *See, e.g.,* War Claims Act, 50 U.S.C. App. §2017m (1990) (10% of award).

Both the state and federal percentage caps are instructive, for they represent constraints on the fee a lawyer may recover in certain legal arenas. Sometimes, the maximum allowable percentage then becomes the market norm in that arena, rather than merely the upper ceiling. . . . At the same time, I recognize that there is no statutory cap for attorney fees in civil rights cases like this one.

(2) Awards in Other Cases. For other strip search class actions resulting in a common fund settlement, the lowest percentage awarded as a fee that I have discovered was 16% ($1 million of a $6.25 million common fund). The highest percentage explicitly awarded by a court was 33.33%, or $3,833,333 of an $11.5 million fund.

Median attorney fee awards in other class actions generally (*i.e.*, not limited to strip searches) range within a few percentage points on either side of 30%. Thus, a survey of 1,120 common fund class actions found that the median award of attorney fees and expenses was 31.6% of the fund for cases in which the class recovery ranged from $3 million to $5 million. . . . Thomas E. Willging & Shannon R. Wheatman, An Empirical Examination of Attorneys' Choice of Forum in Class Action Litigation 52 (2005). . . .

(3) The Award Here. Maine practice is certainly relevant. This is a Maine lawsuit, with a Maine defendant, and mostly Maine plaintiffs. . . .

The above analysis leads me to an attorney fee award here of 25% ($825,000). This percentage is at the higher end of the federal statutory limitation range, somewhat above the effective Maine malpractice limit, much higher than the Maine workers compensation percentage, lower than the standard one-third contingent fee and lower than the two fee agreements entered into before this became a class action. The percentage is in the mid-range of court awards in strip search cases, and it is more than 6% lower than the average award in general class actions with recoveries of this size. . . .

I am not confident that 25% truly is a good approximation of the market-mimicking rate. I could be wrong in either direction. On the information I have, I just don't know. Ironically, therefore, on this record my use of the Seventh Circuit's market-mimicking analysis may not be much better than the multifactor approach. But I hope that it will generate better evidence of the attorney fee market in future cases and more rational and predictable awards.

My reduction from the lawyers' requested 30% is no reflection whatsoever upon the quality of representation, or the nature of this litigation; these lawyers were excellent. Further, it is not a criticism of the percentage that they requested, given the precedents that they cite from other jurisdictions.

In future class actions that involve court-awarded attorney fees from a common fund, I will expect to receive evidentiary materials bearing on what lawyers negotiate for contingent fees or otherwise in comparable cases. I may well request detail about the percentages that would apply at different settlement stages of the case. I may also consider using my authority under Fed. R. Evid. 706 to appoint an expert to advise me on the attorney fee market. Finally, I may at least consider ordering lawyers to propose fee arrangements at the outset.[43] . . .

APPENDIX I

Here, for what it is worth, is the multifactor reasonableness analysis, drawn from the factors common to all Circuits that use this method.

1. The size of the fund created and the number of persons benefited. The common fund created by the settlement agreement totals $3.3 million, plus interest now approaching $70,000. It will be distributed in its entirety after payment of fees, costs, claims administration expenses, and incentive payments. Although not part of the common fund created, there is additional value in the requirement that York County

maintain a written policy prohibiting challenged strip searches, value akin to that of injunctive relief, which will benefit future arrestees.

There are approximately 7,500 class members. From claims filed it appears that with a participation rate of approximately 17.78%, over 1,300 persons will directly benefit from this common fund. The participation rate is particularly noteworthy as it was revised upward from an earlier estimate of 12-13% during the class notice period, indicating that even more people will benefit than had previously been thought.

2. The presence or absence of substantial objections. I have previously addressed the issue of objectors to the settlement. Due to the nature of this lawsuit and its potential for embarrassment in publicly stepping forward, I do not consider the relative absence of objections to settlement a significant factor.

3. The lawyers' skill and efficiency and the quality of representation. I have previously noted the skill of class counsel in this case, and there is no need to recite this aspect again. I do take additional note of class counsel's "considerable and highly successful effort" to reach as many class members as possible during the notice period. This effort resulted in an upwardly revised participation rate estimate, which in turn contributed directly to the number of people benefited by this common fund.

4. The complexity and duration of the litigation. This litigation lasted two years and occasioned extensive

---

43. That has been the recommendation of two Third Circuit Task Forces. *2002 Task Force Report*, 208 F.R.D. at 340-341; *1985 Task Force Report*, 108 F.R.D. at 255-56. Under Rule 23, however, no attorney fee computation can be final until the reasonableness review at the end of the case.

discovery. There were significant factual disputes as to whether the corrections officers actually viewed the arrestees' naked bodies while they changed into Jail clothing. There was additional complexity due to the individualized nature of the alleged dignitary harm, which could have made the damages stage of the case procedurally complicated if the defendant moved to decertify the class on the this issue. Further, class certification was not guaranteed, and was in fact vigorously disputed by York County all the way through appeal.

5. *Contingency and risk of non-payment.* Class counsel in this case faced a substantial risk of nonpayment. The Jail contested liability factually from the outset, and there was a "serious risk" that a jury would credit the corrections officers' testimony over that of the arrestees. Even if liability were established, it would still have been difficult for the plaintiffs to prove and recover damages for harms that were often dignitary rather than pecuniary. York County was reluctant to engage in settlement discussions, and even after two lengthy mediation sessions, the two parties remained far apart. Finally, the risk of nonpayment was increased substantially by the fact that the settlement was funded largely by insurance, and the amount available to fund it was finite and declined as York County spent more on defense costs.

6. *The amount of time devoted to the case by plaintiffs' counsel.* There is no doubt that class counsel devoted a long period of time to this litigation. The lodestar figure (the product of reasonable hours worked times the reasonable hourly rate) shows that in June, 2005, class counsel estimated that it would spend in total an amount somewhat less than $520,000.00 worth of time on this case, at least 4,084 hours, over 2 years.

7. *The awards in similar cases.* In the main body of this Order, I have compared at length the percentage awards in other cases. Suffice it to say that the cases that are most similar (strip search common fund settlements) range from 16% to 33%.

I can assess the lodestar cross-check similarly. The 25% awarded here represents a lodestar multiplier of approximately 1.6. Of the analogous strip search class action cases I reviewed for which lodestar data was available, I found a multiplier range from 1.19 to 2.68. For class actions generally, in 142 cases with a class recovery ranging from $3 million to $5 million the median multiplier was 1.89. But these averages and medians are of limited utility because the multiplier appears to differ greatly from case to case, based on the size of the fund and the type of class action.

The 1.6 multiplier in this case is lower than all but one of the strip search cases, and lower than the average multiplier of 1.89 found in class actions generally, and thus it is not unreasonable.

I conclude that under a multifactor approach to determining the reasonableness of a percentage fee, the preceding factors fully support an award of 25% from a common fund of $3.3 million, as well as many other percentages.

■ Practice Pointers:
Fee Agreements

The materials in this chapter demonstrate that the reasonableness requirement in Model Rule 1.5 applies to every kind of lawyer fee.[1] Statutes, case law, administrative regulation, and court rules all assume that lawyers may bargain for, charge, and collect fees, but only within limits. This reasonableness limit essentially becomes an implied term in every lawyer-client fee agreement. When it is exceeded, lawyers cannot collect the fee they bargained for, and may be subject to professional discipline as well.[2]

Legal Regulation of Lawyer's Fees

Although professional discipline is not common in fee cases, *Fordham* illustrates that it is possible whenever expert witnesses will testify that a fee is unreasonable.[3] *Nilsen* cites statutes and regulations that directly control the amount of the fee in an increasing number of cases.[4] It also cites cases where statutes provide for fee shifting, that is, the statute specifically entitles a prevailing plaintiff to recover "reasonable fees and expenses of attorneys" directly from an unsuccessful defendant in addition to other damages.[5]

Fee-shifting provisions typically are found in statutes that encourage private attorneys general to assist in enforcing a statutory policy, such as securities, antitrust, environmental, and civil rights laws.[6] The Supreme Court has held that recovery of reasonable fees under federal fee-shifting statutes requires a lodestar method of calculation (reasonable hourly rate times reasonable number of hours expended) and does not allow for any contingency enhancement beyond the lodestar amount.[7]

Every state has similar statutes and regulations that control lawyer's fees, both in certain kinds of representations such as workers' compensation, and by providing for fee shifting in statutory actions such as consumer or securities fraud.[8] Each jurisdiction has developed its own jurisprudence about the meaning of a "reasonable attorney's fee" under these statutes. Some courts allow for contingency fees or contingency enhancements in addition to a lodestar amount. Others mirror federal jurisprudence, relying solely on lodestars. *Nilsen* also cites state statutes that limit the amount of all contingent fees. Some of

---

1. RLGL §34.
2. *See, e.g.,* Robert L. Rossi, *Attorneys' Fees* (2d ed., Thomson 1995).
3. *See* Dale R. Agthe, *Attorney's Charging Excessive Fee as Ground for Disciplinary Action,* 11 A.L.R. 4th 133 (1982).
4. *See* Rossi, *supra* note 2, at Chapter 10; Gisbrecht v. Barnhart, 535 U.S. 789 (2002) (statutory "reasonable fee . . . not in excess of 25% of . . . the past due benefits" allows for lawyer-client contingent fees subject to court review of reasonableness).
5. *See, e.g., Gisbrecht, supra* note 4, construing the EAJA which allows the United States to avoid fees by showing that its position in the litigation was "substantially justified," a provision not commonly found in other fee-shifting statutes.
6. For a list of federal statutes with fee-shifting provisions, *see* John W. Toothman & William G. Ross, *Legal Fees: Law and Management* 351-407 (Carolina Academic Press 2003).
7. Burlington v. Dague, 505 U.S. 557 (1992).
8. *See, e.g.,* Roa v. Lodi Med. Group, 695 P.2d 164 (Cal. 1985) (citing representative statutes); Rossi, *supra* note 2, §§11:79-11:87.

these regulations also provide that a lawyer who charges more than the regulated amount will be deemed to have charged an unreasonable fee within the meaning of Model Rule 1.5.[9] Violations of these provisions not only subject a lawyer to discipline, but also create the basis for the client to argue that the fee contract is illegal and therefore unenforceable.[10]

Nilsen illustrates that courts also have jurisdiction to consider the reasonableness of the fee because of other obligations. In class actions, court approval is required for fees because of the common fund doctrine, which obligates courts to approve the amount and expenditure of any amounts that come from a common fund generated by settlement or judgment.[11] *Nilsen* indicates the range of approaches the Circuits have used because the Supreme Court has not yet settled the issue of the proper calculation of a reasonable class action fee. Similarly, bankruptcy proceedings require judicial approval of lawyer's fees because the court supervises the costs of administering the estate.[12] In state courts, lawyers who serve as fiduciaries are subject to the power of a probate court to examine and approve expenditures against an estate.[13] In cases that involve juveniles or other persons who lack legal capacity, courts also have a responsibility to approve fees as part of their *parens patriae* power to protect the ward.[14]

Apart from statutory and common law powers, courts have no general ability to supervise lawyer fees.[15] But courts adjudicate fee disputes brought to them in suits by lawyers to recover unpaid fees,[16] or client suits or counterclaims that

---

9. *E.g.*, N.J. Ct. R. 1:21-7 (2007); N.Y. Jud. L. §474-a (2007); Fla. R. Prof. Conduct 1.5(f) (2006). Some states also require a prescribed closing statement that regulates the calculation of the contingent fee. *See, e.g.,* Ohio Rev. Code §4705.15 (2007).

10. *See, e.g.,* Fourchon Docks, Inc. v. Milchem Inc., 849 F.2d 1561 (5th Cir. 1988) (limiting a liquidated damages clause of $216,000 for lawyer's fees in a lease to a reasonable fee of $57,750); Starkey, Kelly, Blaney & White v. Estate of Nicholaysen, 796 A.2d 238 (N.J. 2002) (oral contingent fee contract not enforceable, but recovery allowed in quantum meruit); White v. McBride, 937 S.W.2d 796 (Tenn. 1996) (lawyer who charged excessive contingent fee loses both contractual rights and quantum meruit recovery); American Home Assurance Co. v. Golomb, 606 N.E.2d 793 (Ill. App. 1992) (lawyer who charged fee in excess of that allowed by state statute in medical malpractice cases barred from recovering any fee, including quantum meruit). *Cf.* Winkler v. Keane, 7 F.3d 304 (2d Cir. 1993) (lawyer's use of an illegal contingent fee in a criminal case was not grounds for reversing conviction for ineffective assistance of counsel absent actual prejudice to the defendant).

11. *E.g.*, Lealao v. Beneficial Cal., Inc., 97 Cal. Rptr. 2d 797 (Cal. App. 2000) (trial court had discretion to adjust lodestar in successful $14 million consumer class action by applying a multiplier where necessary to ensure that the fee awarded would be within the range of fees freely negotiated in the legal marketplace in comparable litigation); Bowling v. Pfizer, Inc., 922 F. Supp. 1261, 1283 (S.D. Ohio 1996), *aff'd,* 132 F.3d 98 (6th Cir. 1998) (lawyer's fee in successful and valuable class action reduced by two-thirds because work was "not even remotely commensurate" with the amount requested). For a discussion of particular applications of this doctrine, *see* Rossi, *supra* note 2, at Chapter 6.

12. *See, e.g.,* Watkins v. Sedberry, 261 U.S. 571 (1923); Rossi, *supra* note 2, at §§10:10-10:15.

13. Rossi, *supra* note 2, §§11:39-11:60.

14. *E.g.,* Hoffert v. General Motors Corp., 656 F.2d 161 (5th Cir. 1981) (upholding trial court's reduction of 40 percent contingent fee contract for a minor to 20 percent of the recovery). Recall that in Spaulding v. Zimmerman, *supra* p. 204, the court relied on this same *parens patriae* power to justify reopening the judgment under the Minnesota equivalent of Fed. R. Civ. P. 60.

15. Gagnon v. Shoblom, 565 N.E.2d 775 (Mass. 1991) (trial judge has no power to raise issue of excessive fee *sua sponte*).

16. *See, e.g.,* Jane Massey Draper, *Excessiveness or Inadequacy of Attorney's Fees in Matters Involving Commercial and General Business Activities,* 23 A.L.R.5th 241 (1994); Jane Massey Draper, *Excessiveness or Adequacy of Attorneys' Fees in Domestic Relations Cases,* 17 A.L.R.5th 366

claim refunds or disgorgement of fees already paid. Model Rule 1.6(b)(5) recognizes the right of a lawyer to use confidential information to bring such a suit, and many lawyers successfully recover sums from clients who unjustly refuse to pay. [17]

All of this legal regulation means that many fees routinely are reviewed by courts or are subject to explicit legal regulation by statute or court rule. Beyond this specific oversight, any fee also can come to a court's attention by virtue of a suit to recover a promised or already paid fee. Many jurisdictions have established fee arbitration systems to promote alternatives to formal lawsuits.[18] Like the judges called on in lawsuits to decide when fees are payable or refundable, the arbitrators who rule or make recommendations in these cases also rely on the factors set forth in Model Rule 1.5.

Fee Agreements

The best way to avoid fee disputes is to communicate the basis or rate of the fee and the client's responsibility for costs and expenses in a written document. Model Rule 1.5 requires written contingent fees agreements, but only prefers rather than requires a writing for other fees agreements. Some jurisdictions go further, requiring that *all* fee agreements be reduced to a writing.[19] This is because fee disputes are not uncommon, and written documents not only may avoid them but also clarify the respective rights of both client and lawyer if they do occur. For example, one case upheld a jury verdict of breach of fiduciary duty against a lawyer who failed to reduce a fee agreement to writing after his client requested a written document. The lack of documentation cost the lawyer all but $11,000 of the $100,000 fee to which he claimed entitlement.[20] Thus, the best practice is to provide your clients with a written document that communicates both "the scope of the representation and the basis or rate of the fee and expenses

---

(1994); John E. Theuman, *Excessiveness or Adequacy of Attorneys' Fees in Matters Involving Real Estate—Modern Cases*, 10 A.L.R.5th 448 (1993).

17. One constant problem with fee suits is procedural: Any invocation of the court's jurisdiction can result in a counterclaim for other behavior the client might not otherwise have contested. For example, clients have raised claims about sexual misconduct in the context of a fee suit, and counterclaims for malpractice also are common. *See, e.g.*, Barbara A. v. John G., 193 Cal. Rptr. 422 (Cal. App. 1983); McDaniel v. Gile, 281 Cal. Rptr. 242 (Cal. App. 1991); Ronald E. Mallen & Jeffrey M. Smith, *Legal Malpractice* §15.9 (West, 2007 ed.).

18. *See, e.g.*, ABA Model Rules for Fee Arbitration (1995); Fla. Bar Reg. Rule 14-5 (2007). *See also* Disc. Counsel v. McCord, 770 N.E.2d 571 (Ohio 2002) (lawyer who failed to return fee following an arbitration award to his client suspended for six months for conduct prejudicial to the administration of justice); Guralnick v. N.J. S. Ct., 747 F. Supp. 1109 (D.N.J. 1990), *aff'd*, 961 F.2d 209 (3d Cir. 1992) (N.J. system of compulsory binding arbitration for lawyer-client fee disputes not unconstitutional).

19. Alaska R. Prof. Conduct 1.5(b) (2007) (over $500); Cal. Bus. & Prof. Code §6147 (2007); Colo. R. Prof. Conduct 1.5(b) (2007); Conn. R. Prof. Conduct 1.5(b) (2007); D.C. R. Prof. Conduct 1.5(b) (2007); N.J. R. Prof. Conduct 1.5(b) (2007); N.Y. DR 2-106(c)(2)(ii) (domestic relations matters); Pa. R. Prof. Conduct 1.5(b) (2006); R.I. R. Prof. Conduct 1.5(b) (2007); Utah R. Prof. Conduct 1.5(b) (2007) (over $750). The ABA has twice refused to amend Model Rule 1.5(b) to require a written communication of every fee. The ABA House of Delegates defeated both the Kutak Commission proposal in 1983 and the Ethics 2000 proposal in 2001 that would have required a written communication to the client about the scope of the representation and the basis or rate of the fee. Can you make a principled distinction between this outcome and the requirement that conflicts waivers by "confirmed in writing"?

20. Frazier v. Boyle, 206 F.R.D. 480 (E.D. Wis. 2002).

for which the client will be responsible."[21] The effort you invest in providing such a writing will more than be repaid in client understanding and goodwill, and if necessary, in forming the basis for the resolution of a fee dispute.

A written fee agreement also gives clients and lawyers the opportunity to consider alternative fee structures. This chapter focuses primarily on the common fee arrangements: hourly, contingent, and flat fees. Lawyers and clients are becoming increasingly creative in blending these options. Some adopt blended hourly fees, where the client pays a set rate regardless of which lawyer performs the work. Others prefer retainer plus fees, which supplement monthly retainers with an hourly fee when the lawyer works more than an agreed-upon number of hours per month. Task-based fees, which break or unbundle a representation into different legal tasks, such as complaint drafting, negotiation, or interrogatories, also are becoming more common, along with work-unit fees, which allocate flat fees by a client-determined unit such as number of lots sold.[22]

Finally, lawyers who amend fee contracts after the representation has commenced are subject to conflicts of interest rules, including the law of undue influence designed to enforce their fiduciary obligations to clients. This means that changes to initial agreements are presumed the product of undue influence by the lawyer and voidable by the client.[23]

Fee Collection

Of course, lawyers not only must provide clients with clear fee agreements, but also abide by their provisions in charging and collecting their fees, and provide clarifications where necessary.[24]

Lawyers who execute otherwise valid fee contracts sometimes engage in what ABA Opinion 93-379 called "problematic billing practices." Unfortunately, some of these practices include fraud. For example, Professor Lerman has documented the practices of 16 well-respected lawyers who engaged in blatant billing and expense fraud.[25] Another survey finds that more subtle

---

21. MR 1.5(b).

22. *ABA Panelists Look into Whys and Hows of Moving to Different Fee Arrangements*, 18 ABA/BNA Lawyers' Manual on Prof. Conduct 485 (2002).

23. Brown & Sturm v. Frederick Rd. Ltd. Partn., 768 A.2d 62 (Md. Ct. Spec. App. 2001); Mallen & Smith, *supra* note 18.

24. Cox's Case, 813 A.2d 429 (N.H. 2002) (lawyer who failed to respond to client's request for accounting data reprimanded for violating MR 1.4 and 1.15(b)).

25. Lisa G. Lerman, *Blue-Chip Bilking: Regulation of Billing and Expense Fraud by Lawyers*, 12 Geo. J. Leg. Ethics 205 (1999). For example, one judge described the practices of one of these lawyers as "almost fictional," because they included nearly $100,000 billed for services that were never performed, nearly $500,000 for work done by paralegals that was actually performed by secretaries and a receptionist, and $66,000 for legal research that cost the firm $395. His partners helped cover up the fraud when complaints were made. *Id.* at 238. *See also* Dresser Indus. v. Digges, 1989 U.S. Dist. LEXIS 17396. Because the conduct was fraudulent, a later case determined that the law firm's insurer had no contractual obligation to pay the judgment the client obtained against the firm. St. Paul Fire & Marine Ins. Co. v. Dresser Indus., 1992 U.S. App. LEXIS 18561 (4th Cir.). The lawyer pled guilty to one count of mail fraud, was sentenced to 30 months in prison, and ordered to pay $1 million in restitution to the client and a $30,000 fine. Lerman, *supra,* at 264.

deception, ranging from performing unnecessary work and "estimating" billable hours to deliberately padding bills or expenses, occurs more than occasionally.[26] Of course, if deliberate, these practices constitute fraud,[27] and if done repeatedly, may rise to the level of mail or wire fraud under state and federal criminal statutes.[28] We have seen that a clear and serious violation of a lawyer's duty to a client also constitutes grounds for total or partial fee forfeiture.[29] Further, sloppy or negligent billing that does not accurately reflect the agreement or the time spent may be grounds for a breach of contract, malpractice, or breach of fiduciary duty claim.[30]

Lawyers and law firms must monitor the accuracy of fee billings to prevent both intentional and inadvertent wrongdoing. The power of clients to discharge lawyers at any time discussed in *Malonis* and *Sather* means that regardless of the nature of the fee agreement, every lawyer must keep records of time actually spent on each matter to be able to establish the alternative basis for quantum meruit recovery.[31] Billing systems should include efficient and nearly simultaneous recording of time. Good recordkeeping also serves to document adherence to contractual terms, and provides the basis for lawyers to recover fees against clients who refuse to honor their own obligations. In law firms, no lawyer should have carte blanche to send out any bill he or she wishes.[32] Lawyers who lose their fees or are subject to damages in civil actions usually bind their law firms as well. Model Rule 5.1 also makes supervisory lawyers responsible for violations by other lawyers in their firms.

Many jurisdictions recognize retaining or charging liens to secure a lawyer's fee. Retaining liens are nonconsensual and allow lawyers to retain a client's papers and funds in the lawyer's possession until the client pays the bill.[33] The Restatement adopts the minority view, which recognizes retaining liens only where legitimated by statute, because the lawyer's refusal to turn over the client's files may harm the client's interests, including the client's right to fire

---

26. *See* William G. Ross, *The Honest Hour: The Ethics of Time-Based Billing by Attorneys* 23-38 (Carolina Academic Press 1996); Lisa G. Lerman, *Lying to Clients*, 138 U. Penn. L. Rev. 659, 705 (1990). The bill padding was accomplished by billing for hours not actually worked, or by "premium billing," which adds lump sums to a bill based on the lawyer's subjective determination of its value. *Id.* at 709-715.

27. *See, e.g.,* Ratcliff v. Boydell, 674 So. 2d 272 (La. App. 1996) (lawyer who misrepresented amount of client's annuity at settlement to increase his contingent fee and later sued client for defamation and malicious prosecution liable for fraud, intentional infliction of emotional distress, and abuse of process); Cantu v. Butron, 921 S.W.2d 344 (Tex. App. 1996) (lawyers who increased fee from 40 to 45 percent liable for fraud and breach of fiduciary duty, including punitive damages).

28. Lerman, *supra* note 26, at 263-271 (detailing criminal prosecutions of nine lawyers for billing fraud); *id.* at 282-287 (detailing civil penalties in 16 cases of billing fraud).

29. *E.g.,* Golomb, *supra* note 11 (total fee forfeiture of illegal fee that violated state statute); The Law Governing Lawyers: *Loss of Fee or Other Benefits, supra* p. 339.

30. *See, e.g.,* Lerman, *supra* note 27, at 696-698; Cripe v. Leiter, 703 N.E.2d 100 (Ill. 1998) (citing cases).

31. RLGL §40.

32. Ross, *supra* note 27, at 249-260.

33. The lien does not include any property held in safekeeping for the client. Ronald D. Rotunda & John S. Dzienkowski, *Legal Ethics: The Lawyer's Deskbook on Professional Responsibility* §1.8-10(a) (West 2007).

the lawyer.[34] The Restatement does recognize the legitimacy of charging liens, because they are created by contract with a client, and provide for the lawyer's right to a fee out of funds recovered for the client.[35] Lawyers also may secure a client payment by taking a security interest in other client property, as long as they remember that they are engaging in a business transaction with a client subject to the stringent requirements of Model Rule 1.8(a).[36]

To sum up: Lawyers have every right to be compensated for their work, as long as the compensation is reasonable. To protect yourself, and increase your chances of avoiding or winning a fee dispute, you should reduce fee agreements to a writing or include them in written retainer agreements,[37] and you should keep accurate records of the time you spend on each client matter. The time these tasks take will more than repay you in client goodwill,[38] and eventual recovery of adequate compensation.

---

34. RLGL §43. *See also* Sage Realty Corp. v. Proskauer Rose Geotz & Mendlesohn L.L.P., 689 N.E.2d 879 (N.Y. 1997) (client presumptively entitled to entire file, but law firm may charge for cost of assembling and delivering documents to client). RLGL §43 does allow a lawyer to withhold a particular document (such as a will) drafted for the client until the client pays for it, as long as retaining the document would not unreasonably harm the client.
35. RLGL §43(2).
36. RLGL §43(4).
37. *See* Practice Pointers: *Engagement, Nonengagement, and Disengagement Letters, supra* p. 107.
38. *See, e.g.,* Avi Azrieli, *Your Lawyer on a Short Leash: A Survivor's Guide to Dealing with Lawyers* 125-138 (Bridge St. 1997).

Chapter 11

Ending the Client-Lawyer Relationship

We have seen that fiduciary duties generally do not attach until a lawyer agrees to represent a client, and when a lawyer completes a client matter, most, but not all fiduciary duties, end. In Chapters 6 and 7, we addressed the continuing duties of confidentiality to former clients. In Chapters 8 and 9, we identified specific rules that govern conflicts of interest concerning former clients. In Chapter 10, we saw that the lawyer's fee agreement may be invalidated when a client fires a lawyer. In this chapter, we review the various ways a client representation can end, including termination by the client and withdrawal from the matter by the lawyer. We also focus here on situations where the client's activity may force a lawyer to resign, and whether a lawyer faced with such a circumstance can seek any remedy.

Problems

11-1. Martyn & Fox has been handling a litigation matter for a client for several years. Last September, the client stopped paying Martyn & Fox's bills, and has given one excuse after another. May Martyn & Fox resign?

11-2. Client admits she doesn't pay Social Security for her daughter's "wonderful" nanny, an illegal alien who might then get in trouble. Martyn & Fox informs Client, "If you don't report her income and pay the tax, the firm can't prepare and sign your income tax return." "That's okay," says the client. "You just prepare it; I'll sign it. Then the risk's on me." Are we safe?

11-3. Martyn & Fox have counseled Big Pharma that it must disclose recent problems with defibrillators manufactured and implanted five years ago. Big Pharma refuses. Pharma CEO explains: "It will cause a panic and the global risk to patients is greater in having the defibrillators replaced than just living with a few defective ones." May (must) Martyn & Fox resign? What if Martyn is inside counsel to the corporation?

11-4. Martyn, as an army reservist, is enlisted to represent a detainee at Guantanamo. The detainee thanks Martyn but says he does not want to be represented because it would lend legitimacy to the proceedings. Martyn judges the detainee to be totally competent. Martyn reports this to her superior, who explains that under Guantanamo rules no one may represent himself. What should Martyn do if the detainee persists in his original view?

Consider: Model Rules 1.2, 1.6, 1.7, 1.16
         Model Code DR 2-110
         RLGL §§14, 32, 33

Gilles v. Wiley, Malehorn & Sirota
783 A.2d 756 (N.J. App. 2001)

PRESSLER, P.J.A.D.

Plaintiff Denise Gilles appeals from a summary judgment dismissing her legal malpractice complaint against defendants, the law firm of Wiley, Malehorn & Sirota, and its partner, Arthur L. Raynes, who had represented her. The gravamen of her complaint is that Raynes, voluntarily and without good cause attributable to her, terminated the representation without adequately protecting her against the running of the statute of limitations, thus causing her to lose her medical malpractice cause of action. . . .

. . . Plaintiff's asserted medical malpractice cause had its genesis in a colonoscopy she underwent on February 26, 1996, to determine the cause of occult bleeding. . . . The gravamen of the asserted medical malpractice was that the physician who performed the . . . colonoscopy perforated her colon, requiring her to undergo an emergency surgical repair that day. During her week-long hospital stay following the surgery, she developed a right hydropneumothorax that retarded her recovery. She apparently did, however, fully recover.

Persuaded by advice she had received from a physician family member that the perforation resulting in the emergency surgery was caused by malpractice, she consulted Raynes in early April 1996. . . .

. . . At Raynes's instruction, plaintiff obtained and delivered to him the relevant medical records. Raynes explained to her that before suit could be commenced, he would need a report from a medical expert opining that she had been the victim of malpractice. Accordingly, he sought an opinion from a forensic gastroenterologist, Dr. Andrew Lo of Beth Israel Medical Center in New York, who reported to him that he believed there had not been malpractice. By letter dated March 24, 1997, Raynes advised plaintiff of Dr. Lo's opinion but added that:

Let me make clear that the above opinions on your care are those of Dr. Lo, and not of this office. We are willing to pursue your case further. However, in order to make this case viable, we will need to find an expert witness who can testify authoritatively that the care you received did not meet acceptable medical standards. If we do proceed with your case, we will need to lay out additional monies to potential witnesses in order to find one who agrees that you have received substandard treatment. This means that you will incur several hundred more dollars of expenses.

The letter concluded with Raynes's request that plaintiff telephone him to "discuss this further and decide whether you want us to continue to search for an independent expert." Plaintiff communicated her desire to proceed and agreed to pay the expenses involved.

A little over three months later, Raynes received a report dated July 3, 1997, from Dr. Lawrence B. Stein, a board-certified gastroenterologist, who opined that... [the medical technique used]... "greatly increased the likelihood of creating a colonic perforation and is a deviation from acceptable medical practice." Raynes mailed a copy of Dr. Stein's report to plaintiff on July 18, 1997, under cover of letter simply referring to it and making no further comment thereon.

On October 20, 1997, Raynes wrote to plaintiff again complaining that she had not yet paid the $1,204 she had been billed to cover expenses. The letter noted that the last payment he had received from her was the previous May. He then went on to say that:

I understand that you want us to continue representing you in this matter; if that has changed, please advise us accordingly. In any event, you must reimburse us for the monies we have disbursed in working on your case thus far, as well as any expenses which may result from future work on your case. We cannot continue as your attorneys unless you fulfill that responsibility.

I would ask that you pay us in full by no later than October 31, 1997. If we do not receive payment from you by that time, we may reconsider our

representation of you in this matter. . . .

Although there was some dispute as to when that $1,204 was paid and as to just what the installment arrangements, if any, had been, Raynes agreed in his deposition testimony that by the beginning of January 1998 the balance due had been reduced to something just under $125.

Despite the favorable report from Dr. Stein, Raynes did not file a medical malpractice complaint. Some six months had gone by after his receipt of that report, when, on January 6, 1998, Raynes wrote the following letter to plaintiff:

This is to advise that our firm has taken a new direction, away from most plaintiffs' malpractice cases. I therefore need to tell you that we will not be in a position to file suit on your behalf.

The work that we have done for you, in obtaining a report from a reputable expert, Dr. Stein, will be useful to you with your next attorney. I enclose a copy of that report for you. Your next attorney will know to obtain the required affidavit from Dr. Stein.

You have two years from the incident of malpractice to file suit. This should afford you sufficient time to obtain another attorney. Failure to file suit within the two year period will likely result in your losing your right to sue. I suggest that you contact another attorney immediately to protect your rights.

There are numerous attorneys who handle medical malpractice cases. I recommend Tom Chesson of Porzio, Bromberg and Newman, whose telephone number is (973) 538-4006, or Adrian Karp, whose telephone number is (973) 267-7787.

We have not charged you at all for our legal time. We have only charged you for reimbursement to us of our expenses.

Best of luck to you.

Several comments must be made about that letter. First, at his deposition, Raynes explained that the firm had had some financially negative experience with contingent fee cases and while some were retained and some new ones being undertaken, they were not regarded as a desirable type of business. He then went on to explain that plaintiff's case was not as good—presumably in terms of damages—as he had originally thought and that Dr. Stein's report was not as strong as he had hoped for. He also suggested that plaintiff's failure to make prompt payment of the bill for expenses played a part in his decision to terminate the representation, although this had not been expressed to her and although her balance at the time of the termination was relatively insignificant.

In any event, the letter, which referred to the two-year statute of limitations but did not expressly state the date on which it would expire, came as a complete surprise to plaintiff, who, as she testified, was away on a trip when it was sent and did not believe that she actually received it until the end of January 1998. She did not, upon its receipt, immediately attempt to communicate with another lawyer, either one of the lawyers mentioned by Raynes or anyone else. As she testified on her deposition, she thought that if Raynes were sending her to another lawyer, then he should have made the referral himself and that in any event, she was so upset when she did receive his letter that she was unable to mobilize herself to take further steps although she did see another lawyer after the statute ran, some three or four weeks later. . . .

. . . Plaintiff asserts that Raynes breached his duty to her by unreasonably terminating the attorney-client relationship so soon before the running of the statute of limitations and without adequately protecting her interests in preserving her cause of action.

The Rules of Professional Conduct (R.P.C.s) speak to termination of the representation. And while we recognize that a cause of action for malpractice cannot be based exclusively on the asserted breach of an R.P.C., nevertheless it is clear that the R.P.C.s may be relied on as prescribing the requisite standard of care and the scope of the attorney's duty to the client. . . .

[The court cites Model Rule 1.16 (b)(1) and (d).] The issue then, as we view it, is whether in the totality of the circumstances, Raynes's withdrawal, considering both the manner in which it was done and its timing, was accomplished without "material adverse effect" on plaintiff's interests in that it was attended by those steps "reasonably practicable" to protect her interests.

The trial judge concluded that Raynes had, beyond any question of material fact, acted reasonably. The sole basis of that conclusion was our decision in Fraser v. Bovino, 721 A.2d 20 (N.J. App. 1998), in which we held that in the circumstances there an attorney's termination of the attorney-client relationship "several weeks" before the statute of limitations had run was reasonable in that it afforded plaintiff adequate time to obtain another lawyer. We did not, however, in Fraser establish a bright-line rule that a withdrawal several weeks before the running of the statute of limitations is reasonable as a matter of law. We reached that conclusion there based on the operative facts in that case including the plaintiff's sophistication as a business man having regular dealings with lawyers, including such dealings with respect to the basic transactions in controversy; his having failed to raise the issue of possible litigation with defendant attorney until five years and nine months of the six-year statute of limitations had elapsed; and the brief period, some three months, during which the defendant-lawyer reviewed and studied the file. We note further that the defendant-lawyer there had denied that he had ever undertaken the representation.

Clearly the determination of reasonableness is ordinarily circumstantially dependent, and we are satisfied that a finder of fact would be justified in finding from the circumstances here that the timing and method of withdrawal were not reasonable. The facts here are very different from those in *Fraser*. Here, unlike *Fraser*, there was never a disavowal during a twenty-one month period of representation that Raynes represented plaintiff. As he said in his deposition, "I was her lawyer." For a six-month period he had all the information he needed not only to commence an action but also to have reached the conclusion that he eventually did reach respecting the probable unprofitability of the representation, a conclusion that evidently was the primary reason for the withdrawal. Plaintiff, on the other hand, was an unsophisticated lay person unaccustomed to legal dealings. The letter of termination, moreover, while it referred to the two-year statute of limitations and "suggested" plaintiff contact another lawyer immediately, did not specify the critical date. Finally, a fact-finder could also conclude that the period of time left to plaintiff before the statute of limitations had run was unreasonably short,

particularly in view of the preceding six-month period following Raynes's receipt of Dr. Stein's favorable report. In this regard, we note that medical malpractice cases are ordinarily difficult representations and are not lightly or casually undertaken by serious and responsible lawyers. It is by no means clear that plaintiff could have obtained a new lawyer who, in three weeks, would have been able to review her file, make the necessary evaluations, and agree to file a complaint, particularly after knowing that her previous lawyer, who had represented her for twenty-one months, had suddenly declined to continue. After all, it apparently took Raynes six months after having reviewed the medical records and experts' reports to decide that he was no longer interested. Finally, and most significantly, a finder of fact could have found that Raynes failed to take those steps "reasonably practicable" to protect her interests, a matter we address hereafter.

Plaintiff supported her resistance to the summary judgment motion by submission of a report from an expert, a member of the bar of this State. The report opined that defendant, after his almost two years of representation, should not have terminated the relationship by a letter sent by ordinary mail but rather should have explained the situation and its imperatives to the client or, at the least, sent her his withdrawal by certified mail both to assure its timely receipt and to impress upon her the urgency of the situation. He also opined that considering the late withdrawal, reasonable steps to protect her interests would have required him to prepare for her a pro se complaint which she could have filed to avoid the danger of the statute running. . . .

The point, of course, is that plaintiff perceived herself as having been abandoned by defendant too late in the day to enable her to protect herself, and we do not regard that perception as prima facie unreasonable. We addressed the issue of abandonment in Kriegsman v. Kriegsman, 375 A.2d 1253 (N.J. App. 1977). Although we were there dealing with an attorney's motion for leave to withdraw from a matter already in litigation, what we said there is equally apt to an attorney's prelitigation obligations. Thus, in affirming the denial of that motion, we started from the premise that "when a firm accepts a retainer to conduct a legal proceeding, it impliedly agrees to prosecute the matter to a conclusion. The firm is not at liberty to abandon the case without justifiable or reasonable cause, or the

consent of its client." . . . [O]ur rationale in Kriegsman remains as relevant today as it was then in defining the attorney's duty. As we explained:

> We are not unmindful of the fact that the Rose firm has performed substantial legal services for plaintiff and clearly is entitled to reasonable compensation therefor. Nevertheless, an attorney has certain obligations and duties to a client once representation is undertaken. These obligations do not evaporate because the case becomes more complicated or the work more arduous or the retainer not as profitable as first contemplated or imagined. . . .
>
> Whether Raynes's withdrawal afforded plaintiff a reasonable opportunity in the circumstances to protect her cause of action was, in our view, at least a question of fact precluding summary judgment dismissing the complaint. . . .

Crews v. Buckman Laboratories International, Inc.

78 S.W.3d 852 (Tenn. 2002)

WILLIAM M. BARKER, J. . . .

The sole issue in this case is whether an in-house lawyer can bring a common-law claim for retaliatory discharge when she was terminated for reporting that her employer's general counsel was engaged in the unauthorized practice of law. The trial court dismissed the plaintiff's complaint for failure to state a claim, and the dismissal was affirmed by the Court of Appeals. We hold that in-house counsel may bring a common-law action for retaliatory discharge resulting from counsel's compliance with a provision of the Code of Professional Responsi-

bility that represents a clear and definitive statement of public policy. . . .

According to the allegations of the complaint, the plaintiff was hired by Buckman in 1995 as associate general counsel in its legal department, and while working in this capacity, she reported to Buckman's General Counsel, Ms. Katherine Buckman Davis. Sometime in 1996, the plaintiff discovered that Ms. Davis, who "held herself out as a licensed attorney," did not possess a license to practice law in the State of Tennessee. The plaintiff became concerned that Ms. Davis was engaged in the unauthorized practice of law, and she discussed her suspicions with a member of Buckman's Board of Directors.[1]

Ms. Davis eventually took and passed the bar exam, but the plaintiff learned some time later that Ms. Davis had yet to complete the requirements for licensure by taking the Multi-State Professional Responsibility Examination. The plaintiff informed Buckman officials of the continuing problem, and she advised them on how best to proceed. On June 17, 1999, Ms. Davis allegedly entered the plaintiff's office, yelling that she was frustrated with the plaintiff's actions. The plaintiff responded that she also was frustrated with the situation, to which Ms. Davis remarked that "maybe [the plaintiff] should just leave." The plaintiff declined to leave, and she later received a below-average raise for the first time during her tenure at Buckman, despite having been told earlier by Ms. Davis that she was "doing a good job in position of Associate Counsel."

In August, the plaintiff sought legal advice concerning her ethical obligations, and based on this advice, she informed the Board of Law Examiners of Ms. Davis's situation. The Board later issued a show-cause order asking Ms. Davis to clarify certain facts in her bar application. Upon receipt of the order, Ms. Davis demanded to know from the plaintiff what information the Board possessed in its application file. The plaintiff stated that she knew nothing of the file, and she told Ms. Davis that her actions were threatening and inappropriate. Ms. Davis then apolo-

gized, but she immediately proceeded to schedule the plaintiff's performance review.

The plaintiff then informed Mr. Buckman and the Vice-President of Human Resources that "the situation [had become] untenable and that she could not function under those circumstances." They agreed that the plaintiff should be immediately transferred to a position away from Ms. Davis's supervision and that she should eventually leave the company altogether within six to nine months. However, while the plaintiff was "in the midst of working out the new arrangement," Ms. Davis informed her that her services would no longer be needed. More specifically, Ms. Davis told her that "since [the plaintiff] had given her notice of resignation, it was logically best to end the Plaintiff's association with Buckman." Although the plaintiff denied that she had resigned, her computer was confiscated; she was placed on personal leave; and she was given a notice of termination.

On April 10, 2000, the plaintiff filed suit against Buckman in the Shelby County Circuit Court, alleging a common-law action for retaliatory discharge in violation of public policy. . . .

IN-HOUSE COUNSEL AND THE TORT OF RETALIATORY DISCHARGE

Tennessee has long adhered to the employment-at-will doctrine in employment relationships not established or formalized by a contract for

---

1. This Director then requested an opinion from the Board of Professional Responsibility based on a hypothetical scenario mirroring the situation at Buckman. The Board replied that a person without a Tennessee law license may not be employed as general counsel in this state and that the failure to have such a license constitutes the unauthorized practice of law.

a definite term. Under this "employ-ment at will" doctrine, both the em-ployer and the employee are generally permitted, with certain exceptions, to terminate the employment relation-ship "at any time for good cause, bad cause, or no cause." . . .

However, an employer's ability to discharge at-will employees was sig-nificantly tempered by our recognition in Clanton v. Cain-Sloan Co., 677 S.W.2d 441 (Tenn. 1984), of a cause of action for retaliatory discharge. Since that time, we have further rec-ognized that an at-will employee "generally may not be discharged for attempting to exercise a statutory or constitutional right, or for any other reason which violates a clear public policy which is evidenced by an un-ambiguous constitutional, statutory, or regulatory provision." . . .

DECISIONS OF OTHER STATES RELATING TO DISCHARGE IN VIOLATION OF PUBLIC POLICY

Several jurisdictions have grappled with how to balance the competing interests involved in these types of cases. Although the rationales often differed, most of the earlier cases on this subject held that a lawyer could not bring a retaliatory discharge ac-tion based upon the lawyer's adher-ence to his or her ethical duties. *See, e.g.,* Willy v. Coastal Corp., 647 F. Supp. 116 (S.D. Tex. 1986); McGonagle v. Union Fid. Corp., 556 A.2d 878 (Pa. Super. Ct. 1989); Herbster v. North Am. Co. for Life & Health Ins., 501 N.E.2d 343 (Ill. App. Ct. 1986). This line of cases culmi-nated in Balla v. Gambro, Inc., 584 N.E.2d 104 (Ill. 1991), in which the Illinois Supreme Court reviewed the other cases and set forth several rationales why in-house counsel should not be permitted to assert an action for retaliatory discharge. These rationales included (1) that because "in-house counsel do not have a choice of whether to follow their eth-ical obligations as attorneys licensed to practice law," lawyers do not need an action for retaliatory discharge to encourage them to abide by their ethical duties; and (2) that recogniz-ing such an action would affect the foundation of trust in attorney-client relationships, which would then make employers "naturally hesitant to rely upon in-house counsel for advice re-garding [the employer's] potentially questionable conduct."

In more recent years, however, other states have permitted a lawyer, under limited circumstances, to pur-sue a claim of retaliatory discharge based upon termination in violation of public policy. The principal case permitting such an action is General Dynamics Corp. v. Rose, 876 P.2d 487 (Cal. 1994), [and] . . . GTE Pro-ducts Corp. v. Stewart, 653 N.E.2d 161 (Mass. 1995) . . .

Finally, . . . [i]n Burkhart v. Semi-tool, Inc., 5 P.3d 103 (Mont. 2000), . . . the court reasoned that "by making his or her attorney an employee, [the employer] has avoided the traditional attorney-client rela-tionship and granted the attorney protections that do not apply to in-dependent contractors, but do apply to employees. . . . " Moreover, unlike the previous cases recognizing such an action, the *Burkhart* Court per-mitted lawyers to disclose the employer's confidential information to the extent necessary to establish a retaliatory discharge claim.

REJECTION OF THE RATIONALES ADVANCED BY *BALLA* AND OTHER CASES

Considering these two general approaches to retaliatory discharge actions based upon termination in violation of public policy, we generally agree with the approaches taken by the courts in *General Dynamics, Stewart,* and *Burkhart.* The very purpose of recognizing an employee's action for retaliatory discharge in violation of public policy is to encourage the employee to protect the public interest, and it seems anomalous to protect only non-lawyer employees under these circumstances. Indeed, as cases in similar contexts show, in-house counsel do not generally forfeit employment protections provided to other employees merely because of their status or duties as a lawyer.[2]

Moreover, we must reject the rationales typically set forth by *Balla* and the Court of Appeals in this case to generally deny lawyers the ability to pursue retaliatory discharge actions. *Balla's* principal rationale was that recognition of a retaliatory discharge action was not necessary to protect the public interest so long as lawyers were required to follow a code of ethics. . . .

. . . It is true that counsel in this case was under a mandatory duty to not aid a non-lawyer in the unauthorized practice of law, *see* Tenn. Sup. Ct. R. 8, Model Rule 5.5(b), and

the intermediate court was also correct that lawyers do not have the option of disregarding the commandments of the Disciplinary Rules. . . .

Ultimately, sole reliance on the mere presence of the ethical rules to protect important public policies gives too little weight to the actual presence of economic pressures designed to tempt in-house counsel into subordinating ethical standards to corporate misconduct. Unlike lawyers possessing a multiple client base, in-house counsel are dependent upon only one client for their livelihood. As the *General Dynamics* Court acknowledged, the economic fate of in-house attorneys is tied directly to a single employer, at whose sufferance they serve. Thus, from an economic standpoint, the dependence of in-house counsel is indistinguishable from that of other corporate managers or senior executives who also owe their livelihoods, career goals and satisfaction to a single organizational employer.

The pressure to conform to corporate misconduct at the expense of one's entire livelihood, therefore, presents some risk that ethical standards could be disregarded. Like other non-lawyer employees, an in-house lawyer is dependent upon the corporation for his or her sole income, benefits, and pensions; the lawyer is often governed by the corporation's personnel policies and

---

2. For example, courts have permitted in-house lawyers to sue for age and race discrimination in violation of federal law, Stinneford v. Spiegel Inc., 845 F. Supp. 1243, 1245-47 (N.D. Ill. 1994); Golightly-Howell v. Oil, Chem. & Atomic Workers Intl. Union, 806 F. Supp. 921, 924 (D. Colo. 1992); to sue for protections under a state "whistleblower" statute, Parker v. M & T Chemicals, Inc., 566 A.2d 215, 220 (N.J. App. 1989); to sue for breach of express and implied employment contracts, Chyten v. Lawrence & Howell Invs., 46 Cal. Rptr. 2d 459, 464-65 (Cal. App. 1993); Nordling v. Northern State Power Co., 478 N.W.2d 498, 502 (Minn. 1991); and to sue based on implied covenants of good faith and fair dealing, *Golightly-Howell,* 806 F. Supp. at 924.

employees' handbooks; and the lawyer is subject to raises and promotions as determined by the corporation. In addition, the lawyer's hours of employment and nature of work are usually determined by the corporation. To the extent that these realities are ignored, the analysis here cannot hope to present an accurate picture of modern in-house practice. . . .

We also reject *Balla*'s reasoning that recognition of a retaliatory discharge action under these circumstances would have a chilling effect upon the attorney-client relationship and would impair the trust between an attorney and his or her client. This rationale appears to be premised on one key assumption: the employer desires to act contrary to public policy and expects the lawyer to further that conduct in violation of the lawyer's ethical duties. We are simply unwilling to presume that employers as a class operate with so nefarious a motive, and we recognize that when employers seek legal advice from in-house counsel, they usually do so with the intent to comply with the law.

Moreover, employers of in-house counsel should be aware that the lawyer is bound by the Code of Professional Responsibility, and that the lawyer may ethically reveal client confidences and secrets in many cases. Therefore, with respect to the employer's willingness to seek the advice of the lawyer for legally questionable conduct, the nature of the relationship should not be further diminished by the remote possibility of a retaliatory discharge suit. In fact, "there should be no discernible impact on the attorney-client relationship [by recognition of a retaliatory discharge action], unless the employer expects his counsel to blindly follow his mandate in contravention of the lawyer's ethical duty." Therefore, we conclude that little, if any, adverse effect upon the attorney-client relationship will occur if we recognize an action for discharge in violation of public policy.

Finally, we reject *Balla*'s assertion that allowing damages as a remedy for retaliatory discharge would have the effect of shifting to the employer the costs of in-house counsel's adherence to the ethics rules. The very purpose of permitting a claim for retaliatory discharge in violation of public policy is to encourage employers to refrain from conduct that is injurious to the public interest. Because retaliatory discharge actions recognize that it is the employer who is attempting to circumvent clear expressions of public policy, basic principles of equity all but demand that the costs associated with such conduct also be borne by the employer. . . .

. . . Therefore, we hold that a lawyer may generally bring a claim for retaliatory discharge when the lawyer is discharged for abiding by the ethics rules as established by this Court.

PROPER STANDARD TO APPLY IN TENNESSEE

In Tennessee, the elements of a typical common-law retaliatory discharge claim are as follows: (1) that an employment-at-will relationship existed; (2) that the employee was discharged, (3) that the reason for the discharge was that the employee attempted to exercise a statutory or constitutional right, or for any other reason which violates a clear public policy evidenced by an unambiguous constitutional, statutory, or regulatory provision; and (4) that a substantial factor in the employer's decision to discharge the employee was the employee's exercise of protected rights or compliance with clear public policy.

However, as we have noted throughout this opinion, this case does not present the typical retaliatory discharge claim. Consequently, while the special relationship between a lawyer and a client does not categorically prohibit in-house counsel from bringing a retaliatory discharge action, other courts have held that it necessarily shapes the contours of the action when the plaintiff was employed as in-house counsel. For example, the courts in *General Dynamics* and *Stewart* held that a lawyer could pursue a retaliatory discharge claim, but only if the lawyer could do so without breaching the duty of confidentiality. Indeed, the California Supreme Court went so far as to forewarn lawyers that those who revealed confidential information in a retaliatory discharge suit, without a basis for doing so under the ethics rules, would be subject to disciplinary proceedings. . . .

If we perceive any shortcomings in the holdings of *General Dynamics* and *Stewart*, it is that they largely take away with one hand what they appear to give with the other. Although the courts in these cases gave in-house counsel an important right of action, their respective admonitions about preserving client confidentiality appear to stop just short of halting most of these actions at the courthouse door. With little imagination, one could envision cases involving important issues of public concern being denied relief merely because the wrongdoer is protected by the lawyer's duty of confidentiali-

ty. Therefore, given that courts have recognized retaliatory discharge actions in order to protect the public interest, this potentially severe limitation strikes us as a curious, if not largely ineffective, measure to achieve that goal.

. . . Model Rule 1.6(b) permits a lawyer to reveal "information relating to the representation of a client" when the lawyer reasonably believes such information is necessary "to establish a claim or defense on behalf of the lawyer in a controversy between the lawyer and the client. . . . " Although some commentators have asserted that this provision merely permits lawyers to use confidential information in fee-collection disputes as under the Model Code, the plain language of the Model Rule is clearly more broad than these authorities would presume. In fact, at least one state supreme court has held that this language permits in-house counsel to reveal confidential information in a retaliatory discharge suit, at least to the extent reasonably necessary to establish the claim. *See Burkhart*, 5 P.3d at 1041.

We agree with the approach taken by the Model Rules, and pursuant to our inherent authority to regulate and govern the practice of law in this state, we hereby expressly adopt a new provision . . . [that] parallels the language of Model Rule of Professional Conduct 1.6(b)(2), and we perceive the adoption of a similar standard to be essential in protecting the ability of in-house counsel to effectively assert an action for discharge in violation of public policy. Nevertheless, while in-house counsel may ethically disclose such information to the extent necessary to establish the claim, we emphasize that in-house counsel "must make every effort practicable to avoid unnecessary disclosure of [client confidences and secrets], to limit disclosure to those having the need to know it, and to obtain protective orders or make other arrangements minimizing the risk of disclosure." Model Rule 1.6 Comment 19.

ANALYSIS OF THE COMPLAINT IN THIS CASE

Having found that in-house counsel are not categorically prohibited from maintaining retaliatory discharge actions against their former employers, we now examine whether the plaintiff in this case has stated such a claim in her complaint. As for the first element, the existence of an at-will employment relationship, . . . we will presume that the plaintiff intended to allege an at-will employment relationship. . . .

The next issue, then, is whether the complaint alleges the existence of a "clear public policy which is evidenced by an unambiguous constitutional, statutory, or regulatory provision." To establish this second element, the plaintiff argues that the ethical rules relating to the unauthorized practice of law—such as Disciplinary Rule 3-101(A), which places upon lawyers a mandatory ethical duty "not [to] aid a non-lawyer in the unauthorized practice of law"—are for the protection of the public interest and may serve as the basis for a retaliatory discharge action. We agree. . . .

Although we need not conclude today that every provision of the Code of Professional Responsibility reflects an important public policy, there can be no doubt that the public has a substantial interest in preventing the unauthorized practice of law. As this Court has acknowledged, "the purpose of regulations governing the unauthorized practice of law is . . . to serve the public right to protection against unlearned and unskilled advice in matters relating to the science of the law." . . .

To be clear, although the plaintiff was not under a mandatory ethical duty to report Ms. Davis's alleged unauthorized practice of law to the Board of Law Examiners, she certainly possessed a permissive duty to report Ms. Davis's conduct.[6] . . . [G]iven the clear expression of this permissive duty, combined with the clear expression of public policy in Disciplinary Rule 3-101(A), we hold that the complaint has sufficiently alleged the existence of a clear public policy evidenced by an unambiguous provision of the Tennessee Code of Professional Responsibility.

Next, we examine whether the complaint has sufficiently alleged that the plaintiff was discharged from her employment with Buckman. With regard to these allegations, we note that the plaintiff has asserted that she was constructively discharged from her position as in-house counsel. . . .

Here, we find that the complaint has fairly raised an allegation that the plaintiff did not voluntarily leave her

---

6. Disciplinary Rule 1-103(A) imposes a mandatory duty to report clear violations of Disciplinary Rule 1-102, which itself prohibits violations of a Disciplinary Rule. However, Rule 1-102 applies only to violations by lawyers, and because Ms. Davis was not yet licensed at the time the plaintiff reported her conduct to the Board of Law Examiners, it appears that the plaintiff's only mandatory duty here was to refrain from furthering Ms. Davis's application for admission to the bar under Disciplinary Rule 1-101(B).

employment with Buckman. Importantly, after her final encounter with Ms. Davis, the corporation is alleged to have removed the plaintiff's computer; to have placed the plaintiff on temporary leave; and to have given the plaintiff a notice of termination. Under these circumstances, the allegation is fairly raised that a reasonable person would have felt compelled to resign, and we therefore conclude that the plaintiff has sufficiently alleged a termination of employment necessary to state a claim for relief.

Finally, we examine whether the complaint alleges that a substantial factor in Buckman's decision to discharge the plaintiff was her adherence to her ethical duties under the Code of Professional Responsibility. Here, the plaintiff alleges that the sole motivation for the constructive discharge was her adherence to her ethical duties to report the unauthorized practice of law to the Board of Law Examiners. Accordingly, we conclude that the existence of this element has likewise been sufficiently alleged in the complaint and that, consequently, the plaintiff has stated a cause of action for retaliatory discharge in violation of public policy. . . .

▦ Lawyers and Other Professionals: *Wrongful Discharge*

In the last chapter, we saw that an implied condition of every client-lawyer contract is the client's right to discharge the lawyer at any time, for any reason. *Crews*, on the other hand, tells us that one group of lawyers—those who are employees of the client they serve—may bring claims for wrongful discharge similar to those of other employees under certain circumstances.

Employment-At-Will

Most lawyers are independent contractors. When a client hires a lawyer to perform legal services, the lawyer becomes an agent, but not a servant or employee of the client. Most lawyers also serve a multiple client base.

After World War II, corporations began to follow the lead of government units by hiring more inside lawyers as employees.[1] Unlike lawyers in their own practices, these inside lawyers had only one client and were full-time employees who depended on a corporation or government for benefits and terms of employment. For the most part, they performed legal tasks similar to lawyers in outside practices, but often concentrated on providing advice and counsel to prevent or solve legal issues rather than litigation services after a controversy arose. As the value of these services to large organizations increased, more and

---

1. In 1951, about 3 percent of all lawyers worked directly for private industry, and 10 percent worked for various levels of the government. *See* Reginald Heber Smith, *The Second Statistical Report on The Lawyer of the United States* 2 (ABA 1951). By 1960, 10 percent of all lawyers worked for private industry. *See* Barbara A. Curran, *The Lawyer Statistical Report: A Statistical Profile of the U.S. Legal Profession in the 1980s*, at 12 (Am. Bar Found. 1985). Since then, these percentages have remained about the same for both private industry and government lawyers (both about 8 percent in 2000), although the total numbers in each category have risen, from about 28,000 in 1960 to 89,300 in 2000. *Id.; ABA Lawyer Demographics* (2006). Available at *http://www.abanet.org/marketresearch/lawyer_demographics_2006.pdf*. Last visited July 31, 2007.

more legal work has been moved inside organizations. Today, inside lawyers often manage nearly all of the legal matters that confront the organization, and usually decide when to hire outside lawyers for specific tasks.

While this move to inside counsel was developing, courts in most jurisdictions were beginning to develop exceptions to the employment-at-will doctrine. Developed in the latter part of the nineteenth century, this doctrine provided that absent contractual agreements to the contrary, both employer and employee were free to terminate the employment relationship at any time.[2]

Wrongful Discharge

A California court created the first exception to the employment-at-will doctrine in 1959, in a case where an employee was fired for refusing to commit perjury when his employer ordered him to do so. The court provided the employee with a cause of action for wrongful discharge, holding that the at-will doctrine was limited by important public policies.[3] This public policy exception has gained wide recognition under a variety of appellations in the past 20 years.[4] Federal and state statutes, often called "whistleblowing" provisions, create similar rights for employees in both the public and private sectors.[5] Beyond statutory rights, courts also have recognized the rights of employees to sue in tort for retaliatory discharge, wrongful termination, and wrongful discharge, and in contract for breach of express and implied provisions in employment contracts, as well as on the basis of an implied covenant of good faith.[6]

Public Policy

The public policy exception recognizes that employers are not free to fire employees because they report or refuse to engage in illegal activity, exercise a statutory or constitutional right, or perform a duty required by law. All three of these categories of public policy exceptions were implicated in *Crews.*

Both common law and statutes protect whistleblowers. Some states construe the public policy exception narrowly, limiting it to situations where the employer instructs the employee to commit a crime.[7] Others extend it to tortious acts as well,[8] and some grant the cause of action to employees who refuse to commit a violation of administrative regulations.[9] Jurisdictions differ on whether the unlawful activity must relate to public health and safety, and whether the employee must actually report the activity outside the organization.[10] In *Crews,* the court found that although not every provision of the law-

---

2. Mark A. Rothstein et al., *Employment Law* §8.1 (2d ed., West 1999).
3. Petermann v. Teamsters Local 396, 344 P.2d 25 (Cal. App. 1959).
4. *See* Lionel J. Postic, *Wrongful Termination: A State-by-State Survey* (BNA 1994).
5. *See* Daniel P. Westman & Nancy M. Modesitt, *Whistleblowing: The Law of Retaliatory Discharge* (BNA 2d ed., 2004).
6. *See* Rothstein, *supra* note 2, at §§8.2-8.6.
7. *See, e.g.,* Sabine Pilot Service v. Hauck, 687 S.W.2d 733 (Tex. 1985).
8. *See, e.g.,* Delaney v. Taco Time Intl. Inc., 681 P.2d 114 (Or. 1984) (potential defamation).
9. *See, e.g.,* Minn. Stat. §181.932 (2003); N.Y. Lab. Law §740 (2003); Tenn. Code §50-1-304 (2003).
10. Rothstein, *supra* note 2, at §§8.10-8.11.

yer's code might reflect an important public policy, refusing to assist in the unauthorized practice of law certainly qualified.

Statutes and case law also recognize that employees who exercise a statutory right, such as the right to seek workers' compensation for a workplace injury, also are protected from retaliatory discharge.[11] Crews alleged, and the Tennessee Supreme Court agreed, that she had a right to report her supervisor's conduct.

Finally, many courts and statutes create a public policy exception for the performance of a public duty. *Crews* points out that the plaintiff was under no such obligation to report her supervisor's conduct, because the latter was not yet a lawyer subject to the state professional code. Similarly, very few public reporting obligations create mandatory duties. Nevertheless, the courts have not hesitated to protect employees who were fired because they were called to jury service, or insisted on obeying a subpoena, or reported child or elder abuse.[12]

Professional Code Violations

Many courts have recognized that refusal to violate a professional ethics code may qualify as an important public policy.[13] These courts agree with *Crews* that not all professional code provisions qualify as important public policies, either because they may lack a clear mandate to act[14] or because they may have been created to serve primarily the profession's *own* interests rather than the public's.[15]

Similarly, ethical code provisions that rest on the judgment of professionals do not constitute a clear mandate of public policy unless they require a specific action.[16] So, for example, a pharmacist who alleged that state regulations would be violated if he were forced to close a pharmacy on a holiday stated a cause of action.[17] The same was true of an accountant who alleged that he was terminated for objecting to an employer's accounting practices because they misrepresented facts in contravention of a specific provision in the State Board of Accountancy Rules of Professional Conduct.[18]

---

11. *See* Theresa Ludwig Kruk, *Recovery for Discharge from Employment in Retaliation for Filing Workers' Compensation Claim*, 32 A.L.R.4th 1221 (1984).

12. Rothstein, *supra* note 2, at §8.13.

13. *See* Genna H. Rosten, *Wrongful Discharge Based on Public Policy Derived from Professional Ethics Codes*, 52 A.L.R.5th 405 (1997).

14. Pierce v. Ortho Pharm. Corp., 417 A.2d 505 (N.J. 1980) (physician who disagreed with drug company's decision to test a new drug could not prevail because she did not allege any violation of federal or state law or a specific provision of the AMA Principles of Medical Ethics).

15. *E.g.,* Warthen v. Toms River Community Meml. Hosp., 488 A.2d 229 (N.J. App. 1985) (provision in nurse's code of ethics, excusing nurses from administering treatment if personally opposed to the delivery of care, protected nurses, not the public, and was therefore not a mandate of public policy).

16. *E.g.,* Lay v. St. Louis Helicopter Airways, 869 S.W.2d 172 (Mo. App. 1993) (Code of Ethics of Helicopter Assn. Intl. requirement that pilots use their "best judgment" was not a clear mandate of public policy); Birthisel v. Tri-Cities Health Servs. Corp., 424 S.E.2d 606 (W. Va. 1992) (provisions in social worker's administrative regulations that stated that a social worker should act in accordance with the highest standards of professional integrity, and that social worker's primary responsibility was to clients were not "substantial public policies" that provided specific guidance to social workers).

17. Kalman v. Grand Union Co., 443 A.2d 728 (N.J. App. 1982).

18. Rocky Mt. Hosp. & Med. Serv. v. Mariani, 916 P.2d 519 (Colo. 1996).

Crews agrees with these decisions, finding first, that the unauthorized practice rules were intended to protect the public, and second, that they provided a permissive duty combined with a clear public policy. Other courts also have found clear public policies in lawyer professional codes. These include Model Rule 1.2(d)'s prohibition against counseling or assisting fraudulent client conduct,[19] ethical considerations that entitle citizens to consult with lawyers,[20] Model Rules 3.3 and 3.4, which prohibit the submission of false evidence,[21] and Model Rules 1.5, 7.1, and 8.4(c), which prohibit fraudulent billing.[22]

Discharge

The plaintiff in a wrongful discharge case must prove not only that she sought to vindicate an important public policy, but also that she was fired for doing so. When an employee like Ms. Crews resigns or quits her job, the implication is that the employer did not discharge her. The Tennessee court recognizes the doctrine of constructive discharge in her situation, where facts indicate that the plaintiff did not voluntarily leave her job, but felt compelled to resign because of the employer's actions. Most courts agree with *Crews* that intolerable employment conditions created by the employer, which essentially force the employee to quit, constitute constructive discharge. On the other hand, single instances of demotion, unfavorable performance reviews, or dissatisfaction with assignments are not enough.[23]

Are Lawyers Different?

When lawyer employees initially sought court recognition of a wrongful discharge cause of action, courts reasoned that the right of clients to fire lawyers at any time should trump any contrary employment law doctrine. *Crews* illustrates how several state courts over the past decade have moved away from that notion and have begun to emphasize the similarity between lawyer-employees and other employees protected by the wrongful discharge doctrine.

With respect to confidentiality, *Crews* applies the self-defense exception to client confidentiality in the Tennessee lawyer code to justify the disclosure necessary to establish a cause of action.[24] Recognizing such an exception par-

---

19. O'Brien v. Stolt-Nielsen Trans. Group, Ltd., 2003 Conn. Super. LEXIS 1763; Burkhart v. Semitool, Inc., 5 P.3d 1031 (Mont. 2000) (refusing to prepare fraudulent patent applications); Shearin v. E. F. Hutton Group, 652 A.2d 578 (Del. Ch. Ct. 1994) (refusing to be part of material misrepresentations to banks and securities regulators); Parker v. M & T Chemicals, Inc., 566 A.2d 215 (N.J. Super. 1989) (objecting to "unlawful and fraudulent conduct" of client).
20. Thompto v. Coborn's Inc., 871 F. Supp. 1097 (N.D. Iowa 1994) (nonlawyer employee fired when she threatened to consult with a lawyer).
21. Paralegal v. Law., 783 F. Supp. 230 (E.D. Pa. 1992) (paralegal fired for notifying her employer's lawyer that her employer submitted false evidence).
22. Brown v. Hammond, 810 F. Supp. 644 (E.D. Pa. 1993).
23. *See, e.g.*, GTE Prod. Corp. v. Stewart, 653 N.E.2d 161 (1995) (inside counsel who quit his job not constructively discharged because conditions under which he would have been forced to work were not so intolerable that a reasonable person would have felt compelled to resign).
24. The California court in *General Dynamics* similarly relied on the statutory exceptions to the attorney-client privilege found in its evidence code to provide the basis for a cause of action. Gen. Dynamics v. Sup. Ct., 876 P.2d 487, 503 (Cal. 1994). A subsequent California court ruled that a

allels the situation of other employees who also have confidentiality obligations as a matter of common law fiduciary duty.[25] When these employees become whistleblowers, they are permitted to use some of this sensitive information to prove that they had a good faith belief that their employer was engaged in wrongful activity.[26] The ABA Ethics Committee recently reached the same result for lawyers, finding that wrongful discharge actions by inside counsel fall within the meaning of the term "claim" in Model Rule 1.6(b)(5) and that in pursuing such a claim "the lawyer must limit disclosure of confidential client information to the extent reasonably possible."[27]

Of course, the real policy debate in all of the lawyer cases is whether the right of clients to fire lawyers should override other employment protections. *Crews* begins by pointing out that inside counsel do not forfeit other statutory employment rights simply because they are lawyers. Other professionals along with lawyers have long been accorded rights under a myriad of these provisions.[28] Once a court recognizes that a lawyer-employee may sue her employer for race, age, or gender discrimination, the public policies inherent in other employment laws, such as federal and state whistleblower statutes, become equally easy to follow.[29]

The last vestige of the employment-at-will doctrine concerns lawyers like Crews, who have no statutory or contractual cause of action against their employers. Their claims raise the issue of the relationship between the lawyer codes and employment law, which may incorporate other conflicting public policies. *Crews* indicates that the early cases, such as Balla v. Gambro,[30] rejected any cause of action for wrongful discharge by lawyer-employees, even where another professional employee, such as an engineer, would be granted a cause of

---

lawyer who seeks legal advice about whether to bring a wrongful discharge suit may disclose relevant facts to her own lawyer, including employer confidences and privileged communications. Fox Searchlight Pictures, Inc. v. Paladino, 106 Cal. Rptr. 2d 906 (Cal. App. 2001).

25. For example, the common law duty not to divulge trade secrets can be remedied by injunctive relief by the organization. *See, e.g.,* Webcraft Tech. v. McCaw, 674 F. Supp. 1039 (S.D.N.Y. 1997).

26. *See* Westman, *supra* note 5, at 22-44.

27. ABA Formal Op. 01-424; *see also* Spratley v. St. Farm Mut. Auto Ins. Co., 78 P.3d 603 (Utah 2003) (insurer's inside counsel lawyers who alleged that they quit their employment because insurer required them to violate ethical duties to insureds could disclose matters relating to their representation of insurer, but not insureds, to prove their claim for wrongful discharge).

28. *See, e.g.,*EEOC v. Sidley Austin, 437 F.3d 695 (7th Cir. 2007), *cert. denied,* 127 S. Ct. 76; Sonja A. Soehnel, *Sex Discrimination in Employment Against Female Attorney in Violation of Federal Civil Rights Law—Federal Cases,* 81 L. Ed. 2d 894 (1999); Gregory G. Sarno, *Liability Under Racketeer Influenced and Corrupt Organization Act (RICO) (18 U.S.C. §§1961-68) for Retaliation Against Employee for Disclosing or Refusing to Commit Wrongful Act,* 100 A.L.R. Fed. 66 (1990); Daniel A. Klein, *Whistleblowers' Protection Under Energy Reorganization Act (42 USCA §5851),* 79 A.L.R. Fed. 631 (1986).

29. *See, e.g.,* In re Newark, 788 A.2d 776 (N.J. App. 2002) (unionization of nonmanagerial lawyers employed by city permitted under state public employment law). Federal and state whistleblower statutes provide protection mainly for public sector employees who disclose illegal acts of their government employers. Some also protect private sector employee from retaliation. *See* Rothstein, *supra* note 2, at §8.17. A number of cases have raised the question whether federal statutes that include antiretaliation provisions preempt state law. *See, e.g.,* Gregory G. Sarno, *Federal Pre-Emption of Whistleblower's State-Law Action for Wrongful Retaliation,* 99 A.L.R. Fed. 775 (1990).

30. 584 N.E.2d 104 (Ill. 1991). *See also* Meadows v. KinderCare Learning Ctrs. Inc., 2004 U.S. Dist. LEXIS 8770 (D. Or.); Ausman v. Arthur Anderson LLP, 810 N.E.2d 566 (Ill. App. 2004), *appeal denied,* 823 N.E.2d 962.

action if fired for making the same disclosure. These courts reasoned that a lawyer who discovers that a client insists on pursuing illegal activity must either convince the client to stop or leave the employment. Even where disclosure was allowed or required by lawyer codes to prevent harm to others, lawyers could disclose for that purpose, but were not free to use the same client confidences to create a cause of action against their employer.

These decisions stressed the need for organizations to be able to trust their lawyers, the need for confidentiality to foster that trust, and the social value of encouraging organizations to seek legal advice. Recognizing a cause of action for wrongful discharge ultimately would lead organizations to avoid sharing information about sensitive or questionable activity with their legal staff. This avoidance would in turn erase opportunities for inside lawyers to counsel their clients about better means of complying with legal requirements.

Crews represents the opposite and emerging point of view: that conduct giving rise to a cause of action by other organizational employees also ought to extend to a cause of action for wrongful discharge by lawyer-employees.[31] The client remains free to discharge the lawyer, but may have to suffer a monetary penalty for punishing lawyers who refuse to violate clear mandates in their professional rules. Inside counsel are more like other employees than they are like other lawyers, because they depend on their one client/employer for their livelihood. Expecting inside lawyers to adhere to professional codes in the face of the economic pressure of losing their job undervalues lawyer professionalism, as well as the important public policy in other law that these lawyers help implement. Allowing such a cause of action also deters the employer that seeks to engage in clearly unlawful activity.

One thing is certain. Competent lawyering requires any lawyer who disagrees with a decision by corporate management first to determine the basis for the disagreement. The lawyer or other professional who can articulate a clear public policy, embodied in a specific statute, regulation, professional code, or constitutional provision, should communicate that policy to responsible decision makers. If at that point the professional loses her job, she will have created a record that her discharge was caused by her insistence that the organization not violate the articulated public policy.

Whether a court will recognize such a cause of action for lawyers depends on that court's view of the realities of the role of inside counsel. Those who see organizations as reliant on legal advice and worry about the pressure to conform will agree with the rationale in *Crews*. Those who wish to promote open communication with inside counsel may be willing to risk the economic pressures on such lawyers, hoping that the threat of professional discipline will adequately protect the public interest. Ultimately, the best result will be a function not only of the equities in a particular case, but also the incentives those equities create in the ongoing relationship between inside counsel and their clients.

---

31. *See, e.g.,* Heckman v. Zurick Holding Co. of Am., 242 F.R.D. 606 (D. Kan. 2007); Alexander v. Tandem Staffing Solutions, Inc., 881 So. 2d 607 (Fla. App. 2004); Spratley v. St. Farm Mut. Auto. Ins. Co., 78 P.3d 603 (Utah 2003).

Part III

Lawyers and Justice:
The Limits of Advocacy

Chapter 12

The Bounds of the Law

*"If you want justice, it's two hundred dollars an hour.
Obstruction of justice runs a bit more."*

A. Introduction

Problems

12-1. How do you advise Martyn & Fox's client who just told us that an otherwise perfectly legal $10,000 political contribution to the Republican Party will guarantee issuance of a building permit six months sooner, saving our client hundreds of thousands of dollars? What if our client asks us to buy five of the ten $1,000 tickets to the County Lincoln Day Dinner necessary to complete the transaction?

12-2. Martyn & Fox's client in a criminal matter brings an $11,000 cash retainer to the office. He reminds Fox that unless he is indicted, he does not want the fact that he retained us or his identity disclosed. Do we have any problem meeting this request?

12-3. Martyn & Fox take on the pro bono representation of a detainee at Guantanamo. Thereafter it is disclosed that the government is conducting warrantless surveillance of e-mails and telephone calls between the United States and overseas countries. Martyn & Fox have regularly been contacting the detainee's relatives and friends in Yemen. The DOJ refuses to assure Martyn & Fox that lawyer calls are exempt from the surveillance. What should Martyn & Fox do?

Consider: Model Rules 1.2(d), 1.6, 8.4
Model Code DR 1-102, 4-101, 7-102(A)(7)
18 U.S.C. §201

▓ The Bounds of the Law: *A Reprise*

Up to this point, we have been traversing the ethical minefield of fiduciary duty. We have examined the contours of the 5 Cs: control, competence, communication, confidentiality, and conflict of interest resolution. Along the way, we have come across a number of legal constraints that impose equally important limits on a lawyer's fiduciary duty or advocacy on behalf of a client.

These legal responses create additional minefields waiting for the lawyer unaware of their existence or unclear about their relevance in a given case. In previous notes and cases, we have identified some of these limits or bounds of the law that restrain unfettered client allegiance. We have encountered both lawyer and client fraud and criminal conduct, court orders that require or limit lawyer advocacy, procedural requirements that require disclosure of information, and federal and state conflict of interest statutes that limit the advocacy of former government lawyers. We begin this chapter by pausing to identify the bodies of law that create these restraints. We have already encountered at least seven distinct kinds of legal constraints that can limit a lawyer's advocacy on behalf of a client:

1. The law of **tort**, such as the law of **fraud** that created a duty to a third party in Greycas v. Proud; or, the law of negligence, which potentially

can create a duty to third parties in a *Tarasoff*-like case, as discussed in Hawkins v. King County.

2. The law of **evidence,** which can create exceptions to confidentiality enforced through court orders, like the crime-fraud exception to the attorney-client privilege, discussed in Purcell v. District Attorney and United States v. Chen.

3. **Court orders**, issued pursuant to the **inherent power** of a court, that can require a lawyer to provide representation, as discussed in Bothwell v. Republic Tobacco; enjoin a lawyer from further representation, as occurred in Maritrans GP Inc. v. Pepper, Hamilton & Sheetz; disqualify a lawyer whose representation will taint the trial, as in Eastman Kodak Co. v. Sony Corp. and Mitchell v. Metropolitan Life Insurance Co; provide for contempt if a lawyer refuses to obey an order, as occurred in Hughes v. Meade; or, impose sanctions against lawyers who disregard their obligations of candor to the court, as occurred in United States v. Shaffer Equipment Co.

4. Procedural rules of **civil or appellate procedure**, which provided the basis for relief against an opposing party in Matter of Hendrix.

5. Civil and criminal provisions in state and federal **securities law**, such as the provisions that afforded relief to third parties in Meyerhofer v. Empire Fire & Marine Ins. Co. and In re American Continental Corporation/Lincoln Savings & Loan Securities Litigation.

6. General **criminal statutes**, such as the prohibition against criminal impersonation, which created a limit on the lawyer's advocacy in People v. Casey, or the prohibition against obstruction of justice, which was not transgressed by the lawyers in People v. Belge. We also encountered criminal laws that limit the practice of former government lawyers in the note about government lawyers in Chapter 9.

7. The provisions of **insurance law**, which enforce contractual duties to insured persons, such as the law of bad faith discussed in Wolpaw v. General Accident Insurance Co. and the note about insurance defense lawyers in Chapter 8.

All of this generally applicable law served as the basis for limiting what a lawyer was able to do on behalf of a client. Each legal provision also created substantial penalties or other ramifications for the lawyers unaware of the relevant limit.

In some instances, the lawyer or law firm involved paid substantial damages to third parties or a court for violating relevant legal prohibitions. In *Greycas*, for example, the court upheld a judgment against an opposing party's lawyer for $833,760. Even more daunting was the result in *ACC*, where the law firm eventually settled the bondholder's claims for $24 million and the government's claims for $51 million, $20 million of which was paid personally by law firm partners. You might also recall that the government lawyers in *Shaffer Equipment* were ordered to pay personal sanctions of $2,000 each.

Several of the cases listed above also illustrate that a lawyer who ignores a relevant limit on advocacy often buys his or her client extended future litigation. For example, the insurance company that hired the lawyers in *Spaulding* probably regretted relitigating its exposure, and may actually have ended up paying more than if it initially had disclosed the fact of Spaulding's injury. Contrast the lawyer in *Meyerhofer* who tried to change several clients' conduct before they violated federal securities laws. The law firm fired him, only to subject itself and its clients to subsequent securities liability.

In other cases such as *Casey,* the lawyer's violation of a criminal statute resulted in discipline for an indictable offense. On the other hand, acceding to the appropriate limit on advocacy resulted in quashing the criminal indictment in *Belge.*

And finally, consider the consequences to the lawyers in *Eastman Kodak* and *Mitchell.* Although it may have been worth their time to litigate the question of whether they or their law firms could represent a client against a former client, both of these cases resulted in eventual disqualification, after the firms and their clients had spent a great deal of time and money defending the motions.

Additional Legal Limits

The application of general legal provisions to lawyers continues in many arenas. For example, the court in Anderson v. O'Brien held the defendant lawyer responsible for damages under the state unfair trade practices act. Other prominent examples have involved federal law.

Form 8300 In 1984, Congress imposed an IRS reporting rule on a "trade or business" that receives more than $10,000 in cash.[1] A number of federal courts have considered the effect of this federal anti-money-laundering statute on the practice of criminal defense lawyers. These cases agree that, absent very narrow special circumstances,[2] lawyers who accept more than $10,000 in cash from clients must report the transaction to the Treasury Department, may not withhold the client's name, and are liable for substantial fines up to $25,000 per violation.[3] Similarly, lawyers hired to foreclose on mortgages have been held to be "debt collectors" within the meaning of the Fair Debt Collection Practices Act.[4]

The USA Patriot Act The USA Patriot Act was passed after September 11, 2001 to respond to terrorist activities. One goal of the law was to strengthen the previously existing Financial Action Task Force on Money Laundering (FATF), an intergovernmental body designed to promote national and international policies to combat money laundering. A new undertaking of this group, called the "Gatekeeper Initiative," is directed at professionals, including lawyers, whose clients engage in domestic and international financial transactions and

---

1. 26 U.S.C. §6050I (2006) and 26 C.F.R. §301.6721.
2. Only one case has found such special circumstances. United States v. Sindel, 53 F.3d 874 (8th Cir. 1995). The courts seem to agree that the statutory filing must amount to something like the facts in *Belge,* a coerced confession of criminal activity, disclosure of which would violate the client's Fifth Amendment right against self-incrimination. *See, e.g.,* Gerald B. Lefcourt, P.C. v. United States, 125 F.3d 79 (2d Cir. 1997), *cert. denied,* 524 U.S. 937 (1998).
3. *Id.; cf.,* St. ex rel. Triplett v. Ross, 855 N.E. 2d 1154 (Ohio 2006) (discussing applicability of Ohio Patriot Act disclosure requirements to lawyers).
4. Sayyed v. Wolpoff & Abramson, 485 F.3d 226 (4th Cir. 2007).

business. Should this initiative become law, lawyers could be required to submit Suspicious Activities Reports (now required of financial institutions)[5] regarding client activities, and lawyers would be prohibited from telling their clients they had done so. In some countries, such obligations already apply to lawyers who manage client money or who assist in the planning or execution of transactions for clients concerning any financial or real estate transaction.

The ABA House of Delegates has taken the position that requiring lawyers who receive or transfer funds on behalf of clients "to verify the identity of clients, maintain records on domestic and international transactions, and develop training programs that would help attorneys identify potential money laundering schemes" was appropriate.[6] The same group strongly opposed the so-called tip off provisions, which would require lawyers to submit Suspicious Transaction Reports to government authorities based on a mere suspicion that the funds involved in the client's transaction stemmed from illegal activity, and also opposed preventing lawyers from telling their clients they had done so.

The Bounds of the Law and Client Advocacy

Proposals like these continue the debate about the appropriate scope of client advocacy. Taken together, these requirements remind lawyers that neither they, nor their clients, are exempt from general legal requirements, some of which create limitations on client advocacy. These legal limits also can create affirmative duties to third parties, such as the obligation to disclose a client's confidential information. In short, general law does, on occasion, make lawyers gatekeepers.[7] This is not an unfamiliar role, as lawyers have always been in the business of advising clients to avoid illegality. We probably should be most wary of these efforts, however, when the government seeks to make lawyers agents of its law enforcement efforts. On the other hand, we probably should welcome limits on advocacy when they seek to provide a fair and accessible justice system.

This chapter sheds light on additional examples of these legal limits on client advocacy that may ensnare an unenlightened lawyer. These bodies of law also create the potential for criminal, civil, disciplinary, or procedural sanctions. We begin by considering a variety of procedural rules and inherent powers that provide the basis for monetary sanctions against lawyers who file frivolous lawsuits or evade discovery obligations. We then turn to consider limitations imposed on lawyers by laws that prohibit bias, such as civil rights provisions and the ADA. Near the end of the chapter, we focus on additional professional rules that prohibit or limit communication with represented and unrepresented persons, judges, and jurors. Finally, we examine the scope and application of professional code provisions that prohibit lawyers from appearing as witnesses in clients' cases.

---

5. 31 U.S.C. §5318(g) (2006).
6. ABA Task Force on Gatekeeper Regulation and the Profession, Comments of the ABA Task Force on Gatekeeper Regulation and the Profession on the Financial Action Task Force Consultation Paper dated May 30, 2002, at 10 (2002).
7. Fred Zacharias, *Lawyers as Gatekeepers*, 41 San Diego L. Rev. 1387 (2004).

B. Frivolous Claims

Problem

12-4.   Martyn & Fox filed a lawsuit against Chemco one week before the
        statute of limitations ran on behalf of three children born with birth
        defects, alleging that the birth defects were caused in utero by their
        mother's exposure to poisonous chemicals Chemco emitted into the
        air near their homes. Ten months later, Martyn & Fox consulted an
        expert for the first time, who told them there was no way to prove
        that Chemco's chemicals caused the birth defects in question.
        Martyn & Fox then voluntarily dismissed the claim, after Chemco
        had spent thousands of dollars on its own experts. Is Martyn & Fox
        in trouble?

    Consider: Model Rules 3.1, 3.4
               Model Code DR 7-102(A)(1)
               Federal Rule of Civil Procedure 11

Christian v. Mattel, Inc.

286 F.3d 1118 (9th Cir. 2002)

McKEOWN, Circuit Judge:

It is difficult to imagine that the Barbie doll, so perfect in her sculpture and presentation, and so comfortable in every setting, from "California girl" to "Chief Executive Officer Barbie," could spawn such acrimonious litigation and such egregious conduct on the part of her challenger. In her wildest dreams, Barbie could not have imagined herself in the middle of Rule 11 proceedings. But the intersection of copyrights on Barbie sculptures and the scope of Rule 11 is precisely what defines this case.

James Hicks appeals from a district court order requiring him, pursuant to Federal Rule of Civil Procedure 11, to pay Mattel, Inc. $501,565 in attorneys' fees that it incurred in defending against what the district court determined to be a frivolous action. Hicks brought suit on behalf of Harry

Christian, claiming that Mattel's Barbie dolls infringed Christian's Claudene doll sculpture copyright. In its sanctions orders, the district court found that Hicks should have discovered prior to commencing the civil action that Mattel's dolls could not have infringed Christian's copyright because, among other things, the Mattel dolls had been created well prior to the Claudene doll and the Mattel dolls had clearly visible copyright notices on their heads. After determining that Hicks had behaved "boorishly" during discovery and had a lengthy rap sheet of prior litigation misconduct, the district court imposed sanctions.

We hold that the district court did not abuse its discretion in determining that the complaint filed by Hicks was frivolous under Rule 11. In parsing the language of the district court's sanctions orders, however, we cannot determine with any degree of certainty whether the district court grounded its Rule 11 decision on Hicks' misconduct that occurred outside the pleadings, such as in oral argument, at a meeting of counsel, and at a key deposition. This is an important distinction because Rule 11 sanctions are limited to misconduct regarding signed pleadings, motions, and other filings. Fed. R. Civ. P. 11. Consequently, we vacate the district court's orders and remand for further proceedings consistent with this opinion. In so doing, we do not condone Hicks' conduct or suggest that the district court did not have a firm basis for awarding sanctions. Indeed, the district court undertook a careful and exhaustive examination of the facts and the legal underpinnings of the copyright challenge. Rather, the remand is to assure that any Rule 11 sanctions are grounded in conduct covered by Rule 11 and to ensure adequate findings for the sizeable fee award.

BACKGROUND

I. PRIOR LITIGATION BETWEEN MATTEL AND CDC

Mattel is a toy company that is perhaps best recognized as the manufacturer of the world-famous Barbie doll. Since Barbie's creation in 1959, Mattel has outfitted her in fashions and accessories that have evolved over time. In perhaps the most classic embodiment, Barbie is depicted as a slender-figured doll with long blonde hair and blue eyes. Mattel has sought to protect its intellectual property by registering various Barbie-related copyrights, including copyrights protecting the doll's head sculpture. Mattel has vigorously litigated against putative infringers.

In 1990, Claudene Christian, then an undergraduate student at the University of Southern California ("USC"), decided to create and market a collegiate cheerleader doll. The doll, which the parties refer to throughout their papers as "Claudene," had blonde hair and blue eyes and was outfitted to resemble a USC cheerleader.

Mattel soon learned about the Claudene doll . . . [and] commenced a federal court action in 1997 in which it . . . alleged that CDC infringed various of Mattel's copyrights. At the time, Claudene Christian was president of CDC and Harry Christian was listed as co-founder of the company and chief financial officer. CDC retained Hicks as its counsel. After the court dismissed CDC's multiple counter-claims, the case was settled. Mattel released CDC from any copyright infringement liability in exchange for, among other things, a stipulation that Mattel was free to challenge CDC's alleged copyright of the Claudene doll should CDC "or any successor in interest" challenge Mattel's right to market its Barbie dolls.

II. THE PRESENT ACTION

Seizing on a loophole in the parties' settlement agreement, within weeks of the agreement, Harry Christian, who was not a signatory to the agreement, retained Hicks as his counsel and filed a federal court action against Mattel. In the complaint, which Hicks signed, Christian alleged that Mattel obtained a copy of the copyrighted Claudene doll in 1996, the year of its creation, and then infringed its overall appearance, including its face paint, by developing a new Barbie line called "Cool Blue" that was substantially similar to Claudene. Christian sought damages in the amount of $2.4 billion and various forms of injunctive relief. In an apparent effort to demonstrate that the action was not a sham, Claudene Christian and CDC were also named as defendants. . . .

Two months after the complaint was filed, Mattel moved for summary judgment. In support of its motion, Mattel proffered evidence that the Cool Blue Barbie doll contained a 1991 copyright notice on the back of its head, indicating that it predated Claudene's head sculpture copyright by approximately six years. Mattel therefore argued that Cool Blue Barbie could not as a matter of law infringe Claudene's head sculpture copyright. . . .

At a follow-up counsel meeting required by a local rule, Mattel's counsel attempted to convince Hicks that his complaint was frivolous. During the videotaped meeting, they presented Hicks with copies of various Barbie dolls that not only had been created prior to 1996 (the date of Claudene's creation), but also had copyright designations on their heads that pre-dated Claudene's creation. Additionally, Mattel's counsel noted that the face paint on some of the earlier-created Barbie dolls was virtually identical to that used on Claudene. Hicks declined Mattel's invitation to inspect the dolls and, later during the meeting, hurled them in disgust from a conference table.

Having been unsuccessful in convincing Hicks to dismiss Christian's action voluntarily, Mattel served Hicks with a motion for Rule 11 sanctions. In its motion papers, Mattel argued, among other things, that Hicks had signed and filed a frivolous complaint based on a legally

meritless theory that Mattel's prior-created head sculptures infringed Claudene's 1997 copyright. Hicks declined to withdraw the complaint during the 21-day safe harbor period provided by Rule 11, and Mattel filed its motion.

Seemingly unfazed by Mattel's Rule 11 motion, Hicks proceeded with the litigation and filed a motion pursuant to Federal Rule of Civil Procedure 56(f) to obtain additional discovery. . . . The district court summarily denied the motion. . . .

Hicks then began filing additional papers that were characterized by frequency and volume. Following official completion of the summary judgment briefing schedule, Hicks filed what was styled as a "supplemental opposition." In those papers, Christian asserted for the first time that the head sculpture of Mattel's CEO Barbie (which was created in 1998) infringed Christian's copyright in the Claudene doll. He did not, however, move for leave to amend the complaint.

Hicks later filed additional papers alleging that several additional Barbie dolls infringed the Claudene sculpture. . . . [N]o motion for leave to amend the complaint was filed. . . .

III. THE DISTRICT COURT'S ORDERS

The district court granted Mattel's motions for summary judgment and Rule 11 sanctions. The court ruled that Mattel did not infringe the 1997 Claudene copyright because it could not possibly have accessed the Claudene doll at the time it created the head sculptures of the Cool Blue (copyrighted in 1991). . . .

Having rejected Hicks' reasons for eschewing a fees award, the district court made the following observations and findings:

> The court has considered whether an award of monetary sanctions less than the fees actually incurred would represent an appropriate sanction. The court has concluded that it would not. There is no dispute that Mr. Hicks was directly responsible for filing and pursuing this frivolous suit. Nor is there any dispute that the fees sought were actually incurred and paid. *Moreover, the court is satisfied from the documentation provided by Mattel's counsel that the fees incurred were reasonable.* While recognizing the significant burden this award imposes, the court has concluded that in light of Mr. Hicks' failure to respond to lesser sanctions and his continuing disregard for the most basic rules governing an attorney's professional conduct, the costs of his unacceptable behavior should fall squarely on him. Finally, while the court may reimburse an adverse party for expenses incurred in disposing of frivolous litigation, it can never compensate the judicial system for the time spent to dispose of an action that should never have been brought. The court can only hope that a sanction of this size will, at last, put a stop to Mr. Hicks' continuing pattern of abuse. Emphasis added....

The court is satisfied that the other attorneys' fees Mattel has claimed are both reasonable and proximately caused by Mr. Hicks' pursuit of this frivolous action. [T]he Court *grants* Mattel its attorneys' fees in the amount of $501,565.00.

DISCUSSION...

II. IMPOSITION OF RULE 11 SANCTIONS...

A. General Rule 11 Principles

Filing a complaint in federal court is no trifling undertaking. An attorney's signature on a complaint is tantamount to a warranty that the complaint is well grounded in fact and "existing law" (or proposes a good faith extension of the existing law) and that it is not filed for an improper purpose.

Rule 11 provides in pertinent part:

> (a) Signature. Every pleading, written motion, and other paper shall be signed by at least one attorney of record in the attorney's individual name....
> (b) Representations to Court. By presenting to the court (whether by signing, filing, submitting, or later advocating) a pleading, written motion, or other paper, an attorney or unrepresented party is certifying to the best of the person's knowledge, information, and belief, formed after an inquiry reasonable under the circumstances...
> (2) the claims, defenses, and other legal contentions therein are warranted by existing law or by a nonfrivolous argument for the extension, modification, or reversal of existing law or the establishment of new law;
> (3) the allegations and other factual contentions have evidentiary support or, if specifically so identified, are likely to have evidentiary support after a reasonable opportunity for further investigation or discovery[.]

The attorney has a duty prior to filing a complaint not only to conduct a reasonable factual investigation, but also to perform adequate legal research that confirms whether the theoretical underpinnings of the complaint are "warranted by existing law or a good faith argument for an extension, modification or reversal of existing law." Golden Eagle Distrib. Corp. v. Burroughs Corp., 801 F.2d 1531, 1537 (9th Cir. 1986). One of the fundamental purposes of Rule 11 is to "reduce frivolous claims, defenses or motions and to deter costly meritless maneuvers, . . . [thereby] avoiding delay and unnecessary expense in litigation." Nonetheless, a finding of significant delay or expense is not required under Rule 11. Where, as here, the complaint is the primary focus of Rule 11 proceedings, a district court must conduct a two-prong inquiry to determine (1) whether the complaint is legally or factually "baseless" from an objective perspective, and (2) if the attorney has conducted "a reasonable and competent inquiry" before signing and filing it.

B. The District Court's Findings Regarding the Meritless Claim

1. Did Hicks Have an Adequate Legal or Factual Basis for Filing the Complaint?

Hicks filed a single claim of copyright infringement against Mattel. The complaint charges that the Cool Blue Barbie infringed the copyright in the Claudene doll head. . . . Hicks cannot seriously dispute the district court's conclusions that, assuming the applicability of the doctrine of prior creation, Christian's complaint was legally and factually frivolous.

Indeed, as a matter of copyright law, it is well established that a prior-created work cannot infringe a later-created one. *See* Grubb v. KMS Patriots, L.P., 88 F.3d 1, 5 (1st Cir. 1996) (noting that "prior creation renders any conclusion of access or inference of copying illogical").

Copyright infringement requires proof that a plaintiff owns a valid copyright in the work and that the defendant copied the work. . . . By simple logic, it is impossible to copy something that does not exist. Thus, if Mattel created its doll sculptures before CDC created Claudene in 1994, it is factually and legally impossible for Mattel to be an infringer.

The record of creation is telling and conclusive. The Cool Blue Barbie doll uses the Neptune's Daughter doll head which was created in 1991, some six years before the Claudene doll. . . . Hicks should have been well aware of the prior creation, not to mention that the copyright notice (including date of creation) appears prominently on the back of the dolls' heads. . . .

Consequently, in the face of undisputed evidence concerning the prior-creation of the Barbie dolls, the district court did not abuse its discretion by ruling that the complaint was frivolous.

2. Did Hicks Conduct an Adequate Factual Investigation?

The district court concluded that Hicks "filed a case without factual foundation." Hicks, having argued unsuccessfully that his failure to perform even minimal due diligence was irrelevant as a matter of copyright law, does not contest that he would have been able to discover the copyright information simply by examining the doll heads. Instead he argues that the district court did not understand certain "complex" issues. Simply saying so does not make it so. The district court well understood the legal and factual background of the case. It was Hicks' absence of investigation, not the district court's absence of analysis, that brought about his downfall.

The district court did not abuse its discretion in concluding that Hicks' failure to investigate fell below the requisite standard established by Rule 11.

III. THE DISTRICT COURT'S ADDITIONAL FINDINGS REGARDING MISCONDUCT

Hicks argues that even if the district court were justified in sanctioning him under Rule 11 based on Christian's complaint and the follow-on motions, its conclusion was tainted because it impermissibly considered other misconduct that cannot be sanctioned under Rule 11, such as discovery abuses, misstatements made during oral argument, and conduct in other litigation.

Hicks' argument has merit. While Rule 11 permits the district court to sanction an attorney for conduct regarding "pleadings, written motions, and other papers" that have been signed and filed in a given case, Fed. R. Civ. P. 11(a), it does not authorize sanctions for, among other things, discovery abuses or misstatements made to the court during an oral presentation. . . .

In its January 5, 2000, order, the district court cited multiple bases for its Rule 11 findings. . . .

In connection with the conclusion on boorish behavior, the court cited Hicks' conduct ("tossing Barbie dolls off a table") at a meeting of counsel and his interruption of a deposition following a damaging admission by his client. The charge of misrepresentation of facts was based on a statement made at oral argument that he had never seen a particular catalogue while a videotape of exhibit inspections showed him "leisurely thumbing through the catalogue." Hicks' conflicting representations in pleadings as to the identity of allegedly infringing Barbie dolls was an additional example of misrepresentation noted by the court. Finally, the court determined that Hicks made misrepresentations in his briefs concerning the law of joint authorship in the copyright context. . . .

The laundry list of Hicks' outlandish conduct is a long one and raises serious questions as to his respect for the judicial process. Nonetheless, Rule 11 sanctions are limited to "papers" signed in violation of the rule. Conduct in depositions, discovery meetings of counsel, oral representations at hearings, and behavior in prior proceedings do not fall within the ambit of Rule 11. Because we do not know for certain whether the district court granted Mattel's Rule 11 motion as a result of an impermissible intertwining of its conclusion about the complaint's frivolity and Hicks' extrinsic misconduct, we must vacate the district court's Rule 11 orders.

We decline Mattel's suggestion that the district court's sanctions orders could be supported in their entirety under the court's inherent authority. To impose sanctions under its inherent authority, the district court must "make an explicit finding [which it did not do here] that counsel's conduct constituted or was tantamount to bad faith." We acknowledge that the district court has a broad array of sanctions options at its disposal: Rule 11, 28 U.S.C. §1927,[11] and the court's inherent authority. Each of these sanctions alternatives has its own particular requirements, and it is important that

---

11. Section 1927 provides for imposition of "excess costs, expenses, and attorneys' fees" on counsel who "multiplies the proceedings in any case unreasonably and vexatiously."

the grounds be separately articulated to assure that the conduct at issue falls within the scope of the sanctions remedy. . . . On remand, the district court will have an opportunity to delineate the factual and legal basis for its sanctions orders.

IV. THE DISTRICT COURT'S DECISION TO AWARD ATTORNEYS' FEES

Hicks raises various challenges to the quantum of attorneys' fees. Because we are vacating the district court's Rule 11 orders on other legal grounds, we express no opinion at this stage about the particular reasonableness of any of the fees the district court elected to award Mattel. We do, however, encourage the district court on remand to ensure that the time spent by Mattel's attorneys was reasonably and appropriately spent in relation to both the patent frivolousness of Christian's complaint and the services directly caused by the sanctionable conduct.[12] See Fed. R. Civ. P. 11, advisory committee notes, 1993 Amendments, Subdivisions (b) and (c) (noting that attorneys' fees may only be awarded under Rule 11 for those "services directly and unavoidably caused" by the sanctionable conduct).

CONCLUSION

We vacate the district court's Rule 11 orders and remand for further proceedings consistent with this opinion. . . .

C. Discovery Abuse

Problem

12-5. An associate at Martyn & Fox believes the firm must produce certain damaging documents in a product liability case. Fox insists they not be produced because the documents came from the client's subsidiary in Germany, and it would be burdensome to search the German subsidiary's warehouse. "Let's just object to producing any of the subsidiary's documents," Fox instructs the associate. May the associate accept direction from Fox, the experienced partner? What if documents from the subsidiary have not been requested?

Consider: Model Rules 3.2, 3.4, 5.2
Model Code DR 7-106(A) and (C), 7-109(A)
Federal Rules of Civil Procedure 26, 37

---

12. For example, because the action was frivolous on its face, why would Mattel's attorneys need to spend 700 hours ($173,151.50 in fees) for the summary judgment motion and response? Although Hicks clearly complicated the proceedings through multiple filings, Mattel's theory and approach was stunningly simple and required little explication: (1) Mattel's Barbie dolls and face paint were prior copyright creations that could not infringe the after-created Claudene doll and (2) Christian was neither a contributor to nor owner of the copyright. This is not to say that Hicks' defense of the motion necessarily called for a timid response, but neither does it compel a bazooka approach.

In re Tutu Wells Contamination Litigation
120 F.3d 368 (3d Cir. 1997)

BECKER, Circuit Judge.

This is an appeal from an order of the district court imposing heavy sanctions upon a law firm, several of its partners, and its client for discovery violations in connection with a large environmental lawsuit. The client, Esso, is charged in the underlying complaint with having "poisoned the wells" in the Estate Tutu area in the eastern end of St. Thomas by releasing from the Esso Tutu service station petroleum hydrocarbons and chlorinated hydrocarbons into the Tutu aquifer which supplies drinking water to much of the east end of the island. The discovery abuse primarily involves the alleged suppression by Esso's former counsel in the litigation, the San Juan, Puerto Rico law firm of Goldman, Antonetti, Ferraiuoli & Axtmayer, of a report by Jose Agrelot, a professional engineer, summarizing the results of soil and liquid tests he had performed at the Esso Tutu site in December 1989. The suppression of this report is claimed to have dramatically increased the discovery time and expense for other parties in connection with their prosecution of the case. . . .

What specially marks this case is the character and magnitude of the sanctions imposed. Eschewing the auspices of Fed. R. Civ. P. 37, which authorizes sanctions for failure to make disclosure or cooperate in discovery, the district court imposed the challenged sanctions under its inherent power. The sanction imposed on the lawyers was suspension from practice in the District Court of the Virgin Islands: Jose Cepeda and Francis Torres for three years, and Eugenio Romero for one year.[4] The sanction imposed upon Esso was the payment of $750,000 to a "Community Service Sanction Account" to be utilized to fund construction of a halfway house on St. Thomas, the training of inmates, and renovation of the St. Thomas Criminal Justice Complex. The sanction imposed upon Goldman Antonetti was the payment of $250,000 to the Community Service Sanction Account (for the same purpose), and the sum of $120,000 as counsel fees and costs ($30,000 incurred by each of four moving parties for time they spent in connection with the sanctions proceedings themselves). Esso was similarly assessed a sanction of $30,000 to be paid to each of four other movants, but Esso has paid that sum and does not challenge it on this appeal.

Goldman Antonetti, its three named partners, and Esso appeal the sanctions imposed against them on a variety of grounds. . . .

I. FACTS AND PROCEDURAL HISTORY

A. Background and Overview

In the summer of 1987, a water well owner noticed the smell of gasoline

---

4. Romero and Torres were admitted to practice before the court *pro hac vice*. There is some dispute as to whether Cepeda was technically admitted. . . .

emanating from his well. He contacted local environmental officials
who, with the help of the federal government, began an investigation into
possible contamination of the Tutu
aquifer. Investigators discovered the
presence of gasoline and chlorinated
organics in the aquifer. Government
officials thereafter closed many of the
wells.

The discovery of the contamination led to a number of private lawsuits. Detailed explication of the
anatomy of the various suits is unnecessary; it is sufficient to note that
the private litigation seeks to assign
responsibility for the contamination
between and among a number of
possible contaminators, including
but not limited to two automobile
service stations, an automobile deal-
er, a shopping plaza, a dry cleaner,
and a former textile plant. That private litigation also includes claims for
contribution under CERCLA. The
parties in the litigation include both
possible contaminators and businesses and landowners allegedly
harmed by the contamination. The
law firm of Goldman, Antonetti,
Ferraiuoli & Axtmayer ("Goldman
Antonetti") represented Esso for
much of the period in question but
no longer does so.

Discovery began in 1989. During
this discovery, Esso and Goldman
Antonetti employed practices the
district court found to be sanctionable. In its three opinions regarding
the sanctions, the district court
grouped the discovery violations into
three categories. First, the court
found that Esso and its attorneys
engaged in a strategy that kept the
various other parties in the litigation
from obtaining needed information in
a timely fashion. . . . Without delving
into the specifics of individual abu-

ses, the court noted that Esso and
Goldman Antonetti met many
discovery requests with legal tactics
intended to delay, oppress, or harass
their opponents. Often, Esso and
Goldman Antonetti would refuse to
turn over requested documents until
forced to do so by court order.
According to the court, the level of
judicial involvement in the discovery
process was consequently unusually
high, requiring the court unnecessarily to devote significant resources
to resolving ordinary discovery disputes.

Second, the court focused on the
handling of the so-called Agrelot
memorandum. In December 1989,
Soil Tech, a company that specializes
in environmental analyses of soil,
took samples from the soil at the Esso
Tutu Service Station ("ETSS") and
from liquid in a holding tank at
ETSS. Soil Tech sent those samples
to the Environmental Testing and
Certification Corp. ("ETC") for
analysis. ETC returned the results of
the investigation to Soil Tech shortly
thereafter. The results revealed some
contamination. Jose Agrelot, President of Soil Tech, received the preliminary results and summarized
them in a memorandum, which he
forwarded to Goldman Antonetti in
anticipation of a meeting in January
1990. ETC produced the final results
of the testing shortly after the meeting had occurred. Agrelot testified
that he discussed the memorandum
with attorneys at Goldman Antonetti,
including Jose Cepeda and Francis
Torres. . . .

Although for the most part the
Agrelot memorandum merely summarized the information contained in
the ETC findings, the memorandum
did include a map pinpointing the
locations of the soil borings from

which the tested soil was taken. It appears from the record that, without the Agrelot memorandum, someone examining the ETC data could not determine with precision the location of the borings. The record does, however, give some indication that there is enough information in the ETC supporting data that was made available to determine that the ETC analyzed soil from ETSS rather than from some other location above the Tutu aquifer. Esso and its attorneys produced the full ETC report on which the Agrelot memorandum was based.

However, neither Esso, Goldman Antonetti, nor Soil Tech turned over the Agrelot memorandum during discovery until October 1993. Prior to that time, various parties had specifically requested all reports generated from soil and groundwater testing in the Tutu area, but the responses to such requests, either signed by or reviewed by Esso employees or Goldman Antonetti attorneys, made no mention of the Agrelot memorandum. The reasons for this omission are not clear. Lawyers from Goldman Antonetti testified that the Agrelot memorandum had been indexed incorrectly in their computer database; Agrelot himself testified that the memorandum had been labeled incorrectly and therefore misfiled in his office. The district court found that the failure to produce the Agrelot memorandum was intentional. At all events, only after Agrelot had searched his files in the fall of 1993 to assist Esso in negotiating a case management order did he find the memorandum and turn it over to Esso, who revealed it to its new counsel Archer & Greiner. It was Archer & Greiner that finally notified the other parties of its existence.

The third category of violations occurred in connection with an attempted inspection underneath the surface of the ETSS site. In particular, the plaintiffs wished to determine whether an underground storage tank was located on the site, and also to trace the pipes leading out of the oil/water separator located on the site. The parties refer to this aspect of the discovery as the "anomaly investigation." In May, 1992, the plaintiffs employed ground penetrating radar ("GPR") to examine the area beneath the ETSS. The GPR turned up an anomalous shadow in the corner of the site, possibly indicating the presence of an underground storage tank. Esso claimed that the GPR produced a false result because of interference from overhead power lines or from a reinforcing bar in a nearby retaining wall. The magistrate judge ultimately ordered an excavation of the site to determine once and for all if such a tank existed. It did not.

Excavation of the site was to occur in accordance with the magistrate judge's order. However, according to the district court, Esso failed to comply with this order. . . . This failure led to months of wrangling among the parties and between Esso and the court until Esso finally conducted the investigation to the satisfaction of the court, nearly 10 months after the investigation was scheduled to be completed. . . .

II. SUSPENSIONS OF ATTORNEYS CEPEDA, ROMERO, AND TORRES . . .

Cepeda, Romero, and Torres submit that their suspensions cannot stand because the district court did not afford them particularized notice of the form of the sanctions they faced. They had no way of knowing, they contend, that the possibility of suspension as a sanction existed. Therefore, they conclude, their right to due process was infringed. . . .

In considering the suspension of an attorney as a sanction, courts must provide the attorney with due process. Although the precise contours of the process that is due varies given the particular context, "the fundamental requirements of due process—notice and an opportunity to respond—must be afforded before any sanction is imposed." Similarly, prior to the suspension of an attorney from practicing before the District Court of the Virgin Islands because of misconduct as defined by local rule, an attorney must be provided "notice and an opportunity to be heard." D.V.I. R. 83.2(b)(4)(A).

The party against whom sanctions are being considered is entitled to notice of the legal rule on which the sanctions would be based, the reasons for the sanctions, and the form of the potential sanctions. . . .

In the present case, neither Cepeda, Romero, nor Torres received particularized notice that the court was contemplating suspending them from practicing law as a sanction. . . . As far as we can tell, the possibility of suspension arose for the first time in the court's third and final published opinion on the matter, when the court actually imposed the suspensions. Neither did the parties moving for sanctions seek suspension; their papers

before the district court sought only monetary sanctions and dismissal. . . .

. . . Put differently, had Cepeda, Romero, and Torres been on notice that they faced suspension, they doubtless would have utilized their opportunity to be heard to raise different matters. As it happened, because of the lack of notice, the attorneys' opportunity to be heard was less than meaningful; they were not given the appropriate opportunity to present relevant defenses to the penalties which they were ultimately assessed. . . . Because their rights to due process were violated, we will vacate that portion of the order on appeal suspending them from practice in the District Court of the Virgin Islands.

III. THE COMMUNITY SERVICE SANCTION . . .

As previously noted, the district court employed its inherent powers to sanction Esso and Goldman Antonetti. A threshold question, then, might be whether the court's resort to the inherent powers, in lieu of the rule-based and statute-based sanctions—e.g., Fed. R. Civ. P. 11, 16, and 37, or 28 U.S.C. §1927—was appropriate.[13] We need not reach this question, however. As we shall discuss more fully below, the court had no authority under its inherent powers to impose the type of sanction it did.

The Supreme Court has furnished us with at least a partial list of a court's inherent powers. Employing

---

13. In Chambers v. NASCO, Inc., 501 U.S. 32 (1991), the Supreme Court discussed at length the inherent powers of a court to sanction and their relationship to rule-based and statute-based powers to sanction, e.g., Rule 11, Rule 16, Rule 37, and §1927. To oversimplify somewhat, the Court held that the existence of rule-based or statute-based powers does not preclude a court's employing its inherent powers. The Court observed, but apparently did not require, that normally a court should look first to those rule-based or statute-based powers before turning to its inherent powers, reserving the inherent powers for instances in which the rule-based or statute-based powers are not "up to the task."

its inherent powers, a court can control admission to its bar, discipline attorneys, punish for contempt, vacate its own judgment upon a finding of fraud, bar a criminal defendant from a courtroom for disruptive behavior, dismiss a suit on forum non conveniens grounds or for failure to prosecute, and assess attorney's fees. *See* Chambers v. NASCO, Inc., 501 U.S. 32 (1991).

In addition to those mentioned by the Supreme Court, other inherent powers include the power to fine, to disqualify counsel, to preclude claims or defenses, and to limit a litigant's future access to the courts. With these many bows in their sanctioning quivers, courts have frequently invoked their inherent powers "to regulate the conduct of the members of the bar as well as to provide tools for docket management." Notwithstanding the variety of tools available to a court under its inherent powers, we believe that an order directing a party to the litigation to remit funds to a third party is outside the scope of a court's inherent powers. We begin our analysis by noting that "because of their very potency, inherent powers must be exercised with restraint and discretion." *Chambers*, 501 U.S. at 44. That "inherent powers are shielded from direct democratic controls" makes this exercise of restraint and discretion even more important. Roadway Express, Inc. v. Piper, 447 U.S. 752, 764 (1980). . . .

. . . [I]nherent powers fall into three distinct categories: powers arising from Article III, powers arising from the nature of the court, and powers arising from historical notions of the courts of equity.

No matter where one places their origin, it is clear that the power exercised in this case cannot be derived from a court's inherent powers. The district court's actions are essentially legislative in nature. Although we recognize that the line between a judicial act and legislative act is difficult to fix with certainty, the district court's sanction here falls on the legislative side of whatever line we may draw. The court ordered the reallocation of resources from private entities to an agency of the public sector not a party in the case. . . . In so doing, the court ventured well beyond the case and controversy before it.

We do not find persuasive the argument that a court's inherent powers include the wielding of what is essentially a legislative power. We believe that it is not in the nature of courts of justice normally to engage in the redistribution of wealth to parties outside of the litigation. We find nothing in Article III that allows for such a power. Further, we do not believe that such a power is necessary for the efficient functioning of a court. Fines made payable to the court would do just as well in ensuring that parties do not interfere with that functioning. From the standpoint of the sanctioned party, the disciplining effect of a fine made payable to the court is no different from the disciplining effect of a sanction made payable to some third party; the sanctioned party is out of pocket the same amount either way. Finally, we have been directed to no historical evidence demonstrating that courts of equity had this power, and given that the inherent powers must be exercised with restraint, we see no reason to permit this power now. . . .

We appreciate the sense of outrage that motivated the district court's decision to impose the community service sanction. The contamination of the Tutu aquifer was tragic, and the delay in determining responsibility for that contamination is doubtless frustrating. The community service sanction, at least on its face, is attractive because it seeks to punish those who have caused, at least in part, that delay and assist those who might have been harmed by the contamination. In that sense, the district court's actions were admirable. However, a court does not always do well by doing good. Though we applaud the district court's motives, we are constrained to find fault with its remedy.

In sum, we hold that the district court's inherent powers cannot support the imposition of the community service sanction.[18]

IV. MONETARY SANCTIONS . . .

Was the Monetary Sanction Appropriate?[21] . . .

Goldman Antonetti argues that the district court impermissibly awarded sanctions based on the costs and expenses arising from the sanctions proceedings themselves. In the firm's submission, such an award constitutes improper fee shifting. We disagree. It is beyond dispute that attorney's fees are, in certain circumstances, properly awarded as a sanction. . . . The time, effort, and resources expended in bringing sanctionable conduct to light would have been unnecessary had the sanctionable conduct never occurred. These costs are as much a harm to a party in the litigation as is the delay in the litigation or the substantive prejudice caused by the conduct. If we exclude from a possible award the costs of sanctions proceedings, we would undermine the compensatory goal of a sanctions award.

Further, if a party is aware ex ante that the costs he incurs in exposing sanctionable conduct will never be recouped, that party may decide to forgo a sanctions proceeding altogether. . . . In doing so, however, that party might allow otherwise sanctionable conduct to go unaddressed. In such cases, the deterrent goal of a sanction award has been lost; parties who know that the likelihood of facing a sanction proceeding are low may engage in sanctionable conduct more often. . . .

Goldman Antonetti is correct in pointing out that the district court did not identify with specificity many of the acts that caused it to infer that Esso and Goldman Antonetti were engaged in a pattern of delay. The court did, however, make extensive findings as to the Agrelot memorandum and the anomaly investigation. With respect to both of those matters, the district court's findings were not unreasonable. The undisputed fact is that the Agrelot memorandum

---

18. Moreover, we have serious doubts that one could plausibly argue that Congress provided the courts—by statute or by rule—the power to impose the type of sanction imposed here. In order to provide such power, we believe three criteria must be satisfied: (1) this must be a power that Congress can constitutionally delegate to a coordinate branch; (2) Congress must clearly indicate its intent to delegate this power; and (3) Congress must provide intelligible principles to guide the courts in the exercise of this power. None of these criteria is satisfied here.

21. The analysis that follows in the text does not make a distinction between inherent powers sanctions and statute-based or rule-based sanctions. In respects relevant to our discussion, the sanctioning tools are the same.

did not surface until well after discovery had begun and until well after parties to the litigation had made repeated requests that clearly covered the document.

Goldman Antonetti advances a plausible explanation for why the Agrelot memorandum was produced so late in the litigation. It is certainly possible that no attorney from Goldman Antonetti knew of the Agrelot memorandum until it was found in October 1993, notwithstanding testimony to the contrary; it is equally possible that the Agrelot memorandum was misfiled by both Soil Tech and by Goldman Antonetti. That is not to say, however, that the court's findings, which are based on an inference that Goldman Antonetti intentionally withheld the Agrelot memorandum, are unreasonable. There is evidence in the record that Goldman Antonetti attorneys knew of the memorandum's existence. Those same attorneys responded to the discovery requests covering such memorandum, and yet the document was not produced.

With respect to the anomaly investigation, our analysis is similar. Goldman Antonetti relies on a report by a magistrate judge concluding that the firm's actions during the investigation amounted to nothing more than zealous advocacy in representation of its clients and therefore did not warrant sanctions. The firm submits that the district court had no basis to disagree with the magistrate judge's conclusions. However, the district court in that instance did not owe the magistrate judge any deference. Further, the undisputed evidence makes it clear that it was not unreasonable for the district court to conclude that the delays in the investigation were willful and in bad faith. The investigation began late, was aborted prematurely because of the failure of the parties to arrive with appropriate equipment, and was not completed for many months.

Goldman Antonetti's next argument—that the failure to produce the Agrelot memorandum caused no harm to the other parties in the litigation—suffers the same fate. . . . The ETC report was both complex and voluminous. Examining it required significant costs. A summary prepared by an expert would have reduced these costs and identified the problems that could only have been discovered by imposing a considerable burden on those examining the report for the first time. We concede, as did the district court, that the summary, timely produced, might have provided the parties to the litigation with less assistance than they claim. Still, it would have provided assistance, and that is the crux of the harm caused by the failure of Esso and Goldman Antonetti to produce the Agrelot memorandum. . . .

In sum, we are satisfied that the district court did not abuse its discretion in concluding that Goldman Antonetti is subject to some form of sanction and that $120,000 was an appropriate sanction. . . .

Having held that the discovery violations caused harm, the court examined the papers these parties submitted that purported to describe the extent of that harm. The court believed that the papers "suffered from two shortcomings." First, the papers did not adequately categorize the claimed harm within the framework the court had created for addressing the sanctionable conduct. The court found it difficult to determine whether the moving parties were seeking costs and expenses from (1) discovery violations related to the search for evidence of contamination at ETSS; (2) the failure to disclose the Agrelot memo; or (3) the sanctions proceedings themselves, the three broad areas into which the court held sanctionable conduct fell. Second, the court faulted the parties for their general failure to provide it with documentation "that adequately and efficiently explained to the court how those expenses could be justified as a sanction."

These shortcomings led the court to award only a portion of the sanctions sought. The court declined to scrutinize the voluminous submissions of the parties in order to perform the categorization it had requested the parties to perform. Instead, the court simply denied the award of sanctions arising from (1) discovery violations related to the search for evidence of contamination at ETSS; and (2) the failure to disclose the Agrelot memo. The court did, however, award sanctions arising from the sanctions proceedings themselves. The court set a uniform level of sanction award based on L'Henri's request. The court did so because it believed that L'Henri's

request was clear, well supported, and, in all, "unassailable." . . .

We believe that the district court was well within its discretion to deny the requested sanctions based upon the parties' submissions. . . .

. . . Although a court is free to do so, it is not incumbent upon a district court to devote its own valuable time, energy, and resources to remedy the shortcomings of movants' submissions if that assistance falls short. . . .

According to the court, L'Henri's counsel, Nancy D'Anna, submitted well-reasoned, thoroughly researched, and adequately documented material to the court throughout the sanctions proceedings. What is more, the court continued, L'Henri produced such material efficiently and relatively cheaply. In deciding to base the uniform level of sanction on L'Henri's request, the district court implicitly found that each party could have produced similarly well-reasoned, thorough, and adequately documented material for no greater cost than that incurred by L'Henri. We believe that it is not an abuse of discretion for the district court to assume that all parties can produce work of L'Henri's quality for approximately the same cost. . . .

D. Bias

Problem

12-6. Martyn is furious with opposing counsel, who happens to be one of the most highly regarded male lawyers in town. In the course of a recent deposition, this lawyer referred to Martyn as "office help," and repeatedly called her "sweetheart," "dear," and raised his voice to drown her out, which required Martyn to stop talking until he was finished and then inquire if she could be heard. What do you advise?

Consider: Model Rules 4.4, 8.4
          Model Code DR 7-101
          Model Code of Judicial Conduct Rule 2.3

In re Charges of Unprofessional Conduct Contained in Panel Case No. 15976

653 N.W.2d 452 (Minn. 2002)

PER CURIAM.

... Respondent's client sustained serious permanent physical injuries that disabled him when a school bus hit and ran over him with a rear tire while he was riding a bicycle in South Minneapolis. The accident crushed his pelvis, and left him in a coma for approximately 1 month. By the time of trial, the client was able to walk with the assistance of a cane. Before the accident, the client was employed as a checker and bagger at a grocery store and as a greeter at a restaurant. His employment background consisted of similar unskilled and physical labor positions. At trial, the client asserted that his permanent injuries prevented him from performing physical-labor-type jobs and that he did not qualify educationally or intellectually for other types of employment. Therefore, he sought damages for future loss of wages and future diminished earning capacity.

[Judge Franklin J. Knoll, the complainant in this disciplinary proceeding,] presided over the personal-injury action and assigned one of his two law clerks to assist with the action. The clerk assigned by complainant to assist in this case is physically disabled. He is paralyzed from his mouth down and has difficulty breathing and speaking. He performed his duties as a law clerk with the assistance of a large wheelchair, respirator and full-time attendant. The disabled clerk was present in the courtroom at the outset of the personal-injury trial, assisted with jury selection, and remained in the courtroom throughout the trial.

On the first day of trial, respondent's client expressed reservations about his ability to receive a fair trial grounded on the fact that if the disabled law clerk continued to work in the courtroom, the jury would compare the clerk who was more severely disabled yet able to work, to himself, who was less severely disabled and claiming an inability to work. Later that same day respondent made an oral motion outside the presence of the jury, "for a mistrial and another panel of jurors without your law clerk present or in the alternative that this case be assigned to another judge." Respondent gave the following explanation for his motion:

> I will be asking the jury to award future loss of wages, future diminished earning capacity. I do not believe a jury when they look at the comparison with your law clerk, who's obviously gainfully employed, working in the courtroom under great handicap and great duress, will be able to award anything to my client under those circumstances.

Respondent stated that he brought the motion with "great reluctance" and acknowledged that the motion was "outrageous and distasteful for the court." He did not support his motion with any legal authority. Stating that the motion was "un-American," complainant denied the motion.

The jury found in favor of the defendant on the issue of liability. Subsequently, respondent brought a written motion for a new trial. Respondent asserted the presence of the disabled clerk in the courtroom as one basis for the motion. Respondent again stated that his objection to the clerk's presence in the courtroom was made with "the greatest reluctance," but he argued that the jury would compare the disabilities of the law clerk with the injuries of his client. Again, respondent failed to cite any legal authority in support of his position. . . .

In In re Panel File 98-26, 597 N.W.2d 563 (Minn. 1999), we issued an admonition to a prosecutor for making a motion to exclude a public defender from participating in a trial based solely on his race. After accepting a position as a special assistant county attorney, the prosecutor was assigned to take over the prosecution of an African-American male charged with two counts of felony robbery of a Caucasian couple. The prosecutor previously assigned to the case left a memorandum in the case file explaining that the public defender felt race was an issue in the case and planned to recruit an African-American public defender to try the case. Subsequently, the prosecutor brought a motion in limine requesting:

> An Order from this Court prohibiting counsel for the defendant to have a person of color as co-counsel for the sole purpose of playing upon the emotions of the jury.

Two workdays after filing the motion, the prosecutor realized the gravity of her mistake, withdrew the motion, and apologized to both public defenders. She also implemented measures to prevent reoccurrence of the misconduct. . . .

On review, we rejected the Panel's determination that the prosecutor's conduct was "non-serious" and unequivocally held that race-based misconduct is inherently serious.

Moreover, we emphasized that race-based misconduct committed by an officer of the court is especially destructive because it "undermine[s] confidence in our system of justice [and] erode[s] the very foundation upon which justice is based." . . .

. . . [W]e emphasized that race should never be used as a basis for limiting an attorney's participation in a court proceeding. We extend this holding to encompass situations where disability is used to limit a court employee's participation in a court proceeding. Neither race nor disability should be used as a means of limiting participation in our courts. Minnesota has adopted legislation prohibiting discrimination against individuals with disabilities. *See* Minnesota Human Rights Act (MHRA), Minn. Stat. §§363.01-363.20 (2000). The MHRA prohibits discrimination against individuals with disabilities in employment, housing, public accommodations, public services and education; the MHRA also prohibits race-based discrimination in these same areas. . . . Therefore, we conclude that the Panel's determination that respondent violated Rule 8.4(d) is not clearly erroneous. . . .

. . . A disabled court employee has a right to perform his job in the courtroom. But here we have the perceived rights of two disabled persons potentially in conflict with one another. Respondent's client also suffers from a disability. Respondent's client was concerned that the jury would compare the law clerk's more severe disability with his less severe disability and that comparison would unduly influence the jury to decide against him on his claims and deprive him of a fair trial. Ironically, the concern of respondent's client, as argued by respondent, was not that the law clerk's disability prevented him from capably performing his job, but that the law clerk's demonstrated capability would diminish the client's disability claim. Respondent's motion can be viewed as an inappropriate attempt to address the respective rights of two disabled persons, rather than elevating the rights of one over the rights of another. If respondent was concerned that the jury might make improper comparisons, respondent could have addressed those concerns during voir dire. Nonetheless, when viewed in context, we conclude that the Panel did not act arbitrarily, capriciously or unreasonably by finding that respondent's

conduct in this particular situation was non-serious.

Any discriminatory effect from the motion was indirect because respondent did not exercise any authority or control over the disabled clerk. In contrast, the prosecutor in In re Panel File 98-26 misused the power of the state by interfering with a defendant's right to counsel in seeking to prevent the public defender from representing the defendant based solely on the public defender's race. Taking into consideration the unique circumstances of this case, we conclude that the Panel did not act arbitrarily, capriciously, or unreasonably by issuing an amended admonition to respondent. . . .

E. Communication with Unrepresented and Represented Persons

Problems

12-7.   Negotiations have been going on for months. Then Martyn receives a call from the potential buyer. "With my lawyer involved, we'll never reach agreement. Let's talk—just you and me." What if buyer announces, "I fired my lawyer"?

12-8.   Martyn & Fox's client is totally frustrated. "I'll bet our settlement offers are not even being passed on to the plaintiff by that shyster lawyer of his. Why don't you just call the plaintiff up yourself and tell him our latest?" What if the client simply asks us to write the lawyer on the other side, with a copy to the plaintiff? What if our client asks us to write a letter for the client to send to the plaintiff?

12-9.   Martyn & Fox's client has a petition for a variance pending. Client tells Fox, "I think if you meet with the Zoning Board Chairman and explain our position, the hearing will go a lot better. That's what the Democratic committeeman told me." What may Fox do?

12-10. An Assistant U.S. Attorney gets a call from a defendant whose trial is now scheduled in six weeks. "I can't stand it," defendant exclaims, "That guy [from Martyn & Fox] the company hired to represent me couldn't care less about my case. All he wants is to make sure the company gets off scot-free. Can we talk? I'll meet you at Local Pub at 11:00 P.M. OK?"

12-11. Martyn & Fox has been representing a corporate client in an SEC investigation, a fact known to the SEC. One Saturday morning, Fox gets a panicked telephone call from our client's sales manager.

The cause: Justice Department lawyers visited at least ten brokers employed by our client this morning. What should Fox do?

12-12. Can Martyn & Fox send a memorandum to all our client's corporate employees directing them not to talk to anyone from the Justice Department?

12-13. The trial is a week away. Can Martyn visit with the other side's expert witness? How about a former employee of the party on the other side? What if the employee was separately represented at her deposition?

12-14. Martyn & Fox's client, an activist vegetarian group, thinks that a national chain is using beef tallow in processing its French fries. They believe the only way to prove this is to get someone hired to work at the national chain's French fry processing center. They ask Martyn & Fox if we will get one of our paralegals to apply for employment at the plant. What should we say?

Consider: Model Rules 4.1, 4.2, 4.3, 5.3, 8.4(a)
           Model Code DR 7-102, 7-104
           RLGL §§99-103

Messing, Rudavsky & Weliky, P.C. v. President & Fellows of Harvard College
764 N.E.2d 825 (Mass. 2002)

COWIN, J.

The law firm of Messing, Rudavsky & Weliky, P.C. (MR&W), appeals from an order of the Superior Court sanctioning the firm for violation of Mass. R. Prof. C. 4.2 . . . [which] prohibits attorneys from communicating with a represented party in the absence of that party's attorney. This appeal raises the issue whether, and to what extent, the rule prohibits an attorney from speaking ex parte to the employees of an organization represented by counsel. . . .

. . . From the stipulated facts, we distill the following. In August of 1997, MR&W filed a complaint against President and Fellows of Harvard College (Harvard) with the Massachusetts Commission Against Discrimination (commission) on be-

half of its client, Kathleen Stanford. Stanford, a sergeant with the Harvard University police department (HUPD), alleged that Harvard and its police chief, Francis Riley, discriminated against her on the basis of gender and in reprisal for earlier complaints of discrimination. MR&W represented Stanford, and Harvard was represented before the commission by in-house counsel, and thereafter by a Boston law firm. Following the institution of the suit, MR&W communicated ex parte with five employees of the HUPD: two lieutenants, two patrol officers, and a dispatcher. Although the two lieutenants had some supervisory authority over Stanford, it was not claimed that any of the five employees were involved in the alleged discrimination or retaliation against her or exercised management authority with respect to the alleged discriminatory or retaliatory acts.

In response to a motion by Harvard, the commission [and later, the Superior Court,] ruled that MR&W's ex parte contacts with all five employees violated rule 4.2, [and] . . . prohibit[ed] MR&W from using the affidavits it had procured during the interviews, and award[ed] Harvard the attorney's fees and costs it had expended in litigating the motion, in a later order calculated as $94,418.14.[3] . . .

. . . [R]ule [4.2.] has been justified generally as "preserving the mediating role of counsel on behalf of their clients . . . protecting clients from overreaching by counsel for adverse interests," and "protecting the attorney-client relationship."

. . . When the represented person is an individual, there is no difficulty determining when an attorney has violated the rule; the represented person is easily identifiable. In the case of an organization, however, identifying the protected class is more complicated.

Because an organization acts only through its employees, the rule must extend to some of these employees. However, most courts have rejected the position that the rule automatically prevents an attorney from speaking with all employees of a represented organization. . . .

According to comment [7] to rule 4.2, an attorney may not speak ex parte to three categories of employees: (1) "persons having managerial responsibility on behalf of the organization with regard to the subject of the representation"; (2) persons "whose act or omission in connection with that matter may be imputed to the organization for purposes of civil or criminal liability"; and (3) persons "whose statement may constitute an admission on the part of the organization."

. . . The [Superior Court] judge held that all five employees interviewed by MR&W were within the third category of the comment. He reached this result by concluding that the phrase "admission" in the comment refers to statements admissible in court under the admissions exception to the rule against hearsay. The Commonwealth's version of this rule . . . is identical to Fed. R. Evid. 801(d)(2)(D). Because the comment includes any employee whose statement may constitute an admission, this interpretation would prohibit an attorney from contacting any current employees of an organization to discuss any subject within the scope of their employment. This is, as the Superior Court judge admitted, a rule that is "strikingly protective of corporations regarding employee interviews." . . .

Some jurisdictions have adopted the broad reading of the rule endorsed by the judge in this case. *See, e.g.,* Weibrecht v. Southern Ill. Transfer, Inc., 241 F.3d 875 (7th Cir. 2001); Cole v. Appalachian Power Co., 903 F. Supp. 975 (S.D. W. Va. 1995); Brown v. St. Joseph County, 148 F.R.D. 246, 254 (N.D. Ind. 1993). Courts reaching this result do so because, like the Superior Court, they read the word "admission" in the third category of the comment as a reference to Fed. R. Evid. 801(d)(2)(D) and any corresponding State rule of evidence. This

---

3. Harvard claimed fees of $152,255.96. The judge reduced this amount after deducting fees incurred in the proceedings before the commission, and subtracting a portion of the billing rate as excessive.

rule forbids contact with practically all employees because "virtually every employee may conceivably make admissions binding on his or her employer." . . .

At the other end of the spectrum, a small number of jurisdictions have interpreted the rule narrowly so as to allow an attorney for the opposing party to contact most employees of a represented organization. These courts construe the rule to restrict contact with only those employees in the organization's "control group," defined as those employees in the uppermost echelon of the organization's management. *See* Johnson v. Cadillac Plastic Group, Inc., 930 F. Supp. 1437, 1442 (D. Colo. 1996); Fair Automotive Repair, Inc. v. Car-X Serv. Sys., Inc., 471 N.E.2d 554 (Ill. App. 1984) (applying rule only to "top management persons who had the responsibility of making final decisions"); Wright v. Group Health Hosp., 691 P.2d 564 (Wash. 1984) (applying rule only to "those employees who have the legal authority to 'bind' the corporation in a legal evidentiary sense, i.e., those employees who have 'speaking authority' for the corporation").

Other jurisdictions have adopted yet a third test that, while allowing for some ex parte contacts with a represented organization's employees, still maintains some protection of the organization. The Court of Appeals of New York articulated such a rule in Niesig v. Team I, 558 N.E.2d 1030 (N.Y. 1990), rejecting an approach that ties the rule to Fed. R. Evid. 801(d)(2)(D). Instead, the court defined a represented person to include "employees whose acts or omissions in the matter under inquiry are binding on the corporation . . . or imputed to the corporation for pur-

poses of its liability, or employees implementing the advice of counsel." Other jurisdictions have subsequently adopted the *Niesig* test. In addition, the Restatement (Third) of the Law Governing Lawyers [§100 comment e] endorses this rule.

. . . We adopt a test similar to that proposed in Niesig v. Team I, *supra*.

We . . . interpret the rule to ban contact only with those employees who have the authority to "commit the organization to a position regarding the subject matter of representation." Restatement (Third) of Law Governing Lawyers, at §100 comment e. *See also* Ethics 2000 Commission Draft for Public Comment Model Rule 4.2 Reporter's Explanation of Changes (Feb. 21, 2000) (recommending deletion of the third category of the comment). . . .

This interpretation, when read in conjunction with the other two categories of the comment, would prohibit ex parte contact only with those employees who exercise managerial responsibility in the matter, who are alleged to have committed the wrongful acts at issue in the litigation, or who have authority on behalf of the corporation to make decisions about the course of the litigation. This result is substantially the same as the *Niesig* test because it "prohibits direct communication . . . 'with those officials . . . who have the legal power to bind the corporation in the matter or who are responsible for implementing the advice of the corporation's lawyer . . . or whose own interests are directly at stake in a representation.'"

Our test is consistent with the purposes of the rule, which are not to "protect a corporate party from the revelation of prejudicial facts," but to protect the attorney-client relationship and prevent clients from making ill-advised statements without the counsel of their attorney. . . .

While our interpretation of the rule may reduce the protection available to organizations provided by the attorney-client privilege, it allows a litigant to obtain more meaningful disclosure of the truth by conducting informal interviews with certain employees of an opposing organization. Our interpretation does not jeopardize legitimate organizational interests because it continues to disallow contacts with those members of the organization who are so closely tied with the organization or the events at issue that it would be unfair to interview them without the presence of the organization's counsel. Fairness to the organization does not require the presence of an attorney every time an employee may make a statement admissible in evidence against his or her employer. The public policy of promoting efficient discovery is better advanced by adopting a rule which favors the revelation of the truth by making it more difficult for an organization to prevent the disclosure of relevant evidence. . . .

Our decision may initially result in some increased litigation to define exactly which employees fall within the bounds of the rule. Although "a bright-line rule" in the form of a "control group" test or a blanket ban on all employee interviews would be easier to apply, the rule we adopt is, as discussed above, fair, and will allow for ex parte interviews without prior counsel's permission when an employee clearly falls outside of the rule's scope.

. . . The five Harvard employees interviewed by MR&W do not fall within the third category of the comment as we have construed it. As employees of the HUPD, they are not involved in directing the litigation at bar or authorizing the organization to make binding admissions. In fact, Harvard does not argue that any of the five employees fit within our definition of this category.

The Harvard employees are also not employees "whose act or omission in connection with that matter may be imputed to the organization for purposes of civil or criminal liability." Stanford's complaint does not name any of these employees as involved in the alleged discrimination. In fact, in an affidavit she states that the two lieutenants "had no role in making any of the decisions that are the subject of my complaint of discrimination and retaliation," and Harvard does not refute this averment. All five employees were mere witnesses to the events that occurred, not active participants.

We must still determine, however, whether any of the interviewed employees have "managerial responsibility on behalf of the organization with regard to the subject of the representation." Although the two patrol officers and the dispatcher were subordinate to Stanford and had no managerial authority, the two lieutenants exercised some supervisory authority over Stanford. However, not all employees with some supervisory power over their coworkers are deemed to have "managerial" responsibility in the sense intended by the comment. "Supervision of a small group of workers would not constitute a managerial position within a corporation."

Even if the two lieutenants are deemed to have managerial responsibility, the Massachusetts version of the comment adds the requirement that the managerial responsibility be in "regard to the subject of the representation." Thus, the comment includes only those employees who have supervisory authority over the events at issue in the litigation. There is no evidence in the record that the lieutenants' managerial decisions were a subject of the litigation. The affidavits of the two lieutenants indicate that they did not complete any

evaluations or offer any opinions of Stanford that Chief Riley considered in reaching his decisions.

. . . Because we conclude that rule 4.2 did not prohibit MR&W from contacting and interviewing the five HUPD employees, we vacate the order of the Superior Court judge and remand the case for the entry of an order denying the defendant's motion for sanctions. . . .

F. Communication with Judges and Jurors

Problem

12-15.   Martyn lost a jury verdict Fox assured her she was certain to win. In an effort to understand what happened, Martyn phoned three jurors at home after the trial and she hopes to catch the trial judge tomorrow morning in chambers to chat about the case. Any problem?

Consider: Model Rules 3.3(d), 3.5
                 Model Code DR 7-108, 7-110
                 Model Code of Judicial Conduct Rule 2.9

In the Matter of Disciplinary Proceedings Against Ragatz
429 N.W.2d 488 (Wis. 1988)

PER CURIAM . . .

In early 1986, Attorney Ragatz, as a member of the Foley and Lardner law firm, undertook to represent the estate of Marie Swerig in a will contest filed in Dane county circuit court by the law firm of Clifford and Relles on behalf of the decedent's son. Soon thereafter, Attorney Ragatz filed an action, entitled Bennin v. Swerig, claiming equitable adjustment with respect to the will contestant's indebtedness to his parents, indebtedness which had been discharged in bankruptcy prior to the commencement of that action. The lawsuit was

intended to reduce the amount the son might receive in the event he prevailed in the will contest.

The Clifford and Relles law firm moved to dismiss the equitable adjustment action and have it declared frivolous, thereby entitling its client to payment of costs and attorney fees. Foley and Lardner agreed to dismiss the action but opposed the motion to hold the action frivolous. Oral argument on the frivolousness issue was made to the court, the Honorable Paulette Siebers presiding, and written briefs were then filed. Bennin remained pending in that court when John Aulik succeeded Judge Siebers to the bench. . . .

In late October or early November, 1986, Judge Aulik met Attorney Ragatz by chance and in a brief conversation told him that the judge's law clerk had stated to the judge that *Bennin* might indeed be frivolous. Attorney Ragatz responded to the judge's remarks, maintaining that the law clerk was in error and that the action was not frivolous. Opposing counsel was not present during that conversation or thereafter advised that it had occurred.

Shortly after that conversation, Attorney Ragatz received by mail a document "in the form of a proposed decision in the *Bennin* case" indicating a ruling that the lawsuit was frivolous. Attorney Ragatz had not solicited that document and correctly assumed it had been sent by Judge Aulik.[1] After Attorney Ragatz ascertained the contents of the document he received from Judge Aulik, he met with Attorney David Reinecke, the attorney in his office who had been assigned to work on *Bennin* under his supervision, and directed him to prepare a response. Attorney Reinecke did so, citing authority and making legal arguments "intended to influence the Court in its decision." Attorney Ragatz reviewed and edited that letter, changing the salutation from "Dear Judge Aulik" to "Dear Jack" and signing it "Tom." Attorney Ragatz also added a paragraph stating that it was unlikely either side would appeal the judge's ruling on the frivolousness issue and pointed out that argument in the will contest was scheduled for November 26, 1986,

and a ruling in that case from the bench or shortly after argument was possible. He wrote that, if successful in the will contest, he believed he could reach a compromise in *Bennin*. Attorney Ragatz then had the letter marked "Confidential" and sent to Judge Aulik, but he did not provide opposing counsel with a copy of it. Moreover, Attorney Ragatz did not intend that opposing counsel be aware of the existence or contents of it.

The related will contest was tried to another branch of Dane county circuit court and in late November, 1986, the court ruled in favor of the will proponent, Foley and Lardner's client. . . .

In late January or early February, 1987, Attorney Reinecke initiated contact with the Clifford and Relles law firm attempting to resolve all pending litigation between the parties. By February 4, 1987 Attorney Ragatz himself attempted to pursue settlement negotiations in those matters. At no time during conversations with that law firm did Attorney Ragatz or Attorney Reinecke disclose the fact that ex parte communications had taken place with the judge or that Attorney Ragatz had submitted legal arguments to the judge in response to the "proposed decision" favoring Attorney Clifford's client.

On February 5, 1987, Attorney Clifford examined the court file in *Bennin* and in it discovered the letter Attorney Ragatz had sent to the judge in November setting forth legal arguments on the frivolousness issue. He asked the judge's clerk for a copy of the letter, but the clerk stated that

---

1. We considered the judge's conduct in this matter in Disc. Proceedings Against Aulik, 429 N.W.2d 759 (Wis. 1988). [Ed. Note: Judge Aulik was suspended from the bench for 90 days for violating a provision substantially the same as current Model Code of Judicial Conduct Rule 2.9 (A).]

she could not provide him one without the judge's authorization, as it had been marked "Confidential." The clerk took the letter to the judge, who was elsewhere in the courthouse, relaying Attorney Clifford's request for a copy. Judge Aulik retained the letter, and when the clerk returned to Attorney Clifford without either the letter or a copy, Attorney Clifford went to see the judge. When Attorney Clifford found him, the judge was engaged in a telephone conversation. Unbeknownst to Attorney Clifford, Judge Aulik was telling Attorney Ragatz that Attorney Clifford had found the letter. However, the judge did not tell Attorney Clifford to whom he had been talking or the subject of the conversation.

Attorney Clifford then returned to his office without having obtained a copy of the Ragatz letter, whereupon he called Attorney Ragatz. During the ensuing conversation, Attorney Ragatz did not reveal the fact that the judge had called him and he denied familiarity with the letter, stating that he would attempt to find a copy of it. The next morning, Attorney Ragatz telephoned the judge and suggested that he schedule a conference with counsel. That request was not made through the judge's clerk, nor was it made in a telephone conference call with Attorney Clifford participating. Judge Aulik told Attorney Ragatz in that conversation that he had already determined to schedule such a conference for that morning.

That conference was held in the judge's chambers, at which time Judge Aulik signed and distributed copies of his decision on the frivolousness issue, which was in favor of Attorney Clifford's client. During the conference, Attorney Clifford renewed his request for a copy of the Ragatz letter,

but Judge Aulik stated that he was no longer in possession of it and Attorney Ragatz said that he had not yet been able to locate a copy.

During the conference in the judge's chambers, both Attorney Ragatz and Judge Aulik urged Attorney Clifford to settle the pending litigation, as Judge Aulik's decision had not awarded a specific amount of attorney fees to the Clifford firm and that issue remained to be addressed. Attorney Clifford stated that he was not comfortable settling the matter until he had received a copy of the Ragatz letter. A file copy was later found in Attorney Ragatz's office and a copy of it was sent to Attorney Clifford. . . .

. . . The referee considered Attorney Ragatz's letter to be "an advocacy piece" which "could have no possible intended purpose but to influence the outcome of litigation." In the referee's view, whether Attorney Ragatz was successful in having the judge decide the matter in favor of his client or in using his knowledge of the proposed decision to gain a favorable settlement did not alter the wrongfulness of the conduct. While on the basis of the character testimony presented on Attorney Ragatz's behalf the referee expressed a willingness to believe that his misconduct was "out of character," she considered it serious nonetheless.

The referee concluded that, by directing the preparation of the letter on the frivolousness issue and causing it to be sent to the judge without disclosing its contents to opposing counsel, Attorney Ragatz violated SCR 20: 4.4(2), which prohibits a lawyer from engaging in ex parte communications on the merits of a case with a judge before whom that case is pending, with exceptions not here relevant.

We adopt the referee's findings of fact and conclusions of law and accept the recommendation for discipline. It is significant that in neither of the two instances of ex parte communication did Attorney Ragatz bring up the subject of the pending litigation. Rather, he was responding to communication from the judge: in one instance, to remarks concerning the judge's law clerk's conclusion on the frivolousness issue; in the other, to a proposed decision on that issue the judge had sent him, apparently without having sent a copy to opposing counsel. Nevertheless, the proscription against ex parte communications between a lawyer and a judge on the merits of a pending adversary proceeding applied here.

Attorney Ragatz had the duty to either refrain from participating in those communications or provide a copy of his response to opposing counsel. His refusal to do so was a serious breach of his professional responsibilities. He permitted ex parte information from the judge on a contested issue and additional ex parte argument to the judge on that issue to influence the outcome of litigation. In so doing, he acted contrary to the objectives of our court system, a system in which he, as attorney, serves an integral role. In effect, his actions denied one party to that litigation a full and fair hearing on the merits of the controversy.

As it violated a fundamental principle of our justice system, Attorney Ragatz's misconduct warrants severe discipline—a suspension of his license to practice law. In determining the appropriate length of that suspension, we take into account the fact that Attorney Ragatz did not initiate the ex parte communications but, rather, responded to communications initiated by the judge and the fact that this is the first time Attorney Ragatz has been the subject of a disciplinary proceeding.

IT IS ORDERED that the license of Thomas G. Ragatz to practice law in Wisconsin is suspended for a period of 60 days, commencing November 7, 1988. . . .

G. Lawyer as Witness

Problem

12-16. Martyn actively negotiates a business deal for Client with Third Party. Two years later, Third Party sues Client to rescind the deal, alleging that Client committed fraud during the negotiations.

  (a) Can Martyn defend Client in the rescission action? Does it matter if Client is now terminally ill? Can Martyn do pretrial work only?

  (b) Can Fox represent Client in the rescission action? Does it matter if Martyn's recollection of the facts might not support Client's position?

  (c) What if Third Party calls Martyn to the stand during the trial? Can Martyn & Fox continue the representation?

Consider: Model Rule 3.7
       Model Code DR 5-101(B), 5-102

D.J. Investment Group, L.L.C. v. DAE/Westbrook, L.L.C.

147 P.3d 414 (Utah 2006)

DURRANT, Justice . . .

BACKGROUND

. . . SunCrest seeks to disqualify Snuffer and his firm, Nelson, Snuffer, Dahle & Poulsen, P.C., from representing D.J. as an advocate at trial based on Snuffer's involvement in a November 16, 2000 settlement agreement ("the Agreement") between SunCrest and D.J. that is now a subject of dispute in the present case.

The Agreement was intended to resolve an October 2000 lawsuit brought by D.J. against SunCrest for an alleged trespass. . . . Snuffer acted as D.J.'s lawyer at all times during these events and has continued to represent D.J. through the present proceedings. The extent of his involvement in negotiating the November 2000 Agreement is disputed.

A short time after the parties signed the Agreement, the dispute between the parties was rekindled. . . . On May 7, 2001, D.J. filed the present lawsuit. It seeks to rescind the Agreement and brings multiple claims against SunCrest.

On February 19, 2004, over two and one-half years after D.J. filed its complaint, SunCrest moved pursuant to rule 3.7 of the Utah Rules of Professional Conduct to disqualify Snuffer from representing D.J. at trial, arguing that Snuffer is a necessary witness in the case. SunCrest alleges that Snuffer played an important role in drafting [a] provision of the Agreement and that his testimony regarding the intent of the parties will be crucial. In turn, D.J.

argues that Snuffer was not present when [the] provision was drafted and disputes Snuffer's value as a witness. . . .

[T]he district court . . . decline[ed] to disqualify Snuffer and his firm from representing D.J. at trial. It reasoned that it need not determine whether Snuffer was likely to be a necessary witness because his disqualification would cause substantial hardship to D.J. and thus fell within the exception provided by rule 3.7(a)(3). After noting that it had weighed the interests of the two parties in accordance with the comments to rule 3.7, the district court stated,

> [T]he parties have conducted a significant amount of discovery in connection with this litigation. Most, if not all, of the key witnesses have been deposed and written discovery has been sent out and answered by both parties. . . . Indeed, the Court file now fills seven exceptionally thick folders and addresses some very complex legal issues. . . . Under these circumstances, the Court doubts that another attorney could be brought up to speed in this matter and recognizes that such an effort would require D.J. to expend an exorbitant amount of time and money.

. . . Ultimately, the district court concluded, "Because disqualifying Denver Snuffer from the case at bar would result in significant financial and tactical prejudice to D.J., and in light of [SunCrest's] untimely filing of its Motion to Disqualify, this Court rejects [SunCrest's] motion and declines to disqualify Denver Snuffer from this litigation." . . .

ANALYSIS . . .

Rule 3.7(a)(3) provides an exception to the advocate-witness prohibition where "disqualification of the lawyer would work substantial hardship on the client," but its plain language does not indicate how much hardship may be imposed on a client before the hardship becomes "substantial." . . .

In applying the substantial hardship exception to the facts of this case, the district court focused its analysis on the fourth and fifth factors mentioned in . . . comment [[4] to Rule 3.7]. The district court first discussed the complexity and length of the litigation, the size of the record filed with the court, and the expense and time that would be required for D.J. to bring new trial counsel into the case—all of which are relevant to the hardship imposed on D.J. The court then discussed SunCrest's culpability in contributing to D.J.'s hardship by failing to file its motion to disqualify Snuffer earlier in the parties' preparations for trial. The district court observed that "[SunCrest's] own pleadings intimate that [SunCrest] has 'reasonably foreseen,' since the initiation of this litigation[,] that Snuffer might be called as a witness in the case at bar." . . .

. . . [T]he district court's interpretation of the factors in the context of this case appears to be quite reasonable.

A delay in filing a motion to disqualify counsel or in notifying opposing counsel that a motion to disqualify is likely raises concerns that the party who delays may be using the motion as a manipulative litigation tactic. This concern naturally enters into the balancing of interests and is addressed, in part, by the "foreseeability" factor from . . . comment [4] to rule 3.7. In Zions First National Bank v. Barbara Jensen Interiors, Inc., 781 P.2d 478, 480-81 (Utah App. 1989), the court of appeals stated that "[a] motion to disqualify counsel must be immediately filed and diligently pursued as soon as the party becomes aware of the basis for disqualification, and it may not be used as a manipulative litigation tactic." . . .

SunCrest claims that the district court erred because it simply assumed that Snuffer's testimony was necessary under rule 3.7 rather than making a specific factual finding to that effect. SunCrest argues that, by doing so, the court inevitably gave too little weight to SunCrest's interests, which depend in part on "the importance and probable tenor of the lawyer's testimony" and "the probability that the lawyer's testimony will conflict with that of other witnesses." We do not agree. The district court advanced judicial economy in the face of a complex factual dispute by making only those findings that were dispositive to its balancing of interests and assuming that other facts favored SunCrest.

Second, SunCrest argues that monetary hardship should never be sufficient to support a finding of "substantial hardship." However, there is nothing in the language of rule 3.7 that requires the potential hardship to the client to be unique or of a nonmonetary nature, only "substantial."

Third, SunCrest argues that the district court misunderstood the scope of the disqualification required by rule 3.7 and that this misunderstanding led the district court to ascribe too much weight to D.J.'s interests. Although SunCrest is likely

correct that rule 3.7 would not require a lawyer to be disqualified from
the case altogether, but only from
acting as trial counsel, the district
court's written decision . . . gives no
indication that the district court
misinterpreted the extent of Snuffer's
disqualification when it weighed the
interests of the parties.

. . . In sum, we hold that the court
of appeals correctly concluded both
that the district court's decision
contained adequate findings to support its substantial hardship determination and that the district court
did not abuse its discretion in finding
that D.J. would suffer substantial
hardship if Snuffer were disqualified.

Part IV

Lawyers and Society: The Profession

Chapter 13

Self-Regulation

Part IV of this book offers us an opportunity to examine additional issues about the structure, function, and regulation of the legal profession itself. In this chapter, we address subjects that raise the question whether the legal professional truly can be considered self-regulating. We begin by looking at restrictions on the ability of lawyers to organize their practices. We then reexamine the inherent powers of courts, this time with a focus on whether the judicial branch can prevent the regulation of lawyers by other branches of government. We move next to consider the impact of federal law on the business practices of lawyers, and end the chapter by considering the current regime of unauthorized practice restrictions that both exclude nonlawyers from legal practice and prevent lawyers from practicing across state boundaries.

A. Restrictions on Practice

Problems

13-1. Martyn & Fox is worried about the firm's new lease obligation. What if the firm says that "any lawyer who leaves the firm and practices within 100 miles must pay the firm his last year's draw"? "Forfeits his pension"? "Owes the firm 25 percent of all fees generated by former Martyn & Fox clients"?

13-2. Martyn & Fox's manufacturing client is fed up with repetitive product liability suits over allegedly defective forklift trucks brought by one law firm over the last decade. "Tell them we'll settle with their latest client for an extra $100,000, if they promise never to sue us again," CEO tells our lawyer. Is this a great idea?

Consider: Model Rules 1.17, 5.6
              Model Code DR 2-108

B. Inherent Power

So far in these materials, we have had at least eight examples of the inherent power of the judicial branch of government:

1. *Bothwell* (inherent power to compel an unwilling lawyer to accept a civil appointment);
2. *Converse* (bar admission);
3. *Busch* (bar discipline);
4. *Chen* (contempt power);
5. *Shaffer Equipment* (sanctions against lawyers for failing to mitigate client perjury);
6. *Eastman Kodak* and *Mitchell* (disqualification);
7. *Mattel* (sanctions for frivolous lawsuit); and
8. *Tutu Wells* (sanctions for discovery abuse).

These are all examples of *positive* inherent powers, that is, power the judicial branch of government finds necessary to perform its constitutionally required functions.

This chapter begins by examining a different but related facet of the inherent powers doctrine: *negative* inherent powers. When a court exercises a negative inherent power, it finds the judicial branch's constitutional power to regulate the bar sufficiently powerful to nullify another branch of government's exercise of a similar power. Courts exercise a negative inherent power when they declare a legislative enactment unconstitutional because it infringes on a judicial prerogative.

Problem

13-3.   The State Trial Lawyer's Association recently retained Martyn & Fox because it wants to do something about recent tort reform legislation that caps contingent fees in state medical malpractice and worker's compensation actions. What advice should Martyn & Fox give its new client?

Consider: Model Rule 1.5
           Model Code DR 2-106

C. Advertising and Solicitation

Problems

13-4.   Can Martyn & Fox advertise their new phone number as "1-800-HonestL"? What about "1-800-PIT-BULL"?

13-5.   Can Martyn & Fox use *www.superlawyers.com* as its URL or website address?

13-6.   Can Martyn & Fox e-mail families of a recent accident to inform them of their need for counsel? Can Fox follow up on e-mail responses with phone calls? Can he follow up using real-time electronic exchanges?

13-7.   Can Martyn & Fox advertise "Law for You" seminars where Martyn touts the advantage of living trusts? Can Martyn hand out business cards to those who attend the seminars? Advertising brochures?

13-8. Can Martyn ask those who attend the seminar to hire the firm to draft a living trust? Does it matter if the seminar is sponsored by a local not-for-profit organization?

13-9. While visiting her father at a local hospital, Martyn warns the person in the next bed not to sign an insurance settlement form until she speaks to a lawyer. Can Martyn & Fox take the case?

Consider: Model Rules 7.1-7.5, 8.5
Model Code DR 2-101-2-105

Florida Bar v. Went For It, Inc.
515 U.S. 618 (1995)

Justice O'CONNOR delivered the opinion of the Court.

Rules of the Florida Bar prohibit personal injury lawyers from sending targeted direct-mail solicitations to victims and their relatives for 30 days following an accident or disaster. This case asks us to consider whether such Rules violate the First and Fourteenth Amendments of the Constitution. We hold that in the circumstances presented here, they do not.

I

In 1989, the Florida Bar (Bar) completed a 2-year study of the effects of lawyer advertising on public opinion. After conducting hearings, commissioning surveys, and reviewing extensive public commentary, the Bar determined that several changes to its advertising rules were in order. In late 1990, the Florida Supreme Court adopted the Bar's proposed amendments with some modifications. Two of these amendments are at issue in this case. Rule 4-7.4(b)(1) provides that "[a] lawyer shall not send, or knowingly permit to be sent, . . . a written communication to a prospective client for the purpose of obtaining professional employment if: (A) the written communication concerns an action for personal injury or wrongful death or otherwise relates to an accident or disaster involving the person to whom the communication is addressed or a relative of that person, unless the accident or disaster occurred more than 30 days prior to the mailing of the communication." Rule 4-7.8(a) states that "[a] lawyer shall not accept referrals from a lawyer referral service unless the service: (1) engages in no communication with the public and in no direct contact with prospective clients in a manner that would violate the Rules of Professional Conduct if the communication or contact were made by the lawyer." Together, these rules create a brief 30-day blackout period after an accident during which lawyers may not, directly or indirectly, single out accident victims or their relatives in order to solicit their business.

In March 1992, G. Stewart McHenry and his wholly owned lawyer referral service, Went For It, Inc., filed this action for declaratory and injunctive relief in the United States District Court for the Middle District of

Florida challenging Rules 4-7.4(b)(1) and 4-7.8 as violative of the First and Fourteenth Amendments to the Constitution. . . .

The District Court . . . entered summary judgment for the plaintiffs, relying on Bates v. State Bar of Ariz., 433 U.S. 350 (1977), and subsequent cases. The Eleventh Circuit affirmed on similar grounds. . . . We granted certiorari, 512 U.S. 1289 (1994), and now reverse.

II

A

Constitutional protection for attorney advertising, and for commercial speech generally, is of recent vintage. Until the mid-1970's, we adhered to the broad rule laid out in Valentine v. Chrestensen, 316 U.S. 52, 54 (1942), that, while the First Amendment guards against government restriction of speech in most contexts, "the Constitution imposes no such restraint on government as respects purely commercial advertising." In 1976, the Court changed course. In Virginia Bd. of Pharmacy v. Virginia Citizens Consumer Council, Inc., 425 U.S. 748, we invalidated a state statute barring pharmacists from advertising prescription drug prices. At issue was speech that involved the idea that "'I will sell you the X prescription drug at the Y price.'" . . . Striking the ban as unconstitutional, we rejected the argument that such speech "is so removed from 'any exposition of ideas,' and from 'truth, science, morality, and arts in general, in its diffusion of liberal sentiments on the administration of Government,' that it lacks all protection."

. . . In Bates v. State Bar of Arizona, *supra,* the Court struck a ban

on price advertising for what it deemed "routine" legal services: "the uncontested divorce, the simple adoption, the uncontested personal bankruptcy, the change of name, and the like." Expressing confidence that legal advertising would only be practicable for such simple, standardized services, the Court rejected the State's proffered justifications for regulation.

Nearly two decades of cases have built upon the foundation laid by *Bates.* It is now well established that lawyer advertising is commercial speech and, as such, is accorded a measure of First Amendment protection. *See, e.g.,* Shapero v. Kentucky Bar Assn., 486 U.S. 466, 472 (1988); Zauderer v. Office of Disciplinary Counsel of Supreme Court of Ohio, 471 U.S. 626, 637 (1985); In re R. M. J., 455 U.S. 191, 199 (1982). Such First Amendment protection, of course, is not absolute. We have always been careful to distinguish commercial speech from speech at the First Amendment's core. "'Commercial speech [enjoys] a limited measure of protection, commensurate with its subordinate position in the scale of First Amendment values,' and is subject to 'modes of regulation that might be impermissible in the realm of noncommercial expression.'" Board of Trustees of State Univ. of N.Y. v. Fox, 492 U.S. 469, 477 (1989), quoting Ohralik v. Ohio State Bar Assn., 436 U.S. 447, 456 (1978). . . .

Mindful of these concerns, we engage in "intermediate" scrutiny of restrictions on commercial speech, analyzing them under the framework set forth in Central Hudson Gas & Elec. Corp. v. Public Serv. Comm'n of N.Y., 447 U.S. 557 (1980). Under *Central Hudson,* the government may freely regulate commercial speech that concerns unlawful activity or is misleading. Commercial speech that falls into neither of those categories, like the advertising at issue here, may be regulated if the government satisfies a test consisting of three related prongs: First, the government must assert a substantial interest in support of its regulation; second, the government must demonstrate that the restriction on commercial speech directly and materially advances that interest; and third, the regulation must be "'narrowly drawn.'"

B

"Unlike rational basis review, the *Central Hudson* standard does not permit us to supplant the precise interests put forward by the State with other suppositions," Edenfield v. Fane, 507 U.S. 761, 768 (1993). The Florida Bar asserts that it has a substantial interest in protecting the privacy and tranquility of personal injury victims and their loved ones against intrusive, unsolicited contact by lawyers. This interest obviously factors into the Bar's paramount (and repeatedly professed) objective of curbing activities that "negatively affect the administration of justice." Because direct mail solicitations in the wake of accidents are perceived by the public as intrusive, the Bar argues, the reputation of the legal profession in the eyes of Floridians has suffered commensurately. The regulation, then, is an effort to protect the flagging reputations of Florida lawyers by preventing them from engaging in conduct that, the Bar maintains, "'is universally regarded as deplorable and beneath common decency because of its intrusion upon the special vulnerability and private grief of victims or their families.'"

We have little trouble crediting the Bar's interest as substantial. . . .

Under *Central Hudson*'s second prong, the State must demonstrate that the challenged regulation "advances the Government's interest 'in a direct and material way.'" . . . That burden, we have explained, "'is not satisfied by mere speculation or conjecture; rather, a governmental body seeking to sustain a restriction on commercial speech must demonstrate that the harms it recites are real and that its restriction will in fact alleviate them to a material degree.'" In *Edenfield*, the Court invalidated a Florida ban on in-person solicitation by certified public accountants (CPA's). We observed that the State Board of Accountancy had "presented no studies that suggest personal solicitation of prospective business clients by CPA's creates the dangers of fraud, overreaching, or compromised independence that the Board claims to fear." Moreover, "the record [did] not disclose any anecdotal evidence, either from Florida or another State, that validated the Board's suppositions." In fact, we concluded that the only evidence in the record tended to "contradict, rather than strengthen, the Board's submissions." Finding nothing in the record to substantiate the State's allegations of harm, we invalidated the regulation.

The direct-mail solicitation regulation before us does not suffer from such infirmities. The Florida Bar submitted a 106-page summary of its 2-year study of lawyer advertising and solicitation to the District Court. That summary contains data—both statistical and anecdotal—supporting the Bar's contentions that the Florida public views direct-mail solicitations in the immediate wake of accidents as an intrusion on privacy that reflects poorly upon the profession. As of June 1989, lawyers mailed 700,000 direct solicitations in Florida annually, 40% of which were aimed at accident victims or their survivors. A survey of Florida adults commissioned by the Bar indicated that Floridians "have negative feelings about those attorneys who use direct mail advertising." Fifty-four percent of the general population surveyed said that contacting persons concerning accidents or similar events is a violation of privacy. A random sampling of persons who received direct-mail advertising from lawyers in 1987 revealed that 45% believed that direct-mail solicitation is "designed to take advantage of gullible or unstable people"; 34% found such tactics "annoying or irritating"; 26% found it "an invasion of your privacy"; and 24% reported that it "made you angry." Significantly, 27% of direct-mail recipients reported that their regard for the legal profession and for the judicial process as a whole was "lower" as a result of receiving the direct mail.

The anecdotal record mustered by the Bar is noteworthy for its breadth and detail. With titles like "Scavenger Lawyers" and "Solicitors Out of Bounds," newspaper editorial pages in Florida have burgeoned with criticism of Florida lawyers who send targeted direct mail to victims shortly after accidents. . . .

In light of this showing . . . we conclude that the Bar has satisfied the second prong of the *Central Hudson* test. . . .

In reaching a contrary conclusion, the Court of Appeals determined that this case was governed squarely by Shapero v. Kentucky Bar Assn., 486 U.S. 466 (1988). Making no mention

of the Bar's study, the court concluded that "'a targeted letter [does not] invade the recipient's privacy any more than does a substantively identical letter mailed at large. The invasion, if any, occurs when the lawyer discovers the recipient's legal affairs, not when he confronts the recipient with the discovery.'" In many cases, the Court of Appeals explained, "this invasion of privacy will involve no more than reading the newspaper."

While some of *Shapero*'s language might be read to support the Court of Appeals' interpretation, *Shapero* differs in several fundamental respects from the case before us. First and foremost, *Shapero*'s treatment of privacy was casual. . . . Second, in contrast to this case, *Shapero* dealt with a broad ban on all direct-mail solicitations, whatever the time frame and whoever the recipient. Finally, the State in *Shapero* assembled no evidence attempting to demonstrate any actual harm caused by targeted direct mail. The Court rejected the State's effort to justify a prophylactic ban on the basis of blanket, untested assertions of undue influence and overreaching. Because the State did not make a privacy-based argument at all, its empirical showing on that issue was similarly infirm. . . .

Here . . . the harm targeted by the Florida Bar cannot be eliminated by a brief journey to the trash can. The purpose of the 30-day targeted direct-mail ban is to forestall the outrage and irritation with the state-licensed legal profession that the practice of direct solicitation only days after accidents has engendered. The Bar is concerned not with citizens' "offense" in the abstract, but with the demonstrable detrimental effects that such "offense" has on the profession it regulates. Moreover, the harm posited by the Bar is as much a function of simple receipt of targeted solicitations within days of accidents as it is a function of the letters' contents. Throwing the letter away shortly after opening it may minimize the latter intrusion, but it does little to combat the former. . . .

Passing to *Central Hudson*'s third prong, we examine the relationship between the Florida Bar's interests and the means chosen to serve them. *See* Board of Trustees of State Univ. of N.Y. v. Fox, 492 U.S. at 480. With respect to this prong, the differences between commercial speech and noncommercial speech are manifest. In *Fox*, we made clear that the "least restrictive means" test has no role in the commercial speech context. "What our decisions require," instead, "is a 'fit' between the legislature's ends and the means chosen to accomplish those ends," "a fit that is not necessarily perfect, but reasonable; that represents not necessarily the single best disposition but one whose scope is 'in proportion to the interest served,' that employs not necessarily the least restrictive means but . . . a means narrowly tailored to achieve the desired objective." . . .

III

Speech by professionals obviously has many dimensions. There are circumstances in which we will accord speech by attorneys on public issues and matters of legal representation the strongest protection our Constitution has to offer. *See, e.g.*, Gentile v. State Bar of Nevada, 501 U.S. 1030 (1991); In re Primus, 436 U.S. 412 (1978). This case, however, concerns pure commercial advertising, for which we have always reserved a lesser degree of protection

under the First Amendment. Particularly because the standards and conduct of state-licensed lawyers have traditionally been subject to extensive regulation by the States, it is all the more appropriate that we limit our scrutiny of state regulations to a level commensurate with the "'subordinate position'" of commercial speech in the scale of First Amendment values.

We believe that the Florida Bar's 30-day restriction on targeted direct-mail solicitation of accident victims and their relatives withstands scrutiny under the three-pronged *Central Hudson* test that we have devised for this context. The Bar has substantial interest both in protecting injured Floridians from invasive conduct by lawyers and in preventing the erosion of confidence in the profession that such repeated invasions have engendered. The Bar's proffered study, unrebutted by respondents below, provides evidence indicating that the harms it targets are far from illusory. The palliative devised by the Bar to address these harms is narrow both in scope and in duration. The Constitution, in our view, requires nothing more.

The judgment of the Court of Appeals, accordingly, is *Reversed*.

Justice KENNEDY, with whom Justice STEVENS, Justice SOUTER, and Justice GINSBURG join, Dissenting

Attorneys who communicate their willingness to assist potential clients are engaged in speech protected by the First and Fourteenth Amendments. That principle has been understood since Bates v. State Bar of Arizona, 433 U.S. 35 (1977). The Court today undercuts this guarantee in an important class of cases and unsettles leading First Amendment precedents, at the expense of those victims most in need of legal assistance. With all respect for the Court, in my view its solicitude for the privacy of victims and its concern for our profession are misplaced and self-defeating, even upon the Court's own premises.

I take it to be uncontroverted that when an accident results in death or injury, it is often urgent at once to investigate the occurrence, identify witnesses, and preserve evidence. Vital interests in speech and expression are, therefore, at stake when by law an attorney cannot direct a letter to the victim or the family explaining this simple fact and offering competent legal assistance. Meanwhile, represented and better informed parties, or parties who have been solicited in ways more sophisticated and indirect, may be at work. Indeed, these parties, either themselves or by their attorneys, investigators, and adjusters, are free to contact the unrepresented persons to gather evidence or offer settlement. This scheme makes little sense. As is often true when the law makes little sense, it is not first principles but their interpretation and application that have gone away.

Although I agree with the Court that the case can be resolved by following the three-part inquiry we have identified to assess restrictions on commercial speech, Central Hudson Gas & Elec. Corp. v. Public Serv. Comm'n of N.Y., 447 U.S. 557, 566 (1980), a preliminary observation is in order. Speech has the capacity to convey complex substance, yielding various insights and interpretations depending upon the identity of the listener or the reader and the context of its transmission. It would oversimplify to say that what we consider here is commercial speech and nothing

more, for in many instances the banned communications may be vital to the recipients' right to petition the courts for redress of grievances. The complex nature of expression is one reason why even so-called commercial speech has become an essential part of the public discourse the First Amendment secures. If our commercial speech rules are to control this case, then, it is imperative to apply them with exacting care and fidelity to our precedents, for what is at stake is the suppression of information and knowledge that transcends the financial self-interests of the speaker. . . .

In the face of these difficulties of logic and precedent, the State and the opinion of the Court turn to a second interest: protecting the reputation and dignity of the legal profession. The argument is, it seems fair to say, that all are demeaned by the crass behavior of a few. . . . While disrespect will arise from an unethical or improper practice, the majority begs a most critical question by assuming that direct-mail solicitations constitute such a practice. The fact is, however, that direct solicitation may serve vital purposes and promote the administration of justice, and to the extent the bar seeks to protect lawyers' reputations by preventing them from engaging in speech some deem offensive, the State is doing nothing more (as amicus the Association of Trial Lawyers of America is at least candid enough to admit) than manipulating the public's opinion by suppressing speech that informs us how the legal system works. The disrespect argument thus proceeds from the very assumption it tries to prove, which is to say that solicitations within 30 days serve no legitimate purpose. This, of course, is censorship pure and simple; and censorship is antithetical to the first principles of free expression. . . .

It is telling that the essential thrust of all the material adduced to justify the State's interest is devoted to the reputational concerns of the Bar. It is not at all clear that this regulation advances the interest of protecting persons who are suffering trauma and grief, and we are cited to no material in the record for that claim. . . .

. . . The accident victims who are prejudiced to vindicate the State's purported desire for more dignity in the legal profession will be the very persons who most need legal advice, for they are the victims who, because they lack education, linguistic ability, or familiarity with the legal system, are unable to seek out legal services. *Cf.* Trainmen v. Virginia ex rel. Virginia State Bar, 377 U.S. 1, 3-4 (1964).

The reasonableness of the State's chosen methods for redressing perceived evils can be evaluated, in part, by a commonsense consideration of other possible means of regulation that have not been tried. Here, the Court neglects the fact that this problem is largely self-policing: Potential clients will not hire lawyers who offend them. And even if a person enters into a contract with an attorney and later regrets it, Florida, like some other States, allows clients to rescind certain contracts with attorneys within a stated time after they are executed. *See, e.g.,* Rules Regulating the Florida Bar, Rule 4-1.5 (Statement of Client's Rights) (effective Jan. 1, 1993). . . . The very fact that some 280,000 direct-mail solicitations are sent to accident victims and their survivors in Florida each year is some indication of the efficacy of this device. . . .

It is most ironic that, for the first time since Bates v. State Bar of Arizona, the Court now orders a major retreat from the constitutional guarantees for commercial speech in order to shield its own profession from public criticism. Obscuring the financial aspect of the legal profession from public discussion through direct-mail solicitation, at the expense of the least sophisticated members of society, is not a laudable constitutional goal. There is no authority for the proposition that the Constitution permits the State to promote the public image of the legal profession by suppressing information about the profession's business aspects. If public respect for the profession erodes because solicitation distorts the idea of the law as most lawyers see it, it must be remembered that real progress begins with more rational speech, not less. . . .

Utah State Bar Ethics Advisory Opinion Committee
*Opinion No. 99-04**

General Issue: What are the ethical considerations that govern a lawyer who wishes to conduct legal seminars; provide legal information to groups of retirement-home residents; host open houses; set up information booths at trade shows; participate in Bar-sponsored question-and-answer programs; or make in-person contacts with prospective clients at the request of their friends or relatives?

---

* Ed. Note: Portions of this opinion have been reordered for clarity.

Summary: This Opinion analyzes and decides a range of related questions that have arisen in connection with lawyers' marketing and solicitation activities. In general, we find that lawyers may make their services known through a variety of methods that do not involve uninvited, one-on-one approaches, discussions or solicitations. On the other hand, where monetary gain is a significant motivation, lawyers may not generally engage in uninvited, direct in-person communications with prospective clients in order to indicate the lawyer's availability to accept professional employment.

Issue No. 1: May a lawyer sponsor and advertise a free seminar on legal issues to be presented in a group setting to members of the public and (i) offer literature or videos discussing the legal topic, either with or without fee, to attendees of the seminar, (ii) give a business card to attendees who request one, and (iii) accept employment to provide legal services to an attendee who initiates a request for professional services?

Opinion: Yes . . .

Rule 7.3(a) prohibits in-person and telephonic communication directed to a specific recipient with whom the lawyer has no family or prior professional relationship soliciting professional employment when a significant motive for the lawyer's doing so is pecuniary gain.

Unlike the rules in some other states, the Utah Rules of Professional Conduct do not define the term "solicit" as this term is used in Rule 7.3(a). We believe that "solicit" in this context means a communication initiated by the lawyer with respect to the lawyer's availability to provide or to accept professional employment.[3] The term "solicit" necessarily includes an offer initiated by the lawyer to provide or to accept professional employment and the unrequested advice or recommendation of the lawyer that the lawyer be engaged to provide professional services.

Rule 7.3 prohibits only solicitations to provide legal services. An invitation to attend a law-related seminar without any communication of the lawyer's availability to accept professional employment is not a solicitation of professional employment. Therefore, a lawyer may invite attendance at a law-related seminar sponsored by the lawyer or by others by telephone or by direct in-person communication, so long as the lawyer does not communicate a message or offer concerning the availability of the lawyer to accept professional employment. If the invitation contains such a message or offer, the invitation must be made by mail and must comply with Rules 7.1, 7.2 and 7.3(b).

A lawyer may appear and make presentations at a law-related seminar provided he does not engage in in-person solicitation prohibited by Rule 7.3(a). Therefore, a lawyer may not communicate the lawyer's availability to provide professional employment, offer to provide or accept professional employment or recommend that the lawyer or the lawyer's firm be employed to provide legal services.[7] The lawyer may distribute or offer in person to each attendee of the

---

3. *See* Cal. R. Prof. Conduct, Rule 1400(B)(1) ("solicitation" is any communication "concerning the availability or professional employment of a member or law firm in which a significant motive is pecuniary gain").

7. Some state bar associations have allowed lawyers to make generalized statements at law-related seminars regarding their availability to accept professional employment. *See, e.g.,* Ohio St. Bar

seminar, with or without fee, literature or video tapes concerning the legal issues addressed at the seminar that may state the lawyer's name, firm affiliation, address and telephone number.[8] Literature or video tapes offered in person to each attendee may not communicate the lawyer's availability to provide or accept professional employment.[9] Therefore, the lawyer's business card, brochures or other endorsements of the lawyer or the lawyer's law firm should not be generally distributed in person to attendees of law-related seminars.[10] If an attendee of a law-related seminar initiates a request to the lawyer to receive literature or video tapes that communicate the lawyer's availability to provide or to accept professional employment, the lawyer may ethically provide such materials to the attendee. Letters and brochures offering the lawyer's legal services may be mailed by the lawyer after the seminar to the attendees of the seminar.[11]

A lawyer may not provide individualized legal advice during the course of a law-related seminar.[12] By doing so, the lawyer would be providing legal services. In response to questions by attendees, the lawyer must endeavor to respond generally so as to create no impression that the lawyer has accepted professional employment on behalf of an attendee. While the lawyer may not initiate a recommendation of the lawyer's engagement by any attendee of the seminar, he may recommend, when appropriate, that an attendee of the seminar consult with a lawyer of the attendee's own choosing.

A lawyer may meet one on one with an attendee of the seminar, when such a contact is initiated by an attendee. In private sessions with attendees, if a request for individualized legal advice is initiated by the attendee, the lawyer may provide individualized legal advice. The lawyer may accept professional employment offered by an attendee of the seminar, either offered privately at the seminar or after the seminar, provided the lawyer has not initiated the offer by engaging in in-person solicitation in violation of Rule 7.3(a).

Some state bar associations have placed additional restrictions on lawyer participants at law-related seminars. The Committee chooses not to adopt these additional restrictions. . . .

Assn., Op. 94-13, ABA\BNA Lawyer's Man. on Prof. Conduct 1001:6862 (Dec. 2, 1994); Ariz. St. Bar Assn., Op. 87-23, ABA\BNA Lawyer's Man. on Prof. Conduct 901:1408 (Oct. 26, 1987). Arizona allows lawyer presenters at law-related seminars to offer to provide legal services with or without fee, if no pressure or coercion is exercised upon attendees at the seminar. We do not agree with these opinions. We believe such conduct constitutes in-person solicitation prohibited by Rule 7.3(a).

8. Ill. St. Bar Assn., Op. 96-01, 1996 WL 466449.

9. Mass. St. Bar Assn., Op. 86-3, ABA\BNA Lawyer's Man. on Prof. Conduct 901:4601 (Nov. 25, 1996); L.A. County Bar Assn., Formal Op. 494.

10. The Committee does not believe that Rule 7.3(a) precludes lawyer sponsors or presenters at law-related seminars from leaving business cards, brochures or other literature communicating the lawyer's availability to accept professional employment at tables where these materials may be picked up by any attendee choosing to do so. However, the lawyer may not in any way promote or encourage attendees in person to pick up such written materials.

11. S.C. St. Bar Assn., Op. 97-05, ABA\BNA Lawyer's Man. on Prof. Conduct 1101:7904 (April 1997).

12. Ohio St. Bar Assn., Op. 94-13, ABA\BNA Lawyer's Man. on Prof. Conduct 1001:6862 (Dec. 2, 1994); Ala. State Bar Assn., Op. 87-119, ABA\BNA Lawyer's Man. on Prof. Conduct 901:1032 (Sept. 29, 1987); Pa. St. Bar Assn., Op. 93-42A, ABA\BNA Lawyer's Man. on Prof. Conduct 1001:7326 (June 2, 1993).

Issue No. 3: If a lawyer purchases booth space at a trade show, may the lawyer (i) discuss legal topics one-on-one with persons who voluntarily visit the lawyer's booth and (ii) accept legal engagements offered by attendees of the trade show who visit the lawyer's booth and engage in one-on-one discussions with the lawyer?

Opinion: Yes, so long as the lawyer complies with the requirements of Rule 7.3(a) and does not engage in in-person solicitation of professional employment. . . .

It is not unethical for a lawyer to purchase booth space at a trade show. So long as advertisements attached to or near the booth space comply with Rules 7.1 and 7.2, it is not unethical for the lawyer to display print advertisements of the lawyer's availability to accept legal employment. This is equivalent to outdoor advertising authorized by Rule 7.2. What distinguishes booth space at a trade show from outdoor advertising is the presence of the lawyer at the booth to engage in one-on-one oral communications with attendees of the trade show.

Other state bar associations are divided on what activities a lawyer at a trade show booth may ethically engage in. . . .

The Committee believes that visits to a lawyer's trade show booth should be likened to visits to a lawyer's office during an advertised open house. Non-clients who attend an advertised lawyer open house do not reasonably anticipate that they will be subjected to in-person solicitation of professional employment.[19] For this reason, it is unethical for lawyers to engage in in-person solicitation of such persons.[20] These occasions afford the lawyer the opportunity to meet prospective clients and for prospective clients to meet the lawyer. The lawyer may discuss legal topics with the attendees and may, when the request is initiated by the prospective client, privately provide individualized legal advice.[21] . . .

The Committee believes that the same analysis applies to trade-show booths. The lawyer may get acquainted with those who visit the booth, may discuss legal topics generally and may, when the request is initiated by the prospective client, privately provide individualized legal advice. The lawyer may not initiate in-person communications about the lawyer's availability to accept professional employment. The lawyer may not in person distribute business cards, brochures or other literature communicating the lawyer's availability to accept professional employment unless the person visiting the booth initiates the request for this information. So long as the lawyer does not engage in

---

19. This Opinion assumes that the invitation to a lawyer's open house does not specifically invite the public to attend for the purpose of being solicited to provide professional employment to the lawyer. The Committee believes that non-clients who attend an open house in response to an invitation that states that the non-clients will be solicited have, in turn, invited the in-person solicitation. It would, therefore, not be unethical for a lawyer to make an in-person solicitation to such a person.

20. N.C. St. Bar Assn., Op. 146, 1992 WL 753128 (Jan. 15, 1993); Or. St. Bar Assn., Op. 1991-35, 1991 WL 279176 (July, 1991); *see also* R.I. St. Bar Assn., Op. 89-14, ABA\BNA Lawyer's Man. on Prof. Conduct 901:7805 (July 20, 1989) (lawyer may attend social gatherings to meet prospective clients, but may not engage in in-person solicitation).

21. When providing individualized legal advice, the lawyer must comply with all Rules of Professional Conduct, including the conflict-of-interest Rules 1.7, 1.9 and 1.10 and Rule 1.6 concerning client confidences.

in-person solicitation in violation of Rule 7.3(a), he is free to accept professional employment offered by those who visit the booth.

Issue No. 4: May a lawyer volunteer to set up a table in a common area of a retirement or senior center in order to meet one on one to discuss legal topics with residents of the center who voluntarily visit the lawyer's table, and may the lawyer accept legal engagements proposed by residents of the center who visit the lawyer's table and voluntarily engage in one-on-one discussions of legal issues with the lawyer?

Opinion: Yes, so long as the lawyer complies with the requirements of Rule 7.3(a). . . .

The Committee believes that a table set up by a lawyer at a retirement or senior center for the purpose of meeting with residents of the center who voluntarily visit the lawyer's table to discuss legal topics is indistinguishable from a lawyer's open house or a booth set up by a lawyer at a trade show. The analysis of this issue is the same as the analysis of Issue No. 3, and the ethical restraints on the lawyer's conduct are the same as the restraints on a lawyer's holding an open house or setting up a trade-show booth.

Issue No. 5: May a lawyer volunteer to provide one-on-one consultations with residents of a retirement or senior center concerning legal topics, initiate one-on-one in-person communications with residents of the center in their rooms or common areas to discuss their legal questions or concerns, and accept legal engagements proposed by such residents who discuss legal topics one on one with the lawyer?

Opinion: No. . . .

The lawyer's conduct in initiating uninvited communications with residents of the senior center, whether in their rooms or in common areas of the center, is distinguishable from establishing a table in a common area of the senior center. When the lawyer initiates the contact, the resident is subjected to the uninvited presence of the lawyer in a one-on-one encounter. This situation is "fraught with the possibility of undue influence, intimidation and over-reaching."[23] The residents of the senior center are subjected to "the private importuning of a trained advocate, in a direct interpersonal encounter" which was wholly uninvited by the resident. Because the communications are private and oral and not visible or otherwise open to public scrutiny, it is nearly impossible for the lawyer's conduct to be regulated. The potential for abuse inherent in this situation justifies a prophylactic prohibition of the acceptance of legal representation offered by the residents of the senior center under these circumstances, unless the representation is *pro bono*.[25]

It may be argued that such uninvited one-on-one contact to discuss legal topics of interest to the residents of the senior center is not solicitation unless the lawyer communicates his availability to accept legal employment. . . . While

---

23. Rule 7.3 cmt.
25. Ohralik v. Ohio State Bar, 436 U.S. 447 (1978) (prophylactic rule against in-person solicitation does not violate the rights of free expression afforded by the First and Fourteenth Amendments of the United States Constitution even in the absence of a showing of any specific harm to the prospective clients). *Accord* Shapero v. Kentucky Bar Assn., 486 U.S. 466 (1988). If the representations are accepted on a *pro bono* basis, then Rule 7.3(a) would not be applicable. The primary motive of the lawyer would not be pecuniary gain.

the one-on-one communications at the lawyer open house, lawyer trade-show booth and discussion table are also fraught with the danger of undue influence, intimidation and over reaching, and are also private and not open to public scrutiny, they are at least invited communications. . . .

In Shapero v. Kentucky Bar Association, the United States Supreme Court distinguished solicitation by targeted mail from in-person solicitation, stating: "In assessing the potential for over reaching and undue influence, the mode of communication makes all the difference." We agree, but further note that uninvited one-on-one communication is fraught with the most danger of abuse. It is this form of communication to attract professional employment that Rule 7.3(a) was intended to prevent. A lawyer may not accept professional employment resulting from such uninvited one-on-one contacts, unless the representation is solicited and provided on a pro bono basis.

Issue No. 6: If a lawyer volunteers to answer questions of members of the public participating in a Utah State Bar-sponsored one-on-one question-and-answer session, such as a Bar-sponsored telethon (in-person telephonic contact) or the Bar-sponsored Tuesday Night Bar (face-to-face contact), may the lawyer provide to a member of the public his name and telephone number during the Bar-sponsored communication and accept professional employment for a fee offered by a member of the public during or after the Bar-sponsored communication?

Opinion: No. . . .

Bar-sponsored telethons and the "Tuesday Night Bar" result in in-person communications by members of the public with lawyers similar to the lawyer open house, trade-show booth and discussion table communications discussed earlier in this Opinion. There is, however, one important distinction. These events are sponsored and advertised to the public by the Bar. Lawyers volunteering to participate in these Bar-sponsored programs are, therefore, subject to the Bar's rules, regulations and policies regarding the program, in addition to the Utah Rules of Professional Conduct.

Each participant in the Tuesday Night Bar Program receives a policy statement which describes the program as being designed to provide preliminary counseling and general legal information and, if appropriate, referral to a lawyer using the Bar's Lawyer Referral Service. The policy statement further states: "[The program] is not intended to create an on-going attorney-client relationship between the participants. . . . Attorneys shall not take clients and\or cases from the Program unless the attorney does so on a pro bono basis." The Bar has also informally indicated it intends to apply a similar policy statement regarding Bar-sponsored telethons. . . .

If there were no Bar policy preventing a lawyer participant from accepting professional employment on a for-fee basis from members of the public with whom the lawyer has made contact during a Bar-sponsored program, the lawyer would be governed by the same limitations as discussed previously in this Opinion with respect to communications at lawyer open houses, trade-show booths and discussion tables.

Issue No. 7: If a relative or close friend of a prospective client requests that the lawyer telephone the prospective client to offer to provide legal representation, is it ethical for the lawyer to telephone the prospective client and to offer to provide legal representation?

Opinion: Generally no, unless the relative or friend of the prospective client requesting the lawyer to make the contact is the agent of the prospective client. . . .

Rule 7.3(a) states in part: "A lawyer may not solicit in person, professional employment from a prospective client with whom the lawyer has no family or prior professional relationship, when a significant motive for the lawyer's doing so is the lawyer's pecuniary gain." Thus, the lawyer may not generally communicate in person with the prospective client and offer to provide legal services, even if the lawyer has been requested by a friend or close relative of a prospective client to make the communication.[27]

However, if the person requesting the lawyer to contact the prospective client is the prospective client's agent, . . . the in-person contact has been invited by the prospective client. To satisfy this requirement, a lawyer must make an objective, reasonable good-faith determination that the person is actually the agent of the prospective client.

In these circumstances, it would be best for the lawyer to advise the person referring the prospective client that the prospective client should contact the lawyer and request the lawyer's professional services. Otherwise, the lawyer runs the risk that the prospective client's friend or family member is not authorized by the prospective client to request the lawyer's direct in-person communication with the prospective client.

▪ The Bounds of the Law:
The Constitution

In previous notes, we have examined legal constraints that limit a lawyer's advocacy on behalf of a client, such as the law of fraud, the criminal law, court orders, and procedural sanctions. *Went For It* illustrates another legal boundary. There, lawyers claimed that the federal or state constitution created a decisive limit on the law governing lawyers itself. They argued that constitutional provisions protected their advocacy on behalf of clients, and prevented state regulation or limitation of lawyer behavior.

The First Amendment: Lawyer Speech and Prospective Clients

The result in *Went For It* belies the vitality of the First Amendment as a means of overturning state regulation of lawyer speech. In a series of cases over the past four decades, the Supreme Court has forced the rewriting of traditional rules that

---

27. Norris v. Ala. St. Bar, 582 So. 2d 1034 (Ala. 1991) (lawyer suspended from practice for two years after delivering to a funeral home a funeral wreath and a letter addressed to the widow offering assistance after having received an anonymous telephone call from someone purporting to be a friend of the widow stating that she required legal services and did not have sufficient funds for a funeral wreath); Spence, Payne, Masington & Grossman, P.A. v. Gerson, 483 So. 2d 775 (Fla. App. 1986) (unethical in-person solicitation for a lawyer to send an investigator to obtain a retainer agreement from a widow after receiving a telephone call from a client of the lawyer and a close friend of the widow requesting that the lawyer offer to provide professional services to the widow).

prevented advertising and solicitation by applying the First Amendment to lawyer speech. In doing so, the Court has labeled some lawyer speech "political," some "commercial," and some as "unprotected." The following chart categorizes these cases and the current professional rules that these cases have shaped.

FIRST AMENDMENT REGULATION OF LAWYER ADVERTISING AND SOLICITATION

Level of Constitutional protection	Traditional First Amendment Protection	Commercial Speech (intermediate level scrutiny)	Unprotected Speech (no Constitutional protection)
Kind of speech	Political speech, speech that seeks access to the courts	Speech that proposes a commercial transaction	Speech that proposes an illegal activity; Misleading commercial speech
Governmental interest necessary to justify regulation	Compelling govt. interest; Regulation must be the least restrictive means to promote governmental interest (no prior restraints)	Substantial govt. interest; Speech restriction must directly and materially advance govt. interest and regulation must be narrowly drawn (prior restraints allowed)	Govt. interest presumed; Complete ban allowed
Cases	NAACP v. Button, 371 U.S. 415 (1963); Bhd. of R.R. Trainmen v. Va., 377 U.S. 1 (1964); United Mine Workers v. Ill. St. Bar Assn., 389 U.S. 217 (1967); United Trans. Union v. St. Bar of Mich., 401 U.S. 576 (1971); In re Primus, 436 U.S. 412 (1978)	Bates v. St. Bar. of Ariz., 433 U.S. 350 (1977); In re RMJ, 455 U.S. 191 (1982); Zauderer v. Disc. Counsel of S. Ct. of Ohio, 471 U.S. 626 (1985); Shapero v. Ky. Bar Assn., 486 U.S. 466 (1988); Peel v. Atty. Registration & Disc. Commn., 496 U.S. 91 (1990); Fla. Bar v. Went For It, Inc. 515 U.S. 618 (1995)	Ohralik v. Ohio St. Bar Assn., 436 U.S. 447 (1978)
Challenged Rules	MR 7.3; DR 2-103, 2-104	MR 7.1, 7.2, 7.4; DR 2-101, 102, 105	MR 7.3(a); DR 2-103, 104

Political Speech   The second column of the chart includes cases in which the Supreme Court has afforded lawyer speech the highest level of First Amendment protection. Here, the Court allows an overbreadth analysis and requires a compelling interest to justify the restriction on speech. In addition, the regulation must be the least restrictive means to promote the governmental interest, and, to prevent chilling fragile First Amendment interests, no prior restraints are allowed.

In *Button*, for example, the court overturned a Virginia antisolicitation regulation that had been applied to prohibit NAACP lawyers from general solicitation of persons to serve as plaintiffs in constitutional challenges by the NAACP to segregated education. The Court held that the regulation violated the NAACP's First and Fourteenth Amendment rights by "unduly inhibiting protected freedoms of expression and association." It characterized the NAACP's litigation activity as "political expression," which "may well be the sole practicable avenue open to a minority to petition for redress of grievances."[1]

In the next three cases, the court applied the same level of constitutional protection to the activities of labor unions that sought to provide low cost legal services to their members. These decisions culminated with the statement in *United Transportation Union*: "the common thread running through our decisions in NAACP v. Button, Trainmen, and United Mine Workers is that collective activity undertaken to obtain meaningful access to the courts is a fundamental right within the protection of the First Amendment."[2]

In *Primus*, the Court returned to a distinction it had first made in *Button* between private pecuniary gain and political expression to overturn an attempt by South Carolina to prohibit an ACLU lawyer from soliciting civil rights plaintiffs. The Court found that the ACLU, like the NAACP, used litigation as a "form of political expression," not as a means to resolve private differences. Responding to the state's argument that the ACLU's policy of requesting attorney's fees took the case outside of political expression, the Court found that such a possibility was not sufficient to equate the work of these lawyers "with that group that exist for the primary purpose of financial gain through the recovery of counsel fees."[3]

Commercial Speech The third column of the chart includes a line of cases in which commercial, rather than political, speech is at stake. Here, the speech proposes a purely commercial transaction, such as "I will sell you the X prescription drug at Y price."[4] *Went For It* indicates that the First Amendment also protects commercial speech, but common sense differences between political and commercial speech justify a different level of constitutional scrutiny. Thus, a substantial, rather than compelling, governmental interest must be shown to uphold the regulation. Further, the regulation need not be the least restrictive means of promoting the governmental interest so long as it directly and materially advances the interest and is narrowly drawn. Prior restraints (such as requiring a bar ethics opinion before releasing an advertisement)[5] are allowed. Further, to prevent fraud, states can require lawyers to add disclaimers to their communications, such as "Advertising Material."[6] Finally, constitutional challenges to professional advertising can be made only as applied to the conduct of the person regulated. An overbreadth analysis is not available to challenge every

1. NAACP v. Button, 371 U.S. 415, 429-430 (1963).
2. United Transp. Union v. St. Bar of Mich., 401 U.S. 576, 585 (1971).
3. In re Primus, 436 U.S. 412, 428, 431 (1978).
4. Va. Pharm. Bd. v. Va. Consumer Council, 425 U.S. 748, 761 (1976).
5. C. Hudson Gas & Elec. Corp. v. Pub. Serv. Commn. of N.Y., 447 U.S. 557, 571 (1980).
6. MR 7.3(c).

conceivable application of the regulation because the commercial motive makes such speech likely to recur.[7]

This extensive line of cases means that states cannot completely prohibit advertising, but can regulate it to prevent false, fraudulent, or misleading statements. *RMJ* and *Shapero* made clear that "advertising" includes targeted mail as well as mass media communications. *Peel* addressed claims of certification in a letterhead, holding that states could not categorically ban lawyers from honestly advertising a certification granted by a national organization, but were free to prevent potentially misleading certifications from private organizations by creating official state specialty designations.[8] In the context of a partial, time-based prohibition, *Went For It* adds the protection of personal privacy and, where empirical evidence exists, the reputation of the profession as justifiable state interests.

Unprotected Speech   Despite its extensive application of the First Amendment to lawyer speech, the Supreme Court has characterized one form of lawyer speech—in-person solicitation for pecuniary gain—as unprotected by the First Amendment. The right column of the chart summarizes this decision, referred to in *Went For It*. When lawyers seek employment by speaking face to face with potential clients, the state may presume harm and prohibit speech in order to prevent it. In *Ohralik*, the court upheld a complete ban on in-person solicitation by lawyers, finding that that type of speech was a subordinate part of a purely commercial transaction. Unlike media advertising, the pressure of in-person solicitation often demands an immediate response, not leaving the recipient free to evaluate the speech. The evils of fraud, undue influence, intimidation, and overreaching in such a circumstance can be presumed as so likely to occur that the state can prohibit all in-person solicitation by lawyers to prevent them. No actual injury need be shown to justify a complete ban on speech in this circumstance.[9]

Although it is now clear that the First Amendment applies to lawyer advertising and solicitation, some issues remained unresolved. The Supreme Court has not yet addressed radio and television or e-mail, but the Model Rules include them in the advertising category.[10] On the other hand, because it demands a more immediate response, real-time electronic or telephone contact is included in the ban on in-person solicitation in Model Rule 7.3.[11]

Other First Amendment Issues

The First Amendment also has been instrumental in a number of other challenges to regulations of lawyer speech, including restrictions on pretrial publicity, criticism of judges, the use of mandatory bar dues, and gag rules on the litigation activity of legal services lawyers.

Model Rule 3.6, which governs trial publicity, has been rewritten following the Supreme Court's decision in Gentile v. St. Bar of Nevada.[12] There, the Court

---

7. Bates v. St. Bar of Ariz., 433 U.S. 350, 380-381 (1977).
8. MR 7.4 represents the ABA response to *Peel*.
9. Ohralik v. Ohio St. Bar Assn., 436 U.S. 447, 466 (1978).
10. MR 7.2.
11. MR 7.3; Fla. St. Bar Assn., Op. A-00-1 (2000).
12. 501 U.S. 1030 (1991).

unanimously upheld the "substantial likelihood of material prejudice" test in the rule as "designed to protect the integrity and fairness of a state's judicial system." At the same time, a majority of the Court found that part of the rule was void for vagueness as applied to Gentile, because its provisions failed to give him adequate warning or a principle for determining "when his remarks pass from the safe harbor of the general to the forbidden sea of the elaborated." As a result, the ABA rewrote Model Rule 3.6 in 1994 to eliminate the qualifying terms the Court found misleading and to authorize a lawyer to respond to adverse publicity initiated by others.

Free speech also collides with the integrity and fairness of the judicial system when lawyers criticize judges. Model Rule 8.2 recognizes that judges are public officials by restating the First Amendment standard required in defamation cases: a lawyer can be disciplined only for making a false statement (not opinion) about a judge if he or she knows the statement is false or acts in reckless disregard of the truth.[13] Several courts have held that an isolated incident of rude comment should not be enough to warrant discipline under this or more general provisions such as Model Rule 8.4(d) (conduct prejudicial to the administration of justice).[14] Untrue statements have resulted in discipline, however, where the criticism could have been investigated first, or raised with judicial disciplinary authorities rather than in court proceedings or with the press.[15] Similarly, a number of courts have upheld discipline where lawyers have made repeated untrue and derogatory statements about judges.[16]

The First Amendment further has played a role in reining in the power of state bar associations that use mandatory dues structures to fund not only admission and discipline, but also to promote political viewpoints with which individual members may disagree. In Keller v. St. Bar of Cal., the Supreme Court held that the State Bar's compulsory dues could only be used to fund activities "justified by the State's interest in regulating the legal profession and improving the quality of legal services."[17] Although the precise line may not be easy to ascertain, ideological activities such as lobbying for or against state legislation or funding state initiatives not reasonably related to legitimate state goals violates the First Amendment.[18] Subsequent cases have determined that blanket challenges to lobbying efforts cannot be maintained,[19] and that bar dues

---

13. For a discussion of the constitutional application of this rule, *see* In re Shearin, 765 A.2d 930, 937-938 (Del. 2000); In re Palmisano, 70 F.3d 483, 487-488 (7th Cir. 1995); Standing Comm. on Disc. v. Yagman, 55 F.3d 1430, 1438 (9th Cir. 1995).

14. *See, e.g.*, In re Snyder, 472 U.S. 634 (1985); St. Bar v. Semann, 508 S.W.2d 429 (Tex. Civ. App. 1974); Justices of App. Div. v. Erdmann, 301 N.E.2d 426 (N.Y. 1973).

15. *See, e.g.*, In re Becker, 620 N.E.2d 691 (Ind. 1993); Matter of Holtzman, 577 N.E.2d 30 (N.Y. 1991), *cert. denied*, 502 U.S. 1009 (1991); In re Lacey, 283 N.W.2d 250 (S.D. 1979).

16. *See, e.g.*, Comm. on Leg. Ethics of W. Va. v. Farber, 408 S.E.2d 274 (W. Va. 1991), *cert. denied*, 502 U.S. 1073 (1992); St. ex rel. Neb. Bar Assn. v. Michaelis, 316 N.W.2d 46 (Neb. 1982), *cert. denied and appeal dismissed*, 459 U.S. 804 (1982).

17. 496 U.S. 1, 13-14 (1990).

18. Morrow v. St. Bar of Cal., 188 F.3d 1174 (9th Cir. 1999), *cert. denied*, 528 U.S. 1156 (2000) (requiring membership in State Bar that takes positions on public issues is not unconstitutional so long as members who dissent can obtain a refund of the portion of their mandatory dues used for that purpose).

19. Popejoy v. N.M. Bd. of Bar Commrs., 887 F. Supp. 1422 (D.N.M. 1995).

may fund public relations activities that advance the understanding of law,[20] or *pro bono* legal services to military reservists.[21] Funding for non-ideological activities such as the provision of office space for state bar employees,[22] or awarding journalists for writing on law-related topics also have been upheld.[23] A state bar also has been allowed to fund a campaign advocating voter approval of two initiatives concerning the merit selection and retention of state judges because it related to improvement of the function of the judicial system.[24] In addition, a state bar was allowed to fund lobbying activities concerning the regulation and discipline of lawyers, client trust accounts, and the availability of legal services.[25] The same jurisdiction was barred, however, from using dues to pay for lobbying on child welfare or family wellness matters.[26]

Finally, in Legal Services Corp. v. Velazquez, the Supreme Court invalidated a gag rule that restricted Legal Service Corporation lawyers from challenging existing welfare laws when representing clients seeking welfare benefits.[27] The court held that the LCS Act funded constitutionally protected expression, including welfare representation, and that this restriction on speech was an attempt to "exclude from litigation those arguments and theories Congress finds unacceptable but which by their nature are within the province of the courts to consider."[28] In invalidating the restriction, the Court relied not only on the First Amendment, but also on constitutional separation of powers principles. The legislatively imposed restriction on Legal Services lawyers threatened "serious impairment of the judicial function" because it prohibited "expression upon which the courts must depend for the proper exercise of the judicial power."[29]

Beyond the First Amendment

Other fundamental constitutional provisions have played a role in shaping the legal regulation of lawyers. For example, the state separation of powers doctrine that parallels the federal law relied on in *Velazquez* has provided the basis for overturning legislative intrusions on judicial regulation of lawyers.[30] We have

---

20. Gardner v. St. Bar of Nev., 284 F.3d 1040 (9th Cir. 2002).
21. *Popejoy, supra* note 19.
22. *Id.*
23. Thiel v. St. Bar of Wis., 94 F.3d 399 (7th Cir. 1996).
24. Alper v. Fla. Bar, 771 So. 2d 523 (Fla. 2000).
25. Fla. Bar re Schwarz, 552 So. 2d 1094 (Fla. 1989).
26. Fla. Bar re Frankel, 581 So. 2d 1294 (Fla. 1991).
27. 531 U.S. 533 (2001).
28. *Id.* at 546.
29. *Id.* at 545.
30. *See, e.g.*, Gmerek v. St. Ethics Commn., 807 A.2d 812 (Pa. 2002) (evenly divided court upheld trial court's decision that lobbying disclosure act controlled the conduct of lawyer when rendering legal services and therefore infringed on the supreme court's exclusive jurisdiction to regulate lawyers); Irwin v. Surdyk's Liquor, 599 N.W.2d 132 (Minn. 1999) (legislative amendment invalid because it set a "maximum permissible fee" in workers' compensation cases and repealed a prior provision that had allowed judicial review of lawyer's fees and departure from a statutory contingent fee formula in cases involving medical benefits); Cripe v. Leiter, 703 N.E. 2d 100 (Ill. 1998) (Consumer Fraud Act valid, but did not apply to a lawyer's billing of a client for legal services); Succession of Wallace, 574 So. 2d 348 (La. 1991) (statute that provided that an estate executor could discharge a lawyer designated in the testator's will "only for just cause" invalid because it directly conflicted with MR1.16, which grants clients the right to discharge lawyers for any reason); St. of Wis. ex rel. Feidler v. Wis. Senate, 454 N.W.2d 770 (Wis. 1990) (While

also seen how the Supreme Court has interpreted the Privileges and Immunities Clause to overturn residency requirements that limit bar admission.[31]

The Supremacy Clause The Supremacy Clause is the focus of litigation when federal law clearly preempts state provisions to the contrary. For example, a lawyer licensed to practice before the United States Patent Office successfully opposed a state's claim that he was engaged in the unauthorized practice of law. The Supreme Court held that the state unauthorized practice law must yield to incompatible federal legislation, and that the Commissioner of Patents was well within his statutory authority to license nonlawyer patent practitioners.[32] The Supremacy Clause also has played a role in several bankruptcy cases where lawyers have discharged debts such as loans or malpractice judgments that later become relevant in bar admission or disciplinary proceedings. Several state courts have held that the Supremacy Clause prevents the imposition of conditions on admission or readmission that require a lawyer to repay debts discharged in bankruptcy.[33] Others have avoided the Supremacy Clause problem by finding that the debt was not the sole cause for the denial of bar admission,[34] or the repayment was for some purpose other than penalizing the lawyer for discharging a debt, such as protecting the public.[35]

Although Congress has the power to preempt contrary state legislation, in order for the Supremacy Clause to apply, it must do so explicitly. So, for example, when the Department of Justice relied on a general federal "housekeeping statute" that authorizes executive department officials to set up offices and file governmental documents to justify a substantive regulation of lawyer conduct, the Eighth Circuit held that the Department lacked "valid statutory authority" to exempt its lawyers from state professional regulation.[36] Shortly thereafter, Congress passed the McDade Amendment, which specifically requires federal prosecutors to abide by state ethics rules.[37]

Due Process In cases where lawyers have been admitted to the bar and have a vested right to practice law, courts impose procedural due process requirements on limitations of the right. *Tutu Wells*, for example, illustrates that courts must afford lawyers procedural due process rights when considering professional discipline. We also considered the contours of these guarantees in detail in

---

legislature may prescribe minimum standards for eligibility of persons to practice law, judicial branch has exclusive right to regulate the activities of lawyers following their admission to practice. Legislative CLE requirement for lawyers prior to their appointment as Guardians Ad Litem invalid).

31. *See* Lawyers and Other Professionals: *Professional Licensure, supra* p. 29.

32. Sperry v. Fla. ex rel. Fla. Bar, 373 U.S. 379 (1963).

33. *See, e.g.,* Cleveland Bar Assn. v. Gay, 763 N.E.2d 585 (Ohio 2002); In re Batali, 657 P.2d 775 (Wash. 1983).

34. In re Gahan, 279 N.W.2d 826 (Minn. 1979).

35. *See, e.g.,* People v. Sullivan, 802 P.2d 1091 (Colo. 1990); Brookman v. St. Bar of Cal., 760 P.2d 1023 (Cal. 1988).

36. United States ex rel. O'Keefe v. McDonnell Douglas Corp., 132 F.3d 1252, 1257 (8th Cir. 1998).

37. 28 U.S.C. §530B (2006). *See, e.g.,* MR 3.8.

Chapter 2.[38] In Chapter 7, we encountered similar due process guarantees when lawyers or others are held in criminal contempt.[39]

In cases where lawyers seek admission, however, courts are much less likely to impose procedural due process guarantees. So, for example, when a lawyer who is not admitted in a jurisdiction seeks leave of a court for admission *pro hac vice*, the Supreme Court has held that a lawyer has no right to appear and need not be afforded any procedural due process if the motion to appear is denied.[40] Some jurisdictions have created more exacting standards that require a judge to provide substantial justifications for refusing *pro hac vice* admission.[41] In criminal cases where the rights of the defendant rather than the interests of the lawyer are at stake, many courts are more likely to require a judge to provide a legitimate reason why the defendant should be deprived of his choice of counsel,[42] but it is enough if the judge provides notice and an opportunity to show cause why the admission should not be allowed.[43]

Constitutional Power and Client Advocacy

It should come as no surprise that the Constitution, which provides the framework for all law, also has shaped the law governing lawyers. Other notes in this series entitled "The Bounds of the Law" have discussed the limits created by general law that restrict a lawyer's ability to advocate on behalf of a client. In this note, by contrast, we have seen lawyers who seek to expand their right to advocate on behalf of their clients by invoking constitutional rights to restrict the application of other general law, such as professional rules, court procedures, or legislative enactments. In pursuing your law practice, you should be alert to other occasions when state or federal constitutional rights may help you promote legitimate client advocacy.

D. Referrals

Problem

13-10.   Martyn tells Fox she has joined a business referral club. "For only $350, per year, I get to be the only lawyer member of the group along with one each of various other professionals and business people. All I have to do is attend weekly meetings, give 60-second

---

38. *See* Law Governing Lawyers: *Professional Discipline, supra* p. 47.
39. The Bounds of the Law: *Court Orders, supra* p. 211.
40. Leis v. Flynt, 439 U.S. 438 (1979). A California court rule prohibiting *pro hac vice* admission by California residents also has withstood a privileges and immunities challenge, because the state's requirement that residents take and pass the bar examination simply ensures that all residents are treated alike. Paciulan v. George, 229 F.3d 1226 (9th Cir. 2000), *cert. denied*, 531 U. S. 1077 (2001).
41. *See, e.g.*, St. ex rel. H.K. Porter Co. v. White, 386 S.E.2d 25 (W. Va. 1989); Hahn v. Boeing Co., 621 P.2d 1263 (Wash. 1980).
42. *See, e.g.*, Panzardi-Alvarez v. United States, 879 F.2d 975, 980 (1st Cir. 1989); Fuller v. Diesslin, 868 F.2d 604, 607-608 (3d Cir. 1989); *cert. denied sub nom.* Parretti v. Fuller, 493 U.S. 873 (1989); Herrmann v. Summer Plaza Corp., 513 A.2d 1211, 1214 (Conn. 1986).
43. *See, e.g.*, United States v. Collins, 920 F.2d 619 (10th Cir. 1990), *cert. denied*, 500 U.S. 920 (1991).

"commercials" to the group, and provide referrals to other members." Fox checks the Club's website, which says:

Joining us is like having dozens of sales people working for you because all of our members carry several copies of your business card around with them. When they meet someone who could use your products or services, they hand out your card and recommend you. It's as simple as that!

Consider: Model Rules 5.4, 7.2
            Model Code Canon 3

District of Columbia
Opinion 329 (2005)

Inquiry

The inquirer, a District of Columbia non-profit entity, would like to assist day laborers in pursuing small workers' compensation claims. The non-profit has learned from experience that the day laborers have a difficult time finding competent counsel who are willing to provide representation in these types of cases. To help facilitate adequate representation, the non-profit proposes to pay a qualified attorney a $10,000 annual retainer for handling these matters; allow the attorney to take a 10 percent contingency fee from client awards; and then require the attorney to pay the non-profit the first $10,000 he receives in contingent fees each year to permit it to recoup its out-of-pocket retainer costs. Other than recouping out-of-pocket costs, the financial arrangement the non-profit has with the attorney is not in any way tied to the amount of fees collected by the attorney in the representation of a particular client. The non-profit has asked the Committee to opine whether this arrangement complies with the D.C. Rules of Professional Conduct. The Committee concludes that it does for the reasons set forth below.

Discussion

Rule 5.4(a) of the D.C. Rules states that "a lawyer or law firm shall not share legal fees with a non-lawyer" except in certain narrow circumstances not pertinent to this inquiry. This provision could be interpreted to preclude a lawyer from ever sharing a portion of the fees that the lawyer receives from a client with an organization that made the referral. [Model Rule 7.2 (b)(2)] and Comment [6], however, indicate otherwise. . . .

There appears to be an inherent conflict, therefore, between the flat prohibition on fee-sharing between lawyers and non-lawyers found in Rule 5.4 and the implied acceptance of sharing fees with non-lawyers found in Rule [7.2]. Numerous ethics opinions here and in other jurisdictions have examined this conflict to determine whether fee-sharing arrangements are permitted under certain circumstances, . . . and have . . . focused on two . . . policy considerations: 1) whether a proposed arrangement would interfere with a lawyer's independent judgment; and 2) whether refusing to permit the arrangement would result in fewer legal resources being available for those in need of them.

[In Opinion 307 (2001), this Committee opined] that a lawyer may "participate in a federal government referral service that negotiates contracts to provide legal services to federal agencies where that program requires the lawyer to submit one percent of the legal fees received through the service to the government office in order to fund the program." The Committee concluded that the arrangement was acceptable even though it would involve fee-sharing between lawyers and non-lawyers because . . . Comment 6 to Rule [7.2] "suggests that the drafters of the D.C. Rules were not particularly concerned about the manner in which non-profit lawyer referral services structured their fee arrangements; their principal focus was on preventing non-lawyer intermediaries from using their power over lawyers who rely on them for business referrals to influence those lawyers' 'professional independence of judgment'." The Committee then concluded that the proposed arrangement obviated this concern because the inquiring organization presented "no risks of interfering with participating lawyers' independent professional judgment." In addition, the Committee pointed out that the referring organization "is a non-profit service aimed at achieving important public policy objectives, including holding down the cost to taxpayers of legal services provided to government agencies." . . .

Opinion 307 also referred to [other state] opinions which concluded that lawyer referral services operated by local bar associations may accept a percentage of fees earned by lawyers from referred clients. *See* Mich. St. Bar Comm. Prof. and Judicial Ethics Op. RI-75 (1991); Pa. Bar Assoc. Ethics Op. 93-162 (1993); Ark. Bar Assoc. Op. 95-01 (1995); and Va. Legal Ethics Comm. Op. 1744 (2001). These opinions noted that a number of jurisdictions help fund their legal referral services through the return of fees from referred lawyers. . . .

The American Bar Association has on at least three occasions [upheld] similar fee sharing arrangements. In Formal Opinion 291 (1956), the ABA determined that "a bar association may require members of a lawyer referral panel to help finance the service either by a flat charge or a percentage of fees collected." In addition, the ABA concluded that it was "ethically proper" for a lawyer referral service to require attorneys to return all or part of consultation fees, as well as a percentage of fees earned, to the service. ABA Informal Op. 1076 (1966). Finally, Formal Opinion 93-374 noted that a lawyer may perform pro bono litigation services and then share a portion of any court awarded fees with the non-profit organization that referred the lawyer to the client.

The Restatement of the Law Governing Lawyers §10 (3) reflects the same view that concerns about fee-sharing are not present when fees are shared with a referring non-profit organization. . . . [Although the black letter prohibits fee sharing with nonlawyers,] comments to Section 10 indicate that the fee-sharing prohibition should only be interpreted strictly where policy concerns warrant a narrow interpretation. Comment b notes, for example, that "this section should be construed so as to prevent non-lawyer control over lawyers' services, not to implement other goals such as preventing new and useful ways of providing legal services or making sure that non-lawyers do not profit indirectly from legal services in circumstances and under arrangements presenting no significant risk of harm to clients or third persons." In addition, the comments note that although fee-sharing gives power to the non-lawyer referrer, "that incentive is not present when the referral comes from a non-profit referral service." *Id.* at cmt. d.

While these opinions, court decisions, and standards suggest strong support for the proposed arrangement, there is one aspect, namely the fact that the attorney will be representing the day laborers on a contingent fee basis, that requires further analysis. In [Opinion 286 (1998)], this Committee determined that Rule 5.4 precluded a lawyer from making payments to a referral service if the payments are "contingent upon, and tied to, the lawyer's receipt of revenue from the referred legal business and is tied to the amount of those fees." According to this Opinion, the only departure from the ban on fee-sharing that Rule [7.2] permits is the authorization of payments to referring organizations when the payments are non-contingent and "paid regardless of the success or outcome" because that does not represent a division of legal fees.[8] [Opinion 302 (2000)] from this Committee relating to soliciting plaintiffs for class action lawsuits or obtaining legal work through Internet-based web pages expressed approval of this interpretation of the rules (agreeing with the view that "any fee a law firm pays to a service provider [on the Internet] cannot be linked to or contingent on the amount of legal fees the lawyers obtain from a posted project, since such an arrangement would violate D.C. Rule 5.4's prohibition against lawyers sharing legal fees with non-lawyers").

These two opinions could be interpreted to preclude *any* fee-sharing arrangement where the fees are contingent upon a lawyer's receipt of revenue from a referred client. But the opinions are narrower than that and do not address whether a non-profit that refers its clients to lawyers may recoup its out-of-pocket costs in situations where the lawyer collects sufficient funds to pay them from the various contingent fees he or she receives.[9] . . .

It is the opinion of the Committee that Rule 5.4's prohibition on fee-sharing does not preclude a non-profit from recouping its out-of-pocket expenses by requiring a lawyer to whom cases are referred to repay the expenses if sufficient funds are received from contingent fees obtained from various representations. . . .

Because the particular structure of the relationship between the non-profit and the lawyer here is comparable to that which normally exists with a lawyer and a non-profit referral service, the Committee concludes that the Committee's rationale for its Opinion 307 applies equally to this type of arrangement because

---

8. This opinion relied in part on an opinion issued by the Florida Bar Professional Ethics Committee, which held that "a nonlawyer hired to engage in permissible marketing activities on behalf of a lawyer may be paid a straight salary," but that "if commissions would be tied to legal fees derived from business brought to the firm by the nonlawyer's efforts, payment of those commissions would constitute a violation of [the Florida rule that] forbids a lawyer to divide a legal fee with a nonlawyer." Fla. Bar Prof. Ethics Comm., Op. 89-4 (1989).

9. The Committee does not address the question whether the attorney must return any portion of the retainer that is not utilized to provide legal services to day laborer clients. The situations in which all or a portion of the retainer needs to be returned are governed by the Committee's Opinion 264. It is our understanding that this is a retainer to ensure availability which is explicitly permitted in that Opinion.

it: 1) does not interfere with the lawyer's independent judgment;[10] and 2) will benefit the public by facilitating the provision of legal services to those who are in need of them.[11] . . .

As part of the arrangement, however, the inquiring non-profit and the attorney providing the services, must [inform the client of the existence and nature of the agreement].

E. Unauthorized Practice

Problems

13-11. Martyn & Fox represent mortgagees in lending transactions. Martyn & Fox is approached by a group of investors who want to set up a new business, make Martyn & Fox minority shareholders, and enter into a contract with Martyn & Fox that provides that Martyn & Fox will have the new enterprise undertake all of the non-legal aspects of Martyn & Fox's practice (title searches, service of process, advertising foreclosure sales, filing papers, photocopying, messenger services) for the next ten years. "Your clients won't even have to know."

13-12. Martyn & Fox represents a Norwegian company that has subsidiaries in two distant states. Martyn & Fox lawyers travel to both states to negotiate collective bargaining agreements. Has Martyn & Fox engaged in unauthorized practice? Does it matter if the Norwegian company has an office in Martyn & Fox's state?

Consider: Model Rules 5.4, 5.5, 5.7, 7.2, 8.5
Model Code Canon 3
RLGL §3

---

10. That the non-profit in question does not appear to be affiliated with any bar association should not affect the non-profit's ability to receive a portion of fees from referred lawyers. *See* Prof. Ethics Comm. of the State Bar of Tex., Op. 502 (1994) (holding that a non-profit service that was not established by a bar association may refer clients to a lawyer and then receive a portion of the fee collected by the lawyer in part because Texas public policy supports the establishment of lawyer referral services, and the fees received through this arrangement would benefit this policy).

11. It should also be noted that both ethics committees and courts have indicated that if an attorney were to raise a client's fee to cover the cost of returning some of the funds to a referral service, the arrangement would be ethically unacceptable. *See, e.g.,* Cal. State Bar Ethics Op. 1983-70 (1983); *Alpers v. Hunt,* 86 Cal. 78, 88 (Cal. 1890) (holding that a contract made with a non-lawyer through a third party who would receive one third of any recovered funds was invalid in part because "such a practice would tend to increase the amounts demanded for professional services. In such a case an attorney would be induced to demand a larger sum for his services, as he would have to divide such sum with a third person"). In addition, D.C. Rule [1.5] requires that any fee charged to a client be reasonable. However, by allowing an attorney only a 10% contingency fee and by requiring the attorney to return only the $10,000 that had been advanced, the proposed arrangement avoids offending these fee-based concerns.

Birbrower, Montalbano, Condon & Frank P.C. v. Superior Court

949 P.2d 1 (Cal. 1998), cert. denied, 525 U.S. 920 (1998)

CHIN, J.

Business and Professions Code section 6125 states: "No person shall practice law in California unless the person is an active member of the State Bar. . . ." We must decide whether an out-of-state law firm, not licensed to practice law in this state, violated section 6125 when it performed legal services in California for a California-based client under a fee agreement stipulating that California law would govern all matters in the representation. . . .

I. BACKGROUND

The facts with respect to the unauthorized practice of law question are essentially undisputed. Birbrower is a professional law corporation incorporated in New York, with its principal place of business in New York. During 1992 and 1993, Birbrower attorneys, defendants Kevin F. Hobbs and Thomas A. Condon (Hobbs and Condon), performed substantial work in California relating to the law firm's representation of ESQ. Neither Hobbs nor Condon has ever been licensed to practice law in California. None of Birbrower's attorneys were licensed to practice law in California during Birbrower's ESQ representation.

ESQ is a California corporation with its principal place of business in Santa Clara County. In July 1992, the parties negotiated and executed the fee agreement in New York, providing that Birbrower would perform legal services for ESQ, including "All

matters pertaining to the investigation of and prosecution of all claims and causes of action against Tandem Computers Incorporated [Tandem]." The "claims and causes of action" against Tandem, a Delaware corporation with its principal place of business in Santa Clara County, California, related to a software development and marketing contract between Tandem and ESQ dated March 16, 1990 (Tandem Agreement). The Tandem Agreement stated that "The internal laws of the State of California (irrespective of its choice of law principles) shall govern the validity of this Agreement, the construction of its terms, and the interpretation and enforcement of the rights and duties of the parties hereto." Birbrower asserts, and ESQ disputes, that ESQ knew Birbrower was not licensed to practice law in California.

While representing ESQ, Hobbs and Condon traveled to California on several occasions. . . .

ESQ eventually settled the Tandem dispute, and the matter never went to arbitration. But before the settlement, ESQ and Birbrower modified the contingency fee agreement. The modification changed the fee arrangement from contingency to fixed fee, providing that ESQ would pay Birbrower over $1 million. The original contingency fee arrangement had called for Birbrower to receive "one-third (1/3) of all sums received for the benefit of the Clients . . . whether obtained through settlement, motion practice, hearing, arbitration, or trial by way of judgment, award, settlement, or otherwise...."

In January 1994, ESQ sued Birbrower for legal malpractice and related claims in Santa Clara County Superior Court. Birbrower removed the matter to federal court and filed a counterclaim, which included a claim for attorney fees for the work it performed in both California and New York. The matter was then remanded to the superior court. ... ESQ argued that by practicing law without a license in California and by failing to associate legal counsel while doing so, Birbrower violated section 6125, rendering the fee agreement unenforceable. ...

II. DISCUSSION

A. The Unauthorized Practice of Law

The California Legislature enacted section 6125 in 1927 as part of the State Bar Act (the Act), a comprehensive scheme regulating the practice of law in the state. ... Since the Act's passage, the general rule has been that, although persons may represent themselves and their own interests regardless of State Bar membership, no one but an active member of the State Bar may practice law for another person in California. The prohibition against unauthorized law practice is within the state's police power and is designed to ensure that those performing legal services do so competently.

A violation of section 6125 is a misdemeanor. Moreover, "No one may recover compensation for services as an attorney at law in this state unless [the person] was at the time the services were performed a member of The State Bar."

Although the Act did not define the term "practice law," case law explained it as "'the doing and performing services in a court of justice in any matter depending therein throughout its various stages and in conformity with the adopted rules of procedure.'" (People v. Merchants Protective Corp., 209 P. 363, 365 (Cal. 1922).) *Merchants* included in its definition legal advice and legal instrument and contract preparation, whether or not these subjects were rendered in the course of litigation. ...

In addition to not defining the term "practice law," the Act also did not define the meaning of "in California." In today's legal practice, questions often arise concerning whether the phrase refers to the nature of the legal services, or restricts the Act's application to those out-of-state attorneys who are physically present in the state.

Section 6125 has generated numerous opinions on the meaning of "practice law" but none on the meaning of "in California." In our view, the practice of law "in California" entails sufficient contact with the California client to render the nature of the legal service a clear legal representation. In addition to a quantitative analysis, we must consider the nature of the unlicensed lawyer's activities in the state. Mere fortuitous or attenuated contacts will not sustain a finding that the unlicensed lawyer practiced law "in California." The primary inquiry is whether the unlicensed lawyer engaged in sufficient activities in the state, or created a continuing relationship with the California client that included legal duties and obligations.

Our definition does not necessarily depend on or require the unlicensed lawyer's physical presence in the state. Physical presence here is one factor we may consider in deciding whether the unlicensed lawyer has violated section 6125, but it is by no means exclusive. For example, one may practice law in the state in violation of section 6125 although not physically present here by advising a California client on California law in connection with a California legal dispute by telephone, fax, computer, or other modern technological means. Conversely, although we decline to provide a comprehensive list of what activities constitute sufficient contact with the state, we do reject the notion that a person automatically practices law "in California" whenever that person practices California law anywhere, or "virtually" enters the state by telephone, fax, e-mail, or satellite. . . .

Exceptions to section 6125 do exist, but are generally limited to allowing out-of-state attorneys to make brief appearances before a state court or tribunal. They are narrowly drawn and strictly interpreted. For example, an out-of-state attorney not licensed to practice in California may be permitted, by consent of a trial judge, to appear in California in a particular pending action.

In addition, with the permission of the California court in which a particular cause is pending, out-of-state counsel may appear before a court as counsel *pro hac vice*. A court will approve a *pro hac vice* application only if the out-of-state attorney is a member in good standing of another state bar and is eligible to practice in any United States court or the highest court in another jurisdiction. The out-of-state attorney must also associate an active member of the California Bar as attorney of record and is subject to the Rules of Professional Conduct of the State Bar.

The Act does not regulate practice before United States courts. Thus, an out-of-state attorney engaged to render services in bankruptcy proceedings was entitled to collect his fee.

Finally, California Rules of Court, rule 988, permits the State Bar to issue registration certificates to foreign legal consultants who may advise on the law of the foreign jurisdiction where they are admitted. These consultants may not, however, appear as attorneys before a California court or judicial officer or otherwise prepare pleadings and instruments in California or give advice on the law of California or any other state or jurisdiction except those where they are admitted.

The Legislature has recognized an exception to section 6125 in international disputes resolved in California under the state's rules for arbitration and conciliation of international commercial disputes. This exception states that in a commercial conciliation in California involving international commercial disputes, "The parties may appear in person or be represented or assisted by any person of their choice. A person assisting or representing a party need not be a member of the legal profession or licensed to practice law in California." (Code Civ. Proc., §1297.351.) Likewise, the Act does not apply to the preparation of or participation in labor negotiations and arbitrations arising under collective bargaining agreements in industries subject to federal law.

B. The Present Case

The undisputed facts here show that neither *Baron's* definition nor our "sufficient contact" definition of "practice law in California" would excuse Birbrower's extensive practice in this state. Nor would any of the limited statutory exceptions to section 6125 apply to Birbrower's California practice. As the Court of Appeal observed, Birbrower engaged in unauthorized law practice in California on more than a limited basis, and no firm attorney engaged in that practice was an active member of the California State Bar. As noted, in 1992 and 1993, Birbrower attorneys traveled to California to discuss with ESQ and others various matters pertaining to the dispute between ESQ and Tandem. Hobbs and Condon discussed strategy for resolving the dispute and advised ESQ on this strategy. Furthermore, during California meetings with Tandem representatives in August 1992, Hobbs demanded Tandem pay $15 million, and Condon told Tandem he believed damages in the matter would exceed that amount if the parties proceeded to litigation. Also in California, Hobbs met with ESQ for the stated purpose of helping to reach a settlement agreement and to discuss the agreement that was eventually proposed. Birbrower attorneys also traveled to California to initiate arbitration proceedings before the matter was settled. As the Court of Appeal concluded, " . . . the Birbrower firm's in-state activities clearly constituted the [unauthorized] practice of law" in California.

Birbrower contends, however, that section 6125 is not meant to apply to any out-of-state attorneys. Instead, it argues that the statute is intended solely to prevent nonattorneys from practicing law. This contention is without merit because it contravenes the plain language of the statute. Section 6125 clearly states that no person shall practice law in California unless that person is a member of the State Bar. The statute does not differentiate between attorneys or nonattorneys, nor does it excuse a person who is a member of another state bar. . . .

Birbrower next argues that we do not further the statute's intent and purpose—to protect California citizens from incompetent attorneys—by enforcing it against out-of-state attorneys. Birbrower argues that because out-of-state attorneys have been licensed to practice in other jurisdictions, they have already demonstrated sufficient competence to protect California clients. But Birbrower's argument overlooks the obvious fact that other states' laws may differ substantially from California law. Competence in one jurisdiction does not necessarily guarantee competence in another. By applying section 6125 to out-of-state attorneys who engage in the extensive practice of law in California without becoming licensed in our state, we serve the statute's goal of assuring the competence of all attorneys practicing law in this state. . . .

Birbrower alternatively asks us to create an exception to section 6125 for work incidental to private arbitration or other alternative dispute resolution proceedings. Birbrower points to fundamental differences between private arbitration and legal proceedings, including procedural differences relating to discovery, rules of evidence, compulsory process, cross-examination of witnesses, and other areas. As Birbrower observes, in light of these differences, at least one court has decided that an out-of-state attorney could recover fees for services rendered in an arbitration proceeding. . . . (*See* Williamson v. John D. Quinn Const. Corp., 537 F. Supp. 613, 616 (S.D. N.Y. 1982).)

In *Williamson*, a New Jersey law firm was employed by a client's New York law firm to defend a construction contract arbitration in New York. It sought to recover fees solely related to the arbitration proceedings, even though the attorney who did the work was not licensed in New York, nor was the firm authorized to practice in the state. In allowing the New Jersey firm to recover its arbitration fees, the federal district court concluded that an arbitration tribunal is not a court of record, and its fact-finding process is not similar to a court's process. The court relied on a local state bar report concluding that representing a client in an arbitration was not the unauthorized practice of law. But . . . [in this] case, it is undisputed that none of the time that the New York attorneys spent in California was spent in arbitration; *Williamson* thus carries limited weight. . . .

We decline Birbrower's invitation to craft an arbitration exception to section 6125's prohibition of the unlicensed practice of law in this state. Any exception for arbitration is best left to the Legislature, which has the authority to determine qualifications for admission to the State Bar and to decide what constitutes the practice of law. Even though the Legislature has spoken with respect to international arbitration and conciliation, it has not enacted a similar rule for private arbitration proceedings. Of course, private arbitration and other alternative dispute resolution practices are important aspects of our justice system. Section 6125, however, articulates a strong public policy favoring the practice of law in California by licensed State Bar members. In the face of the Legislature's silence, we will not create an arbitration exception under the facts presented. . . .

Finally, Birbrower urges us to adopt an exception to section 6125 based on the unique circumstances of this case. Birbrower notes that "Multistate relationships are a common part of today's society and are to be dealt with in commonsense fashion." . . .

Although, as discussed, we recognize the need to acknowledge and, in certain cases, to accommodate the multistate nature of law practice, the facts here show that Birbrower's extensive activities within California amounted to considerably more than any of our state's recognized exceptions to section 6125 would allow. Accordingly, we reject Birbrower's suggestion that we except the firm from section 6125's rule under the circumstances here.

C. Compensation for Legal Services

Because Birbrower violated section 6125 when it engaged in the unlawful practice of law in California, the Court of Appeal found its fee agreement with ESQ unenforceable in its entirety. Without crediting Birbrower for some services performed in New York, for which fees were generated under the fee agreement, the court reasoned that the agreement was void and unenforceable because it included payment for services rendered to a California client in the state by an unlicensed out-of-state lawyer. . . . The Court of Appeal let stand, however, the trial court's decision to allow Birbrower to pursue its fifth cause of action in quantum meruit.[5] We agree with the Court of Appeal to the extent it barred Birbrower from recovering fees generated under the fee agreement for the unauthorized legal services it performed in California. We disagree with the same court to the extent it implicitly barred Birbrower from recovering fees generated under the fee agreement for the limited legal services the firm performed in New York.

It is a general rule that an attorney is barred from recovering compensation for services rendered in another state where the attorney was not admitted to the bar. The general rule, however, has some recognized exceptions. . . .

We agree with Birbrower that it may be able to recover fees under the fee agreement for the limited legal services it performed for ESQ in New York to the extent they did not constitute practicing law in California, even though those services were performed for a California client. Because section 6125 applies to the practice of law in California, it does not, in general, regulate law practice in other states. . . .

Thus, the portion of the fee agreement between Birbrower and ESQ that includes payment for services rendered in New York may be enforceable to the extent that the illegal compensation can be severed from the rest of the agreement. On remand, therefore, the trial court must first resolve the dispute surrounding the parties' fee agreement and determine whether their agreement conforms to California law. If the parties and the court resolve the fee dispute and determine that one fee agreement is operable and does not violate any state drafting rules, the court may sever the illegal portion of the consideration (the value of the California services) from the rest of the fee agreement. Whether the trial court finds the contingent fee agreement or the fixed fee agreement to be valid, it will determine whether some amount is due under the valid agreement. The trial court must then determine, on evidence the parties present, how much of this sum is attributable to services Birbrower rendered in New York. The parties may then pursue their remaining claims. . . .

---

5. We observe that ESQ did not seek (and thus the court did not grant) summary adjudication on the Birbrower firm's quantum meruit claim for the reasonable value of services rendered. Birbrower thus still has a cause of action pending in quantum meruit.

▓ Practice Pointers:
Multijurisdictional and Multidisciplinary Practice

Unauthorized practice rules, such as those discussed in *Birbrower,* act to restrict lawyers from practicing law in two different ways. First, *Birbrower* illustrates the fact that unauthorized practice rules combine with Model Rule 5.5(a) to keep lawyers jurisdiction-specific and prevent multijurisdictional practice. At the same time, Model Rule 5.5(b) prevents lawyers from aiding the unauthorized practice of law by laypersons. This rule, along with Model Rule 5.4, prevents multidisciplinary practice in most jurisdictions by preventing lawyers from sharing fees and control with nonlawyers. Restrictions on both multi-jurisdictional and multidisciplinary practice have been the subject of increasing attack in the past few decades. Understanding the debate can help you avoid professional discipline and other consequences such as the fee forfeiture that occurred in *Birbrower.*

Multijurisdictional Practice

Current restrictions on the unauthorized practice of law originated about a century ago and apply to both non-admitted lawyers and laypersons. In most states, statutes define the restriction and provide for criminal (usually misde-meanor) penalties,[1] but cases define the scope of the restriction, which is commonly enforced through injunctive relief rather than criminal penalty.[2] Yet, as both individual and corporate clients have become more mobile, they often want to take a trusted lawyer with them. Individuals may live in several jur-isdictions in a given time period and may need legal services in all of them. Many entity clients do business throughout the United States and may wish to con-centrate their legal work with only a few firms. Many are impacted by federal as well as state environmental, labor, securities, and antitrust laws.

  Birbrower states that many jurisdictions have developed exceptions to general unauthorized practice rules. It also shows that a law firm's ability to rely on a safe harbor (such as representation in arbitration matters) that has been accepted in one jurisdiction may not excuse similar conduct in another juris-diction that does not recognize the exception. This confusion about recognized exceptions created a consensus that certain instances of multijurisdictional practice should be explicitly legitimated in the black letter of lawyer codes.

  Model Rule 5.5 allows some, but not all, multijurisdictional practice. The basic rule articulated in *Birbrower* remains the same: A lawyer is not allowed to establish an office or "other systematic and continuous presence" in a juris-diction where he or she is not admitted to practice.

  Two groups of exceptions have been carved out of this basic rule. The first group of exceptions hinges on temporary presence in a jurisdiction to accomplish

---

1. *E.g.,* Cal. Bus. & Prof. Code §6126 (2007); Minn. Stat. §481.02 (2006); N.Y. Jud. L. §478 (2007); Tex. Penal Code §38.123 (2007); Va. Code §54.1-3904 (2007).
2. *See, e.g.,* Disc. Counsel v. Shrode, 766 N.E.2d 597 (Ohio 2002) (nonlawyer enjoined from filing court documents for a corporation as a "statutory agent"); Fla. Bar v. Furman, 376 So. 2d 378 (Fla. 1979) (nonlawyer enjoined from providing legal advice about marriage dissolutions and adoptions).

some specific purpose, such as *pro hac vice* admission, reciprocal admission by motion, the licensing of legal consultants, and temporary practice by foreign lawyers. This group of exceptions also includes temporarily associating with another lawyer admitted in the jurisdiction, practice reasonably related to a matter where the lawyer is admitted to practice, and alternative dispute resolution proceedings that are reasonably related to practice where the lawyer is admitted. Note that these exceptions would not have legitimated the California practice of the New York lawyers in *Birbrower*, because they were not associated with California counsel, the matter apparently was not related to their New York practice,[3] and ADR was not the primary focus of their efforts to resolve the contract dispute.

The second group of exceptions do not rest on temporary presence, but instead acknowledge the need for multijurisdictional services to some clients. Thus, entities can hire inside counsel who do not need to be admitted in the jurisdiction where their office is located, and legal services can be provided in any jurisdiction if they are either authorized by federal law[4] or the law of that jurisdiction.

Once such multijurisdictional practice is accepted, however, another jurisdictional issue arises. Jurisdictions where unadmitted lawyers practice on a temporary or otherwise acceptable basis need the power to discipline a lawyer who provides legal services in that jurisdiction. To accomplish this, Model Rule 8.5 clarifies that such jurisdiction exists, and provides a clearer choice of law provision.[5]

Multidisciplinary Practice

Multidisciplinary practice (MDP) occurs when lawyers and nonlawyers collaborate to provide clients legal and nonlegal services. Examples include mental health counselors teamed with divorce lawyers, real estate brokers and title insurance providers working with lawyers, or social workers associated with criminal defense lawyers. Clients in complex business transactions might benefit from the combined services of investment bankers, lawyers, accountants, and other associated consultants. Under current rules, these associations are perfectly acceptable so long as lawyers and nonlawyers do not share legal fees or work in an organization in which lawyers and nonlawyers share managerial control. In other words, lawyers can hire nonlawyers but cannot be hired by for-profit organizations controlled by nonlawyers to provide legal services to third parties.[6] These restrictions protect clients from harm by preventing economic

---

3. The lawyers had, however, provided legal services to a sister company, Esq. N.Y. This may explain why the California court leaves open the possibility that the firm can recover for legal services provided in New York to the California affiliate. *See* Birbower v. Sup. Ct., 949 P.2d 1, 14 (1998) (Kennard, J. dissenting).
4. *See, e.g.*, In re Desilets, 291 F.3d 925 (6th Cir. 2002) (lawyer licensed to practice in Texas and admitted in a Michigan federal court may practice law in a federal bankruptcy court in Michigan).
5. Several jurisdictions have disciplined non-admitted lawyers. *See, e.g.*, In re Marks, 665 N.W.2d 836 (Wis. 2003); In re Mothershed, 2001 Ariz. LEXIS 63.
6. Lawline v. ABA, 956 F.2d 1378 (7th Cir 1992), *cert. denied*, 510 U.S. 992 (1993) (unincorporated association of lawyers, paralegals, and laypersons that answered legal questions and provided assistance in pro se representation without charge subject to Model Rules 5.4 and 5.5, which bear a rational relation to proper state goals; defendants who promulgated the rule were immune from antitrust and civil rights liability).

coercion by nonlawyers that will inevitably lead to the compromising of clients' interests.

In 1980, the Kutak Commission recommended that these prohibitions be scuttled in favor of multidisciplinary practice, including the sharing of fees and management control, as long as lawyers in such an enterprise remained free to exercise their independent professional judgment and to adhere to all of their professional obligations under the Model Rules. These amendments were defeated in the House of Delegates, and Model Rule 5.4 retained all of the historic limitations on multidisciplinary practice. Model Rule 5.7 did, however, legitimize certain law-related services, as long as lawyers disclosed to clients their interest in the related business.

In 1998, the ABA established a Multidisciplinary Practice Commission to reexamine these issues. The Commission's recommendations, which would have allowed some fee sharing, were soundly defeated once again in 2000 by the House of Delegates. These events have shifted the focus of reform efforts to the individual states, where some are considering rule changes to allow some form of MDP. These proposals include some combination of the following changes:[7]

1. Shared ownership or equity interest in the firm with nonlawyers;
2. Ancillary business ownership by lawyers;
3. Strategic alliances (formal affiliations of law firms and other service providers);
4. Requirements that MDP clients will be governed by the legal profession's confidentiality and conflict of interest rules;
5. Requirements that nonlawyers in MDPs be members of another licensed profession;
6. Disclosure to clients that reveals the extent of shared ownership or contractual agreement to provide nonlegal services; and
7. Permission from the relevant court to establish an MDP.

New York, for example, has amended its professional code, but has also declared: "Multi-disciplinary practice between lawyers and nonlawyers is incompatible with the core values of the legal profession" and therefore requires "strict division between services provided by lawyers and those provided by nonlawyers. . . ."[8] The new rule does allow for business alliances between lawyers and nonlawyers and also mandates that a "Statement of Client's Rights in Cooperative Business Arrangements" be signed by clients to protect them.[9]

States considering MDP reform must face a number of issues. First, empirically, do clients want diversified professional services from one company or firm? Second, if client demand is present, will clients benefit from MDPs? Third, if demand occurs and clients seem well-served, what will happen when a client who receives MDP services claims competence, confidentiality, or loyalty obligations from such an integrated firm? Finally, if lawyers are members of the

---

7. For a more detailed account of current proposals, *see* Robert A. Esperti et al., *Latest Developments on the State of Multidisciplinary Practice*, 29 Est. Plan. 267 (June 2002).
8. N.Y. DR 1-107 (2007).
9. 22 N.Y.C.R.R. 1205.4 (2007). *Cf.*, MR 7.2(b)(4).

MDP firm, will courts impose lawyers' fiduciary duties on the firm's non-legal services, even if other professionals offer a large part of the service?

As you might expect, lawyers differ tremendously over the answers to these questions. Those who favor change dream of "an unregulated marketplace," where "clients would have the choice of hiring a single firm that provided all of these services or multiple firms that specialized in some subset." These proponents for change also argue that it is too late to turn back the clock because law firms already are run like big businesses, and self-interested economic behavior furthers social welfare in a market economy.[10] With respect to confidentiality, they maintain that clients can decide when the attorney-client privilege is important enough not to risk an MDP.[11]

As for loyalty, MDPs offer a great opportunity to avoid imputed conflicts rules that restrict law firms from growing to their efficient size.[12] This would mean that MDPs could represent clients with adverse interests as well as those whose interests are adverse to former clients of the firm in the same or substantially related matters. Screens "may not work perfectly" but, along with "structural separations," they would, for the most part, protect clients from information sharing.[13] Further, equity markets could be opened to MDPs, which would create a new mechanism for financing litigation.[14] Overall, lawyers should welcome MDPs as a new economic opportunity. If law firms can't compete with a "Sears MDP," then their "position is exactly analogous to horse and buggy manufacturers faced with the invention of the automobile."[15]

Those who oppose MDPs could not disagree more.[16] They argue that clients already can get the services they need from independent professionals. It is not too late to stop MDPs because a number of core values already restrain the ability of lawyers to compete in an unregulated market. Social welfare is promoted by lawyer pro bono efforts[17] and by the entire law governing lawyers that imposes fiduciary duties on lawyers to assure that client interests curb lawyer economic advantage. Loyalty rules including imputed disqualification mean that lawyers must say "no" to some clients in order to protect the interests of others.[18] Association with other service providers easily could compromise the confidentiality obligations of lawyers because MDPs need shared information among professionals to thrive. Worst of all, MDPs could come to compromise the independent judgment of lawyers in the same way HMOs have come to compromise the independent medical judgment of some physicians. Lawyers may be tempted to cheat on competence if their part of the package is the loss leader that brings in the business but needs to be subordinated to some other service such as the sale of securities or insurance in order to maximize profit.[19]

---

10. Daniel R. Fischel, *Multidisciplinary Practice*, 55 Bus. Law. 951, 957 (2000).
11. *Id.* at 964.
12. *Id.* at 965-967.
13. *Id.* at 966.
14. *Id.* at 968.
15. *Id.* at 972.
16. Lawrence J. Fox, *Dan's World: A Free Enterprise Dream; An Ethics Nightmare*, 55 Bus. Law. 1533 (2000).
17. *Id.* at 1551.
18. *Id.* at 1557-1559.
19. *Id.* at 1546-1547.

Law firms should not compete with "Sears MDPs" because Sears should not be able to practice law. The market does not always provide more consumer choice, but can lead to monopoly power that robs consumers of bargaining power. Witness the former Big 8 accounting firms, which, without limitations on concentration, soon became the Big 5 and, after further losing their way, are now the regulated Final 4.[20]

The Future

The sheer number of jurisdictions considering some change in unauthorized practice rules may mean that some forms of MDPs might emerge.[21] Although some jurisdictions seem to favor fully integrated MDPs, key issues such as profit sharing and management control still will persist.[22] Ultimately, it remains to be seen whether these new structures will attract both lawyers and clients. MDP regulations that subject other professionals to lawyer codes may be seen as too economically restrictive to those who favor fully integrated MDPs.

Provisions that allow full sharing of profits and management initially may be likely to attract new forms of practice. If MDPs grow and multiply, eventually an aggrieved client will bring a malpractice suit, just as aggrieved clients of lawyers and other professionals do. Or an MDP client may seek some other remedy such as professional discipline of disqualification or injunctive relief against the MDP, or fee forfeiture based on similar claims. At that point, courts will have to decide first, whether the law governing lawyers applies, and if so, whether it also creates remedies against the entire MDP. In truly integrated entities, ordinary agency principles of vicarious liability easily could mean that the entire firm would be subject to the law governing lawyers, and that lawyers in the firm also may be subject to additional legal provisions that govern other professionals with whom they are associated.

For example, a lawyer who owned a title insurance company took on a prospective borrower as a client when the borrower sought the title company's assistance with a real estate closing, but needed to probate a relative's estate to obtain clear title for a real estate transaction. In seeking to gain the title insurance income, the lawyer took several shortcuts and erred in significant ways in handling the probate matter. The court found that his personal financial conflict of interest was the "central factor" in his misconduct and suspended him from law practice for six months.[23] Similarly, a British case offers us a glimpse of other litigation that may ensue. There, an accounting firm hired lawyers to offer prelitigation services in teams with other professionals. They

---

20. Lawrence J. Fox, *MDPs Done Gone: The Silver Lining in the Very Black Enron Cloud*, 44 Ariz. L. Rev. 547 (2002).
21. *See* Susan Poser, *Main Street Multidisciplinary Practice Firms: Laboratories for the Future*, 37 U. Mich. J.L. Reform 95 (2003).
22. In Wouters v. Algemene Raad de Nederlandse Orde van Advocaten, 2002 ECR I-1577 (2002), the European Court of Justice of the European Communities upheld a ban on partnerships between lawyers and other professionals adopted by the Bar of the Netherlands. The Court held that despite its restrictive effects on competition, the regulation was "necessary for the proper practice of the legal profession," even though other EU Member States allowed multidisciplinary partnerships.
23. In re Evans, 902 A.2d 56 (D.C. App. 2006).

later took on an audit of a matter adverse to the former prelitigation services client in a substantially related matter. The House of Lords applied the substantial relationship test applicable to lawyers in deciding a loyalty dispute, even though the accounting firm argued that such a standard was not required by accounting profession rules for audit matters.[24] The reasonable expectations of the client, who understood that lawyers were part of the prelitigation services team, trumped the accounting firm's assumption that it could define loyalty and confidentiality obligations by the standards of another profession.

Should more cases produce similar results, professionals in MDPs will have to face the prospect that the legal standards governing all professionals in the group provide a wide range of remedies to their clients. MDPs will then need to reassess whether the expanded liability and range of remedies opened to clients of the firm are worth the prospect of increased profits.

---

24. Prince Jefri Bolkiah v. KPMG, 2 A.C. 222, 2 W.L.R. 215 (H.L. 1998).

Chapter 14

Being a Lawyer

In this chapter we turn our attention to you, asking what kind of a profession you wish to be a part of in the future as well as what kind of person you want to be as you practice law. We begin by returning to a consideration of what it means to be a professional. We then examine lawyer personality and professionalism. We conclude by returning to some examples from this book that may help you find your own way in the world of law practice.

A. Being a Professional

Problems

14-1. Associate tells Fox he has discovered that Martyn has been sending bills to clients charging them for Martyn's services at Martyn's hourly rate for services actually performed by Associate. Fox investigates and tells Associate that, in each instance when this occurred, the client was billed either a fixed fee or a uniform hourly rate regardless of which lawyer performed the work, that Martyn will not repeat the conduct because she is now on medication for her depression, and that Fox considers the matter satisfactorily resolved. What should Associate do?

14-2. Fox tells Martyn that he has just been convicted of drunk driving in a distant state. He admits he may have a drinking problem, but tells Martyn not to worry, "I'll handle it myself." What should Martyn do?

Consider: Model Rules 5.1, 5.2, 8.3, 8.4
Model Code DR 1-102, 1-103

Kelly v. Hunton & Williams
1999 U.S. Dist. LEXIS 9139 (E.D.N.Y.)

GLEESON, District Judge:

Peter M. Kelly brought this diversity action against his former employer, the law firm of Hunton & Williams ("H&W"), alleging that H&W breached implied contractual obligations owed him when it terminated his employment with the firm. Specifically, plaintiff claims that H&W forced him to resign and implicitly threatened to withhold a favorable job reference, in order to impede and discourage him from reporting H&W partner Scott Wolas's billing fraud to the Disciplinary Committee. Hunton & Williams moves for summary judgment. The motion is denied.

FACTS . . .

H&W is a large, prestigious law firm. Founded in 1901 in Richmond, Virginia, it now has 650 lawyers in fifteen offices, five of which are overseas. . . . When plaintiff began with H&W in October 1990, the litigation department in the New York office (which was founded in 1983) consisted of fewer than ten partners and associates. Plaintiff was one of two first-year associates. He worked primarily with Scott Wolas and Franklin Stone, who were partners, and with Christopher Mason, who became a partner in early 1992.

Plaintiff's first-year performance reviews, prepared in June and July of 1991, resulting in favorable ratings but expressed some concern over his not having passed the bar examination. In October 1991, Stone described plaintiff to another H&W partner as "a terrific associate—functioning well above

his second year." The following month, when the favorable result of the bar examination was announced, partner Kathy Robb . . . wrote the following on plaintiff's first annual associate evaluation: "Typical 1st year. Strong 'goods.' Apply with vigor to work. Congratulations on passing the bar. Good potential here." Stone wrote: "Peter does excellent work and is a valuable asset to our team. He brings an intelligence and maturity to his work that is rare in a first year associate." Mason wrote: "Peter has good skills, indeed, very good skills in many ways. . . . I also have a good deal of confidence in his work, confidence beyond his first-year level." Plaintiff received the maximum pay raise for his class.

Earlier in 1991, around April or May, plaintiff began suspecting Scott Wolas of billing fraud. Wolas had billed four hours per day over a two-week period for a particular matter, and plaintiff suspected that Wolas had not worked those hours. He shared those suspicions with another litigation associate, Joseph Saltarelli. In June 1991, Saltarelli informed plaintiff that Wolas had billed fictitious hours on a series of matters. Over the next several months, Saltarelli related to plaintiff other instances of Wolas's improper billing.

In November 1991, Saltarelli told plaintiff that Saltarelli was meeting with B. Carey Tolley, III, the managing partner of the firm's New York office, along with Stone, Mason, and Robb to discuss Wolas's billing practices. . . .

Around this time, plaintiff began socializing with Saltarelli and Hal Geary, a litigation associate hired from another firm in 1991. They frequently lunched together and went out after work for drinks or dinner. The other attorneys on plaintiff's floor, including Wolas, Stone, and Mason, were aware of the close association of plaintiff and Saltarelli. For this reason, and because plaintiff was involved in preparing fee applications (and thus had access to Wolas's billing records), plaintiff asserts that, as early as November 1991, Wolas, Stone, Mason, and Robb knew that plaintiff was aware of Wolas's billing improprieties.

In approximately June of 1992, plaintiff told Mason that Wolas was billing clients for time not worked. Unbeknownst to plaintiff, Mason had been investing heavily (and profitably) through Wolas for nearly two years. In addition to Wolas's status as a "rainmaking" partner at H&W, he solicited investments in his family's liquor business. These so-called investments were actually part of an alleged "Ponzi scheme" Wolas was conducting from his office at H&W. Wolas lent considerable credence to those allegations—in fact, everyone now seems to agree they are true—by absconding in 1995, leaving behind more than 100 investors who claim to have been defrauded of more than $30 million. Mason, however, was not one of the investors who were left holding the bag. To the contrary, he profited enormously from Wolas's scheme; in 1994 alone he earned $2 million. In any event, when plaintiff told him in June 1992 that Wolas was billing for time not worked, Mason responded curtly, telling plaintiff that things are not always what they seem, and that Wolas's billing was not plaintiff's concern.

Before his conversation with Mason about Wolas's billing fraud, plaintiff had not received any substantial negative criticism of his work or work habits. However, shortly after the meeting, Stone began inquiring about plaintiff's whereabouts on mornings when he arrived late to the office. Stone, like Mason, invested heavily with Wolas from 1990 through 1995. In an e-mail to Robb, dated July 24, 1992, Stone wrote that plaintiff's "problems with basic logistics have gotten Scott [Wolas], Chris [Mason] and me pulling our hair out." Robb, like Mason and Stone, had invested substantial sums through Wolas. Four days later, in a July 28, 1992 e-mail to Stone, Wolas, and Mason, Robb mentioned that she had spoken to plaintiff about "his constant tardiness and other inattentions to the administrative aspects of practicing law (e.g., not pursuing finalizing his bar application in a timely fashion)." Robb continued, "I told him that all of you liked him enormously, think he is talented, and view him as having the potential to become an excellent lawyer, but that if he didn't take his inability to get to work consistently seriously, there was a good chance that you were going to boot him out of here."

Meanwhile, after putting Saltarelli off for months, Tolley finally reviewed Wolas's billing records. Tolley refused to approach Wolas for an explanation, but rather told Saltarelli in early August 1992 to raise it directly with Wolas, in a non-accusatory manner, under the guise of asking his help in explaining billing records that might raise questions when cases were settled or fee applications were made to courts. In essence, Tolley told Saltarelli to help Wolas repair billing records that Saltarelli believed were fraudulent.

On September 10, 1992, Robb and Mason spoke further to plaintiff regarding his performance. As a result, plaintiff prepared a memorandum on September 16, 1992, listing ten steps he intended to take to improve his work habits. On November 10, 1992, plaintiff again met with Mason and Robb for his second annual associate evaluation. They informed him that he had received "needs improvement" ratings in several critical categories, that he displayed "poor attention to work" in general. . . .

Over the following months, plaintiff, Saltarelli, and Geary encountered additional evidence of Wolas's systematic overbilling of clients. Sensing that Tolley was not going to deal with the problem, they approached James A. Jones, III, Tolley's predecessor as managing partner, in February of 1993. The three came forward as a group, prompted in part by the advice of a federal district judge whom Geary had served as a law clerk. The judge had further told Geary that he might have an ethical obligation to disclose the billing irregularities to the Disciplinary Committee if appropriate action were not taken by the firm.

Saltarelli, Geary, and plaintiff raised the issue of Wolas's improper billing with Jones in February 1993. Geary brought to Jones documentary evidence of Wolas's fraud, and informed Jones that plaintiff had further evidence of it and was willing to assist the firm in its investigation of the matter. The day following Geary's meeting with Jones, plaintiff met with Tolley to discuss Wolas's billing practices. In the ensuing weeks, plaintiff had additional meetings with Tolley, Jones, and Wolas himself to review Wolas's billing records. In late February, Tolley informed plaintiff that W. Taylor Reveley, the former managing partner of the firm's

Richmond office, would be coming to New York to head the investigation into Wolas's billing. . . .

On February 25, 1993, Stone sent an e-mail to Mason and Robb. She stated, "I want to fire Peter Kelly NOW. He missed his deadline: 10:00 a.m. this morning to give me a draft. . . . Then Peter disappeared all day. He just returned and has nothing more for me. . . . I can't stand it anymore. We must get rid of him now." Plaintiff claims that, in fact, he met Stone's deadline, and that he had worked through the previous night to do so.

On March 1, 1993, the day before Reveley was scheduled to interview plaintiff about Wolas's billing activities, Robb and Mason told plaintiff that he had to leave the firm. They gave him a choice: he could (a) be fired immediately, without severance pay or a favorable job reference; or (b) announce his resignation and stay with the firm the next several months, which would gain him a favorable reference. This was not much of a choice. Plaintiff had no other employment lined up and no other source of income. He would face a difficult job search if he could not obtain a favorable reference from H&W. . . . Consequently, plaintiff chose coerced resignation over being fired.

Before coming to New York to conduct his inquiry, Reveley spoke by telephone with Robb, who disparaged plaintiff and Geary. Stone admits that she "might have" told her partners (presumably including Reveley) before the billing investigation that plaintiff had concocted his allegations against Wolas in order to stretch out his employment at H&W. In any event, Reveley promptly rejected the accusing associates' claims. He interviewed them on

March 2, 1993. He conducted a "hearing" nine days later. Present were the three accusers, Stone (whom Reveley insisted be present because she was "inextricably relevant" to the hearing), Mason, and Wolas. It was not much of a hearing. Reveley denied the accusing associates access to Wolas's written response to their charges and refused to permit them to question Wolas. Stone and Mason sat silently. They did not disclose their separate, investment-based financial interest in Wolas's continued membership in the firm. Indeed, Mason had invested $12,900 with Wolas the day before the hearing, and had received a $35,000 "return of principal" from him just ten days before that. Stone had received $96,200 in "repayments" from Wolas in the seven weeks before the hearing. Indeed, though Mason, Stone, and Robb were all integrally involved as H&W partners in exonerating Wolas and getting rid of plaintiff—Wolas's accuser—none of them revealed to Tolley, Reveley, or Jones their involvement as investors in Wolas's scheme. Indeed, if Mason, Stone, and Robb are to be believed, they never even discussed their financial stakes in Wolas among themselves until 1994 at the earliest.

It took Reveley only one day to decide that Wolas had not committed billing fraud, but he waited almost a month to meet with his accusers. On April 7, 1993, Reveley met with plaintiff, Geary, Saltarelli, and Tolley to discuss his findings. He told them that Wolas was a "sloppy pig, not a dirty rat." The three associates responded by presenting Reveley with additional evidence of fraudulent billing by Wolas. Reveley promised to continue his investigation.

On April 13, 1993, Tolley e-mailed Reveley. The subject was whether the firm or the accusing associates had an obligation to report the facts about Wolas's billing to the Disciplinary Committee. The e-mail made explicit reference to Wieder v. Skala, 609 N.E.2d 105 (N.Y. 1992), the December 1992 New York Court of Appeals decision that is discussed *infra*. Tolley opined that the firm's determination that fraud had not been clearly established extinguished the obligation to report not only for the firm, but for the associates as well. He sought Reveley's counsel on how to tell the associates that they had no obligation to report Wolas. On May 6, 1993, Reveley met with the accusing associates separately and told them they had no ethical obligation to take their accusations further. Although he added that each associate had to make that decision for himself, it was clear that anyone taking on Wolas before the Disciplinary Committee would be taking on H&W as well.

Plaintiff left H&W at the end of May 1993, although he remained on the firm's payroll for another month. In seven letters to prospective employers, dated July 27 through September 3, 1993, plaintiff stated that he left the firm "voluntarily." On November 11, 1993, a partner at another firm in New York contacted Stone seeking a job reference for plaintiff. Stone praised plaintiff's substantive abilities but mentioned that a series of personal problems had negatively affected plaintiff's job performance and attendance. According to Stone, the caller told her that plaintiff had mentioned that H&W let him go because he had blown the whistle on a partner's billing irregularities. Stone informed him that plaintiff's departure from H&W stemmed entirely from plaintiff's performance problems.

Unable to secure work in New York, plaintiff moved to Texas in 1994. On February 28, 1994, an attorney placement firm in Houston contacted Stone with regard to plaintiff. According to Stone, she told the placement firm that plaintiff "was very smart and a very good writer, but that he suffered from performance problems and family crises which severely affected his work."

Plaintiff was admitted to the Texas bar in 1994, and was finally admitted to the New York bar in the summer of 1997. On September 29, 1997, he brought this action.

DISCUSSION...

Plaintiff concedes that he worked at H&W as an employee-at-will, and that, under New York law, an employer may generally terminate such an employee at any time for any or no reason. He contends that his termination fits within the narrow exception to that rule established by the New York Court of Appeals in Wieder v. Skala, 609 N.E.2d 105 (N.Y. 1992).

In *Wieder*, the court held that even though an associate at a law firm was an at-will employee, he had a valid claim against his firm for breach of contract based on the firm's discharging him for his insistence that the firm comply with the Code of Professional Responsibility by reporting to the Disciplinary Committee the professional misconduct of another associate. The court noted that associates at law firms are not only employees, they are also independent officers of the court, responsible in a broader public sense for their professional obligations. The court further stated that

> in any hiring of an attorney as an associate to practice law with a firm there is implied an understanding so fundamental to the relationship and essential to its purpose as to require no expression: that both the associate and the firm in conducting the practice will do so in accordance with the ethical standards of the profession. Erecting or countenancing disincentives to compliance with the applicable rules of professional conduct...would subvert the central professional purpose of [plaintiff's] relationship with the firm—the lawful and ethical practice of law.

As in this case, the particular rule of professional conduct at issue in *Wieder* was DR 1-103(A), which imposes on lawyers a duty to report to the Disciplinary Committee any potential violations of the disciplinary rules that raise a substantial question as to another lawyer's honesty. The court held that the allegation that the firm had placed the associate in the position of having to choose between continued employment and fulfilling this ethical obligation stated a claim for breach of contract based on an "implied-in-law obligation" in the employment relationship. . . .

A. The Availability of a *Wieder* Claim to an Associate Not Yet Admitted to the Bar . . .

It is difficult to conceive of H&W telling its clients what it is now telling me, i.e., that, as far as the firm is concerned, its unadmitted associates are not bound by the disciplinary rules and may knowingly act contrary to them without fear of professional sanction. More difficult still is imagining H&W telling that to the new class of law graduates that joins the firm as unadmitted associates each fall.

In any event, the question whether the *Wieder* cause of action would be extended by New York courts to unadmitted law graduates working as associates in law firms is easily answered. The answer is yes. *Wieder* applies to "any hiring of an attorney as an associate." ... When H&W hired plaintiff, it paid him as an associate, evaluated him as an associate, and gave him assignments as an associate. The only restrictions he faced as an unadmitted associate were that he could neither sign briefs nor appear in court on behalf of clients. In a big-firm practice, those restrictions have little operational significance.

... An associate at a law firm might reasonably believe that his knowing failure to disclose an attorney's fraud would cause the Character and Fitness Committee to recommend the denial of his application for admission to the bar. ...

... Plaintiff was not hired as a paralegal, or to perform administrative tasks. He was hired by H&W for the sole purpose of practicing law. H&W owed him the same implied-in-law obligation it owed its other associates.

Finally, it bears mention that in April 1993, just four months after *Wieder* was decided, H&W itself carefully examined whether the three accusing associates had a duty to report Wolas to the Disciplinary Committee. ... The argument advanced here—that plaintiff, unlike Saltarelli and Geary, was simply a "law clerk" who had no reporting obligation at all—occurred to no one at H&W at the time. This is not because the H&W partners involved are not resourceful lawyers. Rather, it is because the formal, legalistic contention the firm now makes is incompatible with the way associates like Peter Kelly are viewed and expected to act in the real world of big-firm practice.

B. The Other Claimed Limitations on the *Wieder* Cause of Action

The upshot of H&W's other arguments regarding the scope of *Wieder* is surprising. According to H&W, if there is actual fraud at the firm, about which an associate has complained to the firm, the firm can immediately fire the associate in retaliation for complaining and threaten to ruin his future with bad references if he reports the fraud to the Disciplinary Committee. As long as the associate is fired before he threatened to go to the Disciplinary Committee, and if only a favorable reference (i.e., not his job) is conditioned on his continuing violation of DR 1-103(A), H&W asserts that "the *Wieder* case does not create a cause of action in that setting." ...

First, I do not consider the absence of a threat by plaintiff to go to the Disciplinary Committee as raising an open question of New York Law. If a law firm fires an associate in retaliation for reporting a lawyer's misconduct to the firm, its action is inherently coercive and necessarily implies an effort to impede post-termination reporting to the Disciplinary Committee. Thus, a cause of action is available under *Wieder*. The associate's stated intention to go to the disciplinary authorities may be powerful circumstantial evidence of the firm's intent to punish and/or silence him or her, but it is neither dispositive nor necessary to the associate's claim.

H&W's contention that *Wieder* is inapplicable to a law firm's conditioning of a favorable job reference on the attorney's silence arguably raises an open question of New York law, but the question is easily answered. Where, as here, a jury can reasonably infer that a law firm's unfavorable reference can effectively prevent the attorney from obtaining the type of employment he seeks, conditioning a favorable reference on continued silence may properly be found to be "placing him in the position of having to choose between continued employment" and the consequences of failing to comply with DR 1-103(A).

Finally, H&W's reply brief contends that the January 21, 1999 decision of the Appellate Division in Geary v. Hunton & Williams, 684 N.Y.S.2d 207 (A.D. 1999), is "completely dispositive" of this motion. That case held that Geary's breach of contract claim against H&W "was properly rejected on the basis of evidence establishing that defendant terminated plaintiff before plaintiff had raised any concerns about [Wolas's] billing practices with the other partners. A jury could find otherwise here, that is, it could find that the decision to fire plaintiff was made only after he first told Mason about Wolas's billing for time he did not work. . . .

. . . Plaintiff, unlike Geary, claims not only that he was forced to resign in retaliation for blowing the whistle on Wolas, but also that the firm continued to discourage him from reporting Wolas to the Disciplinary Committee even after he was fired. Specifically, plaintiff contends that Reveley's statement to him that he had no ethical responsibility to report Wolas, at a time when Plaintiff sorely

needed a favorable reference from the firm, "was designed to create an appearance of compliance with *Wieder* while simultaneously discouraging me from reporting another attorney's professional misconduct to authorities. . . ."

. . . [T]he Appellate Division's decision states that H&W could not have impeded or discouraged Geary's compliance with the obligation he "did not believe he had, did not express an intent to carry out, and did not carry out." Here, there is evidence from which a jury could infer that plaintiff believed he had such an obligation, including the statements by Reveley that explicitly sensitized the accusing associates to their obligation.

In sum, while I recognize that *Wieder* established a narrow exception to New York's at-will employment law, I decline to give it the crabbed construction advanced by H&W. If the jury resolves the disputed issues of facts in plaintiff's favor, it may properly conclude that H&W breached its employment contract with him. . . .

The rest of H&W's arguments in support of its motion rely on purportedly undisputed facts that are anything but undisputed. It contends that it is undisputed that prior to February 1993 plaintiff had never apprised an H&W partner that he believed Wolas had engaged in billing fraud. But plaintiff testified that he told Mason in June or July of 1992 that Wolas was not working all the hours that he was billing. Billing for hours not worked is fraud. H&W further contends that plaintiff indisputably left H&W voluntarily. But plaintiff asserts that he was forced out by the threat that he would be fired without severance pay or a favorable job reference if he did not resign. A jury could conclude that his departure from the firm was not voluntary. That he told subsequent employers or bar examiners otherwise will be fair ground for impeachment at trial, but it does not warrant summary judgment for H&W. H&W contends that it indisputably did not threaten adverse action to plaintiff if he reported Wolas's misconduct to the Disciplinary Committee. While it is true that the H&W partners studied *Wieder* closely during the events in question and made no explicit threat, a rational jury could conclude that H&W fired plaintiff because he had insisted on airing Wolas's fraud, and implicitly conditioned its favorable references to prospective future employers on plaintiff's keeping quiet about that fraud. . . .

B. Personality and Professionalism

Martin E.P. Seligman, Paul R. Verkuil & Terry H. Kang*
Why Lawyers Are Unhappy
23 Cardozo L. Rev. 33 (2001)

. . . Introduction

Much attention has been paid recently to the disillusionment among lawyers. The New York City Bar Association, a leader among bar groups, has focused upon the lawyer's (especially young associate's) "quality of life." Its Task Force Report cites "unhappiness" among young lawyers and measures its impact. The implication and costs of this unhappiness are significant, as many bright attorneys grow disillusioned and cynical, with diminishing career opportunities. Unhappy associates fail to achieve their full potential at a cost to them, their firms, their clients, and even their families. Invariably many lawyers leave the law firm, and some the practice of law, prematurely, resulting in undesirable turnover, and a loss of talent to the profession.[2]

In this essay we suggest that much of the unhappiness of lawyers can be cured. It stems from three causes: (1) Lawyers are selected for their pessimism (or "prudence") and this generalizes to the rest of their lives; (2) Young associates hold jobs that are characterized by high pressure and low decision latitude, exactly the conditions that promote poor health and poor morale; and (3) American law is to some extent a zero-sum game, and negative emotions flow from zero-sum games. We acknowledge that while the first two causes have well-documented antidotes, the third, the zero-sum nature of law, may be a justifiable aspect of the profession; but even in this case we suggest promising amelioratives. . . .

---

* Martin Seligman is Robert A. Fox Leadership Professor of Psychology, University of Pennsylvania; Paul Verkuil is Professor, Benjamin N. Cardozo School of Law, Yeshiva University, and Terry Kang, J.D., is an Assistant to Professor Seligman.
2. *See* Report of the Task Force on Lawyers' Quality of Life, 55 Rec. Assn. B. N.Y. 755, 756 (2000) [hereinafter N.Y. Bar Task Force Report].

The unhappiness and discontent of lawyers is well documented[3] and much lamented.[4] Since lawyers are members of a "public profession,"[5] their dysfunction entails societal, as well as personal, costs. Indeed, the creation of law itself is in one sense bound up with the health of judges, lawyers, legislators, and academicians. But remedies for lawyer distress and the collective malaise of the profession are harder to identify. The attempts by lawyer groups, even distinguished ones like the New York City Bar, to address the issues seem self-serving and half hearted—driven more by public relations and economic concerns than objective study. . . .

I. Defining the Unhappiness Problem

Practitioners have increasingly acknowledged that law is a profession in crisis,[13] and the crisis they speak of relates to the widespread disenchantment among even the most talented lawyers.[14] . . .

In many cases, the problem is not financial. Associates at top firms can earn (with bonuses) up to $200,000 per year in their first year of practice. . . . The recent pay increases at large law firms are themselves partially caused by lawyer dissatisfaction. The euphemistic "retention bonuses" are awarded to ensure that young associates extend their service beyond two or three years. Combating this desire to leave early is among law firms' highest priorities, since they can only recoup their investment in new lawyers over a longer period of time.

In addition to being disenchanted, lawyers are "in remarkably poor health."[19] They are at much greater risk than the general population for depression, heart disease, alcoholism and illegal drug use. For example,

---

3. *See generally* John P. Heinz et al., *Lawyers and Their Discontents: Findings from a Survey of the Chicago Bar*, 74 Ind. L.J. 735 (1999); Patrick J. Schiltz, *On Being a Happy, Healthy, and Ethical Member of an Unhappy, Unhealthy, and Unethical Profession*, 52 Vand. L. Rev. 871 (1999).

4. *See* Anthony T. Kronman, *The Lost Lawyer: Failing Ideals of the Legal Profession* 13 (1993) (lamenting the "demise of the lawyer-statesman ideal"); *see also* Mary Ann Glendon, *A Nation Under Lawyers: How the Crisis in the Legal Profession Is Transforming American Society* (1994) (characterizing lawyers today as contentious litigators rather than impartial advocates).

5. *See* Charles Silver & Frank B. Cross, *What's Not to Like About Being a Lawyer?*, 109 Yale L.J. 1443 (2000) (reviewing Arthur L. Liman, *Lawyer: A Life of Counsel and Controversy* (1998)). The authors, in defending the public nature of private-sector practice, argue that private-sector lawyers make "an enormous economic contribution to social welfare, including the welfare of the poor. . . . [They] help our economy grow, producing jobs and making people's lives better." *Id.* at 1479; *see also* Amiram Elwork, *Stress Management for Lawyers: How to Increase Personal & Professional Satisfaction in the Law* (1997).

13. *See* Carl Horn, *Twelve Steps Toward Personal Fulfillment in Law Practice*, 25 ABA L. Prac. Mgmt. 36 (Oct. 1999).

14. *See* Robert Kurson, *Who's Killing the Great Lawyers of Harvard?*, Esquire, Aug. 2000, at 82. The author, himself a 1990 Harvard Law graduate, describes the trend among his former classmates: "One after another, those who have left law, especially law firms, seem happy. Those who have not are suffering or, worse, resigned. They talk about losing themselves. . . . More vow to leave the law with the next infusion of cash or gumption." *Id.* at 84. *See also* Note, *Making Docile Lawyers: An Essay on the Pacification of Law Students*, 111 Harv. L. Rev. 2027, 2028 (1998) (documenting the "psychological distress that so often accompanies a Harvard Law School education").

19. *See* Schiltz, *supra* note 3, at 873; *see also* Michael Quinn, *Reality Bites*, Tex. Law., Jan. 31, 2000, at 63 (reviewing Steven Keeva, *Transforming Practices: Finding Joy and Satisfaction in the Legal Life* (1999)).

researchers at Johns Hopkins University found statistically significant elevations of major depressive disorder ("MDD") in only three of 104 occupations surveyed.[20] When adjusted for socio-demographic factors, lawyers topped the list, suffering from MDD at a rate 3.6 times higher than employed persons generally.[21] The researchers noted the possibility that the work environments in these at-risk professions were conducive to depression. Further, they proposed that lawyers and secretaries—two of the three highest risk groups—have little autonomy and control, a factor that has been implicated in depression. These studies confirm the hypothesis that lawyer unhappiness can lead to serious health and social problems that pose a threat to the legal profession.

Unhappy lawyers not only burden their families. Given their role in a public profession they can also injure their clients by failing to provide adequate representation.[23] Unhappiness and depression are intimately associated with passivity and poor productivity at work. Bar associations have the best data on these costs since lawyers who violate their clients' interests often become disciplinary problems. But formal recognition usually comes late in lawyers' careers, after a long period of unrecognized and unaddressed problematic behavior. By that point, inadequate representation may already have caused irreparable injuries to clients and the legal system. The task, then, is to protect the public against harm by addressing potential problems before they rise to the level of disciplinary offenses.

That said, we must remember that not all lawyers are unhappy or dysfunctional; indeed, many are very happy and highly functional. And some may follow the course of Justice Cardozo, channeling their unhappiness into professional excellence or even perfectionism. . . .

II. Psychological Explanations for Lawyer Unhappiness . . .

A. Pessimism

. . . Pessimism is defined not in the colloquial sense: "seeing the glass as half full or half empty" but rather, as a pessimistic "explanatory style." This is the tendency to interpret the causes of negative events in stable, global and internal ways: "It's going to last forever; it's going to undermine everything; it's my own fault."[28] Under this definition, the pessimist will view bad events as unchangeable. The optimist, in contrast, sees setbacks as temporary. That crucial distinction is what connects pessimism to unhappiness.

Research has revealed, predictably, that pessimism is maladaptive in most endeavors: pessimistic life insurance agents make fewer sales attempts, are less

---

20. *See* William W. Eaton et al., *Occupations and the Prevalence of Major Depressive Disorder*, 32 J. Occupational Med. 1079, 1081 (1990) (discussing findings based on interviews of 1,200 workers).
21. The other two at-risk occupations are teachers and counselors, with a depressive rate of 2.8; and secretaries, with a rate of 1.9. *Id.* at 1079.
23. *See* John F. Harkness, Jr., *Lawyers Helping Lawyers: A Message of Hope*, 73 Fla. B.J. 10 (Dec. 1999) (reporting that over half the grievances filed against lawyers have addiction or mental disorder as a significant contributing factor).
28. *See* Martin E.P. Seligman, *Helplessness: On Depression, Development, and Death* (2d ed., W.H. Freeman 1992).

productive and persistent, and quit more readily than optimistic agents. Pessimistic undergraduates get lower grades, relative to their SAT's and past academic record, than optimistic students. Pessimistic swimmers have more substandard swims and bounce back from poor swims less readily than do optimistic
swimmers. Historical research even suggests that pessimistic world leaders take
fewer risks and act more passively during political conflicts than their optimistic
counterparts. In the context of a military crisis and aggression by an adversary,
such passivity can have devastating consequences.

But while pessimists tend to be losers on many fronts, there is one striking
exception: pessimists may fare better in law. . . . In sharp contrast to results in
other realms of life, law students whose attributional style defined them as
"pessimistic" actually fared better than their optimistic peers. Specifically, the
pessimists outperformed more optimistic students on traditional measures of
achievement, such as grade-point average and law journal success.

These data suggest that what is labeled as pessimism is not a detriment and
may even be a virtue for lawyers. Pessimism encompasses certain "positive"
dimensions; it contains what we call—in less pejorative terms—"prudence." A
prudent perspective, which requires caution, skepticism and "reality-apprecia-
tion," may be an asset for law or other skill-based professions. It is certainly a
quality that is embraced in legal education. Prudence enables a good lawyer to see
snares and catastrophes that might conceivably occur in any given transaction.
The ability to anticipate a whole range of problems that non-lawyers do not see is
highly adaptive for the practicing lawyer. Indeed clients would be less effectively
served if lawyers did not so behave, even though this ability to question occasionally leads to lawyers being labeled as deal breakers or obstructionists.

The qualities that make for a good lawyer, however, may not make for a
happy human being. Pessimism is well documented as a major risk factor for
unhappiness and depression. Lawyers cannot easily turn off their pessimism
(i.e. prudence) when they leave the office. Lawyers who can see acutely how bad
things might be for clients are also burdened with the tendency to see how bad
things might be for themselves. . . . In this manner, pessimism that might be
adaptive in the profession also carries the risk of depression and anxiety in the
lawyer's personal life. The challenge is how to remain prudent professionally and
yet contain pessimistic tendencies in domains of life outside the office.

B. Low Decision Latitude

. . . Decision latitude refers to the number of choices one has or, as it turns
out, one believes one has. Workers in occupations that involve little or no
control are at risk for depression and for poor physical health. An important
study of the correlation of job conditions with depression and coronary disease
used two dimensions: (1) job demands and (2) decision latitude. There is one
quadrant particularly inimical to health and morale: high job demand combined
with low decision latitude. Individuals with jobs in this quadrant had a much
higher incidence of coronary disease and depression than individuals in the
other three quadrants.

Nurses and secretaries are the usual occupations falling in that quadrant,
but in recent years, junior associates at major law firms have been added to the
list. These lawyers often confront situations of high pressure combined with low

decision latitude. Beyond the intense job demands of law practice, low decision latitude is also a frequently cited problem. Associates often have little voice or control over their work, only limited contact with their superiors, and virtually no client contact. Instead, for at least the first few years of practice, many remain cloistered and isolated in a library (or behind a computer screen), researching and drafting memos.

In these high-pressure, low decision latitude positions, the associates are likely candidates for negative health effects, such as higher rates of heart disease; and for higher divorce rates. These same associates are, not surprisingly, candidates for early departure from law firms [and] . . . many young lawyers who do leave firms early choose alternative legal careers, such as legal aid or assistant district attorney, where the pay is considerably lower but the decision latitude is considerably greater.

III. Remedies for Pessimism and for Low Decision Latitude

There are well-documented antidotes for the difficulty lawyers face because of their pessimism and low decision latitude. As to pessimism, the antidote is to enlist its opposite dimension: optimism. Optimism is the ability to dispute recurrent catastrophic thoughts effectively, and it can be learned. "Flexible optimism" can be taught to both children and adults to enable them to determine how and in what situations one should use optimism and when to use pessimism. The techniques of "learned optimism," can teach lawyers to use optimism in their personal lives, yet maintain an adaptive pessimism in their professional lives. . . .

Learned optimism recommends that individuals employ a "disputing technique" to control their negative emotions. In the disputing technique, the lawyer first learns to identify catastrophic thoughts she has, and the circumstances under which they occur: "I'll never make it to partner," whenever a senior member of the firm fails to return her greeting. Then she learns to treat these thoughts as if they were uttered by a rival for her job, a third person whose mission is to make her life miserable. She then learns to marshal evidence against the catastrophic thoughts, "Even though he didn't smile when I said 'hi' this morning, he praised my brief in the meeting last week. He probably is on my side and was distracted by the big case he has to argue this afternoon." Credible disputing of pessimistic thinking (unlike, say dieting) is self-maintaining because one feels better at the moment one does it.

As to the high pressure-low decision latitude problem, there is a remedy as well. We accept that pressure is an inescapable aspect of law practice. But high pressure itself does not seem to be the problem; rather, it is the combination of high pressure and low decision latitude that causes negative health effects. By modifying this dimension, lawyers can become both more satisfied and more productive. One solution is to tailor a lawyer's day so there is considerably more personal control over work.[52] . . . Antidotes to associate malaise include

---

52. Volvo solved a similar problem on its assembly lines in the 1960s by giving its workers the choice of building a whole car in a group, rather than repeatedly building the same part. Similarly, a junior associate might be given a better sense of the whole picture by being introduced to clients, mentored by partners, and involved in transactional discussions.

more substantive training, mentoring, a voice in management, and earlier client contact—not expensive dinners or Cuban cigars. Those firms who understand the need to make these changes will benefit. Those who do not so respond, who instead simply throw money at the problem, will continue to see associates vote with their feet. . . .

Law firms should discover the particular signature strengths of their associates.[58] Exploiting them could make the difference between a demoralized associate and an energized, productive colleague. A firm can produce higher morale by setting aside five to ten hours of the workweek for "signature strength time," (i.e., a non-routine assignment that uses the signature strengths).[59] Over time, higher morale will translate into higher billing hours.

Some examples may serve to make the point. If an associate's strengths include leadership he or she could be assigned to associate committee work; or if it is social intelligence, he or she could be exposed to clients at an earlier stage. Originality might send an associate to the library to search out a non-obvious theory to an intractable legal problem. That may sound like the kind of duty all associates should assume; however, the idea of signature strengths is that some associates are indeed better suited to library work, and others to different roles at the firm, even though they must all have a commitment to legal analysis.

IV. The Harder Case: Zero vs. Non-Zero Sum Games

A. Zero-Sum Games and Emotion

A zero-sum game is a familiar occurrence. It is an endeavor in which the net result is zero. For every gain by one side, there is a counterbalancing loss by the other. A sports event is a zero-sum game, in that there must be winners and losers. A non-zero-sum game, in contrast, is an endeavor in which there is a net gain. Reading this essay is a positive-sum game: your exposure to new information does not mean someone else has forgotten an equivalent amount of information. Rather, there are gains on both sides: the reader learns something new, the authors disseminate their ideas, and so forth. . . .

B. The Adversary System as a Zero-Sum Game

The adversary process, which lies at the heart of the American system of law, has long been viewed as a classic zero-sum game: in litigation, one side's gain often moves in lockstep with the other side's loss. Lawyers are trained to be aggressive and competitive precisely because they must win the litigation game. This training, because it is fueled by negative emotions, can be a source of lawyer demoralization, even if it fulfills a social function. One problem with the

---

58. *See http://www.psych.upenn.edu/seligman* for identification of these and other strengths, and a self-test. A law firm can develop an inventory of associate strengths by having associates take tests and assigning duties based on the results. At law schools, the strengths analysis can be used to give students and placement directors a better sense of their career goals.

59. In each of these cases, the five to ten hours an associate devotes to using his or her signature strengths should be considered part of the normal workload, whether or not this time produces billable hours. This is similar to what happens when pro bono hours are calculated into an associate's workweek.

adversarial paradigm, according to leading lawyers like Sol Linowitz, is that "the single-minded drive toward winning the competition . . . will make these young lawyers not only less useful citizens . . . but also less good as lawyers, less sympathetic to other people's troubles, and less valuable to their clients."[64] . . . By understanding the values of the adversary system in terms of its zero-sum nature, we can assess alternatives that seek to soften competition with cooperation. Modifications to our legal system must be justified both in terms of an individual's well-being, and of our system of justice.

C. The Adversary System as a Social Good . . .

An accepted virtue of the common law, adversarial system of justice is that it leaves more control in the parties (through their attorneys). The civil law, accusatory system, on the other hand, places more control on the judge (or other decision-maker). Since control has a salutary psychological effect, the adversary model is one expression of a satisfactory political system. By placing control in the individual over the state the adversary system reflects deeper values of liberalism and even natural justice. In this way, the lawyer has a central role as a public servant, a preserver of the values inherent in our political structure, even when he or she is seemingly only arguing for a client's self-interest. And since the days of Adam Smith, we have believed that self-interest serves the public interest.

The psychological question is whether adversaries can be competitive without being pessimistic. . . .

This is not just a question of positive psychology. Justice Sandra Day O'Connor has asked why the profession envisions litigation as war.[71] The question is, can lawyers serve the adversary system without generating conflict on a personal level? Civility need not weaken the lawyer's commitment to the adversary system. In fact, a growing number of law schools and law firms now recognize the importance of instilling civility and teaching team-building skills. Under this vision, it may be possible to retain the virtues of adversariness while discarding some of its negative dimensions.

We suggest that controlling the intensity of non-zero behavior, like curbing the effects of pessimism in the earlier examples, can serve as a coping technique with positive health effects. Moreover, our initial description of the litigation experience emphasizes a largely limited, if not misleading, reality. The zero-sum effects of the adversary model, in terms of its "winner-take-all" mentality, usually occur where cases are tried to judgment—a small minority of cases. Where settlements occur, both sides frequently have made wise choices that allow them to claim victory.

Outside of litigation, non-zero expectations can play an even greater role. As Dean Clark has noted, most lawyers are not litigators; rather they are specialists

---

64. Sol M. Linowitz, *The Betrayed Profession: Lawyering at the End of the Twentieth Century* 107-08 (1994).
71. *See* Sandra Day O'Connor, Speech, *Professionalism*, 78 Or. L. Rev. 385, 388 (1999). The "war" analogy is deeply imbedded in the litigation world, where dealings with other attorneys are described with terms such as "attacked" and "shot down." *Id.*

in "normative ordering."[75] The notion of normative ordering suggests a role that fits the lawyer-statesman ideal Dean Kronman seeks to revive. When lawyers assume these roles, cooperation challenges the virtue of competition. For example, Ronald Gilson has argued that business lawyers—the deal-makers—can create value in such a way as to eliminate the zero-sum problem altogether.[76] . . .

V. The Role and Responsibility of Law Schools

Law schools are both a source of the problem and a necessary part of the solution. The Socratic teaching method—employed especially in large, first-year classes—cultivates and encourages adversarial thinking by emphasizing zero-sum situations. The students' adversarial skills are honed by withstanding questioning from skeptical interrogators. In this respect, law school pedagogy differs from that of business schools, where cooperative projects and thinking are the rule in leading MBA programs. Moreover, competition for grades, among a group who self selects law for its pessimistic qualities, adds to the challenges. . . . This relationship of success in classroom performance to the litigation model is rarely explored or explained in legal education. Yet the connections between the Socratic method and the adversary system may well set the stage for the kinds of difficulties law students later face as young associates, as well as their successes. We encourage further study into the relationships among teaching style, grading methods, and the pessimistic tendencies of law students.

The connection between law teaching and the demands of practice might be revealed early in the first year, rather than assumed. Such an explanation may not overcome embarrassing moments in the classroom, but it can provide an objective rationale for an experience that some now find alienating precisely because it seems unnecessary or even gratuitous. At the least, explaining that their education serves certain social purposes gives students the illusion of control and also introduces them to the demands they will face in practice.

The subject of positive psychology and lawyer unhappiness deserves exploration in the academic setting. Offering law students a sense of what the lawyer's life demands can increase the feeling of control over their professional lives. With this background, both academic and career choices can be made on a more intelligent and emotionally satisfying basis. In fact, a survey of student strengths at this stage might have considerable value. Some students have talents for litigation, for example, while others lean in the direction of less confrontational forms of practice. Some have signature strengths of valor and originality, others of social intelligence and fairness. These strengths have a real world dimension: they could be factored into the career placement function at law schools in order to provide a better fit between a first job and the talents of graduating students. . . .

---

75. Robert C. Clark, *Why So Many Lawyers: Are They Good or Bad?*, 61 Fordham L. Rev. 275, 281 (1992).
76. *See* Ronald J. Gilson, *Value Creation by Business Lawyers: Legal Skills and Asset Pricing*, 94 Yale L.J. 239, 253-55 (1984) (labeling those lawyers "transaction cost engineers").

VI. Summary and Next Steps

The pervasive disenchantment among lawyers and the concomitant attrition rate among law firms can be remedied. The solutions will be found not by increasing compensation or perks, but instead by using more valuable, but less tangible rewards. This will require changes in law firm culture—greater emphasis on positive-sum games and cooperation—as well as reforms at three levels: individual, firm-wide, and institutional. At the individual level, lawyers must first recognize that pessimism is maladaptive outside of work. Perhaps they then can learn to apply the techniques of flexible optimism in their private lives. At the law firm level, those members with the most power to effect change should actively participate in creating more decision latitude for junior associates. At the least, partners should create mentoring relationships with junior associates. They should also delegate responsibilities and allocate tasks to junior associates that better speak to their signature strengths, thereby providing more control and decision-making power at an earlier stage in their development.

Third, at the institutional level, bar associations that foster and promote civility among their members are on the right track. Judges and counsel who encourage settlement and direct cases toward mediation may deserve credit for dampening the zero-sum nature of practice. The law schools also play an institutional role. They are the entry point to the profession and help shape the system. By assisting new lawyers to adapt to the demands of practice they can become agents for positive change. The goal is clear if elusive: create a psychologically healthier profession while honoring the essential role of lawyers as client representatives. These need not be incompatible objectives.

. . . We suggest that by decreasing pessimism, increasing decision latitude, and leavening zero-sum games with a cooperative dimension, the practice of law can become healthier and no less profitable. Admittedly, this is a challenging agenda. But even if it cannot be fully realized, we have at least helped answer the question why lawyers are unhappy and we have suggested why they need not be in the future.

■ Lawyers' Roles:
Finding Your Own Way

In Chapter 1, we defined legal ethics as the study of what is required for a lawyer to provide a professional service to another. Lawyers' roles are complicated by the facts that clients simultaneously empower lawyers to act and then become subject to the power created by the lawyer's specialized knowledge and ability to access the legal system. Several notes and cases in Chapters 6 and 7 commented on lawyers who apparently assumed directive or instrumental roles, which caused them to risk violating legal norms designed to protect clients or the public.[1] At the end of Chapter 7, we pointed out that most lawyers get it right most of the time by zealously representing their clients within the bounds of the

---

1. Lawyers' Roles: *The Directive Lawyer and Fiduciary Duty, supra* p. 168; Lawyers' Roles: *The Instrumental Lawyer and the Bounds of the Law, supra* p. 225.

law.[2] The cases and materials in the second half of this book illustrate these same themes. Some of the lawyers in these cases acted in directive roles, preferring the interests of third persons or their own interests over those of their clients. Others got into trouble by overidentifying with their clients, by seeing themselves as instrumental cogs in the machinery of the legal system.

Directive Self-Servers

Chapters 8 and 9 offered numerous examples of lawyers who breached fiduciary duty by failing to recognize or respond properly to conflicts of interest. These lawyers underidentified with their clients and fell short of providing zealous representation. They neglected the lessons of fiduciary duty that lawyers serve client interests, not their own, another client's, or the interests of a third party.[3] Chapter 10 also offered examples of lawyers who placed profit maximization above fiduciary duty to their clients. These lawyers failed to recognize that lawyer fees are regulated, and that clients have absolute rights to discharge them at will.[4] Similarly, *Gilles* in Chapter 11 illustrates a lawyer and law firm that failed to view fiduciary duty from the client's point of view, incorrectly thinking they could abandon the client's case without assuring that the client had ample opportunity to find replacement counsel.

Instrumental Cogs

At the same time, Chapter 12 offered new and serious examples of lawyers who understood their role in largely instrumental terms. These lawyers provided zealous advocacy, but failed to recognize a clear legal limit to their representation of client interests, such as those provided by Federal Rules of Civil Procedure 11 or 26. They overidentified with their clients and suffered sanctions, discipline, and disqualification as a result.[5]

Dual Difficulties

Several lawyers in the second half of this book suffered from the excesses of both directive and instrumental role behavior at the same time. For example, the insurance defense firm in *Wolpaw*,[6] like those in *Perez*[7] and *Spaulding*,[8] acted instrumentally toward one potential client, the insurer who hired it and paid the bill, and inappropriately directed the other primary client, the insured, who was equally entitled to representation complete with the full array of fiduciary

---

2. Lawyers' Roles: *Zealous Representation Within the Bounds of the Law, supra* p. 279.
3. *See* Maritrans GP Inc. v. Pepper Hamilton & Scheetz, *supra* p. 285; Monco v. Janus, *supra* p. 294; In re Halverson, *supra* p. 305; Burrow v. Arce, *supra* p. 333; Eastman Kodak Co. v. Sony Corp., *supra* p. 364; Anderson v. O'Brien,, *supra* p. 350; Mitchell v. Metropolitan Life Ins. Co., *supra* p. 373.
4. *See* Matter of Fordham, *supra* p. 405; Malonis v. Harrington, *supra* p. 433; In re Sather, *supra* p. 425.
5. *See* Christian v. Mattel, Inc., *supra* p. 478; In re Tutu Wells Contamination Litigation, *supra* p. 485; In re Charges of Unprofessional Conduct, *supra* p. 493; Matter of Disc. Proceedings Against Ragatz, *supra* p. 500.
6. *See* Wolpaw v. Gen. Accident Ins. Co., *supra* p. 348.
7. Perez v. Kirk & Carrigan, *supra* p. 165.
8. Spaulding v. Zimmerman, *supra* p. 204.

duties. In serving the insurance company, the lawyers in both of these cases breached duties to the insured, and, at the same time, aided the insurer in neglecting its contractual obligations to the insured.

The same duality of role confusion emerges in *Birbrower*.[9] The court there was concerned with protecting the public from unlicensed professionals and made clear that the New York law firm failed to recognize that legal limit on their right to practice law. At the same time, the court characterized the firm's unauthorized practice of law as a breach of a client obligation by granting the affected client a complementary remedy, freedom to avoid its contractual fee.

Getting It Right

At the end of Chapter 7, we noted that most lawyers avoid both of these extremes by acting as collaborators with their clients.[10] Many of the lawyers in the second half of this book also found the right course. For example, the law firm in A. v. B. sought the discretion to disclose material information learned from one client to another.[11] These lawyers did not favor one client over another by automatically disclosing, as occurred in *Perez*. Instead, they recognized that some strong policy must justify limiting their fiduciary duty to one client, then sought and won court approval to rely on an explicit confidentiality exception to legitimate the disclosure.

Consider further the law firm in *Messing*.[12] After being sanctioned nearly $100,000 for unlawful contact with Harvard employees, the firm had to decide whether to recommend an appeal to its client. Although the client's interest in avoiding additional litigation costs and the law firm's interest in reversing the sanction conflicted, ultimately both client and lawyer interests were vindicated on appeal.[13] The law firm took a risk in advising its client to appeal the issue, but also no doubt recognized that the lower court's decision was not universally supported by other courts and had negative policy implications both for its client and others in similar circumstances.

Finally, consider the actions of the lawyers who blew the whistle on employers in *Crews* and *Kelly*.[14] Each understood that lawyers in their offices were engaged in violations of the rules of professional conduct, both understood their own obligation to speak up, and both did so, first to supervisors and eventually to others. Each encountered significant economic, personal, and professional incentives not to speak, or to defer to supervisors who told them that the matter was being handled. Like the lawyer in *Meyerhofer*,[15] both carefully documented the continuing rule violations, and both suffered job loss

---

9. Birbrower, Montalbano, Condon & Frank P.C. v. Superior Court, *supra* p. 535.
10. *See* Lawyers' Roles: *Zealous Representation Within the Bounds of the Law*, *supra* p. 279.
11. A. v. B., *supra* p. 355.
12. Messing, Rudavsky & Weliky, P.C. v. President & Fellows of Harvard College, *supra* p. 496.
13. In fact, the case attracted a number of amicus briefs from other groups including labor unions, which supported the law firm's activity.
14. Crews v. Buckman Laboratories Intl., Inc., *supra* p. 458; Kelly v. Hunton & Williams, *supra* p. 548.
15. Meyerhofer v. Empire Fire & Marine Ins. Co., *supra* p. 243.

as a result. Neither had any assurance that any legal relief would later be available to them for doing the right thing, yet each persevered.

All of these lawyers got it right. They realized that the rules of professional conduct allowed them a great deal of professional discretion to do the right thing. We have seen, for example, that lawyers are free to participate in pro bono and law reform cases, an option open to lawyers in a case like *Messing* when client financial limitations may otherwise prevent full judicial consideration of an important legal issue. Further, lawyers are free to choose the kind of practice they prefer and to decide which cases to take.[16] Lawyers also can limit the scope of the engagement and have a great deal of discretion to counsel clients about moral as well as legal limits to conduct. If a client insists on advocacy arguably or clearly outside of legal limits, lawyers also may or must end the representation.[17] Ultimately, lawyers, like all other professionals, have the option of changing jobs, as *Meyerhofer, Crews,* and *Kelly* demonstrate.

But how did they formulate their chosen course of action? First, each of these lawyers learned from the law of lawyering to avoid the extremes of both instrumental and directive behavior. They avoided instrumental thinking by being aware of the limits of the law and by refusing to "exclude their own personal values from all professional decisionmaking."[18] At the same time, they avoided directive behavior by recalling the dictates of fiduciary duty and by checking their personal beliefs against their professional obligations to represent clients zealously within the bounds of the law. In other words, they relied on both their personal values and their professional obligations "to signal an ethical quandary," and drew on these values to construct a personal goal. In this process, they were continually informed by their responsibilities to clients and the limits of the law to assure them that the action they took was well within the scope of professional discretion "relegated to the lawyer's ungrounded discretion."[19]

Law and Life

In an earlier note, we introduced the idea that lawyers who represent clients zealously within the bounds of the law act as translators or mediators between the private world of clients and the public world of law. The lawyers in these materials who got it right did the same thing for themselves, mediating between their own personal values and the public world of law. They translated the law for themselves, as well as for their clients, and translated their own values into the law they eventually were a part of making. This insight leads us to consider a fuller meaning of the lawyer as translator metaphor, and we defer here to Professor James Boyd White, who created it:

---

16. *See, e.g.,* Patrick J. Schilt, *On Being a Happy, Healthy, and Ethical Member of an Unhappy, Unhealthy, and Unethical Profession,* 52 Vand. L. Rev. 871 (1999).
17. *See* Nathan M. Crystal, *Developing a Philosophy of Lawyering,* 14 Notre Dame J.L., Ethics & Pub. Policy 75 (2000).
18. Bruce A. Green, *The Role of Personal Values in Professional Decisionmaking,* 11 Geo. J. Leg. Ethics 19, 56 (1997).
19. *Id.*

What I suggest, briefly, is this: that the lawyer is not, as we sometimes think, only a cog in a system of social administration, nor simply a profit-maximizing service provider, but a person who meets, who can learn to meet, the moment at which the language of the law—a language that has justice as its aim—is applied to experience, the moment at which it must confront other languages. . . . The lawyer or judge live constantly at the edge of language, the edge of meaning, where the world can be, must be, imagined anew; to do this well is an enormous achievement; to do it badly, a disaster of real importance, not only for the lawyer or judge but for the social world of which they are a part, including the particular people whose lives they affect. . . .

I might sum it up in this way: Of course the lawyer usually knows more than his client about the law, and in some sense has thus already thought about the issue his client presents; but there is always, or almost always, something new and distinctive and problematic about what the client brings him that requires further thought, and often thought of a deep and uncertain kind. . . .

One way to think about the law, in fact, is as an intervention into a world that works largely in nonlegal terms, and for the most part well enough, but that has now suffered a crisis or breakdown calling for its help. . . .

In each case we begin with the life of the world that precedes the lawyer's involvement, where the parties are competent at shaping their own existences; there is then an event that leads one, then the other, to go to a lawyer; there then ensues a lot of activity, mainly in language—followed by an action, or a refusal to act, by the court or by the lawyers in negotiation, and a return to the world of ordinary life, either changed by what has happened, or unchanged. It thus always is—or should be—a question for the lawyer what relation exists or can exist between the language of the law, the language in which he talks and functions, and the experience and life of the world. . . .

[T]he lawyer must perpetually face the relation between legal language and other languages—other ways of representing the situation or the actors in it, other ways of imagining human motive and experience, other ways of shaping the future. In the courtroom and negotiation alike other languages and voices are regularly translated into the law, always with some distortion, sometimes to good effect, sometimes to bad. Sometimes the law itself changes as a result, but in the end it systematically excludes voices, narratives, languages—ways of thinking and talking that it finds irrelevant to its concerns or of which it does not approve. It is thus a constant question for the lawyer how to manage the relation between law and other languages. . . .

Think for example what it would be like to have someone come to you and describe the collapse of a commercial deal, perhaps a partnership or a long-term contract, for which he had once had great hopes, but which has now proven a disaster. How completely could you capture in your own mind what happened in the world, what its significance was, and how would you think about what ought to happen next? How adequate do you suppose the legal language of partnerships or contracts would be to this situation? The language of accounting or economic theory? What place would the voices of languages of the parties, or of outside experts on technical issues, have in what you said or did? This set of questions could be asked about virtually any case—a divorce, an accident, a crime—and they are present not only when the law looks back on past experience, as it does here, but when it tries to shape experience for the future, by drafting a partnership agreement, for example, or a prenuptial contract, or a divorce settlement. . . .

The law is among other things a system for attracting our attention to difficult questions, and holding it there; for stimulating thought of a disciplined and often creative kind, and feelings too, especially . . . the desire for justice that is called into existence by the questions the case presents, by the contrasting views of the lawyers on each side, and by our own inner sense of the reality and importance of what is at stake. The process of legal thought simultaneously resists simplicity and appeals to the side of us that wants to imagine the world, and ourselves and others within it, in a coherent way. A case is a bright moment, at which we have the opportunity to face at once the language we are given to use and the particulars of the case before us, and in both directions we are drawn into real struggles of mind and imagination. The object of law is justice; but the law teaches us, over and over again, that we do not have unmediated access to the pure idea of justice in the heavens, which we can apply directly and with confidence, but rather live in a world in which everything has to be thought about, argued out, and reimagined afresh. It is a lesson in the difficulty of imagining the world, and the self and others within it, in such a way as to make possible coherent speech and meaningful action.[20]

Your Way

Of course, you may not agree with all Professor White has to say, or with our characterization of the lawyers in this book. At the very least, we hope that these materials illustrate for you the wide latitude you will have in practice to establish your own role with clients, as well as the clear dangers you will face if you err too far on either end of the spectrum.

Like some of the lawyers in this book, you can choose a somewhat simplistic but psychologically comfortable role, which tends to emphasize instrumental behavior. You may even delight in thinking of yourself as a hired gun, serving the autonomous interests of each client. You may overidentify with your clients, turning into a "business servant"[21] or become cynical about your client's motives, assuming that most clients do not want to be fair and assisting them in getting away with what they can.

Or, like other lawyers in this book, perhaps you prefer to think of yourself more as a directive lawyer who finds security not in psychological identification with clients but who prefers distance from their needs; a lawyer who runs a business. You may decide that profit is what led you to law school, and that the pursuit of profit will determine what kind of cases you target, what level of service each client gets, and how you bill.

The materials in this book demonstrate that the law governing lawyers has responded to both of these extremes with concrete incentives that steer lawyers away from the minefields of violating fiduciary duty and exceeding the bounds of legitimate advocacy. If you favor or tend toward an instrumental role, you need to be especially alert to the limits of the law that apply to your own conduct as well as that of your clients. The lawyers in this book who evaded those limits suffered tort liability, sanctions for violations of procedural rules, criminal liability, disqualification, and professional discipline. If you favor or tend to lean toward a directive role, you will be wise to recall the lawyers in this book who

---

20. James Boyd White, *The Edge of Meaning* 223-226, 250-251 (U. Chi. Press 2001).
21. Russell G. Pearce, *The Professional Paradigm Shift: Why Discarding Professional Ideology Will Improve the Conduct and Reputation of the Bar*, 70 N.Y.U. L. Rev. 1229 (1995).

ignored fiduciary duty and suffered malpractice liability, disqualification, loss of a fee or contractual benefit, and professional discipline.

Ultimately, these legal rules spring from and dictate ethics: how we ought to respond to those we chose to serve.[22] They require concrete action, not just intent or thought. They also prod you to assess risk realistically. Beyond understanding these rules and assessing the obligations they create, however, the materials in this chapter also ask you to consider how your life as a lawyer will influence the rest of your life and how the rest of your life will influence your practice of law. Most people and most lawyers want to reconcile their personal values with their professional life. To do so requires continuing dialogue between your personal beliefs and your professional practice.[23] Just as representing clients well requires translation of their personal beliefs into the professional language of the law and translation of the moral fabric of legal rules to your client's situation, so also does your sense of self require continuing translation of your professional to your personal self and back again.

In the end, if you hope to develop the ability to serve clients' interests well, to invent and articulate plans for them, or to grease the bearings of social justice by translating their stories into the language of the law, you will need to develop and maintain the ability to mediate between the ordinary world of everyday life and the legal system.[24] If you want to find guidance for the exercise of your own professional discretion, you also will need to mediate between your personal self and the legal world you work in.[25] As you do this, we wish you the blessing of a life that allows you to integrate your personal and professional self. The lawyers able to discover this connection will be most capable of practicing what they advise their clients: moving on with their lives, perhaps with a renewed sense of vision, influenced both by the ordinary world and the lessons of law that support it.

---

22. *See, e.g.,* Anthony E. Cook, *Forward: Towards a Postmodern Ethics of Service,* 81 Geo. L.J. 2457 (1993).
23. *See* George W. Kaufman, *The Lawyers' Guide to Balancing Life and Work: Taking the Stress Out of Success* (ABA 1999).
24. *See* Lawrence S. Krieger, *What We're Not Telling Law Students—and Lawyers—That They Really Need to Know: Some Thoughts-in-Action Toward Revitalizing the Profession from Its Roots,* 13 J. L. & Health 1 (1998-1999).
25. *See, e.g.,* Joseph Allegretti, *Lawyers, Client, and Covenant: A Religious Perspective on Legal Practice and Ethics,* 66 Fordham L. Rev. 1101 (1998).

Chapter 15

Judicial Ethics

Problems

15-1. Martyn is representing a client in an appeal to Judge Jones from an adverse zoning hearing board decision. Martyn's client calls her up in a panic. Client's family was out to dinner in Puerto Rico last week escaping the cold. As the family went to their assigned table in the dining room, they passed a table where Judge Jones, the Solicitor for the Township, and what appeared to be their spouses were seated, clinking champagne flutes. As Client walked past, Judge Jones awkwardly explained they were attending a county association annual meeting. "We're high school classmates, y'know."

15-2. In a local candidate forum for next fall's county elections, the moderator asked the judicial candidates, "What is your opinion on abortion?" "If I had the right case come before me," the Republican candidate replied, "I'd overturn Roe v. Wade in a minute. Worst decision in history," she continued, as the applause from half the attendees drowned out the rest of her speech.

15-3. Fox has a huge contingency practice. When he is nominated to go on the bench, Fox hands off his cases to an old friend, with the understanding that Fox will receive a referral fee. "Don't worry," Fox tells his friend, "I'll help you with these cases since I know them so well." Three of the cases are pending in the same county court where Fox will become a judge.

Consider: Model Code of Judicial Conduct Rules
        28 U.S.C. §455

Cheney v. United States District Court for the District of Columbia

541 U.S. 913 (2004)

Memorandum of Justice SCALIA.

I have before me a motion to recuse in these cases consolidated below.

I

The decision whether a judge's impartiality can "'reasonably be questioned'" is to be made in light of the facts as they existed, and not as they were surmised or reported. The facts here were as follows:

For five years or so, I have been going to Louisiana during the Court's long December-January recess, to the duck-hunting camp of a friend whom I met through two hunting companions from Baton Rouge, one a dentist and the other a worker in the field of handicapped rehabilitation. The last three years, I have been accompanied on this trip by a son-in-law who lives near me. Our friend and host, Wallace Carline, has never, as far as I know, had business before this Court. He is not, as some reports have described him, an "energy industry executive" in the sense that summons up boardrooms of Exxon Mobil or Con Edison. He runs his own company that provides services and equipment rental to oil rigs in the Gulf of Mexico.

During my December 2002 visit, I learned that Mr. Carline was an admirer of Vice President Cheney. Knowing that the Vice President, with whom I am well acquainted (from our years serving together in the Ford administration), is an enthusiastic duck-hunter, I asked whether Mr. Carline would like to invite him to our next

year's hunt. The answer was yes; I conveyed the invitation (with my own warm recommendation) in the spring of 2003 and received an acceptance (subject, of course, to any superseding demands on the Vice President's time) in the summer. The Vice President said that if he did go, I would be welcome to fly down to Louisiana with him. (Because of national security requirements, of course, he must fly in a Government plane.) That invitation was later extended—if space was available—to my son-in-law and to a son who was joining the hunt for the first time; they accepted. The trip was set long before the Court granted certiorari in the present case, and indeed before the petition for certiorari had even been filed.

We departed from Andrews Air Force Base at about 10 a.m. on Monday, January 5, flying in a Gulfstream jet owned by the Government. We landed in Patterson, Louisiana, and went by car to a dock where Mr. Carline met us, to take us on the 20-minute boat trip to his hunting camp. We arrived at about 2 pm., the 5 of us joining about 8 other hunters, making about 13 hunters in all; also present during our time there were about 3 members of Mr. Carline's staff, and, of course, the Vice President's staff and security detail. It was not an intimate setting. The group hunted that afternoon and Tuesday and Wednesday mornings; it fished (in two boats) Tuesday afternoon. All meals were in common. Sleeping was in rooms of two or three, except for the Vice President, who had his own quarters. Hunting was in two- or three-man blinds. As it turned out, I never hunted in the same blind with the Vice President. Nor was I alone with him at any time during the trip, except, perhaps, for instances so brief and unintentional that I would not recall them—walking to or from a boat, perhaps, or going to or from dinner. Of course we said not a word about the present case. The Vice President left the camp Wednesday afternoon, about two days after our arrival. I stayed on to hunt (with my son and son-in-law) until late Friday morning, when the three of us returned to Washington on a commercial flight from New Orleans.

II

Let me respond, at the outset, to Sierra Club's suggestion that I should "resolve any doubts in favor of recusal." That might be sound advice if I were sitting on a Court of Appeals. There, my place would be taken by another judge, and the case would proceed normally. On the Supreme Court, however, the consequence is different: The Court proceeds with eight Justices, raising the possibility that, by reason of a tie vote, it will find itself unable to resolve the significant legal issue presented by the case. Thus, as Justices stated in their 1993 Statement of Recusal Policy: "[W]e do not think it would serve the public interest to go beyond the requirements of the statute, and to recuse ourselves, out of an excess of caution, whenever a relative is a partner in the firm before us or acted as a lawyer at an earlier stage. Even one unnecessary recusal impairs the functioning of the Court." Moreover, granting the motion is (insofar as the outcome of the particular case is

concerned) effectively the same as casting a vote against the petitioner. The petitioner needs five votes to overturn the judgment below, and it makes no difference whether the needed fifth vote is missing because it has been cast for the other side, or because it has not been cast at all.

Even so, recusal is the course I must take—and will take—when, on the basis of established principles and practices, I have said or done something which requires that course. I have recused for such a reason this very Term. *See* Elk Grove Unified School District v. Newdow, 540 U.S. 945 (2003). I believe, however, that established principles and practices do not require (and thus do not permit) recusal in the present case.

A

My recusal is required if, by reason of the actions described above, my "impartiality might reasonably be questioned." 28 U.S.C. §455(a). Why would that result follow from my being in a sizable group of persons, in a hunting camp with the Vice President, where I never hunted with him in the same blind or had other opportunity for private conversation? The only possibility is that it would suggest I am a friend of his. But while friendship is a ground for recusal of a Justice where the personal fortune or the personal freedom of the friend is at issue, it has traditionally *not* been a ground for recusal where *official action* is at issue, no matter how important the official action was to the ambitions or the reputation of the Government officer.

A rule that required Members of this Court to remove themselves from cases in which the official actions of friends were at issue would be utterly disabling. Many Justices have reached this Court precisely because they were friends of the incumbent President or other senior officials— and from the earliest days down to modern times Justices have had close personal relationships with the President and other officers of the Executive. John Quincy Adams hosted dinner parties featuring such luminaries as Chief Justice Marshall, Justices Johnson, Story, and Todd, Attorney General Wirt, and Daniel Webster. Justice Harlan and his wife often "'stopped in'" at the White House to see the Hayes family and pass a Sunday evening in a small group, visiting and singing hymns. Justice Stone tossed around a medicine ball with members of the Hoover administration mornings outside the White House. Justice Douglas was a regular at President Franklin Roosevelt's poker parties; Chief Justice Vinson played poker with President Truman. A no-friends rule would have disqualified much of the Court in Youngstown Sheet & Tube Co. v. Sawyer, 343 U.S. 579 (1952), the case that challenged President Truman's seizure of the steel mills. Most of the Justices knew Truman well, and four had been appointed by him. A no-friends rule would surely have required Justice Holmes's recusal in Northern Securities Co. v. United States, 193 U.S. 197 (1904), the case that challenged President Theodore Roosevelt's trust-busting initiative. *See* S. Novick, Honorable Justice: The Life of Oliver Wendell Holmes 264 (1989) ("Holmes and Fanny dined at the White House every week or two . . . ").

It is said, however, that this case is different because the federal officer (Vice President Cheney) is actually a *named party*. That is by no means a rarity. At the beginning of the current Term, there were before the Court (excluding habeas actions) no fewer than 83 cases in which high-level federal Executive officers were named in their official capacity— more than 1 in every 10 federal civil cases then pending. That an officer is named has traditionally made no difference to the proposition that friendship is not considered to affect impartiality in official-action suits. Regardless of whom they name, such suits, when the officer is the plaintiff, seek relief not for him personally but for the Government; and, when the officer is the defendant, seek relief not against him personally, but against the Government. That is why federal law provides for *automatic substitution* of the new officer when the originally named officer has been replaced. The caption of Sierra Club's complaint in this action designates as a defendant "Vice President Richard Cheney, *in his official capacity* as Vice President of the United States and Chairman of the National Energy Policy Development Group." The body of the complaint repeats (in paragraph 6) that "Defendant Richard Cheney is sued *in his official capacity* as the Vice President of the United States and Chairman of the Cheney Energy Task Force." *Id.*, at 143 (emphasis added). Sierra Club has *relied* upon the fact that this is an official-action rather than a personal suit as a basis for denying the petition. It asserted in its brief in opposition that if there was no presidential immunity from discovery in Clinton v. Jones, 520 U.S. 681 (1997), which was a private suit, "[s]urely . . . the Vice President and subordinate White House officials have no greater immunity claim here, especially when the lawsuit relates to their official actions while in office and the primary relief sought is a declaratory judgment."

Richard Cheney's name appears in this suit only because he was the head of a Government committee that allegedly did not comply with the Federal Advisory Committee Act (FACA), and because he may, by reason of his office, have custody of some or all of the Government documents that the plaintiffs seek. If some other person were to become head of that committee or to obtain custody of those documents, the plaintiffs would name that person and Cheney would be dismissed. Unlike the defendant in United States v. Nixon, 418 U.S. 683 (1974), or Clinton v. Jones, *supra*, 520 U.S. 681, Cheney is represented here, not by his personal attorney, but by the United States Department of Justice in the person of the Solicitor General. And the courts at all levels have referred to his arguments as (what they are) the arguments of "the government."

The recusal motion, however, asserts the following:

> "Critical to the issue of Justice Scalia's recusal is understanding that this is not a run-of-the-mill legal dispute about an administrative decision. . . . Because his own conduct is central to this case, the Vice President's 'reputation and his integrity are on the line.'"

I think not. Certainly as far as the legal issues immediately presented to me are concerned, this *is* "a run-of-the-mill legal dispute about an administrative decision." I am asked to determine what powers the District Court possessed under FACA, and whether the Court of Appeals should have asserted mandamus or appellate jurisdiction over the District Court.[1] Nothing this Court says on those subjects will have any bearing upon the reputation and integrity of Richard Cheney. Moreover, even if this Court affirms the decision below and allows discovery to proceed in the District Court, the issue that would ultimately present itself *still* would have no bearing upon the reputation and integrity of Richard Cheney. That issue would be, quite simply, whether some private individuals were *de facto* members of the National Energy Policy Development Group (NEPDG). It matters not whether they were caused to be so by Cheney or someone else, or whether Cheney was even aware of their *de facto* status; if they *were de facto* members, then (according to D.C. Circuit law) the records and minutes of NEPDG must be made public.

The recusal motion asserts, however, that Richard Cheney's "reputation and his integrity are on the line" because

> "respondents have alleged, *inter alia*, that the Vice President, as the head

---

1. The Questions Presented in the petition, and accepted for review, are as follows:

"1. Whether the Federal Advisory Committee Act (FACA), 5 U.S.C. App. §§1 *et seq.*, can be construed . . . to authorize broad discovery of the process by which the Vice President and other senior advisors gathered information to advise the President on important national policy matters, based solely on an unsupported allegation in a complaint that the advisory group was not constituted as the President expressly directed and the advisory group itself reported.

2. Whether the court of appeals had mandamus or appellate jurisdiction to review the district court's unprecedented discovery orders in this litigation."

of the Task Force and its sub-groups, was responsible for the involvement of energy industry executives in the operations of the Task Force, as a result of which the Task Force and its sub-groups became subject to FACA."

As far as Sierra Club's *complaint* is concerned, it simply is not true that Vice President Cheney is singled out as having caused the involvement of energy executives. But even if the allegation had been made, it would be irrelevant to the case. FACA assertedly requires disclosure if there were private members of the task force, *no matter who* they were—"energy industry executives" or Ralph Nader; and *no matter who* was responsible for their membership—the Vice President or no one in particular. I do not see how the Vice President's "reputation and integrity are on the line" any more than the agency head's reputation and integrity are on the line in virtually all official-action suits, which accuse his agency of acting (to quote the Administrative Procedure Act) "arbitrar[ily], capricious[ly], [with] an abuse of discretion, or otherwise not in accordance with law." 5 U.S.C. §706 (2)(A). Beyond that always-present accusation, there is nothing illegal or immoral about making "energy industry executives" members of a task force on energy; some people probably think it would be a good idea. If, in doing so, or in allowing it to happen, the Vice President went beyond his assigned powers, that is no worse than what every agency head has done when his action is judicially set aside.

To be sure, there could be political consequences from disclosure of the fact (if it be so) that the Vice President favored business interests, and especially a sector of business with which he was formerly connected. But political consequences are not my concern, and the possibility of them does not convert an official suit into a private one. That possibility exists to a greater or lesser degree in virtually all suits involving agency action. To expect judges to take account of political consequences—and to assess the high or low degree of them—is to ask judges to do precisely what they should not do. It seems to me quite wrong (and quite impossible) to make recusal depend upon what degree of political damage a particular case can be expected to inflict.

In sum, I see nothing about this case which takes it out of the category of normal official-action litigation, where my friendship, or the appearance of my friendship, with one of the named officers does not require recusal.

B

The recusal motion claims that "the fact that Justice Scalia and his daughter [sic] were the Vice President's guest on Air Force Two on the flight down to Louisiana" means that I "accepted a sizable gift from a party in a pending case," a gift "measured in the thousands of dollars."

Let me speak first to the value, though that is not the principal point. Our flight down cost the Government nothing, since space-available was the condition of our invitation. And, though our flight down on the Vice President's plane was indeed free, since we were not returning with him we purchased (because they were least expensive) round-trip tickets that cost precisely what we would have paid if we had gone both down and back on commercial flights. In other words, none of us saved a cent by flying on the Vice President's plane. The purpose of going with him was not saving money, but avoiding some inconvenience to ourselves (being taken by car from

New Orleans to Morgan City) and considerable inconvenience to our friends, who would have had to meet our plane in New Orleans, and schedule separate boat trips to the hunting camp, for us and for the Vice President's party. (To be sure, flying on the Vice President's jet was more comfortable and more convenient than flying commercially; that accommodation is a matter I address in the next paragraph.)[2]

The principal point, however, is that social courtesies, provided at Government expense by officials whose only business before the Court is business in their official capacity, have not hitherto been thought prohibited. Members of Congress and others are frequently invited to accompany Executive Branch officials on Government planes, where space is available. That this is not the sort of gift thought likely to affect a judge's impartiality is suggested by the fact that the Ethics in Government Act of 1978, 5 U.S.C. App. §101 et seq., which requires annual reporting of transportation provided or reimbursed, excludes from this requirement transportation provided by the United States. I daresay that, at a hy-

pothetical charity auction, much more would be bid for dinner for two at the White House than for a one-way flight to Louisiana on the Vice President's jet. Justices accept the former with regularity. While this matter was pending, Justices and their spouses were invited (*all* of them, I believe) to a December 11, 2003, Christmas reception at the residence of the Vice President—which included an opportunity for a photograph with the Vice President and Mrs. Cheney. Several of the Justices attended, and in doing so they were fully in accord with the proprieties.

III

When I learned that Sierra Club had filed a recusal motion in this case, I assumed that the motion would be replete with citations of legal authority, and would provide some instances of cases in which, because of activity similar to what occurred here, Justices have recused themselves or at least have been asked to do so. In fact, however, the motion cites only two Supreme Court cases assertedly relevant to the issue here discussed,[3] and nine Court of

---

2. As my statement of the facts indicated, by the way, my daughter did not accompany me. My married son and son-in-law were given a ride—not because they were relatives and as a favor to me; but because they were other hunters leaving from Washington, and as a favor to them (and to those who would have had to go to New Orleans to meet them). Had they been unrelated invitees to the hunt, the same would undoubtedly have occurred. Financially, the flight was worth as little to them as it was to me.

3. The motion cites a third Supreme Court case, Public Citizen v. Department of Justice, 491 U.S. 440, (1989), as a case involving FACA in which I recused myself. It speculates (1) that the reason for recusal was that as Assistant Attorney General for the Office of Legal Counsel I had provided an opinion which concluded that applying FACA to presidential advisory committees was unconstitutional; and asserts (2) that this would also be grounds for my recusal here. My opinion as Assistant Attorney General addressed the precise question presented in *Public Citizen*: whether the American Bar Association's Standing Committee on Federal Judiciary, which provided advice to the President concerning judicial nominees, could be regulated as an "advisory committee" under FACA. I concluded that my withdrawal from the case was required by 28 USC §455(b)(3), which mandates recusal where the judge "has served in governmental employment and in such capacity . . . expressed an opinion concerning the merits of the particular case in controversy." I have never expressed an opinion concerning the merits of the present case.

Appeals cases. Not a single one of these even involves an official-action suit.[4] And the motion gives not a single instance in which, under even remotely similar circumstances, a Justice has recused or been asked to recuse. Instead, the Argument section of the motion consists almost entirely of references to, and quotations from, newspaper editorials.

The core of Sierra Club's argument is as follows:

> "Sierra Club makes this motion because . . . damage [to the integrity of the system] is being done right now. As of today, 8 of the 10 newspapers with the largest circulation in the United States, 14 of the largest 20, and 20 of the 30 largest have called on Justice Scalia to step aside. . . . Of equal import, there is no counterbalance or controversy: not a single newspaper has argued against recusal. Because the American public, as reflected in the nation's newspaper editorials, has unanimously concluded that there is an appearance of favoritism, any objective observer would be compelled to conclude that Justice Scalia's impartiality has been questioned. These facts more than satisfy Section 455(a), which mandates recusal merely when a Justice's impartiality 'might reasonably be questioned.'"

The implications of this argument are staggering. I must recuse because a significant portion of the press, which is deemed to be the American public, demands it.

The motion attaches as exhibits the press editorials on which it relies. Many of them do not even have the facts right. The length of our hunting trip together was said to be several days (San Francisco Chronicle), four days (Boston Globe), or nine days (San Antonio Express-News). We spent about 48 hours together at the hunting camp. It was asserted that the Vice President and I "spent time alone in the rushes," "huddled together in a Louisiana marsh," where we had "plenty of time . . . to talk privately" (Los Angeles Times); that we "spent . . . quality time bonding together in a duck blind" (Atlanta Journal-Constitution); and that "[t]here is simply no reason to think these two did not discuss the pending case" (Buffalo News). As I have described, the Vice President and I were never in the same blind, and never discussed the case. (Washington officials know the rules, and know that discussing with judges pending cases—their own or anyone else's—is forbidden.) The Palm Beach Post stated that our "transportation was provided, appropriately, by an oil services company," and Newsday that a "private jet . . . whisked Scalia to Louisiana." The Vice President and I flew in a Government plane. The Cincinnati Enquirer said that "Scalia was Cheney's guest at a private duck-hunting camp in Louisiana." Cheney and I were Wallace Carline's guest. Various newspapers described Mr. Carline as "an energy company official" (Atlanta Journal-Constitution), an "oil industrialist," (Cincinnati Enquirer), an "oil company executive" (Contra Costa Times), an "oilman" (Minneapolis Star Tribune), and an "energy

---

4. United States v. Murphy, 768 F.2d 1518 (7th Cir. 1985), at least involved a judge's going on vacation—but not with the named defendant in an official-action suit. The judge had departed for a vacation with the prosecutor of Murphy's case, immediately after sentencing Murphy. Obviously, the prosecutor is personally involved in the outcome of the case in a way that the nominal defendant in an official-action suit is not.

industry executive" (Washington Post). All of these descriptions are misleading.

And these are just the inaccuracies pertaining to the *facts*. With regard to the *law*, the vast majority of the editorials display no recognition of the central proposition that a federal officer is not ordinarily regarded to be a personal party in interest in an official-action suit. And those that do display such recognition facilely assume, contrary to all precedent, that in such suits mere political damage (which they characterize as a destruction of Cheney's reputation and integrity) is ground for recusal. Such a blast of largely inaccurate and uninformed opinion cannot determine the recusal question. It is well established that the recusal inquiry must be "made from the perspective of a *reasonable* observer who is *informed of all the surrounding facts and circumstances*." Microsoft Corp. v. United States, 530 U.S. 1301 (2000) (Rehnquist, C.J.).

IV

While Sierra Club was apparently unable to summon forth a single example of a Justice's recusal (or even motion for a Justice's recusal) under circumstances similar to those here, I have been able to accomplish the seemingly more difficult task of finding a couple of examples establishing the negative: that recusal or motion for recusal did *not* occur under circumstances similar to those here.

Justice White and Robert Kennedy

The first example pertains to a Justice with whom I have sat, and who retired from the Court only 11

years ago, Byron R. White. Justice White was close friends with Attorney General Robert Kennedy from the days when White had served as Kennedy's Deputy Attorney General. In January 1963, the Justice went on a skiing vacation in Colorado with Robert Kennedy and his family, Secretary of Defense Robert McNamara and his family, and other members of the Kennedy family. (The skiing in Colorado, like my hunting in Louisiana, was not particularly successful.) At the time of this skiing vacation there were pending before the Court at least two cases in which Robert Kennedy, in his official capacity as Attorney General, was a party. In the first of these, moreover, the press might have said, as plausibly as it has said here, that the reputation and integrity of the Attorney General were at issue. There the Department of Justice had decreed deportation of a resident alien on grounds that he had been a member of the Communist Party. (The Court found that the evidence adduced by the Department was inadequate.)

Besides these cases naming Kennedy, another case pending at the time of the skiing vacation was argued to the Court *by Kennedy* about two weeks later. *See* Gray v. Sanders, 372 U.S. 368 (1963). That case was important to the Kennedy administration, because by the time of its argument everybody knew that the apportionment cases were not far behind, and *Gray* was a significant step in the march toward Reynolds v. Sims, 377 U.S. 533 (1964). When the decision was announced, it was front-page news. Attorney General Kennedy argued for affirmance of a three-judge District Court's ruling that the Georgia Democratic Party's county-unit voting system violated the one-person, one-vote principle. This was Kennedy's only argument before the Court, and it certainly put "on the line" his reputation as a lawyer, as well as an important policy of his brother's administration.

Justice Jackson and Franklin Roosevelt

The second example pertains to a Justice who was one of the most distinguished occupants of the seat to which I was appointed, Robert Jackson. Justice Jackson took the recusal obligation particularly seriously. Nonetheless, he saw nothing wrong with maintaining a close personal relationship, and engaging in "quite frequen[t]" socializing with the President whose administration's acts came before him regularly.

In April 1942, the two "spent a weekend on a very delightful house party down at General Watson's in Charlottesville, Virginia. I had been invited to ride down with the President and to ride back with him." Pending at the time, and argued the next month, was one of the most important cases concerning the scope of permissible federal action under the Commerce Clause, Wickard v. Filburn, 317 U.S. 111 (1942). Justice Jackson wrote the opinion for the Court. Roosevelt's Secretary of Agriculture, rather than Roosevelt himself, was the named federal officer in the case, but there is no doubt that it was important to the President.

I see nothing wrong about Justice White's and Justice Jackson's socializing—including vacationing and accepting rides—with their friends. Nor, seemingly, did anyone else at the time. (The Denver Post, which has been critical of me, reported the White-Kennedy-McNamara skiing vacation with nothing but enthusiasm.) If friendship is basis for recusal (as it assuredly is when friends are sued personally) then activity which suggests close friendship must be avoided. But if friendship is *no* basis for recusal (as it is not in official-capacity suits) social contacts that do no more than evidence that friendship suggest no impropriety whatever.

Of course it can be claimed (as some editorials have claimed) that "times have changed," and what was once considered proper—even as recently as Byron White's day—is no longer so. That may be true with regard to the earlier rare phenomenon of a Supreme Court Justice's serving as advisor and confidant to the President—though that activity, so incompatible with the separation of powers, was not widely known when it was occurring, and can hardly be said to have been generally approved before it was properly abandoned. But the well-known and constant practice of Justices' enjoying friendship and social intercourse with Members of Congress and officers of the Executive Branch has *not* been abandoned, and ought not to be.

V

Since I do not believe my impartiality can reasonably be questioned, I do not think it would be proper for me to recuse. That alone is conclusive; but another consideration moves me in the same direction: Recusal would in my judgment harm the Court. If I were to withdraw from this case, it would be because some of the press has argued that the Vice President would suffer political damage *if* he should lose this appeal, and *if*, on remand, discovery should establish that energy industry representatives were *de facto* members of NEPDG—and because some of the press has elevated that possible political damage to the status of an impending stain on the reputation and integrity of the Vice President. But since political damage often comes from the Government's losing official-action suits; and since political damage can readily be characterized as a stain on reputation and integrity; recusing in the face of such charges would give elements of the press a veto over participation of any Justices who had social contacts with, or were even known to be friends of, a named official. That is intolerable.

My recusal would also encourage so-called investigative journalists to suggest improprieties, and demand recusals, for other inappropriate (and increasingly silly) reasons. The Los Angeles Times has already suggested that it was improper for me to sit on a case argued by a law school dean whose school I had visited several weeks before—visited not at his invitation, but at his predecessor's. The same paper has asserted that it was improper for me to speak at a dinner honoring Cardinal Bevilaqua given by the Urban Family Council of Philadelphia because (according to the Times's false report) that organization was engaged in litigation seeking to prevent same-sex civil unions, and I had before me a case presenting the question (whether same-sex civil unions were lawful?—no) whether homosexual sodomy could constitutionally be *criminalized. See* Lawrence v. Texas, 539 U.S. 558 (2003). While the political branches can perhaps survive the constant baseless allegations of impropriety that have become the staple of Washington reportage, this Court cannot. The people must have confidence in the integrity of the Justices, and that cannot exist in a system that assumes them to be corruptible by the slightest friendship or favor, and in an atmosphere where the press will be eager to find foot-faults.

As I noted at the outset, one of the private respondents in this case has not called for my recusal, and has expressed confidence that I will rule impartially, as indeed I will. Counsel for the other private respondent seek to impose, it seems to me, a standard regarding friendship, the appearance of friendship, and the acceptance of social favors, that is more stringent than what they themselves observe. Two days before the brief in opposition to the petition in this case was filed, lead counsel for Sierra Club, a friend, wrote me a warm note inviting me to come to Stanford Law School to speak to one of his classes. (Available in Clerk of Court's case file.) (Judges teaching classes at law schools normally have their transportation and expenses paid.) I saw nothing amiss in that friendly letter and invitation. I surely would have thought otherwise if I had applied the standards urged in the present motion.

There are, I am sure, those who believe that my friendship with persons in the current administration might cause me to favor the Government in cases brought against it. That is not the issue here. Nor is the issue whether personal friendship with the Vice President might cause me to favor the Government in cases in which *he* is named. None of those suspicions regarding my impartiality (erroneous suspicions, I hasten to protest) bears upon recusal here. The question, simply put, is whether someone who thought I could decide this case impartially despite my friendship with the Vice President would reasonably believe that I *cannot* decide it impartially because I went hunting with that friend and accepted an invitation to fly there with him on a Government plane. If it is reasonable to think that a Supreme Court Justice can be bought so cheap, the Nation is in deeper trouble than I had imagined.

As the newspaper editorials appended to the motion make clear, I have received a good deal of embarrassing criticism and adverse publicity in connection with the matters at issue here—even to the point of becoming (as the motion cruelly but accurately states) "fodder for late-night comedians." If I could have done so in good conscience, I would have been pleased to demonstrate my integrity, and immediately silence the criticism, by getting off the case. Since I believe there is no basis for recusal, I cannot. The motion is denied.

Lawrence J. Fox

I Did Not Sleep With That Vice-President

15 No. 2 The Professional Lawyer 1 (ABA 2004)

One could begin to think, in the terms of my great friend Kathleen Clark,[1] that the Supreme Court has provided us with an "overshare," i.e. more information than we really want to know. For example, several years ago my law firm, Drinker Biddle & Reath, ditched its March Madness Office Pool. Well, we didn't really ditch it. It just went underground, officially expunged but apparently thriving quite well headquartered at a local watering hole. Then we read that no less a personage than the Chief Justice himself, William Rehnquist, was the major domo of an office pool of his own design, this one on the results of certain games of chance otherwise known as national elections. And we learned that the Chief Justice had ensnared many of his supreme colleagues in this enterprise. How could we at Drinker Biddle & Reath snatch from our many employees the opportunity to bet on these 64 basketball games when the Chief himself was presiding over an illegal betting operation, right there in the marble palace of justice where he presides?

But now we have much more. And much worse. Justice Antonin Scalia was the subject of a motion to recuse filed by respondent Sierra Club in an action against one Richard B. Cheney, Vice President of the United States, arising out of the Vice President's role as Chair of the National Energy Policy Development Group. The motion was prompted by the disclosure that Vice President Cheney and Justice Scalia had journeyed together and spent two days duck hunting in Louisiana.

In apparent conformity with Supreme Court practice, the motion was referred to Justice Scalia himself who, on March 18, 2004, issued an extraordinary 21-page memorandum denying the motion. It is the contents of that opinion that prompts my concern about over-sharing and thus this commentary.

---

1. Professor of Law at Washington University in St. Louis.

Why is the Scalia memorandum extraordinary? First, there is the question of its length. As one reads page after page of Justice Scalia's prolix but well balanced sentences, one begins to wonder whether the need to go on at such length suggests, like a too-long summary judgment motion, that Justice Scalia's side of the argument is quite weak. Me thinks the gentleman doth protest too much.

The tone of the memorandum does not help. Justice Scalia is known for his rapier pen. He often demonstrates how clever he is in terms that must leave the litigants with whom he doesn't agree and his fellow Justices in similar circumstances quivering at the poverty of their own cognitive powers. But with his own integrity on the line, one would have hoped—as it turns out, against hope—that Justice Scalia would have adopted a less belligerent, cynical and dismissive voice in defending his willingness to sit on this important case. Instead we get a strident brief, dripping with annoyed sarcasm that anyone would question his rectitude and, as it turns out, one that raises far more questions than it answers, one that highlights the infirmities of the good Justice's self-assured stance.

Make no mistake abut it. Justice Scalia thinks he is a trial lawyer. Right from the beginning he goes for our sympathy vote. How else can one explain Justice Scalia's remarkable narrative which begins by telling us the totally irrelevant fact that the Justice was introduced to the man who hosted this exclusive soirée by a dentist and, drum roll please, a worker in handicapped rehabilitation? With that as a starting point, one cannot help but feeling all warm and fuzzy about the down to earth altruistic folk who brought the Justice and the veep together.

Next, Justice Scalia addresses the issue of his host, Wallace Carline, a magnanimous gentleman, who has been inviting Justice Scalia to Louisiana for years. On this occasion Mr. Carline agreed, at Justice Scalia's request, to invite the Vice-President, an avid duck hunter, as well, an invitation the host permitted Justice Scalia to extend personally.

Justice Scalia tells us a lot more about what the host is not, than what he is. But this must be very important because twice in the memorandum Justice Scalia addresses the issue of how his host makes his less than modest living.

The host is not:

"an energy industry executive,"[2]
"an oil company executive,"[3]
"an oil man,"[4]
"an energy company official,"[5] or
"an oil industrialist."[6]

How "misleading" it is, Justice Scalia scolds, for these supposedly responsible newspapers covering the recusal motion to mischaracterize the host of Justice Scalia and the Vice President as any of these things—particularly since the Vice President is fighting so hard to keep secret the identity of the private

2. Washington Post
3. Contra Costa Times
4. Minneapolis Star Tribune
5. Atlanta Journal Constitution
6. Cincinnati Enquirer

members of the Vice President's Energy Task Force. In fact his host, far from being an oil industrialist—drum roll please—"runs his own company that provides services and equipment rental to"—pause—"*oil rigs*." (Emphasis added).

Certainly doesn't sound like an "oil industrialist" to me. In fact—how could anyone make such a mistake? He was in point of fact an "oil rig and oil equipment industrialist." The gauze is lifted from our eyes.

What Justice Scalia apparently wanted to make clear was that his host was not an "ExxonMobil" or "Con Ed" executive; he apparently was not a Halliburton executive either, though the host's wholly-owned company does sound an awful lot like a competitor of Halliburton. I guess Justice Scalia is asserting that these oil field supply folks, unlike the BP Unocal gang, are totally indifferent to the administration's energy policy, not caring one way or the other whether the Bush-Cheney administration allows off-shore or North Slope drilling for petroleum.

Justice Scalia then tells us—a real confidence builder here—that the trip was set even before certiorari was granted, and was completed long before the case is to be argued. Justice Scalia does not, however, cite any authority for the remarkable proposition that it would be okay to preside over a case involving a litigant with whom you spent the weekend before oral argument, but not okay to arrange for same thing after cert. is granted.

Only then does Justice Scalia address the trip on Air Force Two, the Vice President's personal jet that whisked Scalia and party to Louisiana. One of the most interesting aspects of this disquisition is what Scalia does not address. While later we learn who was with whom during the duck hunt, in the section of the opinion dealing with the sumptuous air travel arrangements, that subject is studiously not discussed. From the opinion, all one learns is that the complement included the Vice President and his staff and security detail, Justice Scalia and his son and son-in-law, quite a cozy group for a multiple-hour plane ride on a Gulfstream jet. Perhaps the cabin was too noisy for any conversation, unlike a duck blind. But we will never know, though somehow we doubt it. In any event, we receive no assurance that the justice was sequestered from the litigant.

But if we were concerned about this omission our fears are quickly put to rest by Justice Scalia's assertion that, when he rode on Air Force Two, the trip cost the taxpayers nothing; the plane was flying there anyway and Justice Scalia received nothing of value when his son, son-in-law and he were offered these otherwise vacant seats on Air Force Two. This is because—damnit—they were only able to hitch a one-way ride with the Vice President. This meant—groan—the Scalia party had to buy one-way tickets back. But since one-way tickets, in addition to being a clear sign that the flyers are terrorists, are so much more expensive than round-trip tickets, the Scalia group bought round-trip tickets and, in violation of the airline's rules, tore up the other half. So the out-of-pocket expense for the Scalia party was the same as it would have been if the Vice President had never offered this little perquisite. In Justice Scalia's flamboyant rhetoric, "none of us saved a cent." End of discussion.

Well, not quite. Not many have flown on private jets. The author was lucky enough to do it once. And let me tell you there is real value to flying in the rarefied world of the dedicated private Gulfstream. The plane leaves when you want. It makes no stops. There is no racing through a hub to change planes. The space is luxurious. The food custom prepared. I can still taste the smoked salmon sandwiches served on monogrammed china aboard the Merrill Lynch Gulfstream. And you land not in New Orleans—how inconvenient—but at a private airport in Morgan City right next to your duck-hunting destination.

Justice Scalia grudgingly recognizes that even if he did not save any money, there was some very small value in what he received. But he wants us to put that value into perspective. He observes that at a charity auction one would bid far more for a dinner at the White House—something typically provided to Supreme Court justices—than a trip on Air Force Two.

Does Justice Scalia think for one minute that this astonishing assertion proves that a trip on Air Force Two is not valuable? I have no idea what people would bid for seats at a Christmas dinner at the White House, but it would certainly be in the thousands. That certainly leaves lots of room to value the Air Force Two trip at a very high number as well—even if it could be snared at a lower dollar figure than dinner at the White House.

Moreover, it is my humble opinion that, given the choice between going to a dinner at the White House with hundreds, a quick photo-op with the President and First Lady, and the President retiring at 9:20, or spending three days with the Vice President, one traveling on Air Force Two, the other two dining, fishing and duck hunting, the auction bids for the latter would be ten times that paid for the White House dinner.

It is so interesting to observe Justice Scalia's embracing a free enterprise way of determining value. He is so at ease thinking in these terms. Yet it is just hard to reconcile his upside-down valuations with this author's view, a view which the author has confirmed repeatedly in a totally unscientific ongoing survey among the author's friends and family—though I must admit that most of those in my informal poll have never seen a duck blind, let alone shot a duck, and really know nothing of the hardships one endures pursuing this activity.

Finally, Justice Scalia addresses the duck hunting itself. We are told there were 13 hunters in all, a group Justice Scalia characterizes as "not intimate," even "sizable," perhaps because he found the flight down so much more *intime*. We learn they took meals together. One day they went fishing—in two boats. And though Justice Scalia studiously fails to tell us whether he was in the Vice President's fishing boat, we know that is where he fished because when it came to the duck hunting, Justice Scalia makes it quite clear that Mr. Cheney and he never shared a duck blind, as it sadly turns out. Finally, lest you were worried about the Vice President having a Clinton problem, we are told that, although virtually everyone shared sleeping rooms, this sharing did not include the Vice President, who was not forced to sleep with Justice Scalia, his son or his son-in-law.

I make light of Justice Scalia's exegesis of the facts. I might even be accused of adopting a Scalia-like tone. But the fact that Justice Scalia spends all this time arguing the facts is really quite informative. Taking the time to share them with us, Justice Scalia must feel that they are critical, if not dispositive to dismissing any allegations that he should recuse himself. But what is he really saying?

If I had been introduced to my host by an oil man, not someone—tears now—who works with the handicapped, then I would have been forced to recuse.

If the host was an oil man and not an oil rig man, then I would have been forced to recuse.

If certiorari had been granted before the trip was set, then I would have been forced to recuse.

If I took a round trip on Air Force Two—and saved the cost of a round-trip ticket—then I would have been forced to recuse.

If I had been in the same duck blind—like he was in the same small plane and same small fishing boat—I would have been forced to recuse.

If I had shared a room with the Vice President, I would have been forced to recuse.

Why *is* Justice Scalia telling us all this? In my view, it demonstrates the weakness of his position. Should any motion to recuse turn on the facts to which Justice Scalia so tenaciously clings? The fact is Justice Scalia spent this huge amount of time with a litigant with a present matter before the court. No amount of tap dancing about who introduced who to whom, whether the host was an oil man or an oil rig man, or whether they were in the same duck blind changes the substance of what occurred. Justice Scalia engaged in conduct vis-à-vis the Vice President that required him to recuse himself. From the point of view of the adverse litigants this situation is intolerable. And no argument about how oblivious Justice Scalia was to the trappings of flying on Air Force Two with his son and son-in-law can change that.

Justice Scalia knows this. He knows that his neutrality was compromised by his sojourn with the Vice President, even if he didn't have to worry whether the Vice President snores. But his memorandum grabs on to one passing lifesaver. For sure if this case were personal to Richard Cheney, he would recuse, Justice Scalia admits. But this case is a suit against Mr. Cheney in his official capacity. And therefore Justice Scalia was certainly required, in his humble opinion, to stay in the case.

It is true that different standards might apply in personal versus official capacity law suits. The Social Security Administrator might well be indifferent to the fact that he or she is sued hundreds of times a month. And the idea that a judge played golf with that administrator while hearing some poor soul's social security appeal might not raise serious questions of judicial ethics. But to analogize such an unremarkable prosaic circumstance to *this* lawsuit against *this* vice president is surely to exalt form above substance.

It is also certainly true, as Justice Scalia repeatedly observes, that the Vice President has been sued in his official capacity. But the concept of official capacity-private capacity cannot be an on-off switch for deciding when a justice must recuse himself. Some official capacity lawsuits are far more personal than lawsuits that are classified as personal. Despite Justice Scalia's naked assertion to the contrary, this lawsuit raises an issue that has garnered significant attention for years—the highly charged question of who was sitting down in secret with the former CEO of Halliburton to decide our country's energy policy. Who were these oil industrialists? Oil men? Energy industry executives? It is an issue on which the Vice President has literally staked his reputation, one that might even affect the Vice President's re-nomination or re-election. And to assert that the Vice President does not have a deep, abiding and personal interest in whether he is going to be forced to share this information with an inquisitive world is to ignore the dozens of editorials that have been written on the topic.

And that is something we know Justice Scalia did not do. Indeed, he proclaims that the unanimous view of these editorial writers, whose facts he so carefully has checked, is not going to persuade him to recuse himself. That lesson is one conclusion of the Justice with which I agree. Just because 20 newspapers say a judge should recuse himself is no reason to do it. But that 20 newspapers thought this case was so important that they commented on the recusal issue demonstrates in a dramatic way that Justice Scalia's attempts to assure his participation in this case on the basis that this case is just like any garden variety run-of-the-mill Social Security appeal does not pass the straight face test.

But I have spent too much time addressing Justice Scalia on his own terms (this is all about the Vice President and me) and not nearly enough confronting the very serious ethical lapse his failure to recuse creates. Imagine you are a lawyer. You are handling a major case for a distraught client. The case will be tried next month to a judge. Your client, on your advice, takes a weekend of rest and relaxation at the Homestead. The client enters the elegant dining room with his wife and, as they are escorted to their table, they notice the judge, the adversary and the adversary's wife hoisting martini glasses filled with a silver liquid, laughing boisterously. As your client passes their way, there is an embarrassed silence followed by the judge's halting comment, "Great to see you, Mr. Jones. Just down here for some trout fishing. Of course, we haven't discussed that little matter."

How does that client feel? How do you feel? What has this done to the system of justice? Can the client ever be convinced that the judge will still be impartial? Should there be a need to convince the client of that fact? Even if you know the judge will be impartial, the appearance of bias is both profound and destructive. There is no place for judges fraternizing with litigants who have matters before them. And that is precisely what Justice Scalia brazenly and insensitively did and yet, when called on it, instead of curing the problem by graciously acknowledging the conflict of interest, he launches a rhetorical broadside that only fans the flames.

This Homestead scenario also highlights how useless is Justice Scalia's reliance on the matter being one in which Cheney is sued in his official capacity. If at our dining room scene our dismayed client had also been told, "Don't worry. The case I'm deciding next week is against my olive-loving friend in his official capacity," do you suppose the client would feel relieved, any lingering concerns evaporating once those words were uttered by the convivial judge? You see the problems with the personal-official distinction, are that (a) the offended party, a layman, will not understand the distinction and (b) even if he did, in the eyes of the offended party the betrayal looks identical. While the judge may think it is perfectly alright to go duck hunting with a litigant whose case is pending before him (so long as he does not occupy the same duck blind) because the matter involves the litigant in the litigant's official capacity, that fact is of no consequence to the litigant who was not invited to join the hunting party.

What does all of this teach us? I think there are two lessons here. First, Supreme Court practice apparently provides that the Justice who is the subject of a recusal motion decides whether the motion should be granted. Thus, we are the recipients of Justice Scalia's twenty page pronuncimento. How much better would it be if every justice but the justice who is the object of attention were to decide this matter? These other justices are fully cognizant of the special considerations that must inform a Supreme Court motion to recuse, given the fact if one Justice steps down there is no one to take her place. Moreover, they are objective in a way that any judge who is the subject of such a motion cannot be. You can be sure that if the present eight Justices, without Scalia participating, had decided this motion, the world would have been treated, in the best sense of that word, to a far shorter and more persuasive opinion—even if the Court decided to deny the motion—than the one Scalia handed down. And the world would also have far more confidence that the result that was reached was a fair one.

Second, we could not find a better poster child than Justice Scalia's conduct and his defense for the importance of maintaining an appearance standard, if not the current appearance of impropriety standard, in our canons of judicial conduct. Since Justice Scalia may be completely unaffected by his sojourn with Dick Cheney, some of us might agree with Justice Scalia's assertion that if a Justice of the Supreme Court could be corrupted by this little fishing adventure then the nation is in real trouble. On the other hand, the appearance that Justice Scalia would be biased as a result of his Louisiana sojourn is something our canons of judicial ethics cannot condone or ignore.

It is true that back in 1983 the ABA slayed the appearance of the impropriety dragon for lawyers with hardly a tear shed. Too subjective, too undefined, too given to the whim of the beholder, the critics cried. And so we jettisoned ancient and hoary tradition in the name of blackletter rules which in most cases provided a better guidance for the practicing bar.

Something was lost. After all, everyone would agree that lawyers should conduct themselves in such a way that the appearance of what they do inspires no less confidence in the integrity of lawyers than its substance. But on balance, and only on balance, one can say that more was gained than was lost. Besides, it was hard to argue that lawyers should keep up appearances when sleazy advertisements for legal services were running during the late show right next to ads for the Veg-O-Matic.

But now the cry has been raised anew. This time the object of attention is not the appearance of impropriety as it applies to lawyers; no, now, the call is heard that the requirement that judges must avoid the appearance of impropriety should be jettisoned. Again we are told the standard is standardless, a trap for the wary, an antiquated and subjective rule whose demise is long past due.

But Justice Scalia's twenty page tirade has convinced me that it would be a mistake to join those critics of the appearance of impropriety rule. That having been said, I think we can craft a rule that captures its multiple beneficial characteristics and at the same time, at least in part, responds to its vociferous detractors.

A discussion of the appearance of impropriety raises two different issues. The first is whether any new disciplinary rule applying to judges should address appearances. As to this I would hope there is no debate. Whatever can be said of the importance to our system of justice of the appearance of lawyers must be multiplied ten fold when it comes to judges. The public's confidence in the independence, impartiality and conscientiousness of judges depends almost entirely on how the judiciary appears to be acting.

Even twelve Bishops from Boston (from the days when they were the gold standard) assuring the public that a given judge's impartiality is beyond question cannot overcome the public's dismay with the disclosure that the judge was seen dining with one of the litigants in a case before her. Nor can uncontradicted testimony of a judge's brilliance overcome the public distrust of a judge who sleeps through oral argument.

In the world of judging, appearances count and anyone who thinks that a requirement that judges be unfettered, honest and erudite in all things is enough, if what the judges appear to be doing goes unregulated, is failing to recognize how fragile is the trust the American public is currently willing to repose in our judiciary.

So we must, I submit, preserve the appearance of something. But "impropriety" apparently will not do. Justice Scalia teaches us that. It's too broad; it's too difficult to define; it's too subjective. One person's impropriety is apparently another person's admirable conduct. Well maybe not quite that. But another person's even marginally permissible conduct.

What is it then that we don't want our judges to appear to be doing, even if they are not in fact doing it? We don't want them to engage in conduct that might lead the public to question their impartiality. We don't want them to engage in conduct that might lead the public to question their independence. We don't want them to engage in conduct that might lead the public to question their honesty. And we don't want them to engage in conduct that might lead the public to question their competence.

Well if those are the key subjects—and this list may not be complete—then why don't we draft a rule that says precisely that?

Canon 1

Conduct in general: A judge shall act with diligence, integrity and independence. Moreover, a judge shall avoid engaging in conduct that would provide the appearance that any of these required standards of conduct have been compromised.

Maybe that formulation does not capture every essential category. More could be added. But my idea is that, while appearance of impropriety could capture something as benign as using the wrong fork or donning a mismatched golf outfit, appearing to engage in dishonest conduct is a concrete standard that will not only put the judiciary on notice of what should not be done, but not let the judiciary hide, like Justice Scalia has done so effectively, by arguing that what the judge did was perfectly "proper." This is because Justice Scalia's adventure with Vice President Cheney not only reflected an appearance of impropriety, but also reflected an appearance that Justice Scalia was not impartial.

He might assert in endless compound and complex sentences that he was uncorrupted as a result of his flight on Air Force 2 and his fishing and duck hunting excursion. He can argue further that what he did was proper. For proof of that proposition look no further than the Justice's total absence of shame. But the one thing Justice Scalia cannot argue is that what he did avoided the appearance that he was biased.

One final observation: it has been said that Justice Scalia finds being a Supreme Court Justice not all that splendid an occupation, an overrated position that is not quite enough of a challenge for this larger than life intellectual giant, though we notice with interest that Justice Scalia would rather complain than give up the position to cure the problem. But even if he does have a dim view of his job, this should not give him permission to cast a shadow of the court. For so many of us, the Supreme Court is the most important symbol of both the separation of powers and the rule of law. Maintaining the Court's dignity is critical to both of its symbolic roles. Gentle reader, please read Justice Scalia's 21 page tirade again. Has Justice Scalia enhanced the dignity of the Court by providing us with this? Do we feel better about the Court knowing that this Justice did not recuse himself because he did not sleep with Vice President Cheney? I don't think so and I'll bet you don't either.

▓ The Law Governing Lawyers: *Judicial Ethics*

Introduction

Judicial ethics is an important topic for lawyers both because most judges are lawyers, and because lawyers interact with judges, and are thereby "indirectly governed" by the law that governs judicial conduct.[1]

Sources of Law

Like lawyers, judges are governed by judicial codes promulgated by the highest courts. These codes apply to all the activities of full-time and some activities of part-time judges,[2] including justices of the peace, magistrates, court commissioners, special masters, referees, and administrative law judges. Like state lawyer codes, state codes of judicial ethics follow national models that have been drafted and recommended by the American Bar Association.[3] Federal judges are subject to the Code of Conduct for Federal Judges, adopted by the United States Judicial Conference.[4] The models for these Codes have been updated and revised over the past 80 years, culminating in the most recent Model Code of Judicial Conduct adopted by the ABA House of Delegates in 2007.

Like executive and legislative branch employees, state and federal judges also are subject to statutory regulations. For example, federal statutes prohibit

---

1. Ronald D. Rotunda & John S. Dzienkowski, *Legal Ethics: The Lawyer's Deskbook on Professional Responsibility* §10.0-1 (West 2006-2007).
2. *See* ABA Model Code of Judicial Conduct (2007), Application, Parts II (Retired Judge Subject to Recall), III (Continuing Part-Time Judge), IV (Periodic Part-Time Judge), and V (Pro Tempore Part-Time Judge).
3. The first Model, the 1924 Canons of Judicial Ethics, was promulgated in response to a scandal created by Judge Kenesaw Mountain Landis, who earned six times his federal judicial salary in the private practice of law while sitting as a federal judge. Rotunda & Dzienkowski, *supra* note 1 at §10.0-2. For a compendium of past Codes and Reporter's explanation of changes, *see* ABA Center for Prof. Responsibility, *Model Code of Judicial Conduct* (2007 ed.), Lisa L. Milord, *The Development of the ABA Judicial Code* (ABA 1992).
4. 175 F.R.D. 364 (1998). Supreme Court Justices are not governed by these rules.

the practice of law by federal judges[5] and create standards for disqualification.[6] Judges can be disqualified from sitting in a case if they violate these provisions. Both state and federal judges also are subject to criminal sanctions for violation of applicable statutory regulations.[7]

Unlike lawyers, however, judges are absolutely immune from civil liability for their official duties, even if they act from improper motives.[8] Judicial immunity extends to intentional torts such as defamation and malicious prosecution as well as statutory civil rights actions.[9] The Supreme Court has created this common law immunity to protect judicial independence, and to encourage judges to decide all contested and controversial cases without fear of later legal retribution from the parties. An independent judiciary also promotes public confidence in the courts and the rule of law.[10]

Judges who leave the bench are subject not only to lawyer code provisions such as Model Rule 1.12, but also to court rules that regulate their subsequent practice. For example, United States Supreme Court Rules prevent law clerks from participating in any case before the Court for two years after they leave government service.[11] Model Rule 1.12 regulates the conduct of former arbitrators and mediators as well as that of former judges. Lawyers who serve in these capacities also may be subject to more stringent standards under state law or the code of ethics of a private organization, such as the American Arbitration Association or the Society of Professionals in Dispute Resolution.[12]

Judicial Discipline

Judicial disciplinary procedures begin by the filing of a complaint by another judge, lawyer, or any member of the public. Lawyer and judicial codes create an obligation to report another lawyer's or judge's impairment or misconduct to the appropriate authority.[13]

Nearly every state has created a judicial disciplinary commission empowered by constitutional amendment or statute to discipline sitting judges.[14] Disciplinary sanctions range from private and public reprimands to deprivation of salary to removal from office.

In the federal courts, Article III judges can be removed from office only by impeachment, a seldom-used remedy.[15] In 1980, Congress created judicial councils in each circuit and empowered them to take disciplinary action short of

---

5. 28 U.S.C. §454 (2006).
6. 28 U.S.C. §144 (2006) (bias or prejudice of a judge); §455 (2000) (disqualification).
7. Jeffrey M. Shaman, Steven Lubet & James J. Alfini, Judicial Conduct and Ethics §14.11 (3d ed. Matthew Bender 2000).
8. Mireles v. Waco, 502 U.S. 9 (1991), Stump v. Sparkman, 433 U.S. 349 (1978), Pierson v. Ray, 386 U.S. 547 (1967).
9. O'Brien v. Chandler, 352 F.2d 776 (10th Cir. 1965), *cert. denied,* 384 U.S. 926 (1966), Garfield v. Palmieri, 297 F.2d 526 (2d Cir. 1962), *cert. denied,* 369 U.S. 871 (1962).
10. Shaman, Lubet & Alfini, *supra* note 7 at §14.01.
11. U.S. Sup. Ct. R. 7 (2003); *see also* John Paul Jones, *Some Ethical Considerations for Judicial Clerks,* 4 Geo. J. Legal Ethics 771 (1991).
12. *See* MR 1.12, Comment [2]; MR 2.4, Comment [2].
13. Code of Judicial Conduct Rules 2.14, 2.16. *Cf.* MR 8.3.
14. Shaman, Lubet & Alfini, *supra* note 7 at §1.03.
15. *See* Mary L. Volcansek, *Judicial Impeachment: None Called for Justice* (U. Ill. Press 1993).

removal from office.[16] Disciplinary sanctions range from private and public censure to temporary suspension of a judge's caseload. Judicial councils also can ask judges to retire and recommend impeachment to the Senate.[17] A recent study committee chaired by Associate Justice Stephen Breyer reported on the effectiveness of these procedures in regulating the ethics of federal judges. The committee concluded that the vast majority of complaints filed against federal judges were properly reviewed and resolved, but it did recommend additional procedures to reduce a higher error rate in high-visibility cases.[18]

The Judge's Role

We have seen that the lawyer's role is partisan: to represent a client's interests zealously, within the bounds of the law.[19] The touchstone ethic for judges is impartiality, not partisanship. Like lawyers, judges have obligations of communication, competence, confidentiality, and conflict remediation, but these judicial obligations are intended to promote confidence in the independence, integrity, and impartiality of a public tribunal.[20] The Model Code of Judicial Conduct begins with this goal and promotes it by requiring compliance with the law,[21] avoiding impropriety and the appearance of impropriety,[22] and prohibiting abuse of the power of the judicial office.[23]

Judicial Behavior

While performing judicial duties, judges must be mindful of their obligations to act impartially, competently, and diligently. Competence and diligence require that judges give priority to judicial duties,[24] exercise necessary skill in a prompt and timely manner,[25] and properly hire and supervise court staff.[26] To promote impartiality, Canon 2 of the Model Code requires judges to "uphold and apply the law";[27] act without bias, prejudice, or harassment;[28] ensure each person the right to be heard;[29] act in a patient, courteous manner;[30] and avoid *ex parte* contact with parties[31] as well as extrajudicial statements on pending matters.[32]

---

16. Judicial Councils Reform and Judicial Conduct and Disability Act of 1980, 28 U.S.C. §§331, 332, 372, 604 (2006).
17. Shaman, Lubet & Alfini, *supra* note 7 at §1.04.
18. Judicial Conduct and Disability Study Committee, *Implementation of the Judicial Conduct and Disability Act of 1980: A Report to the Chief Justice* (2006).
19. Model Rules Preamble [8].
20. ABA Code of Judicial Conduct Canon 1.
21. CJC Rule 1.1.
22. CJC Rule 1.2.
23. CJC Rule 1.3. *Cf.* MR 3.5.
24. CJC Rule 2.1.
25. CJC Rules 2.5 and 2.7. *Cf.* MR 1.1 and 1.3.
26. CJC Rules 2.12 and 2.13. *Cf.* MR 5.1 and 5.3.
27. CJC Rule 2.2. *Cf.* MR 8.4.
28. CJC Rule 2.3. *Cf.* MR 8.4 Comment [3].
29. CJC Rule 2.6. Part (B) of this rule distinguishes between encouraging and coercing parties to settle a matter. *See, e.g.,* Problem 7-15, *supra* p. 251.
30. CJC Rule 2.8. *Cf.* MR 4.4.
31. CJC Rule 2.9. *Cf.* MR 3.5 (b), In re Ragatz, *supra* p. 500.
32. CJC Rule 2.10. *Cf.* MR 3.6.

Impartiality also requires that judges disqualify or recuse[33] themselves whenever their "impartiality might reasonably be questioned."[34] Rule 2.11, which identifies a number of recurring circumstances in which this general standard applies, is used as the standard for both judicial discipline and disqualification.[35] A majority of states and the federal government also have adopted statutory standards for judicial disqualification.[36] While a minority of states allow for peremptory disqualification based on the simple motion of any party, most jurisdictions require that good cause be shown to require disqualification.[37]

Substantively, good cause for disqualification requires a determination that a judge's impartiality "might reasonably be questioned."[38] This standard has been construed in hundreds of cases, the general nature of which are identified in Rule 2.11 of the Code of Judicial Conduct. A judge's impartiality might reasonably be questioned in these circumstances but the impartiality standard is not, limited to only these categories:

- Personal bias or prejudice concerning a party, the party's lawyer, or personal knowledge of the facts in dispute.[39] Many courts add that the source of bias must be extrajudicial, that is, personal, rather than originating in the judicial proceeding itself.[40]
- Relatives of the judge who are parties, managers of parties, lawyers in the proceeding, likely to be a material witness, or who have more than a *de minimis* interest that could be substantially affected by the outcome of the matter.[41]

---

33. "Disqualification" and "recusal" are used interchangeably in the Code of Judicial Conduct. CJC Rule 2.11 Comment [1]. Historically, however, recusal meant voluntary withdrawal from a case, and disqualification referred to removal of a judge following the motion of a party. Richard E. Flamm, *Judicial Disqualification: Recusal and Disqualification of Judges* §1.1 (2d ed., Banks & Jordan Law Pub. 2007).

34. CJC Rule 2.11. The federal disqualification statute uses the same "impartiality might reasonably be questioned" standard. 28 U.S.C. §455 (2006). For an analysis of the federal cases, see Alan Hirsch & Kay Loveland, *Recusal: Analysis of Case Law Under 28 U.S.C. §§455 and 144* (Fed. Jud. Center 2002).

35. Shaman, Lubet & Alfini, *supra* note 7 at §4.01.

36. Flamm, *supra* note 33 at §2.4.

37. *Id.* at §3.1.

38. CJC Rule 2.11(A). *Cf.* MR 1.7(a).

39. CJC Rule 2.11(A)(1).

40. *E.g.*, Farmer v. State, 770 So. 2d 953 (Miss. 2000) (trial judge who took guilty plea overturned on appeal not disqualified from case on remand absent showing of extrajudicial source of partiality or bias). The Supreme Court prefers to call the extrajudicial source doctrine a "factor" in determining whether bias or partiality was present. Liteky v. United States, 510 U.S. 540 (1995) (judge's opinions did not amount to bias or partiality unless they displayed a deep-seated favoritism or antagonism that would make fair judgment impossible). *See also* United States v. Microsoft Corp., 253 F.3d 34 (D.C. Cir. 2001) (judge who gave private interviews to reporters that were very critical to the defense disqualified for lack of impartiality; extrajudicial source rule inapplicable). *Cf.* St. ex rel. McCulloch v. Drumm, 984 S.W.2d 555 (Mo. App. 1999) (judge who told parties he had made up his mind about the validity of the defense prior to retrial disqualified because of the appearance of impropriety). *See also* Flamm, *supra* note 33 at §4.6, Shaman, Lubet & Alfini, *supra* note 7 at §4.05.

41. CJC Rule 2.11(A)(2). *E.g.*, Matter of Johnson, 532 S.E.2d 883 (S.C. 2000) (judge who failed to disqualify herself in grandson's criminal case publicly reprimanded).

- Economic interests of the judge or judge's household in the subject matter of the proceeding.[42]
- Receipt of donations to the judge's election campaign made by parties or their lawyers in excess of a stated amount.[43]
- Prior public statements by the judge that appear to commit him or her to reach a particular result or rule in a particular way in a proceeding or controversy.[44]
- Prior service as a lawyer, judge, material witness, or government employee or agent in the same matter.[45]

Once a judge is subject to disqualification, two events can override such a result. First, the rule of necessity—that no judge has the requisite impartiality to decide the matter—can prevail over an otherwise substantive basis for disqualification.[46] If there is some other judge that can act in the matter, however, disqualification is required.[47] Second, a disqualification not based on personal bias may be waived by the parties as long as they make such a decision to waive outside the presence of the judge.[48]

Extrajudicial Conduct

A judge's impartiality obligation reaches into his or her extrajudicial life. Judges must avoid participating in activities that can often lead to disqualification, or undermine their independence, integrity, or impartiality.[49] For example, judges cannot appear voluntarily before a legislative body or accept governmental appointments, except in connection with matters concerning the legal system

---

42. CJC Rule 2.11(A)(3). *E.g.,* Huffman v. Arkansas Jud. Disc. and Disability Commn., 42 S.W.3d 386 (Ark. 2001).
43. CJC Rule 2.11(A)(4). *E.g.,* Mackenzie v. Super Kids Bargain Store, Inc., 565 So. 2d 1332 (Fla. 1990) (reasonable persons would not perceive judge biased in favor of litigants based solely on fact litigants made a campaign contribution in a jurisdiction where state constitution requires election of certain judges), Barber v. Mackenzie, 762 So. 2d 755 (Fla. App. 1990) (judge's disqualification required where counsel who represented party in matrimonial action before judge were members of the committee to re-elect the judge, whose campaign was vigorously opposed).
44. CJC Rule 2.11(A)(5). *E.g.,* United States v. Norton, 700 F.2d 1072 (6th Cir. 1983) (judge who opposed racism of Ku Klux Klan and Nazi Party not disqualified from actions where those groups are parties). *Cf.* Public Utilities Commn. v. Pollak, 343 U.S. 451, 467 (1952) (*sua sponte* recusal by Justice Frankfurter in a case involving radio programs played on public transit in Washington D.C., because his feelings were "so strongly engaged as a victim of the practice in controversy").
45. CJC Rule 2.11(A)(6). *E.g.,* Lee v. State, 735 N.E.2d 1169 (Ind. 1999) (judge who gained information from prior proceeding involving accomplice not required to recuse). *Cf.* Village of Exeter v. Kahler, 606 N.W.2d 862 (Neb. App. 2000) (judge who gained information from an earlier proceeding involving the same party disqualified).
46. For example, if all members of an appellate court would be disqualified in a case that challenges legislative pay raises for judges, utility rate increases, or state bar actions, the rule of necessity would override disqualification. Shaman, Lubet & Alfini, *supra* note 7 at §4.03. *See* Williams v. United States, 48 F. Supp. 2d 52 (D.D.C. 1999) (recusal not required where federal judge ruled on meaning of statute that affected federal judicial salaries).
47. Flamm, *supra* note 33 at §20.2.3.
48. CJC Rule 2.11(C). *Cf.* MR 1.7(b), 1.0(e). *E.g.,* Matter of Platt, 8 P.3d 686 (Kan. 2000) (judge whose waiver procedure required non-consenting parties to fire counsel or seek statutory disqualification publicly censured for improper coercive procedures).
49. CJC Rule 3.1.

or administration of justice.[50] Nor may they affiliate with discriminatory organizations.[51] To avoid misuse of judicial power or prestige, judges cannot voluntarily testify as character witnesses,[52] or use nonpublic information for a purpose unrelated to judicial duties.[53] To avoid disqualification, judges cannot accept fiduciary appointments,[54] serve as arbitrators or mediators,[55] practice law,[56] serve as an officer or director of any for-profit business entity, or engage in any other financial activities that will interfere with proper performance of judicial duties.[57] Service on nonprofit boards is allowed, as long as those organization's activities do not frequently come before the judge or the court of which the judge is a member, or otherwise undermine the judge's impartiality.[58] To maintain judicial independence, a number of rules regulate extrajudicial compensation, basically limiting it to reasonable honoraria, reimbursement of expenses, or the acceptance of "ordinary social hospitality."[59] Public reporting of extrajudicial compensation also is required.[60]

Judicial Selection

Judicial selection is governed by federal and state constitutional and statutory provisions. The U.S. Constitution requires that federal judges be appointed for life with the advice and consent of the Senate.[61] Alexander Hamilton recommended life tenure as a means to insulate judges from the "encroachments" of Congress and the "occasional ill humors in the society."[62] States have preferred two other methods: merit selection and judicial election.[63]

Canon 4 of the Code of Judicial Conduct regulates a judge's campaign activity in the majority of jurisdictions where judicial election is a reality. It allows judges to participate in legally approved campaign committees and activities,[64] but requires judges who become candidates for nonjudicial offices to resign.[65]

In campaigning for judicial office, judges are prohibited from using court staff to campaign or raise money, from seeking endorsements from or making speeches on behalf of political organizations, and most controversially, from

---

50. CJC Rules 3.2 and 3.4. *Cf.* MR 3.9.
51. CJC Rule 3.6.
52. CJC Rule 3.3. *Cf.* MR 3.7.
53. CJC Rule 3.5. *Cf.* MR 1.6, 1.8(b), 1.9, and 1.11(c).
54. CJC Rule 3.8.
55. CJC Rule 3.9.
56. CJC Rule 3.10.
57. CJC Rule 3.11.
58. CJC Rule 3.7.
59. CJC Rules 3.12-3.14.
60. CJC Rule 3.14.
61. *See* Lee Epstein & Jeffrey A. Segal, *Advice and Consent: The Politics of Judicial Appointments* (Oxford 2005), Sheldon Goldman, *Picking Federal Judges: Lower Court Selection from Roosevelt Through Reagan* (Yale 1997).
62. Alexander Hamilton, *Federalist Papers No. 78, available at: http://thomas.loc.gov/home/histdox/ fed_78.html.*
63. *See generally* Daniel R. Pinello, *The Impact of Judicial-Selection Method on State-Supreme-Court Policy* (Greenwood Press 1995).
64. CJC Rules 4.2-4.5.
65. CJC Rule 4.5.

making "pledges, promises or commitments that are inconsistent with the impartial performance" of judicial office.[66]

This "pledges, promises and commitments" clause language has been more narrowly interpreted after the Supreme Court relied on the First Amendment to overturn a state rule of judicial ethics that prohibited judicial candidates from announcing their views on disputed legal and political issues.[67] The Court found the state prohibition was not sufficiently cabined to serve an otherwise legitimate state interest in the impartiality of judges, defined as lack of bias for or against particular parties to particular proceedings.

Comments [11] through [15] to Rule 4.1 are intended to "encourage adoption of an appropriately narrow interpretation" of the clause, which produces the result that a judicial candidate does not compromise impartiality by announcing personal views as long as the announcement does not "demonstrate a closed mind on the subject" or include "a pledge or a promise to rule in a particular way if the matter comes before the court."[68] However, a judge who "commits or appears to commit" to a particular result about issues that later come before the court will be subject to disqualification.[69]

The Future

The ideals of impartiality and independence remain the primary goal of judicial ethics, embodied in both codes of judicial conduct and relevant statutory regulations. Judges should suspend judgment until all of the evidence has been introduced, and if they cannot act in an unbiased manner, they should disqualify themselves from the case. Yet, the last eight decades have shown that the obligation of avoiding bias and promoting impartiality and independence are not self-executing. Like the law that governs lawyer conduct, the law governing judicial conduct has continually been refined, and will continue to evolve in the future.

---

66. CJC Rule 4.1.
67. Republican Party of Minn. v. White, 536 U.S. 765 (2002).
68. Model Code, *supra* note 3 at 147.
69. CJC Rule 2.11(A)(5).

Appendix

Applying the Law Governing Lawyers

A. Problems

Select one of the following problems as the basis for your research following the guidelines in this appendix:

A-1. Martyn & Fox has decided to open a new office in the jurisdiction where you intend to practice law. Select any problem in this book, and research the answer to that problem in that jurisdiction.

A-2. Interview a practicing lawyer, asking him or her to identify an ethics issue he or she has faced in practice. Research the answer to the lawyer's problem in the jurisdiction where that lawyer practices, or in the jurisdiction where you intend to practice law.

A-3. Videotape a legal ethics problem presented in a movie or television program. Research the answer to that problem in the jurisdiction where the lawyers in the program practice law or in the jurisdiction where you intend to practice.

B. Written Assignment

Goals:

Your ultimate goal should be to produce a paper sufficiently informative that a lawyer could rely on your advice in practice.

1. To do this, you will need to select a problem, identify issues, learn some advanced research techniques, and use and improve your analytical and writing ability.
2. Your grade will be based on the quality of your research, organization, use of authority, analysis, and writing.

Writing and Analysis Outline:

1. Use an interoffice research memo format. Direct the memo to the senior partner in Martyn & Fox who asked you for advice.
2. Begin by describing the facts of the problem you have selected. Next, discuss the relevant law in the following order:

A. The professional rules that govern in your jurisdiction.
B. The case law in your jurisdiction.
C. Any state or ABA ethics opinions that address the issue.
D. The rules, case law, and other authorities in other jurisdictions. Here, you should focus on whether and how your jurisdiction's result is consistent with the rules and case law in most other jurisdictions.

You can learn more about any or all of these Research Resources in the introduction to your Law Governing Lawyers supplement.

Overall Requirements:

1. *Length:* Your paper should be about 10 double spaced pages including footnotes, which should be used for citations to authorities. Footnotes can appear at the bottom of each page, or at the end of the paper.
2. *Citations:* Use the ALWD, Bluebook, or local rules for citation form. When referring to primary source material (statutes, cases, court rules, etc.) always go to the material itself. Do not rely on quotations from other authors.
3. *Plagiarism:* When you quote, paraphrase, rely on, or are influenced by someone else's ideas, cite that author. Ideas taken from another source, even if expressed in your own words, also must be cited to avoid misrepresenting the work as your own. As a rule, if you are in doubt, footnote the material.

Table of Cases

Table of Model Rules, Restatements, and Other Regulations

State Rules, Statutes, and Ethics Opinions

Miscellaneous

Index